ARIOSTO'S BITTER HARMONY

ALBERT RUSSELL ASCOLI

ARIOSTO'S BITTER HARMONY
Crisis and Evasion in the Italian
Renaissance

PRINCETON, NEW JERSEY
PRINCETON UNIVERSITY PRESS

1987

To Mary and Sam Ascoli,
who came in the middle of this book,
but now come before it

CONTENTS

ACKNOWLEDGMENTS

This book began as a paper on canto XXI of *Orlando Furioso* in a seminar on Ariosto and Tasso taught by Walter Stephens, who introduced me to many of the basic texts and problems of the Italian Renaissance. It was first written as a dissertation, in which canto XXI survived only as a series of lengthy footnotes, under the patient, generous, and brilliant direction of Giuseppe Mazzotta. Without his teaching I would be a poorer critic and no scholar at all. Much of the research, and a crucial piece of the writing, were carried out in Italy from January to August 1981 with the support of a Fulbright-Hayes grant. From that period I owe special debts to the hospitality and friendship of Guido and Daniela Fink, Lina Baraldi Dessi, Maria Baraldi, and the late, dear, Antonio Rinaldi; to Riccardo Bruscagli for the care he took of us during our stay and for a different view of Ariosto; to John Freccero's informal Stanford Villa seminar; and to Eugenio Garin, for two precious conversations. Back in Ithaca, Carol Kaske kept me as faithful to the Renaissance as she could. Jonathan Culler offered tools for understanding how unfaithful the Renaissance could be to itself and then gave a thesis the push it needed to become a book. The process of transformation, carried out at Northwestern University in the last two years, was aided by the comments and encouragements of colleagues and friends who read some or all of the manuscript. I owe particular thanks to Tim Bahti, Leonard Barkan, Albert Cirillo, Larry Lipking, Patricia Parker, Elizabeth Chesney Zagura and, especially, Daniel Javitch. Parts of the last sections of Chapters 3 and 4 were presented at a conference organized by Larry Silver at the Newberry Library in March 1984. Cynthia Falzer prepared portions of the manuscript for me, a process aided by a modest grant from Northwestern's Research Grants Committee. Tom Stillinger gave Chapter 3 critical and useful editorial scrutiny. Diana Robin gave me expert help with some of the Latin translations. I owe thanks as well to my Princeton editors—Marjorie Sherwood, as well as Marilyn Campbell, and, especially, Charles Purrenhage for his sympathetic, yet rigorous, copyediting. Above all, David Quint was the Aesculapian

ACKNOWLEDGMENTS

genius of the recomposition process—I hope I have made the best of his many, incisive, suggestions. Finally, Julie Drew Ascoli saw and survived it all. She helped bring forth this twice-born work both by her patience and her impatience. I thank her as best I can.

Evanston, Illinois
July 1985

NOTE ON TRANSLATIONS

In presenting quotations from Italian and Latin I have adopted, with minor exceptions, the following scheme. Primary texts in Italian are quoted in the original with following parenthetical translation. Secondary texts in Italian and all Latin texts are translated into English, with the original reproduced in a footnote. Translations are my own, with these exceptions:

DANTE ALIGHIERI: *The Divine Comedy,* 3 vols., trans. C. Singleton (Princeton: Princeton University Press, 1970).

LUDOVICO ARIOSTO: *The Satires of Ludovico Ariosto: A Renaissance Autobiography,* ed. and trans. P. Wiggins (Athens: Ohio University Press, 1976).

GIOVANNI BOCCACCIO: *Boccaccio on Poetry; Being the Preface and the Fourteenth and Fifteenth Books of Boccaccio's Genealogia Deorum Gentilium,* ed. and trans. C. Osgood (Indianapolis and New York: Bobbs-Merrill, 1956; first published 1930).

DESIDERIUS ERASMUS: *The Praise of Folly,* trans. H.H. Hudson (Princeton: Princeton University Press, 1941; repr. 1969).

LORENZO VALLA: *Dialogue on Free Will,* trans. C. Trinkaus, in E. Cassirer et al., eds., *The Renaissance Philosophy of Man* (Chicago: University of Chicago Press, 1948).

When, in rare cases, I disagree with one of the translators or feel a different emphasis is required, emendations are inserted between brackets.

ARIOSTO'S BITTER HARMONY

Aspro concento, orribile armonia
(*Orlando Furioso* xIV.134.1)

It is as if you were to match one magician against
another, or as if one charmed sword should fight
with a man whose sword also happened to be
charmed. It would be nothing but reweaving the
web of Penelope.
(Erasmus, *Praise of Folly*)

Too real is this feeling of make-believe
(Buck Ram, "The Great Pretender")

I

THE ORLANDO FURIOSO AND
THE POETRY OF CRISIS

The famous "sorriso" of Ariosto; the remote, fantastic settings and events of his narration; the remarkable fluidity of the "ottava d'oro": all of these have seemed to thwart from the beginning any attempt to find in the *Orlando Furioso* a sense of the problematic in poetry and history, a troubled awareness of the interrelated crises of faith, of politics, and of culture which cry out in the principal documents and events of Italy in the early *Cinquecento*.[1] The painfully acquired political stability and independence of the Italian peninsula in the 1400s was shaken in 1494 with the invasion of Charles VIII of France, suffered through the Spanish and French interventions in the early years of the new century (to which the *Furioso* makes such frequent reference), and received an emblematic death blow with the sack of Rome in 1527. As the poem was being written, Italy was also undergoing a "crisi religiosa," alive with mystical, post-Savonarolian currents of reform, while the Reformation itself was just exploding

---

[1] Eugenio Garin, *Ritratti di Umanisti* (Firenze: Sansoni, 1967), puts it this way: "Il Rinascimento italiano è una splendida stagione della storia del mondo, non una stagione lieta. Savonarola e Machiavelli, Leonardo e Michelangelo, hanno aspetto tragico, non gioioso . . . . I paesaggi incantati della Firenze del Magnifico, le immagini di Botticelli e Poliziano . . . costituiscono una sorte di incantesimo per sfuggire alle ferite della realtà" (p. 187). This reading of Poliziano has been applied to Ariosto as well, as we shall shortly see. For a recent anthology of views on several aspects of crisis see Christian Bec, ed., *Italie 1500–1550: Une Situation de Crise?* (Lyon: L'Hermès, 1976). Even Jacob Burckhardt, *The Civilization of the Renaissance in Italy* (New York: Harper, Colophon, 1958), vol. 2, p. 427, speaks of a "grave moral crisis," which was also political, at the beginning of the sixteenth century. In point of fact, Burckhardt's theory of the historical emergence of the individual and of creative consciousness in this era depends on a series of ruptures between the self and those institutions and ideologies which, Burckhardt would say, had incorporated the self during the Middle Ages: faith and its institutions; political rule by law; the family. For Burckhardt, the self-consciousness and creative energy of artist and tyrant alike came from a breakdown in belief, a collapse of the medieval corporate political state, and, often enough, illegitimate birth—all of which tended to throw the self back on its own resources in the face of desperate crisis. See n. 38 below on the myth of a corporate, "epic," consciousness.

further to the north.[2] Finally, the *Quattrocento* revolution in educational and epistemological methods, as well as the ideology of man's dignity and infinite possibility with which Eugenio Garin and others have associated it, continued to constitute a crisis in human self-perception which was often as maddening as it was liberating.[3] God, man, and *corpus politicum* were all at risk in the multiple and widening crises of the "High Renaissance." Nonetheless, Benedetto Croce, whose enduring influence on the course of Ariosto criticism is coextensive with his dominance of much of Italian literary study for the last fifty years, describes an Ariosto "not anguished by doubts, not worried about human destiny," the poet laureate of a cosmic *Armonia*.[4]

Croce's romantic formulation has since been "secularized" for modern taste.[5] It has also been revised in terms of the musical cosmography of Ariosto's own day: the vision of a divinely harmonizing One which tunes the spheres, discovering concordant unity

[2] See, for example, Delio Cantimori, *Eretici Italiani del Cinquecento* (Firenze: Sansoni, 1939), for some of the "voci religiose della crisi italiana" (p. 14). See also Carlo Dionisotti, "Chierici e Laici," in *Geografia e Storia della Letteratura Italiana* (Torino: Einaudi, 1967), pp. 45–73, for the literary reflections of the "crisi della chiesa" (p. 59) in the early *Cinquecento*, including Ariosto. Lauro Martines, *Power and Imagination: City States in Renaissance Italy* (New York: Knopf, 1979), offers a useful overview of the religious upheaval in a larger context, esp. p. 279 ff.

[3] The theme of philological and educational revolution is repeatedly developed by Garin. See especially *L'Educazione in Europa 1400–1600* (Bari: Laterza, 1957), as well as his splendid anthology of *Quattrocento* didactic writings, *Il Pensiero Pedagogico dello Umanesimo* (Firenze: Sansoni e Giuntine, 1958). See also Joseph Mazzeo, *Renaissance and Revolution: The Remaking of European Thought* (New York: Pantheon, 1965), esp. chap. 1, "Renaissance Humanism and the New Education."

[4] Benedetto Croce, "Ariosto," in *Ariosto, Shakespeare e Corneille,* vol. 11 of *Opere di Benedetto Croce* (Bari: Laterza, 1968), pp. 23–25. The original Italian phrase is "non angosciato dai dubbi, non pensoso del destino umano" (p. 40). Though he gave the theme its fullest development, it was not entirely new with him. Cf. Ugo Foscolo, "Poemi Narrativi," in C. Foligno, ed., *Saggi di Letteratura Italiana* (Firenze: LeMonnier, 1958), pt. 2, p. 124.

[5] Among the notable "secularizers" and revisers of Croce's romantic deity are Giorgio DeBlasi, "Ariosto e le Passioni," pts. 1 and 2, *Giornale Storico della Letteratura Italiana* 129 (1952) and 130 (1953); Lanfranco Caretti, "Ariosto," in *Ariosto e Tasso* (Torino: Einaudi, 1961); and Walter Binni, *Metodo e Poesia di Ludovico Ariosto* (Messina: G. D'Anna, 1947), esp. p. 89. DeBlasi and Caretti focus on the psychological equilibrium and ethical "harmony" of the poet, while Binni demonstrates the musical harmony of the versification. See also Chapter 4, nn. 166–67, below.

in the discordant multiplicity of creation.[6] Nor is it my intention to deny that these applications of *armonia* to the poem, particularly the last, are appropriate. There is no doubt, in fact, that the poem's light tone, fluid prosody, and imaginative subject matter are designed specifically to elicit such a response, or that Ariosto is openly aware of constructing a festive art of " 'l canto e l'armonia" ("song and harmony" XLII.81.4), one which he likens to the successful blending of disparate sounds by a musician:[7]

> Signor, mi far convien come fa il buono
> sonator sopra il suo instrumento arguto,
> che spesso muta corda, e varia suono,
> ricercando ora il grave, ora l'acuto.   [VIII.29.1–4]

Lord, I must do as the good player does upon his keen instrument, often changing chord and varying sound, seeking now the solemn, now the sharp.

On the other hand, perhaps readers of the poem have underestimated the complexity and sophistication which marks Ariosto's understanding of the musical cosmology of his day, have failed to note his sense of its limits as a model either for his own artistry or for the grandly tormented world in which he lived.

Thus rather than rejecting the critical concept of *armonia* out

---

[6] For traditional concepts of *armonia*, see Leo Spitzer, *Classical and Christian Ideas of World Harmony* (Baltimore: The Johns Hopkins University Press, 1963). For classical and Renaissance ideas of poetic and musical harmony applied specifically to the *Furioso*, see Robert Durling, *The Figure of the Poet in Renaissance Epic* (Cambridge: Harvard University Press, 1965), pp. 123–24 and p. 251 (nn. 7–10). For the presence of the theme in a variety of Renaissance poetics, see Concetta Greenfield, *Humanist and Scholastic Poetics, 1250–1500* (Lewisburg, Pa.: Bucknell University Press, 1981). In addition to the sources listed by these three, see Augustine, *Confessions* VIII. 3; Baldassare Castiglione, *Il Libro del Cortegiano*, in C. Cordié, ed., *Opere di Baldassare Castiglione, Giovanni della Casa, Benvenuto Cellini* (Milano and Napoli: Ricciardi, 1960), I.xlviii; Cristoforo Landino, "Proemio al Commento sopra la *Commedia* di Dante," in *Scritti Critici e Teorici*, ed. R. Cardini (Roma: Bulzoni, 1974), vol. I, p. 120. For additional sources and discussion, see Chapter 4, sec. iii.

[7] Ludovico Ariosto, *Orlando Furioso*, ed. L. Caretti (Milano and Napoli: Ricciardi, 1954). Consult also the diplomatic-critical edition of Santorre DeBenedetti and Cesare Segre (Bologna: Commissione per i Testi di Lingua, 1960). All references to the third and final version of the poem (1532) are to the former edition; all references to the first (1516) or second (1521) versions are to the latter edition.

of hand, one might pursue Ariosto's treatment of it a little further
to find the moments when the tranquil exhilaration of "'l canto e
l'armonia" gives way to "aspro concento, orribile armonia" ("bitter
unison, horrible harmony" XIV.134.1). I want to argue that Ariosto
does sing his great song, with at least superficial success, as a means
of evading, domesticating, and/or dominating impending crises of
the self, the city, and the temple. But I also claim that an attentive
listener might sense a bitter edge, a disturbing crack, in the singer's
voice—one which betrays awareness of a poetic project doomed to
failure and to being swallowed by the madness and death it so yearns
to transcend. I will do this by a close reading of the poem, its images
and metaphors, its narrative and other structures, in terms of texts
and events of the time, as well as of the peculiar and contradictory
responses the *Furioso* has evoked in readers over the centuries. As we
shall see, even the apparently "modern" theme of *crisis* has its specific
textual (even etymological) equivalent in the opposition between
"errore" and "giudizio." In the last chapter I will show how the
various thematic and structural crises of the poem are ultimately
related to a complex Ariostan poetics (revealed in brief glimpses
throughout the *Furioso*) of concord and discord, one and many, har-
mony and dissonance: a poetics which continually metamorphoses
"discordia concors" into "concordia discors" (and vice versa) and
which enters into crisis in the very act of fleeing from it.

That the poem's strongest impulse is toward evasion from histor-
ical claims of church and state is clear from the first. The poem
begins with a thematic swerve from epic "arm*e*" toward romance
"amori," from the besieged city of Paris, capital and last outpost of
Charlemagne's Christian Empire, into the dark forest of imagination
and desire:

> [*pazzia*] *è come una gran selva, ove la via*
> *conviene a forza, a chi vi va, fallire:*
> *chi su, chi giù, chi qua, chi là travia.*   [XXIV.2.3–5]

[love madness] is like a great forest, where the path deceives whoever
goes there: one up, one down, one here, one there—all stray.

And as the heroes of the poem depart from historical "impegno" in
their world, the poem takes a distance, both spatial and temporal, on
the world of its author. Even the usual strange and desolate haunts

of romance wandering are sometimes abandoned for places beyond all charted geographies and all readerly credibility: the fantastic island of Alcina; the splendid lunar surface itself. Purporting to be a Virgilian epic of genealogical and political origins, where past should be prologue to the historical moment of writing, the poem more often than not seems to be ridiculing any such connection—for instance by its insistent reference to the transparently bogus authority of Bishop Turpin—and to be seeking refuge from an unsettled present in a purely mythical past.[8] The famous narrative strategy of deferral and interlacing matches the deferrals by characters, particularly Ruggiero and Orlando, of all definitive choices and commitments: of political and military duty, of religious faith, and of marriage. The incessant interruptions of adventures at their midpoint, the practice of putting off from one canto to the next the conclusion of a narrative sequence, the immediate passage of heroes and heroines from the end of one adventure to the beginning of another, even more threatening, the potentially endless proliferation of events, characters, landscapes, and so on: all these contribute to the sense that no final closure will ever be reached, no decisive contact between poem and reality made.

It is this technique of narrative, thematic, and structural evasions which led Attilio Momigliano to his brilliant comparison of the poem to the labyrinthine palaces of Atlante where "donne e cavallieri" wander endlessly after the magical figments of their own fantasy and desire, where they, and especially Ruggiero, Atlante's beloved adopted son, are sheltered from the encroachments of time and from the brutal, treacherous death which inevitably attends the young knight's conversion and marriage to Bradamante.[9] As I will show, however, the poet as an Atlante is early set against another prophet-poet-magician, Merlin: a principle of evasion from history and its threatening crises encounters and is countered by a prophetic

---

[8] See Durling, *The Figure of the Poet*, p. 250 (n. 4), for a list of the (mostly ironic) references to Turpin as historical *auctoritas*. Refer to nn. 53 and 55 below on the general question of Ariosto's imitation and/or originality in the use of sources.

[9] Attilio Momigliano, *Saggio sull' "Orlando Furioso"* (Bari: Laterza, 1928), pp. 7–50. For the view that Atlante stands not for Ariosto, but for his predecessor, Boiardo, in the *Furioso*, see David Quint, "The Figure of Atlante: Ariosto and Boiardo's Poem," *MLN* 94 (1979), to whose views I will return in Chapter 4.

celebration of political dynasty and active heroism.[10] For most of the poem Ariosto seems indeed more closely tied to the former than to the latter, to be a poet of aesthetic delight more than of moral utility, of fantastic departure from, rather than allegorical commentary on or mimetic representation of, "reality." Atlante, however, is a poet somewhat different from the one described by Croce—his retreat is motivated precisely by his anguish, while his evasions are strategies to impede a destined, tragic, reality all too clearly foreseen. In other words, he takes his flight *in relation to* crises already on the horizon. If this line were followed, and it will be, we would learn that Ariosto is a poet oppressed by an awareness of crisis and moved by an overwhelming desire to stand outside of it, to interpose an aesthetic distance between himself and his age, himself and God, himself and himself, yet frankly aware of the futility of such a project. The first focus of this study will be the "crisis of identity," but it will appear soon enough that this crisis cannot be separated or judged apart from the religious beliefs and institutions or from the political commitments and events which both threaten the autonomy of the individual person and yet offer it definition and self-realization.

Until recently, if some readers have been willing to find in the *Furioso* the traces of an historical upheaval, these were always taken to be, as it were, negative and involuntary, never to be mistaken for profound creative engagement with history or a genuinely anguished scrutiny of the self by itself. G.W.F. Hegel, in a famous passage from his *Aesthetics,* links Ariosto's name to that of Cervantes as the ironic devastators of the medieval chivalric tradition and its values.[11] Francesco DeSanctis refines the brief Hegelian characterization to discover an Ariosto who takes refuge in the tranquil domain of "pure art," from which is excluded any reference to politics, ethics, or religion.[12] Both Hegel and DeSanctis make Ariosto

[10] Merlin is introduced in the crucial canto III, while Atlante makes his first major appearance in canto IV. They are clearly linked by their involvement, at opposite extremes, in the genealogical plot.

[11] G.W.F. Hegel, *Aesthetics* (Oxford: The Clarendon Press, 1975), vol. 1, pp. 591–92, 605; vol. 2, pp. 1107–1108.

[12] Francesco DeSanctis, "Ariosto," in M.T. Lanza, ed., *Storia della Letteratura Italiana* (Milano: Feltrinelli, 1964), vol. 2, pp. 451–52, 468. Cf. Momigliano, *Saggio,* p. 292, on "la consonanza del *Furioso* con il suo secolo."

the uncritical reflector of a certain historical crisis of values, the epitome of what they take to be the "Spirit" of his age. The critique which DeSanctis aims at Ariosto is, at the broadest level, indistinguishable from that which he directs at Boccaccio, and at the Renaissance in general.[13] Nonetheless, "Ludovico della tranquillitate," heir apparent of "Johannes tranquillitatis," has, like his genial predecessor, now begun to be spoken of in contemporary criticism as a poet of historical and personal crisis.[14]

Even before the recent attempts to represent Ariosto's "seriousness," most critics recognized one work in his canon as the reflection of a violent crisis, even as they denied that the *Furioso* was in any sense contaminated by this moment in Ariostan poetics. The *Cinque Canti*, written for inclusion in the *Furioso* and yet finally omitted by the poet, even from the third and last edition of the poem (1532), have often been cited as evidence that Ariosto recognized how alien their bleak and desperate spirit was to the dominant tones and themes of the *Furioso*.[15] The "dark" elements of Ariosto's poetic consciousness were thus consistently relegated to a

---

[13] This study is influenced throughout by work done by Giuseppe Mazzotta on the *Decameron*. See in particular his articles: "The *Decameron:* The Marginality of Literature," *University of Toronto Quarterly* 42 (1972); "The *Decameron:* The Literal and the Allegorical," *Italian Quarterly* 72 (1975); and "Games of Laughter in the *Decameron*," *Romanic Review* 69 (1978). Of immediate pertinence here is Professor Mazzotta's exploration of the complex significance of the flight of the storytellers from plague-ridden Florence, a symbol of the historical realities of pestilential disease and death, into the temporary refuge of pastoral life, from which perspective, nonetheless, they continue to reflect upon the world they have abandoned. Ariosto too is concerned with the marginal situation of literature, its double, and duplicitous, character as gloss on and departure from history. Thus, if I partly subscribe to the notion of Ariosto as the heir of Boccaccio (and Ovid), it is not in opposition to the "high seriousness" of Virgil, Dante, and Milton.

[14] For the transfer of epithets, see Antonio Baldini, "Ludovico della Tranquillitate," in *Ariosto e Dintorni* (Caltanisetta and Roma: Salvatore Sciascia, 1958).

[15] This judgment is almost universally repeated in twentieth-century criticism of Ariosto. The following passage from Giorgio Petrocchi, "Lettura dell'*Orlando Furioso*," in *I Fantasmi di Tancredi* (Caltanisetta and Roma: Salvatore Sciascia, 1972), is representative in pointing out "quegli elementi di crisi e di disagio che segnarono il passaggio dal pieno al tardo Rinascimento, e dei quali Ludovico Ariosto ebbe in qualche senso a soffrire negli ultimi anni della sua vita, riflettendone il clima di dubbio nei *Cinque Canti*" (p. 282). For a survey of some of the important studies on the *Cinque Canti* see Caretti, *Ariosto e Tasso*, pp. 159–60.

lesser work, thereby, as one hoped, dialectically excluding or exorcising them from the poet's most famous text. But the critical winds have shifted dramatically of late. In an early essay, Lanfranco Caretti defines the *Cinque Canti* as "different and more serious than the first, more authentic, inspiration of the poem," precisely because they foreshadow the "profound crisis" which was about to destroy an already fragile political equilibrium.[16] In a recent, palinodic "Codicillo," however, he concedes that in the 1532 edition the *Orlando Furioso* too is marked by the uneasy awareness of political turmoil and by a series of disillusioning personal experiences, notably the brutal period passed by the poet as governor of Garfagnana.[17] Caretti still rescues the picture of a sunny, untroubled, affirmative Ariosto, wholehearted celebrator of the Estense court and author of an "unified image of life," although only by narrowing its existence to the first edition, published in 1516. It may eventually be shown, though if this study does so it will be only incidentally, that even this further retrenching cannot be sustained and that the Ariostan sense of crisis goes stubbornly beyond the various historical and autobiographical schemes which have been imposed on it.

As early as 1952, Giorgio DeBlasi published a brilliant though uneven essay which focused on the poem's dramatizations and thematizations of the psychological limitations of man—his blindness and irrationality—even though he then went on to argue that those perceptions of mental and moral crisis were recontained and overcome in the very act of recognizing their existence.[18] Giorgio

---

[16] "Ariosto," p. 40: "diverso e 'seriore' rispetto alla prima e più autentica ispirazione del poema." An earlier version of the essay appears as the introduction to Ludovico Ariosto, *Opere Minori,* ed. C. Segre (Milano and Napoli: Ricciardi, 1954), from which all citations of the poetic works of Ariosto other than the *Furioso* itself will be taken.

[17] Caretti, "Codicillo," in *Antichi e Moderni* (Torino: Einaudi, 1976). For the stormy years in Garfagnana and other biographical questions, first consult Michele Catalano, *Vita di Ludovico Ariosto* (Genève: Leo S. Olschki, 1930–1931). See also the *Lettere,* ed. A. Stella (Verona: Mondadori, 1965). For a provocative reading of the *Lettere* as sublimated expression of psychological/linguistic/cultural crisis, see Neuro Bonifazi, *Le Lettere Infedeli* (Roma: Officina Edizioni, 1975), pp. 1–80.

[18] In "Ariosto e le Passioni," DeBlasi sees the recuperation of value and stability taking place through the rhetorical poet-figure who is able to recognize his own and others' limits and thus partially to escape them. His work seems to me, as to

Padoan and Vittore Branca confirm that today the image of Ariosto as a poet caught up in a far-reaching political and cultural crisis, and, to a lesser extent, a crisis of the self and its identity, is gradually winning favor.[19] Branca attacks in particular the view of the *Furioso* as "a masterpiece apparently sunny and apollonian, unproblematic and disengaged" and wishes to place it in the context of a Renaissance "troubled and anxious, on the edge of infernal or apocalyptic abysses, obsessed by irrationality and folly" although he still sees Ariosto as a (besieged) defender of the values of the Renaissance as they and it have been traditionally understood.[20] Eduardo Saccone, who himself draws a sharp line between the *Furioso* and the *Cinque Canti,* nonetheless accurately describes how a crisis of the poet's sense of himself may be reflected in a crisis of poetics: "the greatest novelty in the *Cinque Canti* . . . is the crisis of a poetics understood as demiurgic ordering, building out of chaos, and a consequent . . . transformation [of poetry] into humble and resigned witness, a difficult and risky writing."[21]

Coordinate with this substantial reduction of the quasi-divine powers claimed by the poet-narrator for himself from the *Furioso* to the *Cinque Canti,* Saccone discovers in the latter work alone a pointed attack on the Renaissance vision of integral and autonomous human selfhood. In particular, the insidious metamorphoses

---

Durling (*The Figure of the Poet,* p. 252, n. 20), the most important precursor of the best recent American critics of the poem, including A.B. Giamatti's chapter on Ariosto in *The Earthly Paradise and the Renaissance Epic* (Princeton: Princeton University Press, 1966).

[19] Padoan, "*L'Orlando Furioso* e la Crisi del Rinascimento," in A. Scaglione, ed., *Ariosto 1974 in America* (Ravenna: Longo, 1976). Branca, "Ludovico non della Tranquillitate," *Veltro* 19 (1975), contests Baldini's characterization.

[20] Branca, "*Ludovico,*" pp. 75–76: the *Furioso* is a "capolavoro apparentemente solare e apollineo, aproblematico e disimpegnato" but actually reflects a Renaissance "turbato e ansioso, sull'orlo di abissi infernali o apocalittici, ossessionato dall'irrazionale e dalla follia."

[21] Eduardo Saccone, "Appunti per una Definizione dei *Cinque Canti,*" in *Il Soggetto del "Furioso" e Altri Saggi tra '400 e '500* (Napoli: Liguori, 1974), p. 132 (first published in *Belfagor* 20 [1965]): "la novità maggiore dei *Cinque Canti* . . . [è] la crisi di una poetica intesa come demiurgica ordinazione, architettura del caos, e il conseguente . . . trasformarsi [della poesia] in testimonianza umile e rassegnata . . . un poetare difficile . . . e rischioso."

of the demon Vertunno are taken to represent a crisis of human identity itself.[22] This reading shifts attention from the question of objective conditions of political turmoil to the question of the subjective self in crisis. In a later essay the same critic begins to suggest how the same concern is addressed in the greater work, though in a far more affirmative key.[23] Nor should this seem like such a surprising discovery in a poem which in its title and throughout focuses on the related themes of madness and the loss or acquisition of identity.

In the last fifteen years, the imaginative barrier between the *Cinque Canti* and the *Furioso* has been repeatedly breached. The poem has been seen as a reflector of the great epistemological crisis of its age and as the site of a complex crisis in the language which mediates between psyche and society.[24] Above all, Eugenio Donato has most cogently and effectively illuminated the darker side of the *Furioso* with a brilliant demonstration of the "centrality" to the poem of the self caught and dispersed in the errors of decentering desire and of the deceptive language which expresses it.[25] Donato draws heavily on René Girard's analysis of novelistic treatments of deceit and desire, although he believes that Ariosto subverts the optimistic Girardian model of an "autobiographical" narrative which begins by expressing its own entrapment in desire's illusions but ends with a liberating perspective outside of passion. In stark contrast then is the inconclusive Ariostan narrative which never claims to emerge from the toils of error, never constitutes its author as a coherent and masterful "io."[26] In Donato's version of the *Furioso*, the representation of political crisis is all but for-

---

[22] Ibid., pp. 133-35.

[23] Saccone, "Il Soggetto del *Furioso*," in *Il Soggetto*, pp. 201-247.

[24] The first position is that of Elizabeth Chesney, *The Counter-Voyage of Rabelais and Ariosto: A Comparative Reading of Two Renaissance Mock Epics* (Durham: Duke University Press, 1982). The second is that of Bonifazi (*Le Lettere*, pp. 81-120).

[25] "'Per Selve e Boscherecci Labirinti': Desire and Narrative Structure in Ariosto's *Orlando Furioso*," *Barroco* 4 (1972). Regrettably the limited diffusion of this Brazilian periodical in the United States has kept Donato's article from receiving the recognition it deserves.

[26] Ibid., p. 31. See also René Girard, *Deceit, Desire and the Novel* (Baltimore: The Johns Hopkins University Press, 1965).

gotten: it is a "self-referential" narrative, and not one which suc-cessfully refers to the author's self *or* to the "real world."[27]

In spite of the fundamental value of this analysis, a number of objections may be raised against it. Since, in fact, the poem does finally, at least superficially, appear to predict an escape from nar-rative error (XLVI.1) and does clearly attempt to shape a masterful "figure of the poet," it might be better to speak not of its refusals to make these claims, but rather of its resistance to and reversal of its own claims. At the same time, in order to avoid anachronism, and to reveal more fully the intertextual play of the *Furioso*, one might wish to refer the Ariostan perspective on language and desire not only to Derrida and Girard but also, more persuasively, to the traditions available to the author: rhetorical humanism, neo-Platonism, and even the Augustinian discourse on language as agent of absence and desire—which, as we shall see, are extraordinarily problematic in their own right.[28] Most important, although the discovery of a crisis within Ariosto's language may appear to be relatively, if not radically, new, the formulation of "self-referential narration" remains within the DeSanctian tradition of "art for art's sake," even when it ostensibly serves a frontal attack on Croce's vision of the divine totality of the poet's perspective. DeSanctis furnishes the hint that Croce develops into the image of Ariosto as omniscient God; while Donato says that the *Furioso* subverts any "theological concept of the book."[29] DeSanctis, however, closes on a seemingly opposite note with which Donato would be likely to agree: "the creator has disappeared into the creature."[30]

[27] Donato, "Desire," p. 32.

[28] Donato himself, in a note (ibid.), raises the possibility of consulting neo-Platonic sources to elucidate the "selva" of passionate error, but then demurs, calling for a study of the *Furioso* based on a "yet to be elaborated" theory of the intertexuality of the poem, its playful twisting and revision of the traditions. In this regard, see Giamatti's suggestive invocation of the Platonic tradition of the "horses of desire" in his "Headlong Horses, Headless Horsemen: An Essay in the Chivalric Romances of Pulci, Boiardo and Ariosto," K. Atchity and G. Rimanelli, eds., *Italian Literature: Roots and Branches* (New Haven: Yale University Press, 1976). For Augustine on the relation between language and desire, see *Confessions,* bk. 1, chaps. 6–8.

[29] Croce, "Ariosto," p. 46. Cf. DeSanctis, "Ariosto," p. 453, and Donato, "Desire," p. 31.

[30] DeSanctis, "Ariosto," p. 471: "il creatore è scomparso nella creatura."

And one is even tempted to refer both of them back to perhaps the earliest of Ariosto's critics, G.B. Giraldi-Cinzio, who wrote that "like the chameleon, which takes its color from whatever it leans against, so Ariosto adapts his style to each thing he wishes to treat."[31] The image of the chameleon in turn reminds us that Pico della Mirandola, thirty years before Ariosto first published his poem, had imagined man as chameleon, a creature whose very ability to lose himself in an infinite series of identities is precisely that which offered him the possibility of approaching the comprehensiveness and oneness of God himself. Thus the Renaissance was certainly *able* to set side by side, as part of a single dialectic, the dispersal and constitution of the self. And the *Furioso* was therefore in a position to sustain both theological and anti-theological interpretations, while calling both into question—making affirmative reference to its "divine" author *and* subverting both his identity and its own power to refer to him.

The critical question of the referentiality of the *Furioso*, especially of its references to crises of one kind or another, cannot be resolved simply, or perhaps at all. In many ways, however, this is precisely the question to which my book will be addressed, implicitly and explicitly, throughout. Whether it will ever reach that address, much less answer the question fully on arrival, is not something I am prepared to decide. What I am interested in, and I believe Ariosto was as well, is the troubled itinerary of reference: whether of the text to its author, of the text to "history," including its readers, or of the text to "itself." In the last instance, one might ask whether the text is always, or ever, "self-identical" in such a

---

[31] Giambattista Giraldi-Cinzio, *Lettera a G.B. Pigna*, March 28, 1554, partially reprinted in A. Borlenghi, *Ariosto* (Palermo: Palumbo, 1961), p. 125: "come il camaleonte, che, come egli da quella cosa prende colore alla quale si appoggia, cosí l'Ariosto da ogni cosa che vuole trattare addatta . . . lo stile." For the *topos* of writer as chameleon, see Landino, "Proemio," p. 120, where it is applied to Alberti. A similar note is in fact struck by DeSanctis in treating Ariosto: "il suo ingegno è trasmutabile in tutte guise . . . secondo la varia natura delle cose" ("Ariosto," p. 253). The same thought reappears in Croce, "Ariosto," p. 43. For additional material on the image of the chameleon in the Renaissance (esp. in England), see Jonas Barish, *The Antitheatrical Prejudice* (Berkeley: University of California Press, 1981), pp. 98–112.

way as to permit "self-referential" narration, since to speak of a
self is to attribute *a priori* to the text a certain unity, which in the
case of Ariosto at least has always had to be laboriously and doubt-
fully reconstructed. Perhaps an insistence on this devious referential
process will turn out to be something like an answer, after all.

For the moment, an heuristic survey of some of the prominent
names of Ariosto criticism has furnished three versions of crisis to
which the *Furioso* may be referred: crises of an historical epoch
(whether political, cultural, or religious), crises of the self caught
in its temporal predicament, and crises of the process of reference
itself. The first two of these are, in a sense, already thematically
juxtaposed in Ariosto's canon. The life of Ariosto, or rather his
"autobiographical" writings (the *Satire*, not to mention the *Lettere*),
reflects the tension, crucial for so many Renaissance authors, be-
tween the active life and the contemplative, though one might
prefer to use the humanistic categories of *negotium* and *otium* in
order not to confuse Ariosto's desire for time to write poetry with
the defense by Cristoforo Landino and others of neo-Platonic
spiritual ascent by contemplation.[32] This oft-cited passage from
one of the *Lettere* exemplifies a recurrent theme:[33]

[32] On this subject, generally, see Segre, "La Poesia dell'Ariosto," in *Esperienze
Ariostesche* (Pisa: Nistri-Lischi, 1966), p. 9, first published as the introduction to
Ludovico Ariosto, *Orlando Furioso* (Milano: Mondadori, 1964). See also the *Lettere*
and the *Satire*, which give the clearest first-person image of Ariosto's discontents. In
particular, see *Satira* I, entire, and *Satira* VI, line 238, with its bitter complaint against
Ippolito who "di poeta cavallar mi feo" (cf. Chapter 4, sec. V, below). A recent
article by Caretti, "Autoritratto Ariostesco," in *Antichi e Moderni*, pp. 109–120, and
first published in *Terzoprogramma* 2–3 (1974), maintains that the *Lettere*, unlike the
Satire, are not conscious and artful fictions of the self, and thus offer a more "direct"
and "spontaneous" view of Ariosto. In addition to a cautionary note regarding the
patent artfulness of most epistles in the Renaissance (witness Petrarch, and even
Machiavelli), one would also hesitate to assume that *any* form of writing offers
unmediated access to its author's "frame of mind." In Ariosto's case, one almost
supposes that the author is most himself when he is being most coy and is most
carefully veiling himself in disingenuous fictions. Finally, for the active vs. contem-
plative debate, see Landino, bk. 1 of the *Disputationes Camaldulenses*, ed. P. Lohe
(Firenze: Sansoni, 1980), pp. 3–49, which is also excerpted, with facing-page Italian
translation in E. Garin, ed., *Prosatori Latini del Quattrocento* (Napoli and Milano:
Ricciardi, 1952).

[33] This and all future citations of the *Lettere* are from Stella's edition.

*È vero ch'io faccio un poco di giunta al mio Orlando Furioso, cioè io l'ho
comminciata; ma poi da l'un lato il Duca, da l'altro il cardinale, havendomi
l'un tolto una possessione che già più di trecent'anni era di casa nostra, l'altro
un'altra possessione . . . m'hanno messo altra voglia che di pensare a favole.*

[xxvi.4–5]

It is true that I am making a little addition to my *Orlando Furioso;*
that is, I began it; but then the Duke, on the one hand, and the Cardinal,
on the other, the former having taken from me a property which had
been in our family for more than three hundred years, the latter another
property . . . , have given me other things to think about than fables.

The early humanist proposal of a balance between public engage-
ment and private study, which was in jeopardy from the 1440s on
in any case (as the myth of a Florentine Republic gave way in-
creasingly before the fact of Medici domination), though in a sense
reproposed by such neo-Platonist bureaucrats and diplomats as
Bembo and Castiglione, is clearly in trouble for Ariosto.[34]

The tendency, however, has been to see the dialectic as a stable
one: Ariosto's unhappy life as an Estense official, on the one hand,
and his private world of poetic fantasy on the other. But the *Furioso,*
which in this scheme should be the inviolate *locus amoenus* of litera-
ture, reproduces within itself a thematic tension between public
and private (as well as between outer and inner, words and inten-
tions, etc.). In particular, at the narrative and thematic levels of the
poem, "public" trauma and private crises of desire and identity are
inextricably intertwined and in fact seem to determine one another.
This is certainly true in the case of Orlando, whose solitary pursuit
of Angelica and consequent fall into madness are among the princi-
pal causes of the aggravation of the public crisis in Paris under siege.
In fact, as we shall see later on, the madness is doubly attributed
to the "private" causes of Angelica's betrayal (xxiii.128) and to
the "public" cause of Orlando's failure to honor commitments to

[34] See the selection from Matteo Palmieri's *Della Vita Civile* in C. Varese, ed.,
Prosatori Volgari del Quattrocento (Napoli and Milano: Ricciardi, 1955), p. 359, for
a classic example of the *topos* of writing as the fruit of the brief intervals of "ozio"
afforded by a life of active civic commitment. For the retreat from civic humanism
into a purely "academic" philology and philosophy under the rule of Lorenzo de'
Medici, see, for example, Garin, *L'Umanesimo Italiano* (Bari: Laterza, 1952), esp.
chap. 3, sec. 1, "La Crisi della Libertà."

Carlo, to Christendom, and to God (IX.1; XXXIV.63–64). By the same token, Ruggiero's protracted dilemma is first enacted as a choice between situations of crisis: the private world of Atlante's labyrinthine castle (or of Alcina's island), where he will live long but never win public identity, or the historical world into which his marriage and conversion will lead him, conferring a name on him at the cost of his premature death.

On the one hand, the "separation" of self from the city leads toward the generalized dissolution of the community and the disappearance of the self into forgetfulness and/or madness, while, on the other, the inevitable reclaiming of the self by a series of authoritarian structures (from Carlo's empire to God's) has a devastating effect on the private identity, equaling its death. It is within the perspective of this awkward play between history and subjectivity that one ought to place the *Cinquecento* debate, largely inspired by the *Furioso,* on the existence or nonexistence of a genre of narrative plurality and subjectivity which is complementary to the unified public world of epic, that is, the *romance.*[35] One might even say that the poem was written to generate the critical controversies which immediately began to swirl around it. For that matter, one might say that it was written proleptically as a critique of the distinction made by Lukács between epic and novel: the one the document of an unreflective self in harmony with its culture, whose

[35] See, of course, G.B. Giraldi-Cinzio, *Discorso Intorno al Comporre dei Romanzi* and G.B. Pigna, *I Romanzi.* For the unfolding of the controversy throughout the *Cinquecento* and its importance for the later Ariosto/Tasso polemic, see Bernard Weinberg, *A History of Literary Criticism in the Italian Renaissance* (Chicago: University of Chicago Press, 1961), esp. vol. 2, pp. 954–1073. Patricia Parker, in her fine chapter on Ariosto in *Inescapable Romance* (Princeton: Princeton University Press, 1979), begins by emphasizing the elements of romance in the *Furioso,* but goes on to show how the poet juxtaposes epic and romance elements to undercut or qualify *both* genres (p. 44). See Quint ("Atlante"), who has argued instead that Ariosto imposes epic closure on the open-ended romance form of Boiardo. See Pio Rajna, *Le Fonti dell' "Orlando Furioso,"* ed. F. Mazzoni (Firenze: Sansoni, 1975), for the romance sources of the poem and for the opinion that Ariosto's only "originality" consists in his fusion of medieval romance with the Latin classics (pp. 37–38). See Daniella DelCorno-Branca, *L' "Orlando Furioso" e il Romanzo Cavalleresco Medievale* (Firenze: Leo S. Olschki, 1973), for an instance of the laudable trend toward taking the presence of the romance tradition in the poem more seriously (cf. Chapter 3, n. 69, below).

voice it makes its own; the other the record of an alienated and
inauthentic self, forever "separated" from its cultural context.[36]
Ariosto instead reveals what may have been implicit in the epic
from the beginning: the splits within the self, within the city, and
between the two of them. The *Aeneid,* as modern criticism has
recognized, has as its itinerary the suppression of an individual and
his desires in order to found a nation, even as it mourns the violence
of that suppression.[37] Even the *Iliad,* upon which almost all theories
of "pure" epic and unified cultural consciousness come to rest,
narrates precisely the "crisis" of Achilles' separation from the Greek
camp and consequently from his own apparent destiny, which
causes *and* reflects a crisis in the Achaian war effort.[38] It is one of
the little ironies of the history of criticism that the first "romance,"
the *Odyssey,* which traces the "errors" of the ironic hero *par excel-
lence,* culminates, as the *Iliad* clearly does not, in a relatively suc-
cessful reintegration of self, family, and community. To the extent
that the *Furioso* repeats or discovers the common feature of prior
epics, one is moved to inquire further as to whether the represen-

[36] Georg Lukács, *The Theory of the Novel* (Cambridge: MIT Press, 1971).

[37] W.R. Johnson, *Darkness Visible* (Berkeley: University of California Press,
1976). See also Adam Parry, "The Two Voices of Virgil's *Aeneid,*" *Arion* 2 (1963);
as well as Parker, *Inescapable Romance,* pp. 42–43, who, though contrasting Ariostan
error with Virgilian epic, still notes the Odyssean, erroneous, element in Virgil.
Though William Kennedy, *Rhetorical Norms in Renaissance Literature* (New Haven:
Yale University Press, 1978), observes that "as in Virgil's poem, the chief source of
drama is between role and selfhood" (p. 138), he follows up with a discussion of
the discrepancy between the desires and the powers of the self, which is not the
same thing. He does suggest that this tension exists within the poet's dual role as
celebrant of the Este and as private ironist (p. 142).

[38] From at least Vico on, a vision of the primitive poets, and Homer above all,
as "unreflective," integrated wholly with their cultural and natural surroundings,
as yet untainted by the modern fall into ironic self-consciousness and alienation, has
circulated in Western thought, although often modified in interesting ways. One
influential twentieth-century version is Erich Auerbach, "Odysseus' Scar," in *Mimesis*
(Princeton: Princeton University Press, 1953). The same, questionable, interpretation
can be seen in C.M. Bowra's distinction between "authentic" and "literary" epics,
in *From Virgil to Milton* (Toronto: Macmillan, 1945); and in C.S. Lewis' separation
of "primary" from "secondary" epics in *A Preface to "Paradise Lost"* (London:
Oxford University Press, 1942). For a very useful survey of critical attitudes toward
Homer from Plato forward, see Fausto Codino, *Introduzione ad Omero* (Torino:
Piccole Edizioni Einaudi, 1965).

tation of these two kinds of crisis and their relation is "public" or purely conventional, or whether it reflects the "private" and troubled consciousness of its author. Ultimately the dialectic here elaborated might be supposed to inhere in the fabric of language itself, understood as a contradictory structure which functions only because it is available to a whole community regardless of internal differences and specificities but which is, at the same time, a series of expressions by individuals, provoked by their thoughts and desires. Thus the representations of crises point toward a crisis within language in general and within Ariosto's poetry in particular.

In the light of these observations, my recently proposed division of crises into historical, subjective, and referential appears to be contrived and even deceptive, since every crisis of the self is enacted in terms of the self's relation to the otherness of history, while every generalized historical crisis is documented and filtered by the reactions of individuals to it. As Lauro Martines, an acute historian of the Renaissance, puts it: "historical crisis is at once in the mind and outside of it."³⁹ Nor can the first two sorts of crisis ever really be separated from the last one, since they are always mediated by, represented within, a text or series of texts (or within such related semiological systems as painting, architecture, and so on, which yield up their reference to crisis only when translated by and into an interpreting language) which are themselves torn between the subjective origin and the objects of representation. Nonetheless, the tripartite scheme has its uses, as long as it is thus qualified, since it reflects and at the same time limits the theses of several generations of Ariosto criticism and since the text deploys such oppositions itself only to collapse them. It allows us to see, for example, that one would err in excluding public crisis, just as one would err in insisting only on moments of historical upheaval. The special task of this study, in any case, will be to chart the devious paths between the attempted representations of external or internal crises and the "crises of representation" which inform, limit, and perhaps even defeat such attempts.

The primary guide to this exercise in "mapping" the *Furioso* will be the *Furioso* itself, in imitation of Ariosto's final, emphatic, de-

---

³⁹ Martines, *Power and Imagination*, p. 297.

claration to the "donne e cavallieri" who are both his subject (I.I.I) and his audience (XLVI.3.I–2):

> Or se mi mostra la mia carta il vero
> non è lontano a discoprirsi il porto;
> sì che nel lito i voti sciioglier spero
> a chi nel mar per tanta via m'ha scorto;
> ove, o di non tornar con legno intero,
> o d'errar sempre, ebbi già il viso smorto.   [XLVI.I.I–6]

Now, if my chart tells me the truth, the port will reveal itself before long, so that I hope to fulfill my vows to the one who accompanied me during the long sea-journey—though I had earlier paled with fear that I would not return with a sound vessel, or that I would wander forever.

The "sea of error" from which the poet escapes by ending the poem is the labyrinthine structure of the poem itself (and he clearly did not escape it so easily, since for the remaining sixteen years of his life after its publication he continued to rework it). But the "carta," "chart" or "map," but also "paper" and thus traditionally "poem" as well, by which he charts his way out of the poem is also the poem. Few other poetic images have more powerfully evoked the necessities and the perils of reading as of writing.[40] Or

---

[40] The uses of "carta," Latin "charta," meaning primarily "paper," as a synecdoche for "poem" are helpfully documented by E.R. Curtius, *European Literature and the Latin Middle Ages* (Princeton: Princeton University Press, 1953), pp. 309, 329. Curtius also documents numerous medieval and classical sources for the equation of writing and nautical voyages (pp. 128–30). Curiously enough, the intersection of "carta" as chart or map and "carta" as a poem does not appear in any of the passages cited by Curtius (if anything, it is the double sense of "velum" as veil or poetic surface and as "sail" around which the image turns). Parker, *Inescapable Romance*, pp. 16–17, points to the evident double meaning of "carta," but does not trace its sources. The importance which I attach to the image might be compromised if Ariosto's use of it proved to be merely a repetition of those sources, but, at least in the two most promising analogues (Dante's *Purgatorio* I.I–5 and *Paradiso* 2.I–7, 13–15, as well as Boccaccio's *Filostrato* IX.3–4), key elements are missing. Neither uses the word "carta." In Boccaccio, the closer analogue of the two, it is the object of his desire which is his guide across the sea (the boat/book is also the "legno dei nostri amori"). In Dante, it is the poet who guides and the reader who risks losing himself forever. Both, however, do create complex images of the poet/poem, poem/reader relations. See also Boccaccio, *Filocolo* V.97.I; Pulci, *Morgante* I.4, II.I, III.I, XXVIII.2–3, 146; *Mambriano* XV.I.

rather, of writing which is also a reading: for to end his poem, Ariosto "reads" it to discover where he/it is. The author is a writer and a reader of his own writing, and between the two halves of this doubled self is a text which is both sea, the realm of error, and the mapping of a sea, the means of escaping out of error into a fixed and coherent location. This conflation of functions, of course, makes error and the interpretation of error "literally" indistinguishable, even synonymous. The use of the reflexive "discoprirsi" to indicate a self-discovery or revelation makes this process of doubling all the plainer. Such, I would suggest, is also the fate of the interpreters of Ariosto, condemned to illuminating some part or all of the *Furioso* by referring to some other part, as I am doing now, only to discover that the "chart" has suddenly itself become "sea" and must then be reviewed from another perspective and so on infinitely, or rather, indefinitely. By the same token, the critical reading must itself be read and subjected to "erroneous" interpretations. If the "charting" of interpretation seems to close, or to desire to close, the meaning of the *Furioso* and thus to avoid the risk of "erring forever," nonetheless, the task of traversing the enormous sea of the longest poem in Italian literature protracts the process of interpretation into inconclusive wandering, thus giving extraordinary force to the dubious "se" with which Ariosto opens the stanza cited above.[41] One would be tempted to assume that the glossing of the poem by the poem is precisely that "self-referentiality" which has been the constant theme of the poem's critics. But the circuit of reference, as we have just seen, is hardly direct, much less closed,

---

[41] See Parker for an especially acute exploration of the theme and poetics of error in the *Furioso*. The theme of error, however, has been reiterated in criticism of the poem from the *Cinquecento* to the present, as Parker herself observes. Also of interest is D.S. Carne-Ross, "The One and the Many: A Reading of the *Orlando Furioso*, Cantos 1 and 8," *Arion* 5 (Summer 1966), esp. pp. 198–200 and p. 232 (n. 2), with its list of literary and philosophical sources for the image. As a source for Ariosto one should add his friend Pietro Bembo's *Gli Asolani*, in *Opere in Volgare*, ed. M. Marti (Firenze: Sansoni, 1961), esp. bk. 1, pp. 11–13, 19, 84–85, 90 (cf. Chapter 3, n. 149, below). Recent elaborations of the concept of error can be traced in part to Friedrich Nietzsche; see, for instance, *The Birth of Tragedy and the Genealogy of Morals* (Garden City, N.Y.: Doubleday, Anchor, 1956), p. 10. I owe a particular debt to Mazzotta's elegant treatment of poetic and interpretive error in *Dante: Poet of the Desert* (Princeton: Princeton University Press, 1979).

and is therefore so liable to invite straying that one might almost be afraid that one was actually interpreting the poem as something else entirely while passing it off as a reference to itself. DeSanctis, for example, might think that he was referring to the poem's autotelic nature, whereas in fact he was assuming that the poem refers, *avant la lettre,* to an eighteenth-century theory of aesthetics, perhaps to Kant's definition of the work of art as a "purposive object without purpose."[42] If, as I shall argue below, the *Furioso* anticipates and dramatizes such critical blindspots in its readers, Ariosto will appear not only as a reader of his own poem, but of its numerous critics as well, *avant la lettre* indeed.[43]

It is clear that within the terms of the extended metaphor which opens canto XLVI the only assured destination of the poem is precisely its audience, the "donne" and "cavallieri" who await the poet on the liminal shoreline, a powerful figure for the ambiguous zone of contact between any text and its readers. By including this review in the poem, Ariosto seems to be trying, as poets regularly do, to enclose and create his readers within the world of the poem, thus escaping the violence of (mis)interpretation and arrogating a godlike mastery.[44] Thus the poem seems more than ever determined to refer only to itself. But there is a second moment, later in the canto, which revises the first, and makes such a conclusion problematical. The contemporary knights and ladies reading the *Furioso* find an echo in the analogous viewers and readers of the

[42] Immanuel Kant, *Critique of Judgment,* excerpted in H. Adams, ed., *Critical Theory since Plato* (New York: Harcourt Brace Jovanovich, 1971), p. 384.

[43] Northrop Frye, *Anatomy of Criticism* (Princeton: Princeton University Press, 1957), announced, in one of the best known phrases of recent theory, that "criticism can talk, and all the arts are dumb" (p. 4). I obviously disagree with this statement, which represents a great body of critical-aesthetic opinion, including Croce's, and which simultaneously exalts and trivializes poetic language. For me, the poem is both "sea" and "chart," both object of commentary and a commentary in its own right. On the theme of poetic silence, see Chapter 4, sec. iii, below.

[44] See, for example, the critical attention which has been given to Dante's attempt to constitute the reader within the *Commedia:* especially Auerbach, "Dante's Addresses to the Reader," *Romance Philology* 7 (1954); and Leo Spitzer, "The Addresses to the Reader in the *Commedia,*" in *Romanische Literaturstudien 1936–56* (Tübingen: Niemeyer, 1959). More recently, see Mazzotta, *Dante.* For Ariosto, cf. Chesney, *Rabelais and Ariosto,* p. 167.

tapestry of Cassandra:[45]

> Le donne e i cavallier mirano fisi,
> senza trarne construtto, le figure;
> perché non hanno appresso che gli avvisi
> che tutte quelle sien cose future.
> Prendon piacere a riguardare i visi
> belli e ben fatti, e legger le scritture.
> Sol Bradamante da Melissa instrutta
> gode tra sé; ché sa l'istoria tutta.   [98]

The ladies and knights gaze intently at the figures, though without understanding them because they have no one to alert them that these are things to come. They take pleasure in looking at the faces, lovely and well-crafted, and in reading the inscriptions. Only Bradamante, taught by Melissa, delights inwardly because she knows the whole story.

These readers treat the canvas as a pure, self-enclosed, aesthetic object, which refers, as far as they can tell, to nothing beyond itself. In fact, however, as the exceptional complicity of Bradamante reveals, the tent is not only not self-referential, but also refers precisely to its readers and their descendants. Even as it attempts to define its readers, the poem hints that it will always be misconstrued by them.

Bradamante's delightful knowledge seems to leave open a place for a privileged reader who sees how the poem opens onto the self and its place in history. Nonetheless, her reading is in some ways the most perverse of all, since her delight implies a willful blindness to the violent truths of history which the tapestry unfolds: the "tradimento" ("treachery" XLVI.95) within the very Este family which should be the climactic genealogical product of her marriage

---

[45] Elizabeth Welles, "Magic in the Renaissance Epic: Pulci, Boiardo, Ariosto, Tasso" (Diss. Yale 1970), takes the tapestry as a figure of the poem (p. 124), as does Mary M. Farrell, "Mentors and Magi in Ariosto and Rabelais" (Diss. Yale 1976). Farrell takes it as the image of self-referential art for its own sake; Welles sees the festive reading of the tent as partly undercut by the violent battle which follows, but does not inspect closely either its "con-tents" or its "author," and overemphasizes its optimistic side. See Chapter 4, sec. v (esp. n. 224), below, for the conclusion of this discussion.

to Ruggiero. Bradamante can gloss the tapestry because in canto III Merlin and Melissa had given her a magical preview of her illustrious progeny. That "rassegna," however, opens with a clear reference to Ruggiero's demise by "tradimento" and closes with the same treachery of Ferrante and Giulio d'Este which the tapestry evokes (III.24, 60–62).[46] In fact, Bradamante comes to the cave in the first place because of Pinabello's treachery (II), while in canto IV Atlante reminds her of the treachery which will destroy her beloved. Thus the motif of celebration is placed within a frame of treacherous violence.

For the reader of the *Furioso*, who shares Bradamante's special insight, the implication of violence should be all the more evident since she or he has recently been reminded of Ganelon's treacherous intentions toward Ruggiero (XLVI.67) and has just been told that the first owner of the pavilion, Hector, whose armor Ruggiero typologically bears, "a tradimento ebbe la morte" ("died by treachery" 82.1), just as Ruggiero will shortly after his marriage.[47] The world of civil war, deceitful intentions, and a dissolution of order in death and madness, which is painfully explicit in the *Cinque Canti,* is already an implicit presence, and all the more insidious for its implicitness, in the *Furioso.* It is near this point, in fact, that the *Cinque Canti* were to have been inserted. The poem both stages the collapse of untroubled genealogical celebration into a crisis of political violence and, at the same time, dramatizes a crisis of reading—since the readers of the tapestry, and by analogy the readers who await the *Furioso* on the shore, fail to discern the signs of crisis which the text subtly offers them and thus, in their own way, do violence to poem and poet. In the terms of the *Furioso* itself, therefore, the failure of generations of critics to go much beyond Momigliano's description of the poem as the bearer of "wisdom without problems" and to recognize it as a text of crisis is unsurprising.[48] After all, one aspect of the crisis it represents is

[46] For the historical background of the plot of the Este brothers and an interpretation of Ariosto's developing attitude toward the episode, see Riccardo Bacchelli, *La Congiura di Don Giulio d'Este* (Milano: Mondadori, 1958).

[47] The specifically non-Homeric detail of Hector's death by Achilles' treachery comes from Dictys Cretensis, *De Bello Troiano,* bk. III.

[48] Momigliano, *Saggio,* p. 293: "sagezza senza problemi."

an interpretive blindness, an inability of the self to see itself or history reflected in poetry, or if it does see, its obstinate refusal to perceive tragedy beneath a comic surface. The author is found and lost in the sea-map which is his poem, and the poem depicts itself read and misread by its readers. But we have not yet exhausted the possibilities of understanding how the author appears as a reader, the poem as reading. There is a passage in Ariosto's own *Satira* III, written well after *Furioso* XLVI.1, which picks up the imagery of maps and sea voyages, deploying them in a context primarily of reading rather than of writing, and which is clearly a companion to and a gloss on the longer work:

> *Questo mi basta; il resto de la terra,*
> *senza mai pagar l'oste, andrò cercando*
> *con Ptolomeo, sia il mondo in pace o in guerra,*
>   *e tutto il mar, senza far voti quando*
> *lampeggi il ciel, sicuro in su le carte*
> *verrò, più che sui legni, volteggiando.*   [61–66]

[This is enough for me: I will search through the rest of the earth in Ptolemy's company, without ever paying an innkeeper, whether the world is at peace or at war; and I will traverse the seas secure, without making vows when the skies flash lightning, on charts rather than on ships.]

These lines have often been cited as a sign of Ariosto's "disimpegno," as a retreat from the risks of reality into the fantastic security of literature. At the same time, the safety he claims to enjoy in this domain, the lack of vows and of other commitments, seems to deride the sense of risk which in XLVI.1 is associated with the adventure of poetry. In these lines there appears an Ariosto embarked on a journey of reading, who might be said to have himself fallen into the complacencies of the readers who, from the security of a shoreline or marginal position, interpret the poem as delightful map rather than as difficult sea.

We thus have two images of the poet and his poetry: one of precarious crisis; one of comfortable complacency. In this double focus we can localize the dilemma of a poem which both obviously engages in Atlantean evasions and yet persistently, if obliquely, effects

a serious exposé of those evasions and of the dangers, both histor-
ical and psychological, which provoked them. It may be helpful
here to to recall Roland Barthes' opposition of the "lisible" to the
"scriptible," the former applied to conventional works which offer
themselves to the reader's complacencies, the latter to texts which
turn the act of reading into the adventure of writing.[49] In the
"writerly" moment of XLVI.1, the points of perilous resemblance
between the two experiences, textual and nautical, are emphasized,
while in the "readerly" image of Satira III, it is the soothing differ-
ence which emerges. Taken together, and this is really the point,
the passages suggest a complex relation of figurative resemblance
and difference between "text" and "reality," as well as between
"reading" and "writing." In fact, even taken alone Satira III may
seem to imply this complexity, since the "carte" are both a repre-
sentation of and an escape from the perilous world of geography,
and since the trip Ariosto takes with his atlas is sufficiently unspec-
ified as to allow it to be read either as the reading of the books of
others or as the writing of his own.

In any case, just as the Satire imply and perhaps constitute read-
ings not only of the Furioso, but also of Horace's Satires, of Dante's
terza rima, and of other works and styles, so the Furioso, to adapt
its own metaphor, weaves, or is woven together out of, strands
furnished by the reading of an enormous number of authors, an-
cient and contemporary. Many of the prospective readers in the
final canto of the poem are themselves authors, whom Ariosto in
his turn had read, as for example, Pietro Aretino, Bernardo Tasso,
Girolamo Fracastoro, Iacopo Sannazaro, Gianfrancesco Pico, Pietro
Bembo, and many others. Bembo is an obvious case of a reader of
Ariosto who is also partly responsible for the writing of the poem.
The reference to him was added only in 1532, after a process of
revision which critics have generally agreed was inspired by his

---

[49] Roland Barthes, S/Z (New York: Hill & Wang, 1974), p. 4. Barthes' opposition
is troublesome because it is never clear whether the adjectives are supposed to denote
qualities intrinsic to texts or whether they apply to modes of reading those texts.
Nonetheless, the value of the terms, for me, lies precisely in this ambiguity, since
it illustrates the key point that the line between passive reader and active text (or
between active reader and passive text) is always "under erasure."

Prose della Volgar Lingua.[50] His earlier *Asolani,* as we will see, also had a pervasive influence on the thematics and poetics of the *Furioso.* There are also certain contemporaries of Ariosto whose absence from the list speaks more loudly than their inclusion would have, the most obvious example being Machiavelli.[51] Thus even as the poet seems to master his readers and their writings by circumscribing them within his text, the roles are suddenly reversed, and the *Furioso* appears as itself a collage of other texts, not only literary, to which it refers, or perhaps, passively, to which it is to be referred, and into which its own originality and integrity may begin to disappear. In this suspension of the poem between creative revision and passive reflection of prior texts can again be seen the problematic triple structure of crisis discussed above. In fact, by posing from the beginning as the continuer of Boiardo's *Orlando Innamorato* (which he nonetheless coyly refrains from naming), Ariosto has de-

[50] See especially Gianfranco Contini, "Come Lavorava l'Ariosto," in *Esercizi di Lettura,* 2nd ed. (Torino: Einaudi, 1974). See also Bembo, *Prose della Volgar Lingua,* in Marti edition. Caretti, in the "Codicillo," advances the suggestive proposal that Ariosto's new adherence to Bembo has not only a stylistic, but a political-cultural significance as well, insofar as the conversion to a "national" language is a way of battling the political fragmentation and subjection of Italy after 1527 (p. 107). For the successive revisions of the poem, see the DeBenedetti-Segre edition.

[51] Machiavelli was himself an admirer of the *Furioso* and attached no little significance to being omitted from the list in canto XLVI: "Io ho letto ad questi dì *Orlando Furioso* dello Ariosto, et veramente el poema è bello tucto . . . se truovi costì, raccomandatemi ad lui, et ditegli che io mi dolgo solo che, havendo ricordato tanti poeti, che m'habbi lasciato indreto come un cazo" (*Lettera a Lodovico Alamanni,* December 17, 1517, in *Tutte le Opere,* ed. M. Martelli [Firenze: Sansoni, 1971]). That Machiavelli expected to be included at all suggests that Ariosto indeed knew some of his work, though it is not clear which—the *Principe* being one possibility, given Ariosto's close connections with the Medici circle. See Giambattista Salinari, "L'Ariosto fra Machiavelli ed Erasmo," *Rassegna di Cultura e Vita Scolastica* 21 (1957), nos. 10–12, for a few, relatively uncertain, echoes. See also Charles Klopp, "The Centaur and the Magpie: Ariosto and Machiavelli's *Prince,*" in A. Scaglione, ed., *Ariosto 1974 in America.* The only certain allusion that I know of comes in *Satira* IV. 94–102 (composed 1523), where the combination of a reference to Lorenzo de' Medici (the one to whom the *Principe* was dedicated), with an allusion to *Inferno* 27.73–75 (echoed famously by Machiavelli in Chap. 18) and a truly Machiavellian description of princely behavior is very persuasive. See also Peter DeSa Wiggins, ed. and trans., *The Satires of Ludovico Ariosto: A Renaissance Autobiography* (Athens: Ohio University Press, 1976), p. 112 (n. 12).

liberately sacrificed his "title" to originality, although in the very boldness of this gesture he may seem to be all the more in charge of this threat to poetic identity.[52]

Pio Rajna, whose classic source study, *Le Fonti dell'"Orlando Furioso,"* is as unsophisticated from an interpretive standpoint as it is valuable from a scholarly one, took the vast extent of Ariosto's debts to other authors as proof of his unoriginality.[53] There is by now widespread agreement that the poet's use of his sources is

---

[52] Riccardo Bruscagli points out this significant omission in his fine study, "'Ventura' e 'Inchiesta' fra Boiardo e Ariosto," in C. Segre, ed., *Ludovico Ariosto: Lingua, Stile e Tradizione* (Milano: Feltrinelli, 1976), p. 111, now in *Stagioni della Civiltà Estense* (Pisa: Nistri-Lischi, 1983). One wonders, idly, whether the importance given to the wise horse, "Baiardo," in canto 1 is not meant as a sly pun on "Boiardo," whom Ariosto is "following" much as Rinaldo pursues his (apparently errant, actually purposeful) steed.

[53] Rajna, *Le Fonti*, pp. 33–39. Beginning with the echo of Boiardo in the title and the extravagant claim of representing "cosa non detta in prosa mai né in rima" (1.2.2)—itself an "unoriginal" claim, borrowed from Dante's *Vita Nuova*, chap. 42; cf. Milton's *Paradise Lost* 1.16—Ariosto forces the issue of origin and originality upon his readers. Ugo Foscolo, poet and critic, long ago made the best defense of Ariosto's creativity: "il n'y a peut-être pas de poète qui ait plus imité qu'Ariosto, et il n'y en a aucun qui, en ajoutant aux inventions des autres, et en s'en servant en conquérant victorieux . . . ait mérité plus de lui nom de créateur" ("Poemi Narrativi," p. 126). Parker, *Inescapable Romance*, p. 39, offers an up-to-date version of the same theme. According to her, the poet discredits the priority and authority of any single predecessor by the habitual conflation of two or more sources (the most obvious examples being the Boiardo-Seneca mixture in the title and the Dante-Virgil combination in the first line. Also of interest in this regard is Daniel Javitch, "The Imitation of Imitations in *Orlando Furioso*," *Renaissance Quarterly* 38 (1985). No one, to my knowledge, has situated the poem in close relation to the polemics on imitation and originality which were still going on as it was being written and which, in one especially famous case, involved his friends Bembo and Gianfrancesco Pico. See Giorgio Santangelo, ed., *Le Epistole "De Imitatione" di Giovanfrancesco Pico della Mirandola e di Pietro Bembo* (Firenze: Leo S. Olschki, 1954). For this and other quarrels and a general survey of the problem in the Renaissance, with special attention to the metaphors of digestion and assimilation of borrowings (e.g., the bees distilling honey from flowers), see Thomas Greene, *The Light in Troy* (New Haven: Yale University Press, 1982). See also Quint, *Origin and Originality in Renaissance Literature* (New Haven: Yale University Press, 1983); as well as G. W. Pigman III, "Versions of Imitation in the Renaissance," *Renaissance Quarterly* 33 (1980). For an anti-imitation polemic by one of the period's most successful assimilators of sources, see Angelo Poliziano, *Lettera a Paolo Cortese*, in E. Garin, ed., *Prosatori Latini*, pp. 902–904.

"creative" and often polemical, but the infinitely complicated question of the *Furioso*'s relations with other texts is still wide open. Is Ariosto reducing recognized texts of crisis—the Virgilian epic of political collapse and renewal, the Dantean comedy of spiritual struggle and ascent, the Petrarchan lyric pursuit of poetic identity— to the status of "mere" literature, deluded projects of "engaged" writing or "humanae litterae" in the sense of the civic humanists, which appear through the *Furioso* as delightful fictions and nothing else? Is he, instead, or in addition, taking seriously the failures of previous poets of crisis to represent adequately, much less to influence or resolve, various moments of crisis, and thus, as we have already suggested, not only showing his own awareness of the crises of self and history, but also of a crisis in the function of poetry itself? And further, is it legitimate to pose the questions, as I have done so far, exclusively in terms of Ariosto's masterly rewriting of other texts? Is it not equally true that the *Furioso* is a pastiche, at times complacent indeed, of the Barthian *déjà lu,* the intersection of the literary, philosophical, historical, and other codes which are its context? Merely the reflection and typification of a certain time and place, a particular cultural patrimony, and not their ironic critic? These are questions which it will take the whole of this study (at least) to consider, but the *Furioso,* at least in the few stanzas so far examined, seems to sponsor the asking of them.

In any case, the methodological implications of these reflections are plain enough. It is not sufficient to found an analysis exclusively on the devious relations which the poem establishes between itself and itself, itself and its author, itself and its readers. One must also take Ariosto seriously as a reader of other poetic and nonpoetic works, and especially of the canonical "texts of crisis," and try to place the *Furioso* within a network of writings and events which form part of its historical context (and at the same time see how the poem metaphorically places or displaces those writings and events within itself).[54] In the wake of Rajna there have been nu-

---

[54] In the list of relations to be considered may be discerned the well-known scheme of M.H. Abrams, *The Mirror and the Lamp* (New York: Oxford University Press, 1953), pp. 3–29, which divides critical orientations into four categories which he orders historically as well as conceptually: (1) "mimetic," text as imitation of "nat-

merous source studies as well as occasional attempts to show how the poem faithfully mirrors, without critical reflection, certain motifs and values of the Italian Renaissance. On the other hand, the efforts directed toward exploring the extensive, ironic, critical engagement of the poem with the *topoi,* the motifs, the intellectual and ethical systems of the epoch in which it was composed, have been relatively modest. And this is not really so surprising since if the paths which lead between the *Furioso* and itself are as contorted as suggested, the ways in which the poem reads and/or rewrites other works will be at least as devious, perhaps more so. This supposition is borne out by a simple survey of the incredible variety of Ariostan sources: dozens of French and Italian romances (including Pulci and Boiardo); the "Three Crowns" (Dante, Petrarch, Boccaccio) of the early Italian tradition; Latin and Greek lyrics, epics, and dramas; Alberti's *Intercenali;* Poliziano; Castiglione; Bembo; the hermetic philosophers; the magical and astrological

---

ure"; (2) "pragmatic," text's influence on its readers; (3) "expressive," text as reflection of its author's consciousness; (4) "objective," text as object with intrinsic significance. Compare this scheme with Roman Jakobson's six-fold description of the communication situation (addresser, addressee, context, message, contact, code) in "Linguistics and Poetics," in T. Sebeok, ed., *Style in Language* (Cambridge: MIT Press, 1960). Though Jakobson has clearly been attentive to the detail of communication (Abrams collapses the last three elements into his fourth, "objective" category), he limits his treatment of poetry to the "poetic" function; i.e., to the highlighting of the "message as such." Abrams' more limited descriptive model, on the other hand, opens onto a broader concept of literature which can be examined from any one of four (or six) perspectives, each of which has been the point of departure for a poetics in the course of literary history. It is clear by now that I do not believe these aspects can ever be fully and successfully separated in reading a text; nor am I convinced that the poetics of the Renaissance are exclusively "pragmatic" in the way that Abrams indicates, though the rhetorical approach certainly does receive considerable emphasis. Although I begin my discussion of methodology by adopting the "objective" approach which is characteristic, in very different ways, of both Abrams and the "New Criticism," I hope the development of the argument has taken me beyond that position. Like Abrams, however, I am particularly interested in the poetic metaphors which govern the logic of criticism. For me, this involves the further step of considering how criticism fails to obtain the detached authority of objective "statement" and is continually implicated in the imaginative crises of the literature that it reads. I try to explore criticism and criticized objects as a semiological complex, unfolding in history, which even as I analyze, I enter into.

traditions; and so on, quite endlessly. By establishing himself as the author of a sequel, Ariosto may have surrendered his own claim to being an "origin," but his use of an astounding mixture of sources in any given episode makes it nearly impossible to determine, even momentarily, one external authority upon which the poem depends.[55] My own method will be to move between a more traditional history-of-ideas (and images) approach, using certain key Renaissance texts to illustrate and define problems which find parallel treatments in the *Furioso*, and a study of "intertextuality," the direct or oblique relations which the poem establishes with many of the same texts.

In the three longer chapters which make up the balance of this study, I will try to suggest more specifically how the *Furioso* defines itself as a text both of crisis and of evasion from crisis, as both Merlinesque and Atlantean, and how it inevitably does so in relation to classical and contemporary "texts of crisis." Chapters 2 and 3 will focus on the permutations of a certain key Renaissance theme, and its

[55] A perfect example is the Alcina-Logistilla sequence, to be examined at length in Chapter 3, which, for the motif of metamorphosis alone, draws on Ovid, Virgil, Dante, Petrarch, and others. For this technique, see n. 53 above. In general, studies of the poem tend to assign priority to one source or another in a given textual circumstance. Even Parker and Javitch are talking about the controlled play of two easily opposable sources, for instance Virgil and Ovid. Notwithstanding Parker's excellent discussion of the romance elements of the poem's structure, she also participates in the widespread practice (at least among American critics) of neglecting Ariosto's use of hundreds of specific medieval and Renaissance, French and Italian, romance sources. What I am getting at is the existence of a major difficulty for the "intertextual" reader (such as myself) who is in hot pursuit of elaborately, but not *too* elaborately, anguished traces of an "anxiety of influence," "burden of the past," or "polemical revision." The multiplicity of echoes may cleverly decrease the poet's specific indebtedness to precursors, but it also makes it harder to locate a definite object-of-interpretation, intention or structure as this may be. At a certain point, only the "simple-minded" positivism of a Rajna can cope with the proliferation of "facts" in the text, facts whose sheer number makes any operation beyond simple cataloguing an instance of reductive speculation. In any case, one must agree with C.P. Brand, *Ludovico Ariosto: A Preface to the "Orlando Furioso"* (Edinburgh: Edinburgh University Press, 1974), that "the literary tradition is in some sense the subject of the poem" (p. 56). Whether this means that the poet is writing, deliberately and masterfully, a kind of perverse "literary history," or whether it means that language itself has taken the place of authorial subjectivity, so that "speech speaks," would be difficult to say.

corresponding poetics: education, the programmatic "formazione" of the self, represented in and potentially effected through poetic form. The last chapter will then concentrate on the counterthemes and structures which continually haunt the possibility of education and which offer both negative subversions of and positive alternatives to it: on the one hand, the threats of madness and death to the well-formed Renaissance self, the collapse of allegorical reference into fantastic nonsense, the sharp contrast between poetic characters and the historical personages they are meant both to represent and to instruct; on the other, the hope of a wise folly, *in bono*, and the resurgence of faith in a life beyond physical death, the recovery of the divine Word which transcends the failures of human language, as well as the possibility of a triumphant intersection of poetry and history at poem's end.

Chapter 2 will prepare a double context, before and after, for the *Furioso:* in the first place, an introduction to Renaissance texts and traditions of education of which it is an engaged reader (sections i and ii); in the second place, a survey of the critical tradition which has read it and hypothesized a variety of apparently contradictory links between it and the Renaissance (sections iii and iv). The goal of this chapter is twofold, in keeping with the double method of contextualization just defined: both to assemble the historical tools and terms which *my* reading of the poem requires and to suggest that the poem itself is a reading, a series of readings actually, and not just of precursor texts of crisis, but also, proleptically, of the possible critical responses it will call forth.

The first section shows how deliberately the *Furioso* in its very title, and through its two principal male heroes, is connected with a crucial and extraordinarily complex emblem of choice (will) and understanding (intellect): Hercules. Around this figure, as we shall see, clusters a great deal of humanistic discourse on autonomous human identity, as well as the rhetorical–pedagogical formation thereof. For instance, the son of Jove is allegorically appropriated both by "civic humanist" promoters of the active (political) life and by neo-Platonic polemicists in favor of contemplative transcendence. At the same time, however, Hercules also bears within himself the potential for madness which is the limit and threat to either kind of education. From the very first, the poem links itself to the interpenetrating questions of folly and self-fashioning as posed throughout the early and high Renaissance in Italy. The following section goes on to elaborate further (though still incompletely, symptomatically) a Renaissance context of self-definition through reading and writing. It does not do this by giving fixed images of *the* Renaissance idea of pedagogy, but instead by turning to a number of key authors and crucial motifs who (and which) not only provide a variety of models for poets to use or abuse, but also themselves already both problematize models alternative to their own and give rise to obvious internal contradictions. If I then focus on the "impegno civile" of rhetorical culture and the neo-Platonic return to philosophical mysticism as the two poles of "humanistic" discourse in the age of Ariosto, it is only with the awareness of various intermediate gradations and with the knowledge that historical practices often contradicted the theoretical pronouncements of either camp. In this section I will make only perfunctory gestures toward tying these ideas, values, and texts to the *Furioso* itself since (a) the title alone suffices for that purpose and (b) the subsequent chapter will take up that task with a vengeance.

The second half of Chapter 2 turns from what Ariosto was reading and rewriting to the maze of readings of the poem which have linked it with one or another aspect of historical context, whether as exemplar or ironic subverter, whether as engaged educator or purveyor of nonsensical folly. I will then suggest that this heterogeneous assemblage of contextualizations is strong evidence that the poem in fact incorporates a wide variety of Renaissance positions into a powerful dialectical structure which supports an equal variety of (partial) interpretations. Finally, in the fourth section, I will turn to another of Ariosto's works, his *Satira* vi, which explicitly addresses the theory and practice of education (and its relation to poetry) in the Italian Renaissance. This section will in a sense duplicate, but also elaborate, the function of the first section: to assess and delineate Ariosto's engagement with the key issues of education. But it will also have another function: to argue that this poem actually constitutes a critical, and in some ways quite ungenerous, reading of the *Furioso* as failed didactic instrument—to show that Ariosto himself was the first critic of the poem to raise the issue of whether it is neo-Platonic or secularly humanistic in orientation, whether it proposes to effect ethical-metaphysical instruction or to indulge in aesthetic retreat from any didactic engagement with the reader and the world.

Taken in its entirety, this chapter opens the way to an interpretation of the *Furioso* both as retrospective reading of its historical-textual context and as prospective prophecy of how it too will be read. At the same time, though from the opposite direction, it will show the written boundaries which have "determined," before and after, the meanings of the poem, circumscribing its freedom to signify. Strange as the concept of the poem prophesying the criticism which will be written about it may seem, it is actually only an extension of the assumption that if a poet sets out to change and educate his readers, he must have an implicit idea of how they will go about reading it. In the case of this poet and poem, as we already saw in relation to Cassandra's tapestry, that idea is a difficult and not wholly positive one—just as the poem's vision of *itself* as reader and rewriter allows for the same unoriginality and willful blindness that it attributes to its critics and predecessors.

Chapter 3 takes up this challenge by examining in detail a single, protracted, narrative segment of the poem: the Alcina-Logistilla sequence, usually known as the "Alcina episode" for reasons which will be examined. In those pages readers are confronted with the extended schooling of one of the poem's main characters in the reading of the "texts" both of history and of poetic fantasy. Ariosto defines the acquisition of knowledge of self and others as a problem of interpretive epistemology, and hence of reading in the broadest sense. Thus as Ruggiero's education is dramatized (and subverted), it will also reflect on Ariosto's own situation as poetic pedagogue, as well as on those of other poets, critics, and educators, not to mention his and their own readers. The episode contrasts the "seduction" of Ruggiero into stuporous erotic oblivion by Alcina with his subsequent "education" by Melissa and Logistilla to self-awareness and virtue. Both, in a sense, are attempts to *protect* a part of his identity with the sacrifice of another: the first, a vain effort to forestall death and the loss of physical being; the second, an attempt to promote displaced survival in name and family at the cost of a premature demise on the literal level. At the same time, at least two versions of educational formation clash around Ruggiero, making the crisis of choosing between them as pressing as that of turning toward reason as against folly and forgetting. In fact, each of these programs thinks of the other precisely as seductively utopian madness. On the one hand is the neo-Platonic project, culminating in Ficino and Landino, of a solitary, inward, contemplative *paideia*, a self-realization first by self-knowledge and then, paradoxically, by self-forgetfulness in a union with God, which requires that the self be sheltered from contaminating, fragmenting contact with history (including marriage, political and marital duty, and so on). On the other hand are the civic humanists for whom education is precisely the bringing of the individual into dynamic, creative relation with its community and the abandonment of empty philosophical speculation and sterile isolation. Both, however, lead again to the paradox of an identity formed by means of a certain *loss* of self, in others, or in the Other. The chapter's focus will thus be on the construction of a self, but in terms of its relation (negative or positive as may be) to "reality," whether material and historical or intellectual and transcendent, and above all its relation to the images, signs, words which always mediate any encounter with either of these realities. I will thus be concerned with how evasion and crisis are represented, but also with the status of representation itself—how it too is a form of crisis and evasion for poet and readers alike. The question, however, is not merely *how* a crisis in language envelops poetic representation, but how, paradoxically, that representation clearly refers to the crisis which threatens to overtake it. I will thus, in a sense, refuse to privilege the "metarepresentational" over the "representational," the structural over the thematic, as "postmodern" criticism has taught us to. Instead I see them as engaged in a dialectic and convergence in which the structural is brought within the domain of the thematic (if not by the poet, then by the critic) while representation is being examined critically in terms of the structures that both comprise and compromise it.

Chapter 4 will "conclude," though not definitively or briefly, by trying to show both how the "Alcina" episode and the earlier chapters dedicated to it give us a way of reading other segments of the poem *and* the poem "as a whole" and how readings of those segments then qualify, perhaps even abolish, that earlier perspective. Thus each narrative area is seen as both interpreted by and the interpreter of the other zones of the poem. The first two sections of this chapter focus, respectively, on Astolfo's revision of Ruggiero's education and the cure of Orlando's madness in the "lunar episode," and on that same folly of Orlando which destroys utterly all the values of reason and of language so explicitly developed through Astolfo and Ruggiero. Astolfo and Orlando set the extreme limits of transcendence and madness to Ruggiero's journey. The next two sections, then, will focus in on the poet-narrator, no longer as "teacher" or "entertainer" trying to form his readers' identities or to help them forget themselves, but rather as a man trying to express his own identity, or to create it, through poetic language, himself menaced by the two main threats to human selfhood—madness and death. There I will suggest that poetry becomes equally a way for the authorial self to survive psychic crisis and physical demise *and* a sign of its unarrestable disappearance into a *furor poeticus* and a symbolic tomb. Finally, the chapter will return to the poem's last canto in order to test the narrator's claim to have brought his literary vessel safely into the port of history, for a decisive encounter with the readers who are also its subject matter. The figure of Ippolito d'Este, patron and privileged audience of the poem, ostensibly the climactic product of its genealogical plot, becomes the key to understanding the limits of that claim. Ippolito's life, celebrated in Cassandra's tapestry, gathers to itself the accumulated series of genealogical *encomia* and historical panegyrics, but also crystallizes the underlying sense of political-ethical crisis in early *Cinquecento* Italy. Above all, Ippolito's name becomes the focal point of the celebration and critique of *cavalleria* as horsemanship and heroic selfhood, kept alive through the poem-long imagery of horses reined and running mad, by its tacit and yet immensely powerful evocation of the tragic myth of Hippolytus.

In the first place these readings will afford me the luxury of expanding still further beyond the basic theme of selfhood realized and evaporated, respectively, in education and madness to show more fully the importance of other areas of thematic and textual crisis: particularly those of the religious faith and/or political engagement of the poem and poet. The poet's role as legitimate celebrator of a political dynasty and commentator on contemporary political events is tested against the possibilities of lying poetic flattery and deliberate falsification of history (caused *either* by the poet's desire for economic gain *or* by his fear of harsh political repression). Similarly, faith, which is a mode of knowledge alternative to reason and which, in some sense, can combine deepest blindness with profoundest insight, is itself encroached upon by a widening ironic skepticism which not only undermines our faith in the authority of the poet who employs it, but even threatens to engulf the Gospels themselves, only to discover that a radical skepticism throws open the doors once more to faith.

And, as the last chapter widens the thematic horizons of the poem, it will also widen our sense of the variety of poetic possibilities entertained or enacted in the *Furioso,* particularly by its survey of disparate figures of the poet, reader, and poem. Throughout, and most particularly at the end, this study is in a relation of polemic and development with one of the important treatments of the *Furioso* in the last twenty years: that of Robert Durling in *The Figure of the Poet in Renaissance Epic,* with its pioneering description of the poet-narrator's self-presentation within the confines of the text itself.[56] That book, in a sense, both epitomizes and transcends the repeated efforts of critics to find a single coherent character, or group of characters linked by a single coherent perspective, which embodies the unity of the poem. Momigliano makes the labyrinthine castle of Atlante into a figure of the poem, and Atlante into the figure of the poet. A.B. Giamatti sees Astolfo as the blithe double of Ariosto.[57] Mary M. Farrell finds a series of "mentors and magi" standing in for the poet, although all seem to converge on a theory of poetry not so far from that of Giamatti's Astolfo.[58] Saccone, in one of the more surprising and suggestive moments of recent criticism, wishes to see the constantly scattered and recomposed Orrilo as the figure of the poet repeatedly turned into an idol or fetish by his readers and thereby dismembered.[59] Most important of all, however, is Durling's essay, which concentrates on the explicit appearances and interventions of the narrator in the poem and unifies that rhetorical presence around the concept of the

[56] One of Durling's special contributions was to take up the hint of DeBlasi and, for the first time, systematically identify the rhetorical appearances of an "I" in the text. In doing so, he also made remarkably useful strides in the way of showing the crucial role played by proems, which introduce each canto with an authorial comment or aside.

[57] Giamatti, *The Earthly Paradise,* pp. 140–41.

[58] Farrell, "Mentors and Magi," p. 75 et passim.

[59] Saccone, "Il Soggetto," p. 242.

author as creative Demiurge, giving immanent textual substance to Croce's transcendent author-God.

On the other hand, if Durling offers a proper correction to Croce's anachronistic Hegelian metaphysics of *Armonia* and poetic transcendence, Croce provides a view of the poet's relationship to his characters and his text that, in turn, invites modifications of *The Figure of the Poet*. Croce argues that the names which populate the poem are not properly characters at all, but fragmented and partial "figures," heterogeneous metaphors for the many aspects of a single integral self which authored the poem.[60] With this analysis I would agree, while quarreling with its directionality. It seems to me, with Durling, that it is not possible to arrive at the extratextual One who subsumes the intratextual Many. But it also seems to me, with Croce, that, though the poetic "I" of the rhetorical narrator may be the most explicit poet-figure, it is by no means the only one, nor does it dominate all the others (in fact, it is frequently subverted by them). Saccone's essay, "Il Soggetto del *Furioso*," plays on the multiple meanings of the word "subject" to show that if the poet is a controlling subjective creator, in either Durling's sense or in Croce's, he is also the "subject" matter of the poem and is subjected to and dispersed throughout the work.[61] I will be arguing, in a related vein, that the "unified" figure of the poet is constantly disappearing into the multiple and radically divergent versions of the author scattered through the text, among which are figures of blindness and betrayal profoundly at odds with the usual effortless, godlike, mastery assigned to Ariosto. At the same time, no one of these characters escapes the ironic qualifications of the narrator to become itself *the* figure of the poet. And as the "figures of the poet" are dispersed precisely by the ironic relations between them, so too they tend to disappear into the equally numerous figures of the text: Atlante into his labyrinth, Alcina behind her veil, Astolfo into a tree, Merlin into his tomb. Special importance will be given to the recurrent image of poem as tomb which both serves as a monument

[60] Croce, "Ariosto," pp. 49–50.

[61] More generally on the problem of the "subject(s)" of writing, see Jacques Derrida, "Edmond Jabès and the Question of the Book," in *Writing and Difference* (Chicago: University of Chicago Press, 1978), esp. p. 65.

to the memory of its author and marks definitively his absence from the text, the death which long ago sealed the separation of living self from its written creation. And in canto XLVI we will see the last and perhaps most curious of Ariosto's estranged and "buried" doubles: Cassandra, weaver and prophetess; to her Trojan "readers," a comical madwoman. She and her pavilion, like Ariosto and his poem, are doomed to misinterpretation. At the same time, the reader loses himself in what he reads: Orlando is driven mad by his reading of the poem written by Medoro. Thus the representations of representation succeed only in opening up an extended series of related crises of representation. The last question of all will be whether or not the final canto permits us to close the book in any but a literal sense and end our interpretation by assigning a definitive meaning, or lack of meaning, to the *Furioso*. I will be considering what "end," both as "closure" and as "purpose," is offered to Ariosto's long wanderings away from and into crisis. To the very last I will be asking: Is there a perspective of critical judgment from which evaders can be brought back to confront the truth and from which crisis can be measured and resolved?

In the course of these pages, the reader will have noted, the word "crisis" has appeared repeatedly, and perhaps by very force of repetition this already too familiar concept may have begun to lose its customary sense. At any rate, I both hope and fear that this is the case, because it is precisely the relation of crisis to meaning that is at issue here.[62] Does a crisis jeopardize meaning or produce it? Does it produce meaning *by* jeopardizing it? It will become increasingly apparent in the next three chapters that there are many ways in

---

[62] Among the many influences on my use of the word "crisis" are Frank Kermode's *tour de force*, *The Sense of an Ending* (New York: Oxford University Press, 1967); the concept of "sacrificial crisis" developed by René Girard in *Violence and the Sacred* (Baltimore: The Johns Hopkins University Press, 1977); and Paul DeMan's subtle essay, "Criticism and Crisis," in *Blindness and Insight* (New York: Oxford University Press, 1971). All three approach crisis as a threat to and/or producer of meaning. Kermode talks about how literary closure, on analogy with Biblical Apocalypse, imposes a retrospective order or meaning for the modern consciousness which dwells in the ambiguities of ever-impending crisis. Girard argues that sacrificial crisis really conceals a crisis of communal and individual identity, and that it is by asserting one's difference from the sacrificial victim that one (arbitrarily) restores the hierarchy of

which poetry can be said to be "of crisis" and that there are many ways in which the *Furioso* invites and refuses that qualification. The title of this prelude to my study is designed to leave the relation of the poem to crisis suspended between metonymy and metaphor (as Jakobson defines them), the conjunctive "and" sponsoring either an arbitrary, even antithetical, juxtaposition or an imaginative identification of the two.[63] Here again, however, we may be confronted with a false alternative and be forced to admit that much recent criticism has erred as seriously in insisting on crisis as the "(dis)content" of the *Furioso,* as earlier critics did in contentedly dismissing it as the poem of pure art and sweet harmony.

In defense of DeSanctis' position it can (and will) be shown that the *Furioso* deliberately flaunts its differences, by allusion if not by outright parody, from more engaged poetics—such as the humanists' linking of "litterae" and "impegno civile," with its attendant rhetorical didacticism—as well as from the esoteric tradition (culminating with Pico, Landino, Ficino) of the poet as theologian, and from poems, such as the *Commedia,* of explicit political and spiritual crisis. Even if this is so, however, the travesty of crisis may itself be the naming of a crisis: a calling into question of that poetry which repeatedly fails in its earnest attempts to act constructively on history, or even to refer accurately to it, and which, try as it may to instruct its readers by showing them an exemplary picture of themselves, is constantly reduced by them to an occasion for

---

difference which gives sense to the political order and the individual self within it. Thus crisis is both the threat that meaning will disappear in undifferentiation as well as the stratagem by which meaning is renewed. DeMan argues that "crisis" is the structure of the self and of language, both dwelling in a condition of "separation." The self is "separated" from the language it deploys (through which it hopes to "identify" itself), and language is separated from the reality to which it claims to refer. Thus, "crisis" is the condition in which "meaning" exists and acknowledges its own precariousness and contingency.

[63] For the pairing of metaphor and metonymy in this way, see Jakobson, "The Metaphoric and the Metonymic Poles," in Jakobson and Halle, *Fundamentals of Language* (The Hague: Mouton, 1971). For a more complex treatment of the question, see DeMan, "Semiology and Rhetoric," *Diacritics* 3 (1973), and now in his *Allegories of Reading* (New Haven: Yale University Press, 1979).

self-forgetful entertainment. And this ironic and critical meditation upon crisis informs the poet's attitude toward itself as well, so that the *Furioso* is in many ways its own harshest critic. What the poem reflects upon is in fact the self-reflexive fracture within the poem, making criticism and crisis, as Paul DeMan has suggested, simultaneous, just as the poet images his poem as both map *and* sea.

The etymon of "crisis," Greek κρίσις, means both "separation" and "judgment," or "interpretation" (from which, naturally, comes "criticism"). So defined, the word may refer both to the fact of a rupture, an ambiguous and decisive moment, and also to the interpretive perspective which recognizes, defines, and resolves that moment. As a rupture, crisis is a threat to meaning, but as judgment or interpretation, it is that which discovers or invents meaning. It is, variously, the turmoil separating the irretrievable past of a culture from an uncertain future, and also the clear interpretive line drawn by the historiographer—for example, between the Middle Ages and the Renaissance. Or it is, at one and the same time, the paralysis of a divided consciousness and the act of judging will by which the self recognizes and asserts its identity. Finally, it is the chasm between the individual life and its death, as well as between human existence in general and apocalyptic destruction, on the one hand, and, on the other, the Last Judgment of God by which the dead are raised to eternal life and the void is filled again by "new heaven and new earth."

By jeopardizing meaning, in other words, meaning may be produced. And since it is only by interpretation that crisis as ambiguity or crux is discovered, the two can never truly themselves be separated; that is, judiciously and critically distinguished. The concept of crisis itself is in crisis. In fact, as René Girard has suggested, in another context, crisis as judgment may not elucidate a crisis which exists, but instead invent a crisis (for him the "sacrificial crisis") precisely in order to resolve it. I believe that Ariosto explores with uncommon acuity the ways in which poetry and other modes of writing, including history and philosophy, may manufacture crises for just this purpose: to recover, arbitrarily, an order and a clarity, "the sense of an ending," which cathartically, momentarily, frees poet and reader alike from the awareness that "to live is to live in crisis."[64] He suggests how the representation of crisis may become a screen to hide genuine dangers. Thus, as Girard too goes on to say, the need to discover a fictional crisis is the sign of a very different, and hidden, crisis within those who judge: within the poet who critically reads his literary and political context, and within the readers of the poet's reading. Even as "crisis" is reduced to insubstantial fiction, that fiction becomes the evidence of a "true," if always elusive, crisis. "Crisis" as such is always on the verge of entering the scene and yet never quite makes its appearance, because there is always some doubt as to the authenticity of the critical language in which it was first discerned.

Seen from this (also uncertain) perspective, perhaps the best approach to crisis is an evasive flight in the opposite direction, as in the *Furioso*. Perhaps Ariosto's literary retreat into fantastic fictions operates, as DeMan would have it, to "demystify" the inauthenticity of all language, of all human consciousness, by revealing the essential condition of separation between word and intention or word and referent, and between a self and itself. But there is more, as even DeMan's essay can be made, all unwilling, to say. DeMan seems to be positing literature as a crisis which imperils meaning or which reveals how meaning is always imperiled from within; but, as he does not go on to point out, literature can be said to jeopardize all language only if we assume that it successfully refers its own fictionality to that language, and if he, DeMan, a critic, has successfully referred to that process of reference. Meaning gives way to crisis gives way to meaning. Perhaps DeMan too is in the business of generating fictional crises in order to make some sense. In any event, it seems that it will not do to privilege the "crisis of reference" in Ariosto over possible references to various crises—historical, psychological, or literary as they may be—since any hierarchy is bound to be undercut from within. Nor will it do to assume that "crisis" in *either* sense takes precedence over, and escapes from, a counterpoetics of unjudgeable evasions.

[64] Kermode, *The Sense of an Ending*, p. 56.

2

CRITICAL READINGS OF THE
ORLANDO FURIOSO

The first impulse of this reader and this reading of *Orlando Furioso* is formalist: a rarely repressed tendency to the pleasures of close textual analysis. Nonetheless, recent critical events have made it very difficult to move directly to a thematic and/or structural interpretation of the poem's treatment of human selfhood. The last twenty years have seen the development of strong concepts of intertextuality, along with, more recently still, the emergence of a modified, "new," historicism. A literary text, we feel compelled to recognize, is composed of readings—it is the composite transcription and revision of the classical, medieval, and Renaissance texts and other cultural discourses available to it. The text is thus not "individual" in the sense of remaining intrinsically separable from its precursors, contemporaries, or sequels—what identity it has is positional, contextual, social—just as human "individuals" exist only as a confusing nexus of social, semiotic, and psychological experiences. The question is particularly pressing when dealing with the Renaissance, which has most commonly been defined precisely as a crisis in older models of human identity opening onto the felicitous discovery by European culture of the human self as creative self-consciousness, no longer the Other or shadow of divine totality. In such a view, the proof of a new "individuality" comes exactly in a perception of textual and artistic innovation: the self's failures and successes at being and becoming uniquely itself are acted out in the words of Pico's *Oratio* and the images on the Sistine Chapel ceiling.

All of these considerations militate against moving directly to a protracted study of the metaphors and narrative sequences of the *Furioso* which deal most directly with emergent or defeated selfhood. Instead, I will try to prepare a symptomatic context for the poem in the psychological/textual "identity crisis" of Ariosto's age. To begin with, this means pointing to key texts which both describe and act out the problem of human identity. It means recognizing that there has, in fact, been an ongoing crisis both in Renaissance scholarly-critical attempts to isolate the specific character of "the discovery of the self" and in efforts to define Ariosto's exact relationship—positive or negative, active or passive—to any such discovery. I will suggest, for instance, that there are at least two major versions of the educational acquisition of identity at work in the period: one, rhetorical and ethical, emphasizing the corporeal and civic life of man in this world; the other, philosophical and spiritual, emphasizing the inner intellectual life which aims to lift man beyond this world into a realm of incorporeal divinity. In addition, one cannot afford to ignore the intense awareness in the age and in the poem of that which most threatens the emergence of coherent self-consciousness under either regime: blind madness. In then preparing to apply these themes to a reading of the *Furioso,* one should not forget that the poem not only reflects or represents varieties of education and madness, but may also be said, on the evidence of Renaissance poetics, to embody or effect them. That is to say, in the first place, that for the Renaissance, education is a process of learning to read the world, one's mind, and the words which pass between them interpretively and of then expressing such acquired knowledge in speech and writing. In the second place, it is to remember that books, especially literary works, were the mediators used by teachers to effect such education. And, finally, it is to draw the obvious conclusion that Ariosto's poem almost certainly sees itself either as a successful instrument of readerly education or as its failed double, an agent of the madness which results when the educational process breaks down. In other words, not only am I going to be reading the *Furioso* through Renaissance themes, but in doing so I am going to be recognizing that interpretive reading itself is *a,* if not *the,* theme of the Renaissance and of the *Furioso.* And in this respect, one might suppose, the *Furioso* has as much to say about us as readers as we about it as reading.

The recognition that the poem might be quite aware of its rhetorical situation, its inevitable production of and subjection to the responses of a variety of readers, suggests a second way in which a text may be said to be composed of readings. In other words, even as the *Furioso* gathers together the many strands of precursor texts and codes, it is also dispersed, unraveled, into the "world, the texts, and the critics" which lie beyond itself. In particular, the poem is by now inseparable from the critical traditions which have expanded and appropriated it across the centuries. However, as with the texts which gave rise to it, so with the texts it in turn gives rise to: the *Furioso* is not merely passive; it furnishes us, as I believe, with images of a number of hypothetical readerly responses to itself—hypotheses which in the event have proven uncannily accurate. And it is for this reason that this chapter in particular, and in fact the book as a whole, dwells insistently upon the criticism of the poem—not so much as a way of defining the history of the production of my own study (its debts, its pet peeves), but rather as a means of giving evidence about the relationship between the text and its readers. I will show, on the one hand, how readerly blindness has often "deformed," however brilliantly, the themes and structures of the *Furioso* and how, on the other, the *Furioso* both deliberately provokes a range of readerly responses and then quietly comments upon the situations and the motives of critics who choose this or that partial response which the text, with such apparent generosity, makes available to them.

The bivalent genitive of my chapter heading points to the *Furioso* as a piece of writing which both reads and is read. We can use Renaissance texts as a means of reading the poem, but the poem is also a critical reading of those same texts. By the same token, critics have made readings of the *Furioso,* but the *Furioso* has its own theories about its future readers. I am attempting, in this chapter, to arrive at an understanding of the poem as "inter-text" in the widest possible sense—a text dwelling between texts, past and future. The texts are around it, as con-texts which determine and bound its significance; but, surprisingly, they are also within it, absorbed as co-texts: cited and staged, faithfully or parodically re-presented, approvingly or polemically interpreted. The four sections of this chapter dedicated to Renaissance pre-text and to critical post-text will, yes, prepare us to explore the theme of education-as-reading developed in the *Furioso.* But it will also, perhaps even more importantly, allow us to see the *Furioso* as an act of reading-as-writing, writing-as-reading which names and judges crises, even as it is being critically judged.

i. *Ariosto and the Renaissance Hercules*

In discussing the problem of selfhood in the Renaissance it always makes sense to begin with Jacob Burckhardt, who is more responsible than any other post-Renaissance author for our understanding of that epoch and even for our belief (however embattled and qualified) that such a period or event actually took place at all. It is he who most forcefully contends that Italy from the fourteenth century on was the scene of the birth, or rebirth, of the individual as autonomous, self-aware shaper of his own destiny. Curiously, and brilliantly, he associates that birth with an outburst of illegitimacy, both genealogical and political. Bastard artists (e.g., Alberti, Leonardo, and so on) and usurping princes seem to him to occupy places outside the impersonal medieval structures of family, state, and church, throwing them back on the resources of individual consciousness and personal force.[1] That these resources seemed to include the frequent use of tyrannical violence and to imply the abandonment of conventional ethics and Christian faith appeared a regrettable and yet unavoidable side-effect to Burckhardt. And if Ariosto is at all a sponsor of Burckhardtian humanism, it is only with a firm understanding of these complications and qualifications.

For a less intrinsically problematic image of the crisis in and displacement of Western selfhood in the Renaissance, one might cite, symptomatically, Georges Poulet's phenomenological thesis from *The Metamorphoses of the Circle*. He argues that the medieval, Dantean model of a theocentric and "deiform" universe in which God is a "sphere whose center is everywhere and whose circumference is nowhere" is gradually exchanged for one in which *anthropos* is the hub and pivot of his own existence, the point of reference for all other modes of being.[2] An even more comforting revision of

---

[1] Burckhardt, *Civilization,* vol. 1, pp. 27–29; vol. 2, p. 426 ff.; passim. Such figures were typically obsessed with achieving legitimacy and integration. Witness Alberti's *Libri della Famiglia,* with all the historical pathos and irony of Alberti's ill-treatment by his relatives, as well as the genealogical myths fostered by great ruling families, including the Este, and propagated by poets and scholars, for instance Ariosto.

[2] Poulet, *The Metamorphoses of the Circle* (Baltimore: The Johns Hopkins University Press, 1966), p. xvii ff. For the human body as metaphorical point of reference for describing the cosmos in the Renaissance, see Leonard Barkan, *Nature's*

Burckhardt allows for the emergence of human personality without the loss of Christian faith in deity. Charles Trinkaus has cogently fastened on the metaphor of man formed "in the image and likeness" of God to temper and perhaps to overthrow the claim of a radical shift in perspective from the God who becomes man to the Renaissance man who becomes, or rather makes himself, a god.[3] One might add that the very concept of Renaissance is itself in part an appropriation and transfiguration of a (not exclusively) Christian motif of resurrection.[4] In any case, for Trinkaus this image of creation allows the humanistic exaltation of man insofar as he is a distant figure of true divinity, which continues to be the one true source of identity.

In spite of the impressive mass of evidence assembled by Trinkaus for his claim, it is nonetheless true that there is an easy parodic inversion which might be made (and some Renaissance authors, Pico for example, might seem to have made it), so that God suddenly appears as the image and likeness of man, the cosmic projection of human form and human aspirations to totality. Ariosto criticism has, in any event, tended to associate its *auctor* with the theory of a radical break, as in these words of Caretti: "for medieval theocentric cosmography, Ariosto definitively substituted an anthropomorphic cosmography in which the center is, at any moment, freely variable."[5] Begging for

---

Work of Art (New Haven: Yale University Press, 1975). By a curious historical irony, soon after man is supposed to have displaced God from the center of the universe, a (related) cosmological revolution resulted in the replacement of the earth by the sun (traditional figure of deity) at the center of the physical cosmos. Cf. Chapter 3, n. 109, below.

[3] Trinkaus, *In Our Image and Likeness* (Chicago: University of Chicago Press, 1970), esp. vol. I, pp. xiii–xxiv. By tracing the tradition of *dignitas hominis* back to Saint Augustine, Trinkaus demystifies its alleged origins in classicist secularism.

[4] See, as one good example out of many, Leonardo Bruni Aretino, *Dialoghi,* in Garin, ed., *Prosatori Latini,* esp. p. 46. Bruni, following a medieval *topos* common to Chaucer, Boccaccio, and Dante, sets his work in the Easter season, the time of Christ's Resurrection, but in such a way as to make the metaphor reflect on the rebirth of books and of classical learning. See also nn. 56 and 85 below.

[5] I translate from Caretti, "Ariosto," p. 35. On the question of Ariosto's religiosity or lack thereof, see Chapter 4, sec. i (esp. nn. 31, 45), below. In the next chapter I will show that the *Furioso* itself deploys the image of the circle ironically (cf. Chapter 3, nn. 105–109 and 155–156, below).

the time being the question (to which I will return in Chapter 4) of whether Ariosto in some way recuperates a stable origin for the self outside of the circlings of Time and Fortuna, one must now ask whether his apparent reflections of and on the crisis in medieval models of effaced selfhood are actually accompanied by the positive emergence of a (semi)autonomous Renaissance self.

The obvious place to begin discussing the representation of human identity in the *Furioso* is with the question of characterization. If one does so, however, a problem arises almost immediately, and it comes from an unexpected source: Burckhardt himself. Burckhardt draws evidence for his thesis from numerous areas of human endeavor (not only political and artistic, but economic, ethical, and so on), but literature seems to present him with special difficulties. Petrarch and Dante provide relatively strong, though still contestable, pre-Renaissance proofs in a chapter entitled "The Discovery of Man: Spiritual Description in Poetry."[6] But the assertiveness of this claim is undermined precisely when he arrives at the "High Renaissance," the time when "individualism" should have been at its apogee, and Burckhardt is forced to confess that "the chief reproach made against the heroic poetry of Italy is precisely on the score of the insignificance and imperfect representation of its characters."[7] It further turns out that Ariosto, as the greatest poet of the period, is also the most notable example of this apparent failure (p. 322), which might instead be interpreted as a failure in, or at least an invitation to the modification of, Burckhardt's thesis. Surely more evidence is required before accepting the great historian's summary judgment of the *Furioso*. It is worth noting, however, that if he is accurate, or at least relevant, it means that when we speak of a "crisis of identity" in the poem, it is no longer just the self's identity, but also, in some sense, the identity of an historical epoch, both as it was then perceived and as it is now.

In a number of ways the critics of Ariosto have reaffirmed, though

---

[6] Vol. 1, pp. 303–23.

[7] Vol. 2, pp. 303, 318. For a survey of the chronological development of the concept of a Renaissance, in historical writings from Petrarch to the present, see Wallace Ferguson, *The Renaissance in Historical Thought* (Boston: Houghton-Mifflin, 1948).

usually in more euphemistic terms, the judgment of Burckhardt on the failures of or indifference to characterization in the poem.[8] It is one of the commonplaces of the criticism that Orlando's role is noticeably diminished with respect to Boiardo's treatment of him (he makes his first real appearance of the poem in the eighth canto), while his place as hinge of the plot is at least partly appropriated by Ruggiero. Ruggiero, however, is something of a cypher, a frequently mechanical hero whose subjectivity is generally closed to the reader and whose heroic deeds never really lift him beyond the mass of lesser heroes in the poem, who are distinguished one from the other primarily by name.[9] Angelica, so vividly present in the *Innamorato*, has here become "that obscure object of desire," having, even when stark naked, no special identity beyond the projected images of her many lovers' blind longings. Even Rodomonte, the arch-pagan, is subject to radical shifts in mood and behavior, apparently according to the poet's whim and the logic of the narration. Locally, each of these judgments can be contested, and there are numerous characters and episodes which could be cited as counterexamples, although fairly subtle critical reasoning is required.[10] Nonetheless, the very multiplicity of characters, and the general predominance of narrative exigencies over autonomy of characterization, militate against the emergence in the *Furioso* of a "fully represented self."

More to the point, the *Orlando Furioso* takes a spectacular failure of identity as the occasion for its title. The argument that this title is inappropriate for the work as a whole, first raised by the *Cinquecento* commentators of Ariosto,[11] rather than vitiating this observation, merely signals another notably schizophrenic feature of the text,

---

[8] See, for instance, Greene, *The Descent from Heaven* (New Haven: Yale University Press, 1963), esp. pp. 129, 141; Carne-Ross, "One and Many," p. 225; Caretti, "Ariosto," p. 31.

[9] As early as Foscolo, "Poemi Narrativi," pp. 130, 146, we find a lament for the woodenness of Ruggiero, Bradamante, and the whole genealogical plot.

[10] Peter DeSa Wiggins makes a spirited assault on the standard judgment of Ariostan characterization in "Galileo on Characterization in the *Orlando Furioso*," *Italica* 57 (1980).

[11] E.g., Simone Fornari, "Apologia," in *Spositione sopra l'"Orlando Furioso"* (Firenze: 1549), p. 43.

jeopardizing the poem's "identity" along with that of its characters. In any case, there is one central episode of the poem, Orlando's lapse into folly, which certainly does confound both of the classical signs of human distinctiveness and dignity: *oratio* and *ratio,* speech and reason.[12] This madness is, in both narrative and numerical terms, recounted at the very center of the poem (cantos XXIII–XXIV of forty-six).[13] Thus, the poem not only confirms Burckhardt's judgment about its failure to represent individuality, it does so explicitly and deliberately, implying that this apparent failure is actually a successfully realized artistic choice.

Ironically, this very deliberateness, this evident choosing, seems to allow for a swing back in the opposite direction, in support of Burckhardt's broader hypothesis. We have already seen in the previous chapter that, for Croce, Ariosto's characters are not properly characters at all, but fragmented and partial "figures." He then as-

[12] See Chapter 4, secs. ii–iii, below, for a closer examination of this question. In general for the motif of *oratio/ratio* (or eloquence/wisdom, or word/idea) in the Renaissance, see Jerrold Seigel, *Rhetoric and Philosophy in Renaissance Humanism* (Princeton: Princeton University Press, 1968). On p. xi, Seigel shows that at various times Cicero, key figure for the humanists, defined man by both of these terms (cf. *De Oratore* I.viii, *De Officiis* I.50) and usually insisted on the need to unite rhetorical eloquence with wisdom (Seigel, pp. xv, 7–8; cf. Curtius, *European Literature,* p. 70). In the *Phaedrus,* Socrates advocates roughly the same thing, but in the context of an anti-Sophist, anti-rhetoric polemic. These are the terms in which the early humanist antiphilosophy, pro-rhetoric polemics (especially that of Lorenzo Valla) should be seen, as well as the later *Quattrocento* efforts to unite poetic-rhetorical surface and hidden philosophical content in a "theologia poetica" (cf. Landino, "Proemio," p. 118, on "sapienza" and "eloquenza" together as the proper of man). Even the neo-Platonists, however, had, in a sense, to admit that speech alone was unique to man (the angels, creatures of pure *ratio,* having no need for language). The parodic flip-side of these attempts to define the "human" is the Aristotelian characterization of man as the animal who laughs (*Parts of Animals,* trans. A.L. Peck [Cambridge: Harvard University Press, 1961], bk. III.10) which has its most famous Renaissance reprise in Rabelais, "Aux Lecteurs" preceding *Gargantua* (see *Oeuvres Complètes,* ed. P. Jourda [Paris: Garnier, 1962], vol. 1, p. 3).

[13] The episode is alone at the center only in the third and final edition of the *Furioso.* In the forty-canto 1516 and 1521 editions, the madness of Orlando commences in canto XXI, rather than XXIII. The original canto XX (which in 1532 becomes XXII) focused on Ruggiero and Bradamante, climaxing with the latter's mad vengeance on Pinabello. Thus, the first center of the poem was designed to balance the two main plot lines (which the last edition does by other means), even as it was already zeroed in on the representation of folly.

serts that "the characters of Ariosto take liberties with themselves, according to the situations they run into."[14] Curiously, Croce's use of the word "libertà" may suggest that fragmentation and the possibility of self-contradiction are actually conditions of one sort of freedom: the freedom of self-difference which is in fact a prerequisite for the "freedom of choice" by which the coherently integrated self is constituted. And this is precisely the tack that Croce implicitly takes in asserting that the many "figures" within the poem are metaphors for aspects of the single integral self which produced the *Furioso*. To put it in slightly different terms, the very act of choosing to reflect upon madness suggests the existence of a free will and a lucid understanding, an autonomous authorial self. In this way, madness would be excluded in the process of elegantly and rationally naming it. Perhaps by subjecting the claims of other Renaissance authors about human rationality and dignity to the degradation of bestial *furor,* Ariosto both subverts and obliquely confirms them.

I will come back later and often to the many post-Crocean attempts to submit the multiplicities of the text and its characters to the oneness of the author, as well as to the few critics who, like Donato, have questioned the phenomenological leap from plural text to unified consciousness. For now, however, it is enough to notice, on the one hand, that the text repeatedly dramatizes madness as the dissociation of the self from itself ("non son, non sono io quel che paio in viso" XXIII.128.1) and from its language, suggesting possible ruptures between the author and *his* linguistic products. On the other hand, one also has to admit that the text itself is subject to a further split: even as it represents Orlando's madness as a possible version of Ariosto's, it also charts the education, the apparent self-becoming, of Ruggiero.[15] In fact, madness and education, the loss and acquisition of human identity, contribute to defining each other throughout the poem and the Renaissance. Inhuman, bestial madness is what one escapes in a successful human-

---

[14] I translate from Croce, "Ariosto," pp. 49–50.

[15] Giamatti, "Headlong Horses, Headless Horsemen," is one of the two critics most successful in establishing the connection between the two heroes (who, after all, are the foci of the two main narrative lines of the poem). Saccone, "Il Soggetto," is the other. In Chapter 4 I will add to their accounts and factor in Astolfo as a third term.

istic education. The self acquired or remembered through education is what one forgets in order to go mad. And of course some authors, St. Paul for example, and Ariosto's contemporary, Erasmus, are perfectly capable of conflating the two, both in the mad wisdom of the philosophers and in the wise folly of the Christians, as we shall see more clearly in Chapter 4. They suggest provisionally what the following pages hope to show: namely, that the two activities never quite fight clear of one another, each remaining as an immanent possibility within, and as a condition of possibility for, the other, in a perpetual dialectic of reason and irrationality, speech and silence, humanity and monstrosity.

One can give preliminary definition to the symbolic relation between Orlando and Ruggiero by showing that, for all their obvious differences, they are bound together in a single emblematic silhouette: the towering figure of Hercules, through which are acted out the dialectic of education and madness, the convergence of the poem and its epoch, and, finally, the union of the two main characters, all at once. The emblematic force of Hercules for the Renaissance has been amply charted and celebrated. Perhaps more than any single figure, Hercules displays the qualities which scholars repeatedly seize on as exemplary of the "novelty" of a supposed cultural rebirth, which is also a birth of consciousness. Panofsky's classic iconographical study, *Hercules am Scheidewege,* has been followed up on by the books and articles of several important historians and literary critics who have continued to bring out the multiple aspects under which the strongest of human heroes is represented throughout the period.[16] What makes Hercules such a potent figure? First of all, he is the divinized man, a man who reaches heaven and immortality by force of his own *virtus;* that is

[16] Erwin Panofsky, *Hercules am Scheidewege* (Leipzig: B.G. Teubner, 1930). See also, Franco Gaeta, "L'Avventura d'Ercole," *Rinascimento* 5 (1954); G.K. Galinsky, *The Herakles Theme* (Totowa, N.J.: Rowman & Littlefield, 1972), esp. pp. 185–230; Marc-René Jung, *Hercule dans la Littérature Française du XVIe Siècle* (Genève: Droz, 1966); T.E. Mommsen, "Petrarch and the Story of the Choice of Hercules," in *Medieval and Renaissance Studies* (Ithaca: Cornell University Press, 1959). Also of interest are E. Tietze-Conrat, "Notes on Hercules at the Crossroads," *Journal of the Warburg and Courtauld Institutes* 14 (1951); and Eugene Waith, *The Herculean Hero* (London: Chatto & Windus, 1962).

according to the etymology of the day, by his own male human-ity.[17] His apotheosis leaves room for the interpretations either of secular humanism or of neo-Platonism. As the successful completer of twelve (actually many more) onerous labors, Hercules stands out as the active worker *par excellence,* whose labor for the earthly community brings him humanistic "gloria."[18] In the *Momus* of Alberti, Hercules is borne to heaven by Fama, his eternity appar-ently consisting in a nominal survival of his glorious name.[19] Landino, instead, represents him as the allegorical achiever of true spiritual nobility through philosophical askesis. Part of his power is as a figure who combines active engagement in civic affairs with a reflective philosophical intelligence, capable of resolving the con-troversy over the relative values of active and contemplative lives, as well as those of virtue and knowledge.[20] Above all, however, he dramatizes over and over again, for both camps, the force of

[17] Mommsen, "Choice of Hercules," p. 194, cites Petrarch's appropriation for the new humanism of Cicero's etymological derivation of *virtus* from *vir,* so that virtue equals (male) "humannness" (see *Familiares* XIII.2 in *Rerum Familiarum Libri,* eds. V. Rossi and U. Bosco, vols. 10–13 in Edizione Nazionale delle Opere di Francesco Petrarca [Firenze: Sansoni, 1933–1942]; cf. Cicero, *Tusculan Disputations* II.xviii.43). See also Saccone, "Il Soggetto," p. 219; Galinsky, *Herakles,* p. 190, on Hercules as "exemplar virtutis," with a long list of mythographical sources for that epithet. The shift from the Hercules of the Middle Ages to that of the Renaissance is usually seen as one from an allegorical emblem of Christ, the God become man, to a figure of man's potential for realizing the divine in himself. See Jung, *Hercule,* p. 7 (citing Pierre Bersuire, *Ovidius Moralizatus*) for the medieval position, as well as Garin, *L'Educazione in Europa,* pp. 91–92. For Hercules' qualified status as man-god, in pious deference to the one true God and even the angels, see Coluccio Salutati, *De Laboribus Herculis,* ed. B.L. Ullman (Zurich: Thesaurus Mundi, 1951), bk. III.v (vol. 1, pp. 176–77). See also n. 21, below.

[18] Felice Battaglia, "Introduzione," in *Il Pensiero Pedagogico del Rinascimento* (Firenze: Sansoni e Giuntine, 1960), pp. 23–24. Cf. Gaeta, "Ercole," p. 227 ff.

[19] Leon Battista Alberti, *Momus,* ed. and trans. G. Martini (Bologna: Zanichelli, 1942), pp. 43–45. For the parodic force of this episode see Chapter 3, sec. iv, below.

[20] Cristoforo Landino, *De Vera Nobilitate,* ed. M. Lentzen (Genève: Droz, 1970), esp. pp. 107–110, where he employs Hercules as an emblem of contemplative askesis. Cf. *Disputationes,* Lohe edition, p. 32, where he has "Lorenzo" use Hercules as a figure of the active life in his debate with "Alberti." Cf. Salutati, *De Laboribus Herculis* III.xi (vol. 1, pp. 211–12), where he allegorizes the killing of Chiron as the ascent from active to contemplative lives.

the human will in shaping its own destiny, particularly through the well-known allegory of a youthful moral choice at a crossroads between Virtue and Vice, a choice which seems to exceed, even to contradict outright, the Christian notion that human will originally fell out of edenic perfection exactly because of misguided choice and excessive human aspiration. Perhaps it was precisely this emphasis on will, however, which attracted the "father" of Christian humanism, Coluccio Salutati, to dedicate to Hercules his *magnum opus* (incomplete), the *De Laboribus Herculis*.[21] The multitude and relative incoherence of Hercules' deeds apparently make him a far less tractable object of allegorizing than most Ovidian characters, or than the epic heroes, Ulysses and Aeneas, for that matter. Mythographers from Cicero to Boccaccio speculated that there was really more than one "Hercules" responsible for all the various legends.[22] On the other hand, this very multiplicity in the figure, ranging from philosophical wisdom to brute force, from apotheosis to bestial madness, also makes it a strong symbol of human comprehensiveness, of man's ability to extract unity from a variety of outer experiences and inner contradictions.

[21] The importance of Hercules *in bivio* and the related image of the Pythagorean "Y" was established by Panofsky. See also Mommsen and Tietz-Conrat. The standard source is Cicero, *De Officiis* I.xxxii.18 (cf. III.v.25), who cites Xenophon, *Memorabilia* II.i.21–24, who in turn cites the pre-Socratic Prodicus. The most commonly cited literary use of the image is Aeneas' choice between Orcus to the left and the Elysian Fields to the right (*Aeneid* VI.540–43; cf. Landino's reading of the *Aeneid* in *Disputationes*, bks. III–IV, esp. p. 247 in Lohe edition). According to Mommsen, Petrarch was the first to conflate the two images ("Choice of Hercules," p. 181). For versions of the motif, see Petrarch, *Secretum*, in *Prose*, ed. G. Martellotti (Milano and Napoli: Ricciardi, 1955), bk. III, p. 130; in the same volume, *De Vita Solitaria* I.ii.2 (p. 332) and II.xiii.4 (p. 550). See also Salutati, *De Laboribus Herculis* III.vii, xi, xv (vol. I, pp. 182, 214, 249). Regarding possible anti-Christian implications of the figure, see Panofsky, *Hercules*, p. 164; Mommsen, "Choice of Hercules," p. 194; Mazzeo, *Renaissance and Revolution*, p. 55. Trinkaus, *Image and Likeness* (vol. 1, p. 194, and vol. 2, p. 660), objects that the Renaissance emphasis on will was neo-Augustinian and hardly precluded Christianity, as Salutati's attempts to reconcile the two demonstrate. For overviews of Salutati's philosophy of the will and its importance for the period, see Garin, *L'Umanesimo*, pp. 35–42; and Trinkaus, *Image and Likeness*, vol. 1, p. 51 ff.

[22] Cicero, *De Natura Deorum* III.xvi; Salutati, *De Laboribus Herculis* III.i (vol. I, pp. 164–66); Boccaccio, *Genealogie Deorum Gentilium Libri*, ed. V. Romano (Bari: Laterza, 1951), bk. II.ix (vol. I, pp. 80–81) and bk. XIII.i (vol. 2, p. 638).

The importance of Hercules for the *Furioso* was apparently first noticed by one of Ariosto's earliest critics, G.B. Pigna, in *I Romanzi*. Pigna, as various modern scholars have reminded us, identified a clear echo of Seneca's *Hercules Furens* (alongside that of Boiardo's poem) in the title.[23] Orlando, in effect, is under the sign of Hercules from the very beginning of the work. Moreover, as Saccone has recently made apparent, Hercules is a focal point of the poem-long dialectical relationship, of analogy and opposition, between Orlando and Ruggiero.[24] As we shall see later on, both heroes are allusively identified with a number of mythological and literary figures (notably Perseus), while their dialectic is structured not only through mythic echoes, but also through parallel experiences, settings, imagery, and so on. Nonetheless, the Herculean chiasmus of the title has the privilege of inaugurating and forecasting much that is to follow.

The assimilation of Ruggiero to Hercules, though it commences later than Orlando's, is no less clear. It has been known since the *Cinquecento* that Ruggiero's choice between the easy, if "sinister," road to Alcinian vice and the rightward, right-thinking mountain path to Logistillan virtue recalls the Pythagorean "Y" and Hercules at the Crossroads (VI.55), and also that his effeminate collapse in the hands of Alcina is akin to Hercules' subjection to Omphale, queen of Lydia.[25] Saccone accurately, though sketchily, places these iconographical moments within a larger pattern of the pursuit of identity via a kind of education, arguing that Ruggiero's story as a whole is a kind of *Bildungsroman avant la lettre*. As I will show in Chapter 3, Ruggiero rehearses didactic patterns more peculiar to the Renaissance and its literature in the course of a full-blown "allegory of education," and in doing so adds a significant number of twists and turns to the basic Herculean scheme. That model,

---

[23] Rajna, *Le Fonti*, p. 67, points out that a number of *Cinquecento* commentators, beginning with Pigna, identified the Senecan echo.

[24] Saccone also cites Pigna, arguing that "L'Ercole del titolo genera i due eroi, le cui traiettorie sono insieme analoghe ed opposte " ("Il Soggetto," pp. 217, 222).

[25] For echoes of Hercules *in bivio* in the *Furioso*, see also VI.60, VII.42, XV.92–94, XXVI.66–68. Among the *Cinquecento* commentators (conveniently compiled in Ariosto, *Opere*, S. Orlandini, ed. [Venezia: 1730]), Toscanella and Porcacchi note the use of the Pythagorean "Y" in their allegories of canto VI, while G. Bonomone's *Allegoria* which prefaces the same edition calls Ruggiero "questo nuovo Ercole."

however, is clearly the proper point of departure for dealings with Ruggiero as well as for those with Orlando.

A number of details, with one major, pervasive, connection, bring home this point in the Alcina-Logistilla sequence and throughout the *Furioso*. For instance, Ruggiero reaches Alcina's island precisely by exceeding "il segno che prescritto / avea già a' naviganti Ercole invitto" ("the sign that invincible Hercules once set up for sailors" VI.17.7–8). Most important, however, is the fact that the young knight's mentor and protector is Atlante (i.e., Atlas), who in both Boiardo and Ariosto is not a giant but an elderly magician.[26] Numerous allegorizations of the Herculean labor involving Atlas and the garden of the Hesperides take the sought-after golden apples as a form of wisdom (usually astrological) to be detached from a tree of knowledge *in bono*. They read the bearing of the heavens on one's shoulders as the possession of such wisdom. This interpretation is often extended, by Landino in the *Disputationes*, for example, into an allegory of Atlas as the tutor of young Hercules.[27] Within the Alcina episode, Melissa, disguised as Atlante, makes this connec-

[26] Saccone again provides useful references (*Il Soggetto*, p. 159): a long-standing tradition dating from Augustine, *De Civitate Dei* XVIII.8 (which in turn cites Pliny, *Historia Naturalis* VII.lvi.283), interpreted the giant Atlas of mythology as an astrologer, even a philosopher, linked with the ancient Egyptian wisdom of Moses, Hermes Trismegistus, Prometheus, and Hercules himself. The information is passed on in a more positive light by Ficino in the preface to his translation of the hermetic *Pimander*. As Saccone explains, the tradition was known to the young Ariosto, who makes explicit reference to it in the (fragmentary) verse oration *De Laudibus Sophiae*, with which he introduced the scholastic year at the *Studio* in Ferrara, and in which he links Atlas, as astrologer, to Moses and Hermes as possessors of mystical knowledge (ll. 31–33). See also Salutati, *De Laboribus Herculis* III.xxiii–xxiv, xlii (vol. 1, pp. 297–99, 307, 309, 311, 313–14; vol. 2, p. 418), and Boccaccio, *Genealogia* IV.xxxi (vol. 1, pp. 189–90). I regret that Marianne Shapiro's meticulous article, "From Atlas to Atlante," *Comparative Literature* 35 (1983), which is destined to be a primary resource for students of Ariosto's Atlante, came into my hands too late to influence my argument.

[27] Lohe edition, p. 32 (cf. n. 20, above). Salutati, calling Atlas a philosopher because of his knowledge of the heavens (which, as a giant, he literally bore on his shoulders) sees him as the teacher who made Hercules into a philosopher in his own right (*De Laboribus Herculis*, vol. 2, pp. 633–34); cf. Boccaccio, *Genealogia* XIII.i (vol. 2, p. 641). Jung (*Hercule*, pp. 9–10, 21–23) cites a number of Renaissance examples, notably Enrique de Villena, *Los Doze Trabajos de Hercules* (1417) and Raoul LeFèvre, *Receuil des Hystoires de Troie* (1464), otherwise known as the *Roman de Fort Hercules*.

tion explicitly, referring to tutoring the infant Ruggiero: "t'ho . . . /
fanciullo avezzo a strangolar serpenti" ("I accustomed you, in your
youth, to strangle serpents" VII.57.3–4), a clearly Herculean activity.
What then is the force of the *rapprochement* of the two heroes
through the figure of Hercules? What it most obviously does is
draw upon two usually distinct sets of associations among the multi-
ple Renaissance myths of Hercules in such a way as to compromise
his standing as a symbol of autonomous *humanitas* and, at the same
time, to jeopardize the clear opposition between education and
madness which is necessary for the emergence of human identity.[28]
In short, by conflating two moments in the mythographical career
of Hercules, his youthful choice *in bivio* and his mature lapse into
folly, Ariosto collapses the conventional temporal continuum in
the emergence of personality, reverses the usual division of the
human life into adolescent folly and mature prudence, and generally
works to abolish any clear hierarchy, or even differentiation, be-
tween education and madness.[29] The fact that Ruggiero's education

[28] This discussion is indebted to Saccone, who makes the following contrast
between the two heroes, though without extensive textual grounding: "se Ruggiero
è da un lato un Ercole giovane in cerca della sua via (la quale non sarà trovata una
volta per tutte, come mostra già ciò che accade dopo il rinsavimento e la fuga da
Alcina a Logistilla), Orlando dall'altro, il 'senator romano,' il savio e maturo eroe,
ribadisce, senza possibilità d'equivoco che la virtù come s'acquista, così si perde"
("Il Soggetto," pp. 222–23). Inserting this dialectic into a larger pattern of un-
resolved oppositions which he sees in the poem, he then argues that "la sanità confina
con la pazzia, è dietro, o è l'ombra della pazzia" (p. 243). My discussion will test
Saccone's point in a more detailed reading of the heroes' adventures in the poem to
suggest that Ariosto uses them for deliberately polemical purposes—against human-
istic didacticism, as well as against specific historical-political targets (see n. 31 below).

[29] We have already seen that Hercules tends to be a "double man," associated
both with youth and age, labor and contemplation, strength and virtue, education
and madness, deity and humanity. The following passage from Plotinus, *Enneads,*
4th ed., trans. S. MacKenna, revised by B.S. Page (London: Faber & Faber, 1969),
exemplifies this doubling which seems both synthetic and schizophrenic: "the poet
too, in the story of Hercules, seems to give this image of separate existence; he puts
the shade of Hercules in the lower world and Hercules himself among the gods:
treating the hero as existing in two realms at once, he gives a twofold Hercules"
(I.i.12). Plotinus identifies the split with the active and contemplative sides of the
figure. For the youth/age allegory see, for instance, Dante, *Convivio* IV.xxviii.13–19.
Cf. Mazzotta, *Dante,* pp. 39–41, for a useful discussion of Dante's more complex
treatment of young and old in the *Commedia.* See also Curtius, *European Literature,*
pp. 98–101.

by Logistilla is followed by his furious attempt to rape Angelica, and that Orlando's madness is apparently followed by a restoration to full command of his wits (and then by a little-noticed relapse), emphasizes the cyclical play of identity and self-difference. This mingling is further heightened by a curious tendency to assimilate key conflicts—in which now Orlando, now Ruggiero, participate—to Hercules' struggle with Anteus (always glossed as Virtue's victory over earthbound Vice), but then to compare the heroes to *both* of the mythical combatants, mixing the *virtus* of "Alcide" with the *furor* of Anteus.[30] Such conflations, such reductions of hierarchy, make attempts to find a positive and dominant value of didacticism, for instance in a differential superiority of Ruggiero's acquisition of control to Orlando's "sfrenatezza," questionable indeed. The power of these suggestions is further amplified if we remind ourselves that the privileged audience of the poem, the Este family, had frequently availed itself of the name of Hercules and its mythological baggage, as the poem reminds us with great regularity. The most famous instance is the initial designation of Ippolito d'Este, Ariosto's sometime patron, as "generosa Erculea prole" ("generous offspring of Hercules" 1.3.1), for his father, Ercole I, duke of Ferrara, and alleged descendant of this same (Herculean) Ruggiero.[31]

I will show in Chapters 3 and 4 how consistently Ariosto hints at the darker side of these genealogical myths—not only that of Hercules, but that of Hippolytus as well. The figure of Hercules is

---

[30] See *Furioso* IX.56.1–2, 77.5–8 (cf. 78–79); XXIII.85.6–8, 87–88; XLVI.124–25, 133. I will return to some of these scenes later on. For the standard allegorization of Anteus vs. Hercules, see Salutati, *De Laboribus Herculis* III.xxviii (vol. 1, p. 322) and *Prima Editio* (vol. 2, p. 633); Landino, *De Vera Nobilitate,* p. 108. See also Saccone, "Il Soggetto," p. 219.

[31] Here is an incomplete list of references to Ercole I and II d'Este in the poem: III.46, 49, 50, 58, 62; XIII.71; XXXVII.12–13; XL.1; XLI.67; XLIII.59; XLVI.87. The symbolic value of the name of Ercole I had earlier inspired an Este courtier, Pietro Andrea de' Bassi, to compose *Le Fatiche d'Ercole* in honor of his birth. The work was not published until 1473, some fifty years after its composition. Jung, *Hercule,* pp. 8–9, and Galinsky, *Herakles,* pp. 194–95, discuss it briefly. Other works on the Hercules theme were written by Este courtiers later on: Lilio Gregorio Giraldi, *Vita Herculis* (published in Ferrara, 1539; composed ca. 1514); G.B. Giraldi-Cinzio, *Dell'Ercole Canti 26* (Ferrara, 1557; incomplete).

an obvious vehicle for carrying out a tacit polemic not only with
the political purposes to which the Este were putting it, but also
with the humanistic conceptions of man's dignity and power on
which they were trading when they adopted it. Nonetheless, a
number of additional questions should be raised which will show
how firmly Ariosto's versions of Hercules are tied into a classical
and Renaissance understanding of education and the acquisition of
identity, into the formulation of a poetics of education, and into
the designation of the Renaissance itself as a singular period or
event.

One should begin by considering the details of the relationship
between the *Furioso* and the Senecan drama from which it partly
takes its title. To date, little has been done beyond noting the simple
fact that there is such an echo. Of course, this lacuna in the criticism
may stem from the obvious generic differences between late classical
tragedy and the odd blend of epic and romance elements that com-
pose the *Furioso*. With some justification, readers have almost always
felt that Ariosto's poem was fundamentally alien to tragedy, even
the rhetorical and "baroque" tragedy of Seneca. On the other side,
I will eventually argue that the obvious suppression of tragic ele-
ments, their relegation to oblique echoes such as that in the title,
does not at all mean that they are irrelevant to an understanding
of the poem; that, in fact, the opposite claim is much closer to the
truth. More specifically, however, there is also a seemingly radical
difference in kind between the madness of Seneca's Hercules and
that of Orlando which stands squarely in the way of critical studies
comparing them. The latter folly has as its primary cause an erotic
contretemps, the discovery of Angelica's "infidelity," and, in the sec-
ond place, is a divine punishment for Orlando's neglect of duty to
God and country (XXIII.102; XXXIV.62−66). The former also has a
double attribution, but is apparently divorced from *eros.* It springs
instead from Juno's jealousy of Hercules' achievements and/or from
Hercules' sudden desire to storm heaven by force in order to make
himself the equal of the gods (ll. 1−124, 953−75). It has apparently
not been noticed that this ambiguous double attribution—madness
coming from within vs. madness imposed by a divinity from
without—is a common feature of the two works. Nor has it been
observed that Orlando's failure to recognize his once-beloved

Angelica and his subsequent attempt to destroy her are analogous
to Hercules' more successful assault against his unrecognized loved
ones. The key terms of Orlando's madness and its cure repeatedly
echo the Senecan drama, as do the lines (1.56.7–8) which give para-
digmatic expression to the human dilemma of illusory vision and
blind desire that is at the center of the *Furioso*.[32]

In any event, a single echo, when located in the title, would
alone justify a more careful thematic comparison, and a serious
consideration of what relation Ariosto's "sunny" (or "loony") poem
has to the drama of tragic crisis. This is especially true considering
how well immersed Ariosto must have been both in classical drama
and in the culture of neo-Stoicism. The *Hercules Furens* was certainly
available in the pioneering Este library.[33] The Este court's innovative
role in the renewal of classical drama (comedy in particular), and
Ariosto's part therein, are well known.[34] The Stoic tendency in hu-
manist thought is prominent, ranging from the "Stoical" Augustine
in Petrarch's *Secretum* to Poggio Bracciolini's "Stoic" polemics
against Valla's supposed Epicureanism, even to Castiglione's courtly
version of the ethical imperative of Stoic self-sameness. Finally, the
Stoic fondness for Hercules, because of his mastery of the passions
and the dignity and force of his human will, is obvious not only

[32] All references are to Seneca, *Tragedies,* vol. 1, ed. and trans. F.J. Miller
(Cambridge: Harvard University Press, 1917). Saccone sees VII.55 as echoing both
Hercules Furens (468–70) and Ovid, *Heroides* IX.57–60 ("Il Soggetto," p. 222). More
convincingly, Parker, *Inescapable Romance,* p. 248 (n. 27), observes that the reference
to the Silenus at the curing of Orlando's madness (XXXIX.60) echoes not only Virgil,
Eclogues VI.24, but also *Hercules Furens* 1063: "solvite tantis animum monstris . . . ."
The Virgilian echo is more direct, but the Senecan echo refers specifically to the
cure of a madness and so cannot be discounted. I believe that Orlando's folly also
begins with an echo from *Hercules Furens* 1043–48, which prefigures the head
slumping on the breast in *Furioso* XXIII.112.5, as well as the crucial tree imagery of
that passage. It is clear that 1.56.7–8 comes from *Hercules Furens* 313–14: "quod
nimis miseri volunt / hoc facile credunt."

[33] See Giulio Bertoni, *La Biblioteca Estense e la Coltura Ferrarese* (Torino: Loescher,
1903), esp. pp. 107, 216–17, 251. See also Marvin Herrick, *Italian Tragedy in the
Renaissance* (Urbana: University of Illinois Press, 1965), p. 3, on the Este's possession
of two manuscripts of Seneca's tragedies.

[34] See Herrick, *Italian Tragedy,* as well as Catalano, *Vita,* vol. 1, pp. 116–26.

in the Senecan drama, but in Seneca the moral philosopher as well, and continues into the Renaissance.[35]

Hercules Furens begins with an account of Hercules' descent into and return from hell, and in this sense is a humanistic celebration of triumphant *virtus* (cf. ll. 645–829). But the focus of the story is instead a degradation into inhuman, bestial madness: How can the apparent contradiction be reconciled? The first and most extensive Renaissance treatment of Hercules, Salutati's *De Laboribus Herculis,* in fact has its origin in response to a friend's perplexity over this very point: How could the greatest of heroes, emblem both of virtue and of wisdom, model of an educational itinerary, possibly lapse into madness? In the letter to Giovanni da Siena from which the longer treatise was developed, this doubt is the clear point of departure.[36] When the *De Laboribus Herculis* itself was composed, it had been set aside, or repressed, as it seems to me, in favor of a more general defense of (pagan) poetry as the allegorical bearer of instructive truths (and thus the opponent of the very idolatry and madness which it superficially seemed to represent). Even more important, the two principal episodes of Hercules' folly, the subjects of the two Senecan plays (*Hercules Oetaeus* as well as the *Furens*), remain outside the unfinished treatise, constituting precisely that which was never written.[37] Thus the greatest work by one of the "founders" of humanism originates in and yet finally defers the intuition that the figure *par excellence* of "divine" *humanitas* may be marked from within by madness.

By thus returning to a play which both stands as the product of the most famous Stoic, and yet seems to raise serious questions about the Stoic ideology of human integrity, and by refusing to recur to available allegorizations of Herculean *furor* as the Platonic *furor divinus,*[38] Ariosto discovers within Stoic humanism its own critique, its own lapse into the unnatural and the inhuman. At other points

[35] Cf. Waith, *Herculean Hero,* pp. 30–31. For Castiglione, see *Cortegiano* i.xvii.

[36] This letter is published as the *Prima Editio* of the treatise at the end of vol. 2, Ullman edition.

[37] Salutati, *De Laboribus Herculis,* vol. 2, p. 585.

[38] Cf. Landino, *De Vera Nobilitate,* p. 109; *Cortegiano* iv.lxix. This reading is already explicit in Seneca's *Hercules Oetaeus.*

in the poem, for example in the proem to canto XXI, the neo-Stoic ethic of self-sameness is advanced only to be quickly undermined by the context.[39] It is not stretching a point, however, to argue that the *Hercules Furens,* by the contradictions it dramatizes, already predicts and criticizes the excesses of a certain humanism. Though Hercules is destined for divinity, though he has helped to resist the mad assault of the giants against heaven, now he himself, spurred somehow by Juno, sets aside piety and a sense of human limit and madly aspires to make himself a god by force. The consequence can only be a fall below the human and a severing of connections with the human family and its values (he literally destroys his family). As Juno says, the divine man, defeater of the monstrous and the inhuman, is defeated by his own internal contradictions, realizing his own capacity for monstrosity, incidentally leveling the Stoic project of rational self-restraint and the humanist project of auto-divinization. *Virtus,* humanity, disappears in a monstrous furor. In this perspective it is not surprising that Erasmus, the other great "fictor" of madness in the early *Cinquecento,* and a possible source for the *Furioso,* also takes the folly of the Stoics as a principal target in the *Encomium Moriae.* Erasmus goes on to recuperate a kind of madness as quintessentially *human* and as a key value in his Christian humanism. It remains to be seen in Chapter 4 whether or not madness assumes such a value for Ariosto.[40] More commonly, as we shall shortly see, Ariosto critics have identified the amorous furor of

[39] The proem to canto XXI (stanzas 1–2) insists upon an absolute, uncorrupted ethics of faithfully keeping one's promised word which derives, ultimately, from the Stoics. Saccone, "Clorindano e Medoro, con Alcuni Argomenti per una Lettura del Primo *Furioso,*" in *Il Soggetto,* asserts that this is *the* definitive value for Ariosto, though in "Il Soggetto" he implicitly reverses himself by arguing that any critic attempting to isolate a privileged "subject" of the poem reifies and dismembers it like Orrilo (cf. Chapter 1, n. 60, above). In the case of canto XXI, the story-within-a-story which follows the proem seems first to exemplify its precept; but, in fact, the "faithful" blindness and inflexibility of Filandro is exactly that which the faithless Gabrina manipulates to get him to violate his pledged word by killing her husband and marrying her. Zerbino hears the story from Filandro's noble brother, Ermonide, whom he has just mortally wounded in the process of keeping *his* promised word to this same Gabrina (who then "repays" him by attempting to have him executed in canto XXII). For more on the theme of faith see Chapter 4, nn. 44–45, below.
[40] On Ariosto and Erasmus, see n. 115, below and Chapter 4, nn. 43, 131–33.

Orlando as a parody and critique of *stilnovist* and neo-Platonic versions of a redemptive erotic madness, a love through which the old self is lost only in order that a higher state of spiritual perfection may be attained (usually without remarking that the beginnings of such a critique are already visible in the open Petrarchan dialectic between spiritualizing and degrading love). Orlando, far from such an exaltation to "angelic" status, slides into bestiality. My reading, however, suggests that the secular humanism to which such critics usually turn as the alternative ideology promoted by the poem (an ideology which the text does approach at several points) may be equally a target for ironic subversion, equally a form of degrading madness.

A close look at Salutati's treatise may bring the importance of Hercules into even sharper focus.[41] For Salutati, Hercules is an example both of practical, active virtue and of philosophical wisdom: "Hercules is the pinnacle of genius and of every virtue" (III.xxiii, p. 298).[42] Fighting Anteus, he is virtue personified (III.xxvii); defeating the Hydra, Platonic symbol of sophistry, he is a "philosophus" (III.ix, pp. 192–93). But he is more, a virtual synecdoche for all of classical culture, insofar as he is chosen as the exemplary vehicle for a defense of pagan "litterae." By emphasizing now virtue, now wisdom, Salutati straddles the issue (later developed by Landino) as to whether Hercules' deeds sponsor the *vita activa* or *vita contemplativa*.[43] In effect, the multiplicity of deeds does allow the emergence of a many-faceted hero who might embrace all that is human, thereby displacing the human, but only metaphorically, by "similitude," toward the divine (III.v, pp. 176–77).

---

[41] Since the *De Laboribus Herculis* apparently did not circulate widely in the Renaissance (cf. Jung, *Hercule*, pp. 7–8), I make no claims for its direct influence on Ariosto. Nonetheless, the treatise has great value as a compendium of *topoi* and motifs largely diffused both before and after it. Ariosto's sometimes close associations with the Medici and their circle make it conceivable that he knew the work from their great collection. On the other hand, in Chapter 4 I will argue that Ariosto clearly knew Boccaccio's *Genealogia* (bks. XIV and XV) and alluded to it specifically and polemically in writing canto XXXV.1–31.

[42] *De Laboribus Herculis*, vol. I, p. 298: "Hercules et ingenii et omnis virtutis sublimitas est."

[43] See Galinsky, *Herakles*, pp. 196–97, citing Salutati, III.xv–xvi, xxvi–xxviii, xxxiii, xxxvi.

In the course of an allegorical education which is dramatized, variously, by the choice *in bivio,* by the single labor of Atlas and the Hesperides, or by the composite series of labors taken as a whole,[44] Hercules is said to acquire both wisdom and virtue. His identity, however, does not then consist only in a wise and virtuous mode of being. He also gains a *name,* which is both virtue's *telos* and an etymological dramatization of the relation between virtuous being and glorious name. Following a longstanding tradition, Salutati repeatedly etymologizes Hercules' (Alcides') two names as follows: "the name of Hercules is more perfect than that of Alcides. The latter is from 'alce,' which means 'virtue;' the former is from 'eris' and 'cleos,' that is 'glory from struggle' . . . which is indeed the prize and reward of virtue" (III.xi, p. 214). Elsewhere he repeats: "'Heris' means 'struggle,' 'cleos' means 'glory,' as if to say 'glorious on account of struggle'" (II.xvi, p. 141).[45] Hercules wins a glorious name by virtue; and that name is precisely "virtue" and "glory," a veritable allegory of winning a name through deeds. Besides, as the first citation suggests, there is a hierarchization of the two attributes, with glory ranking higher. Salutati again hedges his bets by sometimes leaving the *gloria* in question suspended between nominal fame and the ontological glory of Christian redemption (II.xvi, p. 141), but in general both Salutati and other readers of Hercules' life tend toward the former. Even Bernardus Silvestris, whose neo-Platonic, spiritualizing tendencies are well known, takes *gloria* in this way, as the enduring product of earthly *fama* (pp. 73, 75, 105).

Hercules' name, thus expounded, is also exemplary of the Renaissance concept of the symbiotic relationship of virtue and glory,

---

[44] This last is the case in Landino's *De Vera Nobilitate.*

[45] *De Laboribus Herculis,* vol. 1, p. 214: "Plus enim perfectionis sonat Herculis nomen quam Alcyde. Hoc enim ab 'alce,' quod est 'virtus,' dictum est; illud ab 'eris,' 'cleos,' id est litis gloria . . . que quidem est premium remuneratioque virtutum." Cf. vol. 1, p. 141: "'Heris' enim 'lis' est, 'cleos,' 'gloria,' quasi 'ex lite gloriosus,'" as well as III.ix (vol. 1, p. 203). The etymology is a standard of mythographical treatises. Bernardus Silvestris, *Commentary on the First Six Books of the "Aeneid,"* eds. J.W. Jones and E.F. Jones (Lincoln: University of Nebraska Press, 1977), glosses Hercules as "her lis, cleos gloria" (p. 56) and Alcides as "quasi fortis et formosus. Fortis notat virtutem, formosus gloriam" (p. 87). Boccaccio, *Genealogia,* offers the same etymology along with several others in XIII.i (vol. 2, p. 638).

being and name, and of the educational poetics which derives from it. Petrarch, for example, in his well-known epistle to "Laelius," recounting his visit with the Emperor Charles, envisions a double function of poetry which, by recording famous deeds, stimulates princes to imitate virtue and, simultaneously, is the end to which virtue is the means, honoring it with fame.[46] Literature, thus understood, is both the *arche* and the *telos* of virtue, rewarding it with the same kind of fame that stimulates it. Thus the aesthetic realm influences the ethical, while the ethical strives to transform itself into the aesthetic—at least within Petrarch's self-aggrandizing literary logic. Salutati argues something quite similar in the following passage: "Clio is first among the Muses. . . . Clio comes from 'cleos' which means glory. Just as glory is the end which scholars seek for their labors, even so it is uppermost in the mind of the student who submits himself to his labor. Thus, as Cicero said, 'honor nourishes the arts, and all men are enflamed for studies by glory'" (i.ix, pp. 42–43).[47] When compared with the various etymologies of Hercules' name, these words reveal that, for Salutati, Hercules is not only a hero represented by poetry, but is in fact "synonymous" with one of the Muses, and is himself a figure for and of writing (historical, but also poetic) as well as being a *philosophus* (for Salutati, in any case, a poet is a philosopher is a theologian).[48]

Hercules bears within his name, as understood in the Renaissance, the seeds of a poetics by which the realms of literature and of life

---

[46] *Rerum Familiarum Libri* XIX.3. See also Mommsen, "Choice of Hercules," pp. 194–96. Cf. Silvestris, *Commentary*, p. 75: "Boreas [gloria] Zeti et Calais pater est quia gloria poematis et egregii operis est causa. Virtutis enim fructum multi ponunt in gloria."

[47] *De Laboribus Herculis*, vol. 1, pp. 43–44: "Prima quidem Musarum est Clyo. . . . Unde Clyo a 'cleos,' quod est 'gloria,' dicta est. Sicut enim gloria finis est quem studiosi assequuntur in ultimis post laborem, ita primum est in intentione studentis propter quam subicit se labori. Nam ut dixit Cicero (*Tusc. Disp.* 1.4): 'Honos alit artes, et incenduntur omnes ad studia gloria.'"

[48] Clio, of course, is the Muse of History, rather than one of the poetic genres, but from the humanistic perspective the poetic and the historical do approach identity under the rubric of exemplary *litterae* and in their glory-conferring functions, for which see n. 75, below. For the *Furioso*'s dramatization of poetry's (and its own) claims to historiographical verity, see Chapter 4, sec. i (esp. n. 29), below.

are bound together in a complex circular relationship both of reference and of mutual influence: language as statement *and* as action. Of course, the first book of Salutati's treatise, and part of the second, is in fact a poetics (What is poetry? How should it be written?) and a hermeneutics (How do we read poetry?) which justifies his interpretations of the labors of Hercules and of which those interpretations are an exemplary illustration. As is well known, Salutati, like most humanists, assimilated poetry to oratory and assigned to it the educative function of persuading to virtue and dissuading from vice by exemplary representations of both.[49] The question he examines most extensively, however, is one of reference rather than of persuasion. How can pagan poetry, and poetic figures such as Hercules, be said to carry out this function when they explicitly seem to represent a plurality of gods, mad idolatry, and a belief in man's capacity literally to make a god of himself, all of which tenets are unacceptable in Christian terms. As Charles Trinkaus points out, Salutati first considers idolatry itself as a possible origin of poetry, perhaps constituted by the attempted conflation of image and essence (he even cites the famous passage from the *Asclepius* in which Hermes Trismegistus speaks of attracting gods into statuary images), but comes to the conclusion that poetry's true origin is exactly the opposite, having been founded by Enoch in recognition of the fact that no single name can ever designate God *properly* and that therefore it would only be "appropriate" to designate Him metaphorically by a multiplicity of improper, figurative names.[50] The plurality of gods can then be reinterpreted as metaphorical aspects of a single deity, and Hercules' divinity can be seen as figurative rather than as proper or essential: plurality and idolatry become

[49] Salutati, *De Laboribus Herculis* I.ii (vol. 1, pp. 10, 14–15) and I.xii (pp. 63, 67). According to Jung, *Hercule,* p. 9, de' Bassi also dedicates the first part of his work on Hercules to poetry. There is a longstanding tradition of Hercules' binding of Cerebrus as a figure of eloquence (and thus of poetry, given the Renaissance tendency to ally literature and rhetoric). Typically the hero is represented with a golden chain emerging from his mouth, an image which derives from Lucian, "Heracles," in *Works,* vol. 1 (Cambridge: Harvard University Press, 1961), pp. 256–59. See also Silvestris, *Commentary,* pp. 87–88.

[50] Salutati, *De Laboribus Herculis* II.i (vol. 1, pp. 76–87); Trinkaus, *Image and Likeness,* vol. 2, pp. 697–98.

unity and piety. On these grounds Trinkaus claims that Salutati sponsors what I would call a "nominalist poetics," which postulates a gap between words and essences (signifiers and signifieds) which is only bridged improperly and metaphorically (by the alienated references of an always allegorical and "self-consuming" writing).[51]

Such a "nominalist poetics" might create, implicitly at least, some problems within the poetics of *cleos* previously described. How properly can glory, the name exalted in poetic writing, reflect virtuous being? What is the relation between the Hercules of poetry and some possible historical creature? The result of such an approach is an allegorical poetics of hermeneutic freedom: since the literal level is always improper, plural, and tendentially idolatrous, the reader can (must, in fact) always invent or rediscover a proper, single, pious meaning, even if the text clearly originated elsewhere. But if the text cannot teach the reader without his already having recognized that it does not mean what it says, but something else altogether different, how effective an educational tool can it be? Just as Hercules' potential madness is repressed within the text, so an idolatrous or demonic origin of textuality is envisioned and then repressed. Perhaps indicative of this repression is the extraordinary effort, even among allegorizers, in iii.xlii (esp. pp. 416–17) to interpret the evidently maddening and demonic Medusa, Dantean symbol of reification, idolatry, and/or heresy, as salutary eloquence.[52] In this way the Pegasus, which arises from her blood and which originates the wellspring of poetry, may have an origin itself *in bono*. There is a clear anxiety to explain the birth of poetry's emblematic creature (evidently evoked by Ariosto's hippogryph) out of demonic, petrifying folly, which parallels the drive to turn reifying idolatry into vitalizing piety.

To what extent then are the themes of identity through a glorious

---

[51] Trinkaus, *Image and Likeness,* vol. 1, pp. 63–66.

[52] For the Medusa in the mythographical and hermeneutical traditions and in Dante, see John Freccero, "Medusa: The Letter and the Spirit," *Yearbook of Italian Studies* 2 (1972). See also Mazzotta, *Dante,* pp. 163–64, 277–86; Durling, "Introduction," in *Petrarch's Lyric Poems* (Cambridge: Harvard University Press, 1976), pp. 29–33, as well as his bibliography for additional references. In the following chapter I will discuss some ways that the Medusa myth makes itself felt in the *Furioso,* especially via related figures such as the Pegasus and Perseus, not to mention Atlas.

name, the poetics of Herculean education that this implies,[53] and the
hermeneutics of allegorical didacticism relevant to Ariosto's specific
use of the figure of Hercules and to the *Furioso* in general? To what
extent is the figure of Hercules both an emblematic version of he-
roic education and, simultaneously, the representative of a certain
hermeneutics and poetics? To what extent, finally, are both the
heroic individual and the poetics of heroic education subjected to
crisis, to the threats of madness and of aesthetic self-enclosure which
are already detectable (albeit negatively) in Salutati? It should be
mentioned right away that, as far as I know, the etymology of
"Hercules" given above is never directly mentioned by Ariosto,
though he frequently depends on the etymological resonances of
names, as we shall see. The concept of a "nominalist poetics" is,
however, thematically crucial to such a key episode as the lunar
allegory of fame won by earthly deeds, which also makes reference
repeatedly to at least one key defense of poetry, Boccaccio's. What
Salutati's "Hercules" tells us about poetry and education is some-
thing that the Renaissance said in many ways. And there can be
no doubt that Ariosto listened very carefully to more than one ver-
sion of it.

To the extent that Ariosto does eventually appear to be reflecting
on a certain concept of ideal selfhood and a related poetics of educa-
tion, he must also be engaging the Renaissance's concept of itself (or
rather, of several related concepts and metaphors which the writers
of the time quite deliberately applied to it and to themselves as part
of it). By complicating the figure of Hercules as deployed by other
Renaissance authors, I also aim to complicate the understanding of
numerous critics for whom that hero has been an especially potent
emblem of the existence and character of a "Renaissance." Panofsky
is the most obvious such scholar, arguing that the mythic choice
of Hercules, along with the frequent use of that motif throughout
the period, demonstrate a new concept of human freedom radically
divergent from the medieval picture of man almost totally depen-
dent on God's determining grace. Panofsky's view, as mentioned
earlier, has been repeated and modified frequently, by Mazzeo and
Trinkaus, for example. Jean Seznec saw the reappearance of a "real-

[53] Cf. Landino, *De Vera Nobilitate,* p. 107: "est . . . Hercules imitandus."

istic" Hercules in his original classical trappings (loincloth and club) as illustrative of the period's new historical sense and its classicism.[54] Garin sums it up in claiming that "Salutati proposed Hercules as the ideal of free humanity, the hero who defeated the monsters and tamed nature," recalling as well Hercules' special role as symbol of Florence, itself in turn a symbol of humanism and rebirth.[55] It is thus singularly appropriate that the image of a restoration of life to dead culture, re-naissance, is frequently expressed in terms alluding to Hercules' successful foray into the Land of the Dead, his restoration of life to Theseus and Pirithoos (*after* which the events of the *Hercules Furens* are said to take place).[56] Hence, my interest in Ariosto's use of this figure does have a double edge. Not only does a reading of the *Furioso* gain from probing the mythic and mythographical background on which the poet is drawing, but, in fact, we also learn that Ariosto's appropriation of Hercules may become in turn a commentary on, a reading of, his epoch's investment in the political, cultural, philosophical, and ethical significations of the myth. Through Hercules he implicitly engages even the very concept of historical rebirth: the Renaissance's identity as a period of productive crisis in human identity.[57] He also engages (obliquely, as it must be) his own specific historical situation as dependant of a family which turned the myth of Hercules into its very own.

---

[54] For Panofsky, Mazzeo, and Trinkaus, cf. nn. 16 and 21 above. Seznec, *The Survival of the Pagan Gods* (Princeton: Princeton University Press, 1953), pp. 184–85.

[55] Garin, *L'Educazione in Europa,* p. 81. See also his "Le Favole Antiche," *Rassegna della Letteratura Italiana* 57 (1953), esp. p. 412. For Hercules as symbol of Florence, see also Landino, "Proemio," p. 128.

[56] E.g., Landino, "Proemio," p. 119: "Merita adunque la nostra repubblica buona grazia da tutta l'Italia, poiché in quella nacquero e' primi che l'una e l'altra eloquenzia, non solo morta ma per tanti seculi sepulta, in vita ridussono e dalle tartaree tenebre in chiara luce rivocarono." The two main models for *successful* rescues from hell are Christ's harrowing thereof and Hercules' rescue mission.

[57] On the question of what the Renaissance was and/or whether it was at all, begin with Ferguson, *The Renaissance,* and Panofsky, *Renaissance and Renascences in Western Art,* 2nd ed. (Stockholm: Almquist & Wiksell, 1965). My own approach is to insist on the metaphorical, "literary," nature of the period; i.e., on the choice of the metaphor of rebirth by writers of the time and since to describe, but also in a way to create fictively, an identity for an enormous stretch of time and for an apparently infinite body of often recalcitrant facts.

To qualify what has just been said: I would prefer not to identify myself fully either with an attempt to make Hercules a perfect synecdoche for the Renaissance or with that of making Ariosto's title a perfect synecdoche for the work as a whole—particularly since the question at hand is precisely that of wholeness and identity, and of the possibility that they may slip into the domain of the partial and the fragmentary. Since the preceding discussion suggests that the relationship between the thing itself and the celebrated name by which it is identified may be crucial and problematic, the *Cinquecento* debate over the impropriety of the poem's title may be especially significant. The title then seemed, and even now may seem, to identify inadequately the work it is placed over and before: Orlando's story is only one of many, and madness is by no means the only prominent theme; there is no hint at the central narrative of genealogical foundation (so that the title conceals the poem's claim to "historicity"). Chapters 3 and 4 will pose and explore this question in greater detail. Meanwhile, it will be worth the trouble to give a broader context to the problems and motifs of a Renaissance "crisis of identity" into which the *Furioso* might fit either passively or polemically. Needless to say, very small parts will still have to be taken as representatives and representations of an irreducibly vast scene.

ii. *Education as "Insegnamento" and "Formazione"*

The "private" problem of acquiring personal identity through literary education was a truly public matter in the Renaissance. Nor is there any doubt that Ariosto and his poem were perfectly positioned in time and space to feel the full force of the intellectual and rhetorical polemics that were being put to the proof in the new educational curricula, introduced during the *Quattrocento* in place of authoritarian medieval models. Early in the *Quattrocento*, Ferrara had been the adopted home of Guarino Veronese who, with Vittorino da Feltre, had been the most influential of early humanist educators and whose presence was felt in the *Studio* long after his death in 1460. Until his own father's death forced him to abandon his academic passions, Ariosto too was a frequenter of the *Studio*. But civic-rhetorical humanism was by then joined to new currents, especially the mystical-philosophical tendencies emerging from the Florence of Lorenzo and Ficino, and from the hand of Pico della Mirandola. There will be ample occasion to see how full the young Ariosto's access would have been to the texts, doctrines, and disciples of neo-Platonism (and to the reactions against it embodied by the Ferrarese Savonarola and Pico's nephew, Gianfrancesco), and to decide exactly how he positioned himself among the various ideologies and practices available to him. First, however, it will pay to look further into some of the basic themes of Renaissance selfhood as they alternately diverge and converge among the many humanisms of the day, particularly as they are expressed in theories and practices of education through the reading of literature.

Where better to begin than with the figure most often cited as *the* theoretician of human nature in the Renaissance and also, rarely though quite interestingly, adduced as a model *both* for what Ariosto is and what he is not.[58] Among *Quattrocento* texts, Giovanni Pico della Mirandola's *Oratio,* by others entitled "On the Dignity of Man," is almost always taken as an especially emblematic point of reference for a (re)new(ed) vision of human dignity and identity, because of its grand synthetic attempt to valorize and unite the multiplicity of human possibilities. In fact, however, Pico tells us as much about the Renaissance by his departures from the mainstream as he does by his embodiment of it. Similarly, his usefulness for criticism of the *Furioso* is equally divided between his possible function as a source or analogue and his obvious status as a polemical target: in either case, however, he defines issues which are basic, not least of all by demonstrating that Ariosto was certainly not the first author of his age to generate a multiple and conflicted representation of human being.

The *Oratio* treads a fine line between the hubristic rupture with

[58] For instance, DeBlasi, "Ariosto," pt. 2, p. 203, assimilates Ariosto to Pico as promoter of the human, though without taking stock of Pico's obvious distance from Ariosto's "humanism of limits." Croce's notion of the poem as *alter universus of Armonia* and Durling's of the poet as *alter Deus* are both developed without reference to Pico, although he, with Landino, is the most obvious *Quattrocento* focal point for these concepts (cf. Chapter 4, n. 67, as well as Chapter 1, n. 6).

Christian humility discerned by Burckhardt and others (as well as by the papacy in Pico's own day!) and a renewal of the forms and insights of Christian piety seen by Trinkaus. Pico, as is well known, rewrites the Genesis myth *ad hoc* in the beginning of his work, significantly omitting any reference either to creation "in the image and likeness" of God or to a subsequent fall of human nature into sinfulness and irremediable self-division.[59] God is still man's creator, according to Pico's account, but He has made man as self-creator, existing initially and uniquely without any particular attribute except the protean, chameleonic power of conferring on himself any form of being that he chooses in the universal order. He may descend, metaphorically, into the senseless being of a rock or tree, or ascend by force of will and intellect beyond the angels to perfect identity with God, who is Identity, Oneness, Being itself. Man, for Pico, is "in the middle of the world [i.e., of the universe]"—he is a microcosm in the novel sense that he bears universal, cosmic possibility within himself. In the economy of divine creation and human re-creation it becomes truly difficult to fix the actual import of Pico's conception of human identity. He leaves room both for the claim that his conception is "orthodox," insofar as man is said to be created by, subordinated to, and derived from divinity, and for the accusations of heresy which dimly recognize the peril of admitting that man could be his own work of art, a "fiction" of his own making. From the latter "Pico" it is not so far as it might seem to the post-Hegelian assertion that man is a fictional construct, a concept whose only substance is its existence as concept, its reality *qua* fiction. Michel Foucault, for example, thinks it possible to assert now that "man is only a recent invention . . . a new wrinkle in our knowledge, and . . . will disappear again as soon as that knowl-

[59] Giovanni Pico della Mirandola, *"De Dignitate Hominis," "Heptaplus," "De Ente et Uno," e Scritti Varii*, ed. E. Garin (Firenze: Vallecchi, 1942), pp. 102–164, esp. 104–106. I do not believe Trinkaus takes into sufficient account the importance of these omissions in attempting to bring Pico back within the fold of Christian humanism. The *Heptaplus*, which is a reading of Genesis, apparently in the Augustinian tradition (cf. *Confessions* XI–XIII and *De Genesi ad Litteram*), does try to make amends by specifically referring to the Fall, though it is not necessarily orthodox even so. Pico *was* linked closely with Savonarola in the last years of his brief life, but, of course, this hardly proves his *orthodoxy*.

edge has discovered a new form."[60] Perhaps less adventurously it might also be remembered that the great celebrator of man has seemed to some scholars to run the risk of falling into an earlier (prepoststructuralist) antihumanism: Averroism (in which the "possible intellect" is to individual instances of thought as "langue" is to "parole" for Saussure and his followers).[61] Thus Pico could be not only the describer of this new epoch of human consciousness, but in fact also one of its inventors, by virtue of that description, and one of its most powerful subverters, because of the transparent fictionality of that invention.

Perhaps a more detailed reading of Pico than can be offered here would be required to defend such claims as these. It will be simpler to show that Pico's vision of human centrality, and of the harmonious synthesis of human knowledge (the "unity of truth"), is menaced and limited from within. For Pico, what makes man a "great miracle" is his protean lack of specific identity. As A.B. Giamatti has convincingly shown, the figure of Proteus is employed in the Renaissance both as the positive emblem of man's creative capacity and as the demonic figure of multiplicity understood as deceptive evil or destroying madness.[62] I would argue that this second side

[60] Foucault, *The Order of Things* (New York: Random House, Vintage, 1973), p. xxiii. See Jonathan Culler, *Structuralist Poetics* (Ithaca: Cornell University Press, 1975), pp. 27–30, for a brief but incisive account of the contemporary "antihumanism" of Structuralism and after. See Greene, "The Flexibility of the Self in Renaissance Literature," in P. Demetz et al., eds., *The Disciplines of Criticism* (New Haven: Yale University Press, 1968), for an humanistic recuperation of the same theme and for these words quoted from Erasmus: "homines non nascuntur sed finguntur." Though Pico does not play a role in Stephen Greenblatt's *Renaissance Self-Fashioning* (Chicago: University of Chicago Press, 1980), the book is brilliant in its judicious applications of Greene's categories as well as Foucault's to a variety of Renaissance fictions of the self.

[61] For an introduction to Saussure, see Culler, *Ferdinand de Saussure* (New York: Penguin, 1977). For Pico's possible Averroistic tendencies, see Trinkaus, *Image and Likeness,* vol. 2, pp. 505–506, 759–60, and relevant notes; see also Bruno Nardi, "La Mistica Averroistica e Pico della Mirandola," in E. Castelli, ed., *Umanesimo e Machiavellismo* (Padova: Liviana, 1949). The irony for Pico is that his treatment of man seems to approach simultaneously the opposite limits of apotheosis and disappearance. In the lunar episode, Ariosto too seems to be flirting, though curiously, with Averroism (cf. Chapter 4, n. 41, below).

[62] Giamatti, "Proteus Unbound: Some Versions of the Sea God in the Renaissance," in Demetz et al., eds., *The Disciplines of Criticism.* For Pico's Proteus, see the

of the image is potentially present in the oration, though it explicitly embraces the first. Before the harmony of synthesis must inevitably come a violent analytical fragmentation—a point made by Pico himself when he uses the myth of Osiris (violently dismembered and then recomposed as Horus by Isis) as the image of the "dialectic of dialectic," of analysis followed by synthesis (p. 116). With a further step it becomes clear that Pico in writing the treatise (and the nine hundred theses it introduces) aspires to enact the very protean universality that he describes. He is a sort of Aesculapius stitching together the torn body of universal truth, reconciling Plato and Aristotle, and so on. This image is hinted at in the text itself, since it begins with a reference to Asclepius (whom Pico would have thought of as a lineal descendant of the physician-god) and makes use of the Isis-Osiris myth which partly doubles that of Aesculapius-Hippolytus.[63] Here again, however, it is worth remembering both that Aesculapius was mythically imprisoned in hell for usurping as a man the life-giving role of a god and that Pico was, with obvious irony, attempting to demonstrate the unity of truth by recourse to nine hundred separate theses, appearing most fragmented, most intellectually violent when making the greatest claims for integrity and concord.

A counter-reading of Pico thus already foreshadows grave difficulties within the view of harmonious, integral selfhood, unmarked by violence, fragmentation, or madness. It is, besides, increasingly

---

Oratio (Garin edition, p. 106). For further discussion of Proteus' significance for the Renaissance, especially in England, see Barish, *Antitheatrical Prejudice,* pp. 98–112 (cf. Chapter 1, n. 31, above).

[63] Boccaccio, *Genealogia* v.xx–xxi (vol. 1, pp. 254–55) reports skeptically that Augustine, *De Civitate Dei* VIII.xxvi, quotes the *Asclepius* to the effect that the titular character is the grandson of the physician-god, the human inventor of medicine who was subsequently deified. The two names, in Greek, are actually one. Pico (Garin edition, p. 126) does make reference to Aesculapius. Boccaccio, in his proem to bk. 1, refers to himself as "quasi Aesculapius alter," collecting the scattered body of pagan mythology (vol. 1, p. 9), a task not so far removed from Pico's own. For the myth of Hippolytus reborn as Virbius as figure of "re-naissance," see Giamatti, "Hippolytus among the Exiles: The Romance of Early Humanism," in *Exile and Change in Renaissance Literature* (New Haven: Yale University Press, 1984), pp. 12–32, as well as Greene, *The Light in Troy,* pp. 162–70 and p. 321 (n. 34).

clear that Pico's vision of man is not of a piece with those of most of his contemporaries, precisely because of the violence which he does as he attempts to incorporate them within his own totalizing discourse. The *Oratio* begins to seem less like the emblem of the "unity" of an era and more and more like a fragment expressing a daring and desperate desire for an absent integrity. For this and other reasons, the illustrative juxtaposition of Pico and Ariosto is as problematic as it is suggestive. What relation does Pico's work bear to Ariosto's poem of cosmic "armonia" and mad collapse of self? And which of the several possible Picos are we invoking? Does he offer a model for the *Furioso*'s humanistic values? A source for the paired concepts of poem as *alter universus* and poet as *alter Deus*? A target for polemical reading—a foil to the vision of identity, human and cosmic, dispersed in multiplicity? There are only a few points in the *Furioso* where one would wish to claim direct echoing, to whatever end, although one of Ariosto's least-known works, the *Erbolato,* seems to me a point-by-point travesty of the *Oratio.*[64] Otherwise, Ariosto seems almost scrupulous in avoiding any of the obvious Piconian implications: his magicians are always "demonic," never "natural"; his "Proteo" does not have the same emblematic force as Pico's; he never mentions Aesculapius, although one of the key figures in the poem is named Ippolito (d'Este) and one of the key thematic complexes involves the irrational, passionate violence of horses and their riders. Above all, human dignity is repeatedly caught in degrading lapses through the *Furioso:* Astolfo becomes a

---

[64] Some points of polemical resemblance or oblique parody will be raised as I proceed. Ariosto was well acquainted with Pico's nephew, Gianfrancesco Pico, who is mentioned at XLVI.17.1–2 among the friends waiting on the shore: "Veggo sublimi e soprumani ingegni / . . . il Pico e il Pio." The *Erbolato* may be consulted in Ariosto, *Opere Minori,* ed. G. Fatini (Firenze: Sansoni, 1915). It was first published well after the poet's death. The work is an oration, a sort of "dramatic monologue" *avant la lettre,* which includes a reference to "la dignità dell'uomo" in a subtitle. Just as with Pico's work it has been argued that this subtitle was a later, nonauthorial addition; but it is clearly an appropriate one. Its speaker, one Antonio Faentino, doctor, begins with a celebration of medicine which invokes Aesculapius, not as curer of souls but as healer of bodies, and then reveals Faentino as a charlatan, a hawker of patent medicines. I hope at a later date to publish a complete analysis of the parodic relation between the two texts.

tree; Orlando is reduced to stoniness and then bestiality. The inversion of Pico's positions in the *Furioso* may begin to seem systematic after a while. In any case, the common reluctance of critics to set Pico and Ariosto side by side, even where there are clear points of negative, and occasionally positive, overlap suggests to me the avoidance, witting or not, of a confrontation which could only accentuate Ariosto's departures from Piconian humanism—the slide from harmony into violence, the repeated lapses of man's divine attributes into bestial folly. Whatever the specifics of Ariosto's feelings about Pico, the *Oratio* clearly points in the direction of themes and texts which are more clearly addressed in the *Furioso*.

Both in Pico and in the figure of Hercules at the Crossroads, the question of the human will is paramount. Both are "at one" with a thematic complex canonically associated with much of the early Renaissance. From Petrarch to Salutati to Valla, and beyond, Renaissance authors sustain the priority of will over intellect, of ethical action over metaphysical abstraction.[65] In effect, this is simply another version of the question of identity, since the possibility of willed choice is the constituent moment of freedom and, therefore, of identity. A crisis in the concept of the will is a "crisis of crisis," since, as mentioned earlier, "crisis" implies a point of reintegrating choice or judgment as well as a destabilizing split. Crisis, as it were, is always structured as the very moment of binary Herculean choice.

---

[65] For Salutati, see n. 21, above. See also Lorenzo Valla, *De Libero Arbitrio,* in Garin, ed., *Prosatori Latini,* pp. 524–65, and the relevant discussions in Garin, *L'Umanesimo,* and in Trinkaus, *Image and Likeness.* The tendency is to connect humanistic discourse on will to the Franciscan movement, with its polemics against the intellectualizing of Dominican Thomism, and thence to Augustine's critique of Platonism in terms of the fallen will. This genealogy puts in focus the key omission from Burckhardt's discussion of the centrality of will in the Renaissance: namely, that the emphasis falls on that faculty not because it is superior to intellect, but because it is man's weakest point in Christian terms (whereas for the Platonist, to know is already to choose and to love). For another, quite dramatic, staging of the problem, see Petrarch's *Secretum,* with its contrast between "Augustinus" who adopts a Stoic ethic and "Francesco" who understands what he should do but cannot, even at the last, resolve his conflicting desires. For the thesis that "Francesco" actually appropriates for himself the position of the historical Augustine, see Trinkaus, vol. 1, p. 5 ff., as well as Klaus Heitmann, "Insegnamenti Agostiniani nel *Secretum* del Petrarca," *Studi Petrarcheschi* 7 (1961).

Nevertheless, to choose *will*, for the humanists, did not necessarily mean to opt for a self-resolving, constructive crisis, by which the individual and the age each easily acquires a new identity. The priority given to will over intellect often implies precisely the ambiguous, divided, irresolute character of the former. In the case of Petrarch, as we know, the attention given to the will puts in relief not its integrity and centeredness, but rather its inner, neo-Augustinian split: "veggio 'l meglio, et al peggior m'appiglio" ("I see the better and cleave to the worse" *Rime* CCLXIV.136).[66] In Valla's *De Libero Arbitrio*, will's superiority over intellect (and rhetoric's over philosophy) appears, paradoxically, in philosophical reason's failures to prove the existence of free will—but one is then left with only blind faith that man's will actually is free and not predetermined.[67] Implicitly, will's ability to choose is left in doubt to the extent that it has no secure intellectual means of distinguishing among its options. Thus, to favor will may mean either to undermine it implicitly or to assume a stable, penetrating intellect which offers clear-cut options to choose among. It is little wonder then if the neo-Platonist heirs of the humanists slip easily over into what appears to be an exactly opposite position—as Castiglione's "Bembo" does, for instance, when he argues that if the truth is known (but *hic est labor*) it cannot help but be loved and chosen.[68] The force of the image of Hercules *in bivio*, then, may not be simply as emblem of ethical choice, but as a dramatization of the vexed dialectic of knowing and choosing: one must know in order to choose, but unless one makes choices, how is one to know? When Ruggiero comes to his "Y" in the Alcina episode he fails twice: unable, on the one hand, to impose his will by force against

[66] Even the source of the thought is divided. Its use links it to St. Paul, Romans 7:15 ("non enim quod voli bonum, hoc age; se quod odi malum, illud facio"), but it obviously derives more directly from Ovid, *Metamorphoses* VII.20–1: "video meliora proboque, / deteriora sequor."

[67] Valla, *De Libero Arbitrio*, esp. pp. 558–64.

[68] See the *Cortegiano* IV.li: "perchè il desiderio non appetisce se non le cose conosciute, bisogna sempre che la cognizione preceda il desiderio: il quale *per sua natura vuole il bene*, ma da sé è cieco e non lo conosce." Compare, however, IV.xiv–xvii, and particularly Bembo's distinction between intemperance and incontinence: the latter being a condition in which evil appetite prevails in spite of reason's better judgment. The contradiction with his later position is evident.

the allegorical vices which he recognizes as such, he then interprets
the two women who offer him aid as (pseudo-)Platonic ideals (VI.69)
when they are in fact agents of Alcina's corrupting seduction.
Fortitude and wisdom, as will and intellect, thus appear to be inter-
dependent and equally fallible. In fact, throughout the poem, intel-
lectual blindness leads into illicit desires as often as illicit desires
provoke willful blindness. The moment of choice becomes a point
of radical suspension of the hierarchy of faculties through which
human consciousness is interpreted in the Renaissance.

Linked closely with the apparent shift from intellect to will is a
marked humanistic preference for rhetoric over dialectic in the
trivium of academic subjects. Dialectic might hope to teach sight
and understanding, but rhetoric persuades the will to act upon what
it knows, to turn words and ideas into realities. And given the
Pauline-Augustinian-Petrarchan critique of human will and its
failings, rhetorical persuasion takes on special importance in moral
education. Unlike dialectic, it attempts to turn to good account the
several appetites and the corrupted will by luring them, in spite of
themselves, toward virtue and truth. The basic principle is that of
an *education* by *seduction,* imaged vividly by the Lucretian assimila-
tion of poetry to a sweetener which lures a child to take bitter
medicine.[69] In fact, poetry, with its aesthetic delights, becomes a
privileged instrument of utilitarian didacticism in a Renaissance
version of the Horatian dictum of "delight with utility," which,
however, imposes a more rigid hierarchy in favor of usefulness than
exists in the *Ars Poetica.*[70] And because this model valorizes the
"pleasures of the text," more than one critic has seen it as a means

[69] Lucretius, *De Rerum Natura* 1.936–50. For notable Renaissance versions of the
image, see Castiglione, *Cortegiano* IV.x, and Tasso, *Gerusalemme Liberata* 1.3. For
a similar, Biblical, motif of interpretive digestion, see Revelation 10:9–10 and
Ezechiel 3:1–4. More generally, poetics such as Boccaccio's *Genealogia* (XIV.xvi)
counter the accusation that poetry seduces with the argument that poets lure men
toward virtue.

[70] *Ars Poetica* 333–46. The rhetorical counterpart is Cicero's widely cited formula
of "delectare, docere, muovere" (e.g., *Brutus* xlix.185). The "dulcis utile" of rhe-
torical humanism also has a Platonically derived analogue in the poetics of "serio
ludere" (see n. 115 below) which is crucial for the *Furioso.* See Phillips Salman,
"Instruction and Delight in Medieval and Renaissance Criticism," *Renaissance Quar-
terly* 32 (1979), for a recent approach to the question in light of a faculty psychology
of reading.

of recuperating a didactic intention for the *Furioso*.[71] Whether in the general rhetorical or in the specifically poetic version, however, the notion of seduction as education is not without obvious problems and risks, a point made already by Plato in the *Phaedrus* and by Augustine, and oft repeated in the Renaissance.[72] Since the rhetorical seducer *in bono* deploys the same earthly delights that his counterpart *in malo* does, how can he be sure that the results will be any different—or even that his own intentions are actually pure? In the *Furioso*, Alcina's seductions are what disrupt Ruggiero's education. In fact, as we shall see, she reverses the sequence, making

[71] See especially Margaret Yoeman, "Allegorical Rhetoric in *Orlando Furioso*" (Diss. University of California–Irvine 1978). Yoeman is strongest in describing a single Renaissance tradition which she assumes to be valid for the *Furioso qua* Renaissance text.

[72] See Plato, *Phaedrus*, esp. 258e and ff., for the dismissal of rhetoric as a spurious seducer (for an ironic modern gloss on the relation of rhetoric and seduction in the *Phaedrus*, see Thomas Mann, *Death in Venice*). See also the attacks on poetry as seducer rather than as educator in *Republic* bks. II, III, X. For Augustine, see the *Confessions* (esp. I.10, 13, 17, 19; III.2, 6), which Christianizes the Platonic objections in asserting that artistic representation and human imagination are conducive to self-forgetfulness and sin rather than to self-remembrance and virtue. The Augustinian hermeneutics of "uti et frui" translates the pragmatic rhetorical approach of Horace into semiological and metaphysical terms (*De Doctrina Christiana*, esp. bk. I). Like Horace, he sees texts (more broadly defined, to include even the Book of Nature!) as either delightful ends in themselves or as useful means to ends beyond themselves— but he then goes on to point out that only complete metaphysical Being (God) can be intrinsically delightful. Thus, to dwell on the "pleasure of the text" is to become an idolator, treating the book as God, taking signs (*verba*) for "things in themselves" (*res*). For Augustine, it is up to the "reader" whether he is going to be educated (led behind the signs) or seduced (drawn into them). For the philosophical attack against rhetoric in the Renaissance (in effect, a counter-reaction against Vallian humanism) see Garin, *L'Umanesimo*, esp. pp. 119–23. He cites a letter by Giovanni Pico to Ermolao Barbaro dated June 9, 1485 (in Pico, *Opera Omnia*, ed. E. Garin [Torino: Bottega d'Erasmo, 1971], vol. I, pp. 351–58) in which Pico argues that rhetoricians, historians, and poets separate *res* from *verba*. He also argues specifically against the Lucretian poetics of medicinal sweetness (p. 355). The letter is partly translated into Italian in E. Garin, ed., *Filosofi Italiani del Quattrocento* (Firenze: LeMonnier, 1942). See also Gianfrancesco Pico della Mirandola, *De Studio Divinae et Humanae Philosophiae* (bk. I. chap. 6), in *Opera Omnia*, ed. E. Garin (Torino: Bottega d'Erasmo, 1972): "nec temere multis invenies qui pulchra alioquin poemata spurcitiis libidinibusque non foedaverunt: Quare scribit Isodorus ideo christianis prohiberi legere figmenta poetarum quia per oblectamenta fabularum excitant mentem ad incentiva libidinum" (cited by Weinberg, *History*, vol. I, pp. 255–57).

education the pretext for seduction. Just how different are her "poetics" from Ariosto's?

The shift from dialectic toward rhetoric also points toward a revolution in the definition of man's special place in the order of creatures: now, rather than primarily *ratio,* or reason, it is *oratio,* or speech, which is most peculiarly and most saliently human.[73] Through speech, man communicates with and acts persuasively upon other men; through speech he shapes the community he lives in and becomes, implicitly, the teller of his own tale, the author of himself and his fellows. As soon as the distinction is made, however, a split between knowledge and speech becomes a possibility and a threat.[74] The certainties of *ratio* disappear into the realm of language in which strategies of persuasion, emerging from the speaker's desire to shape the listener's desire, predominate and seem to preclude any direct access to the subjective truth of the self or the objective truth of the universe. Again, choices may be more easily enacted by force of rhetoric, but insight into the terms of a choice is correspondingly clouded. For this reason, there is a risk that man's tale of himself may slide from "storia" as history to "storia" as fiction (and self-delusion), parallel to the danger that education may degenerate into seduction. Some of the leading humanists were themselves acutely aware of the risk involved. Leonardo Bruni, the civic humanist *par excellence,* first great exemplar of the "new" historiography, acknowledges and embraces the poet's license to misrepresent his own beliefs in dialogue.[75] The rhetorical "formazione" of man and his city, which has seemed to many to blend ethics and aesthetics in the single category of "litterae," thus hovers dangerously between ethical historicity and aesthetic, irrelevant, self-reference. The only

[73] See n. 12, above and consult Seigel, *Rhetoric and Philosophy,* p. vii et passim. Poliziano seems to take this position in his oration on Quintilian and Statius, in Garin, ed., *Prosatori Latini,* pp. 880–85.

[74] Seigel, *Rhetoric and Philosophy,* pp. 6–7 (cf. pp. xiv–xv), cites Cicero, *De Inventione* i.i.i to the effect both that wisdom requires eloquence, and vice versa, *and* that such a union is nearly impossible. Pico, in the letter to Barbaro, replies to the accusation that philosophers separate their wisdom from eloquence by charging that poets, rhetoricians, and historians separate their eloquence from wisdom.

[75] For the humanistic tendency to group both "poetry" and "history" under the broad category of "humanae litterae," see Garin, *L'Umanesimo,* pp. 25–28, 47–54, passim, and his introduction to *Prosatori Latini,* pp. ix–xix. See also Nancy Struever,

way to rescue rhetoric from such perils is to recuperate it as itself a mode of knowledge, not only a mode of action. This is the powerful argument of Eugenio Garin, and it finds its neatest confirmation in Lorenzo Valla's celebration of the Latin language as a sacrament and as a "god descended from heaven," which enacts a Christlike intersection of sign and Being.[76] Once this tendency becomes clear, however, it seems to justify a return, on the one hand, to an

---

The Language of History in the Renaissance (Princeton: Princeton University Press, 1970), for the proximity of rhetoric (to which poetry was habitually assimilated, as seen earlier) and historiography. For the conceptual and etymological proximity of "story" and "history," via the Latin "historia," see Mazzotta, *Dante*, pp. 66–69 and the relevant bibliography cited there. Fornari, "Apologia," in *Spositione*, p. 47, specifically defends Ariosto's right to call the incredible *Furioso* an "istoria": "raguardando all'origine di questa voce, che altro non importa che raccontare." David Quint, "'Alexander the Pig': Shakespeare on History and Poetry," *Boundary* 2 10.3 (1982), offers a wide-ranging survey of classical and late Renaissance attempts to rescue history from the contaminations of poetic fiction and courtly flattery, and makes an interesting suggestion regarding the effect of that debate on the development of modern historical consciousness. For Bruni, see the *Dialoghi*, which begin as an exaltation of rhetorical exercises for educational purposes, but are structured by the movement from "Niccoli's" attack on Dante in pt. i (for, among other things, historical distortions in the *Commedia*, with the further implication that poetry *should* be historically factual), to his recantatory defense of the same "errors" in pt. ii on the ground that poetry can distort literal to achieve symbolic truth. In his letter to Lorenzo Valla, in *Epistolario* vi.8, in Francesco Luiso, *Studi sull'"Epistolario" di Leonardo Bruni*, ed. L.G. Rosa (Roma: Istituto Storico Italiano per il Medio Evo, 1980) Bruni in effect makes the same claim for the dialogue form itself (which is the most obvious point of convergence between the "literary" and the "historical" in humanistic writing): "scriptores, ii praesertim qui dialogo utuntur, occultant ipsi plerumque sententiam suam, promunt alienam, ut in Platone et Cicerone videmus." Guarino Veronese, *Epistola* no. 27, in Garin, ed., *Il Pensiero Pedagogico*, makes a sharp distinction between history and poetry, the former being "nuntia veritatis" (p. 338), while the latter differs from it: (1) in its (frequently unbelievable) fictions; (2) in its tendency to exaggerated praise and lying adulation. The letter, however, was written to urge a friend to write (for pay) the "history" of a local despot, and Guarino admits that a certain amount of distorting praise is inevitable even here. For Ariosto's treatment of the perverse relationship of poetry to history and historiography alike—especially when filtered through the poet-patron relationship in the lunar episode, see Chapter 4, sec. i, below.

[76] Valla, *Elegantiarum Libri*, excerpted in Garin, ed., *Prosatori Latini*, p. 596: Roman speech "quasi deum quendam e caelo dimissum apud se retinuerunt. Magnum ergo latini sermonis sacramentum est, magnum profecto numen quod . . . sancte et religiose per tot saecula custoditur. . . ."

explicitly metaphysical rhetoric—particularly that of Pico and the neo-Platonists—and even to a belief in magic, which is the literal transformation of words into reality. Thus we find that Pico has exactly reversed Valla's position, attacking rhetoric from the perspective of philosophy in a well-known letter to Ermolao Barbaro.[77] On the other hand, however, it might lead toward a parodic radicalization of the discrepancy between poetic rhetoric and the "realities" of history, such as one will find in St. John's treatment of lying writers in canto XXXV of the *Furioso* (another instance of an apparent Ariostan streak of antihumanism, one to which I will return later).

The themes of freedom, will, and rhetoric can be brought together and localized by reference to Renaissance theories and practices of literary, "liberal," education through which the self is formed, comes into being, by its readings. Among those who argue that a new program of education is a (or even the) definitive characteristic of the period are Mazzeo and, especially, Garin. A recent article has rightly suggested that a wider gap exists between educational theory and the practice of it than Garin is sometimes prepared to admit.[78] In any case, I am interested, precisely, in the "official" ideologies of education and in Ariosto's allusions and reactions to

[77] For the complex relation of continuity/opposition between civic humanism and mystical Platonism, see Garin, *L'Umanesimo*, pp. 17–18, 80 ff.; Greene, "The Flexibility of the Self," p. 252; as well as n. 80, below.

[78] On education as the defining characteristic of the Renaissance, see Garin, *L'Educazione in Europa*, pp. 22, 123, et passim, as well as Chapter 1, n. 3, above For Garin, education is actually one part of the larger "philological" movement toward the historicization of language and texts. See A. Grafton and L. Jardine, "Humanism and the School of Guarino: A Problem of Evaluation," *Past and Present* 96 (August 1982), for a necessary corrective to Garin's tendency to equate humanist practice with humanist theory. This article does not, however, address what I take to be Garin's central, brilliant, point: that the philological pedantry of Guarino and others contains within it, implicitly to be sure, grand intellectual and moral consequences; i.e., that their practice has an important theoretical dimension (cf. *L'Umanesimo*, pp. 1–16 passim). Grafton, in *Joseph Scaliger: A Study in the History of Classical Scholarship*, vol. 1 (Oxford: The Clarendon Press, 1983), esp. pp. 9–44, takes aim at Garin's account of the philological revolution as well, displacing its effective origins forward from Valla to Poliziano. For reasons too numerous to detail here, I feel that Grafton's powerful argument does not address the same questions as Garin's and so cannot be said to have overturned it. Finally, Garin does not himself

them—which in fact tend toward this very sort of demystification. Whether one gives priority in speaking of the Renaissance to the recovery and rereading of certain classical texts, or instead to the theme of will, education becomes a common, reconciling focal point, the crossroads at which the etymological proximity of *leggere* and *eleggere* becomes historically and conceptually significant. Reading is interpretation; interpretation is a kind of choice. Education is a learning to read by choosing, learning to choose by reading. The very concept of "liberal" art ("artes liberales") contains, for the Renaissance, a triple pun which embraces the Latin words for books (*libri*), for children (*liberi*), and for freedom (*libertas;* adjectives: *liber, -era, -erum*).[79] Hence: education of children, through reading of books, to the freedom (consisting in inner self-knowledge or in outward action on, or in concert with, others) which constitutes mature self-realization.

To specify a single program or concept of education as that of the whole era is of course sheerest folly. There are several different lines, and each tends to dismiss its competitors as mad, naming itself as uniquely capable of an educational redemption from folly. Even without Scholastic and other rivals, the Humanist movement itself was divided between neo-Stoics and neo-Epicureans, classicizers and Christians, and so on. Most notably, *Quattrocento* humanism can be divided ideologically and temporally between the "impegno civile"

---

always overestimate the impact of civic humanism on the political-cultural realities of the day. He argues, in fact, that the shift toward neo-Platonism in Fluorence during the second half of the *Quattrocento* signaled a clear retreat by intellectuals into the haven of "academic" life, reflecting their awareness that the ideals of the political humanists were at odds with reality. In this view the "contemplative" Platonists were actually less "utopian" than their "active" counterparts/predecessors (a point with which I believe Ariosto would have agreed); cf. *L'Umanesimo,* p. 94 ff.

[79] Seneca, *Epistola* 88.2: "quare liberalis studia dicta sint vides quia homine libero digna sunt." For the Renaissance pun, see Garin, *L'Educazione,* pp. 25, 116. See also Pier Paolo Vergerio, *De Ingenuis Moribus et Liberalibus Studiis,* in Garin, ed., *L'Educazione Umanistica in Italia* (Bari: Laterza, 1966), bk. 1, chap. 1 (p. 82), and Garin's note; as well as bk. 11, chap. 11 (p. 94). Cf. Plutarch, *De Educatione Liberorum,* and Mafeo Vegio, *De Educatione Liberorum.* In light of what happens to the model of education in Ariosto's hands, it is interesting to note a fourth possible pun: on the proper name, Liber, another Latin version of Bacchus.

of the earlier civic humanists and the later emphasis on contempla-
tive, neo-Platonic spirtuality by Landino, by Ficino, by Pico.[80] The
distance between the "two humanisms" can be heuristically mea-
sured, for instance, by comparing Pico's contemplative variant of
the *dignitas hominis* to Manetti's earlier treatment of the theme
which emphasized and celebrated the *vita activa*.[81] Of course, the
opposition is not as rigid as it has sometimes been made out to be,
as we have already seen in discussing the metaphysical implications
of Vallian rhetoric, and as we shall continue to see in reading the
Furioso.[82] In any event, by Ariosto's time it is not surprising to find
the two tendencies jarringly juxtaposed in a single text, as, for in-
stance, they are in book IV of the *Cortegiano,* where the Courtier's
duties as practical educator of his prince are set side by side with
Bembo's vision of Platonic *raptus* which leads (*e-ducit*) the soul out
of the material world of politics into the realm of pure spirit.[83] For
that matter, Salutati, over a hundred years before, places his Her-
cules now in one camp, now in the other. To deal effectively with
Ariosto's treatment of a "crisis" in education (in the formation of
identity), it will be necessary to situate him alternately in relation
to both of these (already too schematic) models of humanistic edu-

---

[80] For instance, Paul Oskar Kristeller, *Renaissance Thought* (New York: Harper &
Row, Harper Torchbooks, 1961), insists on a radical distinction between the early
rhetorical-philological humanism, on the one hand, and the "true" philosophers of
the Florentine Academy on the other. As Garin points out in *L'Umanesimo* (pp.
7–11), one can also follow Renan in identifying a rivalry between the tendentially
Aristotelian scholars of Padova and Bologna, on the one side, and Florentine neo-
Platonism on the other. Garin gives greater weight to the first opposition, however,
and, in fact, this seems to be Ariosto's tendency as well.

[81] Giannozzo Manetti, *De Dignitate et Excellentia Hominis* (1452). Cf. Garin,
L'Umanesimo, p. 81; Trinkaus, *Image and Likeness,* vol. 1, p. 230 ff.

[82] In emphasizing the continuities and the complementarity, as much as the op-
positions, between the two extreme positions, and thus rejecting Kristeller's rigidly
"disciplinarian" distinction between philosophy proper and other fields of endeavor,
I follow Garin, though I would not go so far as Seigel in arguing for the recon-
ciliation of eloquence and wisdom, rhetoric and philosophy, by the early humanists.
Garin's arguments about the philosophical implications of philology are extremely
suggestive, and they get powerful confirmation from the presence of Poliziano, in
his philological aspect, in the circle of Lorenzo along with Pico and Ficino. The
ideal *telos* of Garin's account is Vico.

[83] See Garin, *L'Umanesimo,* p. 118, on the neo-Platonic concept of "e-ducere" as
a leading out of and from the old self. Cf. Landino, *De Vera Nobilitate,* p. 109.

cation, rather than seeing the poem as decisively for one and against the other, as past critics generally have. It will become especially clear that the tendency to align the poem with a worldly humanism and against mysticism and metaphysics is somewhat misguided: Ariosto turns out to be more than willing to attack aspects of secular humanism and is even capable of leaving open, obliquely, transcendental possibilities.

According to Garin, a key cause and/or result of the humanistic conception of identity realized through rhetorical suasion was a practical program of education which aspired to the "freeing" of man by the study of the liberal arts and which grounded itself in new, philologically oriented, techniques of interpretation and in a new and broader canon of educational texts. Educational treatises, such as the *De Ingenuis Moribus* of Pier Paolo Vergerio, and numerous others helpfully collected by Garin,[84] abound in the early *Quattrocento,* forecasting the better-known efforts of Castiglione, Machiavelli, et al. At the same time, the foremost practitioners of the "new education" were Vittorino da Feltre and Guarino Veronese, whose wide fame among contemporaries begins to suggest the importance of the schools over which they presided. Guarino taught primarily in Ferrara, where his methods predominated down through Ariosto's day, partly owing to the efforts of his son, who succeeded him as head of the *Studio* and who consigned his father's program to a widely circulated treatise, *De Ordine Docendi et Discendi.*[85] Ariosto's well-known regret over the lost occasion for studies in Greek may betray a Guarinian influence.

---

[84] In *Il Pensiero Pedagogico dello Umanesimo,* see especially Vergerio; Vegio; Bruni, *De Studiis et Litteris;* Enea Silvio Piccolomini (Pius II), *Tractatus de Liberorum Educatione.* See also Alberti, *Della Famiglia,* in *Opere Volgari,* vol. 1 (Bari: Laterza, 1960), particularly bk. 1 on the education of sons by fathers, but also the whole treatise understood as an *ad hoc* education of "Battista" and "Carlo" by the older Alberti men while their father lies dying. See also the *Momus qua* treatise for the education of princes.

[85] Also to be found in Garin, ed., *Il Pensiero Pedagogico,* along with an interesting sampling of the elder Guarino's letters. For Ariosto's regrets about his studies in Greek, see *Satira* vi, esp. 130–83. For the rebirth of Greek studies in Europe, see Guarino's letters 2, 29, 30, and 31, with their obvious allusions to Emmanuel Crisolora's first name, in its etymological significance of "redeemer."

For the humanists, "insegnamento" was successful when it ful-
filled, as it were, its etymological destiny as a training in the de-
ciphering of "segni," signs. Garin has argued that philological
education was a process of learning to read signs by submitting
them to their historical origins and to an author whose distinctive
human identity emerged intact from his words, engaging the reader
in "living" conversation.[86] The pupil-reader might then turn wri-
ter, asserting yet another historically distinctive identity to be read
by others who would thereby be shaped into writers themselves.
Alternately, he might become an exemplary ruler whose life would
then be canonized by future poets and historians. Thus education
in the reading of signs had as its goal the production of more signs
(if one became a man of letters) or of turning one's own life and
name into a famous sign. The Renaissance value of glory, as of
honor and fame, is precisely the reverse side of "insegnamento"—
since one masters signs in life and enters into signhood in death.
But of course, this is the same process already ascribed to Salutati's
Hercules and for which Petrarch's letter on his visit with the Em-
peror Charles served as one of many possible examples: life imitates
artistic imitations of gloriously virtuous lives, with the hope of it-
self becoming such a written object of imitation in a vertiginous
game of mirrors which may leave the reader uncertain whether he
is mirror or mirrored, artificial construct or organic being.[87]

---

[86] For this *topos,* see Petrarch's letters to Cicero (*Familiares* XXIV.3–4) and other
ancients, as well as his "Posteritati," in *Prose*; Machiavelli's famous letter to Francesco
Vettori (December 10, 1513), reprinted in *Tutte le Opere*; and San Bernardino of
Siena, quoted by Garin in *L'Educazione in Europa,* p. 94.

[87] For education as reading, see Piccolomini, in Garin, ed., *Il Pensiero Pedagogico,*
pp. 224–25; Alberti, *Della Famiglia,* in *Opere Volgari,* pp. 68–71 (though the ques-
tion of book learning vs. experience is a thorny one throughout the text); as well
as Vergerio, pp. 91–93, and Battista Guarino, p. 452, both in *Il Pensiero Pedagogico.*
For the specific motifs of education by imitation of literary example leading to one's
enshrinement as famous poetic name (and the double educational goal of virtue
and glory), see Vergerio, pp. 69, 71–72, 82, 87; Guarino Veronese, letter no. 22,
pp. 384–86; Alberti, pp. 19, 24–25, 67. Battaglia, ed., *Il Pensiero Pedagogico del
Rinascimento,* p. 25, cites texts of Poliziano and Lorenzo de' Medici on the nature of
history as mirror to be imitated and of glory as inspirer to virtue. In Bembo, *Asolani*
1.i (*Opere in Volgare,* pp. 12–13) we find one of the most vivid such images: ". . . le
lettere e la scrittura, nella quale noi molte cose passate, che non potrebbono altra-

The resurrection of the name in poetic words may seem to re-place, or at least to complement, the ontological glory of the soul redeemed in God's word, constituting a nominal, temporal rebirth (*renaissance*) analogous and/or alternative to the Christian resurrec-tion. Nonetheless, for either the educational reading or the redemp-tive writing to be successful, the possibility of an essential link (a bond of reference, ontologically motivated) between sign and being (between the text's historical author and his words; between the virtuous hero and his heroic name) has to be established. Unless signs are somehow anchored firmly to their origins, the hope of humanistic education becomes a closed circuit of meaningless em-blems: not an ethics at all, but a pure aesthetics. Valla, as already noted, images language as "sacramental," as if to ward off the pessi-mistic conclusions about language toward which his own debunking of the inauthentic language of the *Donation of Constantine* and his painful experiences with plagiary might easily have lead him.[88] From Valla and rhetoric, from the concept of an ethical education to virtue, the theory of education can move in at least these two directions: (1) metaphysical and (2) aesthetic, which sometimes turn out not to be distinguishable at all.

The neo-Platonists, along with Pico, are writers who take the ontological possibilities of the sign to their extreme. For Pico in the *Heptaplus,* earthly reality is a metaphorical system which relates di-

---

mente essere alla nostra notizia pervenute, tutte quasi in uno specchio riguardando e quello di loro che faccia per noi raccogliendo, dagli altrui essempi ammaestrati ad entrare nelli non prima o solcati pelaghi o caminati sentieri della vita, quasi provati nocchieri e viandanti, più sicuramente ci mettiamo." As we know, there are several kinds of imitation in the Renaissance. Recent discussion has focused on imitation of literary predecessors (cf. Chapter 1, n. 53, above), but this already complex subject is further complicated by the addition of (1) textual imitation of "reality" and (2) readerly imitation of texts.

[88] Valla, *Elegantiarum Libri,* in Garin, ed., *Prosatori Latini,* pp. 606, 626. Forgery, passing one's own writing off as someone else's, and plagiary, passing someone else's writing off as one's own, are symmetrical threats to the Vallian notion of an inter-section between an author and his writing, and it is striking that in fact his career is marked by important encounters with both of them. For the theme of forgery in the Renaissance, see Quint, *Origin and Originality,* esp. chap. 1 ("The Counterfeit and the Original"), pp. 1–31, as well as Walter E. Stephens, "Berosus Chaldaeus: Counterfeit and Fictive Editors of the Early Sixteenth Century" (Diss. Cornell 1979).

rectly to two higher levels of reality: the visible cosmos and the invisible heaven of heavens. What is more, as each of these realms implicitly refers its "readers" to the other two, containing them, so to speak, in the same way a book, Genesis in particular, can contain all of them metaphorically and yet truly within itself.[89] Education, askesis, is thus, as it is for the neo-Platonists as well, a series of metaphorical displacements within and without: of the reader recognizing the tacit, ontologically founded, resemblance between the books he reads (including the Book of Nature) and the higher levels of existence; of the self inwardly translated (*translatio* = metaphor) from one state of inner being to a higher one.[90] In a humanistic scheme, books offer transparent views of history, exemplary models for action. In a "Platonic" scheme (and again I am speaking too schematically, though of necessity) history itself becomes a book, a series of metaphors for a further, hidden reality. In either case it is clearly the metaphorical, "imitative" relation between "text" and "reality" which is at issue, while what changes, what is exchanged, is the definition of "text" and of "reality" (suggesting that at base the textual always partakes to some extent of the real, and vice versa). Education in both cases is an "outward" transit made from text to referents, and inwardly a metaphorical movement from one stage of selfhood to another. Or rather, it is the literalization of a metaphor in and by the self: education, a metaphor, is literalized as real displacement of the self, real movement beyond the texts. At the same time, however, education is the antithesis of metaphor; for instead of moving from term X to term Y in a gesture of equivalence and identification, education supposes a split within the person, from past ignorance to present knowledge, from *homo vetus* to the new, and requires a necessary self-alienation before selfhood can be established.

[89] *Heptaplus,* Garin edition, esp. pp. 374–82.

[90] For the universe as a book, see Landino, "Proemio," p. 142. The image of God as poet, universe as poem, is also in the *Heptaplus* and, for that matter, already in Augustine (see Chapter 4, n. 67, below). See Curtius, *European Literature,* pp. 319–26, for the "Book of Nature." Ficino, *De Sole,* in Garin, ed., *Prosatori Latini,* pp. 970–72, explicitly writes his work not systematically and logically, but "allegorically" and imaginatively, because ascent to God must take place through similitudes, not directly. Thus the visible sun is taken as a figure for the greater, invisible One. See Garin, *L'Umanesimo,* pp. 118–19.

The turn to metaphysics which ultimately privileges the hidden reality over the "mere" signs of text and history is paralleled and opposed by a turn toward an "aesthetics" of pure form, which for Garin might be located in a figure such as Ermolao Barbaro or, later, in Francesco Della Casa's *Galateo*. In such a view, signs themselves become the primary object, an end in themselves. For Barbaro, linguistic style is the focus (Garin often cites Barbaro's famous phrase—"I acknowledge two Lords: Christ and letters"— which elevates letters to divine status while effectively trivializing Christ and which, incidentally, seems a natural development from Valla's imagery).[91] For Della Casa, the forms of behavior become all-important: his "etiquette" is the point at which ethics is converted into an aesthetics of formal manners for manners' (and art's) sake. Curiously, however, the "extremes" of metaphysics and aesthetics constantly encounter each other in such key figures (key especially for Ariosto) as Bembo and Castiglione. Bembo who, on the one hand, is the author of *Gli Asolani* and an advocate of Platonic spiritual ascent through love of the Beautiful, is also the author of *Prose della Volgar Lingua,* whose prescriptive, formalist character is well known, and the promoter of a poetic Petrarchism whose criteria are largely stylistic. It is especially significant that critical discussions on the relation of Bembo and Ariosto have focused on the adoption by the latter of the linguistic criteria of the former in successive revisions of the poem, thus continuing implicitly the "aestheticization" of the Ariostan project announced by DeSanctis.[92] Castiglione, perhaps more aware of his paradoxical position, is also more agile in the metaphors with which he unites

---

[91] "Duos agnosco dominos: Christum et litteras." The phrase comes from a letter to Arnaldo of Bost from 1486, reprinted in Ermolao Barbaro, *Epistolae, Orationes et Carmina,* ed. V. Branca (Firenze: "Bibliophilus," 1943), vol. i, p. 96. For a crisis of liberal education in courtly Italy, linked specifically to Della Casa's transformation of ethics into etiquette, see Garin, *L'Educazione in Europa,* pp. 143, 179. For Barbaro, see Garin, *L'Umanesimo,* pp. 84–87. One problem here is that the contrast between Barbaro's aesthetic philology and Poliziano's "ethical" one can be contested, since Poliziano himself, in his poetry at least, is implicated in an "aesthetic" attempt, however unsuccessful, to escape history and death. Cf. Eugenio Donato, "Death and History in Poliziano's *Stanze,*" *MLN* 80 (1965).

[92] See Chapter 1, n. 50, above. I will show in the last section of this chapter that Bembo is the target of thematic polemics on the part of his friend.

and contrasts the two. The explicit enterprise of the *Cortegiano* is the "formazione" of the Courtier, i.e., the drawing of a verbal picture of such a person, including the establishment of educational criteria by which a Courtier might actually be formed, and defining the Courtier himself as the "formatore" or educator of his prince. Finally, the Courtier is to pursue the Platonic "forms" in a triumphant spiritual ascent. These are ethical and metaphysical projects, but by the same token "formazione" in the book is frequently an exclusively "aesthetic" category. The participants in the dialogue periodically consign the Courtier to the realm of ideal, unrealizable, and therefore purely fictional forms. As part of his "formazione" he learns to deploy formal behavior unrelated to inner reality. To take Charles Singleton's famous phrase somewhat out of context: "The fiction is that it is not a fiction."[93] The work hovers between the mere aesthetic formality of game and the ethical and metaphysical shaping of reality.[94]

Garin repeats a truism of the Renaissance when he argues that the humanists' use of poetry, or rather of "litterae" in general, was not aesthetic but ethical.[95] By the same token, from Boccaccio and Salutati to Landino and Pico, various forms of the "poetic theology"

---

[93] Though *Il Libro del Cortegiano* was not published until 1525, it existed in an early draft well before the first edition of the Furioso (1516) and Ariosto might easily have seen it. There is an allusion to Castiglione in XLII.85 from 1516 on, but a second allusion identifying him specifically as author of the *Cortegiano* appears only in the 1532 edition (XXXVII.8.3–4). In *Satira* III.91, which according to Segre (Ariosto, *Opere Minori,* p. 524) could have been composed as early as 1518, Castiglione is referred to as the "formator del cortigiano." For the use of "formazione" and its relatives, see *Cortegiano* I.i, xii; II.xxxiii, xlvi, c; passim. For Singleton's remark, see *Dante's "Commedia": Elements of Structure* (Baltimore: The Johns Hopkins University Press, 1977), p. 62. Singleton specifically contrasts this formula with Ariosto's deliberate exposure of the fictiveness of his own poem. But Singleton, translator of the *Courtier,* must have known that his formula very clearly echoes Castiglione's definition of "sprezzatura," the art that hides itself (I.xxvii).

[94] See Greene's excellent article, "*Il Cortegiano* and the Choice of a Game," *Renaissance Quarterly* 32 (1979). The article is reprinted in R. Hanning and D. Rosand, eds., *Castiglione: The Ideal and the Real in Renaissance Culture* (New Haven: Yale University Press, 1983), along with several other useful articles. See also Wayne Rebhorn, *Courtly Performances: Masking and Festivity in Castiglione's "Book of the Courtier"* (Detroit: Wayne State University Press, 1978).

[95] Garin, *L'Educazione in Europa,* pp. 88–89.

announce poetry as the bearer of a tacit revelation (oxymoronic though this may sound) of philosophical and theological truths.[96] Poetry may be a mode of action or a mode of knowledge, or both. When metaphor becomes the structure of the cosmos, as it does for Ficino and Pico, poetry as the metaphorical language above all others assumes a privileged role. Nevertheless, Garin also sees that, at least in the case of the neo-Platonists, we are rapidly approaching an aesthetic view not only of poetry but of all reality.[97] As poetry is lifted up toward theology, theology may slide down into "mere" poetry. Ariosto's awareness of this possibility informs his treatment of St. John and the poets in the lunar episode, as I will show later on. In fact, as has been suggested, *both* the humanistic project of reading books to see and shape history and the neo-Platonic project of reading history to see and attain a hidden spiritual reality risk lapsing into utopian, aesthetic discourse at the moment when one questions the referential relation of their texts to "reality," objective or subjective, historical or spiritual as it may be. It might be argued that this questioning is anachronistic, but of course it is not. Civic humanists question, if not their own discourse, at least the folly of Platonism in aspiring to unseen, impossible realms, while neo-Platonists attack the mad materialism of a secular humanism.[98] A few simple steps lead to an author such as Ariosto who brings both positions under scrutiny and uses each in turn to criticize the other, revealing a threat of madness which inhabits every project of education.

---

[96] For the poetic theology in general, see Trinkaus, *Image and Likeness,* vol. 2, p. 683 ff.; Garin, *L'Umanesimo,* pp. 105–118; and Greenfield, *Humanist and Scholastic Poetics,* passim. See also D.P. Walker, *The Ancient Theology* (Ithaca: Cornell University Press, 1972). Versions can be found in Pico, *Oratio;* Boccaccio, *Genealogia,* esp. bks. xiv and xv; Landino, *Disputationes;* Salutati, *De Laboribus Herculis;* and so on.

[97] Cf. Garin, "La Letteratura degli Umanisti," in *Il Quattrocento e l'Ariosto,* eds. E. Cecchi and N. Sapegno (Milano: Garzanti, 1965), p. 300.

[98] For the "humanistic" attack on Platonic utopianism see, for instance, Matteo Palmieri, *Della Vita Civile,* excerpted in C. Varese, ed., *Prosatori Volgari,* p. 357 (Palmieri does, however, have his own peculiar mystical-Platonic side which appears in the poem *Città di Vita*). See also Machiavelli's dedicatory letter to *Il Principe* and chap. 15 of the treatise. For the other side, see, for example, Landino's relatively mild critique of the *vita activa* in *Disputationes,* bk. 1.

These arguments might seem to bolster (in a new, more histori-
cized, way) the critical picture of the *Furioso* as a world of pure
literary art reflecting exclusively upon itself, without any didactic
"impegno" or pretenses: a debunking of the claims made for litera-
ture during the previous century, whether as humanistic "letters"
or as "poetic theology." But the situation is far more complicated
since education, as we have seen, may itself become an aesthetic en-
deavor. This is true in at least two senses: on the one hand, a notion
of an artistic "formazione" or molding of the self; and on the other,
the conversion of the living self into a literary name.[99] For that
very reason it is equally difficult to accept with complacency the
counterarguments (which will be encountered in the next section)
that the *Furioso* is not "merely" an aesthetic bauble, but is entirely
caught up in a Renaissance "poetics of education." What should be
pursued, instead, is an understanding of Ariosto's understanding of
the dialectics of education and aesthetics, including both the ten-
dency of education to degenerate into mere metaphors and sheer
rhetoric, and its opposite: the possibility for poetic figures to effect
unexpectedly vital transformations in and of the real. Further con-
sideration may even suggest how this dialectic flirts with two com-
peting notions of human freedom: (1) the freedom which comes
into being in the exercise of choice in history, and (2) the freedom
of imagination conferred precisely by fantastic departures from the
constraints of history, of personality, of transcendental destiny—in
other words, the freedom of play.[100]

In the preceding pages the outline of an historical crisis of iden-
tity, of an epoch which both gives new definition and privilege to
human individuality and, simultaneously, threatens it at every turn,
has been sketched—even as I insisted that it is not so easy to iden-

[99] Mazzeo, *Renaissance and Revolution,* p. 31, recounts (without giving a specific
reference) the following piece of advice from Plotinus, who "told his disciples that
they must be like the coroplast, the maker of decorated statues, and assume as the
task of life the transformation of themselves into works of art. The intellectual and
moral discipline of education, starting with the unadorned clay of childhood, was
to help man model his own statue, to become a harmony of parts and functions, a
work of ideal proportions." Cf. Pico, *Heptaplus,* Garin edition, pp. 300–302, on man
as statue placed by God in the midst of His creation to honor Himself.

[100] Marcello Turchi, *Ariosto, o della Liberazione Fantastica* (Ravenna: Longo, 1969),
esp. p. 9, focuses on the second type of freedom, as, in effect, the DeSanctian-Crocean
tradition has all along. DeBlasi, by contrast, insists on the first type.

tify that epoch in a single or simple way. To this era of crisis, and its texts, the *Orlando Furioso* is linked by temporal and geographical proximity, as well as (if one may judge by the Herculean resonances of the title and a few other hints already offered) conceptually and thematically. It will not be easy to argue (even though this is always the temptation in a study dedicated to a single author or work) that the *Furioso* alone exposes the flaws in the arguments of simple-minded contemporaries, alone masters the intricacies of the crises. A sample of just a few relevant authors and works (when Ariosto drew on hundreds) has suggested that many of them raise questions implicitly or explicitly about the values they are usually thought to embrace wholeheartedly and single-mindedly. Whether Ariosto simply restructured the dilemmas found in other texts or himself opened them for the first time is itself an open question, one which I am not prepared to answer definitively. Because of the confluence in the Renaissance, in Italy, in Ferrara, in the *Furioso,* of such a broad spectrum of voices, images, and ideological tendencies, it is impossible to restate simply *a* crisis which the poem represents or to isolate a single school or limited group of texts in relation to which, either supportively or polemically, it defines itself. More-over, as Chapter 3 will show, the *Furioso* inserts itself into the intel-lectual-rhetorical traditions of education via another, related, poetic tradition—that of the epic "allegory of education," particularly as developed in the *Odyssey,* the *Aeneid,* and the *Commedia,* and, of equal importance, in allegorical readings of epics from the pre-Sophists to Cristoforo Landino. And the *Furioso* draws on at least two tendencies which diverge within the allegorizing tradition: the ethical and political; the spiritual and metaphysical.

Ariosto's poem, as much as its epoch, and as many of the individ-uals and texts within it, is self-contradictory, divided repeatedly against itself in its representations of education and of itself as agent of education (or of madness). The extent and deliberateness of those contradictions will be given their first measurement in the next sec-tion by surveying the multiplicity of critical response to the ques-tion of identity in the poem. Finally, however, only an extended unraveling of the relevant motifs and events, if only in a single epi-sode of the *Furioso,* can begin to give an adequate idea of how ex-tensively, how intimately, such crises are dramatized within the poem and how deeply they penetrate and inhabit its structures.

iii. *Reading the Furioso's Readers*

Has criticism of the *Furioso* truly lacked an awareness of the impor-
tance to the poem either of an internal crisis of individual subjec-
tivity or of the historical literature of crisis which took it as a theme?
Clearly not, as the example of Saccone's treatment of the figure of
Hercules in the poem has already shown. In fact, the critical theme
of education in the poem is not by any means new. Many of the ear-
liest commentators, apologetically or not, insisted on an allegorical-
didactic reading of the *Furioso,* although few moderns are willing to
take their interpretations seriously.[101] Subsequent criticism turned
away from such positions, both because of new, antiallegorical,
antiutilitarian ideologies of poetic and critical function and because
of the evident defects of an allegorical reading which does not also
take into account the poem's ironic twists and turns, its overt eva-
sions of the "serious" in all its forms.[102] After all, even its title is
a parody of a tragic drama. The culmination of such a refusal came
in the twin dicta of DeSanctis and Croce—the former denying the
Furioso in particular any didactic seriousness (pp. 451–52); the latter
going further, to refuse an educational *telos* to poetry in general

[101] See, for convenience, the compilation of *Cinquecento* and *Seicento* commenta-
tors in Orlandini's edition of the *Opere;* vol. 1 contains the *Furioso,* a number of
general readings of it, as well as canto-by-canto glosses of it by several critics (taken
from the commentaries, which may also be consulted individually, of C. Valvassori,
G. Bonomone, T. Porcacchi, L. Dolci, G. Ruscelli, O. Toscanella, and others). Some
recent critics have begun to take much more seriously the critical and scholarly re-
sponses of Ariosto's first readers, both the allegorists and those, like Pigna and Giraldi-
Cinzio, who concentrated on narrative structure and genre. In many ways, Giamatti's
readings of the poems are elaborations of images and themes already dear to the
allegorists. On different tacks are Javitch, "*Cantus Interruptus* in the *Orlando Furioso,*"
MLN 95 (1980); Wiggins, "Galileo"; and Parker's discussion of the *Cinquecento* theo-
rists of romance in *Inescapable Romance.*

[102] Tasso already argues that delight, rather than utility, is the intrinsic end of poet-
ry, though, of course, the history of his criticism, as of his poetry, is that of open
warfare between the two functions. See *Discorsi del Poema Eroico,* in *Prose,* ed. E.
Mazzali (Milano and Napoli: Ricciardi, 1959), bk. 1, pp. 497–500; cf. *Gerusalemme
Liberata* 1.3. See Weinberg, *History,* esp. vol. 1, for the debate over the two ends of
poetry, as well as nn. 69 and 70 above. Ludovico Castelvetro is perhaps the most
prominent defender of pure delight as poetry's proper end in this period. See Abrams,
The Mirror and the Lamp, for a sweeping account of the historical shifts in critical
orientation (cf. Chapter 1, n. 54, above).

(p. 7). In the polemical attempts, which have characterized much of twentieth-century criticism, to redress the excesses of these two imposing figures, the theme of education and of humanistic epistemological values in general has been touched on with relative frequency, sometimes with reference to elements of the historical context (including tacit returns to the *Cinquecento* allegorizers), sometimes by a closer reading of the text itself. These efforts almost always regard the DeSanctian position as merely erroneous. And yet, as shall become clear, there is every reason to believe that the text intermittently characterizes itself precisely as an autonomous world of delightful evasion rather than a serious reflection on the tragic world without. On the other hand, these revisionary efforts have begun to show the radical incompleteness of DeSanctis' view and to indicate some of the ways in which the text confronts its readers and its historical surroundings, and in which Ariosto's epoch denies *a priori* to its poets the possibility of a nonpolemical, nonengaged retreat from reference and from a didactic poetics.

In the next few pages I will try to sketch the range of responses excited by the poem. My purpose is to prepare the way for a reading of the *Furioso* as the convergence of several major threads of Renaissance discourse (many of which were touched upon in the previous sections), and consequently as the disingenuous sponsor of the multiple, often mutually contradictory, interpretations that have been given to it. The assimilations of Ariosto to Renaissance culture range from linking him to a this-worldly ethical humanism to claiming his affinity for the mystical neo-Platonism of his friend, Bembo; from arguing that all humanistic values whatsoever disappear into a world of illusory appearance and blind madness to asserting that madness itself, in Erasmian fashion, becomes an alternative source of understanding and value, through a studied critique of "reason." In the next, and final, section of the chapter, I will take a protracted look at one, perhaps the only, critical reading of the *Furioso* which takes all of these positions into account, holding them together in a tense dialectical suspension. Ironically, that reading is contained in one of Ariosto's own "minor" works, *Satira* VI.

The preceding sections, especially the discussion of the title, began to suggest the existence of an antihumanistic vein in the *Furioso*. But if this is so, it runs contrary to a good deal of textual evidence and a greater deal of critical opinion. Giorgio DeBlasi speaks for a whole generation of critics when he suggests that Ariosto discovers solid values in man and in human liberty.[103] DeBlasi, as previously noted, compares Ariosto to Pico, effectively confusing ethical with metaphysical humanism; but, in point of fact, he is also careful to describe Ariosto's humanism as one which proves itself negatively by a sage recognition of human limits, including those of the author himself, notably in the famous line, "ecco il giudicio uman come spesso erra" ("behold how often human judgment strays" 1.7.2).[104] This sense of limit is what might seem to protect the poet from the accusation of humanistic titanism which contributes to the destruction of Seneca's Hercules and which always haunts Pico. To give DeBlasi his due, which is considerable, the poem does seem to remain circumspectly and persistently within the realm of the human and the natural: even the flight to the moon merely emphasizes a decision not to go beyond the sphere which traditionally marks the breaking point between time and eternity. In fact, the moon's main contents are a mimetic copy of worldly reality and an allegory of human time,[105] seeming thereby to deflect any higher-reaching gaze back toward the terrestrial. Nonetheless, while the Alcina episode *can* be read as confirmation of this tendency, Chapter 4 will show that the poem does, deliberately and extensively, reflect on the status of Christian truth and does, however obliquely, leave open the possibility of a transcending faith. On the other hand, as we shall begin to see, the poet's supposed sense of the limits of man often seems both to narrow into a vision of unrestrained blindness, treachery, and violence and to include man's own inability to perceive or observe limits. Chapters 3 and 4 will demonstrate that the flights of Ruggiero and then Astolfo on the hippogryph both actually put the question of limits to specific tests, as each, for evil or for good, seems to exceed a number of key classical and Christian barriers (the gates of Eden, the mouth of hell, the signs of Hercules).

---

[103] DeBlasi, "Ariosto," pt. 2, p. 187. See also Caretti's less textually detailed version of the same basic point in his "Introduzione" to *Opere Minori*, Segre edition.

[104] Pt. 2, pp. 191–92. Cf. n. 58, above.

[105] See Chapter 4, sec. i, for the "allegory of reference" in the lunar episode.

Two American critics, Giamatti and Durling, have given to DeBlasi's basic argument the kind of systematic textual specification and elaboration that it cries out for. In his article entitled "Headlong Horses, Headless Horsemen," Giamatti fastens brilliantly on the traditional Platonic imagery of horses and reining as a means of contrasting Orlando's "sfrenatura," leading to madness, with Ruggiero's educated restraint, at least at the end of the poem. The imagery of reining confers vivid specificity on the "humanism of limits."[106] In addition, his chapter on the Alcina-Logistilla sequence in *The Earthly Paradise and the Renaissance Epic* demonstrates beyond a doubt that the poem dramatizes, through Ruggiero, a complex educational process moving from initial failure to eventual (qualified) success, and that in so doing it scrutinizes the poet's own role as teacher and the reader's as student. In this case there is no explicit connection made to specific traditions of humanistic education, though the motif of the "earthly paradise" points in the direction of Christian and classical concepts of education as a return to a pre-fallen condition of intellect and will represented, respectively, by Eden and the Golden Age.[107]

Oddly enough, in view of his neo-Crocean argument for the poet as *alter Deus,* Durling too ascribes to Ariosto a limited didactic humanism, partly by insisting that Ariosto's model is not the omnipotence of the Christian God, but the more restricted powers of the Platonic Demiurgos.[108] In studying the explicit rhetorical presences of the poet-narrator, Durling naturally focused a great deal of attention on the proems, where that voice is heard most frequently, and he gives special weight to their ethical-didactic commentary on the narrative. Though it is possible to argue that the proems are more subjected to subversive ironies than he will

---

[106] Cf. "Headlong Horses, Headless Horsemen," p. 295 ff.

[107] On the other hand, the value the essay places on ironic insight has an anachronistic savor of twentieth-century American educational humanism. A metaphor applied to one particularly unhappy moment in Ruggiero's itinerary tends to confirm the presence of this bias: "we are watching a young man flunk his course" (*The Earthly Paradise,* p. 148). See the dissertation of Mary M. Farrell, "Mentors and Magi," for an expanded list of poet-pedagogue figures in the poem.

[108] Cf. Chapter 1, n. 6, above; Chapter 4, n. 67, below.

allow,[109] this work makes it clear that the narrator frequently adopts the guise of a magisterial poet, thus aligning the poem, whether seriously or parodically, with a tradition of literature as metaphorical mediator of education. In addition, Durling's argument that the poem's educational function consists partly in emphasizing the differences between the fantasies of literature and the reader's reality (p. 130) offers a hint as to how one might begin to reconcile DeSanctis' stress on poetic delight and evasion with a rhetorical view of poetry as moral education. Some critics have tried to make a similar argument recently in more historicized terms, by explicitly invoking the rhetorical model (Ciceronian and Horatian) of *dulcis* at the service of *utilis,* of linguistic seduction of the fallen will.[110] As already seen, however, this approach, and finally Durling's as well, are subject to the Platonic objection that if seduction can be used to further education, education can equally be used as a pretext for seduction.

There is another, and in some respects quite convincing, interpretation of Ariosto as humanist which reads the *Furioso* as polemi-

---

[109] I strongly disagree with Durling's assertion that "the moralizing of the exordia is preserved from any corrosion by the famous Ariostan irony" (*The Figure of the Poet,* p. 135). Even *he* makes a number of exceptions, and I believe that these exceptions quickly become themselves a rule (p. 135 ff.). See n. 39 above for an instance of a proem read with deadly seriousness by most readers (e.g., Saccone, *Il Soggetto,* p. 161) and yet clearly subverted by narratives that precede and follow it. For another way of reading Durling's positive example of III.1–4, see Chapter 4, sec. iii, below. In the course of this study alone, ironic problems with the proems to cantos VII, VIII, XXI, XXIII, XXIV, XXXIII, XXXV, XLII, and XLVI will emerge. This blind spot is, I suspect, a consequence of Durling's otherwise brilliantly successful method: by privileging the proems along with all other direct utterances of the poet-narrator at the expense of the narrated tales, he *de facto* establishes an interpretive hierarchy of the former over the latter.

[110] Cf. sec. ii and nn. 69–70, 102, above. Proponents of this position include Yoeman, as well as Vincent Cuccaro, *The Humanism of Ludovico Ariosto: From the "Satire" to the "Furioso"* (Ravenna: Longo, 1981), esp. pp. 141–44. See also DeBlasi, "Ariosto," pt. 2, p. 194, for an earlier assimilation of Ariosto's poetry to the Orphic poetry of civilization and education. For specifications of the well-known Ariostan debt to Horace, see Giorgio Petrocchi, "Orazio e Ariosto," *Giornale Italiano di Filologia,* n.s. 1 (1970); and David Marsh, "Horatian Influence and Imitation in Ariosto's *Satire,*" *Comparative Literature* 27 (1975).

cally anti-Platonic, while at the same time claiming for the poet at least a perfunctory Christian piety. Rocco Montano sees Orlando's madness as a travesty of the redeeming Platonic frenzy of love celebrated by such minglers of Platonic askesis and *stil nuovo* erotic idealism as Leone Ebreo, Bembo, and Castiglione.[111] Though there are problems with his argument, it is clear enough that Orlando's pursuit of a "donna angelicata," Angelica, leads down to carnal desire and folly rather than up to an education in spiritual beauty and goodness. This approach clearly points a way toward further study. It may even suggest a sense in which Ariosto's text is already at work demystifying the cult of pure aesthetic beauty founded by DeSanctis and taken to the limit by Croce in their readings of the poem. Orlando's deluded pursuit of the "ideal" Angelica might seem an uncannily proleptic figure for their interpretive pursuit of the poem as, respectively, "l'arte per l'arte" and ideal *Armonia*.

On the other hand, this position as currently defined does not take a broad enough view of the culture of neo-Platonism or of Ariosto's acquaintance with and use of it. Relatively few critics have countered the "humanism of limits" argument with a vision of Ariosto as bona fide Platonist. More to the point, from all sides evidence is beginning to mount regarding the broadly neo-Platonic culture of Ariosto and the neo-Platonic themes and motifs of his poem. Ariosto's familiarity with such material is attested by the early letter requesting an edition of the works of Ficino from a Venetian publisher and by his youthful fragment, "De Laudibus Sophiae," with its celebration of mystical knowledge. It is supported by his friendship with Bembo, and his admiration for Castiglione (of whose skills in synthesizing "civic" humanism with neo-Platonism I have spoken above). Recent studies have begun to make profound inroads in establishing his acquaintance with various

---

[111] Rocco Montano, "La Follia di Orlando," in *Saggi di Cultura Umanistica* (Napoli: Quaderni, 1962), which is a revised edition of his *Follia e Saggezza nel "Furioso" e nell'"Elogio" di Erasmo* (Napoli: Edizioni "Humanitas," 1942). See Cuccaro, *Humanism*, pp. 62–66, 163, 176–77, passim, for a view very close to Montano's. See also Alfredo Bonadeo, "Note sulla Pazzia di Orlando," *Forum Italicum* 4 (1970), for a more textualized and historicized version of the same. For Ariosto and Bembo, see nn. 142 and 145, below. For Ariosto and Castiglione, see n. 93, above.

mystical currents, pseudo-Egyptian lore, and so on.[112] We are increasingly aware of the pervasive presence of neo-Platonic themes and emblems in the *Furioso* and elsewhere in Ariosto's canon: the *selva,* the chariot and horses of the soul, the artistic Demiurge, the cave.[113] In Chapters 3 and 4 I will suggest just how extensively the Platonist version of the "allegory of education," alongside the ethical-rhetorical variety, informs not only the Alcina-Logistilla sequence but the lunar episode as well. If Ariosto's approach to these matters is indeed subversive, its polemic is far broader and concerns a far more complex version of mystical Platonism than has generally been recognized.

In point of fact, a positive reading of Ariosto as Platonist is beginning to emerge explicitly. If Montano's critique makes it difficult to take too seriously a recent claim that Ariosto is a pure and straightforward poet of Platonic beauty,[114] it is not easy to dismiss hints that the *Furioso* reflects a Platonizing poetics of "serio ludere."[115] The concept of allegorically "serious play" is, in effect,

---

[112] See the letter to Aldo Manuzio of Venice, dated January 5, 1498, no. 1 in *Lettere.* Saccone ("Appunti," pp. 157–60) adds on an especially suggestive appendix on Ariosto's acquaintance with neo-Platonic and other lore. See also Gennaro Savarese, "Ariosto al Bivio tra Marsilio Ficino e 'Adescatrici Galliche,'" *Annali dell'Istituto di Filologia Moderna dell'Università di Roma* (1978).

[113] For the *selva,* see Carne-Ross, "One and Many," pp. 198–200 and p. 232 (n. 2), as well as Donato, "Desire," p. 18 and relevant note. For the horses and chariot of the soul (and its wings) see *Phaedrus* 246a–249b and Giamatti's discussion of them in "Headlong Horses, Headless Horsemen." For the Demiurge in general, see Durling, *The Figure of the Poet,* p. 130, and also Saccone, "Appunti," p. 128, which actually locates the figure in the Demogorgon of the *Cinque Canti.* For suspiciously Platonic caves in the *Furioso,* see XI.10, XII.86–94, XIII.1ff., XIX.35, XXIII.106–107, 130 (cf. *Republic* 514a and ff.). To this list I will add as I go along.

[114] Roger Baillet, *Le Monde Poétique de l'Arioste* (Lyon: L'Hermès, 1977), e.g., pp. 42–43, 189.

[115] Such hints are to be found in Savarese, who links Ariosto to the tradition via his, and Erasmus', friend, Celio Calcagnini (cf. *Furioso* XLII.90, XLVI.14). Calcagnini uses Ariosto's name and voice in the dialogue *Equitatio,* as Savarese points out (unfortunately assuming that this fictional character reflects the views of the real Ariosto directly). His scholarship is wonderfully suggestive, though no direct connection is made to the *Furioso.* Less specific, and yet more comprehensive in its implications, is the hint in this direction dropped by Peter Marinelli, "Redemptive Laughter: Comedy in the Italian Romances," *Genre* 9 (Winter 1976/77), p. 508.

the metaphysical counterpart of the rhetorical poetics of "dulcis et utilis," education by seduction. It is essentially a version of the "poetic theology" in which the pleasurable surface that attracts the vulgar reader conceals intellectual treasures that only the initiated few can arrive at. "Serio ludere" makes the poetic theology more attractive and more practical for the actual composition of literature by linking it directly to the playful Socratic technique of ironic self-effacement in the Platonic dialogues themselves. It differs from the rhetorical model by tending to insist that surface and inner meaning *are* radically at odds—the former an agent of ignorance and self-forgetfulness, the latter of intellectual self-enlightenment. There will be ample occasion in the next two chapters to test just how ironic is Ariosto's relation to this version of philosophical-poetic irony.

An easier claim to make and defend is that, whatever its position in regard to the positive program(s) of neo-Platonism, the *Furioso* does seem to embrace the negative side of the perspective— its critique of the physical world of blindness and delusion and of man's attachments to it. As we shall see, for instance, the image of love as violence and folly can actually be understood not as an attack on neo-Platonism, but rather as a reflection of the point of view of Bembo's *Asolani,* book I, which "deconstructs" one kind of "love," the false and carnal, before moving on dialogically to a version of spiritual love *in bono* by book III. In other words, by taking seriously (but not too seriously) both sides of the argument, we begin to see that the encounter of a "humanism of limits" and a neo-Platonic

---

Marinelli promises a fully documented contextual and critical reading of Ariosto's neo-Platonism in a later work. In general for the concept of "serio ludere," see Edgar Wind, *Pagan Mysteries in the Renaissance* (New York: Norton, 1968), who attaches the strategy to Nicolas Cusanus, Ficino, Pico, and Calcagnini, among others, and sees it as deriving from the Socratic technique of ironic self-effacement (cf. *Republic* 545d; Wind, pp. 236–37). The most striking figure of "serio ludere" in Plato and the Renaissance both is the Silenus of Alcibiades, especially as developed by Erasmus (for which see Chapter 4, sec. iii, below). "Serio ludere" might also be the banner placed over the *Cortegiano,* with its retreat into game in order to deal with genuinely serious issues. For Ariosto it is even more useful than the Horatian "misceat dulce utili," because it suggests precisely that an apparently comic, evasive poem can playfully approach serious, even tragic, concerns.

humanism of amorous and intellectual transcendence in Ariosto may be reciprocal and destabilizing rather than hierarchical and stable. The poem may be debunking not only neo-Platonic exceeding of limits, but also the possibility and/or desirability of remaining within the bounds of the merely human and natural. Ultimately I may want to suggest that the boundary between rhetorical humanism and metaphysical neo-Platonism is breached or exceeded by the poem, especially by the irreducible problem of reading and writing which intervenes before man can approach himself either as creature of history or as spiritual being. The text would thus be a *limit* upon either conception of man—and also a *limit* to be exceeded if one or the other is to be realized.

Looking back over the critical positions described so far, it is strikingly clear that positive claims for Ariostan faith in human reason and will are almost all arrived at indirectly by a trivialization of the superficial contents of the poem or by an approach to the thematics of madness and monstrosity—of the *inhuman*, in other words. Croce's sense of all-encompassing "Armonia" emerges only after the assertion that no individual moment in the poem escapes Ariosto's comprehensive, destroying, irony. More recently, it has been argued repeatedly that by seeing blindness, by speaking of inarticulate folly, the narrator can overcome these dangers and rescue the human powers of mind and language. Giamatti's subtle understanding that within the poem deceit is always countered by deceit, illusion with illusion, is perhaps the clearest instance of how the poet may appear to counter madness and monstrosity from within and emerge at the opposite pole of completed education and confident selfhood. But this negative approach to value is common to DeBlasi, Durling, Montano, and others.[116]

---

[116] While Montano's negative argument is strong, if insufficiently textualized, he never moves on to prove the existence of a positive Christian-humanist perspective from which the writings of Platonism are ostensibly attacked. He relies on Giuseppe Toffanin, "L'Amore Sacro e l'Amore Profano," in *La Religione degli Umanisti* (Bologna: Zanichelli, 1950) and first published in the anthology, *L'Ottava d'Oro* (Milano: Mondadori, 1933), for a suspect opposition between Orlando's (Platonic?) idealism and Rinaldo's (Christian-humanist?) realism, which ignores, among other things, that Rinaldo too goes mad for jealous love (cf. Chapter 4, nn. 123 and 153, below).

The precariousness of this negative argument allows for, almost demands, a further displacement in the reading of the poem, one in which seduction is no longer a vehicle of education, the representation of madness no longer a stratagem of reason, in which desire and folly engulf the perspectives that attempt to master them. The paradoxical dilemma can be seen clearly in this summary of the affirmative position by Elissa Weaver: "the poem teaches distrust of literature because it is fiction and because . . . it has a difficult relationship with reality."[117] The (mad) poem teaches about poetry's madness? Or is it that it is itself an agent of madness in its teachings? One suggestive (alternative) response has come in Saccone's insight into the open and unresolved dialectic of madness and education embodied in the figure of Hercules.[118] The next, and natural, step is that taken by Donato, who sees through the poet and Orlando a "conjunction of literature and madness" (p. 29). In contrast with Croce's hypothesis of a poem full of partial and fragmented characters which are harmoniously subsumed by the single integral self which authored them, Donato questions and reverses the phenomenological passage from plural text to unified consciousness, positing a purely negative relationship between the poetic self and the work through which it might hope either to express or construct itself or both.[119] Similarly, Neuro Bonifazi inverts the usual model to ask whether the lucidity and control of the narration which seem to belie the folly they recount are not themselves challenged, covertly, by the mystified reason and duplicitous speech

---

[117] Weaver, "Lettura dell'Intreccio dell'*Orlando Furioso:* Il Caso delle Tre Pazzie d'Amore," *Strumenti Critici* 11 (1977), p. 398.

[118] If this is the position of "Il Soggetto" (see especially p. 242 and cf. Chapter 1, n. 23, above), however, "Clorindano e Medoro" still calls the *Furioso* "an epic with human reason as its protagonist" (p. 171), while in "Appunti" Saccone sees Ariosto putting human reason in jeopardy only in the *Cinque Canti* (cf. Chapter 1, nn. 21–22, above). Despite these conflicts, or perhaps because of them, Saccone's essays are among the best at revealing the unresolved structural and thematic contradictions of the *Furioso*.

[119] Donato, "Desire," pp. 22–29. Cf. James Chiampi, "Angelica's Flight and the Reduction of the Quest in the *Orlando Furioso*," *Canadian Journal of Italian Studies* 4 (1980/81), who says that "desire in the poem is always desire for identity" (p. 12). His position is close to Donato, "Desire," which he seems not to have known.

which they dramatize for us. The poem then becomes an anti-humanistic undermining of the self and its language, maintaining only superficially the appearance of a celebration of Renaissance value.[120]

Given the suspiciously spiral pattern which we see emerging in the criticism of the *Furioso*, it is no surprise that there is a further interpretive twist to the "poem of folly" reading which returns to a point close to where we began, making a closed circle of the spiral, i.e., a Möbius strip. Giulio Ferroni, in an excellent and perhaps over-looked article, situates the reason/madness dialectic firmly within the Renaissance tradition, aligning Ariosto with Alberti, on the one hand, and more especially with the Erasmus of the *Praise of Folly*, on the other. For him this involves, yes, a contamination of the myth of *dignitas hominis* by moments of error and irrationality, but it also suggests the Erasmian recuperation of a positive perspective on the other side of reason, an almost Nietzschean thematization of the necessity and value of moral-intellectual error.[121] Elizabeth Chesney has elaborated a similar account and taken it to its logical conclusion: madness becomes an "*alter* reason," no longer the "oth-

---

[120] Bonifazi, *Le Lettere,* esp. pp. 110, 119–20, sees the poem as a means of disguising and sublimating, under the mask of urbane control and courtly elegance, the violence of desire and the threat of madness. He asserts that the poem is "un'insidia alla personalità rinascimentale, fatta di fede nel soggetto e in ciò che dice e che fa" (p. 117). C.P. Brand also detects an "antihumanistic note" (*Ariosto,* p. 120; cf. p. 60) in the repeated degradations of man's *dignitas* and the habitual disappearance of Albertian *virtus* in the face of Fortuna's depersonalizing tricks, though he does not elaborate.

[121] Giulio Ferroni, "L'Ariosto e la Concezione Umanistica della Follia," in *Atti del Convegno Internazionale "Ludovico Ariosto"* (Roma: Accademia Nazionale dei Lincei, 1975), p. 74. He argues that "la follia s'insinua nel cuore stesso della ragione" becoming "quasi la contradizione interna che la costituisce" (p. 76). His concept of Albertian-Ariostan illusion works counter to Giamatti—illusion itself is a kind of madness, the loss of self in and through the theatrical masks it assumes (p. 78). If this description suggests a Pirandello *avant la lettre,* it probably should. See Pirandello's interesting, if rather "cavallier," treatment of Ariosto in "L'Umorismo," in *Saggi, Poesie e Scritti Varii,* ed. M. Lo Vecchio-Musti (Verona: Mondadori, 1973). Pirandello denies to Ariosto's mocking irony a capacity for his own version of "serio ludere," namely "umorismo," which I, instead, would attribute to him. It would, incidentally, be worth comparing Croce's approach to Ariostan irony with that of his polemical adversary, Pirandello.

er" of reason but "another reason," which exposes the hidden folly of classical rationality. Ariosto and his characters thus enter into the illustrious line of Renaissance "sophomores," or wise fools.[122] Taken far enough, in other words, the theme of madness apparently restores a positive educational perspective.

An additional turn of the screw reminds us that the objects of Folly's critique, humanistic ethical rationalism and neo-Platonic visionary askesis, are in some ways also its historical source—that both "programs" contain within themselves elements which tend toward their own displacement and even contradiction. In the *Phaedrus,* which Ariosto knew filtered through the commentaries and adaptations of Ficino, Landino, and others, Plato's critique of rhetorical seduction as dangerous folly is accompanied by Socrates' famous enumeration of the four frenzies *in bono* (amorous, poetic, "hieratic," and prophetic)—so that the philosophy of self-knowledge (*nosce te ipsum*) includes as well a valorization of self-loss as self-transcendence (*Phaedrus* 244a–252b).[123] On the other hand, as we have seen, at least one branch of rhetorical humanism regularly included critiques of philosophical reason, making them, in this aspect at least, assimilable to such basic works of antirationalism as Nicholas of Cusa's *De Idiota Sapientia.* In any event, it will be a task of Chapter 4 to show how Ariosto approaches the possibilities both of madness as spiritual ascent and of poetry as madness. There I will be facing two equally vexing questions: whether Ariosto's serene narrative pose can really be a screen for violent madness, and whether the violence and degradation of Orlando's madness really contain within them the promise of a transcending folly *in bono.*[124]

It has been suggested on at least one occasion that the intricately woven themes and structures of the *Furioso* are themselves like a Möbius strip, whose end touches and reverses its beginning.[125] The account I have just given of the criticism of the poem suggests that

---

[122] Chesney, *Rabelais and Ariosto,* esp. chap. 5 ("Folly"), pp. 171–204. Cf. Chapter 4, n. 136, below.

[123] Cf. Chapter 4, sec. iii (esp. nn. 140, 156), below.

[124] Orlando's horrible, though often very funny, madness makes it difficult to subscribe easily to Donato's and Parker's hints that, against Dante and Platonism, Ariosto valorizes the *selva* and the crises it produces.

[125] Saccone, "Il Soggetto," p. 247.

it too has such a form, as Ariostan reason becomes madness and vice versa. It is the effort of my critical account to explore the significance of that parallelism, to suggest that the criticism has generally chosen to take as *the* significance of the *Furioso* moments of meaning which the poem soon enough displaces into their contraries. Rather than critics having comprehended the poem, it is the poem which has comprehended its readers, by making possible, but also dramatizing and criticizing, a series of limited positions which have taken turns at the center of interpretive readings. And what has been said above about the potential analogy between Orlando's infuriating idealism and Croce's is only the first of several examples we shall come across of proleptic figurations of the poem's readers within the poem. In other words, the analogy between the *Furioso*'s circular, plural structures, on the one side, and the maze of critical views provoked by them, on the other, is *causal,* or at least *prophetic.* The poem seems designed purposefully to foster and sustain all of the readings enumerated without decisive contradiction.

To put it in its simplest, though not entirely reductive, form, the *Furioso* has wandered between two poles of critical debate, alternately seen as a poem of vision and sanity—the staging ground for the poet's and/or reader's metaphysical, moral, or psychological transcendence—and as a poem of unadulterated nonsense or violent madness. On the one hand, the fragmentation of partial and embattled identities and multiple narratives within the poem seems to be subsumed under the unified vision of the poet or his rhetorical emanation, the narrating "I."[126] A quasi-divine irony installs harmony; the Many are fully subsumed by the One, in a positively Piconian synthesis.[127] The critic can then reenact that irony by (re)discovering the true unity in apparent chaos. On the other hand, the multiplicity of the text becomes a model for the inevitable fragmentation within its author and its reader: the One is split into the Many; *discordia concors* becomes *concordia discors,* "aspro concento,

---

[126] As we have seen (cf. n. 14, above), this is Croce's view, but it has been variously "secularized," "textualized," and "humanized" by DeBlasi ("Ariosto," esp. pt. 2, p. 180ff.); Durling (*The Figure of the Poet,* pp. 174–75); and Caretti ("Ariosto," pp. 31–32).

[127] For "Armonia" and the "One and the Many," see Chapter 1, n. 6, and Chapter 4, n. 167. For the Piconian element in readings of Ariosto by DeBlasi, Croce, and Durling, see n. 58, above.

orribile armonia." Writerly and readerly irony become double-edged, trapping and involving them in that from which they wish to maintain a critical distance of judgment.[128] We now see that these critical polarities may be continuous with one another, precluding the possibility that one of them may assume an hierarchical dominance.

One final point must be touched on here. This account of the poem and its critics, which claims as it were to have brought the total "Möbic" complex into view, is clearly subject to its own critique of "Aesculapian" reading, the reading which "re-collects" and stitches together not only the body of the poem, but also the fragments of a critical tradition.[129] If the text represents itself as potential agent of madness and/or education in its readers, not only as a representation of those processes, it puts into crisis the critic's privileged role as both interpreter and teacher. The critic too is the potential object (or is it subject?) of the poem's representations and its actions, and this caveat is no less true of this study than of any I have just considered. There can be no resolution of this dilemma, only a confession followed by an accommodation. In this case the accommodation will consist primarily in continuing to weigh equally what the critics say about the text with what the text—potentially, implicitly, and clearly—says about them/us (or those like them/us).

iv. *Satira* vi *and the "Arts That Exalt Man"*

In the course of this chapter I have tried to develop a context, before and after, of the Renaissance texts and traditions of which the *Furioso* is a reading and of the critics who in turn read the *Furioso*.

---

[128] For the notion, running counter to the Romantic irony of a transcendent author-God, of irony as a destabilizing trope which engulfs even the perspective from which it originated, see Paul DeMan, "The Rhetoric of Temporality," in C. Singleton, ed. *Interpretation: Theory and Practice* (Baltimore: The Johns Hopkins University Press, 1969), pp. 173–209; Jonathan Culler, "Literary History, Allegory and Semiology," *New Literary History* 7 (1975/76). Cf. Chapter 3, n. 24, below.

[129] Whether my arguments are "original" or "comprehensive" or both is a question the reader will answer in her/his own way. Like Ariosto, however, I hope to stake my claims both upon a broad admission of indebtedness to predecessors and upon the staging of confrontations between them which sheds new light both on their arguments and on the contents of the poem.

Before moving on to study more specifically how the poem posi-
tions itself in relation to its precursors, how it predicts and resigns
itself to a fate of reading, rereading, and misreading, I will make one
more detour: into a contemporary *Cinquecento* text of humanistic
education which is also, in a very special sense, one of the first criti-
cal readings of the *Orlando Furioso,* Ariosto's own *Satira* VI. It is this
poem, rather than the epic, which contains Ariosto's most explicit
discussion of Renaissance pedagogy. At first blush the *Satira* seems
to valorize the possibility of an humanistic education for Ariosto's
son, Virginio, and to lament the education *manqué* of the poet
himself, all in a verse epistle addressed to Bembo, the personification
of what humanism had become in the early *Cinquecento*. Composed
in the years between the second and third editions of the *Furioso,*
the *Satira* can be related to it as *both* historical "pre-text" and critical
"post-script," as we shall soon see.[130]

One recent asserter of Ariosto's Christian "humanism of limits"
suggests that the explicit values of the *Satira,* what he takes to be its
clearly humanistic ideology, can be used to resolve the dialectic of
reason and madness in the longer poem.[131] Such a reading employs
an inverted logic, *a debiliore* so to speak, to argue that the lesser and
clearer work reveals in a straightforward way the meaning of the
greater and far more ambiguous *poema*.[132] This, however, is to

[130] For the dating of *Satira* VI, see Wiggins' introduction to *The Satires of Ludovico
Ariosto,* pp. xxxvii–xliii; as well as Ariosto, *Opere Minori* (Segre edition), p. 561.

[131] See Cuccaro, *Humanism,* p. 160, on the dialectic of reason and madness in the
poem and, pp. 73, 131, passim, on *Satira* VI as key to reading the *Furioso*. In his
treatment of the *Furioso,* however, Cuccaro does not place it in specific textual
relation to the *Satire* or to other texts of education. For a very interesting counter-
point to his reading of the *Satire,* see Antonio Corsaro, "'In Questo Rincrescevol
Labirinto': Le *Satire* Garafagnine di Ludovico Ariosto," *Filologia e Critica* 4 (1979).

[132] The tendency to assume a continuity of thought between the works of a
single author is belied even (or especially?) in such artfully plotted sequences of
artistic development as Dante's passage from the *Vita Nuova* to the *Convivio* and
thence to the *Commedia,* in which palinodic "overgoing" of one's own prior work
is evident. If the "anxiety of influence" felt by poets in relation to predecessors is
now generally recognized, it has yet to be sufficiently remarked that a poet may
feel the same anxiety or alienation with respect to his own completed work (par-
ticularly in a case like Ariosto's where the movement from *Furioso* to *Satire* marks
a distinct retreat).

deny to the poem precisely that which is most characteristic of it, an ironic obliquity and backhandedness. We will soon discover, in fact, that the relationship between the two works, far from being unambiguously continuous, is rather tortuous, even polemical. Even if one could accept such an interpretive strategy, however, one would soon enough learn that *Satira* vi itself takes a more complex approach to education and literature's role therein than it first seems to.

I begin with those features of the *Satira* which seem most to make it an exemplary paean to pedagogical humanism, which the son is to have and which the father regrets having had only in part. For his son, Ariosto desires possession of all the "arti che essalton l'uom" ("arts that exalt man" 2–3).[133] The teachers of these arts are specifically identified as "umanisti" (one of the first uses of the word, although the *studia humanitatis* had been heralded since the dawn of the Renaissance).[134] It is often argued that "umanista" for the Renaissance had just the limited meaning of "teacher of Latin and Greek." But in this case the "umanisti" are clearly those with "vena di poesia" ("a vein of poetry" 31–32). At the same time, poets are identified as the "scolari" of Quintillian (92–93), thus conflating poetry and rhetoric, celebrating active poetic persuasion to action. The education that Ariosto wishes for Virginio is the literary one he had begun but never finished, one which would include the Greeks: Homer, Hesiod, Pindar, and so on. And poetry, at least one sort of poetry, is not only the subject of the study, but is itself seen as a vehicle of education and of civilizing "impegno civile." Ariosto echoes the commonplace that poets were those who first civilized man, bringing him out of a savage condition into the city of law:

> *Esser tali dovean quelli che vieta*
> *che sian ne la republica Platone,*
> *da lui con sì santi ordini discreta;*

---

[133] Translation mine.

[134] See Kristeller, *Renaissance Thought,* pp. 8–9, 111 (n. 5) and 160 (n. 61), where he convincingly contests the theory that Ariosto was the first to use the term "umanista" in Italian. He also insists, wrongly in this case, that the word refers primarily to teachers and pedants.

> *ma non fu tal già Febo, né Anfione,*
> *né gli altri che trovaro i primi versi,*
> *che col buon stile, e più con l'opre buone,*
>   *persuasero agli uomini a doversi*
> *ridurre insieme, e abandonar le giande,*
> . . . .
>   *e fér che i più robusti, la cui grande*
> *forza era usata alli minori tòrre*
> *or mogli, or gregge et or miglior vivande,*
>   *si lasciaro alle leggi sottoporre,*
> *e cominciar, versando aratri e glebe,*
> *del sudor lor più giusti frutti accòrre.*   [67–81]

Such must have been those . . . to whom Plato denied entrance to that republic, which he invested with such saintly laws. But Phoebus was not so, nor Amphion, nor the others who found the first verses. With their good style, and more with their good works, they persuaded men to join together and to give up eating acorns. . . . They persuaded the more robust, whose strength had thus far been employed in stealing wives and flocks and food from weaker men, to submit to laws and to begin with their plows to turn the soil and to harvest with the sweat of their brows [juster fruits].

Though one sort of poet (specifically those "moderns" who think that a Latinized name will replace years of study as the mark of a poetic vocation) is legitimately excluded from the city by Plato, another kind stands at the very origin and center of it. Ethics and aesthetics do seem to be interchangeable for Ariosto.

At the same time, the poet seems to embrace the specifically humanistic preference for ethics over metaphysics, for will over intellect. The (then already clichéd) words of the great humanistic educator Guarino Veronese, "it is better indeed to be good than learned,"[135] find an echo in these lines describing the sought-for tutor:

> *buono in scienza e più in costumi, il quale*
> *voglia insegnarli, e in casa tener seco.*
>   *Dottrina abbia e bontà, ma principale*
> *sia la bontà: che, non vi essendo questa,*
> *né molto quella alla mia estima vale.*

---

[135] Guarino Veronese, letter no. 16, in Garin, ed., *Il Pensiero Pedagogico*, p. 356: "praestat enim bonos esse quam doctos."

So ben che la dottrina fia più presta
a lasciarsi trovar che la bontade:
sì mal l'una ne l'altra oggi s'inesta.   [14–21]

make sure he is learned and good, but first of all good, for without goodness learning, in my opinion, is worth little. I know indeed that learning is much more quickly to be found than goodness, since these days the one agrees so poorly with the other.

This attitude is amplified to include an attack on the aspirations of an overreaching humanism to pass beyond the limits of human intellect to contain the divine:

perché, salendo lo intelletto in suso
per veder Dio, non de' parerci strano
se talor cade giù cieco e confuso.   [46–48]

when the intellect ascends on high to see God, we must not think it strange if sometimes it falls down blind and bewildered.

These lines address, in particular, the "individualistic" Christianity of Luther *and* the Aristotelian, Averroistic tendencies of the Paduan scholar, Nicholas of Vernia, but they fit just as well the Platonic imagery of intellectual ascent developed by Landino, Ficino, and Pico, not to mention Castiglione's "Bembo" and Bembo himself.

Just such an anti-Bembian note *has* previously been detected, though, curiously, without reference to the very remarkable fact that Bembo is both the much-praised addressee of the poem and the subject of its attack. Even more curiously, the same reader locates the opposition to Bembo not so much in these lines as in the following ones, in which he identifies the "tu" as a reference to Bembo only:[136]

dimmi, che truovi tu che sì la mente
ti debbia aviluppar, sì tòrre il senno,
che tu non creda come l'altra gente?   [55–57]

tell me, what have you found that so confuses your [mind] and so deprives you of your sense that you do not believe as others do?

These lines, however, are actually the climax of a longer passage

---

[136] Cuccaro, *Humanism*, pp. 84–85.

which, when cited in full, makes such an interpretation seem very peculiar indeed:

> Ma tu, del qual lo studio è tutto umano
> e son li tuoi suggetti i boschi e i colli,
> il mormorar d'un rio che righi il piano,
>   cantar antiqui gesti e render molli
> con prieghi animi duri, e far sovente
> di false lode i principi satolli,
>   dimmi . . .   [49–55]

But you, whose study is entirely human, and whose subjects are the woods and hills, and the murmuring of a brook that waters the plain, and whose task it is to sing of ancient deeds, and to soften with prayers inexorable spirits, and to satiate princes with false praises, tell me . . .

While these lines may be read as referring in part to that side of Bembo which composed Petrarchesque and quite secular erotic verse, it is clearly the inverse of the intellectual mysticism of a Pico or a Ficino (as well as of Luther and Vernia), against which it is, in fact, deliberately set off. The lines actually contain a direct attack against that secular humanism which remains totally within the narrowest bounds of *humanitas,* and the "tu" refers to anyone, not merely Bembo, whose study is "tutto umano." The two apparently opposed and equally condemned trends of esoteric spirituality and anthropocentric secularism do actually have an unspoken point of encounter: in their narcissistic dwelling upon the human self, its desires and its powers. This is one of the ways in which neo-Platonism and secular humanism can be said to converge and, perhaps, to be confused. What is *most* strange is that both the exceeding of limits and the refusal to exceed them are presented as quite risky.

The reference to the "arts that [exalt] man" is thus countered by this attack on the "study entirely human," throwing the initial valuing of man and the study of *humanitas* into serious question. One might, however, still wish to recuperate a textual space of limited Christian humanism between the two condemned extremes, although one would have then to account for the trivializing exhortation to "believe what others believe," which reduces Christian transcendence to social conformity. What a prohumanist reading of the poem certainly cannot account for, in any case, is the peculiar

way in which Bembo seems to be the butt of both attacks, as neo-
Platonic theorist and as secular lyricist, and the fact that through
him the two positions are brought uncomfortably close together,
as if they were two sides of a single coin.

Nor can one easily and directly apply the (suddenly far more
problematic) humanism of the *Satira* to the *Furioso*. One cannot,
at least, if one recognizes the obvious: that the *Furioso* itself is being
described in the damning lines 49–54. That *poema,* abounding with
loci amoeni, is unquestionably guilty of singing ancient deeds, solic-
iting a softer attitude on the part of the poet's beloved, and, espe-
cially, of praising to excess the Estense princes. Far from a moral
and didactic poetry, the *Furioso* thus characterized seems to be the
very same sort of verse filled with sensuous delight and self-serving
lies which Plato excluded from the Republic because of Socrates'
belief that poetic fables should not be used for the education of
children.[137] A reading of the *Furioso* may confirm or confute (or
both) this "mea culpa." First, however, it is worth asking whether
the *Satira* actually puts its own values and conceptions of humanism
into question. It becomes obvious early on that the poem takes an
equivocal and often openly hostile attitude toward some aspects
and manifestations of humanistic poetics and practices of education.
Burckhardt, whose one other use of Ariosto was as a striking coun-
terexample to his claims regarding the artistic representation of inte-
gral individuals, makes *Satira* VI the focus of his description of early
Cinquecento attacks on a decadent humanism.[138] The following lines
give justification to his interpretation:

> *O nostra male avventurosa etade,*
> *che le virtudi che non abbian misti*
> *vici nefandi si ritrovin rade!*
> *Senza quel vizio son pochi umanisti*
> *che fe' a Dio forza, non che persuase,*
> *di far Gomorra e i suoi vicini tristi:*

[137] *Republic,* bk. II, 376c and ff.

[138] Burckhardt, *Civilization,* pt. 3, chap. 11, "The Fall of the Humanists in the
Sixteenth Century" (vol. I, pp. 273–74). Corsaro follows Burckhardt in reading
all the *Satire* as an expression of ethical and poetic pessimism.

mandò fuoco dal ciel, ch'uomini e case
tutto consumpse; et ebbe tempo a pena
Lot a fugir, ma la moglier rimase.
    Ride il volgo, se sente un ch'abbia vena
di poesia, e poi dice: "È gran periglio
a dormir seco a volgierli la schiena."
    Et oltra questa nota, il peccadiglio
di Spagna gli dànno anco, che non creda
in unità del Spirto il Padre e il Figlio.
    Non che contempli come l'un proceda
da l'altro o nasca. . . .

. . . .

    ma gli par che non dando il suo consenso
a quel che approvan gli altri, mostri ingegno
da penetrar più su che 'l ciel immenso.   [22–42]

O infelicitous age of ours when virtues that nefarious vices have not
polluted are so rarely to be found! Few humanists are without that vice
which did not so much persuade, as forced, God to render Gomorrah
and her neighbor wretched! He sent down fire from heaven that con-
sumed men and houses all, and Lot had scarcely time to flee, while his
wife remained behind. The vulgar laugh when they hear of someone
who possesses a vein of poetry, and then they say, "It is a great peril
to turn your back if you sleep next to him." And beyond this blemish,
the peccadillo of Spain damns him as well, which does not concede be-
lief in [the unity of] the Father, the Son, and the Holy Ghost; but he
does not trouble to contemplate how one proceeds or is born from the
other. . . . He thinks that, in not giving his consent to what others ap-
prove, he demonstrates such intelligence as must penetrate beyond the
vastness of the heavens.

The list of the failings of "umanisti" of all kinds, but especially of
poets, goes on, with some brief interruptions, through line 129.

    The twofold attack on humanists for homosexuality and for in-
tellectual vainglory takes on special force and pathos when it is
linked to its evident analogue in the *Inferno*, Dante's encounter
with his former teacher, "the dear paternal image" of Brunetto
Latini. Latini, a Ciceronian rhetorician and obvious precursor of
the *Quattrocento*, is one of two famous infernal "humanists" that
Dante encounters (the other is Ulysses, who also figures in this poem
and will occupy our attention in the next chapter). The thematic
links are evident: *Inferno* 15 is concerned with an educator and his

(former) pupil, with a program of humanistic "insegnamento" by which "l'uom s'etterna" (85), not ontologically, but by the nominal salvation which books accord to their perished authors. The specific point of contact, however, is that Latini is found in the circle of the Sodomites, on a fiery plain which recalls the descent of flames on Sodom and Gomorrah. Whether Latini is supposed to be identified literally as a homosexual or not, and the criticism has long debated the point, it is clear that homosexuality functions as "a metaphor for the unnatural act of engaging in sterile and unfructifying actions," equivalent in this way to usury, which occupies the same circle.[139] Thus sodomy is precisely a figure for the humanistic promise of textual eternity, the reproduction of the self by itself on itself in its writings: "Sieti raccomandato il mio Tesoro, / nel qual io vivo ancora" ("Let my Treasure, in which I yet live, be commended to you" 119–120). The same motif, of course, can be extracted from the archetypal poetic myth of Orpheus' self-destructive conversion to homosexuality after failing to bring Eurydice back to life by the power of poetry alone.[140]

Ironically, by an exclusive focus on the human realm and the domain of Nature, Latini invited his own exclusion from the natural and the human: "de l'umana natura posto in bando" ("banished from human nature" 81). As Ariosto says it, he "fe' a Dio forza," not only because the enormity of the crime constrained God to action, but also because homosexuality is understood as a violation, a violent forcing of the human form made in the image and likeness of God's divinity. Either sort of humanism, in its futile attempts to achieve textual and intellectual self-sufficiency, lapses into the inhuman, the unnatural, the monstrous, even as it strives to go above the human into the divine and eternal. *Paideia* may be translated into Latin as *humanitas*, but it always seems to lead away from the human either down into bestiality or up into godhood.[141] The very concept of humanism is forced up against the recognition that

[139] Mazzotta, *Dante*, p. 138. See pp. 138–41 for the exegesis on which mine relies and p. 138 (n. 49) for a list of some of the more useful interpretations of the canto.

[140] See, for instance, Poliziano, *Favola d'Orfeo*.

[141] For the translation of *paideia* into *humanitas* by Cicero, see Mazzeo, *Renaissance and Revolution*, p. 31; see also Battista Guarino, *De Ordine Docendi*, in Garin, ed., *Il Pensiero Pedagogico*, p. 470.

man's nature is enigmatic, that the exact character of the human is uncertain, in a way far less optimistic than Pico would admit. Ariosto twice seems to hint that one best clings to human identity by miming "quel che approvan gli altri" (41; cf. 57), hoping that the mirror of otherness will allow one to discover the unidentifiable self.

In spite of the lengthy catalogue of vices and mystifications of most "umanisti," the implicit attack on Bembo, the allusive recourse to the Brunetto Latini episode, and so on, the *Satira* still seems to hold out hope for an ideal tutor, such as Gregory of Spoleto, Ariosto's own sometime teacher; to display genuine affection and admiration for Bembo,[142] regardless of its criticisms of him; and to set those poets who are properly excluded from the city in striking contrast with the active, Orphic authors who first built it. Even these hopes, however, lie under subtle qualification. The very first line of the poem, "Bembo, io vorrei . . . ," echoes the first line of a famous Dantean sonnet, "Guido, i' vorrei che tu e Lapo ed io . . . ." The poem by Dante yearns for an utopian community, sponsored by white magic, of the three poets and their beloved ladies, adrift together in a boat, moved according to the logic of their desires, freely expressed and perfectly satisfied. There, poetry explicitly dreams an ideal situation for itself and, just as explicitly, acknowledges its impossibility. Thus, the whole of the *Satira* and its project of education into a community of poets, in spite of the apparent "realism" and sense of limits, is from the first put under the sign of utopia, of purely imaginative content. At the same time, Ariosto's account of his personal history reinforces this sense of a failed poetic ideal, by suggesting how the ideal poetic education and career are not, as the civic humanists had argued, compatible with active involvement in civic and family life, but are, in fact, constantly disrupted by the intrusions of historical contingency. "Maria," the

---

[142] Ariosto's long friendship with Bembo dates from the latter's lengthy stays in Ferrara (1498–1500, 1502–1503) and their later encounters in Rome and Urbino. It seems to have survived easily Ariosto's annoyance with Leo X for not patronizing him after acceding to the papacy (for which, see *Satire* II, III, VII), as can be seen from this poem and from a later letter on the same subject (February 23, 1531, no. 190 in *Lettere*, Stella edition). See also Latin Lyric VII, *Furioso* XXXVII.8.3–4 and XLVI.15.2–4. Cf. Catalano, *Vita*, vol. I, pp. 128, 142–44, passim.

contemplative life of poetry and scholarship, was relinquished by Ariosto for "Marta," the economic and other cares of an ersatz *pater familias* which fell on him after the death of his own father. Gregory's career was continually interrupted by political events and ended in his own, futile death in exile. The poet continues to lament his present situation and especially the commissions given to him by his patrons who "di poeta cavallar mi feo" ("from a poet made a horseman of me" 238). Most poignantly of all, the poet's cousin, his companion and rival in studies, died prematurely, unable to realize his own potentially brilliant identity, beyond the power of any Orphic poetry to resurrect.

Even the constructive powers of Phoebus and Amphion, celebrated in an apparently commonplace way, as Boccaccio and others (including Bembo) had already frequently done, are in the end strangely compromised. First of all, since poetry has already been coordinated with utopian desire and the play of imagination, we are perhaps invited to recognize that, even if some poets are allowed into Plato's previously discriminatory Republic, the Republic itself is a no-place too, as practical-minded thinkers such as Machiavelli stated without equivocation.[143] Furthermore, says Ariosto, after successfully persuading the savage men out of the woods and into the newly founded city of law:[144]

> Indi i scrittor féro all'indotta plebe
> creder ch'al suon de le soavi cetre
> l'un Troia e l'altro edificasse Tebe;
> e avesson fatto scendere le petre
> dagli alti monti, et Orfeo tratto al canto
> tigri e leon da le spelònche tetre. [82–87]

Thus writers convinced the unlearned populace that, with the sound of their sweet lyres, Phoebus built Troy, and Amphion, Thebes, and that they caused stones to tumble down from lofty mountains, and that with his song Orpheus lured tigers and lions from their gloomy lairs.

---

[143] Cf. n. 98, above. See also Castiglione's dedicatory letter to the *Cortegiano*, as well as bk. IV.xlii. There Castiglione wavers between representing the ideal, if only as an impossible goal, and criticizing his own project as utopian, like Plato's.

[144] The thought, without the ironic twist, is traceable to Horace, *Ars Poetica* 390–407.

Bembo's Perottino and many others do emphasize the use of seduc-
tive fictions to win irrational and uncivilized listeners to rational
and civilized ways:[145]

> *Trovarono le favole altresì, sotto il velame delle quali la verità, sì come sotto*
> *vetro trasparente, ricoprivano . . . del continuo dilettandogli con la novità delle*
> *bugie, et alcuna volta . . . scoprendo loro il vero . . .*
>
> [*Asolani* 1.xii, p. 29]

They invented fables as well, under whose veil they covered truth, as
if beneath transparent glass, . . . continually delighting [their listeners]
with the novelty of their lies and sometimes . . . uncovering the truth
for them . . .

But Ariosto subtly modifies the conventional picture of salutary
allegorical duplicity: instead of adopting a necessary use of delightful
fiction to achieve ethical aims, poets are seen as having capitalized
on a certain success to mystify and exaggerate their own powers.
The "poetic theology," the attribution to poets of mystical powers
and knowledge thus appears to be an utopian fiction in a less benign
sense than the opening line suggests. Poets are depicted as returning
from an active role in human affairs toward self-aggrandizing lies.
Poetry, in the *Satira,* consistently falls short of an humanistic notion
of practical engagement with history, while at the same time being
even more clearly cut off from the mystical insights and magical
powers which Pico and company had attributed to it: it is at once
evasively utopian and yet caught in historically determined limits.
Ultimately, the product of the humanistic education through and
to literature which the poem details is new poets and more literature,
not at all either the "impegno civile" of civic humanism (inclusion
in which Ariosto resented almost as bitterly as his contemporary,

---

[145] See also *Asolani,* in *Opere in Volgare* (Marti edition), pp. 28, 75–77, 96–97.
For the dates of composition, see Marti edition, pp. 5–8. The work was completed
by 1502 (published 1505); it was thus written in the period when Bembo was in
closest contact with Ariosto. Cf. Boccaccio, *Genealogia* xiv.xvi (vol. 2, pp. 728–30)
as well as xiv.ix (p. 709): "Quid multa? tanti quidem sunt fabule, ut earum primo
contextu oblectentur indocti, et circa abscondita doctorum exerceantur ingenia, et
sic una eadem lectione proficiunt et delectant."

Machiavelli, abhorred his exclusion from it) or the spiritual askesis of Platonism.

Though *Satira* VI initially points in the direction of a poetry which is engaged in education, and is the fruit of that education, it also seems to indict the *Furioso,* and even itself, for erotic and aesthetic mystifications. What then of the *Furioso,* and of the Alcina episode in particular? Does not the paradisical garden in which Ruggiero alights in canto VI anticipate the censured creation of the humanist-poet, "whose study is entirely human, and whose subjects are the woods and the hills, and the murmuring of a brook that waters the plain"—with the curious twist that the landscape is not only the "subject matter" of the writing, but is, in fact, composed entirely of metamorphosed human subjectivities, transformed by a collusion of their bestial desires and Alcina's Circean magic? Is it not thus and truly an example of *humanitas* trapped at once (and unnaturally) within the realms of the natural and of the aesthetic and artificial? Does not the poem, at this point, invite the poet's own later critique in the *Satira* of poetry as aesthetic self-enclosure disguised as "naturalism" (the enclosure, for example, of Astolfo in a "scorza" which is the very figure of poetry itself) and ethical disengagement? If the primary rhetorical and didactic poetics (what Abrams calls the "pragmatic" poetics) of the Renaissance calls for an Horatian mixture of delightful poetic surface and exemplary content,[146] Ariosto himself, in a letter, speaks only of the pleasures of his text: "a work which treats of pleasant and delightful matters in love and war . . . for the solace and pleasure of whoever may wish to read it and may delight in doing so."[147] Or rather, he does also speak of the "bene et utile de le fatiche" ("the good and usefulness of my labors"), but only in terms of the economic utility which will accrue to him as its author, as if he were here specifically ridiculing the notion of moral utility. The letter is all the more curious in this regard, since it is addressed to the Venetian Doge, as a request for protection of his rights to the book, and might therefore be expected to adopt a moralizing pose for official consumption. Thus, apparently, even Ariosto seems to join the chorus of critics

---

[146] Cf. Chapter 1, n. 54, above.
[147] Letter no. 16, in Stella edition (cf. no. 187).

who have seen delightful nonsense, not educational matter, as the primary content of the poem, and thereby to anticipate the historical slide from engaged *litterae* into the pre-Baroque aesthetics of the later Renaissance (as in Castelvetro's, and even Tasso's, claim that delight alone is the intrinsic end of poetry) and thence to the Kantian view of artworks as "purposive objects without purpose," which would eventually become the foundation for Croce's and DeSanctis' interpretations of the poem. The truth of the matter, however, is elsewhere, and far more complex, as the next chapter will demonstrate.

ALLEGORY AND EDUCATION
AT THE ANTIPODES

In spite of the internal and external pressures placed on the reader
to accept the *Furioso* as an escapist flight out of the city into the
selva, out of the present into the past, out of familiar geographies
into alien and fantastic landscapes, out of reality and into "pure"
imagination, there is reason to believe that Ariosto is being disingen-
uous, both in *Satira* VI and in the letter to the Doge, about the lack
of complexity and seriousness in his poem. If he addresses the ques-
tion of Renaissance theories and practices of poetic education ex-
plicitly and directly only in *Satira* VI, that does not mean they are
not pertinent to the greater poem. In fact, the *Furioso's* efforts both
in presenting dramas of education and in placing itself within (or at
least on) the horizon of a didactic poetics has already been established
by my treatment of its treatment of the figure of Hercules. It is
true that in the Alcina episode the explicit moment of Herculean
choice ends in failure, when Ruggiero is lured off to the palace of
the *fata* and into her Lethean embraces. Nonetheless, the episode
then goes on to chart his rescue from her illusions, his journey to
and instruction by Logistilla, "la fata più bella" ("the lovelier fairy"
x.43.4), and to recount his subsequent return to Europe and to the
exigencies of his historical destiny: duty to Agramante (at first), love
of Bradamante, foundation of the Este dynasty. Moreover, the epi-
sode (like the poem) unfolds in close allusive relation to other poetic
representations of successful and unsuccessful learning experiences—
the *Odyssey* and the *Aeneid,* as well as the long exegetical tradition
of interpreting these epics as moral and/or spiritual journeys—and
to the traditional metaphors and figures of education which these
allegories rely on (the Platonic horses, the cave, the circle, the sun,
characters such as Hercules and Ulysses). Finally, all of these tra-
ditions reach Ariosto filtered through Dante's appropriation of
Virgil's voice for revised didactic purposes, as well as his use of
Ulysses as a tragic counterpoint to his own cosmically "comic"

travels.[1] Through these intertextual positionings, and through sub-
tle allusions to the larger context of rhetorical and philosophical
crisis in human identity, the *Furioso* approaches, inquisitively and
doubtfully, the poetic representation of education and the possibility
of education taking place by means of that representation. Given all
of these elements, it will begin to appear that the *Cinquecento* com-
mentators were perfectly justified in finding allegorical-didactic res-
onances in the poem, even if they understated the ironic corrosions
to which these were being subjected by the poet. Even in the face
of such evidence, however, we still require a better understanding
of the motives for Ariosto's attempts to dissimulate and conceal it,
and must thus pursue not only the effaced content of education, but
also the apparently willing complicity of the poet in encouraging
his readers to treat the poem as "mere" entertainment.

i. *Ariosto between Alcina and Logistilla*

Among the primary tasks of this reading is that of exploring the
jarring coincidence of these two aspects of the poem: delightful
flight and earnest pedagogy, which might be labeled, respectively,
Alcinian and Logistillan. A reconciliation might be hoped for, as
earlier suggested, partly in terms of the rhetorical poetics of delight
and utility, or its neo-Platonic relative, "serio ludere," which were
characteristic of figures as diverse, and as important for Ariosto, as
Castiglione's playful formation of the Courtier and Alberti's Lucian-
esque satirical works, notably the *Intercenali* and the *Momus*. On the
other hand, the peculiar familial relations of Alcina and Logistilla
(they are half-sisters, Alcina being the product of their father's
incest—but with whom?) suggest complex and bizarre bonds of
intimacy and conflict between the two moral states and the poetic
functions that they stand for.[2] One must be prepared to account for,

---

[1] *Inferno* 26.136, "Noi ci allegrammo, e tosto tornò in pianto." Mazzotta (*Dante*,
p. 86) notes the echo of the conventional definition of tragedy. See Dante's own,
related, definition of tragedy (as well as of comedy) in the *Letter to Can Grande*, in
R. Haller, ed. and trans., *The Literary Criticism of Dante Alighieri* (Lincoln: University
of Nebraska Press, 1973), p. 100.

[2] For the image of Alcina as incestuously begotten sibling of Logistilla interpreted
as a reflection of an intimate dialectic of madness and reason (as against vice and

or at least to recognize, not only the poem's apparent advocacy of employing the demonic tools of illusion and seduction against themselves, for purposes of arriving at an education to freedom from passion and to the clear perception of truth, but also the dramatization of the reverse. For instance, we will see that Alcina disguises her seductions as a standard itinerary of philosophical askesis. Thus if (poetic) illusion may be the tool of education, the forms of education may, at times, be nothing more than seductive illusions. It is thus difficult to exclude the possibility that Ariosto is offering a version of the Platonic critique of poetry as a subversive substitute for genuinely moral and truthful discourse. It is not enough to show that an allegory or a mimesis of education is underway, though this will be the first step. One must go further to suggest, as the poem suggests, that as a representation of education the episode may seduce its readers, even while as a representation of seduction it may educate them. If such a split or crisis is recognizable within the episode, the bearing of this sequence on the balance of the poem may be even more critical. Does it provide Ruggiero with an impetus to act in a new way in the "historical" setting to which he returns? Does it give the reader a clue as to the import of the rest of the poem? Does it in fact dramatize its referential or antireferential relations to its author, its historical context, and its readers?

Like its structurally and thematically symmetrical companion, the lunar episode, the island of Alcina seems to have simultaneously a radically exemplary and a highly alienated position with respect to the events, geography, and mode of writing prevailing in the balance of the *Furioso*. Thus, in reading it under the sign of "insegnamento" (or of seduction), it will be necessary to be very careful in estimating the general relevance of what has been learned

---

virtue), see Carlo Ossola, "Métaphore et Inventaire de la Folie dans la Littérature Italienne du XVIᵉ Siècle," in the conference proceedings *Folie et Déraison à la Renaissance* (Bruxelles: Éditions de l'Université de Bruxelles, 1976), p. 172. The positing of a shift from moral to intellectual dangers is linked to the movement from Middle Ages to Renaissance in this and other discussions of the theme of madness during this period. I would argue, however, that the episode focuses precisely on the relation *between* seeing and acting, epistemology and ethics. See also the discussion of Orlando's madness in Chapter 4, sec. ii, below.

from it, for fear that it may prove a lesson inappropriate or misplaced with regard to the "whole" of the poem. It is geographically distanced from the poem's "Europe," beyond the clearly signed limits of culture, at the antipodes from (diametrically opposite to) it. At the same time, it is written in an extended allegorical mode which is foreign to the generally "representational" character of most of the text (in spite of some notable exceptions, whose very intrusiveness seems to confirm the basic validity of the opposition). In these terms, the episode seems irrelevant, eccentric with respect to the whole. On the other hand, allegory usually implies a studied alienation for didactic purposes, a gloss on reality from a perspective of distance—"making it strange" so it can be reseen and reunderstood.[3] If the allegory of Alcina and Logistilla, and that of the Senapo, the earthly paradise, and the moon, stand as marginal glosses at the edges of the poem's principal events, that relation of reference forms a curious analogy with the relation of the fantastic poem (which seems mimetic only in regard to its own more alienated moments) to its audience and its historical context.

The reader confronts, in other words, a reproduction of the text/ history relation within the text itself. The poem dramatizes its own condition of marginality and alienation, in a way distantly comparable to the liminal stance taken by Dante at the boundary between life and death, time and eternity, to gloss the significance of history;[4] as well as to the retreat of Boccaccio's storytellers to an utopian site at the margin of plague-ridden Florence, from which they reflect back calmly, though provisionally, on the *eros* and violence of the world.[5] It is, in fact, a concern of mine to ask whether the *Furioso*

---

[3] The notion of "making it strange" dates from Russian Formalism, but in a way it is just a transliteration of Isidore of Seville, *Etymologiarum sive Originum Libri XX,* ed. W. Lindsay (Oxford: The Clarendon Press, 1966), I.xxxvii.22, who defined allegory as "alieniloquium," and a conceptual descendent from the use of allegory, as in *Inferno* I, to reflect the estranged condition of man as *homo viator,* an exile and a pilgrim on earth, a "stranger in a strange land." See also *Letter to Can Grande,* p. 99.

[4] See especially Erich Auerbach, "Figura," in *Scenes from the Drama of European Literature,* trans. R. Manheim (New York: Meridian Books, 1959), as well as Singleton, *Dante's "Commedia,"* and Mazzotta, *Dante.*

[5] Mazzotta, "The Marginality of Literature," takes Victor Turner's definition of "liminality" (in *The Forest of Symbols: Aspects of Ndembu Ritual* [Ithaca: Cornell

is nearer to the transcendent, totalizing gloss of historical realities offered by the *Commedia* from its eschatological margin or to the limited, multiple perspectives of those who are looking at death from the other side (this side) in the *Decameron*. The surprise is that the question is not as quickly resolved in favor of the latter alternative as one usually supposes. In any case, it is no accident that the locales of the Alcina-Logistilla sequence are consistently at the point of crossing between two geophysical areas: between land and sea, mountain and desert, earth and sky. Nor is it casual that the word "margine" itself appears in a couple of key spots (VI.23.7; VII.14.4). The primary question in relation both to the dynamic of Ruggiero's education and to the status of Ariosto's text is whether the island represents a "liminal" or a "marginal" experience. Is Ruggiero undergoing a liminal "rite of passage" (or passage to the right, as Hercules can attest) which will lead him from immaturity into maturity? Or will he remain a perpetual adolescent in the grey zone between virtue and vice, understanding and ignorance? Is the poem's turn toward allegorical fantasy one step on the way back to a better understanding of historical realities? Or does the *Furioso* always remain on the margin of history in a condition of evasion and/or irrelevance?

By virtue precisely of its marginal situation, it seems, the episode has lent itself to the interpretations both of those who wish to see the poem as "outside" of, detached from, any referential project *and* of those who want to see it as referring in a significant way to some "reality." My reading of the episode will furnish a critique of the latter group on the grounds that poetic reference is put into a perpetual state of error and crisis. It will also suggest, however, that the former contingent is wrong to posit a text reflecting only on its own textuality, an art appreciating itself in an antinatural mirror of Narcissus, because to speak of a situation of marginality

---

University Press, 1967], pp. 93–111) as a period of *transition* between one socially integrated state and another and sets it off against a concept of "marginality" as a *permanent* condition of betwixt-and-betweenness which is equally applicable to the relation between individual and society and to that between text and history. A major influence on recent literary-critical uses of the theme of marginality is Jacques Derrida, *Marges de la Philosophie* (Paris: Minuit, 1972).

is already to imply a relation, however tortuous and backhanded, to that which has been abandoned.

The Alcina episode has frequently been granted a synecdochical function, often wittingly, though sometimes not, with respect to the *Furioso* as a "whole." Curiously this is equally true of "anti-referential" and "referential" readers of this episode. Both of them, as it will turn out, are "right" in a restricted sense. There are those for whom the flight of Ruggiero on the hippogryph/Pegasus, in its function as emblem of poetic imagination, should be the perfect figure of an evasive poetry: departing from history, from the credible, from erotic loyalties, from public duties, and, above all, from death, into a realm of superficial, and yet profoundly seductive, delights.[6] For Momigliano, the critic most sensuously, and excessively, aware of these fascinations in the poem, Alcina's island is the utopian, edenic place of art that everyone yearns for in the face of life's unyielding difficulties (p. 25). More curiously, it is not really Ruggiero at all who most often figures the poet as escapist for these critics. It is, instead, Alcina, the seducer, mistress of metamorphoses, who continually lends them metaphors by which to characterize the poet luring his readers with the magical fascinations of his poetic world. Ugo Foscolo, the first "modern" Italian critic, as well as one of Italy's great poets, saw the reader as a fisherman seduced by Circean (or Sirenian) music, metaphors which are obviously borrowed from Astolfo's narration of his seduction

---

[6] Donato, "Desire," p. 32, explicitly takes the position that the hippogryph figures the poem's rejection of all referential connections to nature and reality. Luigi Pirandello, "L'Umorismo," p. 93, takes a similar position much earlier. For the several conflated sources of the hippogryph, see Rajna, *Le Fonti*, p. 114ff. See also Bigi's edition of *Orlando Furioso*, notes to canto IV, for additional possibilities. For critical discussions of the hippogryph as symbol of poetic imagination see Giamatti, *The Earthly Paradise*, p. 150, and, especially, "Headlong Horses, Headless Horsemen," p. 270 et passim; Marianne Shapiro, "Perseus and Bellerophon in *Orlando Furioso*," *Modern Philology* 81 (1983); Valerie M. Wise, "Ruggiero and the Hippogriff: The Ambiguities of Vision," *Quaderni d'Italianistica* 2 (1981). The strongest classical figure evoked by the hippogryph is, obviously, the Pegasus, winged horse of poetry, often allegorized, for instance by Silvestris (*Commentary*, p. 73), as the *fama* which poetry confers and which incites to glory (cf. Shapiro, p. 125). Compare Horace, *Ars Poetica* 1–5. See nn. 22 and 26 below for the ethical and metaphysical symbolism of the hippogryph; see also sec. vi of this chapter.

by Alcina. Momigliano says of the episode that "beneath those magical pages shines the human seduction of forms and the senses." For both DeSanctis and Croce, the genius of Ariosto is able to assume any shape ("trasmutabile in tutte guise"), just like the protean Alcina, and is magical. More recently Donato, who shares the belief that the *Furioso* is self- (or anti-) referential, has claimed that "the poet's artifact . . . fixes in its narrative discourse the desire of the reader," just as Alcina's simulacra fix the desire of Ruggiero.[7]

What is most curious of all is that in every case but the last this metaphorical transfer from Alcina to Ariosto seems to take place without an awareness of the implicit identification of Ariosto's poetics with Alcina's art. Nonetheless, it is clear that to "embrace" art for art's sake, or its intrinsic meanings and pleasures, is to follow precisely in the footsteps of Astolfo and then Ruggiero, both of whom cannot or do not go "beyond the sign" of outer beauty as they embrace Alcina. Alcina in fact is the perfect figure of a microcosmic artistic world (VI.27), as is the first castle of her master, Atlante (IV.32),[8] unifying in herself all of the good scattered here and there throughout the rest of the world (at least in the eyes of her lover-interpreters). So, in effect, the critical theme of the poem as *alter mundus* may be seen as essentially an application to the *Furioso* of Alcinian categories.[9]

Naturally, most of the "Alcinian" critics are rigidly antiallegorical. Momigliano dismissed the Logistilla portion of the episode as "non-poesia" in the following words, which suggest just how thorough the metaphorical reenactment of the episode by its readers can be: "the whole episode of Alcina, wrapped in forgetful magic, . . . is animated by an occult experience of the human senses and emotions, but is dangerously menaced by the moral interpretation

---

[7] Donato, "Desire," p. 24. For the others, see Foscolo, "Poemi Narrativi," p. 124; Momigliano, *Saggio*, p. 7, cf. pp. 276, 299; DeSanctis, "Ariosto," p. 253; Croce, "Ariosto," p. 43.

[8] The Ariosto-as-Alcina vs. Ariosto-as-Logistilla debate is paralleled in the criticism by the contradictory assimilations of Ariosto to Atlante and to Merlin, alluded to in Chapter 1 and further developed in Chapter 4, sec. iv.

[9] Though Durling, *The Figure of the Poet*, pp. 125–26, argues elsewhere against the self-enclosure of the *Furioso*, his application of the quotation from Tasso's *Discorsi* to Ariosto's work does suggest that poet and poem are like Alcina as artistic microcosm.

and by the allegorical opposition of the two sisters. Thus, when the sensuous, malicious theme is interrupted, the poetry vanishes," leaving behind only "the naked allegorical meaning."[10] For Momigliano, clearly, allegorical interpretation is exactly like the ring of Angelica which sees through the primarily Alcinian surface of the poem. More recently, Ariosto has been credited with "anti-allegorical stratagems" which deliberately break down medieval allegorical traditions, especially those of mythography.[11] At stake is the commonplace assumption, easily contestable, that the Renaissance is partly identifiable in its rejection of all ahistorical, allegorical readings and writings in favor of discourse which is mimetically faithful to classical texts and/or historical reality.[12]

If for one group of critics the episode contains a flight both from history and from allegory into pure, self-referential poetic surface, the poet being taken for an Alcina (as she presents herself, not as what Melissa shows her to be), for another group the poet is placed on the other side of the conflict, seen as a sort of Logistilla who offers the reader a chance to reflect on the changing shapes of vice and on the contents of his own soul, and who is therefore an agent of education and consciousness, rather than of seduction and

[10] I translate from *Saggio,* pp. 41–42. A more recent version of the same is in Franco Pool, *Interpretazione dell' "Orlando Furioso"* (Firenze: La Nuova Italia, 1968), p. 36, which complains of the "stuchevole allegoria moralistica."

[11] See especially Daniel Javitch, "Rescuing Ovid from the Allegorizers," in A. Scaglione, ed., *Ariosto 1974 in America,* p. 73. Javitch is discussing Ariosto's reworking of the Perseus and Andromeda episode in canto x, which he takes to be a recovery of the Ovidian original from the moral and religious allegories of the Middle Ages. He does not, however, discuss the placement of the allegedly "antiallegorical" episode at the end of the most heavily allegorical stretch of the poem. Cf. Wiggins, "Galileo," pp. 262–63.

[12] The notion of a "mimetic" Renaissance is discredited by Edgar Wind's works, as well as D.C. Allen, *Mysteriously Meant: The Rediscovery of Pagan Symbolism and Allegorical Interpretation in the Renaissance* (Baltimore: The Johns Hopkins University Press, 1970), and, more recently, by Michael Murrin's discussion in *The Allegorical Epic* (Chicago: University of Chicago Press, 1980). Murrin goes so far as to argue that Landino's reading of Virgil is essentially the correct one. On the other hand, he does not treat the *Furioso.* For the general question of what becomes of myths in the Renaissance, see Seznec, and Leonard Barkan, *The Gods Made Flesh: Metamorphosis and the Pursuit of Paganism* (New Haven: Yale University Press, forthcoming 1986).

"forgetful magic." DeBlasi, for instance, argues that Alcina is precisely what Ariosto is not: "on the outside inviting and joyful, inside all misery and sin and pride." And he also takes the allegory of education to virtue in Logistilla's palace quite seriously.[13] The *Cinquecento* allegorizers, bent on pursuing the moral and/or metaphysical contents of the poem, not surprisingly spend more time on this emblematic episode and on the lunar sequence than on any of the others.[14] The modern critics who argue for a poetics of allegorical education turn immediately to this episode as the most explicit confirmation of a full-blown didactic itinerary.[15] And if they cannot always deny our fascination with the delightful surface of the episode, they are able to invoke the model of education by seduction.[16] By an odd, and yet not coincidental, symmetry, Momigliano argues for precisely the opposite interpretation of the same phenomenon: that Astolfo's attempt to educate Ruggiero about Alcina with an elegant retelling of his own fall merely contributes to his pupil's fascination with and seduction by her.[17]

Thus, if one sort of reader seems blithely unaware that the episode "deconstructs," via Melissa's proddings and the ring's unveilings—the very type of reading which they themselves indulge in and the same sort of writing which they promote—another sort, by contrast, seems particularly insensitive both to the Alcinian allure of the poem and to the ironic nature and consequences of the countertext of Logistillan allegory. Neither sort notices that the two figures have exchanged rhetorical structures by the episode's end. Alcina is unveiled as the duplicitous allegorical sign *par excellence*, while Logistilla is said to realize her being in her surface (her nature and

[13] I translate from "Ariosto," pt. 1, p. 332; cf. pp. 349–50.

[14] See again the collected commentaries in the Orlandini edition of Ariosto's *Opere*.

[15] See again Yoeman and Cuccaro. The latter asserts that Logistilla runs nothing less than an "humanistic school," like those in Ferrara and elsewhere in Ariosto's day (*Humanism*, pp. 200–201).

[16] Yoeman, "Allegorical Rhetoric," p. 157ff., esp. p. 160.

[17] Momigliano, *Saggio*, pp. 29–30. Carol Kaske helpfully called my attention to the relevant passages in Romans (7:5–25) where St. Paul speaks about the law as provocation to the very sins it forbids (since fallen man, like Adam and Eve, is tempted by what is prohibited, and, without Grace's aid, cannot resist the evil urge within himself).

the outer signs of it coincide). The issue of "dulcis et utilis" or "serio ludere" is thus played out unwittingly in the critical debate on this episode as a contest between an Alcinian and a Logistillan "Ariosto." And it is my contention that the episode lends itself to both sorts of reading, playing one off against the other. In this way it deliberately brings into question the status of allegory as a mode of educational discourse, and it raises the question of a difficult relationship between the allegorical region of Alcina and Logistilla and the "other world" of the poem to which Ruggiero returns. That encounter, when explored later in the chapter, will raise the possibility of the coexistence of a poetics of representative surfaces with one of allegorical covering and uncovering, provoking a crisis in which literal and allegorical meet, clash, and, worst of all, mingle.[18] And if such a rhetorical crisis were identified, it would no longer be possible to assure oneself either that education pandered in aid of seduction or that seduction was merely a useful means to didactic ends.

Not that all readers of the sequence have failed to recognize the presence of a referential tension, or have so easily placed Ariosto on the side of *either* Alcina *or* Logistilla.[19] By far the best extended reading of the episode to date is found in Giamatti's chapter on Ariosto in *The Earthly Paradise and the Renaissance Epic*, which is also the most notable example of using Ruggiero's Alcinian sojourn as a synecdoche for the poem as a whole and a model for Ariostan didactic poetics.[20] I noted in the preceding chapter that Giamatti traces the didactic itinerary of Ruggiero to the point of qualified

[18] My reading of the (collapsing) opposition between the two modes of signification is influenced by Mazzotta, "The Literal and the Allegorical."

[19] Binni, for instance, at one juncture places Ariosto between what he calls a Poliziano-like poetics of civilization and an aesthetics of pure form (*Metodo e Poesia*, p. 133), between instruction and delight, limited to neither (p. 103), although he finally goes on to consign the poem to the realm of inarticulate music (p. 176).

[20] This point, valid for *The Earthly Paradise*, calls for some qualification in light of "Headlong Horses, Headless Horsemen." The technique of passing part for whole has been canonized by Auerbach, in *Mimesis*, and Greene, in *The Descent from Heaven*, among others. The analogy of a paleontological reconstruction of dinosaurs from a few bones leaps to mind—but of course these critics are in the happy position of breaking the subject up themselves and then of reconstructing it as they see fit. For the "opposite" technique, see Roland Barthes' remarkable *S/Z*.

success and insists on the poem's educational mission, its desire to instruct readers through the combined examples of Ruggiero and Astolfo. To this extent, Giamatti's Ariosto is "Logistillan." On the other hand, he also recognizes that Logistilla's virtues pale in attractiveness before Alcina's vices; that explicit didactic allegories, such as Ruggiero's combat with the band of monstrous vices and with Erifilla, degenerate from apparent moral victories into panders of deviation and seduction; and that, finally, the hero's triumphs are only partial (as we shall see, they are also only temporary), even though they are modeled on the epic allegories of education, especially the moral reading of Aeneas' return from his passionate interlude with Dido to duty and self-sacrifice.[21]

Giamatti formulates the pedagogical transit from Alcina to Logistilla as a passage from referential and existential duplicity (seeing and being at dangerous odds) to a place where there is "no fatal gap between what seems and what is" (p. 162)—a displacement which I have translated, for my own purposes, into a referential movement from allegory toward mimesis. What enables Ruggiero to make this passage, he argues, is a double change of strategy: from reading deceptive surfaces as literally true to a vigilant, ironic mistrust which spies out hidden corruption; from a reliance on virtue and integrity in the fight against vice to a willingness to combat evil with its own arsenal of magical illusions and disingenuous deceptions. One must adopt the perspective of irony in the interpretation of others, and the stance of irony in representing oneself. What remains implicit in all of this is that to achieve "Logistillan" ethical ends, one adopts Alcinian "aesthetic" means. Though Giamatti sets Astolfo/Ariosto ("gentle master of ironies") and Alcina ("malignant manipulator of illusion") poles apart through his morally charged language (p. 141), he nonetheless attributes to them identical structural and referential situations. Both are equally at odds with Logistillan coincidences of outer surface and inner meaning: "the split [between surface and substance] is the very subject of the poem" (p. 138). This thematic conflation

---

[21] Giamatti, *The Earthly Paradise*, pp. 158–60. These pages implicitly suggest, but do not themselves undertake, a recourse to the allegorizations of the *Aeneid* by Landino, Silvestris, *et alii* and to readings of the episode by *Cinquecento* commentators.

of the Alcinian and Logistillan Ariostos along the internal narrative axis is further projected outward along the author-text-reader axis through Giamatti's reinterpretation of the hippogryph as emblem of Ariostan didactic poetics. To the reading of the Pegasean hippogryph as figure of poetic imagination (and fantastic escapism) he rightly adds the moral and metaphysical overtones of the persistent imagery of horses and reining, as well as the allusive reference to the Platonic "horses of the soul," in order to suggest a controlled, ethically motivated, use of poetry. Thus he attempts to reconcile the aesthetic and the ethical, the delightfully "Alcinian" and the usefully "Logistillan," elements of the poem by the recourse to equine imagery, bringing the two opposite sides into a provisional and tense harmony.[22]

In one sense, then, it will be the aim of this chapter simply to make quite explicit what has already been hinted at implicitly: that Ariosto links himself partly to Logistilla, partly to Alcina, while defining the limits of both "poetics" and with them the interpretive stances which privilege one or the other. In addition, however, I will want to look more closely at some loose ends and unresolved contradictions in the criticism generally and in Giamatti's account in particular. In the first instance, I will want to question whether there actually *is* a successful education represented at the narrative

---

[22] "Headlong Horses, Headless Horsemen," p. 270: "the aesthetic and the moral are united in the imagery of curbing [the horses]." For Giamatti, the hippogryph's unreined flight is only the most prominent moment in the imaginative series of unreined horses (and riders). He gives a very useful list of sources for the equine imagery at the beginning of the essay. Two seem especially relevant: the myth of Hippolytus, of which more will be said in Chapter 4, sec. v, and the Platonic myth of the chariot, charioteer, and two horses of the soul in *Phaedrus* 246a and ff. In the usual gloss of the myth, the charioteer stands for reason, while one horse (the black) represents evil appetite and the other (the white) good desires. The hippogryph fuses elements of this Socratic myth with that of the "wings of the soul" developed in the same passage (esp. 246c–e). For the most important neo-Platonic treatment of the image in the Renaissance, see Michael Allen, ed. and trans., *Marsilio Ficino and the Phaedran Charioteer* (Berkeley: University of California Press, 1981), and Landino, *Disputationes*, bk. III, p. 134. See also Peter Marinelli, "Redemptive Laughter," pp. 519–21. See n. 6 above for the "poetic" symbolism of the hippogryph which is yoked with the moral/intellectual implications of the Platonic imagery. The *Phaedrus*, as a discourse on rhetoric and as the *locus classicus* of the *furor poeticus*, had already juxtaposed the two elements combined by Ariosto in his composite beast.

level.[23] Moreover, granted that a positive educational model were to be represented, it is not clear *how* the reader could learn from it, at least in the terms of the lesson which is ostensibly taught. From Ruggiero's inability to apply the lesson that Astolfo teaches him we are said to learn that no "textual" or abstract instruction can show us how to read beneath the surface—only direct experience develops the requisite ironic mistrust. If we apply *that* model to our reading of Ariosto's or Giamatti's didactic texts, how are we to imagine that they can do for us what Astolfo cannot do for Ruggiero?

In other words, Giamatti may substitute one kind of education for another in the case of Ruggiero—simple-minded, superficial allegory replaced by readerly irony—but his sketchy account of the book's mode of referring knowledge and virtue to its reader returns to the level of simple allegorical modeling. And, in any case, as a subsequent developer of the theme of Ariosto's humanistic irony has pointed out, allegory and irony traditionally have the same structure.[24] His main point is that the Crocean account of irony as the antididactic antithesis of allegory is erroneous,[25]

---

[23] In *The Earthly Paradise*, Giamatti astutely refused to pin his interpretation of the educational possibilities in the *Furioso* on Ruggiero. In the later "Headlong Horses, Headless Horsemen," in fact, he notes (p. 299) that our hero's stay with Logistilla is followed shortly by his attempted rape of Angelica. In the earlier essay, Giamatti recurs now to Astolfo, now to the book's reader, as those who have taken (or may take) Ariosto's teachings to heart (pp. 151–52, 163, passim). For Astolfo, see Chapter 4, sec. i, below. The question of the reader's potential education will be considered immediately.

[24] Kennedy, "Ariosto's Ironic Allegory," *MLN* 88 (1973), esp. p. 45. He shows that the two tropes are traditionally linked by classical rhetoricians in virtue of "saying one thing and meaning another," i.e., in their "duplicity." For a modern theoretical account of the structural relationship between the two, see DeMan, "The Rhetoric of Temporality." In arguing first that ironic reversals blur "any cut and dried didactic allegory" (p. 61), but then that they open up the episode into a complexly "ironic allegory" (p. 67), Kennedy is transposing Giamatti's insights into more precise rhetorical terms which both clarify that position and open the way for disagreements with it.

[25] Kennedy's account of allegory deployed, toyed with, and redeployed at a higher level is a good response to Javitch's thesis and, especially, to Croce, who attempts to use irony to exorcise the spectre of its double, allegory, for literature. In the end, however, the Crocean claim that no utterance in the text is to be taken

but there is an underlying suggestion that Giamatti's version of the agonistic relationship between allegory and irony is equally mistaken—that his own discourse does not escape from the commonplaces of a Logistillan humanism.[26] The conflation of Logistilla and Alcina, Alcinian means to Logistillan ends, risks sliding in the opposite direction as well: if irony can slip into allegory, it can also be confused quite easily with seductive duplicity. The account of Astolfo-Ariosto as a well-intentioned teacher who cannot find adequate expressive means to accomplish his ends needs to be supplemented by a less flattering picture of a disingenuous trickster who deliberately trades on his readers' inability to look past surface appearances in order to pass off seductive intentions as educational ones. In other words, what happens if one applies what Giamatti sees as Ariosto's warning against "taking literature (or life) at face value" (p. 139) to the process of reading the *Furioso* itself? In the one case, a failure of reading blocks education; in the other, an abuse of poetic reference does the same. By positing a difference between Ariosto and Alcina and yet leaving them as structural twins, Giamatti reopens the very crisis of readerly blindness and authorial duplicity which he strives to resolve.

At chapter's end, after an extended probing of Ruggiero's education and its applications to the reader, I will return to the figure which seems to effect emblematically a successful synthesis of the moral and the artistic: the hippogryph. I will want to suggest then

---

seriously in itself, even as behind it looms the goddess *Armonia* and the poet-God, seems precisely allegorical to those not blessed with Croce's faith in neo-Hegelian Spirit.

[26] Kennedy observes that no simple allegorization of the hippogryph is possible ("Ironic Allegory," pp. 65–66), thus applying a version of Giamatti's own critique of the simple-minded allegories of the monstrous vices and Erifilla (*The Earthly Paradise*, p. 151) against the latter's privileged figure for poetic discourse. In fact, the moral-intellectual reading of the Ariostan horses and hippogryph was already well developed by the *Cinquecento* allegorizers. For the horse imagery, see Fornari, *Spositione*, pp. 83–84). In *Opere* (Orlandini edition), see the *Allegoria* of G. Bonomone (which precedes the text of the poem) for a reading of Ruggiero and the hippogryph as allegory of unbridled passion, corrected by a Logistillan education in self-knowledge and the mastery of desire by reason. See as well the *Allegoria* of Valvassori to canto VI, the *Allegorie* of Valvassori, Porcacchi, and Toscanella to canto XXIII, and so on.

that the synthesizing union of contraries effected by that literary
beast is inseparable from a persistent, nagging awareness of its
monstrosity, its ambiguous duplicity; that the Pegasean symbol of
moral poetic imagination is not only the adamant dialectical foe of
chimerical and demonic imagination, but is also precisely, textually,
confused with it—in a catastrophic blurring of the moral and
epistemological boundaries between good and evil, true and false.

Before going on to examine the twin crises of reading and of
reference implicit in Giamatti's interpretation, however, I need to
give a clear and more comprehensive idea of the broad narrative
pattern of educational allegory which informs the episode, to point
out the ways in which the text seems to translate that narrative
into a project for instructing its readers, and, most important, to
suggest what it is that is ostensibly taught and how it bears on the
educational techniques, values, problems, and aims discussed in
Chapter 2.

ii. *The Form of the Allegory*

To begin with, what is the full sequence of events through which
Ruggiero's seduction and education are acted out? Several indi-
vidual moments in his itinerary have already been mentioned, but
the larger outlines, beyond the simple notion of a transit from
Alcina to Logistilla, remain obscure. The problem is created by the
text itself—partly through a number of redundancies and incon-
sistencies detected by commentators (e.g., the repeated defeating of
Alcina's fleet) and partly through the breaks in the narrative. The
episode, in fact, begins in canto IV, stanzas 42–50, skips forward
to VI.17, proceeding more or less continuously from there through
VIII.20 (broken only by a brief return to Bradamante and by the
narrator's proems). It then leaves off again, and its "Logistillan"
portion is picked up only in X.35, from there following Ruggiero
on to XI.20 when, back in Europe, he loses Angelica, the ring, and
the hippogryph. This fragmentation and self-contradiction have
been offered as proofs that the allegory is incoherent and thus,
depending on the critic's tastes, either trivial and negligible or
savagely parodic. Yet very close inspection will reveal unexpected
coherence and direction, both logically and in terms of imagery,

particularly when the shape of the whole journey, and its repetitions of other literary journeys, from Europe to the allegorical islands and back again, are taken into account, as they will be toward the end of this description. It remains to be seen, however, why a relatively systematic allegory of education should so thoroughly repress and disguise itself.

Ruggiero's adventures begin in canto IV. Bradamante, deploying the trickery taught her by Melissa and the magical ring stolen from Brunello, defeats Atlante and rescues her fiancé from a miniature courtly world located somewhere in the Pyrenees in which his mentor has (benignly) imprisoned him. No sooner is he released, however, than a dimwitted curiosity leads him to mount Atlante's flying steed, which immediately, and without his assent, takes off for parts unknown, leaving Bradamante as frustrated and unhappy as ever. As the imagery of "sfrenatezza" suggests, Ruggiero's unplanned flight intimates failures both of a will unable to restrain passions or to contain the imagination's wanderings and of an intellect unable to understand itself or its situation.[27] Though the flight soon bears our nervous hero westward beyond the long-established limits of human experience, though he is compared to a Ganymede borne off by Jove's eagle (neo-Platonic emblem of man lifted beyond the human to Olympian heights),[28] these apparent leaps of intellect and will are reduced to literal and therefore parodic movements through space to which Ruggiero's primary response is barely concealed terror (VI.17). When he finally alights on an island at the other side of the world, he ties the hippogryph to a myrtle tree, only to discover, much to his horror, that the tree houses the soul and voice of the former Astolfo. Astolfo gives him what will turn out to be only the first of several lessons he receives while on the island, narrating his own seduction of and by Alcina, and her subsequent Circean metamorphosis of him, along with infinite other ex-lovers,

[27] Giamatti, "Headlong Horses, Headless Horsemen," pp. 267, 292–94.

[28] See Erwin Panofsky, "The Neoplatonic Movement and Michelangelo," *Studies in Iconology* (New York: Harper & Row, Harper Torchbooks, 1962), pp. 213–18. Panofsky gives a brief but cogent history of the Platonic tendency to read the Ganymede myth as the ascent of the spirit freeing itself from the body. He gives special weight, as I do, to Landino's annotations to *Purgatorio* 9.13–33 and quotes them at length.

into the very landscape in which Ruggiero now stands (cf. VI.51–52). An informed reader should recognize immediately the connection of the metamorphosis to the traditional allegorization of Circe as alluring vice which reduces men to beasts (and other subhuman beings—plants, rocks, etc.).[29] And Ruggiero should recognize the obvious parallel between Astolfo unexpectedly carried off to the island by Alcina and her whale and his own recent surprise departure, but he does not seem to. Nonetheless, he is specifically said to be "dotto et instrutto" ("instructed and wise" VI.56.8) after these warnings, and he takes leave from Astolfo determined not to take a leaf from his book: he will avoid the vicious Alcina and instead seek out her virtuous half-sister, Logistilla. An allegorical journey has begun.

The next step is one already discussed in some detail above. Ruggiero arrives at a Herculean Crossroads, a Pythagorean "Y": to the right he faces a steep and rocky road, combat against a hoard of allegorical vices, and, ultimately, access to virtue on the mountain-top; to the left, instead, an inviting plain, a road "ampla e diritta" ("broad and straight" VI.60.4), and the seductive "golden" heights of Alcina's city. After initially choosing the right path and fighting a holding action against the allegorical monsters whose composite conflations of human and bestial forms suggest the inhuman, un-natural character of vice (just as, more subtly, the metamorphosed lovers also do), Ruggiero is distracted by the arrival of two lovely women. They easily, far too easily, chase off the monsters and lead him back toward the golden city on a hill, the lessons of Astolfo having already been forgotten. The seduction of Ruggiero, as Giamatti has shown, begins as an apparent demonstration of his chivalric virtue in combatting the giantess Erifilla. After this, the jour-

---

[29] See Rajna, *Le Fonti*, p. 175, for Circe as source of Alcina. For allegorical readings of the Circe myth, see Boethius, *De Consolatione Philosophiae*, bk. IV, meter iii, and the gloss which follows in prose iv. See also Boccaccio, *Genealogia* IV.xiv (vol. I, pp. 172–73). On the allegorical tradition of Ulysses and Circe, see Giorgio Padoan, *Il Pio Enea, l'Empio Ulisse* (Ravenna: Longo, 1977), esp. pp. 180–81. Bigi's note to VI.16 adds Calypso, Dido, Boiardo's Falerina (*Innamorato* I.xvii) and Carandina from the *Mambriano* (I.32ff.) as analogues to Alcina. Alcina herself is first mentioned in *Innamorato* II.xiii.55–66, where the story of Astolfo's entrapment is first told.

ney to Alcina's palace mysteriously ceases to be the crossing of a plain and turns into a steep, narrow ascent through a wood and up a mountain (VII.8). The fact that, just before beginning to ascend, Ruggiero encounters Erifilla astride a wolf, who is an obvious relative of the allegorical wolf in *Inferno* 1.49–54 (interpreted in the Renaissance as a symbol of avarice),[30] and that once they are "ascesi in su la vetta" ("ascended to the summit" VII.8.5) he meets a "donna sole" ("lady-sun" cf. 10.8, 12.2) in a "paradiso," confirms that the journey to Alcina echoes and parodies the ascent of a spiritual mountain which the unaided Dante fails to make in *Inferno* I, but which he does initiate successfully under Virgil's tutelage in *Purgatorio* 1–2. Even Ruggiero's forgetfulness makes us remember Dante's purifying immersion in Lethe before crossing over to Beatrice's solar presence (VII.18, 33, 40, 44). Alcina herself clearly recalls the lady whose inner and outer beauty, like Beatrice's, induces virtue and knowledge in the lover. From her mouth, "escon le cortesi parolette / da render molle ogni cor rozzo e scabro" ("emerge the courteous little words which soften any coarse and rude heart" VII.13.5–6). It soon becomes obvious, however, that the ascent was purely fictive and that Alcina does not soften hard hearts to vigilant virtue, but to forgetful *eros* and the parodic "virtute" of an amorous silence (30.4). Thus what appears at first as the form of education and the exercise of virtue does indeed mask a seduction. Soon enough Ruggiero is convinced that Astolfo's advice was a product of mere envy (16) and has forgotten both his loyalty to Bradamante and his role in the historical conflict between Agramante and Carlo (VII.33, 40).

With the intercession of Melissa, the magician, the series of moral and intellectual failures begins to be reversed, and a series of seemingly productive educational moments is initiated. Melissa, who had earlier and successfully left Bradamante "instrutta e dotta" (VII.38.8), as we are reminded by words which also recall the unlearned lesson

[30] For Dante's "lupa" as symbol of avarice, see Landino's annotations to *Inferno* I in *La Divina Commedia* (Firenze: 1481). Renaissance commentaries, for instance Bonomone's *Allegoria* (see n. 26, above), recognized Eriffila as a figure of that avarice which stands in the way of a disbursing of gold for seductive ends. Modern annotators recognize a series of echoes, principally Dantean, which link Erifilla and her wolfish steed to avarice. See, for instance, Bigi's notes to VI.78–80 and VII.3–5.

given by Astolfo to Ruggiero, consoles the abandoned Bradamante and promises to lead, or rather drag, Ruggiero, "per via alpestre e dura / alla vera virtù, mal grado d'esso" ("by a rough and mountainous road to true virtue, in spite of himself" 42.3–4), thus placing him back on the path to virtue abandoned for a similar yet false ascent to Alcina. And as Alcina travesties herself to appear an agent of education, so Melissa adopts a disguise as the figure, Atlante, who most desires that Ruggiero never marry, never act out his glorious destiny in the historical drama. In this guise Melissa reminds Ruggiero of his Herculean and/or Achillean education as a youth (57).[31] She/he then points to his heroic potential (he could be an Alexander, a Scipio, a Caesar [59.3]), the praise and glory he can win, the dynasty he and Bradamante are to found, and thus wakes him out of his erotic stupor. Having revived him, she assumes her own form, adds Bradamante's love to the list of claims on him, and then, with the aid of the magic ring, exposes the age and corruption which lie beneath the artful appearance of Alcina (70–74). As a number of critics have observed, this revelation too has a Dantean cast, since it echoes Dante's dream of the "femmina balba" who becomes a tempting Siren and then has her corruption exposed, again by the intervention of a divine lady (*Purgatorio* 19.7 ff.).[32] Earlier, Astolfo, rehearsing the Boiardan origin of the episode (*Orlando Innamorato* II.xiii.62), reported that he had been lured onto the island/whale by Alcina's promise to show him "una sirena / che col suo dolce canto acheta il mare" ("a siren who quiets the sea with her sweet song" VI.40.1–2). The subsequent events imply that Alcina herself was the enchanting Siren in question, and in retrospect make the allusion to the Dantean episode and to the allegorical tradition of the Sirens as erotic temptresses as plain as the related references to Circe's magic.[33]

[31] Melissa herself has a significant mythological predecessor in the Melissa who nursed and tutored the infant Jove while his mother kept him hidden from the paternal cannibalism of father Saturn. She was subsequently changed into a bee.

[32] Parker (*Inescapable Romance*, p. 49) notices the resemblance and gives an interesting interpretation of the differences between the two episodes.

[33] For the allegorical force of the Sirens as erotic, aesthetic, and/or moral temptresses, see Hugo Rahner, "Odysseus at the Mast," in *Greek Myths and Christian Mysteries* (London: Burns & Oates, 1963), esp. pp. 353–71. See also Pierre Courcelle,

Now "instrutto" (VII.77.3) by Melissa, Ruggiero begins anew his travels toward Logistilla. This preliminary instruction points the way to another instruction in the control of the hippogryph: "e poi sarebbe instrutto / come frenarlo e farlo gir per tutto" ("and then he would be taught how to rein it and make it go anywhere" VII.78.7–8). Between the negative discovery of Alcina's hidden corruption and the acquisition of positive self-knowledge from Logistilla, Ruggiero goes through an intermediate, liminal or threshold, stage, in which he confirms his ability not only to recognize evil when it presents itself, but also to resist it. First he finds himself struggling with four cryptically allegorical figures: Alcina's huntsman and his three animals.[34] Whatever the exact import of the allegory, which commentators have been unable to decipher satisfactorily, the encounter gives Ruggiero the chance to refight the earlier battle with the monstrous vices, and thus to show that he has learned Melissa's lesson in strategic deception by using the dazzling shield that he earlier refused to unveil on the grounds that he wished to use virtue ("virtude") and not fraud ("frodo") (VI.67.8; cf. VIII.10−11).

The next stage of his journey seems to set him back on the harsh

---

"Quelques Symboles Funéraires du Néoplatonisme Latin." *Revue des Etudes Anciennes* 46 (1944). Padoan, *Il Pio Enea*, pp. 200–204, discusses the confusion of Circe and the Sirens (both, in any case, temptations faced by Ulysses). Note that in the *Odyssey* it is Circe who teaches Odysseus how to escape the Sirens. See Rajna, *Le Fonti*, p. 175, on Dante's Siren as source for Alcina. For other Ariostan allusions to the (poetic) dangers of the Sirens, see Latin Lyric XVII (*De Iulia*) and Satira V.140–41. For useful catalogues of Dantean echoes in the *Furioso*, see Cesare Segre, "Un Repertorio Linguistico e Stilistico dell'Ariosto: La Commedia," in *Esperienze Ariostesche*, pp. 51–83, as well as Luigi Blasucci, "*La Commedia* come Fonte Linguistica e Stilistica del *Furioso*," in *Studi su Dante e Ariosto* (Napoli and Milano: Ricciardi, 1969), pp. 121–61. See also Bigi's notes. No critic, to my knowledge, has previously detected the extended pattern of verbal, thematic, and structural echoes of the *Commedia* in the episode that is discussed here.

[34] The allegory remains obscure to me, as well, though there may be Dantean undertones in the assault on Ruggiero's "piede manco" (VIII.8.2), which recalls the "piè fermo" of fallen will in *Inferno* 1.30, and in the three animals which threaten him. For the Dantean passage see John Freccero, "Dante's Firm Foot and the Journey without a Guide," *Harvard Theological Review* 52 (1959).

Herculean path to virtue:

> Tra duri sassi e folte spine gía
> Ruggiero intanto invèr la fata saggia,
> di balzo in balzo, e d'una in altra via
> aspra, solinga, inospita e selvaggia;
> tanto ch'a gran fatica riuscia
> su la fervida nona in una spiaggia
> tra 'l mare e 'l monte, al mezzodì scoperta
> arsiccia, nuda, sterile e deserta. [VIII.19]

Meanwhile, Ruggiero went on between hard rocks and thick brambles toward the wise fairy; from crag to crag, from one road to another—harsh, solitary, uninviting and wild; so that with great effort he finally emerged on a strand between sea and mountain, exposed to the midday sun—scorched, bare, sterile and deserted.

The midday, intermediate landscape in which Ruggiero now finds himself is the lifeless residue of Melissa's "deconstruction" of Alcina's city and garden, the reconversion of the rocks, trees, plants, rivers, etc. which inhabited it into human form. The completion of the "discovery" process initiated with the lifting of Alcina's veil reveals this "spiaggia . . . scoperta," this oxymoronic juxtaposition of desert and sea. The marginal moral landscape is again Dantean, again connected to the two parallel points of departure: *Inferno* 1 and *Purgatorio* 1–2, recalling the "piaggia diserta," the "gran diserto" (*Inferno* 1.29, 64), in which Dante's spiritual crisis opens and the "lito diserto" (*Purgatorio* 1.130) in which his purgation begins.[35] The typological importance of the desert as the spiritual middle ground of the Israelites in transit between the hellish world of Egypt and the Promised Land, between idolatry and true worship, transgression and law, has been brilliantly explored by Singleton and Freccero and understood as a primary metaphor of textual as well

---

[35] The plate is only once referred to as a "deserto," but is, in fact, very obviously a desert (cf. VIII.19, 20, 35, 38–42). When Atlante's castle disappears, it too attracts the adjective "deserto" (IV.35.5–6). For a list of the surprising number of deserts and desertions in the proximate episodes, see Chapter 4, n. 84, below.

as spiritual intermediateness and ambiguity by Mazzotta.[36] Like
Dante, Ruggiero is in suspension between sea and mountain, as well
as "le valli e i monti," "il mare e il cielo" (cf. VIII.20.8). His experi-
ence is evidently a sort of purgation, an assumption reinforced by
the line "saria troppo a far liquido il vetro" ("it would be more than
enough to liquefy glass" 20.4), which distantly echoes *Purgatorio*
27.49−50: "in un bogliente vetro / gittato mi sarei" ("I would have
flung myself into molten glass"), which describes Dante's culmi-
nating purgatorial experience, his crossing of the wall of fire which
separates him from Beatrice and Eden. The final test in this region
comes when three women from Alcina's court appear, offering him
drink, shade, and other delights (x.36−43). His rejection of them
makes amends specifically for his earlier deviation at the behest of
two other Alcinian courtesans, and so goes hand in hand with his
battle against the huntsman. Since there are *three* women sitting on
an *island* just off shore, we should recall the traditional group of
three Sirens, as well as Alcina as Siren on her island/whale calling
to Astolfo on another shore.[37] At the same time, the "coppa di
cristallo" (x.39.3) with which they tempt him is clearly related to
the traditional "cup of Circe," by which men are turned into beasts,
the "enchanted chalice" (x.45.3) with which Alcina does the same.
Thus, in rejecting their "help," Ruggiero displays a new immunity

---

[36] Singleton, "In Exitu Israel de Aegyptu," *Annual Report of the Dante Society in
America* 78 (1960). See also Dunstan Tucker, "'In Exitu Israel de Aegyptu': The
Divine Comedy in the Light of the Easter Liturgy," *The American Benedictine
Review* 11 (1960); Freccero, "The River of Death: *Inferno* II,108," in S.B. Chandler
and J.A. Molinaro, eds., *The World of Dante* (Toronto: University of Toronto Press,
1966); Mazzotta, *Dante*. See Derrida, "Edmond Jabès," for the general question of
the desert as metaphor of writing.

[37] In the *Odyssey* (bk. XII.39 ff., 184 ff.) only two Sirens lure Odysseus, while in
the *Republic* (bk. X, 617b−c) each of the celestial spheres is said to be inhabited by a
Siren which contributes a single note to the perfect harmony of the "music of the
spheres." As Courcelle tells us, these heavenly Sirens, to whom are added three more
Sirenian singers, the Fates, come to be identified traditionally with the (eleven?)
Muses. He also points out, however, that the tradition of *three* Sirens tempting
Ulysses becomes the iconographical standard ("Symboles," p. 78). On this score,
see Fulgentius, *Mitologiarum Libri Tres,* in *Opera,* ed. R. Helm (Stuttgart: B.G.
Teubner, 1970), bk. II, chap. 8; as well as Boccaccio, *Genealogia,* bk. VII.xx (vol. I,
pp. 354−57).

to the Circean and Sirenian lures with which Alcina first netted him.

The third and last of the intermediate steps on the way to haven with Logistilla begins upon the arrival of a boat steered by a "vec-chio nochiero" which will take Ruggiero across "quello stretto, onde si varca / alla fata più bella" ("that strait where one crosses to the lovelier fairy" x.43.3–4). The old oarsman, "saggio e di lunga esperienza dotto" ("wise and by long experience taught" 44.8), be-comes the hero's third tutor since his arrival, mediating the passage from the risks of the desert to the sanctuary of Logistilla's castle, while "ragionando" to pass the time. On the one hand, he whets Ruggiero's appetite for contemplating Logistilla and for her defin-itive teaching (x.47), while, on the other, he defends them both from the onslaught of Alcina's fleet by "discovering" the magical shield once again. He thus operates as a pivot between the negative and the positive, external and internal, stages of the young knight's education. Predictably enough, the scene is Dantean, again echoing the threshold cantos of *Purgatorio:* the sailor is a "galeotto" and thus recalls the angelic "galeotto" whose boat brings the newly dead re-deemed souls from the historical world to their purgation (2.27).[38] At the same time, his age and his role as a guardian evoke Dante's Cato, the other didactic figure in those cantos. The journey of education is then completed by the "insegnamento" of Logistilla, whose miraculous gems offer an allegory of the acquisition of pru-dence through self-knowledge (x.58–59), and who finally instructs Ruggiero in the art of reining and controlling the hippogryph, giving him the means at last to return to history and complete a full solar circle of the world. All of Ruggiero's defects now seem to have been cured, and he is ready to "come into his own."

A still-not-exhaustive retelling of the Alcina-Logistilla episode reveals a far more systematic allegory, though not necessarily a more interesting one, than Ariosto is usually supposed to have writ-ten or, for that matter, to have been capable of writing. And though one may still argue that it was written to be dismissed, there is no

---

[38] The mediating angelic "galeotto" is of course a counterpart to the book as seductive "galeotto" in *Inferno* 5.137. As in the *Commedia,* Ariosto's "galeotto" mediates a desire *in bono* which displaces an earlier one *in malo*.

doubt that it *was* written and that a dismissal after such elaboration is indeed a grandly perverse gesture on the poet's part, one that begs for explanation. In fact, the episode follows the canonical pattern of such narratives: (1) a series of moral and spiritual failures and a consequent descent into hellish vice and corruption, mediated by a spurious model of askesis; (2) an intermediate purgative period in which the hero learns to recognize and combat external hardships and enemies; (3) entrance into a paradisical state (here represented by Logistilla's palace and her teachings) where the hero is apparently confirmed in virtuous self-knowledge and spiritual well-being. In fact, an even broader pattern can be detected which embraces the flight beyond Europe to the islands and then the return, a circular pattern which complicates, but also perhaps centers, the increasingly dense series of Dantean allusions. Though the name of Ulysses is never mentioned in the episode, Ruggiero's voyage is placed, from its inception, in precise relation to *Inferno* 26—to the "folle volo," the mad flight, which the flame-sheathed tongue of Ulysses attributes to itself—and to the series of parallels/contrasts between Dante and the Greek hero which persists even in the upper reaches of *Paradiso*.

At the end of *Satira* VI, the figure of Ulysses emerges to take on a singularly emblematic role in the educational project described by the poet. On the one hand, he wishes a tutor for his son who "ne la propria lingua de l'autore / gli insegnasse d'intender ciò che Ulisse / sofferse a Troia e poi nel lungo errore" ("in the actual language of the author can teach him to understand what Ulysses suffered at Troy and afterward during his long wandering" 133–35). This hope he sets against the circumstances which truncated his own literary education: "allora non curai saper . . . / . . . come Ulisse a Reso / la vita a un tempo e li cavalli ruba" ("But at that time I did not care to know . . . how Ulysses robbed Rhesus of his life together with his horses" 172–74). These explicit references sensitize us to the Dantean echo soon thereafter: "ero in luogo di padre, [a] far l'uffizio / che debito e pietà mi avea commesso" ("I had taken the place of a father . . . to perform the offices that duty and compassion had assigned me" 206–207). These are precisely the restraints which Ulysses ignored in his pursuit of "virtute e canoscenza":

né dolcezza di figlio, né la pieta
del vecchio padre, né 'l debito amore
lo qual dovea Penelopè far lieta,
   vincer potero dentro a me l'ardore   [94-97]

neither fondness for my son, nor reverence for my aged father, nor the
love which would have made Penelope glad, could conquer in me the
longing . . .

Thus, curiously, Ulysses is both the immediate object of Ariosto's
desire for broader humanistic knowledge, while, at the same time,
the poet offers his refusal to exceed the boundaries of human obli-
gation and affection as a direct counterpoint to Dante's Ulysses'
boundless thirst for novel experience. In the *Commedia,* Latini and
Ulysses together constitute the most prominent confrontations with
the seductions of rhetorical and philosophical humanism. In fact,
the rhetoric of Ulysses may be specifically derived from that of the
historical Latini, while their similarly fiery punishments in the
Inferno both allude to linguistic and pedagogical sinning.[39] It is thus
unsurprising that Ariosto should juxtapose them in his own com-
plex examination of humanism, setting both Latini's sterile, possibly
pederastic, pseudo-fatherhood (*Inferno* 15.83; cf. ll. 31, 37) and Ulys-
ses' abandonment of legitimate family ties, over against his own
responsibilities "in the place of the father" to his siblings, as well
as his loving care for the education of his illegitimate son, Virginio.

   The Alcina episode has its beginnings in the shattering of his-
torical boundaries by Ruggiero's Ulysses-like departure. In the first
place, the hippogryph, "per l'aria ne va come legno unto / a cui
nel mar propizio vento spira" ("he goes through the air like a swift
boat, for which a propitious wind blows" iv.50.5–6), an image
which recalls, as it inverts, this line from *Inferno* 26: "de' remi
facemmo ali al folle volo" ("we made of our oars wings for the
mad flight" 125). The particular weight of this line, as Freccero has
shown, comes from its own inversion of the "remigium alarum"

---

[39] See Mazzotta, *Dante,* pp. 78–83. In the *Commedia,* the two share the pain of
fire (and, thus, are also both iconographical parodies of the prophetic descent of
flames on the Apostles at the Pentecost, and of the "ignes in ore" of the inflam-
matory orator), as well as the search for eternity on earth.

("oarage of the wings") which characterizes the flights of Mercury and Daedalus in the *Aeneid* (I.103; VI.19) and is traditionally glossed by Christian and neo-Platonic allegorizers as the flight of the soul toward divinity.[40] Even more prominent is the echo of *Inferno* 26.107–109 in the following lines: "[Ruggiero] era uscito fuore / per molto spazio il segno che prescritto / avea già a' naviganti Ercole invitto" ("he had left far behind the sign that invincible Hercules once set for sailors" VI.17.6–8). The departure beyond the signs set up, "written" ("pre-scritto"), by Hercules, the Straits of Gibraltar, which for Dante was analogous to the "trapassar del segno" (*Paradiso* 26.117) committed by Adam in eating from the tree of knowledge, also marks the beginning of Ruggiero's fall into the trap of Alcina and his acquisition of knowledge from Logistilla.[41] Thus, oddly enough, Ruggiero is aligned both with the humanistic Hercules and with the exceeder of Herculean limits, Ulysses, and is effectively torn between at least two figures and versions of humanism. Unlike Ulysses, his flight is involuntary and fearful, but like the Greek he too abandons civic and amorous commitments (not altogether involuntarily). Above all, beyond all local echoes, the

---

[40] The "oarage of the wings" recurs several times in the *Furioso*. In particular, Parker (*Inescapable Romance*, p. 249, n. 47) finds echoes in the episode of Olimpia (IX.43.7–8; cf. *Inferno* 26.139, 141). The same passage, which is sandwiched between the two parts of Ruggiero's journey, also echoes 26.125; and two stanzas later (45.1–2) there is an echo of 26.206–207. See also *Furioso* XLIII. 52, 56, 63, 67–68, 146. Constance Jordan, "Enchanted Ground: Vision and Perspective in Renaissance Romance" (Diss. Yale 1976), notes that the arc of Ruggiero's flight follows that in *Inferno* 26.100–152 (p. 137). For some other explicit allusions to Ulysses, see *Furioso* (XIII.60, XXXIII.28, XXXVI.70) and *Cinque Canti* (III.41). For Dante's use of the image and further references to the tradition, see Freccero, "Dante's Prologue Scene," *Dante Studies* 84 (1966), esp. pt. 2, "The Wings of Ulysses," pp. 12–25. Freccero, drawing on Courcelle, argues that this passage is the key to interpreting Ulysses' journey as the hubristic neo-Platonic counterpoint to Dante's Christian journey in humility. See also Pico, *Oratio* (Garin edition), p. 122; Padoan, *Il Pio Enea*, esp. pp. 181, 187, 193.

[41] The traditional motif of the geographical journey as figure of the quest for knowledge, as developed in allegorizations of the *Odyssey* and elsewhere, requires special qualification in light of the Renaissance journeys of discovery by Columbus *et alii*, to which Ariosto was a witness. See especially Chesney's stimulating treatment of the "counter-voyage" of Rabelais and Ariosto in this light (*Rabelais and Ariosto*, pp. 18–61).

decisive analogy is that between the ultimate goals of the two journeys: both lead toward mountainous islands at the antipodes, where an earthly paradise, or its simulacrum, may be found. The route of Ruggiero's journey is that both of Ulysses and of the more successful angelic "galeotto" and his passengers. These connections are, of course, reinforced by the repeated allusions to *Inferno* 1 and *Purgatorio* 1–2 already enumerated, and those in turn take their force precisely from the systematic patterning of the episode after the Dante/Ulysses contrast which persists throughout the *Commedia*.[42] For example, introducing the encounter with Ulysses, Dante says "più lo 'ngegno affreno ch'i' non soglio / perché non corra che virtù nol guidi" ("I curb my genius more than I am wont, lest it run where virtue does not guide it" 26.21–22), claiming to have the power of *reining* his imagination and intellect within boundaries which both Ruggiero, at first, and Ulysses so obviously lack. Nonetheless, later on, in *Paradiso* 27.82–87, he will look back at the "varco / folle di Ulisse" ("the mad track of Ulysses") from a point of view beyond a celestial "segno" and at a height far more ambitious than that pursued by Ulysses. If Dante *then* was like Elisha gazing from below at the soaring, sunlike chariot of Elijah, while Ulysses pursued the sun in a presumptuous *imitatio solis,* Dante *now* stands above and beyond the sun.[43] After Ruggiero's initial Ulyssean lapse he blunders on, not into the tragic death of *Inferno* 26, but into the seductive nets of a Circe, a Siren, both traditional nemeses of Ulysses. Strikingly, the Dantean "femmina balba," from whom the scene of Alcina's exposure derives, declares that she is a "sweet siren" who turned Ulysses himself from his journey to hear her song (*Purgatorio* 19.19–23). He then goes on, however, to reach successes like Dante's: climbing the mountain and achieving a "paradise." On his return he completes the circle of the world, and from beginning to end follows the path of the sun westward (IV.50; X.70; passim) to

[42] See Freccero ("Dante's Prologue," p. 15) and the amplification of his arguments by David Thompson, *Dante's Epic Journey* (Baltimore: The Johns Hopkins University Press, 1974), esp. p. 72. This identification/opposition has been, in any case, a standard of Dante criticism.

[43] See Mazzotta, *Dante,* pp. 97–99, regarding the "hidden heliocentric structure" of canto XXVI (esp. lines 26–27, 113–15, 117, 124, 131).

a point near that of his departure, thus completing the project of Ulysses as well as that of Dante.

The complexity of these parallels will require further interpretation at a later point, particularly regarding the completion of a near-perfect circle around the world. It is clear now, at any rate, that the return to a Dantean itinerary is partly informed by parody: the ascent of Ruggiero does not reach the heights of Dante's, nor does his fall hit the depths of Ulysses'. In fact, the "real" Eden turns out to be elsewhere in Ariosto's world—its comic disappearance from the site where Dante left it prepares the way for its later reappearance in Africa during the journey of Astolfo (which revises both Ruggiero's and Dante's travels). On the other side, the figure of Ulysses does seem charged with complex significance for the episode, as an exemplar of a certain mode of education: "l'ardore / ch'i' ebbi a divenir del mondo esperto / e de li vizi umani e del valore" ("the longing that I had to gain experience of the world, of human vice and worth" *Inferno* 26.97–99). Even as he pursues his own instruction, he poses as the rhetorical, anti-Circean instructor of others in virtue and knowledge:

> *fatti non foste a viver come bruti,*
> *ma per seguir virtute e canoscenza.*   [119–120]

> you were not made to live as brutes, but to pursue virtue and knowledge

We have so far seen "Ulysses" evoked in the Alcina episode primarily as "student," and yet the "false counselor," the "maestro" of an enflamed and enflaming rhetoric, whose "contrapasso" is eternal "death" within a tongue of flame, is also indirectly evoked by imagery linked to the transformed Astolfo. Astolfo "inalberato" and the alienated speech he emits derive from Dante's adaptation of Virgil's Polydorus episode (*Aeneid* III.20 ff.) in the forest of suicides and spendthrifts (*Inferno* 13).[44] Ruggiero here stands in the position of witness occupied by Aeneas and then Dante; Astolfo in

---

[44] Kennedy ("Ironic Allegory," p. 46) emphasizes the conflation in the metamorphosis of Astolfo of the Polydorus episode, in *Aeneid* III, and the Pier delle Vigne episode, in *Inferno* XIII, while giving a useful list of other sources. Bigi's notes to VI.27 add two passages from Boccaccio's *Filocolo* (IV.2–5, V.6–12) to the list of sources. Javitch, "The Imitation of Imitations," explores how carefully Ariosto conflates the several sources.

that of Polydorus and Pier delle Vigne. In the economy of *Inferno,* however, Pier delle Vigne and the "false counselors" (especially Ulysses and Guido da Montefeltro) are in strict imaginative and conceptual relation. Most obvious is the shared image of tortured speech emerging from an inhuman sheath covering a human soul (a tree in the one case, flames in the other). The figuration of Pier delle Vigne's utterance as the sputtering product of burning timber anticipates the literal flames engulfing Ulysses and company. And the Ariostan association of Astolfo's woody words with fire bears the same evocative relation to Ulysses that its Dantean precursor image does:[45]

> *Poi si vide sudar su per la scorza,*
> *come legno dal bosco allora tratto,*
> *che del fuoco venir sente la forza* [vi.32.1–3; cf. 27, 46]

> then he saw it sweat through the bark, like a log just brought from the woods which feels the force of fire approaching

The Pier/Ulysses pairing is not merely structural and imagistic; there is also a thematic contrast at work: if Ulysses is a giver of false counsel (and Guido a counselor of the *use* of fraud), Pier was also specifically a counselor, but one whose *true* advice was mistakenly believed to be *false.* The Pier/Ulysses structure of the *Commedia* thus lies behind the Astolfo/Melissa sequence in the *Furioso*—Astolfo teaches Ruggiero truly, but is ultimately dismissed as a liar by his pupil, while Melissa has at least contingent success in teaching Ruggiero to use "frodo" as a supplement to Herculean force. She is, in fact, only the most forceful of the voices at this point in the poem which recommend, or deploy, counterfraud as the best weapon for combatting fraud.[46]

---

[45] The closest Dantean source for these lines is actually *Inferno* 13.40–42, but compare *Inferno* 26.85–90 and 27.4–18. For the "alienated speech" of all three sinners, see Leo Spitzer, "Speech and Language in *Inferno* 13," *Italica* 19 (1942).

[46] On the habitual use of fraud against fraud in the poem see especially Bradamante vs. Brunello and Atlante (iv.1–3 ff., xiii.51–53; cf. xvii.26 ff.), Olimpia (ix.35 ff.). A good example of someone who does not use fraud when he probably should is Filandro in canto xxi. This is Giamatti's educational "ideal": "Ruggiero now uses Alcina's methods on her" (*The Earthly Paradise,* p. 160), and he is supported by Jordan ("Enchanted Ground," p. 169): "'fraude' . . . is aligned with reason, . . . it is a means of unmasking."

Nonetheless, if Astolfo's teaching is tainted by its failure, Melissa's Ulyssean lesson in fraud (which she communicates while herself assuming a counterfeit form, Atlante's) also has its problems. She may adopt this strategy as the only effective means of combatting Alcina's spurious "education as seduction," but one must still ask: Where does a critical line, a crisis of definition, appear to mark the difference between teaching salutary fraud and fraudulent teaching (the "consiglio frodolente" of Ulysses and Guido, *Inferno* 27.116)? Can Ariosto avoid the negative moral consequences of this casuistical argument in favor of using any available means for a positive end? Is Melissa finally in the same position as the Machiavelli of *Il Principe,* trying to prove the truth and value of his counsel for the Medici by counseling the continuous use of fraudulent methods to his Prince?[47] Melissa and Astolfo open up a didactic dialectic which haunts Ariosto's own educational pretensions throughout the poem: the risk, on the one hand, that in counseling deception one becomes no better than Alcina and, on the other, that in speaking the plain truth one will be taken for a fraud *anyway.*

The figure of Dante's Ulysses is crucial to the Alcina-Logistilla sequence not because of any simple one-to-one equation between Ruggiero and Ulysses, but because of the accumulation of verbal and structural parallels between the two books. On the one hand, Ulysses brings with him a large part of his dialectical context in the *Commedia:* Guido da Montefeltro, Pier delle Vigne, and Dante the pilgrim himself. On the other hand, the echoes of the *Commedia* attach themselves to all of the characters surrounding Ruggiero (Melissa, Astolfo, Alcina) as well as to the hero. It might still, however, be objected that Ruggiero is associated with a veritable parade of epic and other heroes besides Ulysses, beginning, as I already did, with Hercules, but also including Achilles, Perseus, and, above all, Aeneas (not to mention more limited parallels to mythic characters such as Ganymede, Arethusa [VI. 19], and, as we shall see,

[47] *Il Principe,* esp. chap. 18, on whether the Prince should keep faith. Compare his description of the perfectly faithful counselor (the role *he* would like to fill) in chaps. 22–23. The famous contrast between foxy and leonine uses of power in chap. 18 is taken, not surprisingly, directly from Guido da Montefeltro (*Inferno* 27.75).

Meleager). The basic genealogical-heroic myth of the poem, which makes Ruggiero a direct descendent of Hector, is forged on analogy with Virgil and the Roman *translatio imperii* (from Troy to Rome, along the westward path of the sun).[48] Within the sequence under examination, the Alcina segment, taken by itself, highlights the Virgilian aspects of Ruggiero: the encounter with Polydorus-Astolfo, the seduction by Dido-Alcina, the reminder of public duty and destiny by Mercury-Melissa. These basic motifs, however, are shot through with allusions to later epic variants (e.g., the *Thebaid*),[49] as well as with the Dantean echoes already noticed, and, above all, with the additional allegorizations provided over the centuries by allegorical readers of Homer and Virgil and then reinscribed in literature by the later epic poets, including Boiardo, Dante, and so on, leading finally to the allegorical epic *par excellence*, Spenser's *Faerie Queene*.[50] The *Furioso*, in fact, is drawing upon two of the three basic types of allegorization, the ethical and the metaphysical, as well as upon the poetry they interpreted and influenced.[51]

With this multiple background of poetic and critical traditions, what justifies the special privilege accorded to the Dantean "pre-

[48] For the *translatio imperii* see W. Goez, *Translatio Imperii* (Tübingen: J.C.B. Mohr, 1958); Curtius, *European Literature*, pp. 29, 389 ff.; as well as Mazzotta, *Dante*, pp. 28, 99.

[49] See Bigi's notes and Javitch, "The Imitation of Imitations."

[50] For the "allegory of education," see Servius, *Vergilii Carmina Commentarii*, especially vols. 1 and 2, and Bernardus Silvestris, as late classical and late medieval, respectively, allegorizers of the Virgilian epic. Others include Macrobius, Fulgentius, John of Salisbury, and Dante (*Convivio* iv). See also Salutati's reading of Aeneas' descent into hell in vol. 2 of the *De Laboribus Herculis*. For the Greek and Roman traditions of allegorizing the epics, see Jean Pépin, *Myth et Allégorie* (Paris: Aubier, 1958), and Plato's *Ion* (for the best-known attempt to discredit this then already well-advanced tendency to turn poetry into a mode of knowledge). For the uses of the tradition by Dante, see Thompson, *Dante's Epic Journey* and, especially, the articles by John Freccero cited above in relation to the figure of Ulysses. For the Renaissance allegorizers in particular, see D.C. Allen, *Mysteriously Meant*. Of particular use to this study have been Landino's annotations to the *Commedia* and his reading of the *Aeneid* in bks. 3 and 4 of the *Disputationes*. See also Murrin, *The Allegorical Epic*, esp. his chapter "Landino's Virgil," pp. 27–50, cf. pp. 197–202. See also, of course, the allegorical commentaries on the *Furioso* in Orlandini's edition of the *Opere* for specific applications of the tradition in and to the *Furioso*.

[51] See Thompson, *Dante's Epic Journey*, p. 17; Allen, *Mysteriously Meant*.

text" and the figure of Ulysses? This privileging is certainly not meant to constitute a denial of other echoes; rather, it is the means by which they are all brought within a larger thematic and structural pattern which spans the arc of the entire sequence. Specifically, we have seen that the journey and the geography are recognizably Dantean, as is the allegorical mode of writing. The figure of Ulysses, moreover, has by itself a privileged place not only in the *Commedia,* but in the epic tradition generally which makes it the perfect focus for a dense pattern of allusions to the main texts and heroes of that tradition. Dante's text is itself already a dialectical rewriting of Virgil's rewriting of the *Odyssey* (and the *Iliad*): the Dantean Ulysses is set in a precise relation to Aeneas. In the Virgilian account of the destruction of Troy through the Greeks' demonic trickery, as well as in the Roman hero's partial retracing of Odysseus' route and his adventures, Aeneas' *pietas* is systematically set over against the amoral deceptions of Ulysses, paradigm of the lying Greek.[52] Dante then, partly modeling his journey on Aeneas' and guided by "Virgil," also adopts Ulysses as a privileged, if unholy, foil to his journey, though refocusing the polemic by adding the journey of discovery beyond the pillars of Hercules and by exalting Ulysses' mendacity to the level of classical philosophy and rhetoric—the noble and yet still, ultimately, ruinous products of pagan humanism. Ruggiero, finally, is heir to the heroes of the *Iliad,* the *Odyssey,* the *Aeneid,* and the *Commedia:* the most recent accretion of a cumulative, composite tradition, whose most striking and constant emblem is the figure of Ulysses/Odysseus. Alcina, for her part, is modeled on Dido, but also on the Homeric precursors of the Carthaginian queen: Calypso, Circe, the Sirens, all of them temptations to Odysseus and all of them filtered through a millennial tradition of allegorization and then further recast in such allegorical seductresses as Boiardo's Falerina and Dante's "femmina balba."

Ulysses, in other words, brings with him to the *Furioso* all the baggage of the epic struggle for identity in a literary tradition whose principal highlights, each present to some degree in this sequence, include Homer, Virgil, and Dante. And little wonder, given that Dante's most prominent Renaissance commentator, Landino,

---

[52] *Aeneid,* bk. 11.44 ff., passim; cf. Padoan, *Il Pio Enea,* p. 171 ff.

specifically argues in his gloss of *Inferno* 26 that the pilgrim Dante
and Virgil's Aeneas both imitated the original allegorical itinerary
of Homer's Odysseus toward "the highest happiness," the metaphy-
sical *patria* figured for neo-Platonism by rocky Ithaca.[53] The Renais-
sance was clearly ready to see the epics and their heroes in strict
relations of repetition and difference one to the other. Ariosto's
wider sense of the tradition and its possible interpretations allows
him to bring into play several versions of epic identity simultan-
eously: rhetorical-political and Christian, as well as neo-Platonic.
At ironic stake for him are, variously, the sacrifice of physical iden-
tity to win a famous name (Achilles, to whom Ruggiero is also
compared); the quest to return home to an original, familial and
political, identity (Odysseus); the sacrifice of personal desires and in-
terests for the sake of a great, impersonal, public good (Aeneas); the
realization of the true self as "image and likeness" of God through
the death and rebirth of the self in Christian conversion (Dante). At
one time or another, Ariosto brings to the fore each of these pos-
sibilities for identity, testing them against each other. And he does
so bolstered by an allegorical interpretive tradition, very much alive
in his own day, which had consistently taken poetic treatments of
identity and brought them within narrower, more formal models
of education—whether rhetorical education to civic virtue, Platonic
nostalgia for original heavenly being, or Christian recovery of Para-
dise through confession and conversion.

Ulysses is a figure which persists in the imagination of all three
of the great "epic" poets, existing as a constant dialectical shadow
of the great epic heroes (including Achilles if one believes, as I do,
that the *Odyssey* is a palinodic revision of the *Iliad,* contrasting
Odysseus' wisdom and ultimate survivability with Achilles' *furor*
and premature death). And Ariosto too takes as the pivot of this
episode a figure who embodies the tradition of allegorical represen-
tation of education for didactic purposes, while at the same time
reading that figure through its most vivid restatement and its sternest
Christian critique, Dante's *Commedia.* The allegorical force of

[53] See also *Disputationes,* bk. I, p. 48, and bk. III, p. 119, for a linking of Ulysses
and Aeneas as twin emblems of the contemplative life. Landino's commentary on
Inferno 26 first valorizes Ulysses' search for knowledge, but finally admits that,
though the goal was good, the road to it was mad. Cf. n. 103, below.

Ulysses, like that of Hercules, is all the greater because in the post-classical Western tradition, until shortly before Ariosto's day, this figure had existed primarily outside the untranslated text of the *Odyssey,* in the allegories which derived from it.[54] By placing the allusions to Dante's spiritual itinerary inside a Ulyssean framework, Ariosto creates a double-edged weapon. By recuperating certain aspects of Ulyssean humanism, he can criticize and parodically diminish the didactic project of the *Commedia,* while at the same time he redeploys some of Dante's judgments against Ulysses. In fact, the precise value of Ulysses in the *Furioso* is never certain: the exceeding of limit, the flight of intellectual hubris, the concomitant abandonment of civic responsibility, all are in various ways under attack, as they are in Dante. By contrast, the "lesson" Ruggiero learns from Melissa is eminently Ulyssean: she teaches the value of "frodo" as a supplement to Herculean force in the struggle against vice, in direct opposition to Virgil's and Dante's condemnation of Ulysses' fraudulent trickery. The power of the figure of Ulysses (in itself and taken in relation variously to Hercules, Aeneas, and "Dante") is precisely its ability to focus attention on crucial historical and/or conceptual oppositions. The "folle volo," "il varco folle," of Ulysses is, for Dante, what becomes of a certain kind of education, a certain approach to the quest for identity. Ulysses, via Dante, embodies the encounter of education and madness, the degeneration of the former into the latter. For that matter, even in the classical myths of Odysseus the theme of madness and effacement of identity is always central. The protected one of Athena, goddess of wisdom, Odysseus at first feigned madness to avoid going to Troy, while in the course of his journey of return he constantly resorted to tactical concealments of identity ("my name is Nobody") in order to impose his will and realize his goals. In these tales, symmetrically opposite to Dante's position, madness is always a disguise assumed by sanity.[55] Even within the domain of competing theories of education, Ulysses seems to contain within himself two distinct and often

[54] See Allen, *Mysteriously Meant,* esp. p. 90, as well as Pépin, Rahner, and Courcelle, on the allegorizations of the *Odyssey.* Pico, *Oratio* (Garin edition), p. 150, claims that Homer represented the totality of knowledge in the voyage of Odysseus.

[55] Compare the discussion of the Silenus and of Cassandra in Chapter 4, secs. iv and v, below.

contradictory positions, conflating, as it were, moral and metaphysical allegorizations of the epic hero. He is the humanist rhetorician promoting (at least "rhetorically") virtue and combatting Circe's enchantment and the Siren's song with his own eloquence. Then again, he is the emblematic pursuer of neo-Platonic knowledge, "canoscenza."[56] He is thus a possible uniter of *oratio* and *ratio,* and yet, as fraudulent counselor, he specifically subverts the relation between word and intention and encourages others to do so as well. By means of Ulysses, Ariosto may station himself in relation not only to Dante, but also to the continuities and discontinuities between civic humanism's project of education and that of their neo-Platonic heirs and critics, as well as basic Renaissance controversies such as the opposition and conciliation of active and contemplative lives seen in Landino and, later, in Bembo, Castiglione, and so on. Finally, by means of Ulysses, Ariosto can focus the primary educational dialectic of teacher/student through a single figure who occupies both roles simultaneously. And thus, by extension, he tacitly points to a doubleness of his text: its characters undergoing educations; its author intent on teaching his readers. He may go even further to suggest the ambiguity of the author-teacher who is also caught at the midpoint of an incomplete and utopian education (the becoming of the self through its writing—the "romanzo dell'Io"), trapped, so to speak, in the very same burning bush from which his divinely authoritative precepts emerge.

[56] Readings of *Inferno* 26 differ substantially regarding the exact status of Ulysses' moral/intellectual enterprise. Padoan's Ulysses, as "fandi fictor," is the parody of a rhetor, though he refers us (*Il Pio Enea,* pp. 180–81) to Giovanni del Virgilio's interpretation of Ulysses defeating Circe as the triumph of both "eloquentia" and "sapientia," i.e., both *oratio* and *ratio.* Freccero, and then Thompson, instead focus almost exclusively on Ulysses' links with the neo-Platonic tradition of misguided philosophical askesis. Mazzotta, while not discounting the motif of *paideia* (*Dante,* pp. 74–76), insists on the "orazione piccola," the references to pursuit of "virtute" as well as of knowledge, the connections to Latini as prehumanist (cf. n. 39, above), as the "trappings" of Ciceronian rhetoric. One might argue that the two elements are deliberately played off against one another, determining each other's failure: on the one hand, the metaphysical pursuit of knowledge involves abandoning the city and the productive use of rhetoric to better the human condition; on the other hand, the substance of that pursuit turns out to be nothing more than empty words, mere rhetoric. Philosophy and rhetoric are implicated in each other's errors, both equally utopian, equally "folli."

The outlines at least of the representation of education in the Alcina episode are by now quite well defined. The last remarks made about Ulysses, however, suggest yet another dimension: the implicit and explicit efforts of the text to define its own educational function for the reader and, what is more, its somewhat skeptical reflections upon the status of that didactic role and of the language through which it is enacted. The most evident attempt to translate Ruggiero's marginal adventures directly into a lesson for the reader comes in the proems to cantos VII (1–2) and VIII (1–2). In canto VII, a relationship between the reader and his or her reality and the world of the text is posited: though it seems to be a pack of lies ("menzogna"), the wise reader will see the "light of the discourse" ("lume del discorso"). By opposing the credulous "vulgo" to the knowing few, Ariosto in effect argues for the conventional structure and readership of mystical allegory, whose secrets will be penetrated only by the elite.[57] As Ruggiero finds a lesson beneath the allegorical "scorza" of a myrtle, so the believing reader will win "the precious fruit" of the poet's labors (VII.2.6). Of course, there are a couple of reservations to be made, whose importance will become clearer later on. The roles of "vulgo" and elite seem to be curiously reversed, insofar as it is the common herd which adopts a skeptical attitude toward the surface, and the privileged reader who is asked to take it as the literal truth. And the phrase "il lume del discorso" seems to be a subtle but significant substitute for the more traditional "light of the intellect,"[58] possibly displacing the light of truth into the (deceptive) brilliance of the poet's rhetoric. Nonetheless, the proem to canto VIII then seems to provide the promised "fruit":

Chi l'annello d'Angelica, o più tosto
chi avesse quel de la ragion, potria
veder a tutti il viso che nascosto
da finzione e d'arte non saria.
Tal ci par bello e buono che, deposto
il liscio, brutto e rio forse parria.

---

[57] See Chapter 2, n. 96, above, on the "poetic theology." Pico's *Oratio* is a good place to start for the notion of a Gnostic/Cabalistic/neo-Platonic knowledge reserved for the enlightened few (though, paradoxically, it is a "universal truth" that he claims to be expounding).

[58] Cf. Dante, *Inferno* 3.18; *Purgatorio* 4.75, 6.45; *Paradiso* 5.8.

Fu gran ventura quella di Ruggiero,
ch'ebbe l'annel che gli scoperse il vero.   [VIII.2]

Whoever should possess the ring of Angelica, or rather that of reason,
could see the true face of anyone, unconcealed by feigning or by art.
Such a one seems fair and good who would perhaps appear ugly and
evil once the cosmetics were removed. It was Ruggiero's great luck to
have the ring which revealed the truth to him.

Ruggiero's escape is allegorized as the insight of reason into lies
and fictions. As Bigi has noted, however, the allegorization is
couched grammatically as a condition contrary to fact, i.e., an
utopian impossibility.[59]

In addition, as the case of Ulysses has already suggested, the nar-
rative contains not only dramatizations of the teacher-pupil relation-
ship, but, in fact, of the text/reader situation as well, so that, more
than just an allegory of education, the poem offers allegories of
reading, allegories of didactic allegory.[60] This education, like both
humanist and neo-Platonic educations, teaches reading by reading,
is an exercise in the formation of an interpreter.

To be more precise, this education teaches the deciphering of
allegorical signs. Ruggiero, figure of the eager and relatively inept
student, has encounters with at least three major magisterial pres-
ences, each of which has a role in some way analogous to the text's
and each of which falls under at least one aspect of the figure of
Ulysses: Astolfo, who teaches by the example of his own failure
(and whose teaching fails); Melissa, who teaches the ambiguous
lesson of combatting fraud with fraud; Logistilla, who teaches
"virtute" by way of "canoscenza" of one's self. The rhetorical-
poetic character of these educations is suggested from the first by
the way in which the whole episode is placed under the comple-
mentary signs of Ulysses, the rhetor, and the hippogryph, with its
obvious associations to the Pegasus, winged horse of poetry. It
comes into unmistakable focus through the speaking tree which

[59] Bigi edition, note to VIII.2.
[60] I allude, of course, to Northrop Frye's famous statement that all critical com-
mentary is allegorical (e.g., *Anatomy*, p. 341), as well as to the title of Paul DeMan's
Allegories of Reading and to the latter's habitual attempt to show that literature, too,
as well as language in general, is always in a condition of allegory and constitutes the
allegorical reading of its erring readers.

contains Astolfo. Several traditions, all associated with poetics, flow together in the sterile and chatty myrtle. The myrtle itself gathers together associations with love, poetry, and death.[61] More important, "liber" derives etymologically from the tree bark out of which paper was made in classical times.[62] Hence the related tradition of pretending that poetry, especially erotic verse, is written on trees, as in this canzone from the *Asolani* of Bembo:[63]

> *Canzon, omai lo tronco ne ven meno,*
> *Ma non la doglia che mi strugge . . .*
> *Ond'io ne vergherò quest'altra scorza.*   [I.xxxii, ll. 66–68, p. 56]

Canzone, I am running out of tree to write on, but not of the sorrow which consumes me . . . so I will begin marking up another trunk.

This motif appears plainly in the poetry written on trees by Medoro in celebration of his love for Angelica, that same poetry which will be read by Orlando and precipitate his madness. The motif of poetic trees is one of the common roots from which both Ruggiero's education and Orlando's madness stem.[64] In a related commonplace, eloquence and rhetoric are represented through organic metaphors, as in these three lines from Petrarch's *Trionfo della Fama:*

> *ed uno al cui passar l'erba fioriva:*
> *quest'è quel Marco Tullio in cui si mostra*
> *chiaro quanti eloquenzia à frutti e fiori . . .*   [iii.18–20]

and one at whose passing the grass flowered; this is that Marcus Tullius in whom is clearly shown how many fruits and flowers eloquence has. . .

---

[61] Virgil places the souls of dead lovers in a "myrtea silva" (*Aeneid* VI.441). Cf. Petrarch, *Trionfo d'Amore,* in *Rime, Trionfi e Poesie Latine,* eds. F. Neri et al. (Napoli and Milano: Ricciardi, 1951), i.150. See also *Furioso* XXIV.61.7–8. The poetic suggestions are less specific, though Ovid, *Amores* I.i.29–30, and Petrarch, *Rime* VII.9, are suggestive.

[62] See C.T. Lewis, *An Elementary Latin Dictionary* (Oxford: The Clarendon Press, 1891; repr. 1975), p. 469: "'liber' . . . of a tree, the inner bark . . . [and] because dried bark was anciently used to write on, 'a book, a work, a treatise.'"

[63] See also *Asolani* I.xxxiii (p. 58) and II.xxviii (p. 111); Ovid, *Amores* I.xii.7–20.

[64] The literariness of the trees in the later episode is more easily recognized, since there is actually writing on them. See Giamatti, "Headlong Horses, Headless Horsemen," p. 298; as well as Donato, "Desire," p. 29; Weaver, "Lettura," p. 395; Bonifazi, *Le Lettere,* pp. 107, 109. Shakespeare's *As You Like It* (III.ii) betrays its debt to Ariosto on this score.

Traditional allegoresis actually has it that Ulysses defeated Circe through Mercury's gift of a flower (*moly*) symbolizing eloquence.[65] Petrarch himself is, of course, responsible for giving new power to the preeminent classical myth of a poetic tree: the conversion of Daphne into the laurel, tree of Apollo, god of poetry; the emblematic sublimation of desire into poetic production. Petrarch's double pursuit of the erotic object and of poetic glory is thus fused together in the single complex of Laura/lauro. Astolfo as myrtle is flanked by a "lauro" (VI.23.8) and surrounded by aural echoes of the laurel (cf. VI.21.1, 22.2, 24.5). In all of these connections, the effect of the vegetable metaphors for writing seems to be that of integrating writing and Nature, conflating and secularizing, as it were, "the two Books of God," the written testament and the "sermons in stone" inscribed in Nature, alluding perhaps both to the book reading of the humanists and the reading of Nature undertaken by Pico and the neo-Platonists.[66] And the question of Nature's relation to writing will return to occupy us later on.

The same point, with complications, may be made by emphasizing again how much this representation of a natural scene, and especially of the tree, is actually a collage of artistic precedents: Dante and Petrarch, as already suggested, Virgil and Ovid, Poliziano, Boiardo, and others as well. The landscape is inhabited by the usual pastoral paradox of intense naturalness linked to the most precious artifice, a juxtaposition which is never quite as harmonious as it seems, and in fact gives rise to the slippage between appearance and reality, art and nature, which is a perennial motif of the Renaissance.[67] Actually, the myrtle is also aligned with yet another traditional metaphor of literature, this one emphasizing precisely the unnatural and alien quality of poetic language. As a "scorza" (VI.30.2, 32.1), the allegorical concealer of Astolfo's true being, the tree is a figure of allegory itself: its bark, like the veil, husk, nutshell,

---

[65] Padoan, *Il Pio Enea*, pp. 180–81, quotes Dante's friend Giovanni del Virgilio for this allegorization.

[66] For the "Book of Nature" see Curtius, *European Literature*, p. 106 ff; George Economou, *The Goddess Natura in Medieval Literature* (Cambridge: Harvard University Press, 1972).

[67] See Giamatti, *The Earthly Paradise*, as well as Edward Tayler, *Nature and Art in Renaissance Literature* (New York: Columbia University Press, 1964), for a basic statement of the problem and its tradition. Cf. n. 121, below.

or "integumentum," is a commonplace image for the poetic outside which hides a valuable didactic inside. Thus the figure of the tree as book is linked to traditions both of the representation of nature (*mimesis*) and of allegorical writing, yoking the two opposed modes in a symbolic complex as oxymoronic as the insertion of Astolfo inside the myrtle itself. The relevance of the figure to Ariosto's own poetic project, if not already sufficiently clear, is announced unmistakably in the words with which Astolfo begins his cautionary tale to Ruggiero:

> *a discoprirti in un medesmo tratto*   [VI.32.6]
>
> to reveal to you at the very same time . . .

In words which echo Ariosto's own introduction to the grand tapestry of the *Furioso:*

> *Dirò d'Orlando in un medesmo tratto*   [I.2.1]
>
> I will speak of Orlando at the very same time . . .

Still more remarkably, as we have already seen, Ariosto later characterizes his poem as a "legno" (XLVI.1.5), conflating arboreal and navigational images of the poetic enterprise.

Though these arguments may at first tend to confirm the view of Astolfo as *the* figure of the poet, while introducing a new note of entrapment and impotence, the figures of the poet, text, and reader in the episode are not confined, by any means, to Astolfo alone. It is not just that by a more productive reading of the "text" of Astolfo's discourse Ruggiero could have seen through Alcina, but that, as the author hints repeatedly, and as Melissa's lessons make explicit, Alcina herself is presented as a kind of deceptive artistic surface, as well as the artist behind it, which must be penetrated and interpreted by the educated reader. And, in a sense, she is even the author of the allegorical book which Astolfo has become. When Alcina first appears to Ruggiero, she seems "tanto ben formata, / quanto me' finger san pittori industri . . ." ("as well formed as ingenious painters know how to feign" VII.11.1–2), and a little later on she is seen "sculpted" in Ruggiero's heart (18.6). Throughout the *Furioso*, of course, the relationship between visual art and poetry is repeatedly explored, and complex, tenuous bonds are established.[68] One of the most potent of these references comes in the following lines from the same canto: "Ruggiero entrò ne' profumati lini / che pareano di man d'Aracne usciti" (Ruggiero slipped between the perfumed linens which seemed to have come from the hand of Arachne" 23.5–6). A later passage makes it clear that Alcina herself is the weaver in question (52.8). Ariosto criticism has long since demonstrated how prevalent the image of the poet as weaver is in the poem. Weaving, of course, furnishes the very metaphor of "textuality," and particularly of the romance text based on the narrative interweaving of "entrelacement."[69] By assimilating Alcina to Arachne, the poem assigns to the former the latter's role as would-be usurper of Minerva's divinity, her double function as goddess of wisdom and of a certain artistry (patroness of Ulysses and of Penelope).

The finest product of Alcina's weaving, the one which makes her too an allegory of allegory, is the veil which covers her, though at

[68] The number of *ekphrases* in the poem is considerable: Merlin's art in XXVI and XXXII–XXXIII; the architecture and statuary at the end of XLII; not to mention the tapestry of Cassandra in XLVI. Of the Ariosto-Cassandra, Ariosto-Merlin parallels, more in Chapter 4. A number of studies recently have begun to examine the relation of the *Furioso* to the visual arts: for instance, Robert Hanning, "Ariosto, Ovid and the Painters," in A. Scaglione, ed., *Ariosto 1974 in America*, pp. 99–116.

[69] Durling points to the two most spectacular such images (*The Figure of the Poet*, pp. 117–18): II.30; XIII.81. There are many more, including XVIII.83; XXIII.105; XXV.50; XXXIII.22; XLV.52, 65. See especially XXXIV.81.3–4, where the poet's weaving anticipates the weaving of the Fates themselves (88–92; XXXV.3). There are also other artist figures engaged in weaving: Cassandra, obviously, as well as Vulcan, whose net appears in XV.56–9. In addition to Alcina as Arachne, there is the usually implicit figure of Penelope, an anti-Arachne, favored by Minerva, who weaves by day and unweaves by night, author of a perennial and inconclusive text. Ariosto refers once to her in a laudatory aside (XIII.60.7–8), accompanying the passage with an allusion to himself as weaver (81). He then, however, has St. John unravel that myth of fidelity (XXXV.27.8). In the "Marzo" of the famous *Mesi* frescoes in the Palazzo Schifanoia in Ferrara, Minerva presides over a group of humanists on the one hand and a group of women weaving on the other. For "entrelacement" in general, see Eugene Vinaver, *The Rise of Romance* (Oxford: The Clarendon Press, 1971), who takes his cue from Ferdinand Lot, *Etude sur le Lancelot en Prose* (Paris: Champion, 1918). See DelCorno-Branca for an earnest attempt to apply the romance structures described by Vinaver to the *Furioso*. See Weaver (who else?) for a much better example of how the poem ties together parallel episodes.

first it is not apparent as such:[70]

> Gli angelici sembianti nati in cielo
> non si ponno celar sotto alcun velo   [VII.15.7–8]

The angelic features born in heaven cannot be hidden under any veil

It emerges only later, now apparently transparent:

> Come Ruggiero abbracciò lei, gli cesse
> il manto: e restò il vel suttile e rado
> che non copria dinanzi né di dietro,
> più che le rose o i gigli un chiaro vetro.   [28.5–8]

As Ruggiero embraced her, the robe gave way; only the sheer and subtle veil remained which covered neither before nor behind any more than clear glass covers roses and lilies.

The veil comes soon enough to stand for the magical surface which Alcina has interposed between her lovers and the ancient, corrupted reality of herself. It suggests allegory passing itself off as mimetic window or mirror. And when the lovely veil is finally stripped from her, we learn that "quanto / di beltà Alcina avea, tutto era *estrano;* / *estrano* avea, e non suo, dal piè alla treccia" ("whatever beauty she had, all was alien / alien beauty she had, and not her own, from toe to head" VII.70.5–7), with the emphasis precisely on the estrangement, the alienation, of allegorical signifiers from their underlying signifieds.

The degree to which this imagery enters directly into a hermeneutical polemic on the nature of allegory can be seen from the passage in the *Asolani,* which I had occasion to quote in Chapter

---

[70] The symbolic relationship between veil and allegory is so firmly established that the instances cited below are purely superfluous: Dante, *Inferno* 9.63, " 'l velame de li versi strani"; Boccaccio, *Genealogia* XIV.vii (p. 701), ix (p. 706), passim. See John Freccero, "Medusa," esp. p. 18, for a concise account of the derivation of Christian hermeneutics of veiled truth from II Corinthians 3:6, 12–16; 4:3, 8; etc. See also Michael Murrin, *The Veil of Allegory* (Chicago: University of Chicago Press, 1969). There are numerous references to "veli" in the *Furioso,* many with "veiled" poetic undertones, including the covered shield discussed below: see, for instance, XXI.1, XXII.39, XXXI.101, XLII.93.5, XLIII.39. The key image is, once again, the description, which conflates the artistic metaphors of veiling and weaving, of Cassandra's tapestry as a "prezioso velo" (XLVI.84.4).

2, describing the attempts of the first poets to educate the mass of uncivilized humankind:

> *trovarono le favole altresì, sotto il velame delle quali la verità, sì come sotto*
> *vetro trasparente, ricoprivano, . . . del continuo dilettandogli con la novità delle*
> *bugie, et alcuna volta . . . scoprendo loro il vero* [I.xii, p. 29]

> They invented fables as well, under whose veil they covered the truth,
> as if beneath transparent glass, . . . continually delighting [their listeners]
> with the novelty of their lies and sometimes . . . uncovering the truth
> for them

This passage might easily be a direct source for Ariosto, but even if not, the degradation and abuse of the strategies of the didactic allegorist by Alcina are "transparent" in the confrontation between the two passages. Given this evidence, it is hardly necessary to remind readers either of the assimilation of Alcina to the Sirens and to Circe (and of these to a certain kind of music and poetry) or of the several explicit references in the episode to seductive poetry, which seems to promote the delightful over the useful.[71]

The lesson which Ruggiero learns from Melissa is one in the "reading" of this self-concealing allegory. The metaphor used is, in fact, specifically one of interpreting a book:[72]

---

[71] For example, Alcina's court poet: "Non vi mancava chi, cantando, dire / d'amor sapesse gaudii e passioni, / o con invenzioni e poesie / rappresentasse grate fantasie" (VII.19.5–8). Literature later mediates more erotic delights: "leggon d'antiqui gli amorosi detti" (31). More subtle are the lines which immediately precede this one: "Non è diletto alcun che di fuor reste; / che tutti son ne l'amorosa stanza," where stanza suggests a poetic strophe as well, implying both erotic and aesthetic self-enclosure. Finally, these lines are the most blatant, and the most subtle, of all: "Del gran piacer ch'avean, lor dicer tocca; / che spesso avean più d'una lingua in bocca" (29), where the linguistic and the erotic literally meet in an amorous encounter which is silent (speech is prevented) and which is sponsored by words ("lor dicer tocca," with a tactile pun). The result is a Babelic and duplicitous ("più d'una") language of secrets and seduction. Parker, *Inescapable Romance*, p. 247 (n. 18), remarks that VI.47 also indicates Alcina's semiotic nature.

[72] Parker, *Inescapable Romance*, p. 31 and relevant note, signals the literary interpretive import of these lines and notes as well that its echo of Petrarch, *Rime* IV.5–6 (where it is Christ who comes to earth to fulfill the Old Testament prophecies) suggests a direct connection between the figural hermeneutics of St. Paul (cf. n. 70, above) and Alcina. Andrew Fichter, *Poets Historical* (New Haven: Yale University

Giovane e bella ella [Alcina] si fa con arte,
si che molti ingannò come Ruggiero;
ma l'annel venne a interpretar le carte,
che già molti anni avean celato il vero.   [VII.74.1–4]

Alcina made herself young and beautiful by art, so she fooled many as
she had Ruggiero. But the ring came along to interpret the pages which
for so many years had concealed the truth.

The ring appears, as it does again in VIII.2, as an allegory of a uni-
versal key, a "discovery procedure" as Jonathan Culler has called
such devices in another, and yet perhaps not so different, context.[73]
Melissa herself, as shape shifter, is clearly caught up in the pattern
of fiction and counterfiction. Described as a gifted rhetorician, she
deploys the ring not only against Alcina, but then against her entire
domain as well. She reduces city and garden to a desert in which
only the chant of the cicadas is heard (VIII.20.6). This image, too,
pertains to rhetoric, having stood, since Plato's use of it in his
critique of rhetoric in the *Phaedrus,* for the pure pleasures of human
vocal prowess devoid of any attachment to sense. Socrates, in fact,
connects the cicada's song directly to the Sirens' (259a). Here it
suggests the nonsensical, sterile "reste" which lies behind the fic-
tional significations of Alcina's veil.[74] Melissa's work thus has the

---

Press, 1982), who reads Ariosto as a Christian apologist, sees this echo of Christ as
a pious gesture (p. 97). Even in Petrarch, however, what stands out is the usual, near-
blasphemous, comparison between Laura and the Savior (unlike Dante suggesting a
Beatrice-Christ analogy, and perhaps in polemic against him, Petrarch always makes
this equation with a very bad conscience). There, in any case, Christ himself is both
the veiled and the unveiler; here what is revealed is not an illuminating Son, but
a stinking hag, forecasting the paradoxical impieties of canto XXXV.

[73] Culler, *Structuralist Poetics,* pp. 20–24. He uses the term in reference to the
structuralist search for a universal descriptive mechanism to unlock human language,
which he goes on to expose, quite convincingly, as utopian, self-generating, and self-
confirming. It joins the list of such doomed encyclopedic projects as George Eliot's
Causaubon's "Key to All Mythologies." It is an especially apt term here, given
the metaphorics of covering and uncovering in this episode (cf. n. 76), as well as the
larger issue of Apocalyptic poetic perspective which will be discussed in Chapter 4,
sec. iv (N.B.: "calypso" = "covering"; "apocalypse" = uncovering, unveiling").

[74] *Phaedrus* 230c, 258e–259d, 262d. Socrates associates the cicadas with the Muses,
and hence with poetry as well as with Sophistical rhetoric, and with the Sirens (cf.

character of an interpretive "deconstruction" (*avant la lettre*, and behind it, too) which reduces garden to desert and situates the reader in a marginal place of "unsignificance," where sound is radically divorced from sense (cf. VIII.14). Nonsense is thus a crucial step on the road to sense.

The ring is only one of two magical (and allegorical) implements at the disposal of Ruggiero and Melissa in combating Alcina, the other being the dazzling shield of Atlante. If the ring has an interpretive role in this episode, the shield too carries poetic associations, though less explicit, within and behind it. The polished shield, usually kept in a cloth sheath, dazzles the eyes of all beholders with its sunlike light. When employed against Alcina's huntsman, it leaves him "deserto" of his senses (VIII.11.5). Its effects thus parallel those of the ring which has left the landscape "deserto" (although originally the use of the ring allowed Bradamante to "see through" the magic of the shield). When its effects are first described to Bradamante by Pinabello, he says that anyone who sees it "cada come corpo morto cade" ("falls like a dead body falls" II.55.7), words which recall Dante's faint after hearing the tale of Paolo and Francesca. The shield is thereby allusively assimilated to a "text" which works as a "counter-galeotto,"[75] terrifying Dante with his own proximity to the situation of the damned lovers and his text's nearness to the role of erotic pander. In the same way, when the shield is restored to Ruggiero by Melissa after he regains his senses, it is covered by a "zendado" which specifically recalls the "zendado," i.e., the "velo," of Alcina (VII.28.2−6, 76.7−8). Near the conclusion of the episode, the cover will actually be referred to explicitly as a "velo" (X.109.7). And the shield is at the very

---

Rahner, *Greek Myths,* p. 355). The sounds of the cicadas in VIII thus anticipate and counter the three Siren-like ladies in X. See also Allen, ed. and trans., *Marsilio Ficino,* pp. 192−99. In the *Phaedrus,* the cicadas are negative: producers of sound without content, set against Socrates' union of eloquence with wisdom through philosophy. Here they represent the exposure of the senselessness of nature and language, which seems to be a provisionally positive step. See also Virgil, *Eclogues* II.13. R.J. Clements, *Picta Poesis* (Roma: Edizione Storia e Letteratura, 1960), p. 82, discusses Alciati's use of the cicada as emblem of music in the *Emblemata* (Paris: 1536), p. 144.

[75] This echo is also detected by Parker (*Inescapable Romance,* p. 50), who puts it to different uses. Cf. n. 38, above.

center of a proliferation of reference to (allegorical) covering and (interpretive) uncovering throughout the episode.[76] Though it is quietly brought within the domain of veiled poetic discourse, it is used twice to counter enemies who hide behind Alcina's "velo," once by Ruggiero and once by the old sailor (a "galeotto" or mediator *in bono*), as well as by Ruggiero again to stun the Orca. The power of the ring in exposing, making visible, artistic trickery, is complemented by the shield's power to blind one's enemies.

As Pio Rajna made clear years ago, the shield is yet another trapping taken from the Perseus myth, and specifically the Andromeda episode which Ruggiero partially reenacts on his way back from the island.[77] For Rajna, the shield combines two elements of the myth: (1) the specular shield given by Minerva to Perseus, so that he can see the Medusa indirectly and kill her without being turned to stone, and (2) the severed Gorgon's head as it is used by Perseus to petrify various foes (among these Atlas, the giant, making Atlante's ownership of the shield here a truly ironic touch). What Rajna does not mention is that the story concludes with the Gorgon's head mounted by Minerva on Jove's shield, the *aegis,* thus bringing the two elements together. Salutati, in the reading of the Medusa episode mentioned earlier, refers this shield to the one used by Jove against the rebellious giants and describes it in terms which come very near to that of Atlante in the *Furioso.* He allegorizes the shield,

[76] Note especially the uses of the words "discoprire," "aprire," "scoprire," and "coprire" (VI.32.6, 34.4, 42.4, 67, 71.3; VII.13.4, 21.6, 28, 35.8, 45.7, 76.8; VIII.2.8, 10–11, 19.7, 34.5–6, 37.3, 81; X.46.2, 48–50, 99.1, 107; XI.13.2, 19.3). See again, in this light, XLVI.1.2.

[77] Rajna, *Le Fonti,* pp. 120–21, cites *Pharsalia* IX.669 and *Metamorphoses* IV.700–701. The shield, as Medusaesque implement, has a petrifying effect (apparently *in bono*), which may be set over against Alcina's transformations of lovers into stones etc. In this connection, see again *Inferno* 9 and the *Rime Petrose,* not to mention Petrarch's puns on his own name (e.g., *Rime* CCXLIII.13, CCCLXVI.III). For the Perseus-Ruggiero equation, see Shapiro, "Perseus and Bellerophon," pp. 118–24; Javitch, "Rescuing Ovid"; R. Hanning, "Ariosto, Ovid and the Painters"; and Barbara Pavlock's chapter on Ariosto in her dissertation "Epic and Romance: 'Genera Mixta' in Vergil, Ovid, Ariosto, Milton" (Cornell 1977). See Parker, *Inescapable Romance,* pp. 41–46, for a more interesting general approach to the Ovidian presence in the poem. See Shapiro, p. 115, and Kennedy, *Rhetorical Norms,* 136 ff., for the contestable view that Ovid is *the* privileged classical model for Ariosto.

as well as Medusa herself, as poetic eloquence, the power of rhetoric both to illuminate and to control.[78] Thus, as the ring offers an interpretive deconstruction of Alcina's cosmetic and geographical rhetoric, so the shield is, in its own oblique way, a counter-rhetoric, an antiseductive poetry. One is tempted to make equations—on the one side, between the enchanted light ("incantato lume") of the shield (IV.21.8; X.110.1) and the "lume del discorso" and, on the other, between the shield shining "a guisa di piropo" ("like a carbuncle" II.56.1) and the specular, radiant stones of Logistilla, also compared to a "piropo" (X.58.4) and also analogous to the sun (X.58–60; cf. X.109.7–8).[79] One strange implication of such equations is that Ariosto's text and Logistilla's teachings might actually blind rather than illuminate their readers, though in the latter case at least the shield's negative power seems to be converted into a positive mirroring function—offering their viewer a reflected vision of himself. Nonetheless, it is not quite safe to read these allegorical emblems in a straightforward way in an episode where allegory is linked to Alcinian deviousness, and where the shield is equally adaptable to Atlante's and to Melissa's (cross-)purposes.

Apparently the episode offers an education which turns around two distinct kinds of poetry, the distinction being that which is commonly made in defenses of poetry, between a poetry *in bono* and one *in malo,* or between Poetry and the degenerate abuses of it. There is a Logistillan poetry which aims at useful education and an Alcinian poetry which aims at delightful seduction: a poetry which "dismantles" dangerous fictions and one which is constantly preparing its lies to snare the unwary. These two kinds of verse might be loosely gathered under what a linguistic, even literalist, philosopher of our own day has called "two kinds of pretending," while repeating the age-old attempt to keep lies and poetic fictions

---

[78] Salutati, *De Laboribus Herculis* III.xlii (vol. 2, pp. 416–22). For the value of the *aegis* as symbol of stunning eloquence, see pp. 416–17. Atlante, incidentally, turns up again at precisely this point in the *De Laboribus.* Ovid says that the Gorgons lived beneath the mountain Atlas (IV.797 ff.—which contradicts his earlier account of Atlas' transformation by Perseus), and Salutati quickly associates the giant, as astrologer, to a perfect blend of eloquence and wisdom (p. 419).

[79] Cf. Petrarch, *Trionfo della Fama* I.i.43: "fiammeggiava a guisa d'un piropo."

separate.[80] In this light, the *Furioso* itself seems to prepare the split between the critics who align Ariosto either with Alcina or with Logistilla. Yet it is still not quite clear which of the two the narrator (much less the poet) aligns himself with, or whether his poem partakes of both and/or neither. And clarification must wait until after the "content" of Ruggiero's education, as it appears both in the teachings of various characters and in the narrator's comments, has been described in even greater detail.

iii. *The Nature of the Education*

What then is the nature of the education Ruggiero seems to undergo, ostensibly in the readers' stead? Is the process of education "natural" in some sense? Is it the realization or fulfillment of human nature? Or does it require the supplementing of fallen nature with graceful human artifice ("grazia" in Castiglione's sense), or with divine Grace? Is it within man's nature, as Pico would have it, to assume with equal ease *any* nature, from rock to godhead, because none is truly proper (natural) to him? Is the *telos* or end of his education a paradisical perfection on earth—a wholehearted enjoyment of nature such as that described by Valla in his Epicurean vein (e.g., *De Voluptate* bk. II)? Is it instead the Christian Eden, once and yet no longer available within the constraints of time and Nature, now only an imaginative way station during the necessary transit from Nature to Grace? Or does it, Platonically, lie entirely beyond the realm of material nature, which is no longer even seen as the once and future locus of perfection ("new heaven and new earth"), but as a disguise for the purest Alcinian corruption and degradation?

Questions of Grace and the transcendence of material nature are secondary in the sequence at hand, though they take center stage in my reading of the lunar episode (the moon which marks the boundary between time and eternity, Nature and Grace). The

---

[80] John Searle, "The Logical Status of Fictional Discourse," *New Literary History* 6 (1975), 324–25. See Derrida's critique of Searle in "Limited Inc abc . . . ," *Glyph* 2 (1977), 250–51. The distinction between a "real" lie intended to deceive and a "fictional" lie which is acknowledged as such can be found in many early defenses of poetry: e.g., Boccaccio, *Genealogia* XIV.xiii (vol. 2, pp. 717–18); Sidney's *Defense of Poesie*. Derrida, on the other hand, joins Plato in asserting that a lie is a lie is a lie.

Alcina-Logistilla sequence focuses almost exclusively on the defini-
tion or lack thereof of human nature: its loss in the subhuman,
matched by a possible "trapasso" beyond to the superhuman.

As we shall soon see, this investigation requires the tracing of a
difficult relationship between man and the natural world, which
might either confirm or put into question the occasional attempts
to appropriate for the *Furioso* the label of "Naturalism" already ques-
tionably applied, though more understandably so, to Boccaccio.[81]
The episode freely mixes elements of Dante's Christian askesis,
Hercules' ethical-humanistic itinerary, and Ulysses' "neo-Platonic"
journey, although the relations between these elements are quite
carefully structured. As this array of possibilities suggests, the poem
must be understood as unfolding not simply in terms of the thematic
rivalry between education and madness, but also in terms of the
competing ideologies and narratives of education. Other Renais-
sance texts may adopt one perspective and reduce its competitors
to the otherness of self-deluding folly, or, often enough, they may
try to reconcile elements of several positions—as Ficino does in
arguing for a *pia philosophia* of Platonizing Christianity, as Pico
does in arguing for the unity of truth (and in seeing every plane
of existence—terrestrial, celestial, empyrean—as a double of and
path toward every other), as Castiglione does in juxtaposing boldly
the active and contemplative functions of the Courtier and the
prince. It remains to be determined exactly what hierarchy or syn-
thesis the *Furioso* aspires to—what methods and values of education
are promoted at the expense of what others, or, alternatively, how
seemingly disparate positions are to be reconciled. There is yet an-
other possibility, one to which this study will eventually subscribe:
that instead of using one position to criticize or incorporate others,
each may instead subvert and be subverted in its turn, leaving the

---

[81] For Ariosto's supposed "naturalism," see, for instance, Luigi Russo, "Ariosto
Maggiore e Minore," *Belfagor* 13 (1958), p. 645. See also Croce's discussion of the
question. If for DeSanctis, however, Boccaccio is a "naturalist" and a sensualist
(*Storia*, vol. 1), Ariosto is outside of nature in a realm of pure art. For a critique of
the "naturalist" reading of Boccaccio by, in addition to DeSanctis, Auerbach ("Frate
Alberto," in *Mimesis*, pp. 202–233) and Aldo Scaglione, *Nature and Love in the Late
Middle Ages* (Berkeley: University of California Press, 1963), see Mazzotta's three
articles on the *Decameron*.

notion of *paideia,* in any form, always at the precipice of formless madness (*mise en abyme, messo al baratro*), while madness itself verges on becoming a mode of knowledge, a locus of positive value.

The most obvious parodic elements in the episode are travesties of the neo-Platonic and mystical traditions of education—a series of related, though hardly identical, positions represented variously by Ficino, by Landino's readings of the *Aeneid* and the *Commedia,* by Pico's *Oratio, Heptaplus,* etc., and, contemporary with Ariosto, by Bembo's *Asolani* and the latter chapters of the *Cortegiano. Satira* VI, we saw, contains an explicit critique of such an intellectual "journey without a guide." And we have also seen the importance of the figure of Ulysses, with its underlying neo-Platonic associations. The notion of Ruggiero's flight as a spiritual journey beyond the confines of history and nature is first suggested, however, by the following comparison of the receding hero, as wistfully viewed by Bradamante, to Trojan Priam's son, "Ganimede / ch'al ciel fu assunto dal paterno impero, / . . . / non men gentil di Ganimede e bello" ("Ganymede who was taken to heaven from his father's realm . . . no less noble and lovely than Ganymede" IV.47.5–8). The comparison is tacitly continued in the later assimilation of the hippogryph to Jove's eagle (which, in myth, bore Ganymede up to heaven, VI.18). The reference to the "paterno impero" marks a departure from any "impegno civile," especially in view of Ruggiero's alleged genealogical connections with the ruling house of Troy. And Ganymede, as we have seen, is an image of the divinized man, man lifted up beyond himself into the celestial and the superhuman. The spurious education which Alcina represents herself as effecting is then enacted in terms of the contemplation of an object which epitomizes and surpasses worldly concerns:

> *Io mi godea le delicate membra:*
> *pareami aver qui tutto il ben raccolto*
> *che fra i mortali in più parti si smembra,*
> *a chi più et a chi meno e a nessun molto;*
> *né di Francia né d'altro mi rimembra:*
> *stavomi sempre a contemplar quel volto*   [VI.47.1–6]

I delighted in the delicate limbs: to me it seemed that here was gathered together all the good which is scattered in many parts among mortals— to one less, to another more, to no one much; nor did I recall France or anything else: I was forever contemplating that face

For Ruggiero, too, a contemplative moment appears as the alter-
native to active moral struggle *in bivio*. While he fights the throng
of vices, two of Alcina's ladies approach him:

> ... *a l'uom, guardando e contemplando intorno,*
> *bisognerebbe aver occhio divino*
> *per far di lor giudizio: e tal saria*
> *Beltà, s'avesse corpo, e Leggiadria*   [69.5–8]

> a man gazing and contemplating would need the eye of divinity to
> judge them: such would be Beauty, if it took a body, and Graciousness

These two clearly seem to be the embodiments of (pseudo-)Platonic
Ideas, although they are, ironically, the Beautiful and the Gracious,
rather than the Good and the Beautiful. They invite ascent by con-
templation, and yet even as they promise transcendence of the hu-
man, the poet imposes a sharp contrast between the limited vision
and judgment of man and the all-seeing "occhio divino."

As pointed out earlier, the trip to Alcina then takes the form of
a spiritualized geography of askesis. Once Ruggiero has arrived,
his reception again suggests a leap from the human to the divine:

> ... *non ne potrian far più, se tra loro*
> *fosse Dio sceso dal superno coro*   [VII.9.7–8]

> they could not have done more had God descended among them from
> the heavenly choir

The "se" of course is openly ironic and points toward the subtler
irony of an ascent ("ascesi" VII.8.5), which actually amounts (mounts
up) to a descent ("sceso"). The parody continues with the reappear-
ance of Ganymede, now as a term of comparison for the sensuously
material banquet prepared by Alcina for Ruggiero:

> *Tal non cred'io che s'apparecchi dove*
> *ministra Ganimede al sommo Giove.*   [20.7–8]

> I do not believe they set such [a table] where Ganymede ministers to
> highest Jove.

A soaring contemplative flight thus ends in corrupting, self-indul-
gent stasis, just as Astolfo's contemplation never actually moved

beyond the fascinating surface of Alcina:

> *ogni pensiero, ogni mio bel disegno*
> *in lei finia, né passava oltre il segno*   [vi.47.7–8]

> my every thought, my every sweet design, in her ended, nor passed be-
> yond the sign

Thus what seems to be a metaphysical project in the Piconian mode, degenerates into its opposite, an aesthetic involvement with the sign in and for itself. What seems to be a gathering of fragments into unity and identity ("pareami aver qui tutto il ben raccolto/che fra i mortali in più parti si smembra"), is just another occasion for the loss of human members in Circean metamorphosis and the loss of memory ("né d'altro mi rimembra"), in a clear parody of Platonic *nostalgia* and "recollection."[82]

Throughout the episode, the human repeatedly seems to be ex-alted beyond itself, Ganymede-like, to the divine (cf. vii.9.8, 15.7). And yet this (super)humanistic excess is revealed almost immediately as usurpation and idolatry. It was precisely the reverse move that Salutati hoped to achieve by displacing poetry from idolatry to-ward allegory and by reducing Hercules from a God proper to a god only by analogy, related to the one true God in whose image and likeness he was formed.[83] Alcina is discovered as a "human," or at least a terrestrial, Arachne who tries to usurp the place of Divine Wisdom, and, like Arachne, her fate is to be defeated and to wither into bestial ugliness. Perhaps even more strikingly, she seems a degraded parody of the Renaissance "self-maker" described by Burckhardt and most vividly depicted in Pico's rewriting of the creation myth as a myth of protean self-creation. If, for Pico, man can make of himself ontologically a beast or a god, Alcina makes herself only superficially a "dea," a "paradiso," reducing the status of the human *fictor* from true creator to author of deceptive aesthetic fictions about an unlocatable self. At the same time, the only "real"

---

[82] Cuccaro, in fact, states flatly that Alcina is the "symbolic incarnation of Platonic love" (*Humanism,* p. 196). Needless to say, Platonic love and incarnation are in oxy-moronic relation to one another here.

[83] Cf. Chapter 2, n. 50. See also the discussions of idolatry and relevant notes in Chapter 4, sec. i.

transformations she effects are not from the human to the super-
human, but from the human to the subhuman and monstrous, sub-
jecting man's "dignity" to great degradation while pretending, like
Pico, to celebrate it.

Through Alcina, Ariosto develops something like the anticipa-
tory countermyth of human fictions and monstrosity which the
"humanist," Alberti, had written long before Pico's day. In the
Momus, Charon tells a fable (hellish, of course) of the Creator's
work in creating man:[84]

> Having completed these works, he [the Creator] saw that some men
> were not always delighted by their own shape; so he ordered that they
> be free to transform themselves, according to their pleasure, into the
> form of any one of the other animals which they judged to be preferable.
> Then he showed them his mansion which lay open upon a nearby moun-
> tain, whose inhabitants would have abundance of every good, and he
> exhorted them to ascend there by a steep and direct trail. . . . Again and
> again they were warned not to enter other paths. . . . The men began to
> ascend, but immediately some foolishly preferred to take the shapes of
> cows, asses, and other four-legged creatures; while others, led on by
> erroneous desires, went raving along side-paths. These, . . . on account
> of the difficulty of the place, were transformed into monsters of various
> kinds. . . . For this reason, having found some mud similar to that from
> which they had been made, they put on fictive masks, exactly like the
> faces of their companions. The artifice of these men intent on masking

---

[84] *Momus,* p. 165: "Quibus operibus confectis, cum vidisset homines aliquos sua
non usquequaque forma delectari, edixisse ut, qui id praestare arbitrarentur, quas
placuerit in alias reliquorum animantium facies se verterent. Dehinc suas quae obiecto
in monte paterent aedes monstravit, atque hortatus est ut acclivi directaque via . . .
conscenderent, habituros illic omnem bonarum rerum copiam; sed iterum atque
iterum caverent ne alias praeter hanc inirent vias. . . . [H]omunculos caepisse con-
scendere, sed illico alios per stultitiam boves, asinos, quadrupedes videri maluisse,
alios cupiditatis errore adductos in transversos viculos delirasse. . . . [P]rae loci dif-
ficultate se in varia vertisse monstra. . . . Ea de re, comperto consimili, quo conpacti
essent, luto, fictas et aliorum vultibus compares sibi superinduisse personas, et crevisse
hoc personandorum hominum artificium usu quoad pene a veris secernas fictos
vultus, ni forte accuratius ipsa per foramina obductae personae introspexeris: illinc
enim contemplantibus varias solere occurrere monstri facies. Et appellatas personas
hasce fictiones easque ad Acherontis usque undas durare, nihilo plus, nam fluvium
ingressis humido vapore evenire ut dissolvantur. . . ."

themselves grew with use to the point that one could hardly distinguish the true faces from the false, unless by chance you should peer very attentively through the holes in the covering masks. Only then did the multiple faces of the monster appear to the beholder. And these masks were called "fictions." And they would last until the shore of Acheron, and no further, since once one entered the river the masks departed in a humid vapor so that they were dissolved. . . .

[*Momus*, bk. iv, p. 165]

Clearly Alberti's version of man the "self-maker" and shape shifter has much more to do with Ariosto's than does Pico's divine chameleon.[85]

In spite of these subversions of the most ambitious metaphysical humanism, a recuperation of human values does apparently take place. In the following passages, Melissa adopts and translates the terms of Platonic idealism to a plea for active engagement in terrestrial living:

> Deh, non vietar che le più nobil alme,
> che sian formate ne l'eterne idee,
> di tempo in tempo abbian corporee salme   [vii.61.1–3]

O, do not forbid that the most noble souls formed among the eternal ideas take on corporeal substance, from time to time

Among those descendants of Ruggiero will be:

> Ippolito e il fratel; che pochi il mondo
> ha tali avuti ancor fin al dì d'oggi,
> per tutti i gradi onde a virtù si poggi.   [62.6–8]

Hippolytus and his brother; for the world has seen few such up to the present day, through all the degrees by which one ascends to virtue

Against the radical Platonic dissociation of corrupt body and pure soul, the same allegorical dissociation which permits an aesthetic surface to pass itself off freely and deceptively as the outer reflector of a metaphysical interior, Melissa argues for the union of soul with

---

[85] See again Ferroni for Alberti on the madness of human masking as a point of reference for the theme of dehumanizing folly in Ariosto. Cf. Chapter 4, n. 22, below, for more on Albertian pessimism and "antihumanism."

body and a descent from the ideal into history, rather than for an ascent out of history into ideality. A graded ascent will take place; but, for the usual neo-Platonic *telos* of spiritual knowledge of the good, ethical *virtus* is substituted.

It is certainly clear that the teachings of Melissa and Logistilla are at least temporarily successful in reconverting the degraded lovers of Alcina from inhuman to human form and in giving Ruggiero self-knowledge, which includes an understanding of his own human limits and capabilities. Melissa's successes begin with her own return from a disguise as Atlante to her original form ("la sua prima forma" vii.66.1), thus anticipating the rescue of the metamorphosed lovers whom she returns to their "prima forma" (viii.15.4), especially Astolfo restored to his native semblance ("ne la sua prima faccia" 17.2). This triumph of the human, at least of human form, seems to be sealed by Ruggiero's first adventure after his return— the defeat of the Orca, a monster whose very measurelessness and lack of even distinctly bestial form (x.100.1, 101.5) contrast exactly with the perfect form of Angelica.[86] It is particularly significant, and perhaps part of the subtle anti-Piconian polemic recently detected, that this shapeless hulk is the supposed agent of the revenge of Proteus, the shape shifter (cf. viii.51–58, ix.44–47), whose gift for adopting extrinsic forms may seem less a Piconian emblem of human potential *in bono* than of the demonic power, shared by Alcina, to alter or assume human form at will (cf. vii.11.1), thus blurring, and even eradicating, any stable notion of human identity.[87] The process of educating Ruggiero seems indeed to be an ethical "formazione" in the sense that Garin gives to the term and in a way

[86] On the relation of the Orca to form and representation, see Pliny, *Historia Naturalis* ix.v.12 ("Orcas . . . *cuius imago nulla repraesentatione exprimi possit* alia quam carnis immensae dentibus truculentae," italics mine); and Silvestris (*Commentary,* p. 7), who etymologizes Phorcys, Greek "Orche," as "formans rerum conceptiones" or "conceptio." The latter reference comes in close proximity to mentions of Perseus and the Pegasus, suggesting why Ariosto should have dubbed the monstrous foe of Ruggiero-Perseus an "Orca" to begin with. Cf. also Jordan, "Enchanted Ground," pp. 142–44.

[87] Cf. Giamatti, "Proteus Unbound." It is also relevant that the monster, like some Platonic cave dweller sunk in the chaos of materiality, should be distracted by the *shadow* of horse and rider, rather than looking heavenward at the real articles (x.102 ff.; from *Metamorphoses* iv.712–13).

related to the project of Castiglione, the "formator del cortigiano" ("the one who formed the courtier" *Satira* III.91; cf. *Furioso* XXXVII. 8.3–4). The "galeotto" says that Ruggiero will return from his stay with Logistilla with "pensier . . . meglio formati" ("thoughts . . . better formed" X.47.3), an ethical, intrinsic "formazione," which will forge a correspondence between inner being and outer actions. Such an ethical formation seems specifically designed to counter the extrinsic and superficial, "aesthetic" formation of Alcinian beauty.[88] A transition seems to be marked by Melissa's adoption of Atlante's "forma," and thus of Alcina's metamorphic methods, only in order to further Ruggiero's formation and Alcina's defeat. The distinction between the two kinds of "formazione" is clearly signaled by the reverse directions of the metamorphoses of Melissa and Alcina. Alcina adopts the form of a beautiful young woman which conceals age and decrepitude, while Melissa puts on the decrepit age of Atlante and is subsequently revealed as a beautiful young woman. Nonetheless, it will eventually be necessary to recognize that the difference between these two notions of "form," as between the two kinds of poetry mentioned above, is not quite as substantial as it first appears.

The shape which Ruggiero then begins to assume under the guidance of Logistilla seems clearly circumscribed within an ethical humanism, excluding, at least for the moment, not only the hubristic transcendence of neo-Platonism, but even the "ascent in humility" of Christianity, and of Dante in particular. Far from Dante's Eden, where the four stars/nymphs representing the cardinal virtues of pagan ethics meet the three "theological" virtues (*Purgatorio* 1.22–27, 31.103–111), here the four worldly virtues alone are represented (X.52).[89] Eden itself is not properly here, where Dante had left it, but elsewhere. Though the soul's experience of Logistilla is contemplative (46.6), countering the pseudocontemplation of Alcina, it is not

---

[88] As Kennedy observes ("Ironic Allegory," p. 51), through Alcina the "ethics and aesthetics of *cortesia* are disjoined."

[89] Fichter (*Poets Historical*, p. 97) comments that Ruggiero learns the four cardinal virtues from Logistilla and later receives the addition of Grace (in canto XLI). There is, however, room for doubt both as to whether he actually learns from Logistilla and as to whether the later episode (or Astolfo's lunar journey) really replaces the pagan perspective with the Christian.

a contemplation for purposes of eventual self-transcendence, but for those of present self-knowledge. It is clearly subordinated to the acquisition of practical virtues and the reimmersion in active living. There are two distinct moments in Logistilla's tutelage: the gaze into the specular stones, followed by the lesson in bridling the hippogryph. The one seems to prepare the other:

> . . . mirando in esse [le gemme],
> l'uom sin in mezzo all'anima si vede;
> vede suoi vizii e sue virtudi espresse,
> sì che a lusinghe poi di sé non crede,
> né a chi dar biasmo a torto gli volesse:
> fassi, mirando allo specchio lucente
> se stesso conoscendosi, prudente.   [x.59.2–8]

. . . gazing into these gems a man sees into the very depths of his own soul; he sees his vices and his virtues plainly, so he no longer believes either in those who flatter or in those who wrongly blame him: gazing into the brilliant mirror he makes himself prudent by self-knowledge.

If Melissa taught him how to recognize the true natures hidden behind objective appearance, Logistilla, through these stones, permits an objective "mirroring" knowledge of the subjective self: allegorizing perfectly the traditional moment of *speculation*, figured, for example, by Dante's Lia.[90] By means of the self-reflecting stones, human identity is apparently made present to itself (paradoxically so, by a process of alienation). Even a sly textual reminder of the parodic doubling of specular self-knowledge in the unconscious self-love of Narcissus does not detract from Ruggiero's experience.[91]

---

[90] Porcacchi (*Annotazioni* to canto xii, in the Orlandini edition) notes xii.82— "virtude andava attorno con lo speglio / che fa veder ne l'anima ogni ruga"—and relates it both to x.59 and to the motto of Apollo's oracle at Delphi: "nosce te ipsum" (cf. *Phaedrus* 230a). See also *Purgatorio* 27.100–108.

[91] As Hanning ("Ariosto," p. 112) observes in another context, Alcina in x.49 is compared to Echo. Thus Ruggiero is an implicit Narcissus. In Ovid's *Metamorphoses*, Narcissus' birth is attended by Tiresias' prophecy that he will live "unless he know himself," and his death comes precisely when he recognizes himself as the beloved object in the pool. The tale is a clear parody of the "nosce te ipsum" (*Metamorphoses* iii.339 ff.). One might speculate further that Logistilla's visionary stones ultimately derive from those in Guillaume de Lorris' version of the Narcissus myth in the *Roman de la Rose* (1439 ff.).

Against the allegorical veil, characteristic of Alcina's deception, Logistilla counters with a "mimetic" mirror, though, oddly enough, while the veil passes itself off as a mimetic surface transparent to its inside, the mimetic mirror shows the hidden inside of the self.

Far from a delphic "Nosce te ipsum" preliminary to a knowledge of deity,[92] however, this knowledge does not perfect the self, but simply identifies it for what it, realistically, is, recognizing both its virtues and its vices, its intermediate humanness. It thereby promotes an active virtue, "prudence" (cf. x.52, 65), which should be the correct remedy to the errors of "guidizio" that are universal in the *Furioso*. Knowledge is at the service of virtue. Prudence, the secular and etymological counterpart of divine "providence," is the virtue of ethical vision, of sight penetrating the barriers of mystified appearance, of future events, and so on, to determine proper courses of action. A version of "providenzia" is also the keystone to the Machiavellian ethics, with its peculiar redefinition of *virtus*.[93] It is the humanized counterpart of the "occhio divino" which had earlier seemed to be the only instrument capable of judging Alcina and her agents (vi.69.6) or of seeing through the complicity of Ruggiero's vicious appetites in his own seduction. It seems to answer simultaneously the needs to know in order to choose and to choose in order to know which we earlier saw as the paradoxical requirements blocking an attempt to establish a hierarchy between will and intellect. Prudence is the critical fountain of criteria by which to resolve the crises of objective perception and subjective willfulness. In effect, Melissa's rhetorical suasions on Ruggiero's will pave the way for his choice to see the truth about Alcina, while, conversely, Logistilla's stones afford Ruggiero a knowledge which furthers his choice of return to active life, as well as his new power of will both to govern his own appetites and to harness the emblematic forces of the hippogryph.

---

[92] Garin, *L'Umanesimo,* paraphrases Ficino's project in the following way: "una conoscenza di sé attraverso la conoscenza di Dio, e vice-versa" (pp. 118–19).

[93] Macchiavelli, *Il Principe,* chap. 3: "quello che tutti e' principi savii debbano fare: li quali non solamente hanno ad avere riguardo alli scandoli presenti, ma a' futuri . . . prevedendosi" with "la virtù e prudenzia loro." Cesare Borgia ultimately fails because of the one circumstance he cannot foresee. The climax comes in chap. 25 with its prudence/fortune opposition. See also the remarks on the unarmed prophet (chap. 6).

More than simply substituting a rhetoric of ethical humanism for that of neo-Platonism, Logistilla seems to reconcile vision and choice, knowledge and will, *sapientia* and *virtus*, contemplation and action, inner and outer.[94] She might even appear to effect the union of the human and the natural with the divine which Alcina had spuriously attempted. Her gems are said to be found here and nowhere else, "se non forse su in ciel" ("if not up in heaven" x.58.8). More pointedly still, the "galeotto" tells Ruggiero that he will learn from Logistilla, "come de la gloria de' beati / nel mortal corpo parte si delibi" ("how the glory of the blessed is foretasted while in the mortal body" x.47.5–6). These words bring Ruggiero very close to the description of Dante's imaginative foretaste of the blessings of Paradise while, apparently, still "in the body" (cf. *Paradiso* 24.1–6). Logistilla's humanistic education may thus extend itself even further, in the direction of a potentially metaphysical ascent. Nonetheless, contemplative knowledge is clearly preliminary to the return to history urged by Melissa, while Logistilla's first teaching is preliminary to her second, which urges his departure from her and the contemplative experience. Ruggiero seems oblivious to all transcendental possibilities; his own "conversion" experience still lies some thirty cantos in the book's future.

The immediate goal of the knowledge Logistilla furnishes and the virtue she inculcates is the other form of "glory," radically secularized. The motives for Ruggiero's return, according to Melissa, are two: the twinned Renaissance versions of eternal life realized within the bounds of time. She first urges upon him the value of "['quel odor'] che tra' l'uom del sepolcro e in vita il serba"("[that fragrance] which raises man from the tomb and preserves him in life" VII.41.7), i.e., fame. These lines echo one of the first and boldest Renaissance celebrations of earthly glory, Petrarch's *Trionfo della Fama* (i.9), and suggest how clearly secular rebirth is announced as a counterpoint to and conceptual derivative from Christ's resurrection.[95] Melissa goes on to contrast her wish for Ruggiero to enjoy "onore," "fama," and "laude," even though

---

[94] See again Giamatti, *The Earthly Paradise*, p. 162.

[95] Petrarch places the *Trionfo della Fama* right after that of *Morte*, emphasizing the victory over death. A later allusion to the "sepolcro di Cristo" (ii.144) emphasizes the secularization of resurrection.

it means his premature death, with Atlante's desire to let him live out his mortal term anonymously (VII.43). On the other hand, she also argues, echoing Mercury's words to Virgil's Aeneas:[96]

> Se non ti muovon le tue proprie laudi,
> e l'opre escelse a chi t'ha il cielo eletto,
> la tua succession perché defraudi
> del ben che mille volte io t'ho predetto[?]
> . . . .
>
> . . . il ciel vuol che sia per te concetto
> la gloriosa e soprumana prole
> ch'esser de' al mondo più chiara che 'l sole   [60]

If your own fame, and the high deeds for which heaven has elected you, do not move you—how can you defraud your descendents of the good I have so often predicted to you? . . . Heaven wills that through you be conceived the glorious and superhuman progeny which will shine more brightly than the sun in this world

She thus combines the value of glory with a version of the notion of eternity through generation ("breed" as Shakespeare puts it), making a doubly strong argument for the humanistic hope of eternity in this world. It is curious that only after she has rein-stilled the value of a name in Ruggiero does Melissa name herself (66).[97] It would seem from this preliminary evidence that humanistic Fama, which Burckhardt saw as one of the identifying innovations of the Renaissance, is an unequivocal value for Ariosto.[98] Though it is not accomplished with specific reference to Hercules' name, Ruggiero's education does seem to embody the same dialectic of virtue stimulated by the hope of glory and finally rewarded with a famous name that we saw in Salutati.

Shortly after the mention of the (ontological, Christian) "gloria

---

[96] Cf. *Aeneid* IV.272–76.

[97] Bonifazi (*Le Lettere,* p. 110) reads the repeated deferral of the first naming of characters throughout the poem as an attack on the conjunction of person and proper name, and hence on the stability of identity.

[98] DeBlasi, "Ariosto," pt. 1, p. 349. Burckhardt, *Civilization,* vol. 1, pt. 2, chap. 3 ("The Modern Idea of Fame," which he sees as beginning with Dante, Albertino Mussato, and, above all, Petrarch).

de' beati," the poet speaks of "quel di eterna gloria degno / Ruggiero" ("that Ruggiero, worthy of eternal glory" x.57.1–2), in a context which leaves little doubt that he is returning to a notion of nominal glory (particularly since the reference comes in close proximity to the pathetic image of the defeated Alcina, whose unhappy fate as a "fata" is to go on living physically forever [x.5]). The Dantean echo heard in x.47 thus acts mainly to displace the eschatological emphasis of the *Commedia* toward the proleptic possibilities of the "mortal corpo" itself. If the education *in bono* of of Melissa and Logistilla then returns to resurrect the lapsed Alcinian promise of access to the superhuman, speaking "d'uomini invitti, anzi di semidei" ("of invincible men, or rather, of demigods" vii.39.4) and of Ruggiero's "soprumana prole" ("superhuman progeny" 60.7), perhaps the difference is that these divinized men aspire to and achieve divinity of a more limited kind (if divinity by definition does not contradict limit), aligned by virtue of their virtue with the active Hercules and by virtue of their fame acquiring not the ontological but the nominal eternity of a god. If man can become in any sense a god, this discreet humanism seems to say, it is only within the bounds of Nature—and in conjunction with his human possibilities—as a contingent intersection of temporality and eternity, Nature and Grace.

The "formazione" of Ruggiero consists both in the formation of a virtuous being and in the acquisition of a formal identity which accurately mirrors that being, ostensibly conferring on the hero the unity of being and seeming, signifier and signified, which the schizophrenic world of Alcina, in fact of allegory in general, precludes. The coincidence of inner and outer, which an antimaterial neo-Platonism rejects as utopian and impossible (outer body being irrevocably alien to inner spirit), is instead the hidden metaphysical aim of philological humanism, the implicit conclusion of Valla's notion that language is potentially sacramental; that long-dead, or only geographically absent, authors can be a "real presence," available in their historical dimensions and intentions in their writings (just as the Eucharist is the site of Christ's "real presence"). Even as Ruggiero takes the form of an identifying sign (the sign understood here as the total complex of signifier and signified by which significance takes place),[99] it is accompanied by a process of "insegnamento," of training in the reading of signs to discover their true origins and destinations. These gifts of critical reading seem to be necessary to heal the allegorical crisis of the self, allowing the inscription of an integral identity.

I have already shown to what great extent the education dramatized consists of training in and by reading, and I have suggested how through prudence and "giudizio" reading liberates the human will, as *leggere* becomes *eleggere*. It is now worth considering a little more carefully how the metaphors of "segni" and "insegnamento" are actually deployed and developed in the episode. At the episode's beginning, Ruggiero's (and Astolfo's) failure is defined in terms of two contradictory errors in the "reading" of signs understood as boundaries or limits to human experience. The first comes with Ruggiero's flight past ". . . il segno che prescritto / avea già a' naviganti Ercole invitto" ("the sign that invincible Hercules once set for sailors" VI.17.7–8). By a transgression of the written signpost which delimits man's historical dwelling place, Ruggiero moves toward an alienated world of pure metaphysics, pure being, beyond the appearances and the words by which men must usually pass on the way to meaning. On the other hand, once arrived, he too, like Astolfo, lapses, assuming that Alcina's "rhetoric," her appearance, is her being: "ogni pensier, ogni mio bel disegno / in lei finia né passava oltre il segno" ("my every thought, my every sweet design, in her ended, nor passed beyond the sign" 47.7–8).[100] The first "excess" of reading seems again to support the case for an Ariostan poetics of limited human significance. The second passage, indicating a failure to exceed a sign, suggests the opposite necessity, that of transgressing human appearances, and this necessity becomes a limit to the value of the humanism of limits. Either to exceed the sign or to remain within it has its dangers. Both the "allegorical" and the "aesthetic" reading seem to lead straight to Alcina, confirming what had already been suggested in the reading of *Satira*

<hr>

[99] See Culler, *Structuralist Poetics*, pp. 16–20, for a clear statement of the Saussurian definition of the double structure of the sign.

[100] Kennedy ("Ironic Allegory," p. 52) also notices the echo from VI.17 to 47, though our interpretations of it differ significantly.

VI. In Chapter 2 I argued that humanistic philology could (and did) slide in two directions: toward a metaphysics which privileges the signified (*res*) and toward an aesthetics which privileges the signifier (*verba*), and sometimes toward both at once, as in cases such as Bembo's and Castiglione's. Here Ariosto dramatizes both of these strayings, even as he reveals that they are two related aspects of a single crisis. In this respect Dante's doomed Ulysses is appropriately designated as both the purveyor of an empty rhetoric and the emblem of false neo-Platonic hopes for transcendence. And it is a fitting punishment for either of these semiotic attitudes that the transgressor be caught permanently in the condition of allegory, in which signifier is "radically" alienated and divided from signified, as in Astolfo's entrapment within the "scorza" of an allegorical Nature.

The cure for this degenerative semiosis is undertaken in terms which allude more or less directly to philological "insegnamento," as outlined in Chapter 2. Through cantos VI and VII, Ruggiero is usually said to be undergoing "istruzione," rather than "insegnamento."[101] In canto X, the emphasis shifts strikingly: of Logistilla the old mariner says to Ruggiero, "t'insegnerà." By the end of her teaching, of course, Ruggiero has apparently been versed in reading signs in order to become "one": i.e., both (a) "a sign" and (b) a unified, self-identical personality. One might easily argue that the desire *in bono* which Ruggiero feels for Logistilla (x.46, 48) is, in fact, nothing less than "philo-logy," love of *logoi*, words, and of *logos*, the Greek word which is translated into humanistic Latin as both "oratio" and "ratio."[102] If her name does possess this double etymological resonance, it tends to reconcile the alternative definitions of man as user of language (rhetorician) and as possessor of reason (logician). The fact that Logistilla, unlike Alcina, simultaneously provokes and satisfies desire, suggests further that in her the (outer) signifier which denotes an absence and awakens or guides desire coincides with the (inner) signified which might answer and gratify that desire by its presence. On Ruggiero's return from Europe, just as the episode of the Orca teases out the consequences of "forma-

---

[101] For "istruzione" see VI.43.7, 44.6, 56.8; VII.38.8, 77.3, 78.7, etc.
[102] Seigel, *Rhetoric and Philosophy*, p. xi; cf. Chapter 2, n. 12, above.

zione," so the review of the English troops which precedes it redramatizes an education in the significance of signs (heraldic "insegne") through which the twinned values of heroic identity and familial identity are celebrated. But the full import of those "insegne" will have to be discussed later on.

A provisional review of my conclusions about the nature of Ruggiero's education may now be in order. The poem suggests a conversion from purely metaphysical education to an itinerary of modified secular humanism which forms human identity by teaching to read deceptive outer surfaces *and* the inner nature of the subjective self, and then to master both by virtuous choice. Ruggiero becomes himself by embracing a destiny of conversion, marriage, dynasty, and premature death. By choosing, the self ensures its continued existence as a famous name which will live on in writing and speech, "fin che 'l sol gira." The possibility of this choice, and the opposition it implies between metaphysical and ethical humanism, seems to be dramatized most starkly in the contrast between the two mythological figures with whom Ruggiero is most closely associated, Ulysses and Hercules. As we have seen, Ulysses' "boundless love of understanding and knowing," in the words of Landino,[103] violates precisely the symbolic boundaries (i.e., the Straits of Gibraltar) erected by Hercules, humanistic hero of the engaged will and civilizing tamer of monstrous excess. In light of what has earlier been said, however, it is equally necessary to go on to qualify the apparent simplicity of this opposition. For one thing, Hercules is allegorized by neo-Platonists, including Landino, as well as by humanists, while Ulysses is a humanistic rhetorician as well as an emblem of philosophical askesis: so that in both there is a way in which metaphysical and ethical humanisms tend to converge, contaminating one another. For another thing, Ruggiero is not an entirely successful Hercules, since he first chooses the wrong road *in bivio,* and must then resort to Ulyssean tactics of fraud to free himself. In fact, by permitting Ruggiero as Ulysses to arrive safely at the island which occupies the "same" space as Dante's *Purgatorio,* and by later enacting his hero's movement from the desert of Alcina's shores to Logistilla's castle in Dantean/Ulyssean terms, Ariosto may even be

---

[103] Landino, annotation to *Inferno* 26.115. Cf. Padoan, *Il Pio Enea,* pp. 187, 193.

reversing Dante's critique of Ulysses. He uses Ulysses to valorize the possibilities of human "virtute e canoscenza," even as he displaces the metaphysical goal for which Dante and Ulysses both strove (Eden, the origin and perfection of human life, timeless in time), thereby diminishing Ulysses' achievement and the possibilities of the human, even as he seems to recuperate them. Thus, in addition to a polemical opposition, Ulysses and Hercules are brought together as aspects of an educational humanism alternative to Dante's Christian project of spiritual ascent to deity. In the logic of the episode, where remaining within limits also has its dangers, Ulysses' semiotic transgression is apparently as necessary as it is risky, leading as much to Logistilla as to Alcina, though it is validated only by a return to history and responsibility, a reinsertion of the self in the domain of active Herculean virtue. In poetic terms, a deviation into allegorical fantasy justifies itself in view of the newly educated reader's return to his or her own "reality," even though it still risks seeming either to be a purely aesthetic, unreal place (as Ariosto's poem has so often to its critics) or to be a fruitless, utopian leap into the metaphysical beyond (as Dante's poem does when thus reduced to the level of the "folle volo" of its own Ulysses).

Even more perplexing to the reader, as he or she tries to approach Ariosto's educational values in a simple, coherent way, is that at the same time as Ruggiero begins the flight back to Europe and makes a series of ethical and political commitments, at another, imaginative level, he seems to be on the verge of realizing Ulysses' grand, metaphysical aspirations. When Dante's Ulysses sets out "di retro al sol" ("following the sun" *Inferno* 26.117) and directs his ship away from the "morning" (124) toward the point of the sun's setting, he is attempting an *imitatio solis,* "a quest for eternity patterned on the cycle of death and resurrection of the sun."[104] The sun's apparent circling of the earth is perpetual and yet constitutes the very measure of time. So it is "natural" that the circle be used as a figure for

---

[104] The phrase is Mazzotta's: *Dante,* p. 98. It is of special interest that Hercules, as the one who draws the earth's boundaries, is traditionally compared to the sun (Mazzotta, p. 97, cites Macrobius, *Saturnalia* I.xx.6; see also Salutati, *De Laboribus Herculis* III.ii [vol. I, pp. 168–69]), while Ulysses, who surpasses those boundaries, falls short of its perfection.

both kinds of "mundane" eternity: fame and family.[105] To follow its track is thus to achieve metaphorically what Melissa promotes: secular, temporal eternity—in effect a spatialization of time whose circular form promises perfect and endless self-identity and onto-logical self-sufficiency which is like a god's.

There is, moreover, an explicitly ontological-metaphysical di-mension to the circular journey. It suggests the "eternal return" of Platonism,[106] as well as the circular motion of the angelic soul which possesses perfect, unmediated intellectual understanding (op-posed by neo-Platonic geometers of the spirit to the "linearity" of human understanding mediated by the senses).[107] It is therefore an

[105] Compare this annotation of Landino to *Inferno* 26: "el dì . . . si può porre per la vita humana: Et la parte occidentale pel fine della vita . . ." (cf. *Furioso* x.62.5–6, "altrove appar come a un medesmo sole / e nasca e viva, e morto il capo inchini"; and Petrarch, *Trionfo del Tempo* 1.61). As Salutati, *De Laboribus Herculis* iii.xxiv (vol. i, pp. 313–14) says of the serpent who rounds the world, the circle is an emblem of time's circularity (and hence of continuous temporal movement from life to death, like Fortuna's wheel as well). On the other hand, it is also a figure of eternity. As Toscanella points out (*Allegoria* to canto iv, Orlandini edition), it is "una figura, che non ha né principio né fine, onde . . . viene . . . a significar Dio." Toscanella, as he allegorizes the ring, also interprets the circular shield as the world and Atlante as the emblem of Time flying (Atlas is, after all, a student of astrology, science of temporality). In any case, the circle and sun are clearly capable of figuring, even simultaneously, divine completeness and eternity *and* human temporality and mor-tality. Somewhere between the two extremes are the two secular metaphors of eter-nity: fame and generation. Clements (*Picta Poesis,* p. 127 and plate 6) points to Alciati's gloss on the circular serpent biting its tail as "ex litterarum studiis immor-talitatem acquiri." Castiglione, on the other hand, figures generation as a circle (*Cortegiano* iii.xiv).

[106] For the "eternal return" of souls to the world in metempsychosis, see *Republic* 614b–621d (the myth of Er), and for the Platonic "Great Year" see *Timaeus* 39d and Augustine, *De Civitate Dei* xii.xiv (which both gives the doctrine its most vivid statement and criticizes it in terms of the Christian doctrine of "linear" history).

[107] For the circularity of pure intellection (proper only to the angels) vs. the linearity of sensually mediated understanding (proper to man), as well as the spiral motion which results as man traverses the distance from sense to intellect in the process of spiritual ascent, see Landino, *Disputationes,* bk. i, pp. 22–23. For a remark-able account of the derivation of this tradition from the *Timaeus,* with its analogy between the three motions of the macrocosm and the three motions of man's micro-cosmic soul, see John Freccero, "Dante's Pilgrim in a Gyre," *PMLA* 76 (1961). For a consideration of these movements in terms of the sun and the other stars, see Freccero, "*Paradiso* x: The Dance of the Stars," *Dante Studies* 86 (1968).

emblem of man *at one* with himself and with the universal order.
In Ficino's *De Sole,* God's knowledge and power are still figured
by the sun's light and heat.[108] For the Christian Middle Ages, God
is the sphere whose center is everywhere and whose circumference
is nowhere ("cuius centrum ubique et circunferentia nusquam").[109]
But in this apparent confirmation of Poulet's spatial metaphor of a
"Renaissance," man has now taken over both sun and circle as
images of himself. And in this way, Ariosto seems to embrace full
identification of himself with this Renaissance image of identity.
Throughout the episode under consideration, solar-circular meta-
phors proliferate. We saw earlier that Ruggiero's first impressions
of Alcina are of a "donna sole" (cf. VII.10.8, 12.2), in another in-
stance of her spurious appropriation of neo-Platonic motifs. But the
imagery attaches itself more consistently, and more authentically,
to Ruggiero himself.[110] He sets out along the path of the sun
(IV.50.3–4) like Ulysses, and, unlike Ulysses, he departs the anti-
podes on his way toward completion of a perfect solar circle:

> . . . *finir tutto il cominciato tondo,*
> *per aver, come il sol, girato il mondo.*   [x.70.7–8]

to complete the circle begun; to have rounded the world, like the sun.

The instruments of Ruggiero's education also partake of solarity.

---

[108] *De Sole,* in Garin, ed., *Prosatori Latini,* p. 990 ("sol statua Dei") as well as pp.
972, 1006. See also the last-cited article of Freccero, as well as Landino, *Disputationes,*
bk. III, pp. 138–39, for the etymological derivation of "sol" from "solus," "unique."
Cf. *Furioso* VII.10.

[109] Poulet (*Metamorphoses of the Circle,* pp. xi–xxvii) cites a number of appear-
ances of this definition of the infinite, from the hermetic *Liber XXIV Philosophorum*
to St. Bonaventura, *Itinerarium Mentis in Deum,* to Nicholas Cusanus. He owes a
considerable debt to Marjorie Nicolson, *The Breaking of the Circle* (New York:
Columbia University Press, 1960), and finds relevant passages in Ficino and Landino,
though he argues that the Renaissance in general joined Pico in placing man "in
the middle of the world." Even Dante, however, admits more than one perspec-
tive, so that when he reaches the Empyrean his vision is radically altered. Man and
earth move from center to periphery, with God assuming His proper centrality.

[110] Jordan, who is the most interesting critic to date on the subject of temporality
in the *Furioso,* has noticed both the cited comparisons between Ruggiero and the
sun and has linked them to a quest for timelessness within time ("Enchanted Ground,"
pp. 141, 147, 174, passim).

Rajna noted long ago that the circular ring which Melissa uses to rescue Ruggiero has a precedent in the "heliotrope" stone of Pliny and the lapidaries, the same which is vainly pursued by Boccaccio's Calandrino and which is so explicitly missing from *Inferno* (24.93). This heliotrope, or "trope of the sun," in addition to miming the circular shape of the sun's path, confers on its possessor the complementary solar powers of invisibility and universal illumination (the same powers which make the sun a figure for the divine).[111] Its wearer becomes an "unseen seer." The stones of Logistilla are also tropes of the sun: "il chiaro lume lor, ch'imita il sole, / manda splendore in tanta copia intorno / che chi l'ha, ovunque sia, sempre che vuole, / Febo, mal grado tuo, si può far giorno" ("their clear light, which imitates the sun, shines so brilliantly around that whoever has it, wherever he may be, if only he wishes, makes day for himself, in despite of Phoebus" x.60.1–4), so the *imitatio solis* extends to include perfect self-knowledge. Finally, the dazzling shield too is compared to the sun: "Sta Ruggiero alla posta, e lieva il velo; / e par ch'aggiunga un altro sole al cielo" ("Ruggiero stands fast and lifts the veil; it seems that he adds another sun to the heavens" 109.7–8). Thus even as the solar journey is an emblem of the glorious eternity of race promised by Melissa (cf. VII.60.7–8, XLI.3.5–8, XLIV.10.3–4), it seems to make bold intellectual and ontological promises about Ruggiero's own identification with the sun's power, light, and perpetuity.

In Platonic allegoresis, education is a "circulation": the soul falls out of perfection into material degradation and then by *paideia* is restored to new spiritual perfection. In Platonic terms, circulation is not only the "form" of *paideia,* it is also the spiritual condition to which the fallen "linearity" of men in the body aspires. In a famous Platonic myth, partial beings wander the world, restless with desire for the lost plenitude of an original, spherical, state of

---

[111] Rajna (*Le Fonti,* p. 140) notes the echo of *Decameron* VIII.3 and refers us to the lapidaries, but misses the Dantean resonance. See also Pliny, *Historia Naturalis* x.xxxvii.165. Compare Ficino, *De Sole* (in Garin, ed., *Prosatori Latini,* p. 992), on solar light as both the clearest and the most obscure (i.e., most difficult to know) of things—that which makes all seeing possible and yet is itself impossible to see directly.

being.[112] Dante's mad Ulysses is destroyed because, in Christian terms, man cannot by his own efforts and nature make himself whole and eternal. Brunetto Latini cannot really teach "come l'uom s'etterna," at least not ontologically. The circle will not be "unbroken" without the intervention of divine Grace. Ironically, after he returns to Ithaca, which is always allegorized as the metaphysical *patria* in which Ulysses' spiritual journey should end, his restlessness is not diminished and his desire carries him back into alien regions toward yet another version of the original home of the human spirit, Eden, of which he nonetheless falls tragically short. But Ruggiero's circular route, which also bears him out of the familiar turf of Europe into an alien place and back again to what is forecast as his true "home," achieves at least the form of rebirth, of individual "renaissance," within history that Ulysses died attempting. Ruggiero's education apparently enacts the very "solarity" which we have seen critics attributing to Ariosto as a world view (and we understand better what large claims for the poet and the poem this metaphor implies), and in doing so not only effects personal rebirth, but also celebrates, in despite of Dante and yet via Dante's own metaphors, the identifying values of the Renaissance: the rebirth of classical notions of both ontological and nominal eternity. Curiously, however, in view of the Platonic model, his circle takes him back to a home, not in spiritual rest and perfection, but rather in the natural, material world which Platonism seeks to abandon. By thus bringing together the metaphysical circle and the ethical return, Ariosto again seems not so much to be entirely dismissing the Platonists' project as to be partially reconciling it with, and subordinating it to, an ethical humanism, perhaps recognizing a metaphysics as the necessary underpinning and precondition for moral being.

The solar circle seems not only to be a natural analogue for the self exiled from its original and true nature into a condition of inner spiritual and outer geographical alienation, and then restored to itself and its *patria,* but also to imply a recovery of harmony

---

[112] *Symposium* 189c–193e, contains Aristophanes' comic myth of the circular "Hermaphrodites."

between man and the natural order. It suggests an edenic chiasmus at which man and nature, human and divine, time and eternity, being and appearance, desire and significance, word and thing, and so on, come together in an inclusive and immanently meaningful unity which Platonism, with its unbridgeable dualism, never believed possible, and which Christianity believes to have been lost forever long ago.[113] It points, allusively, toward a paradisical perfection of nature on earth as the goal and reward of man's existence: a wholehearted enjoyment of nature in and for itself, such as that argued for by Valla in his moments of Epicurean humanism and implicit in his notion of the plenary sacramental sign. For Valla, in this sense the true metaphysical physicist of civic humanism, both writing and nature bear their meanings within themselves: they are not only signs to be used en route to hidden signifieds (as Augustine would have it),[114] but also things to be enjoyed intrinsically. By the same token, man the "reader" of these two "Books" himself approaches within nature the unity of body and soul, human appearance and divine Being, that the Middle Ages would have assigned only to Christ. By recognizing that the perfect union of delight

[113] Thus Dante can pass through the original home of man, Eden, but only as a temporary way station en route to the heavenly Paradise of God. This evokes one of the radical paradoxes of the Renaissance as an historical period and as a locus of speculation about the nature of history. It is usually argued that the Renaissance discovers linear history (see Garin, L'Umanesimo, pp. 7–16, 21–24), sees each moment in its historical uniqueness, and traces a line of progress or development from past to present. Yet its self-chosen metaphor is that of phoenix-like rebirth in history, of circular return to the past (cf. Mazzeo, Renaissance and Revolution, p. 8). As points of departure for exploring the question of time and of history in the Renaissance, see C.A. Patrides, The Phoenix and the Ladder (Berkeley: University of California Press, 1964) and Ricardo Quinones, The Renaissance Discovery of Time (Cambridge: Harvard University Press, 1972).

[114] See Valla, De Vero Bono, in Scritti Filosofici e Religiosi (Firenze: Sansoni, 1953), esp. bks. 1 and 2, as well as Trinkaus' account of Valla's theories of voluptas and fruitio (Image and Likeness, vol. 1, pp. 103–170) relation to Augustine's doctrine of uti et frui, as activities which correspond to encounters with verba and with res (see De Doctrina Christiana, esp. bk. 1). What I feel Trinkaus does not account for is Valla's admission of intrinsic enjoyment of things in nature, where for Augustine the only "thing" that can be legitimately enjoyed is God Himself. At this point, we should get into the question of Valla's dialogical dialectic and the status of the individual remarks on voluptas, but do not have the time or space.

and utility—understood as semiotic experiences which correspond, respectively, to remaining within and going beyond the sign in pursuit of Being—is a feature of Eden or of deity itself, we see not only the extent of the aspirations of the education undergone by Ruggiero, but also of the claims that certain of Ariosto's critics, and apparently the text itself, make when they argue for an unproblematic reconciliation of textual pleasure and ethical utility.

The circle which takes Ruggiero toward a point of origin in nature suggests the metaphorical recovery of edenic self-presence: presence of man to man in his true nature, which by virtue of being presence (presence as *being,* both in time and in place, and hence perfectly represented by the circle which spatializes time) lifts man beyond his human identity toward divinity (defined precisely as unmediated, self-present being). Ruggiero's adventures on the island before return include a graded series of encounters between man and apparently natural landscapes which allude quite directly to the desire to recover Eden and an inwardly edenic condition.[115] Ruggiero alights in the usual *locus amoenus,* the traditional literary simulacrum of Eden and, just as traditionally, the scene of restless desire pursuing absence and of the self's lapse into the final absence of death.[116] In the pastoral world, Adamic deathlessness and perennial fulfillment of identity by and through the accessible Other (not only the beloved, but all of the objective landscape beyond the self, even unto the Creator) always give way to inevitable death and the self's sense of self-absence which fuels the pursuits of desire. And Ruggiero discovers soon enough that, far from possessing the intrinsic significance of an edenic world, the perfect rapport of man and nature, this landscape is actually composed of the eminently unnatural conjunction of human spirits and natural surfaces (VI.51–2; VIII.15). Man, Astolfo in particular, is trapped by his endless desires within an alien landscape. The desire of the subject for an object, of the self for an Other, leads not to the perfect union of the two,

---

[115] Cf. Momigliano, *Saggio,* p. 25, as well as Giamatti, *The Earthly Paradise.*

[116] For pastoral and death, see Sannazaro, *Arcadia,* with its increasingly funereal tone (esp. chaps. 10–12). Regarding Ariosto's special admiration for Sannazaro, see XLVI.17.7–8. See also Panofsky, " 'Et in Arcadia Ego': Poussin and the Elegiac Tradition," in *Meaning and the Visual Arts* (Garden City, N.Y.: Doubleday, Anchor, 1955). For the *locus amoenus,* see Curtius, *European Literature,* pp. 182–202.

but rather to the (t)reification of the subject, the alienation of the self. From another perspective, Alcina's nature is merely a screen, a simulacrum of presence, which may be used to travesty and conceal insatiable desire (VI.51).[117] Not only does the landscape designate human self-absence, but also the fall of the natural world to the point where it is no more than a screen onto and into which desires can be projected: it is the landscape of alienation, of allegory, in which both the human and the natural are betrayed. Thus the Ovidian concept of metamorphosis, allowing a free and natural economy of essence in which one being assumes many guises without essential loss, as subject and object interpenetrate freely, is compromised by the introduction of Virgilian and Dantean elements which "deform" Ovid's metamorphosis into an unnatural and violent process.[118]

In point of fact, the Alcinian landscape could be read as the justification of a Platonic critique of material nature and of Socrates'

---

[117] See Croce, "Ariosto,", pp. 50–51. Objecting to DeSanctis' claim that Ariosto lacked "sentimento della natura," he argues that it was not nature that counted anyway but "atteggiamenti dello spirito umano [le passioni] . . . che l'uomo infonde a volta a volta nella natura, ritrovandoli dopo averli posti" (cf. n. 81, above). Carne-Ross ("One and Many," pp. 107–108) sees the *locus amoenus* in canto I as a projection of Angelica's psychological situation and shows how the imagery of place and person match up precisely; he then shows how the "Angelica" that Orlando pursues is merely a projection of his own "thoughts and needs."

[118] See *Metamorphoses* XV.165–172, esp. 165 ("omnia mutantur, nihil interit") and 168 ("nec tempore deperit ullo"). For the contrast between Dantean and Ovidian metamorphosis, see Spitzer, "Speech and Language in *Inferno* 13." In *The Gods Made Flesh,* Barkan objects that Spitzer oversimplifies the character of Ovid's text, which includes several different kinds of metamorphosis. The Ovidian myth of Hermaphroditus, for instance, is an example of the monstrous conjunction of self and other which is relevant to the present Ariostan context (bk. IV.287 ff.). For a perfect example of the two conflicting readings of metamorphosis, in a passage which *might* have influenced Ariosto, see *Asolani* II.xiv (Marti edition, pp. 86–87). Gismondo defends the "naturalness" of love by recourse to its emblem, the laurel tree. Lavinello says that the love of plants is natural, but that the myth of the laurel is, instead, one of the unnatural metamorphosis of a human into a plant: "Ma la donna non amò già essendo amata . . . la qual cosa per ciò che fu contro natura, forse meritò ella di divenir tronco. . . . E certo che altro è, lasciando le membra umane, albero e legno farsi, che, gli affetti naturali abbandonando . . . dolcissimi prendere i non naturali . . . ? che se questi allori parlassero e le nostre parole avessero intese, a me giova di creder che noi ora udiremmo che essi non vorrebbono tornare uomini, poi che noi contro la natura medesima operiamo . . ." (p. 87; cf. p. 124).

attack on mimetic poetry whose surface copy of a desirable reality is merely a veil over corruption and a seducer of unwary youths. The fallen "anthropos" of neo-Platonic and Gnostic myth was etymologized by Salutati as "arbor conversus," which may be meant to suggest the Platonic vision of a headlong fall into materiality, but could as easily be translated into the image of Astolfo converted into a tree.[119] Thus, oddly, even as Alcina is used to parody positive Platonic aspirations for transcendence, she also suggests indirectly the validity of the negative Platonic critique of natural reality, a fact which will prove crucial later on. Alcina herself is, apparently, the best example of a mirroring and a fusing of living being in an edenic landscape. Her city-garden is described as a terrestrial "paradiso" (vi.72.8), while she herself, in her smile, "apre . . . in terra il paradiso" ("opens . . . a paradise on earth" vii.13.8). She too, at first, seems to embody the felicitous conjunction of the human and the natural. The poet's *effictio* of her makes her the double of the landscape she inhabits (and in fact creates): she is a sun (vii.10.8, 12.1); her skin is like roses and lilies (11.6, 28.8); while her breasts are "due pome acerbe [che] . . . / vengono e van come onda al primo margo / quando piacevole aura il mar combatte" ("two unripe apples [that] . . . rise and fall like waves at shore's edge when a pleasant breeze struggles with the sea" 14.3–5; cf. vi.20–22). Not only does her outside appear to be the mirror of her inside (vii.14.7–8), but it also mirrors the world around. She seems both self-identical and identical with nature. In this "proliferation of identity," Alcina seems to achieve *avant la lettre,* the fusion of consciousness and nature mediated by the Romantic symbol, while in fact existing as what some Romantics took to be the enemy and opposite of the symbol: allegory.[120] "Nature" once again turns out to be a screen for unnatural corruption: both she

---

[119] Salutati, *De Laboribus Herculis* ii.viii (vol. 1, p. 111). Ullman's notes give the source in Averroes as "anthropos, quasi arbor inversus," which would not permit the equivocation noted. For the Gnostic theme of the headlong fall of *anthropos* into materiality, and its traces in Dante, see Freccero, "Infernal Inversion and Christian Conversion (*Inferno* xxxiv)," *Italica* 42 (1965).

[120] For Coleridge on allegory, consult Angus Fletcher, *Allegory: The Theory of a Symbolic Mode* (Ithaca: Cornell University Press, 1964), p. 16. For the inherent instability of the allegory/symbol opposition, see DeMan, "The Rhetoric of Temporality." See also Culler, "Literary History, Allegory and Semiology."

and her landscape are not nature at all, but artful imitations of nature. Art usurps nature's place and, Courtier-like, passes itself off for nature, further justifying a Socratic critique of mimesis. "Nature," or rather the Alcinian mimesis of nature, or rather the Ariostan allegory of the mimesis of nature, is opened by Melissa to reveal a deep chasm between appearance and being, man and landscape, art and nature.

Alcina alone, however, does not exhaust the exploration of man's possible relationships with nature in the episode. As with most of the themes and images seen so far, Melissa and Logistilla echo Alcina's categories, apparently reversing and recuperating them. As we shall see better later on, Ruggiero is offered by Melissa the possibility of becoming, metaphorically, a fruit-bearing tree *in bono*, whose fecundity contrasts favorably with the sterility of Astolfo as myrtle (VII.61–62; cf. VI.54.3–4). With Logistilla, Ruggiero's gaze into himself through the mirror-gems seems an explicit counterpoint to Alcina's unnatural, allegorical entrapping of souls within stones (and other subhuman forms). These natural objects "hold the mirror up to man," who in turn mimes the natural order. Logistilla's garden, though it is ostentatiously *not* called a paradise, possesses the edenic qualities of self-sameness, of eternity compassed within temporal bounds, of the heavenly brought to earth:

> Sopra gli altissimi archi, che puntelli
> parean che del ciel fossino a vederli,
> eran giardin sì spaziosi e belli,
> che saria al piano anco fatica averli.
> Verdeggiar gli odoriferi arbuscelli
> si puon veder fra i luminosi merli,
> ch'adorni son l'estate e il verno tutti
> di vaghi fiori e di maturi frutti.
>
> Di così nobili arbori non suole
> prodursi fuor di questi bei giardini,
> né di tai rose o di simil viole,
> di gigli, di amaranti o di gesmini.
> Altrove appar come a un medesmo sole
> e nasca e viva, e morto il capo inchini,
> e come lasci vedovo il suo stelo
> il fior suggetto al variar del cielo:

ma quivi era perpetua la verdura,
perpetua la beltà de' fiori eterni:
non che benignità de la Natura
sì temperatamente li governi;
ma Logistilla con suo studio e cura,
senza bisogno de' moti superni
(quel che agli altri impossibile parea),
sua primavera ognor ferma tenea.   [x.61–63]

Above the high arches which seemed to support the heavens were gardens so lovely that it would be difficult to find such at ground level. Between luminous battlements one can see the flourishing green of sweet-smelling saplings which are all adorned, summer and winter, with graceful flowers and mature fruits. Such noble trees are not usually to be found outside these lovely gardens, nor such roses, nor similar violets, lilies, amaranths, nor jasmines. Elsewhere it seems that in the span of a single day a flower subject to the changing heavens is born, lives, and bows its head in death, leaving a widowed stem. But here the greenery is perpetual, perpetual the beauty of eternal flowers; not that the benevolence of Nature governs them so temperately, but rather Logistilla, with her care and study, without reliance on the movements of the heavens (which to some seemed impossible), kept her springtime everconstant.

The image of a structure supporting the heavens (61.1), taken together with the gardens, evokes the myth of Atlas and the gardens of the Hesperides which, as we saw in the previous chapter, is glossed by mythographers as the Herculean acquisition of philosophical-spiritual knowledge. Logistilla thus repairs Atlante's mischief "on his own terms." Moreover, both the Hesperides and this garden have the obvious edenic resonance as well. Like a secularized Dante, Ruggiero seems at a crucial moment of his education to regain "Paradise." He does so by a recognition of virtues and vices, of good and evil: ironically, since the loss of Paradise was originally occasioned by the "trapassar del segno" through which fallen consciousness acquired the knowledge of good and evil.

Nonetheless, Ruggiero, again like Dante, cannot remain for long in the terrestrial Paradise regained. The pursuit of a pure encounter of man and nature does not find its fulfillment here after all (only hereafter, if at all). Logistilla's palace, in fact, while not quite heavenly, is not altogether natural either and is, just like Alcina's domain, the product in part of "studio" and artifice (x.60.6, 63.5). Nature itself continues to be characterized as variable, unstable, mortal: in brief, *fallen*. Only in this one site are there such stones (x.58.5–8), such trees (x.62.2). Once it is admitted that Eden is still inaccessible, that nature and human nature remain divided, education cannot be purely natural, but must be an artful supplement (Derrida's Rousseauian "supplément") to imperfect nature, whose means are dangerously near to Alcina's, but whose goal is nonetheless a perfect, undivided naturalness.[121] Though the Logistilla episode dramatizes a symbolic self-presence mediated by the generous otherness of natural objects, it does so allegorically, reintroducing the split of "word" from "reality," whose healing it proposes. That residue of division reveals Logistilla's palace for the literary no-place that it obviously is, requiring us to look elsewhere for the fulfillment of Ruggiero's education. The young hero's return, the images of sun and circle through which it takes place, seem to achieve that fulfillment. Following the sun, he becomes

---

[121] Jacques Derrida, *Of Grammatology*, trans. G.C. Spivak (Baltimore: The Johns Hopkins University Press, 1976), pp. 141–69. Derrida's point, reductively stated, is that for Rousseau education must restore man to primitive nature, rescuing him from the corruptions of culture and artifice, but that, in order for it to do so, it must go beyond the resources of nature alone, which is somehow not in itself adequate to the task of teaching, and supplement it with an additional measure of cultural artifice. That seems to be Ruggiero's predicament as well. I think Derrida, *mutatis mutandis*, offers the beginnings of a new way to talk about the perennial art/nature dialectic of the Renaissance (cf. n. 67 above). This would be the place to state clearly what the differences (or the unexpected resemblances) are between Rousseau's Romantic and Ariosto's Renaissance conceptions of nature, art, and education, but I do not feel qualified to do so yet. There are, in any case, certainly grounds for comparing both Plato's notion of education as a full-circle return to origin *and* the Christian *opus restaurationis* (i.e., the work of restoring man to pre-Fall conditions, though not quite leading him back to Eden as origin) with the project of Rousseau. For the *opus restaurationis*, see Mazzotta, *Dante*, pp. 14–65. Compare also John Milton, *Of Education*, in *Complete Poems and Major Prose*, ed. M.Y. Hughes (Indianapolis: Bobbs-Merrill, Odyssey, 1957), p. 630: "the end then of learning is to repair the ruins of our first parents by regaining to know God aright." Note that in the episode of Orlando's madness, nature and art are conflated in the inscriptions on the trees, forming a "natural writing" which, in fact, corresponds exactly to the truth. That such a writing leads straight to madness is a curious paradox which will be explored in Chapter 4, sec. ii.

like the sun, at one with the order of Nature. Morever, by traversing the gap between the marginal literary experience of allegory and the reality to which it "refers" Ruggiero, the solar circle achieves a motivated relationship between art and life, word and thing, while leaving the distance between them in place. The fact that his roundabout path is compared to that of the Magi (x.69.7–8) suggests both that he is now himself a *magus* (who, according to Pico, "marries heaven to earth" and whose powers derive precisely from an understanding of the forces latent in nature) and that his destination, like theirs, offers a union of man and divinity. Ruggiero's education thus not only consists in the linear, forward-moving displacement of an old, vicious, unconscious self toward a new, virtuous, conscious self, but also returns circularly to an "origin," an original state of being, so that "in his end is his beginning" (because education, whether Christian or Platonic, or, for that matter, Freudian, always pursues an origin).[122] Identity is created by a movement toward self-difference which the self perceives with an ironic retrospective glance at the "I" that was and is no more (in order to become myself I must cease to be myself, and see myself as another).[123] But to avoid the schizophrenic risks of splitting

[122] For the Christian and Platonic searches for origin, see n. 121, above. The Freudian (at least the "vulgar" Freudian) notion of a wish to return to the womb is another version of the desire for return to Eden. One might argue that Eden is just a symbolic sublimation of the womb, but since in either case the pursued locale cannot be achieved and hence is never specifically identified, it seems that any "local habitation" and name which might be assigned to it are necessarily metaphorical and improper, i.e., imaginary. The process of psychoanalysis, with its search for an original psychic event marking a "fall" out of happiness and into *both* alienated consciousness and repression, also restructures the myth of a cosmic Fall at the level of the microcosm. Recent versions of Freud, especially that of Lacan, tend to support the notion that what psychoanalysis has so diligently pursued is also an utopia, a garden, a Romantic pre-fallen childhood (which it ostensibly critiques and perverts, with its very different account of how "the child is the father to the man").

[123] This account owes something to Freccero's discussion of Augustinian conversion (with its own debt to Kenneth Burke, *The Rhetoric of Religion: Studies in Logology* [Berkeley: University of California Press, 1970]) in "Dante's Prologue Scene" and "Infernal Inversion," but in some form it is equally applicable to *any* notion of education, secular or religious. The risk, which is run in any event given the fact of temporal displacement, is that in dying to the old self so that a new one may be born, we will become not so many Augustines, secure in our new life, but Iagos who can say "I am not what I am."

the self from itself, the return to an origin guarantees that an essential continuity of self persists (even as I become what I was not, I am what I always was). The self is displaced by its education and yet remains self-identical. It is educated by metaphors and has the shape of metaphor itself, of identity in difference. It avoids the twin pitfalls implicit in the structure of metaphor—neither remaining exactly the same, nor becoming completely different. It is curious, however, that Ruggiero's education involves *two* returns to *two* origins—the pseudo-Eden of Logistilla as well as the point of departure in Europe—which are literally "poles apart," at the antipodes from one another.

The completion of the circle guarantees that the education in and through metaphors at the literary antipodes finally leads back into historical reality, where its efficacy can be tested, its precepts put into practice. The journey thus allegorizes the translation of historical experience by textual reference (from Europe to the islands) and then the corresponding motion from textual insight back into readerly experience via rhetorical persuasion (from the islands to Europe). It dramatizes the full circuit of linguistic reference and action (the "constative" and "performative" aspects of language).[124] As far as Ruggiero is concerned, the (temporary) defeat of the monstrous Orca and the rescue of Angelica are convincing illustrations not only of heroic "impegno," but also of a new willingness to use the resources of magical imagination, notably the shield, to accomplish worthy goals. The description of Angelica tied to the "nudo sasso" suggests a veritable inversion of Alcinian

[124] For the question of language as reference and action, see not only Burke, *The Rhetoric of Religion*, especially the chapter on "Verbal Action in St. Augustine's *Confessions*," but also John Austin, *How to Do Things with Words*, 2nd ed. (Cambridge: Harvard University Press, 1975), and his follower, John Searle, *Speech Acts* (Cambridge: Cambridge University Press, 1969), as well as Derrida's critique of Austin in "Signature Event Context," *Glyph* 1 (1977) (cf. n. 80 above). What Burke seems to know, and what the other two are less interested in, is that the notion of "language as action" has been the heart of a rhetorical tradition that dates at least to the Sophists, and that the Christian Logos is precisely the unity of linguistic action (creating a universe from nothing with a Word) and linguistic reference (the Word is Truth itself). The quarrel between rhetoric and philosophy could be very reductively characterized as the two halves of an original circular Logos trying desperately to be reunited, even as they deny that they have any need of each other.

"un-nature." In such passages as the following, Angelica is linked directly by textual echoes to Alcina, while at the same time replacing the fairy's mere seeming with real, natural being:

la bellissima donna, così ignuda
come Natura prima la compose.
Un velo non ha pure, in che richiuda
i bianchi gigli e le vermiglie rose,
da non cader per luglio o per dicembre   [x.95.3–7]

the most lovely of women, naked as when Nature first composed her. She lacks even a veil in which to enclose the white lilies and vermilion roses that fall not in July nor in December

She seems at this point to be a composition of Nature itself. Her "meaning" is unveiled, present on the gorgeous surface, without the allegorical depths of Alcina. She brings together an edenic landscape exempt from seasonal change with the perfection of human form. Even as she recalls Alcina and her landscape, she also seems to achieve the timeless perfection of Logistilla. The link between antipodal allegory and historical reality seems clear: Ruggiero has learned from the allegory how to act in and on reality, and yet only in reality does the allegory have its fulfillment, take on its significance.

iv. "I Am Become a Name": The End of Education

Unfortunately, as even the most hardy defenders of Ariosto's didactic intentions have recognized, this elaborate narrative of education, amazingly dense with images, figures, and texts of askesis, culminates not with a humanistic triumph over monstrosity, or access to an image of natural perfection, but with a reversion to unreined desire and passionate self-deception, as Ruggiero attempts to rape the woman he has just rescued.[125] He does so, at first, in full consciousness of his obligations to Bradamante. In fact, it is the memory of his attachment to her that first mediates his desire for Angelica, as

[125] Giamatti, "Headlong Horses, Headless Horsemen," p. 299; Donato, "Desire," p. 26; Brand, *Ariosto,* pp. 69–70; Jordan, "Enchanted Ground," p. 125; Yoeman, "Allegorical Rhetoric," pp. 160, 167–68; Momigliano, *Saggio,* p. 36.

"virtue" in effect panders for "vice" (x.97.1–4). At the beginning
of canto XI, having by now forgotten his true beloved, his inten-
tions of returning to the point in Spain from which he originally
departed, and all of the other obligations in which Melissa had in-
structed him, Ruggiero systematically loses the magical/allegorical
instruments with which his education had endowed him: the ring,
the horse (but not the shield). He becomes himself the very image
of a beast, a "cavallo sfrenato," and wanders anew through a "selva"
of blindness and worldly illusion. Instead of a "nostalgic" return
through memory to the "home" of true selfhood and self-possession,
Ruggiero forgets himself entirely, and implicitly risks becoming
another, monstrous, Tereus (x.113.5–6).

For the moment, and the situation obviously changes radically
from moment to moment in this poetic world, "furia" exceeds
completely the limiting powers of reason, even that of an exemplary
moral philosopher:

> Quantunque debil freno a mezzo il corso
> animoso destrier spesso raccolga,
> raro è però che di ragione il morso
> libidinosa furia a dietro volga,
> quando il piacere ha in pronto; a guisa d'orso
> che dal mel non sì tosto si distolga . . .   [XI.1.1–6]

> Qual raggion fia che 'l buon Ruggier raffrene,
> sì che non voglia ora pigliar diletto
> d'Angelica gentil che nuda tiene
> nel solitario e commodo boschetto.
> Di Bradamante più non gli soviene
> che tanto aver solea fissa nel petto:
> e se gli ne sovien pur come prima
> pazzo è se questa ancor non prezza e stima;

> con la qual non saria stato quel crudo
> Zenocrate di lui più continente.   [XI.2, 3.1–2]

Although a weak rein often gathers in a spirited charger in mid-course,
it is nonetheless rare for the bit of reason to turn back libidinous fury
when its pleasure is at hand, just as a bear is not so easily kept from the
honey. . . . What reason will restrain the good Ruggiero from wishing
to take his pleasure with gentle Angelica, whom he holds, naked, in the
solitary and accommodating grove. Of Bradamante he thinks no more,

who once was fixed in his breast; and even if he does think of her as before, he is mad if he does not value and prize this one too, with whom harsh Zenocrates would have been no more continent than he.

This proem seems a specific reversal of the proem to canto VIII cited earlier, which celebrated the power of reason (figured by the ring) to penetrate Alcinian enchantments and curb Ruggiero's desire. Now will, guided by bestial appetite, overpowers unresisting reason. The moment in which Ruggiero's education should prove its worth is instead the moment when he goes mad, albeit temporarily. Throwing off his armor in passionate and comic haste, he is transported back to the erotic fervor of his sojourn with the "fata" (VII.23 ff.). When last seen in canto XI, he has awoken from his erotic trance, but is now pursuing what will later prove to be a completely illusory image of Bradamante and is headed back into yet another labyrinthine castle constructed by Atlante's magic (XIII.44 ff.; cf. XII.4 ff.), where he will once again be deprived of his liberty.[126] He has completed an entirely different kind of circle than he intended to, finding himself (more exactly, losing himself) in exactly the situation, in exactly the condition, in which he began, untransformed in any way. It is as if he had never left Atlante's first castle.

The questions raised by this lapse are many and startling. How is one to explain the fact that an allegory of the elaborateness found in the Logistilla-Alcina episode—so complex, so thoroughly steeped in the great traditions of literary education (Christian, humanist, neo-Platonic)—can thus be superseded violently and immediately, vanishing without a trace as far as the consciousness and future actions of Ruggiero are concerned? All of a sudden this education, rather than having effected an ontological displacement by and through metaphors, seems instead to have been "metaphorical" in the most trivial sense: purely and merely an empty rhetorical gesture. Why does Ruggiero lose control? Is it that he has forgotten what he has just learned (i.e., the lessons were good, but he does not apply them)? Or is it that what he has learned is in some way irrelevant to the realities he now faces? Both of the alternatives imply failures

---

[126] See Donato, "Desire," p. 25, for an interesting contrast between Alcina's island and Atlante's castles as the "two poles of desire." In the long run, for Donato, they come to the same thing.

of reference and influence, as the world of literary, didactic allegory proves unable to bridge the gap between itself and experience after all. But could it be instead, or in addition, that the education itself was not quite what it seemed, betraying itself by participation in the Alcinian duplicity which it claimed to remedy, leading precisely in the direction of this lapse? Does Ariosto now extend to all poetry, not just Alcina's, the Platonic attack on literature as a "copy of a copy," which seduces while pretending to teach? All three of these alternatives can, in fact, be answered with a qualified affirmative, as shall soon appear.

All of the questions regarding Ruggiero's particular case also point toward the larger issue of the structural and dynamic relations between the allegorical site of education and the historical locale which it apparently glosses and which it proposes to transform by sponsoring a program of action and existence. How accurately does Alcina's fantastic world describe the world of nature and history? Even more important, how can Ruggiero, or the reader, detect those resemblances given the differences in outer appearance between the two? What, for instance, is the structural relationship of Alcina, who inspires Ruggiero's lust with allegorical trickery, to Angelica, who does the same with the bare facts of her dazzling and impenetrable (in several senses) surface? A reexamination of the precepts of Melissa, the consequences they seem to promise for Ruggiero's future existence, and the twin goals of fame and family, seen as means of achieving identity, will show that, even before his return, Ruggiero's difficulties are implicitly foreseen.

As Melissa's prophecy for Bradamante had earlier demonstrated (III.24), as Atlante's pathetic justification of his fatherly deception of Ruggiero had confirmed (IV.29–35), and as Melissa herself knows perfectly well (VII.43–44), there is a strict economy involved in Ruggiero's access to the heroic, genealogical identity which marriage to Bradamante, conversion to Christianity, and foundation of the Este dynasty offer him: the acquisition of these goods is to be accomplished only by suffering a great evil—premature, treacherous death. There is even a legitimate doubt as to whether Ruggiero should not remain safely, albeit ignominiously, with Alcina, or instead follow Melissa's counsel and lose his life. It has been pointed out that Ruggiero is actually the exceptional visitor to Alcina who will never be transformed into part of the landscape, since Alcina, as the reader discovers quite late, is in fact under the magical control of Atlante, who is acting by his lights to protect Ruggiero (VII.43–44).[127] It is possible then that the moral dilemma in which our hero finds himself is merely a screen for another choice, the classic dilemma of the epic hero at the crossroads between two mutually exclusive modes of existence: *either* protracted life in anonymity *or* return to action with concomitant subordination of the self, while still living, to various political and social obligations, and to the guarantee of an early death. The most famous examples of this oft-enacted choice are, of course, Achilles and Aeneas. From this perspective, Melissa is again assimilated to Ulysses' highly ambiguous trickery in locating Achilles and leading him off to the Trojan war.[128] On the other side, Atlante (through his puppet, Alcina) seems not so much to be trying to destroy or corrupt Ruggiero as he is struggling to save a life, an aim he shares with other overprotective mentors in the poem (i.e., Malagigi with Rinaldo; the two fairies with Grifone and Aquilante). He is intent, "solamente / a darli vita . . . / . . . più tosto volea che lungamente / vivesse e senza fama e senza onore / che, con tutta la laude che sia al mondo / mancasse un anno al suo viver giocondo" ("only to give him life . . . [H]e wished rather that he live long, without fame and without honor, than that, even for all the praise in the world, he should lose one year of delightful living" VII.43.5–8). Once this well-intentioned aim, however misguided it may be, is understood, Atlante's enterprise may almost seem to contrast favorably with Melissa's, and even Bradamante's, willingness to sacrifice his life. According to Melissa, secular eternity through fame and family demands a literal "death of the self" before the new, integral "I" is born, just as Pauline, Augustinian conversion requires a spiritual one.[129] In order to judge the significance of this crisis of death, to see whether

---

[127] Kennedy, "Ironic Allegory," pp. 61, 65. As Hanning ("Ariosto, Ovid and the Painters," p. 108) observes, the emotional pathos which attaches itself to the jilted Alcina (esp. x.54–56) also undermines the rejection of her as allegorical Vice personified.

[128] See Chapter 1, n. 37. For the *Iliad/Furioso* parallels, see Chapter 4, n. 151.

[129] See Freccero, "Infernal Conversion" and "Dante's Prologue Scene," and Romans 5–7.

it mediates pure loss and absence, or pure realization of identity, or something in between, I will have to consider more carefully the value and meaning of those remnants which survive the mortal part of man.

The text explicitly shows Melissa offering Ruggiero a name (which is the natural product of his virtuous being), as well as the natural continuity of his life in his virtuous and famous descendants. This natural expression and perdurance of identity is in stark contrast to the unnatural counterpoint of Astolfo be-myrtled, whose name is lost ("il nome mio *fu* Astolfo" vi.33.1) and who is sterile, unable to generate a family (54.3). Melissa emphasizes the apparent contrast by redeploying imagery associated with Alcina and Astolfo in order to correct their failings. Of all these repetitions with a twist, most striking is a quiet application of the imagery of plants and trees to the metamorphosis *in bono* which Melissa projects for Ruggiero. At first Ariosto seems to be offering a version of the humanistic image of education as organic growth, the pupil as plant to be "cultivated."[130] The unnatural metamorphosis of Polydorus, Pier delle Vigne, or Ulysses is exchanged for an organic translation of form more in line with the usual interpretation of Ovid, the flow of being from one shape to another in which, ultimately, nothing is lost, not even Ovid himself, who, in the last metamorphosis of all, becomes his own text.[131] Ruggiero's role as founder of the Este dynasty, as hinted earlier, involves his becoming the root of a family tree:

> Deh, non vietar che le più nobil alme
> che sian formate ne l'eterne idee,
> di tempo in tempo abbian corporee salme
> dal ceppo che radice in te aver dee!   [vii.61.1–4]

---

[130] Cf. Garin, *L'Educazione in Europa,* p. 138.

[131] *Metamorphoses* xv.871–79: "Iamque opus exegi, quod nec Iovis ira nec ignis / nec poterit ferrum nec edax abolere vetustas. / cum volet, illa dies, quae nil nisi corporis huius / ius habet, incerti spatium mihi finiat aevi: / parte tamen meliore mei super alta perennis / astra ferar, nomenque erit indelebile nostrum. / Quaque patet domitis Romana potentia terris, / ore legar populi, perque omnia saecula fama, / siquid habent veri vatum praesagia, vivam!" Jordan ("Enchanted Ground," pp. 139–40) remarks on the vegetation imagery associated with Ruggiero in canto vii.

O, do not forbid that the most noble souls formed among the eternal
ideas take on corporeal substance, from time to time, in that trunk whose
roots begin in you!

> . . . a piegarti a questo tante e tante
> anime belle aver dovesson pondo,
> che chiare, illustri, inclite, invitte e sante
> son per fiorir da l'arbor tuo fecondo   [62.1–4]

The many, many lovely souls which—bright, illustrious, renowned, in-
vincible and holy—will flower from your fecund tree must have due
weight in moving you to this

Previously, the narrator had also used plant imagery in describing
Melissa's fears that Ruggiero's subjugation would deprive him of
his heroic name:

> E così il fior de li begli anni suoi
> in lunga inerzia aver potria consunto
> sì gentil cavallier, per dover poi
> perdere il corpo e l'anima in un punto;
> e quel odor, che sol riman di noi
> poscia che 'l resto fragile è defunto,
> che tra' l'uom del sepolcro e in vita il serba,
> gli saria stato tronco o svelto in erba.   [41]

And thus a knight so noble might have spent the flower of his fair years
in lingering sloth; in a single instant then to lose both body and soul;
and that fragrance, which alone remains of us when the fragile balance
has dissolved, which raises man from the tomb and preserves him in life,
would have been cut off or nipped in the bud.

At first it appears that her concern is for Ruggiero's immortal soul,
but the emphasis quickly shifts to "quel odor," which in this bizarre
mixture of metaphors soon turns into grass or a tree susceptible to
being "nipped in the bud," and which, as we saw earlier, stands
for Petrarchan *fama* (the poet uses the same words to refer to nom-
inal poetic resurrections on at least two other occasions: XXXV.23;
XXXVII.16, 18). The echo of the *Trionfo della Fama* in line 7, con-
nected with the plant imagery, alludes plainly enough to Petrarch's
preferred Ovidian myth, the metamorphosis of Daphne into the
laurel, symbol of poetic glory. A number of other images, puns,

etc. reinforce the assimilation of Ruggiero to a tree both genealogical and literary (cf. 1.4.3–4, VI.17.3–4, VII.37.5, 56.7; as well as XXXV.7, XLI.2–3, XLIV.10, XLVI.81.5) and thus set up the contrast between his metaphorical metamorphosis *in bono* and the unnatural, literal alienation of Astolfo.

The organic, natural continuity between Ruggiero's life and the name and family which survive his physical death is partly founded on the fact that he apparently embraces both goals by his own choice, authenticating and creating the self in its freedom. His act of "giudizio" seems to liberate him from a "fata" ("fairy," but suggesting "fato" and "fatale," i.e., *fatality*) who enslaves him by paralyzing his will. When he blindly pursues Angelica, he seems to fall back into that enslavement, losing all critical facility. One at first assumes that another lesson in the reading of self and others is in order. Curiously enough, however, there is a level at which the poem stresses much less the process of active learning and much more what one is destined to become after death, when the will to action in the human arena has dissolved forever. The genealogical "inalberamento" of Ruggiero may actually imply not active reading and choice, but rather passive acquiescence in a "fiero destino." Bradamante may think, and the reader is at first likely to be convinced, that she and Melissa are trying to restore her fiancé's "libertà" (IV.34.5–6; cf. VII.39.7), but the text repeatedly suggests that his marriage and conversion are causally linked to his death and that all three are predestined, written in the stars (IV.29, 30, 35; VII.58, 60), and that neither he nor anyone else, least of all Atlante, is able to alter matters. The "fata" from whom he was "freed" cannot die (X.56), but *his* "freedom" is indeed fatal. Ruggiero's "choice," and it is not his choice, since Melissa somehow forgets to mention to him the risk he runs, is thus between one form of depersonalization and another, rather than between subjugation and liberty.

The episode, I believe, alludes obliquely to a myth which shifts the focus from the tree as organic expression of continued life back to the tree as unnatural, uncanny emblem of an unnatural dependence of heroic life on an exterior object, whose profoundest meaning is not its survival but its reification and death. At first, this myth is associated only with Astolfo and can be linked only heuristically, or, at best, by remote analogy, with Ruggiero. Only later will I be able to show the subtle and unexpected return of the motif in a context which links it more closely with Ruggiero himself and with the problem of chivalric-humanistic identity in general. We saw earlier that Ariosto's use of the Ulysses and Pier delle Vigne cantos produces the following images of a being trapped within a burning piece of wood:

> Come ceppo talor, che le medolle
> rare e vòte abbia, e posto al fuoco sia,
> poi che per gran calor quell'aria molle
> resta consunta ch'in mezzo l'empìa,
> dentro risuona e con strepito bolle
> tanto che quel furor truovi la via;
> così murmura e stride e si coruccia
> quel mirto offeso, e al fine apre la buccia.   [VI.27]

Like a trunk, sometimes, whose core is hollowed and empty, and which is then placed on the fire—when the moist air that filled its center is consumed by heat, it resounds within and boils uproariously until the fury finds a way out; just so the wounded myrtle murmurs and screeches and mutters angrily and finally barks out its words.

> Poi si vide sudar su per la scorza,
> come legno dal bosco allora tratto,
> che del fuoco venir sente la forza   [32.1–3]

then he saw it sweat through the bark, like a log just brought from the woods which feels the force of fire approaching

In the context of a culture steeped in Ovidian myths, in an episode which alludes to the Ovidian metamorphoses of Daphne, Arethusa (19), Ganymede, and perhaps others, this conflation seems designed to call forth the memory of yet another Ovidian tree myth which is not quite a metamorphosis: the myth of Meleager.

Meleager, classical forerunner of Dorian Gray, was attended at birth by a prophecy that his life would continue only so long as a piece of wood, then burning on the hearth, should remain unconsumed. His mother, Altheae, immediately snatched the burning brand from the fire, extinguished it, and kept it faithfully until, years later, angered by Meleager's slaying of his uncles (her brothers), she threw it again into the fire, thus "truncating" his existence.[132] Associated specifically with Astolfo, the importance of this myth seems limited, serving only to reinforce the already obvious dilemma, where a tree can literally stand for and determine a human life. Ruggiero's tree-ness is not initially associated with flame. Curiously, however, Meleager seems a particularly apt figure for the destined death which awaits him. Like Meleager's, Ruggiero's destiny is linked to a "tree" (the Estense family tree), and, like Meleager, his death is determined by the "rhetorical" substitution of a tree for a life. What is not obvious, but may be subversively implied, is that Ruggiero could be somehow submitted to a horrible alienation and loss of self-control by which the self is effaced rather than constituted. He would then, instead of a Daphne organically transmuted into the tree of poetry and genealogy, become what even in Ovid is an obvious anti-Daphne: Meleager—not freed by arboreal metamorphosis, but trapped by an arbitrary destiny; not living perennially, but only prematurely dead.

Only after Ruggiero's return to Europe does this possibility threaten to become reality, but the prediction of a destined "inalberamento" already does put into jeopardy some of the values and methods of the education which Ruggiero is undergoing. In the logic of the "allegory of education," Ruggiero becomes a "lettore" who can "elect," choosing by interpretation, and he thus escapes the dividedness of allegory and enters a condition where his being is transparently legible in his name, his appearance, his familial offshoots. But the "counterplot" which I am unfolding suggests that, on the contrary, he is not reader and elector, but is himself "prescritto" (IV.35.6), "already written" into an inescapable destiny, and that it is he who is "eletto" (VII.60.2) rather than electing, and thus unable to get outside an inhuman structure which engulfs the self. In structuralist parlance he is merely "parole," subjected to a determining "langue," a rhetoric of the stars.[133] His "death" would then be the unmistakable sign of a return to the

---

[132] Ovid, *Metamorphoses* VIII.270–546, esp. 445–525. There may be an echo of the Ovidian story, as well as of Virgil and Dante in VI.27: see 511–14 for the moaning of the brand as it burns. Compare Bradamante's fears that "alta necessità" "avea *tronca* / . . . la vita lieta" of Ruggiero (VII.37.5–6).

[133] Cf. Chapter 2, n. 61.

condition of allegory, to the separation and alienation of the self from the hidden forces by which it is determined and deprived of free will and from the posthumous marks by which it ought to be identified. He would then be a "tree" not so easily distinguishable from that which encloses Astolfo. Furthermore, if genealogical destiny is a "prescription" of the self, fame is its "postscript." The Petrarchan echoes noted above, along with the close association between trees and writing throughout the episode, make it clear that Ruggiero's second hope to overcome death is to be turned into a famous name celebrated in poetic writing. Throughout the poem, Ariosto links burial and death to fame.[134] The value of the name, *arche* and *telos* of the humanistic scheme of education, depends upon the link of historicity, of propriety, between the name and the being to whom it goes on referring across time and space, across the chasm of death itself.[135] If no such link persists, the "renaissance" of the self after death is fictive and the process of exemplary education is founded on spurious names in lying texts, just as St. John suggests in canto XXXV (stanzas 22–29).

Alcina's metamorphosis of Astolfo may already constitute a subtle critique of the specifically Petrarchan value of poetic fame, since she, like Petrarch, transforms, reduces, the beloved into literature and the poetic laurel, in a process of idolatrous (t)reification which ultimately loses sight of the beloved creature behind or within the "tree"/"text."[136] By apparently celebrating the beloved, Alcina as

[134] For instance in the Clorindano and Medoro episode (XVIII.165.2–5, 168.5–8, 169.1, 169.5–8, 170.7–8, 171.4). See also the connection made between Issabella's death, her famous name, and the monumental sepulcher raised to her by Rodomonte. See again also XXXVII.1.7–8, 10.7–8, 13.8, 16.5–8, 18.5–8. Cf. Chesney, *Rabelais and Ariosto*, p. 158.

[135] For the "impropriety" of the "proper name," see Derrida, *Of Grammatology*, esp. pp. 107–118, as well as "Edmond Jabès," p. 70: "only that which is written gives me existence by naming me. It is thus simultaneously true that things come into existence and lose existence by being named." For a derivative (yet unacknowledged, as if to prove Derrida's point) application of the theme to other aspects of Ariosto's text, see Bonifazi, *Le Lettere*, p. 110. See also Ossola, "Métaphore et Inventaire," p. 186.

[136] For the theme of Petrarchan textual idolatry, see Robert Durling, "Petrarch's 'Giovene Donna Sotto un Verde Lauro,'" *MLN* 86 (1971); Freccero, "The Fig-Tree and the Laurel: Petrarch's Poetics," *Diacritics* 5 (Spring 1975). For the theme and hermeneutics of idolatry as applied to the *Furioso* itself, see Chapter 4, nn. 16 and 60.

Petrarch actually puts him to silence, so that he can never narrate her hidden corruption (vi.51). And as Alcina's spell takes hold of Ruggiero, he undergoes a thorough change within, leaving only his *name* intact: "Non era in lui di sano altro che 'l nome; / corrotto tutto il resto" ("Nothing in him was healthy besides the name, the rest was all corrupt" vii.55.5–6). These words, which echo from Circe's transformation of Picus in *Metamorphoses* xiv.396, climax the narrative of seduction, unfolding at last its full effects. It is in this condition of separation that Melissa finds him and undertakes to make name and being one again. But she begins her own endeavors by making their aims literally, structurally, nominally indistinguishable from Alcina's, just as she makes her appearance indistinguishable from Atlante's: the survival of the *name alone* "poscia che 'l resto fragile è defunto" (41.6). She too assumes the unhealable split of being and name, "il resto" and "l'odor." Melissa, for all her apparent humanism, is in the same business as the antihumanistic Alcina, as the "prehumanist" Petrarch, of promoting signs at the expense of the "rest," the rest being precisely the sum total of physical and spiritual being. She too turns men into names. By failing to acknowledge this fact, and especially by refusing to make it part of Ruggiero's own choice, Melissa is once again disguising allegorical dividedness with a natural mimetic surface which purports to represent inner being exactly. She, like Alcina, intends a depersonalizing reification of the self into a tree; but, unlike Alcina, her metamorphosis presupposes not the concealment, but the literal death of the self so treated.

The possibility of this split, the evident fragility of the "properness" of the proper name, becomes the grounds time and again in the Renaissance for sharp qualification of the value of fame, its function as consequence and reward of virtue. One would expect such qualification from a neo-Platonist such as Landino, who sees Juno (i.e., worldly ambition and the lure of glory) as the greatest of many obstacles to Aeneas' conquest of inner virtue and spiritual knowledge.[137] But it appears as well in the very humanists who

---

[137] Landino, *Disputationes,* gives "aenus," or "praise," as the etymology of Aeneas (bk. iii, p. 128), but goes on to allegorize Juno in the way mentioned (bk. iii, pp. 160 ff., 182, 186).

value fame the most, beginning with Petrarch himself. In the
Secretum, "Augustinus" repeatedly attacks "Francesco" for his pur-
suit of the laurel (p. 138), on the grounds that he is substituting
nominal perdurance and human concerns for ontological salvation
and worship of the divine, that it gives "life" to a mere name while
contributing to the eternal "death" of the soul. He says, following
a classical *topos,* that fame "is nothing other than speech about some-
one made public and scattered through the mouths of many," a
"fickle breeze" (which completes the triple pun of Laura/lauro/auro
and then reduces its value to mere rhetorical wind).[138] Glory should
be the "re-collection" of the self; and yet the repetition of it scatters
it, like Pico's Osiris, makes it irreducibly plural, subjects it to the
whim of gossip, envy, etc., and turns it from proper name into
common property, from unity to multiplicity. Castiglione has
"Ludovico da Canossa" argue forcefully for the value of literary
fame as the best stimulus to imitation of great deeds (1.xliii), but
soon after has him allow for the contradictory recognition that "da
natura tutti siamo avidi troppo . . . di laude, e più amano le orecchie
nostre la melodia delle parole che ci laudano, che qualunque altro
suavissimo canto . . . ; e però spesso, come voci di sirene, sono causa
di summergere chi a tal fallace armonia bene non se le ottura" ("by
nature we are too greedy . . . for praise; and our ears love much
more the melody of words that flatter us than any other song,
however sweet . . . ; and thus they often, like the voices of Sirens,
cause the drowning of whoever fails to stop his ears against such
false harmony" 1.xliv). "Ludovico" then goes on to say that books
do not help to teach us how to distinguish flattery from true praise.
Thus desire for glory which breeds virtue can also lead to self-
deception and a complacent willingness to stay as we are. As Erasmus
also suggested, that very fame with which Melissa tempts Ruggiero/
Ulysses can be a sort of Siren, a destroying singer, like Alcina and

---

[138] "[Fama] nichil esse aliud quam sermonem de aliquo vulgatum ac sparsum per
ora multorum," "aura volubilis" (*Secretum,* in *Prose,* bk. III, p. 190; cf. pp. 166–68).
Note also that the *Trionfo della Fama,* which supersedes that of Death, is itself in turn
superseded by the *Trionfi* of Time and Eternity. See especially *Trionfo del Tempo,*
l. 143 ("chiamasi Fama ed è morir secondo") and l. 145 ("così il Tempo trionfa i
nomi e 'l mondo").

her Sirenian ladies.[139] Then there is Alberti, who at first seems an exemplary humanist, suggesting in the *Della Famiglia* that fathers incite sons to "seguire virtù e fama" ("pursue virtue and fame" bk. I, p. 52). Nonetheless in the *Momus* he represents Fama allegorically as a monster (illegitimate fruit of the rape of Praise by Momus) who "mixes true with false," just like Fraud and, for that matter, just like poets (including Alberti himself); who is as likely to praise as to blame; and who iterates the fictions of idle gossip more often than she reflects the true natures of those whose names she bandies about.[140] Alberti satirizes one of the founding myths of humanism when he has Fama, following the plan of Fortuna, bear Hercules from mortal humanity to immortal divinity, implying, of course, that the story of the hero's apotheosis is pure chatter.[141] Ariosto's awareness of this demonic version of fame can also be detected in *Satira* v: "la fama, / più che del ver, del falso relatrice, / la qual patisce mal chi l'onor ama" ("fame, purveyor more of falsity than truth, hardly tolerable to one who loves honor" 44–46). There were, obviously, ample precedents for a "humanistic" critique of humanistic glory, and Ariosto's text may be merely more thoroughgoing than most in this regard.[142]

I have suggested that Ruggiero's destiny is written and that what

---

[139] *Moriae Encomium, id est Stultitiae Laus,* ed. C. H. Miller, vol. 4, pt. 3 in *Opera Omnia* (Amsterdam and Oxford: North-Holland, 1979), p. 102: "Quid Q. Curtium in specum traxit nisi inanis gloria, dulcissima quaedam Siren, sed mirum quam a sapientibus istis damnata?" Elsewhere we learn that poetic fame is the aspiration of Philautia (self-love) and the gift of Kolakia (flattery), the two greatest follies of all (p. 140).

[140] See *Momus* (Martini edition, pp. 37–49) for the allegory of Fama. For Fraud, Fame, and Momus himself as "vera falsis miscens," see pp. 14, 21, 40, 54, passim.

[141] Ibid., pp. 43–45. See also the later, mocking, episode of the divinized Hercules' defense of man to the gods, especially his comments on the pursuit of glory (pp. 91–94).

[142] Among the critics who have broached the theme of fame in the *Furioso*, see, especially, Jordan, "Enchanted Ground," p. 196. Robert Griffin, *Ludovico Ariosto* (New York: Twayne, 1974), p. 81, briefly traces *fama* in the Renaissance, from Petrarch's desire for it to Sannazaro's condemnation of it, and indicates that Ariosto's attitude toward it was at least ambiguous. Chesney, in her chapter "Time and Art" (*Rabelais and Ariosto,* pp. 135–70, esp. 157–59), also has some very suggestive things to say on the subject. The *locus classicus* for ambiguous or evil Fama is *Aeneid* IV.173 ff.

it writes is that he, like Tennyson's Ulysses, will "become a name," losing liberty to become a *libro*.[143] Given this split between name and being, it is clear that Ruggiero bids fair to become what the reader already in some sense knows him to be: a genealogical fiction for purposes of obsequiously celebrating the Este family. Where poetry seemed to be at the service of ethics, ethical education now appears to be in the business of turning people into fictional texts. Ruggiero's name may ultimately be as distant from the real him as Alcina's island is from the world of the poem, as Ariosto's readers sometimes feel themselves to be from the fantasies of the *Furioso*. What indications, then, are there that this scenario is played out by Ruggiero in the world of "history" to which he returns? And for that matter, is it still not possible to see in this death the fructifying potential of exemplary education of others via the famous name (fictive or no) and of genealogical flowerings? His first activity on returning to *terra cognita* provides a surprisingly clear gloss on the nature and value of nominal and familial identity. The review of the British forces and their "insegne" seems initially to be an instance of the most banal epic formality, one of those passages in the *Furioso* which has consistently been damned as encomiastic fertilizer or worse.[144] In this case, the usual dullness of the troop review is intensified by the fact that its subjects are (by and large) not important participants either in the action of the poem or in the courtly world of the Italian *Cinquecento*. Seen, however, as the first event of Ruggiero's "postgraduate" life (it is, after all, an ascent by degrees), as the first characterization of the reality that he returns to, and as the immediate sequel to Logistilla's island, these stanzas take on a completely unexpected relevance. They become emblems, by virtue of their oblique yet central contribution to the problem at hand, of what may be the most important rules of structure in the poem: the intimate thematic and textual relation of episodes which superficially

---

[143] Compare the suggestive title of Ruggiero Ruggieri's essay on the derivation of the names of characters in chivalric epics, especially the *Furioso:* "I Nomi Parlanti . . ." in *L'Umanesimo Cavalleresco Italiano* (Napoli: Fratelli Conte, 1977), pp. 308–323. See also Croce, "Ariosto," p. 50.

[144] Rajna (*Le Fonti,* pp. 192–94) makes a particularly scathing attack against "la soverchia lunghezza e la stuchevole monotonia" (p. 191) of this conventional troop review.

have nothing in common; the unexpected complexity of the seemingly most trivial details.

The comparison between the just-completed sojourn with Logistilla and the review of the troops is most noticeably marked by a curious verbal echo and a certain structural parallel. Only twenty-six stanzas before the review begins, the "galeotto" announces to Ruggiero that Logistilla "t'insegnerà" (x.47.1). Over the course of those intervening stanzas, as seen above, a complex "insegnamento" is carried out. In this light, the references to the "insegne" and cognates (78.5, 82.5, 85.6, 86.1, 86.8, 90.3) are surely meant to echo this use of the verb for teaching. The question is *why:* What bridge in meaning fulfills the etymological relation between the process of instruction and this proliferation of the cryptic emblems of heraldry? One strange link can be seen in the fact that, even after an instruction in the reading of (obscure) signs, Ruggiero still has to have a lesson in the meaning of the "insegne" (just as Astolfo will later require an explanation of the lunar allegory): "mira le varie insegne e ne favella, / e dei signori britanni i nomi impara" ("he gazes at the coats of arms and comments on them and learns the names of the British lords" 90.3−4). It is indeed odd that in his first moments back in Europe Ruggiero, who had apparently become a "maestro" in his own right (67.7), following the footsteps of the "Magi" (69.7−8), should be in the position of having things (or rather, signs which stand for names) explained to him. In spite of this hint of a retrograde motion in Ruggiero's reading habits, however, the immediate effect of this analogy between allegorical "insegnamento" and historical "signification" is to confirm the goals which Ruggiero's teachers had set for him. Each of the "insegne" represents the *name* of a noble *family*. They are, in effect, the reified symbols of chivalric identity. While Logistilla's "insegnamento" tended toward a reading of inner and outer signs in order to attain and maintain identity, these are the signs which represent achieved identity.[145] What is more, they blend the two possibilities for realizing identity raised by Melissa: name and family. *Reading signs one becomes a sign.* By ethical "formazione" one achieves symbolic form.

---

[145] Porcacchi (in Orlandini edition), *Annotazioni* to canto xiv.33 (in which Orlando adopts a black insignia which hides his true identity, even as it expresses

Chivalric humanism seems to find its realization and highest justification in this tiresome parade of "insegne."

Looked at in this way, the "insegne" are the perfect enactment in history of Melissa's promises on the allegorical margin. But, with deep irony, a series of echoes and parallels point even further back, back to Alcina's rather than Melissa's mode of being. The bizarre truth is that these shields accomplish a truly Circean metamorphosis, representing human beings as birds, beasts, flowers, trees, etc. Alcina confined men to the extrinsic subhuman signs of lower nature, thus "denaturing" them; and, by this satirical juxtaposition, heraldry is given a similarly debasing and antihuman function. Worse still, just as Ruggiero seems to have returned to the domain of mimetic nature and trustworthy appearances, natural objects are again converted into cryptic allegories of human identity which only the initiated can penetrate. History, it appears, may be just as "allegorical," just as persistently split between outer sign and inner being, as Alcina's realm, and is not at all the promised site of the untroubled intersection of virtuous being and famous name. Ruggiero's initial inability to read signs like the one he is fated to generate himself signals an unhappy disjunction between the supposedly interconnected moments of reading and being written.

By haunting the apparent triumph of Melissa with the spectral absent-presence of Alcinian bestiality and duplicity, the episode brings these two contraries into an unanticipated and puzzling identity. Melissa's earlier adoption of Alcina's tactics had been justified with reference to the ends she envisioned, but now that distinction falters. The contamination of Melissa's project suggests the appropriateness of a more thoroughgoing version of Giamatti's (and earlier Momigliano's) argument that apparent moral victories become mere vehicles for vice's triumph. This version, however, would contaminate even the positive lessons which Ruggiero (or the reader) subsequently learns from Melissa and Logistilla. It is in keeping

---

his true feelings), comments that *imprese* are meant to body forth our inner state. He cites vii.4, xvii.72, and xxxii.47 in the same connection. Cf. *Cortegiano* i.ix, and Ariosto's own *Capitolo* iv, for cases of deliberately cryptic *imprese* (which are, nonetheless, not quite the same thing as heraldic *insignia*) which defeat successful interpretation. See also Chesney (*Rabelais and Ariosto*, pp. 49–53)

with Ariosto's oblique sense of irony that in canto XLIII a "Melissa" will again appear, again in the business of exposing the infidelity of an apparently faithful lover, but now motivated by an erotic itch not much different (though less successfully "gratified") than Alcina's.[146] By, on the one hand, assimilating Alcina to the admirable (though obviously utopian) purposes of Atlante and, on the other, assimilating Melissa to Alcina's degrading project of allegorical reification, the poem lowers the boundaries between instruction and corruption, education and seduction, mimesis and allegory, nature and monstrosity, humanity and inhumanity. The distinction made earlier between Alcina's aesthetic, purely outward "formazione" and Melissa's ethical "formazione," which ostensibly shapes an inner virtue to match an outer form and vice versa, is an early casualty of this mingling.

Once such a contamination has been noticed, a certain heraldic image, twice repeated, leaps to the reader's attention:

> Del duca di Chiarenza è quella face:
> quel arbore è del duca d'Eborace   [78.1–2]

That flame belongs to the Duke of Clarence; that tree to the Duke of York

> Ne lo stendardo il primo ha un pino ardente   [88.1]

The standard of the first bears a burning pine

The "rassegna" of "insegne" thus echoes not only the general contours of a Circean landscape, but also Astolfo's entrapment in a tree (cf. 80.6) and the metaphorical flames which envelop it and him. These echoes seal the identification of the emblems with Alcina's island, and they also renew the implicit associations with the myth of Meleager, converting my earlier heuristic recourse to direct allusive relevance. True, they still do not apply directly to Ruggiero,

---

[146] For Melissa turned temptress, see XLIII.21–49, esp. 24, 45–46. For a gallant effort to rescue Melissa from this kind of contamination, see Donato Internoscia, "Are There Two Melissas, Both Enchantresses, in the *Furioso?*" *Italica* 25 (1948). He answers in the affirmative. Nonetheless, after nearly thirty years of writing and revising the poem, Ariosto would doubtless have noticed the confusion and remedied it, if it were not a deliberate strategy.

but they do inform the values of name and genealogy in which he is schooled and which all the tree imagery goes to support. In fact, the lack of direct identification seems a deliberate strategy to illustrate both Ruggiero's and the reader's inability to detect their own schizophrenic situation in the images they see/read. Hidden within the pageantry, which Ruggiero views from the vantagepoint of disinterested admiration, is a sign of his own imminent demise, his own disappearance into the death of allegorical signhood. And the violent bridging of the apparently insurmountable distance between reader and allegorical sign may well suggest by analogy the bored disinterest of most readers of these particular stanzas, their understandable blindness to this segment's relevance both to Ruggiero and to themselves.

This interpretation of the troop review is supported by the poem-long series of chivalric contests revolving around possession of essentially arbitrary emblems of heroic identity—a sword, a suit of armor, a horse, an "insegna." The most striking sequence of this kind is the generalized outbreak of rivalries among the pagans encamped outside Paris. The climactic event is the duel between Ruggiero and Mandricardo over the right to own in its entirety a suit of armor of which each currently possesses a part—and with it, most important, clear title to the silver eagle, "insegna" of the house of Troy from which Ruggiero (and the Este) are supposedly descended (XXVI.98–105; XXX.17 ff.). Now it is Ruggiero's familial-heroic identity which is *directly* at stake in the emblem. And it is particularly, comically, apt that we should be reminded of the eagle's special significance for the house of Troy as "l'augel che rapì in Ida Ganimede" ("the bird that abducted Ganymede from Mount Ida" XXVI.100.2), in light of Ruggiero's earlier Ganymede-like helplessness aboard the hippogryph. Notwithstanding these claims to legitimate ownership of the shield, however, what the episode stresses at every turn is precisely that this or any other identifying emblem is arbitrary and that each hero is right in accusing the other of usurpation (XXVI.104–105). One knight cannot be differentiated from the other (XXX.22.1–2). Random chance constantly intervenes in their contest (22–26, passim). Similarly specious quarrels multiply throughout the pagan camp. Doralice launches a demystifying attack on Mandricardo's fatal obsession with honor and name (32–42).

In short, in every way the poem insists that "their quarrel is a zero" (29.5). What emerges, as Donato has shown, is a perfect instance of what Girard calls "mimetic rivalry," an irrepressible spiral of violence born of attempts to impose differences between self and others where none in fact exist, by means of the possession of arbitrary objects whose value is always and only determined by the desire of the other for it.[147]

It has recently been suggested that the possession of property is a, possibly the, key to the problem of Renaissance chivalric identity in the poem. For the knights, property is ostensibly an extension of the identity of the one to whom it is "proper," even though no object ever really stays attached for long to a single owner. Theft and violence, and even mere chance, are forever dislocating property, undermining the identities of owner and owned alike.[148] It is no accident, for instance, that the outbreak of violence in canto XXVI is prefaced by the viewing of Merlin's allegory of the monster Avarice (30 ff.): the monstrous desire for the possession of money (the arbitrary symbol of value *par excellence*) is depicted in the basrelief as that which knighthood is specifically engaged to combat (as Ruggiero fights the giantess Erifilla/Avarice). But, soon enough, it becomes obvious that avarice in its most generalized form (the

[147] My account is substantially indebted to Donato's Girardian reading of the poem and of this episode in particular ("Desire," esp. pp. 19–22). See also Girard, *Violence and the Sacred*, esp. chap. 6 ("From Mimetic Desire to the Monstrous Double"), pp. 143–68. On the question of chivalric furniture and identity, Sergio Zatti, in an unpublished essay entitled "L'Oggetto dell'Inchiesta," has very interesting things to say. See also DelCorno-Branca, *Romanzo Cavalleresco*, chaps. 2 and 3.

[148] Bonifazi, *Le Lettere*, pp. xxxiii, 112–19. For the most spectacular conflation of familial (i.e., nominal) and economic identity, written by one who was an illegitimate child and who had his inheritance tampered with by members of his own family, see *Della Famiglia*, bk. III ("Economicus"). Bonifazi might have taken the following words of Giannozzo as his epigraph: "cognosco chi getta via il suo esser pazzo" (p. 160). The best Ariostan example, not discussed by Bonifazi, comes in cantos XXXIII–XXXV (see Chapter 4, sec. i, below). One crucial area about which I have had little to say is that of sexual identity and the frequent collapses that the male/female opposition undergoes—for instance, in the Bradamante/Fiordispina/Ricciardetto farce; in anything having to do with Marfisa (especially her activities in the city of homicidal women); in canto XXXVII; etc., etc. This is a topic which has rightly generated a great deal of critical interest in the last few years (cf. Chapter 4, n. 225, below).

desire to constitute the self through possession of material objects) is *the* guiding motive of the chivalric enterprise, in which ethical-chivalric "valore" (valor) has more to do with economic "valore" (value) than one would like to think.

Property is like the name is like the family, all marking the identity of the self from without, all meeting in the "insegna," which thus becomes the perfect symbol both of the acquisition of identity and of its arbitrary, allegorical character. The climax of the treatment of naming and owning as expression of identity comes in canto XXXV, when St. John expounds the allegory of Time and of the poets who rescue names from oblivion after death. Whether or not the Evangelist can redeem what this episode so thoroughly sabotages remains to be seen in Chapter 4.

In any case, even if the truth of the person does not survive in the name, there is still a second, and perhaps stronger, justification for a return to history and for a willing self-sacrifice: the foundation of a line of great rulers. The value of such a gesture depends on at least two factors: on whether the flux and violence of history can really be mastered by the *virtù* of a great family, as the optimistic Alberti of *Della Famiglia* suggests they might; and on whether this particular family, the Este, possesses such a *virtù* (i.e., both the moral virtue to choose responsibly and the force to enact their choices). Chapter 1 already suggested certain resistances on both counts. It showed that this history of the family from Ruggiero to Ariosto's day was marked with violence and betrayal, both from without and, more pertinently, from within. In Chapter 4 the question will be raised and explored again, in much greater depth, with particular reference to Ariosto's deeply subversive treatments of his patron, Cardinal Ippolito d'Este. I can add now, however, that the threats operate in both directions, problems with Ruggiero reflecting on the Este and vice versa. On the one hand, the legitimacy of Ruggiero's choice is made to depend on whether or not the reign of the Estense brothers really justifies, to whatever degree, the poet's description of it as a "new golden age" (III.18, 51, 56). But there are broad hints that this account is merely another of the many encomiastic fictions of the Renaissance, bolstered by the tradition of turning classical scholarship into a tool for self-aggrandizement. On the other hand is the question of the legitimacy of Estense rule,

which should separate them from the dangerously extralegal illegit-
imacy of the tyrant. That legitimacy depends, or is made to depend
by Ariosto, on the legitimacy of Ruggiero as family founder. The
myth of origins which, in one sense, is a way of promoting the
family by giving it special ties to the past, even to Troy itself (as
Augustus was linked to Aeneas by Virgil), is, in another sense, a
way of building up the poet's patrons for a fall—mocking their
authority by tying it to a transparently fictional genealogy, to a
little knight who never was. Has the "family tree" been nourished
with liberal helpings of "organic" fictions? Ariosto, I believe, art-
fully teases out the double, subversive, paradox that Ruggiero's
death is justified by the lives of the family which allegedly derives
from him, while the Este are made to depend on the fiction of
Ruggiero's life, and thus on the kindness of a strange poet.

What seemed at first to be a successful humanistic education has
results, almost point for point, that not only suggest the inability
of humanism to accomplish the goals it sets for itself, but that also
demonstrate the existence of contradictions within those goals
which lead humanism into ultimate complicity in undermining it-
self. If Ulyssean abandonment of responsibility is attacked, by the
same token Herculean activism seems also to be destined for degen-
eration into purely literary irrelevance, if not worse. What begins
as a celebration of free will, of the individual's ability to recognize
vice and virtue and then to choose between them (by its choice
establishing an independent identity), ends with a self lost in erotic
folly and subjected to an impersonal destiny which means its proxi-
mate death. In Melissa's disingenuous hands, the educational project
of self-realization is merely a pretext, a screen, for the teaching of
cultural deceptions and political myths designed to repress and/or
appropriate individual energies and understandings rather than to
release or develop them. But it is not even clear that her scheming
has its intended beneficial effect on the community. *Virtus* and *hu-
manitas* disappear anew into bestial madness and treacherous death,
the two principal threats to individual identity, but also to the "res
publica" as a whole. If education does temporarily produce *virtus*,
its effects are indeed "short-lived": Ruggiero is soon back at the
point of Herculean choice, unable to remember his previous success.
The name is again severed from the inner man, *oratio* divorced from

ratio. No linear progression toward selfhood occurs. The hero circles back to an original condition of blindness and aching desire. But even if the education *did* produce virtue, virtue would not necessarily be faithfully reflected and rewarded by glory. Nor would the fictional example have the redeeming effect of guiding others toward the light, since educational examples keep turning out to be Circean snares. In a drastic parody of philological "insegnamento," the Ariostan self disappears, only to reappear as a "segno," but a "segno" which is at best tangentially related to virtuous being. The double humanistic *telos* of education, virtue and glory, is doubly subverted.

In fact, where neo-Platonism's excesses were successfully criticized as utopian and insane by recourse to humanistic categories, it now turns out that humanism's positive program is equally undermined by adoption of neo-Platonism's critique of corporality and materialism. I earlier argued that the episode of Alcina and Logistilla traces a didactic arc which leads naturally toward the values and practices of a modified ethical humanism, subsuming and appropriating some of the images and aspirations of the very neo-Platonism which it so harshly criticizes. Though that critique of idealism remains in place, a countercritique of man's possibilities in the natural world, begun on Alcina's island but apparently superseded, is renewed in neo-Platonic terms on Ruggiero's return to Europe. I have already shown that some of the poem's images derive from the Platonic tradition. It is no coincidence that at the end of canto X and the beginning of canto XI, and on into cantos XI–XIII as well, just as the "positive" Platonic metaphors (circle, sun, equine flight) are dissolving into parody, the poem offers up an especially dense cluster of images drawn from "negative" Platonism: horses as symbols of unreined animal passion (XI.1, 2, 13; cf. 10, 12); the forest or *silva* of corporality as the scene of human error (XI.15); the darkened cave and twisting labyrinth which are versions of the *silva* (XI.9–10; but also the Atlantean labyrinth where Ruggiero winds up [XII.17 ff.] and the hellish cave where Orlando discovers Issabella [XII.87ff.]); deceiving shadows (X.102). All of these figure forth the blindness, madness, and error which Platonism, and Ariosto, believe to be essential characteristics of life in the body (XI.1–2, 6–7, 9, 13).

Ariosto's most immediate, perhaps his primary, source of "negative Platonism" is the same book whose *positive* program he most directly attacks in his critique of self-transcendence through desire. If most of the references to Bembo's *Asolani* made in this study have tended to emphasize an ironic attack by Ariosto on his friend's spiritualized view of love, nonetheless he seems to owe a considerable debt to that treatise, particularly to the first book, with its metaphors of voyage and deviation and its harsh judgment on the violence and error of corporeal desire.[149] In the *Asolani,* book I is destined to be overcome dialectically in the two succeeding books, but Ariosto never gets beyond Platonism's critique of man in nature.[150] Along with Bembo, however, he does present a view of man trapped between, on the one hand, his own passions, which ensure that "la debolezza de' nostri giudicii è molta" ("the weakness of our judgment is great" bk. III.i, p. 125), and, on the other, the "al vero somiglianti apparenze" ("the true-seeming appearances" I.i, p. 11) which suborn perceptual errors and awaken misguided loves.[151] After being shown by Melissa how to penetrate outer appearances and by Logistilla how to master the self, and thus apparently having been given the critical judgment ("giudizio") which can heal the divisive crises of desire and deluding semblance, Ruggiero returns to the point where both he and the book began: "ecco il giudicio uman come spesso erra" ("behold how often human judgment strays" 1.7.2). Those errors are attributable both to Alcinian deceptions in outer appearance, which blind the intellect, and to the self's appetites, which paralyze the ethical will: "'l miser suole / dar facile credenza a quel che vuole" ("the wretch [the lover] usually gives easy credence to whatever he desires" 1.56.7–8).

---

[149] See *Asolani* I.i (Marti edition, pp. 11–12), for the combination of "errore" and "insegnamento" on the road (or sea voyage) of this life, and especially for the image of man at the crossroads unable to judge which way to turn (cf. I.vi, p. 19; II.xiii, pp. 84–88). See I.xi, pp. 26–27, where Perottino continues with his attack against love as "furore" (cf. I.xiii, p. 30; I.xvii, p. 37).

[150] In bk. II, Gismondo replies to Perottino's attack on "mad love" by offering a positive vision of sexual love. In bk. III, however, Lavinello *agrees* with Perottino that sexual desire is mad, but disagrees that it is truly love. He then offers a version of educational askesis through true spiritual love.

[151] *Asolani*, bk. III (Marti edition, pp. 124–25) and bk. I (p. 11).

Ruggiero cannot control his desire even though he probably does know better (XI.2) and cannot recognize as illusory the figure of Bradamante sent by Atlante. In retrospect, this crisis of judgment may have been signaled soon after he had apparently acquired "giudizio" from Logistilla (X.59). In the very next stanza, the poet remarks that "mal giudicar puossi" whether the natural material or the artifice with which it is elaborated is better (X.60.6–8). In the world to which Ruggiero returns, in any event, both will and intellect falter, both self and other are radically split from within, suggesting that even when we do possess ironic intellectual insight, we may still give in to passion and self-deception. For Bembo, a spiritual remedy remains: to escape from the "outer" deceptions of the body and material appearances into pure undivided innerness; but not for Ariosto. Thus the possibilities for human action and understanding seem bleak indeed, when even a pragmatic limit-conscious humanism is revealed to be as utopian and idealistic as any neo-Platonic idealism. Where Castiglione's agile dialectic *might* seem to accommodate, ever so precariously, both the active life of court and the contemplative path of askesis, in Ariosto the two clash and are reciprocally destabilized. Then again, it is not perfectly clear that even Castiglione finds a way to square the courtly master of political appearances with the rapt meditator on divine Beauty and Truth. Certainly there is no such synthesis imagined beyond the confines of the game and of the fragile Urbino court whose principals were dispersed or dead when the treatise finally appeared, as its author notes more than once.[152] Whatever the case for Castiglione, in the *Furioso* neo-Platonism cannot get beyond the material and the natural, while humanistic naturalism always seems to depends on a concealed, utopian metaphysics. Both are stuck in the no-place of Logistilla's domain and of poetic imagination.

If Platonism usurps an unwarranted divinity for man, that is in part because, given human passions and the illusory appearances of reality, "bisognerebbe aver occhio divino / per far di lor giudizio" ("one would need the eye of divinity to judge them" VI.69.6–7).

---

[152] It is tempting to argue that Ariosto was mocking the utopian fantasies of the *Cortegiano* and the Urbino court in his description of Atlante's first castle with its isolated courtly microcosm, its little world of undisturbed delights (IV.31–32).

No wonder that Ariosto is more tolerant of "Nicoletto" and "Fra Martin" in *Satira* VI than of the otiose humanists. Judgment, the critical facility through which will recognizes and chooses among perceptual and moral alternatives, is systematically called into question by the *Furioso*. A "crisis of criticism" or, even better, a "critique of judgment" is opened. "Giudizio" is in fact the Italian translation of the Greek word for criticism (and crisis). "Greek 'critos' means 'judgment' ['iudicium'] or 'adjudication' ['iudicatio'] in Latin," says Salutati, and the same translation can be found in Landino and doubtless in others.[153] The complex figure of Hercules at the Crossroads finds himself in crisis and makes a judgment which ostensibly resolves the crisis. Now we find that interpretive judgment is itself in crisis and that as Ruggiero/Hercules turned right, he may as well have been turning left, leaving the critics (including this one) to judge his crisis in judgment. By the tacit analogy established between Ruggiero's reading of Alcina and the critics' reading of Ruggiero's reading, it appears that a critic who claims to have extracted the text's meaning from beneath its surface is implicitly accused of usurping the role of God, who is the only legitimate judge of both truth and morality, even as that transgressing usurpation is partly excused as the only possible conduct in a world of intellectual blindness and moral error. Not only does the text represent a crisis in humanistic education, but the interpretation of that representation, by its own logic, is also in crisis, and with it various Renaissance hermeneutics and poetics of education.

v. *From Allegory and Mimesis to Alienation and Mimicry*

I have shown, successively, how Ruggiero's allegorical education contains implicit self-contradictions which involve it in the very same seductive duplicity which it was intended to annul, and how the return to an historical testing ground confirms both the failure of the education to make virtue "second-nature" for our hero and its insidious success in reducing him to a state not unlike that of "Astolfo inalberato." It remains to define more precisely the relation between the antipodal realm and the historical scene of

---

[153] "'Critos' enim Grece, Latine 'iudicium' vel 'iudicatio' dici potest," Salutati, *De Laboribus Herculis* III, xliii (vol. 2, p. 416) and Landino, *De Vera Nobilitate*, p. 109.

Ruggiero's madness and then to understand how that relation glosses the poem's situation vis-à-vis its readers (though not in any "linear" or straightforward fashion). Between the two areas, the poet specifically develops a complex play of resemblance and difference, most notably through the circular movement which binds them together. The uncertainty of this play seems to be fatal for Ruggiero's new-found identity, even as it makes it especially difficult to identify the poem's process of self-reference: i.e., the principle of identity which would bind the multiple work into a harmonious whole. The passage between the remote islands and the European mainland is structured as one between two modes of reference, allegory and mimesis, and, at the same time, is a movement of reference itself, referring allegorical writing to "real" situations. In charting the significance of return, I am also inspecting the very process of signification itself, comparing two textual modes which claim to have motivated relationships with their readers' situations and, simultaneously, observing the dramatization of a return from "story" to "history," which points to our own readings of the poem. To add even more complexity, the two modes, though initially opposed, become less and less distinct the more closely they are observed: Alcina forges an allegory of a seductively mimetic imitation of nature, while in the relatively "mimetic" world of history and nature nothing is quite what it appears to be, as simple surfaces give way repeatedly to allegorical depths. Finally, though the text mimes the relation of readers to itself, it does so always at the level of textuality (of its own, limited, point of view, so to speak), so that the problems both of its true reference to our situations and of our ability to perceive, distort, or blindly ignore that reference remain wide open: decidable only in individual transactions of reading and their aftermaths.

Ruggiero is apparently carried off to an utopian, literary world beyond the semiotic limits of reality. When he arrives, it turns out that this idyllic scene is actually a marginal and alienated gloss on the reality he left behind and that, by leaving history for allegory, he was really bound all along to circle back to what he hoped to escape, wiser then than when he had departed. And yet, by the time he does complete the circle, the referential relation so elaborately established seems to have vanished along with Angelica and her ring. Ruggiero is unchanged. Allegory should be a marginal and unlike version of reality, an Augustinian *regio dissimilitudinis* (the place of antisimile), like Dante's *Purgatorio* an estranged double of history, which allows "Dante" or Ruggiero or the reader to achieve a new and detached perspective on reality. These results, instead, suggest that allegorical literature is perfectly irrelevant to the reality it proposes to gloss: either because the very same superficial unlikeness of appearance which allows a detachment from the familiar world also prevents any systematic transfer of responses, since one is never in a position to recognize similar situations, or because allegory never really is anything but a self-referential aesthetic enterprise, using a didactic pretext for imaginative play.

The failure of this referential drama is actually implicit in the poem's treatment of the very metaphor, the perfect solar circle, which seemed to promise its success. That same circle not only dramatizes the referential process, but also the rhetoric of selfhood achieved through reading. The uneducated self, devoid of reason, is allegorically divided against itself, and the transit from ignorance to knowledge has the same structure as the rhetorical displacement from allegory to symbol: into a state where inner and outer correspond, where human appearance equals spiritual *humanitas*. It is thus that education has the form of a rhetorical trope, as rhetoric has the function of educating. Nevertheless, the connection fails, and the rhetoric of education seems just a fictional construct of a hopeful utopian humanism.

Where the ring allowed the penetration of Alcina by Ruggiero's newly acquired "reason," it now helps Angelica disappear in the face of his erotic madness. The same circular ring which revealed then, now conceals, as insight is traded for blindness. In fact, Ruggiero in his folly parodies the circular motion of self-possession and self-knowledge: "s'aggirava a cerco come un matto" ("he whirled in a circle like a madman" XI.7.2), showing implicitly how the "form" of education and sense easily becomes the "form" of madness and nonsense.[154] In point of fact, I should add, the circle undertaken is never quite brought to its expected close. When Ruggiero is suddenly gripped by desire for Angelica, he is just a short distance from

---

[154] Jordan ("Enchanted Ground," pp. 127–28) specifically contrasts the "grand circle" around the world with this mad circling, and suggests that the circle of eternity within time has been reduced to "the circle of nature's time" (fallen seasonal

the point from which he originally took off and yet:

non più tenne la via, come propose
prima, di circundar tutta la Spagna   [X.113.1–2]

he no longer held to the route he first proposed for himself, to circle all
of Spain

Though in isolation these words suggest merely a "grand tour" of
Iberia, in the larger context they allude to the grander circle which
would be closed by a return to his point of departure on the French–
Spanish border. Ruggiero veers off just short of completing the
circle and of realizing the metaphorical displacement of self which
would also be a completion of the self and its symbolic integration
into the natural and political orders. That skewed circle, that barely
opened spiral, which the text so subtly and yet so powerfully attrib-
utes to Ruggiero, signifies both the mad "repetitions in difference"
(lust for Angelica repeating desire for Alcina) to which the young
hero subjects himself and, at the same time, his inability to achieve
self-coherence. In larger terms, it is a proleptic hint of that "breaking
of the circle" which Marjorie Nicolson placed in a slightly later
epoch.[155] He repeats himself in just such a way as to make those

---

change and natural corruption) and even to the senseless circularity of Fortuna's ran-
dom whirlings. She also observes that Orlando's quest for Angelica is a humanized
version of Ceres' pathetic search for Proserpina, the seasonal myth *par excellence*
(XII.81–2; XIII.1–3). Donato ("Desire," p. 25) talks about "the incessant circular
motion to which the characters are submitted," while Giamatti argues that Ariosto
does value the straight line over the crooked and curved path ("Headlong Horses,
Headless Horsemen," p. 297). Shakespeare's Feste might have the last word on the
subject: "Foolery, sir, does walk about the orb like the sun: it shines everywhere"
(*Twelfth Night* III.i.42).
    [155] Nicolson, and even more Poulet, are interested in the "forms of conscious-
ness," in the sense that consciousness represents and understands itself through forms,
particularly the circle. My interest, by contrast, is not only in the forms deployed by
consciousness in attempting to express itself, but more specifically in the fact that
consciousness is *never* encountered directly, but only in these forms, as limited and
distanced aesthetic projections. The circle may be a metaphor of the self, but the self
inhabits it like Astolfo in his tree-text: unwillingly, and with a sense of helplessness
and even of betrayal. If we keep following out the metamorphoses and "translations"
of the circle to discover the truth of consciousness, we always find ourselves back
where we began, ready to start another ride around the hermeneutic wheel. The
forms of consciousness tend toward self-enclosure and exclusion of the self that made
them, though they continually veer toward it, brushing it tangentially.

repetitions almost unrecognizable, and thus useless as moments of education. From the notion of education as metaphorical displacement into identity, the reader is forced back upon the possibility that metaphor actually indicates no ontological identity or displacement, merely masking an undifferentiated sameness with an empty rhetorical appearance of progress.[156]

In thus attempting to imitate the sun's motion, its illumination and its eternity, Ruggiero is not able to appropriate literally the sun's unique identity and its natural presence.[157] Instead, the "imitation" (x.60.1, 70.8) is precisely an unnatural and fictive one, metaphoric in aesthetic terms, not in the metaphysical ones of Pico's *Heptaplus*. By assuming the semblance of eternity, Ruggiero does not designate his being but his desire (that is, his continued lack of being), just as the "nature" in which Astolfo is caught is a fiction of presence masking the "absence" which directs human desires. The experience of allegory has left no trace behind it on Ruggiero's essence; but, at the same time, his intended return to nature and self-presence actually exposes his doubled, alienated state of being, as imitation turns out to conceal allegory.

So, if in one sense allegory makes no difference for history, in another way history repeats and resembles the allegorical experience in surprising ways. After rescuing Angelica, Ruggiero alights in another wood, by another seashore, in another natural scene, which turns out to be the staging ground for alienating passion. We have already seen how precisely the "insegne" recall Alcina and her island, where men can become beasts and burning trees, where outer sign refers only cryptically to hidden thing (and the thing itself turns out only to be another name, which presumably must then also be deciphered). The "nature" to which Ruggiero returns is infected by distinctly Alcinian "allegorical" splits. Angelica at first seems, as

---

[156] Shoshana Felman, in her reading of Henry James' *Turn of the Screw* ("Turning the Screw of Interpretation," *Yale French Studies* 55/56 [1977], p. 178) gives a brilliant reading of the hermeneutic implications of the spiral motion of the screw which can be roughly applied to Ruggiero's spiral as well. See also DeMan, "Form and Intention in the American New Criticism," in *Blindness and Insight*, pp. 31–33, for the conversion of hermeneutic circle into hermeneutic spiral.

[157] Ruggiero's heliotropic qualities are trivialized soon after they are asserted since his return does not take just one solar day, but rather days, or even months (x.72.3).

said earlier, to echo Alcina's qualities only to give them new authenticity, to express bare nature and nothing but; but within a few lines she too is characterized as a "statua finta" (96.1–4), reintroducing the confusion of artful surface and inner nature (which by now we know extends even to Logistilla). With Angelica, unlike Alcina, the reader and Ruggiero are left uncertain as to whether this enigmatic nudity might or might not hide Alcinian wiles, Alcinian mimetic art. The return does not result in the healing of the alienation of signifier from signified, art from nature, the self from itself and from the other, which the text earlier led us to expect. The allegory of Alcina appears all the more appropriate as a gloss on reality, yet Ruggiero is unable or unwilling or both to understand its relevance. The "literal" world of Europe is exposed as having hidden and dangerous depths. But, at the same time, the world of Alcina and Logistilla seems doomed to be read as merely mimetic, referring to its own superficial events only, metaphorically untranslatable into a profitable allegory of Ruggiero's future ethical existence. Ruggiero has not learned to read analytically; instead he is, unwittingly, rewriting himself as the allegorical cypher that Alcina made of him. In Lacanian terms, allegorical psychoanalysis has been replaced by "mimetic" transfer.[158]

History is allegorical; allegory is taken at face value, becoming extrinsic and literal. Reference "takes place," but its own place is soon taken by forgetfulness and deadly repetition. In this frustrating play of resemblance and difference between the two regions, Ariosto seems to be setting up a deliberate encounter between the two modes of reference—and the two didactic poetics which were derived from them during the Renaissance—in order to critique each with reference to the other (just as he plays humanism off against neo-Platonism). The difficulty in translating allegory into reality can be more clearly "seen" by returning again to the image of the ring. The "literal" function of Angelica's ring is as an extrinsic magical agent of revelation and disappearance. The narrator glosses it allegorically as the "ring of reason," and yet ultimately its allegorical, "subjective" meaning is obstructed precisely by the extrinsicness and

---

[158] On this antisubject subject, see Felman, "To Open the Question," *Yale French Studies* 55/56 (1977), 7–8.

adventitiousness of its intervention (via Melissa) on Ruggiero's be-
half. When the ring passes from him back to Angelica, so does the
divinely solar power of invisible seeing: "così dagli occhi di Ruggier
[Angelica] si cela, / come fa il sol quando la nube il vela" ("Angelica
conceals herself from Ruggiero's eyes, like the sun when veiled by
clouds" XI.6.7–8). Ruggiero, meanwhile, remains blind, yet visible,
to her. The ring still possesses its double function of revealing and
concealing, still represents the structure of allegory itself as revela-
tion which both unveils and obscures truth. Yet it is now revealed,
as if by its own deconstructive powers, as a concretization and liter-
alization of allegory (a hardening of the artistry): not outwardly
representing an intrinsic property of its human possessor, but rather
operating as an extrinsic vehicle of magic irrelevant to other edu-
cations, presumably unavailable anywhere but in the fictions of
Ariosto. By the same token, the stones of Logistilla, which seemed
to externalize the process of self-consciousness, in retrospect lose this
universal possibility. We remember that the poet says they are found
nowhere else on earth—and suddenly they now seem both literal
and utopian. The univocal lesson explicitly taught by Melissa and
the poet is split in two between allegorical and literal: on the one
hand, the possibility that reason, like the heliotropic ring, can inter-
pret all deceptive appearances; on the other, a resigned awareness
that only an impossible magic offers the security of a "discovery
procedure" and that without it man is blind.

The encounter between the two modes of writing, as well as
between the two corresponding hermeneutics, is perhaps most ef-
fectively dramatized, however, by the paradoxical relationship of
Alcina and Angelica. Through them literal and allegorical meet and
contaminate each other.[159] They seem to contrast; they seem to be
identical. The literalness of Angelica's meaning is compromised by
allusions to artifice and yet she remains as pure, represented surface,
never allegorically unveiled as Alcina is, disappearing rather than
appearing. The meaning of Alcina changes radically as magical in-
sight moves from naturalistic surface to allegorical interior. She is
read according to an hermeneutics which St. John will make explic-
it in relation to poetic history: "e se tu vuoi che 'l ver non ti sia
ascoso, / tutta al contrario l'istoria converti" ("and if you wish that

_____

[159] Compare Donato's contrasting of the twin seductresses ("Desire," p. 27).

the truth not be hidden from you, turn all of history upside down" xxxv.27.5–6). St. John's advice is of course caught in the "everything I say is a lie" paradox, a fact which becomes apparent when he identifies himself as just another writer supported by patronage. And the simplicity of the allegorical reading of Alcina is also glossed and reversed by Angelica's irreducible literality: her surface may hint at hidden depths, but it gives no clue to an inner nature. She is a riddle which will never be solved—dispelling any simple allegorical insight into the real and yet preventing the opposite assumption, that things are what they literally seem to be.

Angelica becomes, in this view, the very figure of a text reified and/or re-created by the desires of the interpreter: the text which, nonetheless, always again eludes the grasp of the hermeneut,[160] never permitting a final, violent penetration of the sexual/allegorical veil. The virginity of Angelica, real or imagined (cf. 1.56) is the present-absence which leads on Sacripante, Orlando, Ruggiero, and all the rest.[161] The veil-like hymen is what separates the interpreting lovers from what they desire, but is also what confers meaning and value on it for them. As the next chapter will show, when it is literally removed (by Medoro) the imagined treasures beneath, rather than being revealed at last, disappear forever. The amorous interpreter then turns, as it were, to violent "deconstruction": Orlando rips apart, "deflowers," the *locus amoneus* with which and in which Angelica is identified (xxiii–xxiv),[162] then tries to destroy the "thing herself" (xxix). True, her "unveiling," unlike that of Alcina, does not explicitly reveal the other, repulsive side of the male imagination's understanding of female sexuality; it does not open up the concealed "reality" of gynecological corruption and putrefaction which the fairy's cosmetic art covers.[163]

---

[160] See Bonifazi, *Le Lettere*, p. xxx: "scrittura," like Angelica, "non sarà . . . mai catturata o ridotta a fede" (cf. p. 83).

[161] For Donato, Ruggiero is trying "to grasp the presence of the absence of his desire" in Angelica ("Desire," p. 27).

[162] See Carne-Ross, "One and Many," pp. 207–208; cf. n. 117, above.

[163] For the common *topos* of female sexual beauty stripped away to reveal corruption, see not only Dante's "femmina balba" (*Purgatorio* 19.31–33), but also Machiavelli's grotesque account of his encounter with an old prostitute (clearly a figure of Fortuna) in a letter to Luigi Guicciardini dated December 9, 1509, in *Tutte le Opere*.

It does, however, provoke analogous revulsion and violence. Or rather, it is used as a pretext for the release of such violence by the male lover-reader. Even in canto x, Angelica's enigmatically opaque surface raises the doubt that it is not the text in itself which is allegorically divided and deceptively seductive (or literally true, for that matter); not the writing, but the reader who is divided from within, self-seducing, living in a condition of allegory, which he projects onto/into the blank screen of the text, the other, nature itself.[164]

The arc of Ruggiero's journey from Logistilla to Angelica thus measures a crisis which collapses, but does not bridge, the distance— not only between allegorical and literal writing, but also between the written text and the reading of it. Since categories such as "allegory" and "mimesis" are both those by which we relate this episode to the balance of the poem and those by which a certain stable relationship between the reader's world and the text's may be delimited, any questioning of their relation puts the situation of reference and influence (text to/on reader, reader to/on text) into difficulties which go well beyond the structural splitting of either allegory or irony. By representing the failure of Ruggiero's education, Ariosto is naming the project and the failure of an allegorical poetics, which is, in some measure, both Dante's and the neo-Platonists'. He is revealing, as well, its inextricable dependence on an equally fallible allegorical hermeneutics, such as that advocated by Salutati when faced by pagan texts which literally "meant" the opposite of what he wanted them to mean. The "poetic theology" generally relies on a double text: outer, delightful, imitative surface and inner, instructive, allegorical meaning. It anticipates, correspondingly, two classes of readers to go along with them: the "vulgar herd," which is indulged and corrupted by the surface; the knowing few who are instructed by the allegory. We already saw Ariosto coyly confusing the two classes when he referred to the

---

[164] It is never entirely clear whether allegory is a way of writing or a way of reading (a dilemma broached in Chapter 2 while discussing Salutati's poetics and hermeneutics). It *is* clear that "allegorical" writing can always be taken literally, whereas a "literal" text can always be read allegorically. One is, in the last analysis, led to ask whether, *pace* Frye, *pace* Croce, both reader and text are not always, in some sense, both literal *and* allegorical.

"herd" as skeptical and to the critical elite as true believers in the mimetic truth of his text, treating them like so many Boccaccian Calandrinos (VII.I–2). Now the confusion is more pervasive, as it becomes clear that an idolatrous, seductive surface can be read, erroneously, as allegory, while a didactically intended work can be freely converted by the reader to a mere pretext for his or her foolish pleasures. But if the text seems to attack the allegorical writing and reading of Platonism and the Christian Middle Ages, it does no less damage to the poetics and hermeneutics of rhetorical humanism with its concept of "exemplary imitation," revealing that the doubleness of allegory is in some sense the native condition of literature (and of language) and suggesting that the reader who sees the intention of an author and the substance of history shining through a transparent text may only have erected an allegorical mirror which reflects back an image that, Narcissus-like, he projects, yet cannot recognize as his own.

Thus, among many other questions, the question of the relative efficacy of two partly opposed poetics of education is also raised: on the one hand, the humanistic poetics of education by mimetic examples; on the other, the allegorical poetics of seeking metaphysical meaning beneath a seductive surface. Medieval Christian poetics, Dante's poetics of the four levels of interpretation, posits the compatibility of the various modes of reading.[165] On a more modest scale, so does Landino in his reading of the *Aeneid,* the literal level of which is the narration of an exemplary ethical itinerary leading to the foundation of Rome by Aeneas, while its allegorical level is the journey of the soul to knowledge of the highest good.[166] Nevertheless, though Landino tries valiantly to reconcile literal and allegorical, with their respective active and contemplative contents, he eventually comes to the conclusion, mentioned above, that "Hera," the desire for rule and glory on earth, in effect the *telos* of

[165] *Letter to Can Grande,* in Haller, ed. and trans., *The Literary Criticism,* p. 99. Dante actually posits two basic levels, then subdivides the allegorical into the usual three kinds.

[166] As in bk. I, in bks. III and IV of the *Disputationes,* Landino tries to reconcile active with contemplative (bk. III, p. 161; bk. IV, pp. 220–22), but still ends up equating Aeneas' plague-ridden stopover in Crete with wholehearted commitment to the civic life (bk. IV p. 194). See n. 137, above.

the literal level, is precisely the most powerful seduction away from
the realization of the spiritual journey. More commonly, the seduc-
tions of the mimetic surface are seen as truly dangerous, the covert
enemy of hidden truths.[167] Thus the text appears to be both mi-
metic and allegorical, and is thereby divided against itself.

By the same token, though from the opposite direction, the hu-
manistic hope that aesthetic and ethical levels will literally coincide
(the narration imitating, and evoking the imitation of, the deeds
and characters it represents; the famous name making direct con-
tact with the famous being from which it derives) always ends
up showing the signs of a crucial division: in a recognition of the
ability of poetry to tell lies, distorting history (Bruni); in an angry
awareness of the possibility of plagiary, i.e., the divorce of the name
attached to a text from the true author (Valla); in the blushing re-
course to allegory to explain that the representations of idolatry and
vice do not invite (or define!) imitation (Boccaccio and Salutati).
Late in the Renaissance, the weary Tasso will give up all efforts to
heal what he knows (from experience) to be a genuinely schizo-
phrenic feature of textuality: its double and divided character as mi-
mesis *and* allegory. In Ariosto's poem the problem grows even more
confused as allegories are taken at face value, while the mimetic
world of nature appears to be riddled with allegorical cyphers,
every surface having, or seeming to have, hidden depths, every
depth turning into an imitative and still cryptic surface. Truth re-
cedes as it is pursued: Alcina controls Ruggiero, Atlante controls
Alcina, Melissa Atlante, Merlin Melissa, "Ariosto" Merlin, each
surface effaced to produce more surface, as if in anticipation of the
Peircian model of infinite semiosis.[168]

Ariosto draws a picture of reference in which his own attempts
either to teach or to seduce are as likely as not to have the opposite

[167] E.g., either of the Picos, for their different reasons (cf. Chapter 2, n. 72). The
basic objection to mimesis is still Plato's (and Augustine's).

[168] See Giamatti, *The Earthly Paradise,* p. 157: "Alcina is a slave to Atlante much
as Ruggiero . . . is a slave to Alcina. . . . Magic operates against magic, one illusion
contrasts with another and there is no final reality." For Peirce, see *Collected Papers*
(Cambridge: Harvard University Press, 1931–1958). My analysis relies in part on
Freccero's powerful and lucid account ("Petrarch's Poetics") of Peirce's usefulness
in relation to Augustinian and Renaissance theories of signification.

result. Both didactic modes, allegory and exemplary mimesis, turn out to be potentially futile. They are, however, accurate interpreters of each other, and so the poet is left in an insoluble ironic suspension: allegory designates what it is not, i.e., mimesis, even as mimesis, reflects its opposite, allegory. Just such a confusion crops up again in the allegory of Sdegno in canto XLII (56 ff.), where Rinaldo encounters externalized versions of his own feelings (Envy and Disdain) and takes them to be literal and autonomous. Soon after, the now-purged Rinaldo views a series of specifically "mimetic" (74, 81–82) representations of poets and their ladies, the last of which, however, shows Ariosto's own, here unnamed, lady covered by a "puro velo" (93.5) of concealing allegory. The *Furioso* is thus neither allegorical nor imitative, but is engaged in demystifying both positions, while predicting the failure of its demystifications in the face of readerly allegorizing or literalizing. It can be seen as either Alcinian or Logistillan, either neo-Platonic or humanistic, and so on. With this in mind, I recall the double "failure" of Ruggiero, both in exceeding "segni" and remaining within them. The two end up amounting to the same thing: to think that you have gotten behind a sign is to think that you have finally gotten to something literal and real, and is thus to remain within yet another literal-minded aestheticism. The sign, instead, is a limit of boundary of meaning which must and cannot be exceeded—and in that paradox there may still be as much hope as there is risk.

Up to this point, though venturing deep into questions of referential modes and the readers' relations to them, I have assumed that I was referring accurately to the text's oblique "statements" about its characters and the texts they read and, both explicitly and by analogy, about itself and its readers. I have assumed, in other words, that my own reading is untroubled by such intellectual blindness and willful violence. Concurrently, I posit a situation in which the reader learns successfully from the characters' moral and interpretive failures. And yet the critiques which are directed by the text against reading and writing in the abstract are also constantly, slyly transferred to the actual readers of this text and to its author's own "intentions," with subversive effect. I have already established that Ruggiero's transit to and from the island parallels a possible relation of a reader to the text. By regarding certain critics as exemplary readers, I have previously suggested how (mis)interpretations like theirs are forecast by the text. Rather than it being they who identify the text's significance, the text tends to identify *them* as those who reduce Ariosto to an Alcina or a Logistilla, an Atlante or a Merlin. Instead of analyzing from secure and detached positions they are, in effect, analyzed, drawn into the textuality of the *Furioso* as unwitting participants.[169]

This is true even of Giamatti's analysis, which rightly (if obliquely) depicts an Ariosto who blends elements of both Alcina and Logistilla. The assertion that the poem both possesses and teaches ironic intellectual insight into a world of passion and deception overlooks the fact that, as Ovid, St. Paul, St. Augustine, and Petrarch (to name an important few) knew perfectly well, we can see the good clearly and still choose the evil. Corrupt will makes ironic insight perfectly useless—in fact, worse than useless, since it can actually, by its tempting prohibitions, provoke us to the sin it abhors. Giamatti recognizes the complete failure of Astolfo's didactic retelling of his own seduction and metamorphosis to sway its hearer. I would add that in this way Ariosto is placing his own literary discourse within the same bookish tree that encases Astolfo, in a tacit confession of literature's inability to command the moral attention of its readers or to alter their behavior in any more than a superficial way. That is, if what Giamatti says (what he says Ariosto says) is true, it is bound to fall on deaf ears. His essay clearly shows that the *Furioso* makes an incisive critique of illusory access to paradisal perfection on earth,

---

[169] Felman, "Turning the Screw of Interpretation," esp. p. 184, gives an excellent theoretical and practical account of the ways in which a story may comprehend a reader rather than vice versa. Her model derives from Lacan's interpretation of Freudian "transfer" and from DeMan's *Allegories of Reading*, "Criticism and Crisis," etc. Critics have often enough noted that the *Furioso* mocks some version or other of its readers, dramatizing his/her credulity, blindness, and so on. See for instance Momigliano (*Saggio*, p. 49) on the Alcinian traps laid for the reader by the poet. See also Gherardino, quoted in Borlenghi, *Ariosto*, p. 152: "L'Ariosto fa continuo gioco non men de' lettori che degli eroi." Cf. Durling, *The Figure of the Poet*, p. 114; Parker, *Inescapable Romance*, p. 23; Giamatti, *The Earthly Paradise*, p. 151. Those critics, however, have not seen the wide range of readerly positions taken into account by the text, nor have they included themselves among the ranks of duped and doubled interpreters.

that it mocks all human efforts at self-transcendence. But the poem also contains a complementary, almost prophetic, critique of ironic humanistic "pragmatism," indicting it too, *a priori,* for academic utopianism.[170] Moreover, as we are about to see, the sharp difference which the text seems to posit between duplicity *in bono* (Melissa's, Ariosto's) and Alcinian alienation from the True and the Good is eroded, even effaced. Thus, to the ineffectuality of humanistic education is added the further possibility that it actually operates exactly contrary to its stated aim of virtuous self-knowledge.

Now, I believe that this is true, that the positions of several important critics seem to be subsumed by perspectives which the poem manipulates only to overthrow and limit. Yet, by assigning the text such insight, such critical "giudizio," I subscribe, as it were, to the rhetorical and/or ontological deification of the text and author which has been repeatedly featured in criticism of the poem. What is more, though what the text seems to refer to is aggravated referential failure, the success of that reference to failure, which even seems to be extended, prophetically, into the future, is positively astounding. In this argument, in fact, I may be partly guilty of the same retrospective discovery of past prophecy, the same inventive genealogy, that the text itself uses and demystifies. Similar enterprises stumble because they do not really erase mastery, just displace it onto the text and, incidentally, reflect it back on themselves.[171] In this text, as we have seen, mastery recedes infinitely from character to character, toward a vanishing point which is its author.

It seems to me that the *Furioso* goes out of its way to disclaim such mastery, to refuse the role of a Logistilla's stone which reflects back to the reader, however obliquely and allegorically, a revealing image of him or herself. Just as the relation between Alcina's island

---

[170] The Ariosto chapter in *The Earthly Paradise* does conclude that "the final illusion is to think life would be bearable without illusions" (p. 169) and that Alcina's garden is something intrinsic to human nature which can never be completely left behind. Still, the primary thrust of both his essays is toward the recuperation of humanistic values and educational possibilities.

[171] Notably, Felman's "masterly" reading of *The Turn of the Screw* as a demystification of critical mastery depends upon a tacit and fundamentally unquestioned reliance on James', her own, and Lacan's critical authority.

and "Europe" is uncertain, so the relation between text and readers is indeterminate, and it is only in charting the unchartable that "education" may take place, leading the reader out of the text and beyond the self. What bearing this model may have upon my own text and its readings of the *Furioso* is inevitably left to the readerly imagination. As for the *Furioso*'s "dramatizations" and subversions of its own intentions, however, a great deal more remains to be said. The teachings of Melissa and Logistilla have been compromised, shown to be ineffectual or even "of the Devil's party." The narrator-poet, in his guise as teacher, translated example into precept in VIII.1–2, but then contradicted himself flatly in XI.1–2. Stanzas 1 and 2 of canto VII also seem to make the poet's magisterial, Logistillan role felt, as he prepares to translate the unveiling of Alcina into a moral example for his readers: "a voi soli ogni mio intento agogna / che 'l frutto sia di mie fatiche caro" ("my one intention is that for you alone may be the precious fruit of my labors" 2.5–6). I have already detected some ironic inconsistencies in the didactic model presented in these stanzas. Under close scrutiny they yield further and unexpected density. Two key words, at least, in these lines have ambiguous double senses. "Caro" means both "valued" and "costly," suggesting *either* benefit *or* harm to the reader. "Frutto" is a wonderfully dense metaphor which suggests both "useful product" *and* "object of pleasure": "dulcis utile," if you will. More pertinently, "frutto" is the product of a plant, a tree more often than not, and is therefore implicated in the delightful proliferation of "organic" imagery in these cantos, whose complexity has been probed above. The narrative stanzas which follow return to the image in an unforeseen way. As Ruggiero waits anxiously for Alcina he often fears "qualche impedimento . . . / che tra il frutto e la man non gli sia messo" ("that some obstacle be interposed between his hand and the [desired] fruit" 25.7–8). When Melissa finally exposes Alcina for what she really is, the image returns once more: "Come fanciullo che maturo frutto / ripone . . . / e dopo molti giorni . . . / . . . truova a caso il suo deposto, / si maraviglia di vederlo tutto / putrido e guasto . . ." ("Like a lad who sets aside a ripe fruit . . . and after many days . . . finds by chance his cache, marveling to see it wholly spoiled and putrid" 71.1–6). The proem purports to be glossing the exemplary tale which is told, and yet these lines clearly suggest the reverse—that the explicit lesson of "Ariosto" is drawn back into the ambiguous world of the poem's representations.

The repetitions of the imagery of fruit suggest first that the useful "frutto" of Ariosto's text is in some way like the pleasurable erotic experience desired by Ruggiero. The third image in the sequence explodes with the discovery that what seemed to be healthy, succulent fruit has in fact degenerated into Alcinian corruption: that, in other words, Ariosto may be quietly revealing the possible equivalence of his "intento" and Alcina's (or at least the potential identity of their consequences, regardless of intentions). In retrospect, the reader might notice that the "intento" of the narrator echoes the words "vostro intento" which Ruggiero uses in offering his chivalric services to Alcina's ladies, radically mistaking the true nature of *their* intent (VI.80.4). Given my earlier catalogue of the images of Alcina as artist/artwork, poet/poem, etc., it is clear that such an identification is not casual, especially since both are weavers.[172] The irony of Ruggiero's discovery of Alcina as rotten fruit has further ramifications, since it echoes the metaphor of a child desirous of fruit (itself pregnant with edenic associations) which is applied to Dante's crossing of the wall of flame (*Purgatorio* 27) lured by Virgil's promise of access to the presence of Beatrice on the other side:

> come al fanciul si fa ch'è vinto al pome   [*Purgatorio* 27.45]

> as one does to a child that is won with an apple

> Quel dolce pome che per tanti rami
> cercando va la cura de' mortali,
> oggi porrà in pace le tue fami.   [115–17]

> That sweet fruit which the care of mortals goes seeking on so many branches, this day shall give your hungerings peace.

Ariosto inverts the image *par excellence* of seduction toward the educational goal of perfect happiness and free selfhood in Eden

---

[172] Cf. n. 69, above. One could argue that Ariosto is the anti-Arachne (Penelope), especially in the endless protraction of his textual "entrelacement," but one would then have to reckon with the revelation in XXXV.27.8 that the chaste Penelope was actually a whore. Barkan, *The Gods Made Flesh,* makes a strong case for Ovid's identification of his own artistic project with Arachne's (*Metamorphoses* VI.1 ff.).

recaptured, to show an apparently educational fruit converted to purposes of seduction.

The distinction between two kinds of poetry, seductive and educative, idolatrous and pious, lying and truthful, which the episode, at one level, attempts to invoke, was staggered when Melissa's affinities with Alcina became too apparent, and now it crumbles. All around this central narrative subtle hints at such a confusion can be discovered. For instance, Atlante's use of objectionable simulacra is cleverly assimilated to poetic uses of similes. Meanwhile, in canto VIII, a series of confusions between truth and falsehood ultimately points to a confusion in the poem's own status.[173] Thus the critical balance shifts back toward an identification of Ariosto's poetics with Alcina's lies and trickery. It is by now clear that Ariosto pokes fun at the reader and deliberately misleads him or her with some frequency. Yet the very act of referring to his own Alcina-like deceptions, however subtly done, in a sense contradicts them. Ariosto, in one of his rhetorical guises, makes it a point to "expose himself" to his readers, however morally or aesthetically objectionable such an exposure may be. Perhaps it is more apt to link him with neither Alcina nor with Logistilla, but with another figure entirely: Melissa. Melissa at first seemed to mediate the transition between the "evil" fairy and the "good." Now, however, she appears to have qualities of both. And rather than moving through a liminal landscape from one to the other, she seems to inhabit permanently an ambiguous and marginal locale between them. Melissa teaches deception and deceives as she teaches. Her allegory of eternal being hides death beneath it, and yet it is impossible to reject her values out of hand, since without either Alcina's illusions or her own, all that remains is a desert of insignificance which is as intolerable as any of the other options it deconstructs. "Ariosto" "is" a "Melissa" freeing others from desire, stripping away illusion, and yet not himself above using deceit to compass his own desires, as she does in canto XLIII. Or perhaps "Ariosto" is more like Astolfo: not, as critics have often imagined him, astride a Pegasus, furrowing the skies, but

---

[173] For Atlante and similes, note the uses of the words "finzioni," "simulare," and "assimigliare," in IV.1, 2, 3, 19, 23. For the confusion of "vero" with "falso," see VIII.42, 52, 58, 84 (and VI.71).

rather caught inside the alien surface of his own tree-text, offering didactic advice which he learned too late to help himself, and which may contribute to Ruggiero's seduction rather than oppose it (and which, in any event, is ineffectual). Or, he *is* like the rider of the Pegasus, symbol of poetic imagination *in bono,* but in fighting the Chimera, emblem of demonic and violent imagination, as we shall soon see, he is only fighting an aspect of himself. Or perhaps, as the last chapter will show, he is like the other characters whose voices emerge, like Astolfo's, from alienated containers (e.g., Merlin and Atlante speaking from their tombs) and thus is himself in the predicament which Melissa desires for Ruggiero, existing only as the words of his own text, the monumental allegory of a then metaphorical, now (also) literal "death of the author."

Croce argues that the fragmentary characters are projections, "figures," of the integral authorial personality. And he is right. The text does make such analogies over and over again. Yet it is only through these partial, embattled identities that the authorial identity can be approached, and thus it too is embattled, divided against itself, caught in the predicament of the "student/reader" pursuing elusive selfhood, rather than reflecting masterfully and from afar on a battle already won. According to Castiglione (1.xxvi) the educational transaction is mimetic—the student tries to achieve metaphorical resemblance of, even a metamorphic transformation into, the model teacher. But this is only possible if the *magister* has already "found himself" and achieved the stable perspective on himself and reality toward which Ruggiero, and the reader, aspire. Once that perspective is fragmented and destabilized, the poet becomes an "ignis fatuus" which blindly leads the blind. "Ariosto" is also a Ulysses who leads men toward what is unknown to him as well: toward death, the lesson of absence. Or, to take a more positive view, he is like Dante's "Virgil" for "Statius," himself doomed to darkness and capable of illuminating others.[174] Or he is like Chiron, Achilles' tutor, *the* figure of magisterial doubleness,

---

[174] Without the guarantee of Grace which made Virgil's blind and damned path a way for salvation, according to Dante (*Purgatorio* 22.67–73). Not accidentally, Statius' image of the flickering nocturnal light of Grace in Virgil's text recalls Ulysses' flame in the dark of hell.

a composite of bestial passions and divine intellect.

that neither Logistilla, nor Alcina, nor Astolfo, nor Melissa adequately figures, re-presents, the poet: there is instead a constant metaphorical slippage from character to character, as we saw before in the opened circle of A controlled by B controlled by C controlled by . . . . The episode is characterized by a series of geographical displacements and by other patterns of metaphorical substitution: one lover replaces another for Alcina; Ruggiero is the "successor" of Astolfo; a natural landscape takes the place of the successively displaced lovers; the resulting *locus amoenus* is a substitute for Paradise; Melissa appears in the place of Atlante; Logistilla's palace then replaces Alcina's; the ring passes from hand to hand; and so on. The necessary displacement of self in education is precisely that which threatens it with madness and with death; in the same way, judgment may resolve crisis or *be* crisis. The free play of rhetorical substitutions which confuses identity and travesties the education of the poem's characters also makes Ariosto's position, his true intent and identity, unlocalizable.

This treatment of education in the *Furioso* has isolated a number of paradoxes and contaminations within the structures and values of education: "insegnamento" which teaches self-knowledge through reading, but also the disappearance of the self through writing; "formazione" which aspires to shape a human being and yet risks becoming mere aesthetic formality (where art is not realistic, but reality deceptively "artistic"). Alcina is confused with her half-sister Logistilla; the allegorical infects the literal; sensuous delight overpowers the useful education it was designed to support; education stands at the brink of madness; and *nothing* really escapes the frivolity of the text in which all of these oppositions are represented. The *Furioso* adopts the poetics of "serio ludere," following Castiglione, a certain Alberti, and, perhaps most important of all, Erasmus, and yet it playfully puts them too into serious crisis.[176]

The poem envisions the collapse of two modes of didactic ref-

---

[175] For the ambiguous nature of the magisterial Centaur, see *Il Principe,* chap. 18. See also *Inferno* 12.65 ff.

[176] Not that this poetics was not already in crisis for Castiglione, Alberti, and Erasmus. In the *Courtier,* as we know, the serious matters of life are approached through a game, which is a means both of evading and of approaching harsh realities, of holding the most violent contradictions (real/ideal, active/contemplative,

erence, mimesis and allegory, into deceptive mimicry and uncon-
scious alienation: mimesis deceptive because its readers will not see
the unnatural content hidden behind it; allegory equally deceptive
because it will be taken literally, not translated into the readers'
own lives. The same is true of the two poetic functions, delight and
utility, which are sometimes matched up, respectively, with mi-
mesis and allegory.[177] Though the question of identity is an obses-
sion of the poet, he is left with no means· for approaching it.[178]
Throughout the poem, his own and the characters' narratives have
unexpected and even inverted consequences with respect to those
which were intended. On the one hand, a delightful story like that
of Angelica's happy love for Medoro becomes the provocation to
a tragic madness when it is told to Orlando (xxiii.118); meanwhile,
on the other hand, representations of violent reality are repeatedly
described as inspiring pleasure in their readers—and the narrator
specifically anticipates the same sort of response in his readers as
well![179] In the *De Ordine Docendi*, Battista Guarino reports both

---

male/female, etc.) in a suspension which becomes a way of life. The way of life,
however, had long since ended when it resurfaced in the writing of Castiglione, dis-
persed by the deaths of many of the interlocutors and by the tumult of Italy in crisis.
In the *Courtier* it persists only as a playful allegory of loss and death. The Lucianesque,
satirical allegory of Alberti's *Intercenali* and *Momus* left traces on Ariosto which ap-
pear most prominently in the lunar episode. The narrator of the *Momus* justifies the
detour into bizarre fantasy and poetic delight as a propaedeutic mediation of princely
education. But the narrator repeatedly connects his writing with the tales told and
with the treatise on princely government written by Momus, the fraudulent, flat-
tering epitome of malice. If Ariosto implies his resemblance to Alcina, Alberti
equates himself with the mocker and subverter of all established order, human and
divine. As for Ariosto's relationship to Erasmus, and Erasmus' to his narrative *persona*,
Folly personified, see Chapter 4, sec. iii, below.

[177] It is no coincidence that the poetics of the late *Cinquecento*, based on the newly
rediscovered *Poetics* of Aristotle, with its definition and valorization of representa-
tion as mimesis, also turns increasingly toward delight as *the* product of poetic dis-
course. See Weinberg, *History*, vol. 1. Cf. Chapter 2, n. 102, above.

[178] Cf. Donato, "Desire," p. 24: "Ariosto's narrative cannot tell us the truth about
desire since it is inextricably entwined with it."

[179] In the first category, as Weaver notes ("Lettura," pp. 384–85), also falls the
Gascon's tale which so infuriates Bradamante (xxxii.28–36). In the second category
can be entered the readerly responses verified or predicted in xvi.89, xxxiii 58,
xxxvi.53.3 (cf. 7.6–8), xxxix.85–6, and xl.2, and Bradamante's reaction to the
tapestry in xlvi.65.8: "quasi il gaudio ha la donzella uccisa."

of these responses as truisms of the operation of poetry. In the
first place, poetry which is exquisitely delightful can still provoke
nightmares:[180]

> Of poetry may be said what is said of the octopus' head. Indeed they
> say that this head . . . brings great pleasure when eaten in food, but that
> it then afflicts us with unwholesome dreams and turbulent phantasms.
> Thus, poetry feeds the souls of men with great sweetness and nourish-
> ment, but nonetheless torments them with disturbances and agitations.
> Therefore, in reading, the soul must rein itself in and not let itself be
> carried away by love of fables or take the bare fictions for what they
> seem to be; instead each thing must be examined for whatever utility it
> brings beneath the fiction.

Meanwhile, by contrast, the most unpleasant contents of reality
become unexpectedly delightful when reported in poetry:

> Those things which are said impiously, cruelly, unjustly, and shamefully
> by poets are not to be attributed to vice but are to be considered ex-
> cellences of art, which give to the individual characters their due. Just
> so, we see it happen in other cases where the soul abhors the thing itself,
> but nonetheless hears or contemplates it gladly when it is represented
> fictively. Thus we have heard that our Chrysoloras used to say that the
> same scorpions and serpents which we flee, greatly delight us when we
> see them painted in some true imitation; the grunts of swine, the racket
> of sawing, the hissing of the wind, the din of the sea—when we hear

---

[180] *De Ordine Docendi,* in Garin, ed., *Il Pensiero Pedagogico,* p. 464: "De poetica
quid de polypodis capite traditur, idem ipse sentiat. Aiunt siquidem . . . sumptum
caput illud in cibis plurimum suavitatis afferre, caeterum gravibus insonniis turbu-
lentissimisque fantasmatis sensum afficere. Ita poetica hominum animos maxima
quidem dulcedine alit et pabulo, non minus vero turbarum et agitationis ingerit.
Quo circa inter legendum animi frenis uti opus est, nec ita fabularum studio efferri,
ut figmenta illa sic nuda capiantur, sed ununquodque quid utilitatis sub commento
afferat rimandum est." See also pp. 464–66: "Quae apud poetas impie, crudeliter,
iniuste, turpiter dicuntur, non ea vitio danda sunt sed artis excellentia consideranda,
quae singulis personis decorum suum reddit. Sic enim et aliis in rebus accidere vide-
mus, ut a quibus re ipsa apparentibus animus abhorret, proprie tamen efficta libenter
vel contemplemur vel audiamus. Nam et Chrysoloram nostrum sic dicere solitum
accepimus, scorpios et serpentes quos fugimus, si pictos vera quadam imitatione
viderimus, magno opere delectamur; suis grunitum, serrae stridorem, venti sibilum,
maris strepitum, cum audimus turbamur animo; quae tamen si quis ficta voce imi-
tetur, voluptate quadam afficimur. Quae vero in scriptoribus vitae accommodata
et ad virtutis rationem pertinentia reperiuntur, ea memoriae commendanda sunt."

them our soul is troubled; but if someone imitates them in a feigned voice we are carried away by a certain pleasure. Those things which are found in writers that are apt for life and which pertain to the reason of virtue, these things are to be remembered.

Guarino offers as a "remedy" to these complementary risks a careful screening of poetic works for the purposes of education. Ariosto teases out more amply and far more subtly the implications of this clash, of the interdependence and contamination of the playful and the serious in poetry. And the obliqueness with which he does so is itself one of those implications, a point which will be even more apparent when, in the final chapter, I return to the figure of Cassandra.

If explicitly serious matters are bound to be taken as comic and their relevance to the reader dismissed as negligible, if comic laughter barely covers tragic violence, if truth appears as falsehood and vice versa, the poem seems forever exposed to misinterpretation, no matter how earnest its (inaccessible) intentions for moral instruction might be. It must always approach reality indirectly, always accept its destiny of speaking in a voice which will soothe, flatter, and delight, but never teach. Ariosto does deploy didactic motifs and engage educational traditions in order to act formatively on his readers by representations of personal formation, does explore the relation of the ethical to the aesthetic. Yet a version of didactic humanism is being explored and debunked in the process: it may first slip into an utopian metaphysics of human "Being" and thence into aestheticism, offering an impossible version of poetry's power to represent and shape human perceptions of the world and of the self. So those who have equated Ariosto and Alcina are partly right as well.

The critical uncertainties about the educational aims and the referential/rhetorical status of the poem which I have raised preclude the possibility of any simple interpretive resolution of the poem's meanings and its actions by Herculean choice (or choices). Instead, they reflect the poem's complex attempt at interpreting a crisis, a series of crises actually, which leaves readers continually suspended at the "crossroads" of reading (of which the notion of the textual "crux" is only the most obvious example), aware or not that to choose an answer is simply to reenter the crises depicted in the narration, to opt for one blindness over another. The question of education represented in and effected by poetry is certainly posed, and with it a number of meaningful oppositions are announced and possibly collapsed: ethics and aesthetics, allegory and mimesis, fiction and history, and so on. The theme of education must be explored in the Alcina episode not because education *takes place,* but because its simulacra, the metaphors which *take the place of* education, return obsessively, in a condition of crisis, and because that crisis seems to stem directly from the metaphorical, even fictional, character of education itself. As we saw, Eugenio Garin has argued that the *Cinquecento* brought a crisis to the vital educational revolution of the *Quattrocento,* a degeneration from ethics into etiquette, from philology into a sort of "stylistics," foreshadowing the arrival of Baroque aesthetics. The *Furioso* has sometimes been seen as a passive confirmation of that tendency. Here I have argued, to the contrary, that the poem actively brings out the inner divisions both in the Platonic itinerary of poetic ascent and in the humanistic program for the "formazione dell'uomo" through vigorous development of skills in writing and interpretation. The *Furioso,* by adopting the key metaphors of rebirth—the eternal return of the sun, Hercules (who descended into and returned from the Land of the Dead), the phoenix (emblazoned on Marfisa's shield), name and family as forms of life after death—subverts not only the identity of Ruggiero, not only its own identity as poem of amusement or education, not only the self-concepts of its author and readers, but, finally, some of the identifying features of the Renaissance itself (as seen and defined both by contemporaries and by modern scholars), revealing fictionally the Renaissance as a potent fiction of rebirth.

vi. *Pegasus into Geryon: "Truth with a Lying Face"*

After all the exposition and interpretation of this chapter we are still left at an embarrassing *bivio.* On the one hand, Ariosto seems a despairing and desperate character indeed: dramatizing education as impotent or even pernicious; reducing poetry to a tissue of lies which transmutes harsh reality into poetic pleasure, even as those dreamy pleasures conceal a nightmare of Alcinian vice. On the other hand, in arriving at such conclusions, we have discovered a text so complex, so richly aware of moral and epistemological nuance, so obliquely insightful into itself and others, that a new set of positive values seems to spring up, hydralike, to take the place of those struck down. It seems that discourses about Ariosto are never quite closed, that the *Furioso* always leaves itself ajar to further interpretive prying. In the next chapter, in fact, I will try to see whether such values are more explicitly and/or successfully reasserted by other, later, related episodes. Does Astolfo's allegorical and didactic flight remedy and supersede Ruggiero's? Does Orlando's madness circle back toward selfhood and poetic affirmation after Ruggiero's education has spiraled into a loss of self and poetic negativity? In order both to anticipate further displacements in Ariostan treatments of selfhood and literature *and* to summarize emblematically the fruit of these readings in the Alcina-Logistilla sequence, I now turn briefly to the creature, the hippogryph, whose circular flight spans and defines the whole sequence and whose subsequent return in the lunar episode creates a space for extended comparison between one part of the poem and another.

As mentioned near the beginning of this chapter, the hippogryph is a composite creature in more ways than one. At the narrative level it is the product of the strange union of a mare with a gryphon. Its literary-philosophical parentage is even more mixed: it yokes the mythical Pegasus with the Platonic fable of the horses and charioteer of the soul, both of which were endlessly reelaborated and glossed across the centuries; it also borrows elements from a variety of other sources, most directly the Virgilian line "nam iungentur gryphes equis" ("now horses are joined to gryphons" *Eclogue* viii.26–28). As we also saw, this compositeness is easily translated onto the thematic level. The hippogryph brings together two distinct, if often overlapping, symbolic strands: the ethical-philosophical one deriving from the *Phaedrus* and the imaginative-literary one focused, precisely, on the Pegasus.[181] In addition, as critics have frequently observed, by insisting on the naturalness of this animal alone amidst

---

[181] Cf. nn. 6, 22, and 26, above. As mentioned before, the separation between the two traditions was blurred long before they got to the *Furioso,* for example by the *Phaedrus* itself. The same is true of the Pegasus, which *is* glossed as poetic *fama* but which also, in the episodes of Perseus and Andromeda and of Bellerophon and the Chimera, lends itself to moral glossing (see n. 185, below). Mentions of the Pegasus *qua* figure of poetry come in *Furioso* xlii.91 and xlv.92.

all of Atlante's magical instruments and illusions (IV.18.1, 19.7), and by making it the offspring of one real, one mythic, creature, Ariosto forces the question of the relation between reality and imagination, nature and artifice. By the placement of this double creature at the boundaryline between the real and the preposterous, the poet may seem to effect symbolically and from his own perspective what the narrative, from Ruggiero's perspective, has not: a bridge between the allegorical antipodes of literature and the reality of natural life. In the allegory of poetic reference sketched above, the hippogryph would be precisely that which successfully traverses the distance from historical reality to poetic fantasy and then returns to its point of departure. These synthetic, englobing possibilities lead Giamatti to the supposition that the hippogryph (with the equine imagery generally) fuses composite ethical-intellectual and aesthetic elements to effect their reconciliation in the poet's moral imagination. On the other side, Donato's ironic reading of the "naturalness" of the hippogryph tends—in the exact opposite direction—to suggest that the real and the imaginary are brought violently together precisely to expose the lack of any referential connection of the poem's language to "reality" (p. 32). The question then is whether the "compositeness" and "duplicity" of the hippogryph operate the same kind of magical synthesis between fiction and reality, aesthetics and ethics, that Dante's double-natured Christ-as-gryphon does between human and divine,[182] or whether, on the contrary, it is a form of oxymoron or catachresis, the violent yoking of forever irreconcilable entities.

The question becomes immediately undecidable if one attempts to sum up all of the many allusive overtones (poetic, ethical, metaphysical) which are patched together in the hippogryph. And perhaps that lack of an answer is the right answer, even though I will pursue the matter further. In addition, an attempt to deduce the significance of the beast from its narrative roles meets with equal unsuccess. If Ruggiero-as-Perseus on the hippogryph-Pegasus rescues Angelica-Andromeda in a triumph over protean monstrosity, he is also borne by the same steed to the grove where we saw him so

---

[182] Shapiro, "Perseus and Bellerophon," p. 124, notes *en passant* Dante's gryphon (esp. *Purgatorio* 31.112 ff.) as a possible source for the hippogryph.

eager to play the part of Tereus. Astolfo's later journey on the hip-
pogryph provides an equivalent victory over monstrosity (the
Harpies) without the subsequent fall. In either case, however, the
rider's aims and his skill in controlling the steed are decisive—on
the narrative level the hippogryph is morally and epistemologically
neutral. Like the ring of Angelica (which Ruggiero loses at the same
time), its allegorical force as symbol of intrinsic human nature is dis-
sipated by its clearer function as an extrinsic implement, a sliding
signifier, which can be transferred easily from one "owner" to an-
other, serving a variety of opposed purposes for Atlante, Ruggiero,
Melissa, Ruggiero again, and finally Astolfo. It is capable of run-
ning menacingly out of control and of responding docilely to a
masterful touch. At various stages it appears as symbol and/or agent
of Ruggiero's seduction, of his "successful" reeducation and of the
"re-lapsarian" condition which follows—it is thus a perfectly self-
canceling emblem of the young hero's self-becoming and self-loss.
In this respect it is a fusion of the two Platonic horses of the soul—
black and white, good and evil—into an ambiguous grey which
ensures that the narrative allegory of positive ethical imagination
remains continually unstable, questionable. The significance of the
hippogryph, verbal creature composed of so many other creatures,
is itself resolutely, and yet indeterminately, composite.

Nonetheless, the hippogryph has seemed to many capable of
transcending, as symbol, its narrative role and of becoming a pure
emblem of the poetic enterprise itself, which somehow escapes the
moral and epistemological equivocations that it applies to Ruggiero
and "his" steed, offering a perspective above and beyond the tur-
moil both of our world and the *Furioso*'s from which they can be
viewed, understood, and perhaps even mastered. It would thus re-
semble the lunar surface from which Astolfo reflects back on his-
tory, although, significantly, the hippogryph itself is denied access
to that height (XXXIV.68–69). In any case, it is certainly clear by
now that I would not agree unreservedly to the idea that poetry,
poem, and/or poet escape the dangers they represent by the very
act of representing them. Even if the hippogryph should prove an
unmixedly positive figure of poetry, which it will not, we have al-
ready seen the poem compromised in too many other ways, linked
to too many other equivocal figures, to believe this could be *the*

privileged figure. On the other hand, it would be hard not to accord *some* special privilege as emblem of poetry to a creature as striking as this and as directly derived from the Pegasus, whose hoofprint first opened the "Pierian spring" of poetry on Parnassus. The Pegasus is, of course, most directly evoked by Ruggiero's Perseus-like battle with the Orca.[183] It has recently been argued at length, though with much less direct evidence, that Astolfo on the hippogryph is like the other of the Pegasus' mythological masters, Bellerophon.[184] Even without these specifics, however, the mere fact of winged equine flight is enough to make the Pegasus the strongest and most consistent precursor of the hippogryph. And the association seems to be an entirely positive one. Excluded from the poem are direct references to the two elements of the Pegasus story which give it a darker and ambiguous cast: its birth from the vile blood of the Medusa, and Bellerophon's final fall from the winged horse into blindness and confusion when (like Icarus and Phaeton) he tried to soar too high toward heaven and deity. In fact, as will be noted again in Chapter 4, the poet-narrator does allusively avert from himself a fate like Bellerophon's by a timely descent back to earth after his poetic flight to the moon (xxxv.31). And even the Medusan origin of the Pegasus might furnish an heuristic

---

[183] Cf. n. 77, above. In Ovid, Perseus does not ride the Pegasus but flies with the aid of Mercury's winged sandals (the Pegasus, after all, comes into being only after he slays the Medusa). As Javitch ("Rescuing Ovid," pp. 86–87) and, more elaborately, Shapiro ("Perseus and Bellerophon," pp. 127–28) point out, medieval mythographers soon placed Perseus on the Pegasus, presumably encouraged by the vagueness and confusing order of the tale told by Ovid, and by the clear analogy to the myth of Bellerophon.

[184] See Shapiro, "Perseus and Bellerophon," pp. 113–18. Though her accretion of parallels is interesting, there is none so convincing as the direct imitation of Perseus by Ruggiero. If the myth of Bellerophon enters the poem (or our reading of the poem) as I too think it does, it is mostly through the mere presence of a Pegasus. In fact, Ariosto never mentions the myth of Bellerophon (*Iliad* VI.155–202) directly, as Milton does in *Paradise Lost* VII.17–20. He does allude to it now and again. The fall from intellectual heights in *Satira* VI.46–48 suggests Bellerophon's fall of pride, as does *Furioso* XXXV.31. It is also true, as Shapiro suggests, that the bridling of the hippogryph by Logistilla recalls Minerva (wisdom) bridling the Pegasus for Bellerophon. But, contrary to her assertion, the bridle is given first to Ruggiero, not Astolfo. For a different reading of the extended parallelism between the flights of Ruggiero and Astolfo, see Chapter 4, sec. i, below.

image of demonic nightmare giving rise to sweetest dream through poetry, as Guarino suggests it might.

More to my point, Ariosto also excludes any full reenactment of the battle between Bellerophon mounted on the Pegasus and the Chimera. The myth sets one composite creature of imagination *in bono* off against another *in malo*, offering, potentially, a perfect allegorical figuration of the struggle of the ethical imagination against its demonic opposite and double.[185] The failure of the Chimera to put in an appearance in the poem is an especially curious one, since this is obviously a world woven together out of delusive, "chimerical" semblances, where the monster itself would be perfectly at home. If the Orca which Ruggiero battles and the Harpies routed by Astolfo offer limited analogies to that myth, they are more indebted to others, and in both cases strong qualifications seem to drain the allegorical force of the combat: the decisive battle never comes.[186] And although it is always riskier to explain an absence than a presence, in this case I will attempt to do just that. Or rather, I will suggest that the Chimera, or the next best/worst thing to it, *is* present in the poem, in the place one least expects to find it—*within* the hippogryph itself, where it is (con)fused with Pegasus, just as the two Platonic horses are also yoked together there.

Such a fusion and its meaning are anticipated in one of the secondary allusions which cluster around the beast—that to Horace's "composite monster" in *Ars Poetica* 1–5. This nightmarish creature (likened to "aegri somnia," the "dreams of a sick man," l.7) may be a horse with a human head, a body with limbs drawn from different creatures and then covered with feathers. The proximity of horse and feathered creature suggests precisely a Pegasus turned to Chimera, a Pegasus *in malo* which represents the fantastic art that Horace rejects in favor of the verisimilar (or at least in favor of the poet who mixes "true with false" [l. 15] subtly and without

---

[185] The moral reading of Pegasus vs. Chimera as virtue vs. vice can be found, for example, in Salutati, *De Laboribus Herculis,* vol. 2, pp. 424–25. Cf. Clements, *Picta Poesis,* p. 123.

[186] The problems with Ruggiero's battle we have already seen; those with Astolfo will appear in the next chapter.

detection).[187] If he indeed has this passage in mind, Ariosto is clearly flaunting the absence of verisimilitude in his poem, the incredulity it is bound to excite in its readers. In this sense he would seem not to be subscribing to Horace's critique of fantasy, but rather to be converting Chimera back to Pegasus, or at least to be valorizing the chimerical. But there is a more threatening association lurking in the presentation of the hippogryph—an echo, or rather a long and systematic series of echoes, which link and equate it with the Chimera's kissing cousin, Dante's frightful Geryon.

A survey of a good critical edition of the *Furioso*, Bigi's or Segre's or Caretti's, reveals that the hippogryph's many spiral ascents and descents, even those when Astolfo is the rider, are consistently described in language which recalls directly Geryon, "quella sozza imagine di froda" ("that foul image of fraud" *Inferno* 17.7).[188] There is an additional echo which connects those local spirals, markers of the hippogryph's movements from canto IV onward, to Ruggiero's "gran tondo" around the world (x.70.7; cf. VI.20.5). In other words, the circle of educational and referential perfection did not only degenerate into a spiral at the end of the journey; its failure was actually forecast from the very first time we met the hippogryph.[189] Moreover, the associations to Geryon take on extra force because of their special connection to the other Dantean, Ulyssean echoes of word and structure in the episode. Geryon's flight, like Ruggiero's and like the Dantean Ulysses', is described in terms of marine imagery, as a travesty of the "remigium alarum."[190] In fact, within the economy of the *Inferno*, Geryon's emblematic fraudulence, which introduces the ten ditches of Male-

---

[187] For evidence that the Renaissance saw at least the Chimera in the Horatian monster see Erasmus, *Encomium* (Miller edition), p. 166.

[188] Echoes of Geryon in *Inferno* 16 and 17 (esp. 17.97 ff. and 116) are to be found in *Furioso* IV.24.8, VI.19.3 and 20.5, XXIII.16.2 (cf. *Inferno* 17.115), XXIII.16.5–8, XXXIII.114.2. The "catena" in IV.26.1–4 may echo *Inferno* 16.106–111. Shapiro ("Perseus and Bellerophon," pp. 124–25) notes only the first of the listed echoes.

[189] In *Inferno*, the spiral of Geryon is both a part and a parody of Dante's spiral journey through hell. For the significance of the movement see Freccero, "Dante's Pilgrim in a Gyre" and n. 107, above. It is important for understanding Ariosto that, even as Dante distances his own discourse from Geryon's fraud, he makes of the monster a vehicle for one stretch of his journey.

[190] *Inferno* 16.131–36; 17.5, 9, 19–24, 100–101, 104, 115. Cf. n. 40, above.

bolgia, is an especially clear prolepsis of the eighth *bolgia* and Ulysses' "consiglio frodolente." One final detail makes the monster especially apt for employment in the *Furioso*: its fraudulent appearance is specifically tied by Dante to the woven (Alcinian, Ariostan) art of Arachne (*Inferno* 17.18).

The chimerical attributes of Geryon are obvious: he/it is a composite flying monster with man's head, beast's body, and scorpion's tail (the Chimera being a mixture of lion's head, goat's body, and serpent's tail). Given that Virgil's placement of Geryon's "three-bodied form" in the Underworld comes within a line of a similar mention of the Chimera (*Aeneid* vi.288–89; cf. vii.662, viii.202), one suspects that the latter is a direct subtext for Dante's elaboration of the classical monster. Not only is Geryon the image of fraud incarnate, with its sweet face concealing bestial ugliness and mortal peril, it is also closely linked to the whole question of poetic veracity and mendacity. Against the fraudulent appearance of truth in the monster, Dante sets his *own* representation of the monster in an inverse relation: his writing is "ver c'ha faccia di menzogna," truth with a lying, and fantastic, face (*Inferno* 16.124). In the proem to canto vii, as already seen, Ariosto ostensibly takes up the Dantean position, urging belief in an apparently incredible tale. But, as we have seen earlier, his urgings are transparently spurious, assimilable to Alcina's lies and, as we now see, to Geryon's as well. If the hippogryph bridges literature and reality, in this view, it is only with a deceptive spiral motion, a twisting tale, a trope of fraud. The reason that Pegasus and Chimera do not ever "face off" in the poem is that they actually have the same face all along—the former is hidden within the latter. And if Ariosto is a Bellerophon, what he is combating is an aspect of himself and his poem, one which will never be fully extirpated or externalized.

Much later in the poem, as the poet recounts the outrageous deeds of Marfisa and Ruggiero in their battle against the Maganzesi and the Saracens who are holding Malagigi and Viviano captive, he cites Dante even more directly:

> *e se non che pur dubito che manche*
> *credenza al ver c'ha faccia di menzogna,*
> *di più direi; ma di men dir bisogna.*

Il buon Turpin, che sa che dice il vero,
e lascia creder poi quel ch'a l'uom piace,
narra mirabil cose di Ruggiero,
ch'udendolo il direste voi mendace.   [XXVI.22.6–8, 23.1–4]

And if I did not fear that belief would fail before this truth with a lying face, I would say more: but it would be better to say less. The good Turpin knows he tells the truth and lets us believe what we want: he narrates such miraculous things of Ruggiero that, to hear him, you would think him mendacious.

It is no accident that shortly afterward in the same canto the heroes come upon another of Merlin's prophetic works of art, this one recounting the allegory of Avarizia which is depicted as yet another Geryon-like, chimerically composite monstrosity (XXVI.39 ff.). In any case, by basing the intrinsically suspect account of the battle on the even more suspect authority of Turpin, Ariosto clearly turns this Dantean appeal against itself to suggest that these are indeed not *truths*, but *lies* with a lying face—lies which, however, reveal the truth about themselves to all but the most quixotic readers.

Perhaps the most interesting and elaborate of the allusions to Geryon comes in canto XIV, after the Archangel Michael (another composite creature, customarily represented with wings added to a human form) has begun his search to enlist "Silenzio" in aid of the beseiged forces of Charlemagne. Though he proceeds directly from the Word itself, in opposition to the explicitly Babelic forces of Rodomonte/Nimrod, he is singularly uninformed about the truth of life on earth. Having found "Discordia" in the monasteries where he expected to find Holy Silence, he has to fall back on the counsel of Fraud personified to locate his quarry. The figure of Fraud, again as most commentators have observed, is directly based on Dante's Geryon:

Avea piacevol viso, abito onesto,
. . . .
un parlar sì benigno e sì modesto,
che parea Gabriel che dicesse: Ave.
Era brutta e deforme in tutto il resto . . .   [XIV.87.1–5]

She had a pleasant face, honest garb, . . . speech so benign and so modest
that she seemed to be Gabriel saying "Ave." In all the rest she was
ugly and deformed.

There is a special irony in the evocation here of Gabriel's Annuncia-
tion to the Virgin which first revealed that the Word would be
made flesh, that the Truth itself would come among men. Michael,
himself God's messenger, listens to this mendacious simulacrum of
angelic verity, and "Ben che soglia la Fraude esser bugiarda, / pur
è tanto il suo dir simile al vero, / che l'angelo le crede . . ." ("Though
Fraud is usually a liar, still her speech is so like the truth that the
angel believes her" 91.1–3). The first joke is that the credulous
angel takes verisimilitude for verity, suspect words for the Word
itself. The second, and far more resonant, joke is that Fraud's words
prove, in the event, not only to resemble but to *be* the pure truth.

   The twofold irony of Ariosto's text, an irony within and against
the trope of irony itself, as we shall see, is, on the one hand, that
the truth-telling poetics of Dante is haunted by the nightmare fraud
of Geryon; but, on the other, that the voice of Fraud may speak
truths to which even the angels, traditionally creatures of pure
intellect, and divine messengers, are blind. The relation to, and
extension of, Ariosto's ambiguous use of Dante's fraudulent Ulysses
is clear enough. Time and again, Ariosto valorizes the use of fraud
as a weapon to combat the fraudulent weapons of evil,[191] even
as he leaves the implication that this mimetic use may finally collapse
the distinction between good and evil. Alcina's fraud consists in
making lies appear to be the truth; Astolfo as Pier delle Vigne tells
truths which are taken for lies; Melissa uses fraud to expose the
truth about lying Alcina, but effectively lies to Ruggiero about the
value of a return to history and heroic destiny. Fraud is given posi-
tive, though heavily qualified, ethical status. Now it takes on posi-
tive epistemological status as well: it is both truth's opposite and
itself a mode of truth. In a world where nothing is what it seems
or wants to be, truth is inevitably in disguise—it wears a lying
face.

   When critics have examined the Virgilian words, "nam iungentur

[191] Cf. n. 46, above.

gryphes equis," which are the most direct verbal source for the hippogryph, they have usually read them as a figuration of erotic (and poetic) impossibility exemplary of the *Furioso*'s flight from reference to, and representation of, "truth."[192] In the original context, however, they express the lover-narrator's shocked dismay that the impossible has *actually happened*—his beloved Nisa is marrying the old and disgusting Mopsus. The truth appears to him as the false and fantastic, but it is nonethless true. And even as Ariosto exposes his own and other poetry as lying madness, he doubles back to imply that the very transparency of *his* lying, its superficial fantasy, makes it a possible vehicle for truth,[193] a far more certain one than other texts which strive for verisimilitude, insisting all the while on their own virtue, sanity, and veracity. But this may be to overstate the case in favor of a recuperation of the True and the Good in the *Furioso*. My speculations tend rather to suggest that it is proper *neither* to make the hippogryph (and the poem) an emblem of the subservience of fiction and aesthetics to facts and ethics, *nor* to hold it up as the purely negative symbol of complete referential, representational, breakdown. If anything, Ariosto places the hippogryph squarely between the world of nature and that of poetic fantasy as a way of showing how equivocal are all mediations of imagination between the two—suggesting both that nothing is more *natural* to humankind than evasive flights of imagination and that the artifice of imagination always works upon materials derived from the real and inevitably (if involuntarily) reflects back upon them.

Whatever one's final judgment of the hippogryph's significance and the poem's morality and veracity, I have certainly come to

---

[192] Donato, "Desire," p. 32. Cf. Shapiro, "Perseus and Bellerophon," p. 124. In addition to the obvious applications of the Virgilian passage to the *Furioso,* it also refers to a love triangle not unlike that of Orlando/Angelica/Medoro and anticipates the poem-long themes of erotic infidelity and disillusionment.

[193] Ariosto jokingly asserts/subverts the veracity of his text in a number of famous passages—for instance, in the polemic with Federico Fregoso over the latter's doubts about the truth of the battle in Lipadusa (XLII.20−22); in the three alternative versions of the outcome of the hasty and violent departure of Issabella's hermit from the poem, capped by an offhanded dismissal of the problem ("qual si vuol, la vera sia" XXIX.7.7). See also II.54, VI.71, and the passages listed in n. 173, above.

subscribe to this vivid observation of DeSanctis, if not the conclusions that it serves: namely, that Ariosto creates "an equivocal and shifting atmosphere where vice and virtue, true and false, blur their boundaries" (p. 478). At the end of the final chapter, after I have sought at length to test and to recuperate the values that Pegasus/Geryon both subverts and promises, I will examine the image which most strikingly embodies such confusion: Cassandra, the very emblem of "truth with a lying face," whose prophetic words can never win the credence they demand.

CASSANDRA'S VEIL AND
THE POET'S FOLLY

When, after Ruggiero's ostentatious aerial departure, Astolfo leaves
the island of Logistilla, he does so under the guidance of Andronica
(Fortitude) and by far more conventional means than his friend. He
does take with him, however, two magical gifts which can be used
to master any situation: a book which penetrates all magical illusions
and a horn, distant relative of Roland's Oliphant, whose sound ter-
rifies even the bravest of men or women (xv.13–14). When he
finally reaches Europe again, after a series of adventures, he is, like
Ruggiero, lured by an Atlantean phantom into the labyrinth of de-
sire and self-deception, and he too loses his horse in the process.
Unlike Ruggiero he does keep his magical equipment and uses it
to set himself free and dissolve once and for all Atlante's magic
(xxii.11–23). Each of the two implements is a figure for a certain
function or aspect of poetic language. That of the book is obvious:
it contains words which literally "make sense" of deceptive appear-
ances, allowing its user direct access to reality and a certain amount
of control over it. The horn too has a "linguistic" component
insofar as (a) it is so obviously paired and contrasted with the book,
and (b) it produces intense sound.[1] It too exerts a power over reality,
but an opposite one. Instead of order and clarity, it produces chaos
and blindness, driving all who hear it temporarily mad with fear.
What these tools of sense and nonsense have in common, however,
is an extraordinary notion of the power of language, whether it is
to resolve crisis (for instance, that of an evil such as Orrilo which
can be dismembered but always restores itself to a unity, like a
demonic parody of Pico's Osiris) or to precipitate it (dominating
even the fearless Marfisa).

By contrast, the episode to which I have just dedicated such an
extensive analysis seems to point toward an opposite conclusion:

---

[1] Cf. Bonomone (*Allegoria*, in Orlandini edition), who reads Astolfo as "un
encomio delle lettere, il quale, col risonante corno dell'eloquenzia, e col libro della
sapienza . . . ottiene più egli solo, che tutti gli altri con le armi." See also *Innamorato*
I.xiv.60–62, where Orlando's horn has properties similar to Astolfo's here.

toward the impotence of the poetic domain, its perfect irrelevance to history, whether according to its author's designs or in spite of them. On the one hand, the poetry of Alcina and Atlante is (temporarily) thwarted in its attempts to help Ruggiero evade the consequences of the inevitable series of crises and choices which punctuate and define any human life—marriage, religious commitment, public duty, and, finally, death. On the other hand, Melissa and Logistilla, though they stalemate Alcina, are no more successful in preparing Ruggiero to face, judge, and master these crises than the others are in helping him to escape them. The narrator emerges from the episode with the appearance of one oscillating between the two poetic projects, which are doomed to cancel each other out.

The "completeness" of the episode, its parodic closing of an "hermeneutic" circle which leaves author, character, and interpreter exactly where they began, makes it tempting to generalize conclusions about it synecdochically to the poem as a whole. That, however, would be to forget that in focusing on those narrative segments which together make up the Alcina episode, I have strategically neglected those other threads with which they are so carefully interwoven—particularly that of Orlando, whose erotic subjugation comes into view just as Ruggiero seems to have been freed from his (canto VIII)—and the possible resistances and/or modifications these may offer to my interpretation.[2] It would be to forget as well the later events whose seeds are sown in the Alcina episode, particularly those involving Astolfo. As just seen, Astolfo's return, "tutored and instructed" (xv.13.3), seems to have a far different import than Ruggiero's, presenting a view of poetic possibility drastically opposed to that associated with Bradamante's errant beau. In fact, his return leads directly to the freeing of

---

[2] The technique of reading by the episode, the character, the theme, or the image, rather than by the canto (except in the rare case of single-episode cantos) has been the staple of criticism of the *Furioso*—primarily, I believe, because it "makes the most sense," i.e., generates the most compact and coherent readings. This is, of course, a way of rewriting the poem without the narrative "error" (even if error is the chosen theme), without the subtle juxtapositions of *entrelacement*—a charge to which I too plead occasionally guilty. Two useful exceptions are Carne-Ross and Weaver.

Ruggiero from imprisonment and, with powerful symmetry, his reward for this triumph over Atlantean illusion is possession of the hippogryph previously lost by Ruggiero (XXII.24–30). It would be to forget that the conclusion of Ruggiero's itinerary in the poem is still some thirty-five cantos off when he so fecklessly undoes all the work of Logistilla. Finally, it would be to forget that the arc described by Ruggiero jeers at the idea that one part of the poem's geography can either represent or determine that of any other, that it could be the privileged chart which escapes and defines the sea of verse. To rediscover the conclusions of the previous chapter in other sections of the poem is thus simultaneously to contradict them, since they posit the necessary inconclusiveness of the character's education and the poem's representation.

The discussion which follows, nonetheless, undertakes to "conclude" the narrative of my interpretation and to reach a shoreline, a readerly margin from which both itself and its object may be viewed whole and coherent even as it tries to account for the obstacles which the poem places in the way of such a hopeful effort. Accordingly, I will be tracing out several of the implications of what has already been said for a few crucial segments in the poem which stand to the Alcina episode in a relation of obvious repetition, or polemical revision, or both. One result of these readings will be an expansion of critical horizons—a recognition of a range of themes and areas of crisis in the poem which complement or even supersede the somewhat arbitrary privileging of individual education vs. consuming madness as the controlling question of the *Furioso*. On the one hand, it will become apparent that religious faith, seemingly excluded from the secular ethical/aesthetic focus of the Alcina episode, is a matter which cannot be separated from these at all. On the other hand, the whole domain of political crisis, including the relation of the poem to its reluctant patron and its stance in regard to the devastating epoch from 1494 to 1527, is also very much at issue.[3] The instance of metaphorical education will

---

[3] See Durling, *The Figure of the Poet*, pp. 138–46, for one of the most useful discussions of the political events of the epoch and of Ariosto's critical/patriotic treatment of them and his patrons' policies in the course of the poem. See also Catalano, *Vita*, vol. I; and Luciano Chiappini, *Gli Estensi* (Modena: Dall'Oglio,

survive as privileged and exemplary only insofar as the same oblique approach/avoidance strategies of representation are found in these other areas as well and insofar as they are determined by, but themselves also precipitate and determine, crises in the language through which they are named and judged.

Through each of these readings, therefore, I will be forcing the question of the power or impotence of the poem to refer to and/or transform its readers—on the one hand, either educating them or driving them mad; on the other, failing to signify or to make its significance known to interpreters who match Ruggiero for foolishness or willful misunderstanding. At the same time, I will be closing in on the "figure of the poet" himself, whose plural figures or metaphorical projections may perhaps be reducible to folly or impotence, but who usually seems to escape the net of his own weaving by an awareness of madness which contradicts and transcends its objects as well as by speech which overcomes Folly's silence. This poet-God would be the One whose unity resolves all multiplicity, whose "occhio divino" can judge and resolve the perpetual errors of human judgment throughout the poem. In restating, but also further challenging this theme, I will suggest where the crucial notion of "crisis" ultimately and paradoxically tends—*both* to the insignificant absence of death *and* to the perspective of Apocalyptic judgment— and I will show how Ariosto does, quite deliberately, situate himself within that dilemma, and thus both inside and outside of his representations of crisis.

Specifically, I will examine Astolfo's flight, from the Senapo's palace to hell, Eden, and, finally, the lunar surface, which in its entirety is, for more and less apparent reasons, an important companion piece to Ruggiero's education. The twin questions to be asked here are whether Astolfo's pseudo-Dantean ascent provides the remedy to folly that Ruggiero's does not, and whether Ariosto's poem is not thereby claiming for itself the power of illuminating reflection that it previously refused to assert. In the second place,

---

1967), for a less scholarly survey of the period. For the century preceding, see Werner Gundersheimer, *Ferrara: The Style of a Renaissance Despotism* (Princeton: Princeton University Press, 1973).

I will turn to Orlando, Ruggiero's Herculean double, to see whether, on the contrary, he does not carry Ruggiero's blindness out to its (il)logical conclusion, sweeping away even the poet and his language in an all-engulfing *furore,* and whether, as has recently been suggested, madness itself, while defeating reason and its values, does not install a set of Erasmian countervalues, with Folly becoming another, better, mode of understanding self and world.

The last section of this chapter focuses, appropriately, on the last canto of the poem, where the *Furioso* attempts to effect a coincidence of poetry with history (as the marriage of Ruggiero and Bradamante opens the way to an Este dynasty) and of the poet with audience (as his writerly "legno" reaches the readerly shore). On the one hand, does Ruggiero, protagonist of the "historical" narrative, somehow learn the restraint that his elaborate allegorical education failed to teach him? Has he at last embraced and purified the values of famous name and noble family which were earlier contaminated? And just what sort of dynasty does his personal sacrifice give rise to? On the other hand, does Ariosto, protagonist of the drama of epic writing, fully escape from the endless labyrinthine error of romance into the finality of genealogical epic? The festive tapestried pavilion of Cassandra brings the two lines of questioning together. It celebrates Ippolito d'Este, emblem of the historical present toward which Ruggiero's poetic past gestures (and out of which it was written), even as it lays his apotheosis under subtle qualification. It is also the last of the many figures of the poem. And Cassandra herself is the last, perhaps least expected, and most striking of the poet's "lieu-tenants." Around her and her "velo" gather all the accumulated questions of poetic reference both to the world of history and to the poet's mental state: Does the poet depict a comic or tragic world? Is his vision mad or sane? Finally, with a reading of the contents of canto XLVI comes the question of poetic conclusion itself: Can the discourse ever be fully closed, thus disclosing a definitive significance, resolving every narrative, thematic, and referential crisis with the "sense of an ending"?

Thus, if the initial work of my conclusion follows the conventional strategies of closure, of reaching out from the part to the whole, my second effort will be to write an anticonclusion or, rather, to suggest that the question of closure itself is what the dialectic of representing crisis and evading it is all about, and that any attempt to conclude a discussion of it definitively, or definitionally, would be to betray the constituent openness of the question. There is, however, one point which I believe is "proved" by Chapters 2 and ·3 of this study and to which the rest of Chapter 4 has little to add, except superfluous confirmation: namely, that the *Furioso* has, for all that has been written about it, received far less detailed interpretive exegesis and commentary than it can support. Of all the objectionable statements in Croce's masterful treatment of the poem, the only one with which I find myself in *absolute* disagreement is his claim that the poem presents no further interpretive dilemmas at the level of the text (its words, images, etc.), that its literal sense is perfectly transparent.[4] To the extent, and it is a considerable one, that post-Crocean criticism took this claim seriously, dismissing Rajnaesque scholarship as having done both too much and too little in the way of explaining the poem, his legacy has been a genuinely deplorable one.[5] This objection in fact applies not only to such classically callow readings as that of C.S. Lewis, but in a sense to "postmodern" readers whose techniques permit them to privilege isolated passages or motifs or plays on words as "subversive" without regard to contextual elements which may in turn be subverting those subversions.[6] After all, from what

---

[4] Croce, "Ariosto," p. 3: "[*L'Orlando Furioso*] non ha mai presentato serî ostacoli d'interpretazione."

[5] I am not advocating a return to "positivistic" scholarship, far from it, but rather a new sense of the enormous complexity of inter- and intratextual relationships established by the poem, which necessarily begins with an empirical notation of parallels and echoes. A great deal more could be done in the way of reinterpreting Ariosto's use of the romance sources which Rajna merely accumulates and of more thoroughly investigating such little-explored subjects as the poem's stances in relation to Alberti, Boccaccio, Erasmus, and so on. More basically, Ariosto's syntax tends surprisingly often toward significant ambiguities, cruxes, etc., a few of which will come out in the course of this chapter.

[6] C.S. Lewis, *The Allegory of Love* (London: Oxford University Press, 1936). Contrasting Spenser with Ariosto, Lewis makes the following comparison between the two: "If you stand by Athens and London and Oxford, as I do, then of course Ariosto is not a 'great poet'" though he is technically brilliant (p. 303). In a characteristically vivid image, Lewis gives his ideal circumstances for reading such poems: "Johnson once described the ideal happiness which he would choose if he

we have seen, Ariosto's strategy of writing is precisely that of referring *every* utterance to an almost infinite series of subversive contexts, both inside and outside of his poem.

It is partly on these polemical grounds that I permitted myself the extravagence of reading the Alcina episode in such minute, though certainly not exhaustive, detail. Whether or not the other conclusions are accepted, and to an extent, as just mentioned, I do not accept them *qua* conclusions myself, *this* I believe has been (re-) established—that it is not possible to overestimate the extent of the inter- and intratextual play of the *Furioso*, and that the attempts to see the poem as self-enclosed, "self-referential" (rather than prob- lematically referential), are in part motivated by a desire to control that play, to reduce it to manageable dimensions. And this I would say as much of Donato's "deconstructive" reading as I would of Croce's unreconstructed "spiritual" aesthetics.

i. *Ariosto's Allegory of Poets and Theologians*

The so-called lunar episode of the *Furioso* is, if anything, even more celebrated than the Alcina episode, and it is just as often offered as a synecdoche for the meaning (or spirit or tone) of the poem as a whole, for many of the same understandable yet questionable rea- sons.[7] The two episodes are actually structural and thematic com-

---

were regardless of [i.e., indifferent to] futurity. My own choice, with the same reservation, would be to read the Italian epic—to be always convalescent from some small illness and always seated in a window that overlooked the sea, there to read these poems eight hours of each happy day" (p. 304). In view of the sea/shore metaphor discussed in Chapter 1, we might say that Lewis is one reader who "missed the boat."

[7] Among those who have seen the episode as the epitome of the poem are Momigliano (*Saggio*, pp. 10, 283); Greene, for whom it exemplifies "the cool tranquillity of meaninglessness" (*The Descent from Heaven*, p. 131) and a radical skepticism about life and art; and David Quint ("Astolfo's Voyage to the Moon," *Yale Italian Studies*, o.s. 1 [1977], p. 398), who elaborates Greene's thesis in a close reading of the episode. See also James Chiampi, "Between Voice and Writing: Ariosto's Irony According to St. John," *Italica* 60 (1983), who covers some of the same ground as Quint, whom he apparently had not read. Another good reading of this episode is Mario Santoro, "La Sequenza Lunare nel *Furioso:* Una Società allo Specchio," in *Atti dell'Accademia Pontaniana* (Napoli: Giannini, 1975).

panion pieces: set respectively (and roughly) at the one-quarter and three-quarter points in the poem, like the twin foci of an ellipsis. They resemble each other, and differ from most of the rest of the book, in their exotic geography and, especially, in their use of complex, extended, allegories which gloss both the world of the poem and the poem's mode of reference to worlds beyond itself. The glossatory function is even clearer in this case. The lunar surface, as the poet tells the reader (XXXIV.70–72) and as St. John tells Astolfo (XXXV.18), is the exact double of the earth. At the same time, among the highlights of Astolfo's visit, and closely intertwined with the interpretation of earthly life, is St. John's "defense of poetry," far and away Ariosto's most explicit statement of a poetics, with corresponding hermeneutics.[8] St. John's brief discourse is in fact remarkably comprehensive. It situates poetry in relation to power and economic value, as well as to historical and transcendental truth. It contains a sort of brief "literary history" in the form of allusions to and parodies of poets from Homer to Dante, but it also confronts other modes of writing, notably history and Scripture, which act as foils to poetic reference.

The lunar sequence also repeats the Alcina episode in its double focus on human identity and poetic expression, and on the relation between them. It too concentrates on the two principal threats to human identity: madness and death. St. John's teachings can be divided into two parts, both involving allegorical expositions of the contents of the moon's surface. The first, extending from stanza 75 to 84 in canto XXXIV, catalogues the things lost from the earth, all of which are linked to the vanity of those human hopes and desires on which we try to build a sense of ourselves. It culminates, of course, with the mountain of lost wits which signals the universal madness of life back on earth (81.7–8, 82.5–8). The second, which extends from the end of XXXIV (stanzas 87–92) to the beginning of XXXV (stanzas 3–30), is an allegory of the Fates and of Time, with the inevitable focus on human mortality.

To both of these universal crises, solutions are apparently offered.

---

[8] Both Santoro ("La Sequenza Lunare," p. 347) and Durling (*The Figure of the Poet*, p. 149) note the resemblance of St. John's words to standard humanistic defenses of poetry without going into specific texts or motifs.

Before examining them more closely, however, I would like to suggest in much more detailed terms just how thoroughly Astolfo's adventures here are designed to repeat and perhaps revise those of Ruggiero.[9] The most obvious link between the two is the hippogryph itself, with all its associations to ethics and poetics (and to the didactic project which hopes to connect them). We have seen how calculated is the transfer of the animal from one master to another. Astolfo begins *his* flight one canto later (XXIII), a point roughly equidistant from the two allegorical episodes, in the context of two forceful allusions to Ruggiero's initial, ill-conceived, unbridled, flight (13.7–8, 27.1–2), on the eve of Orlando's own earthbound version of a "folle volo" ("mad flight"). The motive of the journey, like that of Ruggiero on his return, is curiosity, pure desire to see the unknown, the same "concupiscentia occulorum" which proved fatal to Dante's Ulysses (x.69, 70; XXII.26; XXIII.12; XXXIV.48).[10] Like Ruggiero's, the beginning of Astolfo's journey takes the Pyrenees as a point of reference (XXXIII.96.7–8), though unlike Ruggiero, Astolfo does succeed in seeing "tutta la Spagna" ("all of Spain" XXXIII.97.8; cf. x.113.2). Like Ruggiero he comes to "la meta che pose / ai primi naviganti Ercole invitto" ("the boundary post that invincible Hercules set for the first sailors" XXXIII.98.1–2; cf. xv.22); but unlike Ruggiero,

---

[9] The numerous parallels linking theme, image, phrase, structure, etc. have never been catalogued extensively, or even symptomatically, partly because the resemblances become really apparent only when we look at both sequences in their entirety: for Ruggiero, this means beginning in canto IV and continuing through XII; for Astolfo, as a minimum, it means beginning in canto XXXIII (if not in XV or XXII) and continuing through XXXV.31. Already in XV, Astolfo's return by boat with a guide contrasts with Ruggiero's unguided flight. The return, and Andronica's prophesy of the "voyages of discovery," allude specifically to the pillars of Hercules (22.5–6) and contain a series of solar images (18, 21, 26), notably in 22.7–8: "del sole imitando il camin tondo, / ritrovar nuove terre e nuovo mondo." Giamatti assumes the contrast in *The Earthly Paradise,* but speaks only in general terms about the lunar episode. For useful hints, see Weaver ("Lettura," p. 400) and Ossola ("Métaphore et Inventaire," p. 187). The latter makes the very acute general observation that the two journeys are both set in relation to Dante's single ascent: Ruggiero's being an education by "experience," Astolfo's by "revelation."

[10] For the *topos* of the three concupiscences, see 1 John 2:16 and Augustine, *Confessions* x.35–37.

significantly, he turns away, remaining within the confines of Europe and Africa, obeying God's will as Andronica had defined it for him (xv.18−24).[11] The recurrence of the name "Atlante," once as the ocean (xxxiii.98.4) and once as the mountain (100.2), both traditionally linked to the giant/astrologer/tutor, deliberately evokes Ruggiero's mentor, as well as the mythological turning of Atlas into a mountain by Perseus. In fact, these details, taken with the flying horse and the Ethiopian destination, reveal that the model for this passage is the very same Ovidian episode (that of Perseus' rescue of Andromeda) from which Ruggiero's rescue of Angelica is taken.[12] Even though when Astolfo lands in Ethiopia he finds not the fair Andromeda but the pathetic Senapo, he too is called upon to defeat monsters, the Harpies, whose allegorical associations with avarice make them the equivalent of one of Ruggiero's foes, Erifilla.[13]

In fact, Astolfo's journey matches Ruggiero's in pairing the sin

[11] Herculean elements reappear in cantos xxxiii and xxxiv. The Lydia episode recalls Hercules' subjection to Omphale, a Lydian woman. Alcestes' name is the same as a woman rescued from hell by Hercules, and he is forced by his cruel beloved to perform labors more difficult than those of the Greek hero. Most of the mythographical accounts—Salutati, *De Laboribus Herculis* iii.xiii−xv (vol. 1, pp. 235−43); Landino, *De Vera Nobilitate*, p. 109; Silvestris, *Commentary*, pp. 73−75—make Hercules the victor over the Harpies and the freer of Phineus, on whose story the Senapo's is modeled.

[12] Ovid, *Metamorphoses* iv.604−v.249, esp. iv.619−30, 655−69. The parallels with Astolfo's journey are the following: after turning *Atlas* into a stony mountain with the Medusa head (also associated with heresy and reifying *invidia*—see Mazzotta, *Dante*, p. 276 ff., and Freccero, "Medusa"), Perseus flies east toward *Ethiopia* and there finds Andromeda, who is being punished by *Ammon*. The Ovidian episode even contains references to Lucifer (iv.629, 665), and a "Phineus" figures prominently in its latter stages (v.8 ff.). Cf. Shapiro, "From Atlas to Atlante," pp. 331−32, passim. For Ariosto's use of Perseus, see Chapter 3, n. 77, above.

[13] The Harpies are consistently allegorized as a divine punishment for the Senapo's avarice by the *Cinquecento* commentators on the *Furioso*. See especially Toscanella's annotations in the Orlandini edition. This reading is partly based on the textual references to his great wealth and on the obvious analogies to the Midas story. There is a long mythographical tradition of glossing Phineus, model both for the Senapo's affliction with punitive blindness and for his difficulties with the Harpies, as the epitome of avarice (e.g., Salutati, *De Laboribus Herculis* iii.xiv [vol. 1, pp. 236−381]).

of avarice with that of idolatry. Whereas Ruggiero, having vanquished the allegorical giantess, is received as a "Dio sceso dal superno coro" ("a god descended from the heavenly choir" VII.9.8), Astolfo, the potential scourge of the Harpies, is greeted by the Senapo as "Angel di Dio, Messia novello" ("Angel of God, new Messiah" XXXIII.114.5). The idolatrous desire which does not "go beyond the sign" of Alcina's art returns in the Senapo's willingness to build a temple to Astolfo and treat him as a god if he can chase off the monsters. The description of the Senapo as "quel re che nulla vede" ("that king who sees nothing" XXXIII.116.7) clearly refers not only to his literal blindness, but to the blind literality of idolatry as well.[14] And the irony deepens when one recognizes that the Senapo's name probably derives from the Italian *senape* (Latin *senapis*), or mustard, and thus most likely alludes to the Biblical mustard seed of faith. Faith, which sees the invisible, can move mountains, while the Senapo, who tried to ascend God's holy mountain, cannot see at all.[15] On brief reflection, one realizes that avarice itself, the other sin to which the Nubian emperor is closely linked, is a clear subspecies of idolatry, treating arbitrary counters of value as if their worth were intrinsic. It is no accident that the Senapo's kingdom is said to be the source of all the precious metals and substances which are valued in Europe, though in Ethiopia their worth is not relative, determined by scarcity and hence by exchange value, but absolute, determined by their intrinsic natures (XXXIII.103–105). At the same time, the city is compared, favorably, to the center of earthly spiritual values, Jerusalem, and is said to be the locus of another version of Christianity (101–102). And its

[14] A reference to the Temple of Ammon in stanza 100 prepares the theme of idolatry by its allusion to Lucan, *Pharsalia* IX.545–65. Cf. Mazzotta, *Dante,* pp. 62–64

[15] For the "senape"/"Senapo" connection, I am indebted to Walter Stephens. The Biblical reference to faith as a mustard seed which allows its possessor to move mountains is in Matthew 15:17 (see also Matthew 13:31–32, Luke 17:6). *Cinque Canti* IV.82.1–4 reveals Ariosto's particular affection for this passage. Compare *Furioso* XXIII.1.7–8 as well. For the debate over the derivation of the name "Senapo," see also Rajna, *Le Fonti,* pp. 528–33, and E. Cerulli, "Il Volo di Astolfo sull'Etiopia nell'*Orlando Furioso,*" in *Atti dell'Accademia dei Lincei, Rendiconti della Classe di Scienze Morali,* series 6, vol. 8 (1932), who also finds an echo of faith: "At Senap, id est Servus Crucis." Other instances of the faith and blindness intersection can be found in 1.56, XXI.1–2, and frequently throughout the poem.

ruler, when young, imitated Lucifer's rebellion, his fall into idolatrous pride, which is precisely the sin of locating in the self something of absolute value, when in fact the self's true worth is only in relation to its manufacturer, God himself.[16]

These observations about the nature of the place in which Astolfo finds himself point toward an even wider pattern of parallels between the two episodes. Ruggiero's and Astolfo's adventures both have at their dynamic centers a passage from a city-garden *in malo* to one *in bono* which dramatizes a movement of educational askesis. The fabulous, yet useless, wealth of the Senapo recalls and exceeds the seductive "oro" of Alcina's palace. Moreover, as an idolatrous *alter* Jerusalem the Senapo's city, like Alcina's, is an obvious antiparadise. In each case, the hero moves on to a second city-garden which seemingly corrects the first. Just as Logistilla's translucent jewels echo and perfect the deceptive gold and stones of Alcina, so Astolfo in Eden itself finds a garden and a palace, whose natural beauties are more brilliant than gems and whose palace walls are made of a single gem, like that of the New Jerusalem (Revelation 21:10–23), which makes all earthly wealth contemptible (XXXIV. 49–53).[17] Moreover, the contours of this journey from false to true

---

[16] Salutati in fact equates pride with avarice: "Est autem Fineus dives, est et avarus. Per divitias autem intelligo divitiarum effectum, id est superbiam" (*De Laboribus Herculis* III.xiv, p. 241). See also Isaiah 2 for the conflation of idolatry, wealth, blindness, and mountains (all key elements of this episode), especially verses 2–3, 7–8, 14, and, above all, 17–20. See also Isaiah 14:12–13 for Lucifer's pride and fall, and for his desire to sit "in monte testamenti," above the clouds (the Senapo, by the way, is the king of the "Nubi") and equal to the Most High. In this regard, Ruscelli's *Allegoria* to canto XXXIII (in Orlandini edition) equates the Senapo with Nimrod and the building of Babel's tower. Arturo Graf, *Miti, Leggende e Superstizioni del Medioevo* (Torino: Loescher, 1892), pp. 116–20, cites as a possible precedent for the Senapo's mad assault on the Holy Mountain the medieval legend of Alexander the Great's hubristic desire to climb up to see the original Terrestrial Paradise. Finally, the affliction of Phineus in the original myth was a punishment for revealing the secrets of the gods to men (for which, see Valerius Flaccus, *Argonautica* IV.422–84), so that there avarice was juxtaposed with pride.

[17] A comparison of VI.59; VII.3, 8–16; X.57–63; XXXIII.103–106; and XXXIV.49–53, 60 suggests that the larger structure of opposed city-gardens is reinforced by specific echoes and repeated imagery, particularly the gemstones and the references to "paradiso." Of special interest is the return to imagery of fruit and trees in Eden. If Astolfo "inalberato" was a parody of the Biblical tree of knowledge, he now has access to the real thing.

paradise are part of an even larger analogy, similar to that seen in
the Alcina episode, though more explicit and better documented
in the criticism, between Astolfo's ascent to the moon and Dante's
travels through the afterlife. Like Dante's journey, Astolfo's is di-
vided into three distinct stages: first he descends into hell, then re-
turns to the light (where, like Dante, he cleans himself of infernal
stains, XXXIV.47), ascending a mountain to the Earthly Paradise,
and finally is granted a saintly guide who carries him up above the
confines of the earthly and human. Whereas Ruggiero never does
arrive at the true Eden (mischievously removed by Ariosto from
its Dantean site), Astolfo does, and with far less effort. It is at this
point that we should begin to emphasize just how different the two
educational itineraries really are.

The most obvious contrast is that, empirically, Ruggiero is a fail-
ure, Astolfo a success in their respective episodes. The lunar episode
not only names the threats of madness and death, but seems to pro-
vide clear remedies for them. In spite of the universal madness of
earth, Astolfo is permitted to recover and eventually to restore
Orlando's wits (XXXIV.83, 87; XXXIX.36–61) and his own as well.
Furthermore, St. John's exposé of the depredations of time, which
reveals men's mortality and then robs them even of a lingering
existence in a famous name, leads into the defense of poetry on the
grounds that it can give princes/heroes the assurance that

> *Oltre che del sepolcro uscirian vivi*
> . . . .
> *pur che sapesson farsi amica Cirra,*
> *più grato odore avrian che nardo o mirra*   [XXXV.24.5–8]

Not only will they emerge living from the tomb— . . . if only they
know how to make a friend of Parnassus, they will have a name more
pleasing than nard or myrrh

His words quite precisely recall and, apparently, redeem those of
Melissa in canto VII, stanza 41. The choice of the moon, which is
a traditional intersection of time and eternity, as the locale for the
revelation of poetic power is clearly significant, particularly so since
the moon is also conventionally associated with Clio, Muse of His-
tory, whose name according to Salutati and many others, means,

precisely, "Glory."[18] Finally, the most important difference be-
tween the two heroes is that Astolfo does in fact return to earth
and put into effect everything that St. John instructed him to. One
might even argue that just as in the *Commedia* Ulysses' failed journey
to Eden is replaced by Dante's successful transcendence of even that
locale of earthly perfection, so Ruggiero's pointless circling is set
off by Astolfo's brilliant performance. The question, however, is
why this should be.

What is it about "il Duca inglese" and his education that sets them
apart? Is he following the educational model of neo-Platonism? Of
secular humanism? Or of a third mode, Christian faith one might
suppose, which combines and yet transcends the two, escaping the
dangers which we saw linked to them in the Alcina episode? The
possibility of philosophical transcendence, though the upward surge
begins with the characteristic *curiositas* of such flights, can be quickly
dispelled. The failure of the Senapo's unaided, prideful, journey
alone should convince us, particularly if we notice how closely it
recalls the mystical thinkers left "blind and confused" in *Satira* VI.
Astolfo is also clearly parodying an ascent, whose goal is the puri-
fication and rediscovery of the original intellectual self, when he
takes possession of his and Orlando's lost wits, stored in handy
"supermarket" containers. The irony is that he is taking them not
for the purpose of going further upward, but of bringing them
back down to earth. This downward swerve from heaven to earth
can be seen as well in a key passage describing the correspondences,
the resemblance-in-difference, of earth and moon:

> Tu dèi saper che non si muove fronda
> la giù, che segno qui non se ne faccia.

[18] I quote from Salutati, *De Laboribus Herculis* I.x, p. 52: "Penultima vero Musarum,
que dicitur Clyo, a 'cleos,' videlicet Grece, Latine 'gloria,' non inapposite cum lunari
circulo qui quidem infimus est, ipsi lune huius dispensationis ordine sociatur. Fama
namque non famosi sed famam exhibentium attestatione relucet; et ipsa luna non
suo sed alieno splendet a lumine. Nullus enim, quantacunque scientia eluceat, famosus
est nisi quatenus celebratur. Crescit etiam et decrescit lunare iubar, et ipsius fame
fulgor tractu temporis, ut in pluribus, sepelitur et pro celebrantium voluntate nunc
diminutionem patitur, nunc recipit augmentum." His source is probably Fulgentius,
Mitologiarum Libri Tres I.15, in *Opera* (Helm edition), pp. 25–26. Cf. Greenfield,
Humanist and Scholastic Poetics, pp. 138–39.

Ogni effetto convien che corrisponda
in terra e in ciel, ma con diversa faccia.   [xxxv.18.1–4]

You ought to know that down there no leaf stirs without making a
trace up here. Every earthly effect necessarily corresponds to one in
heaven, but in a different guise.

Altri fiumi, altri laghi, altre campagne
sono là su, che non son qui tra noi;
altri piani, altre valli, altre montagne   [xxxiv.72.1–3]

Other rivers, other lakes, other fields are up there than those down here
with us; other plains, other valleys, other mountains

The doctrine of correspondences which metaphorically *and* onto-
logically measure but also bridge the distances between the three
traditional orders of being (terrestrial, astronomical, empyrean),
allowing imaginative (and yet *real*) access from lower to higher,
is a commonplace of *Quattrocento* mysticism. It lies behind Pico's
doctrine of natural magic *in bono* and is fully elaborated in the
Heptaplus.[19] It is restated, in words which might well be Ariosto's
immediate source and polemical target, by Bembo in book III of
the *Asolani*:

> *[con gli occhi dell'animo vediamo] essere un altro mondo ancora né materiale,*
> *né sensibile, ma . . . separato e puro che intorno il [a mostro mondo] sopragira*
> *e che è da lui cercato sempre e sempre ritrovato . . . diviso da esso tutto, e tutto*
> *in ciascuna sua parte dimorante . . . nel quale cielo bene ha eziando tutto quello*
> *che ha in questo, ma tanto sono quelle cose di più eccellente stato, che non*
> *sono queste[:] . . . Per ciò che ha esso la sua terra . . . ha il mare . . . ha l'aria*

---

[19] Pico, *Heptaplus*, esp. II.ii, which makes the hermetic equation between earth
and moon (p. 228). Cf. Sannazaro, *Arcadia* Ecl. 5. See also Garin, L'Umanesimo,
p. 125. For magic and the doctrine of correspondences in general, see D.P. Walker,
Spiritual and Demonic Magic from Ficino to Campanella (South Bend: University of
Notre Dame Press, 1975); Frances Yates, *Giordano Bruno and the Hermetic Tradition*
(Chicago: University of Chicago Press, 1964). Yates points out (p. 442) that the
very late Renaissance linked the *Corpus Hermeticum*, where much of the doctrine
of correspondences is to be found, with the Gospel of John, and even occasionally
equated Hermes Trismegistus to St. John. Farrell ("Mentors and Magi," p. 29) notes
the "neo-platonic derivation of the doctrine of correspondences," and a little later
adds that John dwells like "the neo-platonic *magus*, in a strange limbo between
heaven and earth" (p. 85).

. . . ha il fuoco; ha la luna; ha il sole; ha le stelle. . . . Ma quivi né seccano le erbe, né invecchiano le piante, né muoiono gli animali. . . . Non ha quel mondo d'alcun mutamento mestiero . . . [III.xx, p. 159]

[with the eyes of the soul] we see there is another world neither material nor sensible, but . . . separate and pure, which wheels around and above our world, which is entirely divided from it and which dwells in each part of it. . . . Thus that heaven has everything that this world does, but those things are of a more excellent kind than these. . . . It has its earth, its sea, its air, its fire, its moon, its sun, its stars. . . . But there grass does not dry up, plants do not grow old, animals do not die. . . . That world has no need of any change.

For the neo-Platonist Bembo and his "portavoce," Lavinello, the images of this world become means of "translating" oneself into the hidden world of Ideas that they resemble:

Ma se alcuno Idio vi ci portasse . . . e mostrasseceli, quelle cose solamente vere cose ci parrebbono, e la vita, che ivi si vivesse, vera vita, e tutto ciò che è qui, ombra et imagine di loro essere . . . [III.xx, p. 160]

But if some god should take us there . . . and show us those things, they alone would seem true things to us, and only the life that one leads there would seem true life, and everything that is here would seem shadows and images of their essence

The ironic reversal operated by Ariosto is to make a higher world the means of interpreting the lower and not the other way around. He hints, not too subtly, that the neo-Platonists are really doing the opposite of what they say they are doing, i.e., projecting an anthropomorphic image onto the unknown reaches of the seen and unseen heavens.[20]

Once again we find Ariosto oriented toward a humanism within earthly limits which values the power of *oratio* and the usefulness of practical *ratio* at the service of a public cause, specifically Orlando's service to Carlo's cause. Ariosto's primary source for the allegory

---

[20] This is roughly what Auerbach is attempting to do with Dante in *Dante: Poet of the Secular World* (Chicago: University of Chicago Press, 1961) as well as in "Figura" and *Mimesis.*

of lost things is Alberti's *Intercenale,* the *Somnium,* itself lost for centuries and rediscovered in the 1960s by Garin.[21] The *Somnium,* like much of Alberti's Lucianesque satirical allegory, for instance the *Momus,* contains violent attacks against the pretensions of philosophical learning. But it is also unexpectedly brutal to some aspects of early humanism, especially the hunters after lost books such as Niccoli (and Garin!). Garin has in fact quite effectively demonstrated that a *certain* Alberti, far different from the optimistic humanist of traditional criticism, is as caustic about the civic life (in which man "is a wolf to man") as he is about transcendence, leaving no margin for escape.[22] The question is whether a similar critique lies behind Ariosto's apparent rescue of human *ratio* and *oratio.* A consideration of *ratio* will come in the next section of this chapter, though it is worth noting that Astolfo's success is qualified by the news that he will suffer a second loss of wits in the future (XXXIV.86.7–8).[23] It will, however, come as no major critical revelation that such a critique can be discovered behind the humanistic "defense of poetry."

What so obviously gives St. John's version of the value of poetic fame more authority than Melissa's is that he is the spokesman

[21] The text of the "Somnium" was first published by Garin, "Venticinque *Intercenali* Inedite e Sconosciute di Leon Battista Alberti," *Belfagor* 19 (1964), 390–92. In his *Rinascite e Rivoluzioni* (Bari: Laterza, 1975), pp. 193–96, Garin includes a translation of the work into Italian. Cesare Segre was among the first to address the question of the importance of the discovery for the lunar episode in the *Furioso,* in "Leon Battista Alberti e Ludovico Ariosto," in *Esperienze Ariostesche,* pp. 85–96 (first published in *Rivista di Cultura Classica e Medioevale* 7 [1965], 1025–33). Quint, "Astolfo's Voyage," provides one of the more useful summaries of Ariosto's other sources for the lunar episode (see also Rajna, *Le Fonti,* pp. 528–47; Griffin, *Ludovico Ariosto,* p. 100).

[22] For the attack on Niccoli, see Garin, *Rinascite e Rivoluzioni,* p. 93. For the whole, extremely interesting, question of Alberti's self-contradictory antihumanism, see the passage quoted from the *Momus* in Chapter 3, above, in addition to Garin, "La Miseria e Grandezza dell'Uomo" and "I Morti," in *Rinascite e Rivoluzioni,* pp. 161–82 and 183–92, respectively. For man as wolf, see Plautus, *Asinaria* 494, quoted by Alberti in his *Theogenius* bk. II and in *Profugorium ab Aerumna* bk. II.

[23] This is noted, for instance, by Ossola, "Métaphore et Inventaire," p. 187. The prophecy is then realized in *Cinque Canti* IV.52 ff., when Ruggiero is reunited with Astolfo in yet another Alcinian receptacle, the belly of a whale (which clearly recalls the fishy island which first led to Astolfo's entanglement with the enchantress).

for the Word Incarnate (XXXV.4.8) and divine Truth, and thus his celebration of human words is tantamount to giving them the ontological backing and authentication that they require for signification.[24] However, as most critics of the episode recognize, he almost immediately throws that weight in the opposite direction, problematizing irreparably, as Santoro astutely indicates, "the humanistic model of poetry which educates and civilizes."[25] The distinction made between the poetasters (crows) who flatter lyingly and fail to rescue their patrons and the two swans, or true poets, who make their lords' names live eternally (XXXV.23) is sabotaged in its unfolding: first, through a metaphorics of riches which adheres simultaneously to the intrinsic value of the names ("i ricchi nomi") and to the economic wealth of the patrons as well, so that property parallels and subverts the "properness" of the name; and then explicitly by St. John's devastating revelation that even the "swans" are flatterers who sacrifice the value of historical truth at the altar of economic reward (XXXV.25–28).[26] Ariosto's own encomium of Ippolito disappears into the resultant vortex, which swallows both the prince who is lied about and the lying poet.[27] Along with them goes a series of key "civic humanist" values, particularly that of the modified "impegno civile" of Castiglione's *Cortegiano,* which

[24] On this point as on several others in this reading I am indebted to Quint. Our differences will appear as the argument proceeds.

[25] Santoro, "La Sequenza Lunare," pp. 347–49.

[26] The association is developed first through the motif of the "golden fleece" ("vello"), which designates the life of Cardinal Ippolito d'Este (XXXV.3.3–8, 8.8—see Quint, "Astolfo's Voyage," p. 404, for the Senecan source of the fleece). It is then extended to all the "ricca soma" of names being dumped by Time into the river Lethe (11.8, 13.6, 14.4) and is eventually linked directly to the riches of the sponsoring patrons (23.4, 25.4–7). The question of wealth and avarice is obviously being prepared by the Senapo and by the Lydia episode (Lydia having been the home of Croeseus and being a traditional synonym for wealth; cf. XXXIV.16–22, 35, 36, 77, etc.). See also Ariosto's *Capitolo* IX.16, which defends Endymion from the calumny that he seduced the avaricious moon with the "mercé d'un vello." For the connection of proper name and property, see again Bonifazi, *Le Lettere* (cf. Chapter 3, n. 148, above). See Chiampi, "Between Voice and Writing," for a linkage of avarice and poetry, though *not* in reference to the lunar episode.

[27] Quint, "Astolfo's Voyage," pp. 404–406, shows that Ippolito is allusively connected with the demonic Nero. See also sec. v, below for other Ariostan subversions of the Cardinal.

is assailed (directly or not) by a large number of unflattering refer-
ences to courtly parasitism and princely ingratitude (XXXIV.77–78;
XXXV.20–21, 23).[28] One might hope, at least, to rescue the key
humanistic value of historiography, with all it implies for a vision
of man situated firmly in a coherent and discoverable pattern of
events, as against the distortions of poetry. It seems to me, however,
that St. John's use of the word "storia," with its double sense of
"story" and "history," coupled to the vision of history as a place
of loss, delusion, and madness in XXXIV, leaves precious little room
for such an alternative and truthful mode of human writing, though
the "divine" writing of Scripture may remain intact.[29]

Once again, and how much more explicitly and violently here,
the hope for a poetic celebration of famous names which consoles
the dying and teaches the living is dashed. Poetry again appears as
an allegorical Alcina, hiding the opposite of what it means with-
in it:

> E se tu vuoi che 'l ver non ti sia ascoso,
> tutta al contrario l'istoria converti   [XXXV.27.5–6]

And if you wish that the truth not be hidden from you: turn all of his-
tory upside down

In one phrase John turns the humanist value of man shaping the
historical world into an image of poets reshaping the world by lying

---

[28] Cf. Chapter 2, n. 93, above, for Ariosto and Castiglione. The most important
point, as lines 82–83 of that *Satira* suggest, is that Ariosto was at times part of the
same circle as Bembo and Castiglione, and that he would, in any case, have been
steeped in the theme of the Courtier as educator and/or flatterer of the prince.

[29] In Chapter 2, n. 75, it was suggested that the early humanists, notably Bruni
and Guarino, were themselves forced to make a distinction between history and
story, in spite of their tendency to link all of "humane letters" as part of a single
enterprise, in order to keep the fictions of the one from contaminating the truth of
the other. Ariosto is thus merely repeating a humanistic *topos*, but in so doing he
shows how humanism defeats itself from within, already uneasily aware of what
Kermode calls the "growing [modern] awareness of historiography's irreducible
elements of fiction" (*The Sense of an Ending*, p. 43). Instead of Machiavelli's advocacy
of using fraud to shape history in *Il Principe* (which is based on an assumption that
his historical proof texts are *not* fraudulent), Ariosto suggests that humanistic and
Machiavellian historiography alike are guilty of unavoidable falsifications.

about it and, simultaneously, parodies the neo-Platonic dream of a "poetic theology," hidden beneath the delightful surface of the text. Instead of Logos as foundation of human words, we find a radical contrast between Logos as union of Word and Meaning, essence and articulation, and the pitiful fictions of human language. That contrast may even include Dante's poetics of divine inspiration (words from the Word, articulated in imitation of the Trinity):

> . . . I' mi son un che, quando
> Amor mi spira, noto, e a quel modo
> ch'e' ditta dentro vo significando.   [Purgatorio 24.52−54]

> I am one who, when Love inspires me, takes note, and goes setting it
> forth after the fashion which he dictates within me.

That passage, in a context which emphasizes repeatedly the act of *notation* (lines 11, 56), is noticeably travestied in the references to the "note" on which the names are inscribed and by the swan-poets who "van notando" ("go swimming") in the river Lethe (XXXV.15.5; cf. 12, 19). In fact, the allusion to Dante is ironically twofold. *Purgatorio* 24 is itself typologically anticipated, parodically and negatively, by an episode in hell where the *notare/nuotare* pairing is already in place. When Dante first spies that dreadful bird, Geryon, by now familiar to us as an Ariostan subtext, he compares its flight to swimming: "vidi . . . / venir *notando* una *figura* in suso" ("I saw . . . come swimming upwards a figure" 16.130−31). Later he says: "ella se ne va *notando* lenta lenta" ("he [sic] goes swimming slowly on" 17.115). The first quotation comes right on the heels of Dante's attempt to reassure the reader of the veracity of this incredible representation (this "figura"): "per le *note* / di questa comedìa, lettor, ti giuro" ("reader, I swear to you by the notes of this Comedy" 16.127−29). The conundrum of tautological circularity, of guaranteeing the truth of the *Commedia* by an appeal to the *Commedia,* is precisely what the return to the question of *notation* in *Purgatorio* 24 is designed to resolve, by anchoring the words of the *Comedy* in the Word.[30] What Ariosto does here, however, is once again to elide

---

[30] My discussion of Ariosto's parody of Dante depends heavily on Mazzotta, *Dante,* pp. 192−213. Quint pointed out to me the presence of infernal echoes.

the distinction between Geryon's fraud and Dante's truth by col-
lapsing the narrative order and symbolic hierarchy of the two epi-
sodes which he echoes.

In spite of this tweaking of the Christian poet *par excellence,* the
poem does seem to be opening up a space between, and above, both
secular humanism and neo-Platonic mysticism, from which they
can be seen as identical in their glorifications of the human. That
space is the space of a Christian humanism concentrated around the
figure of St. John himself and founded on divinely originating
values in a newly "deiform" universe.[31] The recognition, quite
shocking, that the attempt to make human names eternal and the
building of a Temple to Immortality where famous names are
affixed to a "simulacro" (a statue or idol of Fame) to be worshipped
"in eterno" (XXXV.16) is indistiguishable from the Senapo's wish
to build a temple to a man he mistook for a god, gives this solution
powerful negative confirmation. It seems to suggest that the truest
difference between Ruggiero's failure and Astolfo's success is that
the former sought a worldly *ethics* on a horizontal journey (moving
circularly around the world toward a never-reached horizon), while
the latter surrendered himself to a transcendent *theology* and was
lifted up to vertical heights.

Ruggiero's education was, we recall, carried out exclusively
under the auspices of the four cardinal, i.e., classical, virtues and of
a figure of virtue gained through self-knowledge, while Astolfo's
tutor is a theologian, the patron saint of theologians, in fact.[32]
From Logistilla, Ariosto shifts to the "scrittore" who celebrated
the Logos itself. As observed earlier, Logistilla's habitation is osten-
tatiously not characterized as edenic, and her teachings prove in-

---

[31] For Ariosto as Christian humanist see again Montano, Cuccaro, and, most
recently, Fichter, *Poets Historical,* p. 72 ff. For the definitive refutation of Burckhardt's
identification of humanism with atheism, see once more Charles Trinkaus, *Image
and Likeness.* According to him, the *dignitas hominis* derives from the resemblance
of man to his Creator, in whose likeness he is formed. Trinkaus offers a strong cor-
rective, but is himself guilty of ignoring the problematizing of the man/God relation-
ship in authors as crucial to his argument as Petrarch, Pico, and Valla, not to mention
Ariosto.

[32] For John as patron of theologians and—of special interest here—of *writers*
generally, see Louis Réau, *Iconographie de l'Art Chrétien* (Paris: Presses Universitaires
de France, 1955–1958), vol. 3, pt. 2, pp. 710–11.

adequate to effect the edenic synthesis of art and nature, name and essence, time and eternity. Now, in Eden itself, such a union is again conceivable: not through the discredited power of human words and the value of fame (xxxv.19, 24), but through the Word made Flesh (4.8). From this angle, what appears to be incomplete in Ruggiero's education is the "humiliation," the "death of the self," which he does eventually undergo in canto xli.46–67, in specific imitation of St. Paul's conversion on the road to Damascus (53; cf. Acts 9:14).[33] Whether this conversion really has the desired effect on Ruggiero or not is a point which will be indirectly addressed in section v of this chapter. It is worth noting, however, that while Paul underwent a change in names to reflect the change in his heart, Ruggiero's name remains the same, even though that of the dynasty he founds *is* altered (65). The implication would be that the real significance of Ruggiero's conversion lies in its effect on a nascent political dynasty, rather than on the hero's immortal soul.

Key events of the poem, which from the perspective of the earth seemed to have been determined by man, are now revealed, *sub specie aeternitatis,* as of divine provenance. Orlando's madness, which he himself attributed to the infidelity of Angelica (xxiii.128; cf. xxix.73–74), i.e., to her failure to keep the "word" she gave her lover, is exposed as a divinely sent punishment for *Orlando's* lack of faith to and in God (xxxiv.62–64; cf. ix.1) and a means of re-converting him, as Samson and Nebuchadnezzer were rescued from their pride and folly. It is crucial that only at *this* juncture does the poet resort to the medieval emblem *par excellence* of madness.[34] By

---

[33] Fichter (*Poets Historical,* pp. 98, 106, passim) insists on the priority of this episode, and he is one of the first to do so (another sign of the reluctance of criticism to deal with the "cantos of resolution" from xxxv to the end). One problem, however, is that he, and that episode too, clearly envision an Augustinian/Dantean reconciliation of Aeneas with St. Paul, of dynastic epic with Christian conversion—and I have already had reason to question Ariosto's commitment to the former of these projects.

[34] See Penelope Doob, *Nebuchadnezzer's Children: Conventions of Madness in Middle English Literature* (New Haven: Yale University Press, 1974). According to Doob, medieval madness always is a divine punishment for sin and a means to possible redemption. Walter Stephens initially called my attention to the importance of the reference and to the possible link between Orlando's dream in viii and the dream of Nebuchadnezzer which forecasts *his* madness. Nebuchadnezzer's fall from pride

the same token, Astolfo's ascent to Eden, which seemed at first to be an act of adventurous spirit and human choice, is also shown to be dependent exclusively on divine intervention (XXXIV.56). Astolfo moves from the Ethiopian king, whose other name is Prester John (XXXIII.106.8), to another John, as Ariosto trades on some traditional associations between the two.[35] He thus transcends the double sin of the Senapo, who is guilty first of Lucifer-like pride, of locating divinity in himself, and who then falls into the inverse and yet identical sin of idolatry, of locating divinity in the human other. Pride and idolatry are thus two sides of the same coin, both forms of worshiping the human, of trying to assign intrinsic value and substance in a world of shifting appearances and uncertain identity.[36]

---

and idolatry into blind fury makes him an analogue both of the Senapo and of Orlando. See also Daniel 4:7–19, where Nebuchadnezzer is figuratively turned from a *tree* of pride into a mad beast. Cf. Richard Bernheimer, *Wild Men in the Middle Ages* (New York: Octagon Books, 1970).

[35] We have already seen that both are situated in city-gardens meant to be compared as type and antitype. Graf (*Miti*, pp. 3, 20) says that legends often placed Prester John's realm near the Terrestrial Paradise. He also cites two parallel legends of "Fortunato" (see n. 47, below, for a connection to Astolfo), one of which takes him to the land of Prester John in Ethiopia, the other leading him almost to the Terrestrial Paradise (pp. 123–25; cf. Rajna, *Le Fonti*, pp. 472–73). In another legendary journey cited, Eden and the kingdom of Prester John are two principal stops. Both of the characters are "synonymous" with faith: Prete Ianni through the etymology of "Senapo"; St. John by his status as Evangelist and particularly as the reporter of the story of "Doubting Thomas." According to the *New Catholic Encyclopedia* (New York: McGraw-Hill, 1967), vol. 11, p. 761, entry for "Prester John," one version of the legend has him guarding precisely the tomb of St. Thomas. Most significant of all, the name "Prester John" may in fact be directly linked to St. John. In the second and third Epistles of John, the author is identified as "elder" (Latin "senior," Greek "Presbyter"), and the relation between this elder John and the "young disciple" of the Gospel was a matter of controversy among early historians of the Church (cf. Eusebius, *Historia Ecclesiastica* III.ix.4). Ariosto's John is in any case represented, in accordance with the iconographical tradition, as being very old. On the other side, "Presbyter" is one of the more likely sources for "Prester." For another literary appearance of Prester John, see the thirteenth-century *Novellino*, novella 2, which contains a precursor of Boccaccio's heliotrope and Angelica's ring.

[36] Carne-Ross ("One and Many," p. 232) makes the argument for a necessary pluralism of vision in a world where error and uncertainty are unavoidable. Describing Orlando as a "single visionary in a world of plurals" (p. 216), he in effect calls him a reifier, an idolator. He does not use the latter word, probably because it would

The episode tends toward a perspective on Astolfo not as forceful shaper of his own destiny and that of others, "the all-knowing omnipotent master of ironies," but instead of "homo fortunatus," moved by the serendipity of fortune and employed as unwitting agent by divine providence.[37]

Thus, if Ruggiero's trip first suggests the degeneration of neo-Platonic love into erotic self-indulgence and then, more subtly, yet quite thoroughly, polishes off the values of ethical humanism, Astolfo's seems to offer, by contrast, the alternative of a Christian perspective, from which the errors of human "giudizio" and the failures of human prudence are seen, punished, and redeemed by the "occhio divino" of Providence, and in which blind faith, as of a mustard seed, can accomplish what lucid reason cannot, thereby installing a certain positive possibility within the characteristic blindness of the Ariostan universe, turning it into faithful insight.[38] Ariosto, I now argue, is critiquing the order of Nature, and the mode of knowledge associated with it, reason, in terms of the order

---

imply, as I am here, that while the sub-lunary world is relativistic, there is a Truth beyond appearances which is not, as well as a "theological" Ariosto who struggles with the relation between the two. For the problem of "pluralistic" epic in the Renaissance, see Carol Kaske, "Spenser's Pluralistic Universe: The View from the Mount of Contemplation," in R.C. Frushell and B.J. Vondersmith, eds., *Contemporary Thought on Edmund Spenser* (Carbondale: Southern Illinois University Press, 1975).

[37] The phrase is Giamatti's (*The Earthly Paradise*, p. 141) and equates Ariosto to Astolfo. By contrast see Santoro, "L'Astolfo Ariostesco: *Homo Fortunatus*" in *Letture Ariostesche* (Napoli: Liguori, 1973). Santoro makes the point that Astolfo comes to Eden because of curiosity and "senza consiglio" (xxxiv.55–56) and that he is completely dependent on St. John for interpretation (pp. 207–208). If there is one "poet figure" in the episode, in fact, it is this same St. John who declares "fui scrittore anch'io."

[38] Compare Jordan ("Enchanted Ground," p. 189) on xliii.7, where a different sort of "Fede" is at issue. In Marfisa's conversion (xxxviii.10–23) "invidia" is specifically replaced by "fede." Shortly thereafter Astolfo restores the Senapo's vision, but the outward restoration of sight is apparently not matched by new inward vision since he still deifies the agent of his cure: "l'adora e cole, e come un Dio sublima" (xxxviii.27.8; this failure, by the way, casts a certain doubt on whether Orlando, another ex-idolator, is more than superficially cured in xxxix). See also Freccero, "Medusa," on the interpretive dialectic of blindness and insight in Christian hermeneutics of faith.

of Grace, which is accessible only through faith. He would thus be clearly opposed to the attempts by Pico, Ficino, and others to reconcile philosophy with theology and to assert "the unity of truth" as enunciated both in the pagan classics and in Christian revelation.[39] By placing the episode in the Heaven of the Moon, traditional boundary between Nature and Grace, reason and faith, he is able to set up a clear confrontation between the two orders which makes final harmonization impossible. On the other hand, it is equally clear, from this intermediate perspective, that the two orders must always be measured and judged against one another, that they cannot be separated into the Averroistic "double truth," which would consider them as distinct and equally valid modes of knowledge.[40] It could be further argued that the literal and complete separation of wits from their owners' bodies revealed on the lunar surface is a broad parody of another and related Averroistic doctrine, that of the "separable intellect." The motif of separation, combined with the allusion to the doctrine of parallel worlds, certainly points

[39] Pico, *Oratio* (Garin edition), p. 139 ff., and Marsilio Ficino, *Theologia Platonica.* Cf. Trinkaus, *Image and Likeness,* pp. 753–60.

[40] For the problem of the "double truth" or, more aptly (since one is hard-pressed to find an unequivocal advocate of the "double truth"), of two competing modes of knowledge and what relation (complementarity, incompatability, incommensurability) exists between them in the late Middle Ages, see Étienne Gilson, *Reason and Revelation in the Middle Ages* (New York: Scribner's, 1938). Pages 54–63 in particular consider the Latin Averroists' possible espousal of a "double truth" or radical separation of philosophical orders of knowledge according to the object of investigation and aspect (natural or theological) under which it is being considered. The issue certainly had not died down by Ariosto's day. Throughout his works, Valla polemicizes against philosophical reason, especially Aquinian and other attempts to reconcile Aristotle with Christian revelation. Pico and others subsequently make even more grandiose attempts at reconciliation. An especially interesting case is that of Pietro Pomponazzi's *De Immortalitate Animae,* trans. in E. Cassirer et al., eds., *The Renaissance Philosophy of Man* (Chicago: University of Chicago Press, 1948). Pomponazzi, influenced by Paduan Averroists such as Vernia, though not unequivocally of their persuasion, argues for the *mortality* of the soul from the perspective of reason—though at the end he shifts his ground, whether sincerely or expediently, to adopt a position close to that of Valla: that faith alone can take us where reason cannot. More than Valla, however, he seems to set two legitimate modes of knowledge on more or less equal footing and to force the issue of their contradictory approaches.

toward the tendency of Pico and the mystical Platonists to institute a division so radical between body and mind that they no longer seem to be part of a single creature, and that they thus contradict implicitly the Christian doctrine of an incarnational union of the total person.[41]

It is an interesting structural irony that two apparently opposite positions, the "unity of truth" and the "double truth" converge around a single thinker, Pico. His thought, as suggested earlier, indeed harbors notable internal contradictions. By asserting a unity of truth which transcends the dimensions of corporality, but is shared by every thinking mind, he ends up positing a transcendent "over-mind" which is absolutely divorced from the specific physical existence of the sensory body in time and space, so that even as all human minds are united into one (the Oneness of deity), the mind is split off from all particular bodies. With Ariosto the case is slightly different. His intermediate lunar surface allows for neither a "double truth" nor for the "unity of truth," but rather juxtaposes faith with reason, Grace with Nature, to create an inexorable dialectic in which, at least at this point in the argument, faith and Grace seem to have the upper hand. He would thus be close to Valla's Christian humanism, with its critique of rational philosophical defenses of free will, which closes with the argument that faith alone leaves room for human freedom. Or he might be assimilable to the fideism of G. F. Pico, with its relentless attacks on the very same texts of pagan philosophy that were so dear to his uncle's heart.[42] In this view, God alone has the light of intellectual truth, while man can only fall back on blind faith. The following quotation from the *Encomium Moriae* both illustrates this position and suggests

[41] Pico's studies in Averroism are well known and there has been considerable speculation as to the extent of his debt to it in propounding the "unity of truth." Cf. Chapter 2, n. 61, and Garin, *Ritratti*, pp. 195–96.

[42] Valla, *De Libero Arbitrio*, in Garin, ed., *Prosatori Latini*, pp. 560–62; trans. in Cassirer et al., eds., *Renaissance Philosophy*. For Valla as Christian humanist, see Trinkaus, *Image and Likeness*, vol. 1, pp. 103–170. For Gianfrancesco Pico's "skeptical fideism," see especially his *Examen Vanitatis Doctrinae Gentium*, in *Opera Omnia*. See also Garin, *L'Umanesimo*, pp. 153–55. Ariosto clearly takes his distance both on the "naturalistic" view of corporeal pleasure to be found in Valla, as well as on the uncompromising skepticism of his friend, Pico.

another possible source for Ariosto's moon:[43]

> Again, when the wise Ecclesiasticus [27:12] said that "the fool is changed as the moon," but that "the wise man is fixed as the sun," what did he intend to show except that the whole human race is foolish, and the attribute of wisdom is meet for God alone? For interpreters always read "moon" as human nature, and "sun," the source of all light, as God.
>
> [Hudson, p. 107]

The passage, first of all, points up the contrast between Astolfo's successful ascent to noble lunacy and Ruggiero's failed imitation of solar divinity. More broadly, it suggests that an oblique counterpoint to Erasmus' and Ariosto's negative assessments of universal human folly might be found in the Pauline notion of Christian Folly *in bono* which specifically sees through the self-deluding madness of the philosophers (Romans 1:22; II Corinthians 1:17–27; passim) who believe themselves capable of seeing truth without God's aid.

It has been repeatedly argued of late that "fede" is a key theme and value for Ariosto. One critic asserts that an *ethical* faith, i.e., the keeping of a given word according to the neo-Stoic code of chivalry, is the poem's definitive value. Another argues just the reverse, that ethical faith is repeatedly subverted, revealing not only the universal inconstancy of the characters and their language, but implicating the self-betraying "lettere infedeli" of the text as well.[44] Given the apparent participation of the lunar episode in the Erasmian critique of Stoic values, the second position seems the stronger.

---

[43] "Rursum sapiens ille Ecclesiasticus, qui dixit 'stultus mutatur ut luna, sapiens permanet ut sol,' quid aliud innuit nisi mortale genus omne stultum esse, soli deo sapientis nomen competere? Siquidem lunam humanam naturam interpretantur, solem omnis luminis fontem, deum," *Encomium* (Miller edition), p. 180. It is noteworthy that, as Santoro, "L'Astolfo," points out, Boiardo describes Astolfo in *Innamorato* II.xii.45.6 as "la luna che debbe scemare." Cf. Doob, *Nebuchadnezzer's Children,* p. 20. It is arguable that Astolfo's character as fool has not changed at all in Ariosto, but that the value and diffusion of such folly have.

[44] In the first instance see Durling, *The Figure of the Poet,* p. 167: "there is hardly an episode of the poem which does not revolve around the theme of fidelity and betrayal" (quoted and elaborated by Saccone, "Clorindano e Medoro," p. 168). Saccone chose an episode with two pagans on center stage where religious faith is only a marginal issue, as it is not at most other points. For the second position, see Bonifazi, *Le Lettere,* pp. 81–120.

What both agree on, however, is that "fede" in Ariosto is explored in purely secular terms, a point with which I take issue. A closer examination of the principal instances of ethical "fede," I believe, would show that it is invariably involved in questions of religious faith, with the suggestion that an ethics of words cannot survive at all without a transcendent guarantor.[45]

It is especially significant in this regard that the lunar episode is stationed so carefully in relation to the *Commedia*. Its closest analogue in Dante's *poema sacro* is, of course, the "Heaven of the Moon" (*Paradiso* 2−5), which is specifically associated with human inconstancy, exploring the situation of those who failed to keep their vows ("voti") to God. In the cases both of Piccarda dei Donati and the Empress Constance (!) vows of celibacy were broken: "fuor negletti / li nostri voti, e vòti in alcun canto" ("our vows were neglected and void in some particular" 3.56−57). The inconstancy of their words is also the backdrop for Dante's exposition of his poetics as an improper (unfaithful) representation of transcendent reality.[46] On the other side, among the vanities heaped up on the lunar surface are "infiniti prieghi e voti . . . / che da noi peccatori a Dio si fanno" ("infinite prayers and vows . . . which we sinners make to God" xxxiv.74.7−8; cf. 82.6), while we have already seen how inconstant poetic representation turns out to be in the view of

---

[45] The theme of Ariosto's lack of interest in or open irreverence toward the Christian religion is a constant one in the criticism (with the exceptions already noted; cf. n. 31, above). See, for instance, Croce, "Ariosto," p. 40; DeSanctis, "Ariosto," pp. 451−52; Greene, *The Descent from Heaven,* pp. 119, 122−23; Donato, "Desire," p. 29; as well as DeBlasi, Caretti, etc. Saccone takes as his epigraph the paean to ethical faith in xxi.1−2. In the story which follows it, an exemplar of faith, Filandro, is manipulated by means of his blind trust into killing the very man to whom he owed his loyalty (see Chapter 2, n. 39, above). The story, furthermore, is heard by Zerbino, whose "faith" has led him to defend the faithless Gabrina and to wound unto death an innocent knight, Ermonide. So far, this suggests that Bonifazi's position is the correct one; but, as the lunar episode suggests, and as readings of cantos xxi, xliii, and others which concentrate on the theme of faith would confirm, Ariosto returns obsessively to the problematic relation between ethical and religious "fede," in terms of the faith of and in language which mediates both kinds.

[46] For Dante's lunar poetics, see Freccero, "Introduction," in Dante, *Paradiso,* trans. J. Ciardi (New York: New American Library, Mentor, 1970). Other possible Dantean sources include the image of Jason and the Golden Fleece in *Paradiso* 2.16−18 and the description of Beatrice as Daniel appeasing the wrath of Nebuchadnezzer, *Paradiso* 4.13−15.

St. John. Ariosto, like Dante, is in fact juxtaposing critically the "fede" of a promised human word with "fede" of and in the Word.

Nonetheless, there is a legitimate question as to whether a negative critique of human will and reason from the perspective of Christian faith is in fact extended positively in the episode and the poem to include the transcendent values of Truth and Love. In fact, I will show, Ariosto is just as willing to operate the inverse critique: that of rational skepticism against the blind trust of the faithful in revealed truth. Indeed, in this world blind faith is as dangerous as arrogant belief in one's own insight. Just as in the previous chapter one mode of humanism appeared to undercut another and vice versa, leaving no unequivocally positive perspective, so here Ariosto uses the lunar surface to show how two modes of knowledge, reason and faith, are both interdependent and mutually subversive, neither fully reconcilable nor clearly separable, since faith always relies on visible (and deceptive) signs, while reason inevitably takes blind leaps in the dark. The key to Ariosto's subversion of faith, as to his valorization of it, is St. John, author of both the Gospel of John and the "oscura Apocalisse," who potentially extends his perspective from the Alpha of creation (John 1) to the Omega of eschatology and Christ's Last Judgment. The allegory of universal earthly vanity he expounds is by no means the child of a *secular* Renaissance, but is compatible with such medieval accounts of human degradation as Innocent III's *De Contemptu Mundi,* which had been the specific polemical target of the first major Renaissance defense of man, Gianozzo Manetti's *De Dignitate et Excellentia Hominis Libri VI,* which antedates Pico by some thirty years.[47] Nonetheless, the same authority which reveals human words and deeds as "vuoti" is eventually turned against itself, putting even Christian faith in crisis.

There is, for instance, the matter of Astolfo snacking on the "fruits of paradise" and concluding that they are "di tal sapor, ch'a suo giudicio, sanza / scusa non sono i duo primi parenti, / se per quei fur sì poco ubbidienti" ("of such a flavor that in his judgment

---

[47] Manetti, *De Dignitate Hominis,* in Garin, ed., *Prosatori Latini,* pp. 422–87. For Manetti's place in the (not exclusively Renaissance) tradition of *dignitas hominis,* see Trinkaus, *Image and Likeness,* vol. 1, pp. 230–70.

our first parents were not without excuse if on account of these they were so disobedient" xxxiv.60.5–8). On a larger scale, there is the matter of an extensive parody of the *Commedia:* the mocking placement in hell of an anti-Francesca condemned for excessive chastity; a brusque abbreviation of the itinerary so that it goes no lower than the first circle of hell and no higher than the lowest of the heavens; the conflation of *Inferno* 16–17 with *Purgatorio* 24 already discussed.[48] When Astolfo flies up to the moon in the Chariot of Elijah, it recalls Dante's reference to Elijah's departure in *Inferno* 26 and thus brings out the paradox, discussed in the previous chapter, of Dante contrasting his humility with Ulysses' pride and then soaring far beyond Elijah himself.

However, even if Dante's privileged perspective as he gazes down and back on "l'aiuola che ci fa tanto feroci" ("the little threshing floor which makes us so fierce" *Paradiso* 22.151; cf. 27.82–87) is ridiculed, that does not change our view of St. John and *his* book.[49] St. John's own words, however, do:

> *Gli scrittori amo, e fo il debito mio;*
> *ch'al vostro mondo fui scrittore anch'io.*
>
> *E sopra tutti gli altri io feci acquisto*
> *che non mi può levar tempo né morte:*
> *e ben convenne al mio lodato Cristo*
> *rendermi guidardon di sì gran sorte.*   [xxxv.28.7–8, 29.1–4]

I love writers, as is my duty, because in your world I was a writer too. And, more than all the others, I made an acquisition which neither time nor death can take from me: it certainly behooved my much-praised Christ to bestow on me a reward of [or *for*] such high destiny.

---

[48] For the contrast with Dante, see especially Quint, "Astolfo's Voyage," and Parker. Ossola ("Métaphore et Inventaire," p. 187) contrasts Dante's voyage toward presence with Astolfo's toward absence and lack, again without substantial textual corroboration. For Dantean echoes in the *Furioso,* see Segre, "Un Repertorio Linguistico," as well as Blasucci, "*La Commedia* come Fonte Linguistica."

[49] Santoro ("La Sequenza Lunare," pp. 207, 209) points out that St. John's words and actions actually resemble those of Dantean figures—specifically Cacciaguida's prophecy to Dante and, especially, St. Peter, "rosso per lo sdegno" in *Paradiso* 27 (see esp. lines 4, 13–15, 19–21, 54). The change in the object of saintly wrath from demonic antipope to ungrateful patron already trivializes both Dante and St. John.

As Quint has so cogently put it, John sets himself and his writing on a level with those he has just discredited, and "the depiction of the Gospel as the product of a patron-writer relationship threatens to reduce its testimony to the status of a literary fiction."[50] Already we had seen that instead of proposing a truly Christian remedy to death and madness, John had veered off into a secular eschatology of nominal eternity. The scandal of such a blasphemous reduction hardly abates when John's irony swallows John himself. It grows even more acute if one notices that the Temple of Immortality not only contains an intratextual allusion to the Senapo, but also parodies a vision of salvation, also expressed in terms of names, from John's own Apocalypse:[51]

> He who shall triumph, I will make him a column in the temple of my God and he will depart no more; and I will write upon him the name of the new city of my God—Jerusalem, which descends out of heaven from my God—and [I will write] my own new name.

[3:12; cf. 3:1, 4–5; 19: 12–13]

In reducing the Bible to the level of poetic lies, Ariosto is extrapolating and reversing one of the standard motifs of the defenses of poetry: the argument that poetry can be rescued from the accusation of lying because the Bible itself uses parabolic fictions and nonliteral symbols, in part because no human words can express the literal reality of deity.[52] Thus we saw Salutati rescuing pagan poets from the charge of literal idolatry by pointing to the consistently improper and metaphorical nature of (their) language. Thus

---

[50] See Quint, "Astolfo's Voyage," pp. 405–406, where the thought is attributed to Voltaire as quoted by Casanova (another clear case of suspect literary authority!). Parker (*Inescapable Romance,* p. 51) echoes this sentiment. The ironic reversal is prepared in canto XXXIV.58, 61, where John's gift of deathlessness is tacitly assimilated to the same gift given by the pagan goddess Aurora to her mortal lover Tithon (who never dies but, like the Cumean Sibyl, continues to age), and in 62.4, which echoes *Inferno* 4.104, i.e., Dante's conversations with the great *pagan* writers in a deathless Limbo.

[51] "Qui vicerit, faciam illum columnam in templo Dei mei, et foras non egredietur amplius; et scribam super eum nomen civitatis Dei mei novae Ierusalem, quae descendit de caelo a Deo meo, et nomen meum novum".

[52] As even Thomas Aquinas, *Summa Theologie,* 1ᵃ, q.1, art.9–10, would have agreed.

Dante, in *his* lunar episode, has Beatrice explain to the pilgrim that
the transparent souls he sees are only fictions, *ad hoc* projections of
souls which really dwell in the Empyrean with God, and the reasons
that this must be so:

> *Così parlar conviensi al vostro ingegno,*
> *però che solo da sensato apprende*
> *ciò che fa poscia d'intelletto degno.*
>
> *Per questo la Scrittura condescende*
> *a vostra facultate, e piedi e mano*
> *attribuisce a Dio e altro intende.*   [4.40–45]

It is needful to speak thus to your faculty, since only through sense
perception does it apprehend that which it afterwards makes fit for the
intellect. For this reason Scripture condescends to your capacity, and
attributes hands and feet to God, having other meaning.

I suspect that Ariosto may be alluding to one particular defense
in this tradition, that made by Boccaccio in books XIV and XV
of the *Genealogia Deorum Gentilium*. There are a number of telling
correspondences. The commonplace assertion that Virgil lied
about Dido makes no connection by itself, but to it we can add
Boccaccio's claim that "the names and distinctions of all kings
really depend upon the suffrage of literary men" (xv.xiii; Osgood,
pp. 138–39), at the very point when he is trying to prove that
the king to whom the work is dedicated is not a fictive product
of his own imagination.[53] Even more important, he elaborates the
defense of poetry first on the grounds that poets are theologians
(xv.viii) and then, extensively, in comparing the fictions of poetry
with those of the Bible (XIV.ix, xii, xiv, xvii).[54] Most important
of all in proving a direct link is the following passage:[55]

---

[53] "Suffragiis enim scriptorum stant insignia et nomina regum," *Genealogia* XV.xiii,
p. 782. For Dido see XIV.xiii (pp. 722–23). The same observation appears in Petrarch,
Seniles IV.5, *Secretum* bk. III, etc.; in Guarino Veronese, letter no. 28 in Garin, ed., *Il
Pensiero Pedagogico*, p. 396; in Leonardo Bruni, *De Studiis*, also in *Il Pensiero Pedagogico*,
p. 166. Guarino gives St. Jerome, *Adversus Jovinianum (Patrologia Latina* 23.273)
as a source for this critique of Virgil's historiography.

[54] For poetry as theology (and the Bible as poetry), see Chapter 2, n. 96. Cf.
Petrarch, *Rerum Familiarum Libri* x.4; Boccaccio, *Genealogia* XIV.iv, vi, vii–viii, x.

[55] *Genealogia*, p. 719: "sed queram . . . quid responsurin sint, quo nomine vocanda
sint ea, que per Iohannem Evangelistam in Apocalipsi mira cum maiestate sensuum,
sed ominino persepe prima facie dissona veritati? quo ipse Iohannes? quo alia aliique,

Rather I will ask them to tell me what name should be applied to those parts of the Revelation of John the Evangelist—expressed with amazing majesty of inner sense, though often at first glance quite contrary to the truth—in which he has veiled the great mysteries of God. And what will they call John himself? What too will they call the other writers who have employed the same style to the same end? I certainly should not dare to answer for them "lies" and "liars," even if I might.

[XIV.xiii; Osgood, p. 64]

In brief, Ariosto's choice of St. John as a defender of poetry seems to have been determined by a reading of Boccaccio, although, unlike Boccaccio, he does dare to imply that the Evangelist was a liar. In doing so he embraces the very modern tendency to shift the terms of Boccaccio's comparison so that instead of dignifying poetry by raising it up to the Scriptures, Scripture is lowered to the level of fiction.[56] Thus, Ariosto parodies in yet another way the Dantean Heaven of the Moon. While Dante includes an account of the creative diffusion from the Logos above which invests our world with essence and significance, deriving the Many from the One (2.112–48), Ariosto, as he did with the neo-Platonists, makes the multiplicity (and duplicity) of John's human words a fictive origin for the Word Incarnate. Poetic theology makes way for theologians who are actually poets. In fact, by assigning a theologian to expound an "allegory of poetry," Ariosto may even have been taking direct aim at Dante's famous distinction between the allegory of theologians and that of poets.[57] In a single episode he has thrown into crisis the

---

qui eodem stilo dei magnalia velavere? Ego quidem mendacia aut mendaces, etiam si liceret, dicere non auderem."

[56] See, for instance, M.H. Abrams, *Natural Supernaturalism* (New York: Norton, 1971); Burke, *The Rhetoric of Religion;* Kermode, *The Sense of an Ending;* Frye, *Anatomy,* as well as *The Secular Scripture* (Cambridge: Harvard University Press, 1976). A tendency to treat Scripture as a human product, at least as far as the actual production and transmission of the written text is concerned, can already be found in the philological studies of the Bible by Valla and Manetti (discussed by Trinkaus, *Image and Likeness,* esp. vol. 1, p. 256) leading up to the work of Erasmus. In Valla and the Reformers it actually precipitated a fervent fideistic reaction in favor of the divinely inspired nature of our interpretive encounters with the Bible, no matter what human mediators (ecclesiastical or otherwise) may intervene.

[57] Dante, *Convivio* II.i.2–4. For the suggestion that St. John was the patron *both* of theologians *and* of other writers, including poets, see n. 32, above.

power of language, any language, to refer truthfully either to human history or to transcendent realities. He has used the Bible to assail poetry, and poetry to undermine the Bible.

What then remains? Two basic readerly responses have been registered to St. John's widely recognized self-betrayal. On the one hand is the argument that this ironic twist cannot be taken too seriously, that a hierarchy of Word over words remains substantially intact.[58] By contrast, one may conclude that the *Furioso* as a whole is "a repository not of meaning but of unmeaning," that it "implicates all texts [particularly Dante's and John's] in its own refusal to open onto meaning," and that, finally, it suggests the self-enclosure of all semiotic systems, including history itself.[59] As is by now predictable with Ariosto, the *Furioso* apparently justifies *both* positions—but only up to a certain point. Of the first reading, one must simply say that it does not detect how elaborately the episode structures its mocking critique inter- and intratextually. On the other hand, it is certainly right to question the absolute privileging of this particular, subversive moment in the poem by those who argue for the second position. That stance, in its strongest form, adopts the theme of the "idolatrous" quality of a self-referential, Petrarchan modernity which deliberately reifies itself, renouncing external reference for permanence *as* object.[60] But I have

---

[58] Durling, *The Figure of the Poet*, p. 149: "To suppose that Ariosto meant to suggest that he was lying in praise of his patrons is tantamount to thinking that he meant to suggest that the Evangelist lied about Christ." He goes on to reject this possibility out of hand, as does Fichter, *Poets Historical*, p. 83.

[59] Quint, "Astolfo's Voyage," pp. 398, 407. He thus joins Donato and Parker in arguing that the poem not only denies its own ability to refer, but also questions that of language in general and of all semiotic systems, including history itself. Quint distinguishes his position from the "regno della pura arte" of Croce and DeSanctis by this claim that the poem's "autonomy" is not a "flight into fantasy and art for art's sake away from the 'real,' human world." But, the question is, how can a poem have an "unmeaning" and dismember the whole of Western literature, history, and metaphysics at the same time? And how can a poem make accurate allusions to Seneca, Lucian, et al. and yet maintain that autonomy and "originality"? I would therefore argue either that Quint takes the same line as the earlier critics or that he assumes the poem to be referential, or both, and in any case puts himself in a double bind.

[60] For Petrarch, see Freccero, "The Fig-Tree and the Laurel." Freccero contrasts Augustine's subordination of the self and its language to God's Word, as final referent

already shown how, in this very sequence, Ariosto "refers" to self-referential idolatry as both dangerous (since it invites divine wrath) and impossible (since objects of idolatrous desire, like Angelica, are phantoms, mere images, which always mean something other than themselves). What is at stake is a version of Salutati's distinction between two possible origins for poetry: in literality and idolatry, or in allegory and hidden, devout significance. And my own impression is that Ariosto implies, by his treatment of idolatry and poets in this episode, that poetry always tries to construct itself as idol, but always fails to do so; that it always means something other than what it says or what its author and readers want it to mean. How, after all, can one accord the highest interpretive privilege to a single ironic reversal (St. John's self-subversion) when every utterance in the poem, every claim to authoritative utterance, is eventually called into question, deprived of final authority over the meaning of the whole? To take the inner contradictions of this position a step further: the argument for idolatrous "unmeaning" depends on a paradoxical willingness to believe that the poem's studied thematics of inauthenticity and self-referentiality in themselves constitute an authentic reference to a universe which is the opposite of Dante's, devoid of all ontological grounds for meaning.

---

and the origin of all signification, with Petrarch's attempt to reduce the words of his text to a pure, meaningless, literality—a "thing in itself," an idol which bears its meaning within itself. Quint's Dante/Ariosto opposition is similar. I would contest two basic assumptions of this position: (1) the notion that Augustine's text, unlike Petrarch's, does not already entertain as a serious possibility its own lapse into self-referential idolatry and that it does claim for itself, intrinsically, the power to avoid that lapse (after all, if the *Confessions* are not idolatrous, as Augustine himself would say, it is because of something God says, not something that Augustine writes); and (2) the supposition that Petrarch could hope to be successful in closing the referential system and arresting the "play" of signification. The most obvious such failure to make reference fail can be seen in Freccero's title, which suggests that Petrarch establishes a clear referential connection between his laurel and Augustine's tree: the idol alludes to what it is not (i.e., faithful deference to and referral of the hidden things of God), and it thus plays itself false *qua* idol by not meaning only itself. For further critiques of this reading of Petrarch and the Renaissance, see Giuseppe Mazzotta, "The *Canzoniere* and the Language of the Self," *Studies in Philology* 75 (1978); Timothy Bahti, "Petrarch and the Scene of Writing: A Reading of *Rime* CXXIX," *Yale Italian Studies*, n.s. 1 (1982); and, especially, Greene, *The Light in Troy*, pp. 112–15.

To argue that divine revelation is decisively compromised in the *Furioso* by being traced back to unstable human language and untrustworthy human authors is to make at least three questionable assumptions: (1) that Ariosto, the author of the argument, deploys a stable and trustworthy language, exempt from its own critique; (2) that in general the trustworthiness of human authors is relevant to deciding whether or not God speaks to others through them; and (3) that the "authoritative" texts of revelation ostensibly subverted have not already made plain their problematic status as the written products of human beings. As we have seen, the first assumption is made patently untenable by the *Furioso* itself. The second is basic to the whole question of Biblical testimony and revelation. Augustine, centuries earlier, made it clear that human authors' intentions, while of interest, have nothing fundamental to do with the Bible's charitable and gracious messages to its readers.[61] As to the third assumption, I will now argue that the lunar episode is, in an important sense, only elaborating a problematic of faith in God mediated by faith in the written word which can already be seen not only in Dante, but also in the Gospel of John itself.

It has been argued convincingly that Dante recognizes the proximity of faith to heresy, as well as the danger that his own text, in its claims to be an authentic human messenger of hidden divine Truth, may in fact be slipping toward the madness of idolatry.[62] We find precisely such a self-effacing recognition of the fictiveness and insubstantiality of poetic images in the passage from *Paradiso* 4 cited above, one which leaves open the possibility that even such an apparently idolatrous claim as Plato's that stars literally contain souls can, by faithful interpretation, become the vehicle to allegorical truths. Furthermore, I would contend, Ariosto's preoccupation

---

[61] Augustine, *Confessions* XIII. 18, 23–25, 30–32.

[62] Mazzotta, *Dante,* chap. 7 ("The Language of Faith: Messengers and Idols"), pp. 275–318. What is at stake here is what Quint calls the "originality" of Ariosto's language of "unmeaning." If we show that the problematic of textual authority originates with St. John and/or Dante, then not only is Ariosto not claiming to be an origin (i.e., a creator *ex nihilo,* like a poet-God), he is also positively referring to what others have said in claiming *and* renouncing that authority for themselves. Ariosto's words appear, as was already suggested in Chapter 1, as a controlled play of other texts, other events; and whatever originality is obtained proceeds from the refusal of any but the most contingent autonomy.

with belief in, and doubt about, human and textual authority which tries to mediate belief in the Logos is shared, obsessively, by the author(s) of the Gospel of John.[63] The Gospel repeatedly alludes to (and Ariosto echoes it—XXXIV.58, 61; XXXV.29) the privileged status of the "disciple whom Jesus loved" (13:23–25; 18:15–16; 20:4, 8; 21:19–27) which culminates in the discovery that this unnamed disciple was the very same John who wrote the Gospel. The desire to establish the special privilege and authority of the human author's perspective is complemented by a long series of references to doubts about and belief in the evidence which suggest that Jesus *is* the Christ, the Word. The book begins by harping on the "testimony" of the *first* John, the Baptist (1:15, 19, 32, 34). It then comes to rest repeatedly on the problem of the *words* (Moses', John's) and *signs* (the miracles) which mediated belief in Jesus for his contemporaries:[64]

> If indeed you believe Moses, then perhaps you will believe me: about me he wrote; if, however, you do not believe his writings, how will you believe my words?   [5:46–47]

The climactic anecdote of Doubting Thomas brings the problem to its natural conclusion, as Christ offers his apostle the chance to indulge his literalist skepticism, but also chides him:[65]

> Because you saw me, Thomas, you believed: blessed are those who have not seen yet have believed.   [20:29]

From this example, the Evangelist turns directly to the question of how his readers, who cannot hope to see Jesus, can believe in the

---

[63] I leave aside the modern scholarly belief that the Gospel of John is the product of several hands and even bracket the medieval-Renaissance hypothesis that there were two Johns—the disciple and the "elder," the latter of whom might have been responsible for some or all of the three Epistles of John.

[64] "Si enim crederetis Moysi, crederetis forsitan et mihi: de me enim ille *scripsit*. Si autem illius *litteris* non creditis, quomodo *verbis* meis creditis?" Cf. 1:12; 2:23–25; 6:26, 30, 31, 35, 36, 40.

[65] "Quia vidisti me Thoma, credidisti: beati qui non viderunt, et crediderunt."

derivative signs of a writing increasingly distanced from the events
and the personages with whom it originated (20:30–31). In fact,
the last verse of the Gospel, following the claim to truth of the
human author's "testimonium," which recalls and completes John
the Baptist's testimony, as much as confesses the inability of the
signs of this writing to contain, except improperly and incompletely,
the Word itself:[66]

> There are many other things which Jesus did which, if they were written
> one by one, I doubt the world itself could contain the books that would
> have to be written.   [21:25]

Thus, since the call for faith in God always necessarily requires a
corresponding doubt in human autonomy, man's power to see and
write the truth, since faith is always blind and gratuitous ("speran-
darum substantia rerum, argumentum non apparentia" Hebrews
11:1), it is still quite possible to imagine a reconciliation between
even such a thoroughgoing critique of textual authority as Ariosto's
and faith in the "invisible things of God."

Now we come to the question of the authority that this same
Ariosto, and his critics, claim for his "deconstruction" of St. John's
authority, which is also the question of *our* belief in Ariosto and
his poem. In tacitly according such a negative and comprehensive
power to Ariosto's irony, it seems to me, these readers in a sense
rejoin the camp of those who make the most extravagantly positive
claims for the *Furioso* as self-contained artistic microcosm presided
over by a smiling poetic deity who judges his characters' flaws—
even identifying himself in them—but who seems to escape the
principal crisis, "error di giudizio," precisely by the accuracy and
comprehensiveness of his judgments on self and others. Whether
the theology is negative or positive, however, it still accords the
poet a mastery which verges on the very idolatry he so thoroughly
rejects.

None of the principal formulators of the poet-God image has un-
covered a direct reference to it in the text, or avoided completely

---

[66] "Sunt autem et alia multa quae fecit Iesus: quae si scribantur per singula, nec
ipsum arbitror mundum capere posse eos, qui scribendi sunt, libros."

the hazards of anachronism in situating it historically.[67] Here, however, I have shown that in drawing an analogy between poets (including himself) and St. John, Ariosto is also comparing his book to God's Book and appropriating the authority, if not of God him-

---

[67] Croce's poet-God ("Ariosto," pp. 40, 46–47, passim), which actually appears first in DeSanctis' reading ("Ariosto," p. 453), specifically lacks any textual grounding and is, as Croce himself states, a cousin of the ironic poet-God of Fichte's Romanticism (p. 47). The lack of textual grounding is, in fact, built into the structure of Croce's concept: the God is transcendent, and what he transcends is precisely the multiplicity of the text (p. 53). The totality of his ironic vision makes it impossible to take anything within the text seriously. In order for us to believe in this deity, therefore, we must first put everything into doubt and take a blind leap of faith in the direction of the absent Presence. When Durling set out deliberately to remedy Croce's evident shortcomings (*The Figure of the Poet*, p. 251), he addressed two problems. First, he reduced the poet as deity to the level of an immanent, purely rhetorical existence named, and not doubtfully, within the text. The only problem with this conception was that he was unable to locate a direct reference to such a figure in the poem and was thus forced to rely primarily on the evidence of the poet-narrator's "absolute control" over characters, narrative, etc. The second gesture was designed to complement the first: he set out to derive the figure from literary-philosophical traditions available to the author of the *Furioso*, as well as to his belated critics. After a very suggestive review of the tradition of the images, both of poem as harmonious microcosm and the poet as divine creator, he settled on the figure of a neo-Platonic *Demiurgos*, an intermediate creator who assumes dominance over the poetic world and yet defers to Renaissance Christianity by submitting to a higher Author still, a creating creature who occupies roughly the place in the neo-Platonic hierarchy that the angels do in the Christian chain of being. But, curiously enough, Durling, like Croce, ends up using as his primary instance an anachronistic passage, taken from Tasso's *Discorsi del Poema Eroico* (in *Prose*, Mazzali edition, pp. 385–88), where it is set in a context specifically condemnatory of Ariosto's *failure* to maintain the unity-in-multiplicity which Tasso feels is proper to the true poet-deity. Moreover, as Saccone ("Appunti," p. 129) would later observe, the "Demiurge" does make one appearance in a poem of Ariosto's, precisely at the beginning of the *Cinque Canti*, in the person of the *Demogorgon* who presides over a maleficent council of fairies and demons. A series of relevant texts contemporary with or just prior to the composition of the *Furioso* were in fact available to Ariosto. There is, for instance, Pico's analogy between God as creator of the universe as Poem (a concept already in Augustine) and the writer (explicitly Moses, implicitly Pico himself) as the author of a work which can, not only metaphorically but actually, contain the totality of the universe (*Heptaplus;* esp. proem to bk. v, pp. 286–88). Durling himself cites M.H. Abrams citing Landino's audacious depiction of the poet as creator *ex nihilo* (Durling, *The Figure of the Poet*, pp. 130, 253; Abrams, *The Mirror and the Lamp*, p. 273 ff.; Landino, "Proemio," pp. 141–42; see also Greenfield, *Humanist and Scholastic Poetics*, p. 226, and

self, at least of a "scriba Dei."[68] It is no coincidence that the famous "riso" or "sorriso" of the poet, which the criticism has repeatedly invoked to characterize both Ariosto's control and his lack of seriousness, but which it has rarely, if ever, localized in the text, actually does appear in this episode, on the inky lips of St. John:[69]

> poi volto al duca con un saggio riso
> tornò sereno il conturbato viso. [xxxv.30.7–8]

then he turned to the Duke with a wise laugh and his perturbed countenance grew serene again.

Once again we find critics picking up one of Ariosto's ironically and precariously situated images and using it for a straightforward, totalizing, description of the poem. The fact that Ariosto is taking for himself this evangelic perspective at the exact moment when he is removing it from St. John, needless to say, leaves one in doubt about the legitimacy of both moves.

On closer inspection, it turns out that the whole arc of the episode, from the beginning of canto XXXIII to the end of the lunar sequence, has, through a subtle but substantial chain of allusions and parallels, been entertaining and demystifying the image of the divinized, angelic man, and particularly of the artist who assumes, or is assigned by his interpreters, the role of immortal intermediary between heaven and earth—in short, of the poet as *alter Deus*. The Senapo's greeting of Astolfo on his winged horse as "Angel di Dio,

---

Curtius, *European Literature*, pp. 397–404, 544–46). These convenient models can not be reconciled with the image of the limited, immanent, rhetorical "figure of the poet" as Demiurge who is consciously defining his own creative boundaries. That figure finally remains outside both text and context.

[68] As seen earlier, the lunar surface enacts the *topos* of poem as *alter mundus*. There are other playful and often self-canceling juxtapositions of God's will and Ariosto's. For instance, in canto XLI.46 and 51–53, Ruggiero's rescue from drowning, leading to his conversion, is first attributed by the narrator to himself and then to God.

[69] Among the critics using the image are Montano, "Follia," pp. 167, 192; DeBlasi, "Ariosto," pt. 1, 332; Momigliano, *Saggio*, p. 8 et passim; Brand, *Ludovico Ariosto*, p. 159; Bonifazi, *Le Lettere*, pp. xxvii–xxix; Turchi, *Ariosto*, pp. 57–59; DeSanctis, "Ariosto," p. 457.

Messia novello" is the obvious focal point of the pattern. Not only does it forecast the idolatrous worship of names preserved in poetic texts, it is also the climax of an earlier sequence. Canto XXXIII begins with a paean to visual artists, ancient and modern (1–2), leading up to an account of the magical, prophetic, art of Merlin. Stanza 1, with its "naive" view of the powers of writers to celebrate their fellow creators, already anticipates what will happen in canto XXXV:

di quai la fama (mal grado di Cloto,
che spinse i corpi e dipoi l'opre loro)
sempre starà, fin che si legga e scriva,
mercé degli scrittori, al mondo viva. [1.1–4]

whose fame, notwithstanding Clotho, who ravaged their bodies and then their works, will always be alive in the world, thanks to the writers, as long as there is reading and writing.

What is crucial for us is that the modern artist whose name stands out most prominently in the list is "Michel, più che mortale, Angel divino" ("Michael, more than mortal, Angel divine" 2.4). Slightly more than a hundred stanzas separate the proem from the point where we finally meet the Senapo; but a striking series of references to heaven and hell, angel and demon (which coalesces around the opposition between the "angelic" figure of Astolfo astride the hippogryph and the demonic birds, the Harpies, and earlier the "mostro" which disrupts the battle between Rinaldo and Gradasso) passes through the three narrative segments that intervene.[70] Mediating the two, implicitly, is the figure of Lucifer, the angel (XXXII.41) become *demon*, as well as the figure of Merlin, "del demonio figlio" ("son of the demon" 9.3), whose art overgoes all the others and who, apparently, is "on the side of the angels" (since in canto III he speaks by "voler divino" 9.1; cf. 19.1). In this way the name of Michelangelo is brought into contact with the Senapo, thus mixing divine with demonic art, and equating the exaltation

---

[70] For the angel/demon, heaven/hell oppositions see especially XXXIII.51.8, 85, 88.7–8, 91.6, 109.5, 111.2. A number of the references explicitly depict a mixing of sacred and profane (esp. 50.1–4, 55.3–4, 86.7). Related episodes and figures include Rinaldo, rescued by an angel *or* demon (XLII.65–66); Melissa, agent of divine will using demons in her magic and, in XLIII, showing some devilish tendencies herself; Angelica, whose being may or may not belie her name.

of artists with the idolatrous mistaking of man for Messiah, implicitly indicating, with Merlin-like foresight, a series of the poem's critics for the same error.

The reference to Michelangelo also echoes significantly in another direction, since it recalls the real Angel Michael, who appears in cantos XIV and XXVII as God's messenger and who is, as Greene implies, making a "descent from heaven" in more ways than one. The inverse symmetry is obvious. As the human artist is apparently lifted upward toward deity, the angel seems all too humanly fallible, particularly when he realizes that this divinely inspired plan for helping the Christians has gone astray: "anzi tutto il contrario al suo disegno / parea aver fatto" ("in fact it seemed that he had done the exact opposite of his design" XXVII.35.7–8). Not coincidentally, the words which identify the angel as blind bungler closely anticipate those in which St. John, in effect, calls all writers (including himself) liars. Moreover, we have already seen the Archangel's credulous response to Fraud's pseudoangelic verisimilitude. So the poem not only blurs the opposition between angel and demon, but also those between human and divine, true and false, and so on.

Paradoxically, it is the very thoroughness of the irony—its willingness to involve even itself in the accusations of poetic lying, bad faith, and demonic pride—which leaves open the possibility that value may be recuperated, language may be rescued, *somewhere,* if not within the confines of the skeptical poem. Consider, for instance, the possibility that Ariosto's demystification of Dante and St. John was itself a knowing lie, an act of bad faith which must be turned by the reader "tutta al contrario." On leaving hell, Astolfo "fabricates" a hedge to keep the Harpies from ever returning to the light to gorge their ravenous bellies (XXXIV.46). The words for hedge ("siepe") and belly ("epe") derive from *Inferno* 30 (lines 102, 119, 123), the canto of Mastro Adamo—whose distorted form falsifies the archetypal human image of Adam—and the forgers. The Ariostan scene itself is patently false, since in the beginning of the canto the narrator describes contemporary Italy once more ravaged by the same monsters that Astolfo allegedly is hedging in forever (recalling canto XXVI, with its ludicrous allegory of the monstrous Avarice slain over and over and over again). The implication is that Astolfo's hedge, and the Ariostan narrative which represents it, and which it represents in turn, are fabrications, forgeries. What they forge is a twisted copy of Dante's hell. The mastery of Ariosto over Dante's poem is replaced by an image of Ariosto misrepresenting his predecessor. So, is the *Furioso* an inverted reading which discovers the bad faith of Dante? Or should one read that reading inversely, according to its own hermeneutic, and discover that its bad faith betrays Dantean truths?

Once we have doubted the authenticity of one moment in Ariosto's representation, it seems that we have no way of preventing the expansion of that doubt to the rest of the poem, including the very phrase which encouraged that mode of reading in the first place. Inverting the superficial claims of a poem in order to discover reality is actually an affirmation of man's power to ground himself in a stable truth, as Pico well knew. Appearances are eminently legible if all one has to do is read them upside down. The trouble is that if we believe St. John when he tells us to invert what we read, we are violating his precept. If we disbelieve it, we are putting it into practice. In Lucian's *Vera Historia,* the narrator declares: "I now make the only true statement you are to expect—that I am a liar."[71] Ariosto's Lucianesque narrator throws even this point into doubt— thereby reopening the way to faith. Belief and disbelief appear to be as inseparable as they are irreconcilable in Ariosto's text.[72] With this in mind I will consider again St. John's self-betraying words. While he does throw the authenticity of his own writing into doubt, and subjects God himself to the vicissitudes of random "sorte" (29.4), he also affirms Christ's power to confer ontological eternity.

[71] Lucian, *Works,* trans. H.W. and F.G. Fowler (London: Oxford University Press, 1905), vol. 2, p. 137.

[72] See Durling (*The Figure of the Poet,* p. 250) for an extensive catalogue of the appearances of the motif of authorial doubt or ignorance. I have already mentioned the Christian-skeptical tradition represented by G.F. Pico, Cornelius Agrippa, and others, in which doubts about the authority of philosophical texts go hand in hand with blind faith in God and His Book. Ariosto's skepticism extends in both directions and yet circles back to doubt even its own right to doubt, leaving open the possibility of belief. Weaver ("Lettura," p. 398) was headed in the right direction when she observed that if we apply John's logic to him, the inversion of history must be reinverted. For doubt and faith in the Renaissance, see D.C. Allen, *Doubt's Boundless Sea: Skepticism and Faith in the Renaissance* (Baltimore: The Johns Hopkins University Press, 1964); Delio Cantimori, *Eretici Italiani,* esp. pp. 7–8.

If we believe in the first of these, our faith in the second is shaken, *and vice versa!* Is John an "imitator di Cristo" (10.1) in the sense that his words are a poetic imitation which create and sustain the fiction of Christ's divinity? Or is he an "imitator di Cristo" in the sense that his words derive from, and point toward, the truth of the "Verbo Incarnato"? At the level of the text, according to the principles of reading that it offers, this double paradox is undecidable: the poem is suspended between inauthenticity and authenticity, blasphemy and belief. One might speak of a blow struck by Ariosto at the secure ontological meanings established by the use of Christian typology.[73] But typology is never conceived of as the *source* or origin of Christian Truth; it is instead a confirmation of it, a visible hint at the invisible, an extended act of interpretation founded on an original and constantly repeated act of faith, a leap into the void. St. Paul says that belief, in reason's terms, is a scandal, a blindness. Paul DeMan urges demonic (hopeless) insight into a never penetrated blindness.[74] The blind spot of the saint might hide a demon, Ariosto says. But he also says that the blind spot of the man may hide an angel. The convergence, the in-difference, of these two spots is acknowledged neither in Croce's metaphysics nor in Donato's deconstruction. And it is this blindness, carried to its extreme in the "eroici furori" of the *Furioso,* that I will be trying, once more, to penetrate in the next section of this chapter.

Just as in Ruggiero's trip around the world, the lunar episode brings the reader "full circle" to a point of beginning, and not of conclusion, where all the interpretive problems open up once more. We have seen that the lunar episode constitutes a problematic gloss on historical and transcendental realities, on the powers of *other* texts to effect such glosses, on the very poetic world on whose margin (but marginality is central to the poem) it is situated. It refers to itself, to other texts, and to "reality," but defers and questions the finality

---

[73] Quint, "Astolfo's Voyage," pp. 400–401.

[74] Paul DeMan, "The Rhetoric of Temporality," esp. p. 203, as well as a number of the essays in *Blindness and Insight.* I would agree that Ariosto is both demystifying faith and demystifying demystification, leaving us at a point of radical uncertainty about what constitutes blindness and what vision: blindness is characteristic both of faith and of idolatry, and because it, and we, are blind, one can never be sure of having ascertained which.

of any such reference. In doing so it presents specific challenges both to those who read the episode and the poem as the accurate reflection of certain ethical, metaphysical, and/or poetic positions staked out by the author and to those who argue that the poem "does not point to anything except itself as narrative."[75]

The essential characteristic of the moon as traditional symbol, and as emblem of Ariosto's poetic situation, is its inevitable bivalence and intermediacy, its station at a distance from either of the two principal orders of significance, reflecting on both. Set at the junction of time and eternity, Nature and Grace, it mirrors the light of the sun (image of God) and also doubles the earth's contents. Clearly, however, the lunar episode does not mediate access to either domain: it reveals the world of Nature as an order of insubstantial appearances, less authentic even than poetic illusion because of a constant failure to recognize itself as a place of absence and loss; on the other hand, the project of transcendence is equally remote from it, being subjected to an almost inevitable downward deflection by blind human desire and blinder human intellect. The poem places itself as language between the diachronic and the synchronic, as between the physical and the abstract. In the domain of the imagination and of memory, poetry frees itself briefly from temporal sequence and from logic, but it never transcends them.[76] It straddles the boundary between madness ("lunacy") and its cure, between blasphemy (the degradation of St. John) and belief (the condemnation of idolatry), between poetry (words) and theology (Word), and so on. It takes

[75] Donato, "Desire," p. 29, who, in this, echoes DeSanctis on "l'arte per l'arte."

[76] The inter-mediacy of the moon can be seen from the variety of symbolic uses to which it is put in the Renaissance. Ficino, *De Sole,* in Garin, ed., *Prosatori Latini,* sees it as "quasi sol alter" and "speculum," deriving its light from the sun, which is an emblem of unity and divinity (pp. 980, 986–92). Landino (*Disputationes,* p. 205) says that the moon is corporeal and inferior, figuring the human rather than the divine. The imagination too is traditionally intermediate between sense and intellect, corporeal and spiritual, and mediates *all* human experience whether it is oriented in one direction or the other. It can thus be seen either as the means for moving up from sense to intellect or the means by which the latter is dragged down to the former. See G.F. Pico, *On the Imagination,* as well as Murray Bundy, *The Theory of Imagination in Classical and Medieval Thought* (Urbana: University of Illinois Press, 1927). For Ariosto, I would argue, it *is* intermediate; but it doubts its own power to mediate, existing as the inevitable place where all human experience wanders, able neither to make direct contact with nature nor to reach pure intellectual ideality.

human crises seriously and laughs at them and itself for doing so.

If it is consistently double in *what* it signifies, it is also double in its mode of signification. Perhaps the most "telling" feature of the moon is the relationship that is established between it and the earth.[77] It is specifically said to duplicate the contents of earthly reality, but it gives *two* versions of how that reference takes place, as a mimetic repetition (XXXIV.70) and as allegorical alienation, masking resemblance under "altra faccia" (XXXV.18). The shift roughly corresponds to Ariosto's changing modes in the course of the poem: from marginal allegory to the basically "mimetic" forms of romance. This doubling leaves the reader, once again, uncertain whether to take Ariosto at "face value" or pursue the hidden truths of a text which here (XXXIV.71.5) echoes Dante's admonition to allegorical interpretation: "Aguzza qui, lettor, ben li occhi al vero" ("Reader, here sharpen well your eyes to the truth" *Purgatorio* 8.19; cf. *Inferno* 15.20, 29.134).

There is, however, one further complication, an extra, typically Ariostan, doubling. While, on the one hand, the moon, allegorical or mimetic as may be, is said to reproduce the contents of the earth, it is also, on the other hand, said to be the site of all that is *lacking* from our world. The two passages come scandalously close together:

> e lo trovano uguale, o minor poco
> di ciò ch'in questo globo si raguna   [70.5–6]

they find it equal to, or little less than, what is gathered together in this globe

> ciò che si perde o per nostro difetto,
> o per colpa di tempo o di Fortuna:
> ciò che si perde qui, là si raguna.   [73.6–8]

whatever is lost, either by our own fault or by that of time or Fortune, whatever is lost here, there is gathered together.

Thus if the moon (emblematic of Ariosto's poetry) stations itself as an ambiguously referential commentary on reality, it is also a place where we go to find what reality can never offer us, where our vain

---

[77] As Weaver aptly puts it: "la corrispondenza luna-terra è esattamente quella significante-significato del parlar figurato" ("Lettura," p. 411, n. 11). As I will show, however, the relation may be exact, but it is hardly straightforward.

desires take on imaginary substance, where poet and reader grate-
fully dip themselves, however briefly, in Lethean oblivion and
Ledean delights, and are freed from the follies of historical existence,
freed from their own inability to claim freedom of choice. The final
ironic gesture of the episode is that even as it offers up a figure of
Ariostan poetry which both flees crisis and judges it, it also reminds
us of its differences from the rest of the poem, and hints that there
are always other scenes, other landscapes, other figures asking for
another interpretation altogether.

ii. *The Signs of Madness*

The "centrality" of the lunar experience to the world of the *Furioso*
undoubtedly and paradoxically derives from its ambiguity and mar-
ginality. Astolfo, the "eccentric" of Boiardo's poem, becomes for
Ariosto in this episode the point of convergence of the titular and
genealogical protagonists (Orlando and Ruggiero, respectively),
and to this extent the special privilege some critics accord him is
justified. He cures the madness of the former and repeats, parodies,
and/or perfects the education of the latter. Besides, he, together with
St. John, and in spite of all the problematic aspects of their experi-
ence, provides an image of the poet blessed with serendipity, able
to maintain a perspective of ironic detachment which places him
well outside the reality he smilingly views, seemingly beyond the
reach of death or madness, even exempt from the main narrative and
thematic crises of his own poem which he solves or dissolves with
a "saggio riso." In other words, this episode, whatever its challenges
to authority and to values, leaves intact the possibility of poetry as
contingent refuge and/or "refrigerio" ("cooling off"), whether in
the mode of evasion from reality or in that of ironically distanced
commentary on it.

As Caretti observes, however, the *Furioso* has no one center, but
many.[78] And the privilege of this critical perspective on the poem's

---

[78] Caretti, "Ariosto," p. 33: "tutti i luoghi della inesauribile geografia ariostesca
divengono . . . temporanei centri della vicenda." I would add, however, that
this pattern subverts not only medieval theocentrism, but also Renaissance an-
thropocentrism.

and the poet's perspective is challenged from without and even from within. St. John's commentary in canto XXXV, for example, is bounded on either side by references to the narrator-poet's position, both of which suggest his own inability to transcend the limits of an earthly love and of human language, to remain outside the reach of erroneous desire and universal madness more than fugitively. In stanza 31, he abandons the moon with the remark that "I can no longer stay aloft on my wings," presumably an allusion to Icarus' abuse of Daedalus' art or to Bellerophon's fall from the horse of soaring imagination. In the proem (1–2) to the canto he once again sees his own love-sickness as potentially analogous to Orlando's and deliberately reproduces the impious error attributed to the Count by taking his beloved and not the heavens as the landscape of his desire, seeing in her and indulgence, rather than in God and abstinence, the cure for his sanity.[79] There is thus a clear suggestion that the lunar perspective is provisional even for the poet and that he is bound to find himself back at ground level, narrating the doings of characters whose blindness and folly he shares, without their hope for rescue by a poet-God in a machine. Irony, with its constituent splitting of self from self, its double perspective, is menaced by, perhaps even confusable with, the doubling of the self in madness, the splitting which is the Renaissance equivalent of schizophrenia.[80] Is the poet outside or inside the poem? Is he the judge of others' crises or an embodiment of crisis himself?

These questions hinge on yet another question, one which is and has been explored, though not decided or perhaps even decidable, by the poem and its critics—whether or not the poet's madness is anything more than "rhetorical," more than mere verbal posturing

[79] Parker (*Inescapable Romance*, p. 27) notes the ironic contrast between the two "cures."

[80] Andrea DiTommaso, "'Insania' and 'Furor': A Diagnostic Note on Orlando's Malady," *Romance Notes* 14 (1972/73), p. 586 (n. 8), comments that whatever other changes there may have been in psychopathology over the centuries, the notion of the divided self has remained a constant. For an exceptional treatment of irony as a doubled perspective of the self on itself as other, see DeMan, "The Rhetoric of Temporality." For the intimate relationship between irony and folly in the Renaissance, see the fundamental article by Robert Klein, "Le Thème du Fou et l'Ironie Humaniste," in E. Castelli, ed., *Umanesimo ed Ermeneutica* (Padova: CEDAM, 1963), pp. 11–25.

divorced from psychological reality. This query in turn invites a larger one: What *is* the relationship between language and madness? Can madness be truly represented or expressed in language? Or are language and madness mutually exclusive, so that a rhetoric of folly is on the side of reason, as it might seem to be in the great text of Erasmus, the *Encomium Moriae?*[81] Or can, instead, the harmonious poetic representation actually *be* the "voice of Folly"?

In order to probe this complex of questions further, I need to turn to yet another "center" of the poem, which might also be thought of as the center of "otherness": namely, Orlando's slide toward and fall into madness. This narrative, source of the poem's nominal identity, pivots around cantos XXIII and XXIV, which are indeed the numerical center of the third and final edition of the poem.[82] Even more than the lunar episode, this unifying center is a parody of itself and of the very concept of centrality, since madness, this madness in particular, is an experience of radical "decentering" and dispersal of the integral self. The lunar episode already seemed to confirm the hypothesis that "furor" in the *Furioso* is primarily understood as negation, as the *other* of reason (*déraison*) and its absence.[83] That understanding in turn seems to justify a critical focus on Ruggiero and education, on the positive search for selfhood from which the definition of madness would proceed as a negative corollary. But the moon also suggested that absence and loss are *the* defining characteristics of the human condition, in which the illusions of the subject and its desires are matched by the vanity of the desired objects. From this follows an additional series of vexing questions about the nature

---

[81] Cf. Montano, "Follia," p. 165: Ariosto "è per i saggi, non per i pazzi." He juxtaposes Ariosto and Erasmus as exemplars of a Christian humanism defeating folly on its own ground.

[82] Observed by Momigliano, *Saggio*, p. 270; Giamatti, "Headlong Horses, Headless Horsemen," p. 297; etc. Cf. Chapter 2, n. 13, above. Compare Dante's centering of his poem numerically and thematically on Virgil's discourse on love and free will in *Purgatorio* 17 (cf. Charles Singleton, "The Poet's Number at the Center," *MLN* 80 [1965]).

[83] Ossola, "Métaphore et Inventaire," pp. 185–86. An extremely suggestive reading which nonetheless avoids treating *the* episode of madness, concentrating instead on Ruggiero and Alcina, and vitiating its conclusion by stating flatly that the *Furioso* is "le plus seren poème de la raison du XVIe siècle" (p. 171).

and status of this all too present absence. Is there in fact ever a "true" reason against which madness can be defined, which cures and escapes it, offers a perspective from which it can be viewed? Or is there a sense, Christian or otherwise, in which folly is not only the other of reason but also an "*alter* reason" which exposes classical *ratio* for a hollow sham, a greater folly than Folly itself? Is there, in spite of the essentially violent and negative depiction of Orlando's madness, a positive folly through which vision, value, and sense can be reinstituted after the disappearance of reason? And if this is so, which of these follies is the poet's? Does his poetry express, cause, cure, or defer madness? Finally, does the centrality of madness suggest that the unity-in-multiplicity of the *Furioso,* attributed to the *Armonia* diffused by an all-seeing poetic deity, is mere illusion? Or does madness itself, the principle of discord and fractured unity, by a strange twist become the principle of oneness-in-nonsense which knits the poem together?

Earlier in this study I suggested that Ruggiero and Orlando, and through them education and madness, were paired, via the figure of Hercules and the symmetrical opposition of their careers, in a dialectic of human identity found and lost. A reading of a notable (though ultimately "inconsequential") segment of Ruggiero's adventures suggested that education to virtue and reason was inhabited by the very madness it sought to master, and that Ruggiero was thus unexpectedly pushed in the direction of Orlandian "furor." The lunar episode, by contrast, gives an account of that "furor" as divine cure, in its effects a mode of education leading to self-discovery and reconversion to duty and faith. There, the opposite is apparently true: madness is infused with didactic and redemptive possibilities. A closer look at the way the parallels and attendant contrasts between the two heroes are developed may suggest which of the two versions is correct, or may force us to entertain them as simultaneous and undecidable possibilities.

The introduction of Orlando at the end of the eighth canto is set in close proximity to Ruggiero's escape from Alcina's palace into the purgative desert in the beginning of that canto. His first adventure is evidently designed to establish the parallel between them. In the third and final edition of the poem, Ariosto added the rescue of Olimpia by Orlando in canto XI, one of whose functions is to repeat and revise Ruggiero's rescue of Angelica, aligning both with yet another mythical hero and destroyer of monsters, Perseus. In this comparison, Orlando's success in definitively doing in the Orca and his lack of erotic interest in Olimpia contrast favorably with Ruggiero's "holding action" with the creature and his "furor" when faced with Angelica's unveiled beauties. The contrast, indeed, is already in place in canto VIII and the first edition. At first, however, it goes in the opposite direction. Both men are leaving cities for a sort of wilderness, but Ruggiero, for the nonce, seems to be headed back to his duty after his "disillusionment" and the testing and reconstruction of his virtue, while Orlando is abandoning his duty to pursue Angelica. Of particular interest is the exact recapitulation of Ruggiero's experience by Orlando's dream:

> Parea ad Orlando, s'una verde riva
> d'odoriferi fior tutta dipinta,
> mirar il bello avorio, e la nativa
> purpura ch'avea Amor di sua man tinta,
> e le due chiare stelle onde nutriva
> ne le reti d'Amor l'anima avinta:
> io parlo de' begli occhi e del bel volto
> che gli hanno il cor di mezzo il petto tolto.

> Sentia il maggior piacer, la maggior festa
> che sentir possa alcun felice amante:
> ma ecco intanto uscire una tempesta
> che struggea i fiori, et abbattea le piante.
> Non se ne suol veder simile a questa,
> quando giostra aquilone, austro e levante.
> Parea che per trovar qualche coperto,
> andasse errando invan per un deserto.   [80–81]

It seemed to Orlando that, upon a green bank painted all with fragrant flowers, he gazed at the lovely ivory and the native crimson which Love had dyed with his own hand and the two bright stars upon which the soul, caught in Love's nets, nourished itself: I speak of the lovely eyes and the lovely face which tore his heart from the midst of his breast. He was feeling the greatest pleasure, the greatest happiness, that any happy lover can: but, lo, a tempest now arises which destroys the flowers and smashes the plants. Such a storm as this is not usually seen when the north, south and east winds joust. It seemed that he went wandering in vain through a desert, seeking some cover.

The Petrarchan beloved ensconced in a *locus amoenus*, herself comparable to the natural setting and deploying a net to snare the lover's heart, recalls Alcina, her garden, and her wiles. More striking still is the effect of the subsequent tempest which has precisely the same "de-constructive" power as the ring on Alcina, and as Melissa on Alcina's landscape: plants and flowers vanish, and only a *desert* remains, through which the disillusioned hero makes his lonely way.[84] What the echoes point up, however, is that while Ruggiero is (temporarily) free from self-delusion, Orlando instead is still deceiving himself with "l'imagin false / quando per tema o per disio si sogna" ("the false images dreamed in fear or desire" 84.1–2), in both the dream of an erotic idyll he has never known and in that of the never-realized death of the beloved lady.[85]

Nonetheless, though the text sets up two antithetical lines of contrast, putting forth first Ruggiero and then Orlando as free from the illusion and desire which imprisons the other, the attempt to sustain such an opposition and a hierarchy from either side is soon compromised by the discovery that *both* heroes, having completed their rescue missions, are drawn by their own deceptive desire and Atlante's deluding magic into another labyrinth of illusions:

> Una voce medesma, una persona
> che paruta era Angelica ad Orlando,
> parve a Ruggier la donna di Dordona,
> che lo tenea di sé medesmo in bando.
> Se con Gradasso o con alcun ragiona
> di quei ch'andavan nel palazzo errando,
> a tutti par che quella cosa sia
> che più ciascun per sé brama e desia.   [XII.20]

[84] The word "deserto" in a variety of acceptances, along with such relatives as "sabbia," appears repeatedly in all the strands woven together through cantos VIII and x in connection with Ruggiero, Orlando, Olimpia, and Angelica: VIII.11, 19, 38, 39, 81 (cf. VII.4, 29) and x.16, 34, 35, 39 (cf. XI.72). They are obviously connected to the imagery of margins and shorelines noted in Chapter 3.

[85] Orlando's dream recalls directly Petrarch's vision of Laura's death (83.5–6 echoes *Rime* CCL.14) and indirectly Dante's dream in *Vita Nuova* chap. 3—ironically so, because Angelica never does die in the poem, though the dream actually is prophetic in predicting a "death of the self" for Orlando. It is this unexpected element of truth that prevents easy acceptance of G. Resta's classic "Freudian" reading of the dream as pure wish-fulfillment, based on 84.1–2.

The same voice, the same person, that seemed Angelica to Orlando, to Ruggiero seemed Bradamante, she who kept him in exile from himself. When it speaks with Gradasso or with anyone of those who wander through the palace, to each it seems that thing which each most covets and desires for himself.

Ruggiero pursues a vain image of Bradamante, and Orlando one of Angelica; but both are equally "in exile from themselves." The equation is implicitly sustained in canto XXIII, as will become increasingly clear as I go along. One obvious signal for us to make the comparison is that among the instances of "furor" (including Bradamante's and Mandricardo's), which lead up to the "gran follia, si orrenda, / che de la più non sarà mai ch'intenda" ("the great folly, so horrendous that no one will ever hear of a greater" XXIII.133.7–8), are the pointed references to Ruggiero's mad flight on the hippogryph which were cited above.[86]

Both in symptoms and in apparent causes, Orlando's madness seems to bear out my characterization of Ruggiero's. Like Ruggiero, Orlando is systematically deprived of all those qualities by which either a secular humanism or a mystical Platonism would define the *dignitas hominis*. As the madness progresses, he is both literally and figuratively stripped of all the signs of his humanity and his own special heroic identity, leaving him, in the end, unrecognizable to *almost* everyone. In a metaphorical transformation reminiscent of Alcina's literal metamorphoses, he slides down the chain of being from man to beast (XIX.42.1) and even to insensible stone (XXIII.III.7–8).[87] Most cogent of all, perhaps, is the image of the magnificent heroic head slumped abjectly on the breast (112.5), clearly echoing and parodying the traditions that the breast is the troubled locus of encounter between passion and intellect, between bestial and divine, in man, and that man's ability to stand erect and gaze at the heavens is a symbol of his dignity and aspiration to

[86] Giamatti, "Headlong Horses, Headless Horsemen," p. 297, notes the prolepsis in XXIII.7. See also 5–6, 19, 31, 48, 84, 85, 86, 91.

[87] Giamatti (ibid.) shows the "overriding" importance of horse imagery for Orlando's madness. See also Giuseppe Dalla Palma, "Una Cifra per la Pazzia di Orlando," *Strumenti Critici* 9 (1975). It is especially significant that, in his mad rush across Europe and Africa, Orlando leaves a trail of dead horses behind him (XXXIX.63, 71; XXX.13).

divinity.[88] The symbolism culminates as Orlando figuratively "loses his head" (121.1–2), a loss prefigured in canto XII when Angelica literally stole his helmet.[89] When the series of blows establishing as a certainty Angelica's marriage to Medoro is complete, Orlando, whose exemplary wisdom and "humanistic" linguistic skills are repeatedly stressed, has lost not only his *ratio,* but also, apparently, *oratio* as well (132.2)—with one stroke deprived of both of the definitive human characteristics.[90]

By now it is well established that Orlando's madness polemically derives not only from Dantean and Petrarchan, but also neo-Platonic, conventions of a redemptive spiritual love.[91] Instead of

[88] On this and a number of points in my reading of Orlando's madness I am indebted to suggestions made by Giuseppe Mazzotta. For the *topos* of man's ability to look upward as a sign of his nobility, see Alberti, *Momus,* p. 100. The imagery of the canto focuses repeatedly on the breast: 105.4, 111.5–6, 112.5–6, 119.5–6, 127.3–4. The Centaur as man-horse, standard image of the human and the bestial in a single being (Giamatti, "Headlong Horses, Headless Horsemen," p. 267), emphasizes, as in *Inferno* 12.83–84, the beast as locus of encounter between the "due nature," sensual and intellectual. See also Machiavelli, *Il Principe* chap. 18.

[89] The occasion is a duel with Ferraù, which reminds the reader of that pagan hero's loss of *his* helmet in canto I. Also relevant is Issabella's *literal* loss of her head in XXIX.22 ff.

[90] Orlando's "alto ingegno" (VIII.63.4) is repeatedly mentioned (e.g., I.2.4, IX.I.4, XXXI.42.7, XXXIV.83.1–4, XXXIX.60–61) as is his linguistic skill (e.g., IX.5.6–8, XXIII.107, 110). Paolo Valesio, "The Language of Madness in the Renaissance," *Yearbook of Italian Studies* I (1971), cites the latter two stanzas and argues that Orlando's madness is "medieval" in the sense that he remains silent throughout it, with only one exception (XXX.5–7). Jordan ("Enchanted Ground," p. 171) follows through on Valesio's analysis. It is certainly clear that Ariosto sets up this contrast, but whether he leaves it in place is another matter. For *ratio/oratio,* cf. Chapter 2, n. 12. The loss of both constitutes, as Ferroni has said, "una crisi interna dei miti centrali dell'antropologia umanistica" ("L'Ariosto," p. 91); cf. Bonifazi, *Le Lettere,* p. xxxiii.

[91] For the anti-Platonic side of Orlando's madness, see again Montano and Cuccaro, as well as Bonadeo who argues that the poem attacks ideal love of all kinds: "cortese, stilnovista e neoplatonico" ("Note sulla Pazzia," p. 41). For Ariosto's thematic anti-Petrarchism (which would also be a slap at Bembo), see especially Giamatti, "Headlong Horses, Headless Horsemen." For his stylistic debts to Francesco, see Emilio Bigi, "Petrarchismo Ariostesco," *Giornale Storico della Letteratura Italiana* 130 (1953). Petrarch himself, in the *Secretum,* provides Ariosto with all the tools he needs for his critique. There "Augustinus" demystifies the dream of the intrinsic educative power of female beauty by arguing that, in the first place, no necessary connection exists between inner and outer beauty and, in the second place,

a "donna angelicata" whose physical beauty exactly reflects tran-
scendental spiritual beauty and lifts the lover out of himself in a
positive way, educating him (as in the *Asolani*, book 3, and the
Cortegiano, book 4), there is Angelica, whose beauty proves detach-
able from any hidden spiritual signifier and leads back in the "love
as *furor*" of the *Asolani*, book 1. But the madness also involves an
abandonment of civic humanism's values, notably duty to the state,
with the implication that transgressive desire will repeatedly render
such values utopian. Moreover, Orlando's scholarly blending of
wisdom and eloquence not only cannot help him *avoid* madness, but
in fact contributes materially to it, allowing him to read Medoro's
poem and confront the facts which are driving him berserk. In
either case, secularly humanistic or neo-Platonic, the semiotic vehi-
cle of education (the *signs* of language or the externalized *image* of
beauty) becomes the gateway to another sort of "leading out," a
journey of the self into a place of estrangement and undifferentiation.

The structure of Orlando's madness also seems to repeat, on a
grand scale, Ruggiero's. The latter goes through *two* madnesses, the
second of which prefigures Orlando's exactly: the complete immer-
sion of the self in the accessible other (Alcina) and the utter loss of
control in pursuit of the unattainable other (Angelica).[92] In either
case, madness is the other or absence of sanity. The self in its exces-
sive desire for another becomes other to itself: "di sé medesmo in
bando" (XII.20.4); "uscito di se stesso" (XII.86.3); "da quel che fu,
tanto diviso" (XII.14.8); "fuor dell'intelletto" (XXIV.50.8). Ironically,
canto XXIII begins with a proemial appeal for self-sacrifice:

> *Studisi ognun giovare altrui; che rade*
> *volte il ben far senza il suo premio fia:*
> *e se pur senza, almen non te ne accade*
> *morte né danno né ignominia ria.*
> *Chi nuoce altrui, tardi o per tempo cade*
> *il debito a scontar, che non s'oblia.*   [1.1–6]

---

even if it did the lover would not necessarily go beyond superficial desire and erotic
furor (see *Prose*, Martellotti edition, pp. 132–54). It is possible to interpret this passage,
in its turn, as a critique of the Dante who wrote the *Vita Nuova*.

[92] Cf. Donato, "Desire," pp. 23–27.

Let everyone take care to help others, since rarely will good deeds go without their reward; and even if they go without, at least death and harm and evil fame will not befall you. Whoever injures another, sooner or later his debt comes due, because it is never forgotten.

The next stanza applies this moral to Pinabello, who now pays with his life for earlier violence to Bradamante, and makes it clear that the one who does not forget is God, who saves the innocent and punishes the guilty. Later on in the canto, Orlando, by rescuing Zerbino from the Conte Anselmo's erroneous justice and reuniting him at last with Issabella, aligns himself with those who aid the innocent others:

> *Ma Dio, che spesso gl'innocenti aiuta,*
> *né lascia mai ch'in sua bontà si fida,*
> *tal difesa [Orlando] gli avea già proveduta*
> *che non v'è dubbio più ch'oggi s'uccida* [53.1–4]

But God, who often aids innocents, and never abandons whoever trusts in His goodness, had already provided such a defense for him that there is no question of his being killed today.

Far from receiving any "premio" for his generous defense, however, Orlando is soon, and apparently blasphemously, rewarded with "danno e ignominia ria." Zerbino thinks that his lady has abandoned him for another, but soon learns the happy truth. Orlando, *au contraire,* tries in every way to fool himself into not believing in such a betrayal, but is quickly faced with its unavoidable reality.

Thus at the beginning of canto XXIV, glossing the preceding events, Ariosto once more finds himself reversing his earlier moralizing, in words once more borrowed from the *Asolani* (I.xxxiii.51–52):

> *E quale è di pazzia segno più espresso*
> *che, per* altri *voler, perder* se stesso? [1.7–8]

And what is a plainer sign of madness than to lose oneself for desire of another?

A few lines later Ariosto implicates himself in this devastating alterity:[93]

> *Ben mi si potria dir: "Frate tu vai*
> *l'altrui mostrando, e non vedi il tuo fallo"*   [3.1 −2]

> Well you might say to me: "Brother, you go around pointing out the
> faults of others and don't see your own"

From sacrifice of self to benefit the other, the focus shifts back to the
self, which may be lost in desiring another and which may deceive
itself about that loss by blaming others for what it too is guilty of.
In the space between these two commentaries, Orlando has gone
mad, has died to himself precisely because of the selfish self-sacrifice
of his love for Angelica, coupled with her surrender of virginity to
"l'altrui . . . fallo." At the height of his anguish Orlando cries (in
a much-quoted stanza):

> *Non son, non sono io quel che paio in viso:*
> *quel ch'era Orlando è morto et è sotterra,*
> *la sua donna ingratissima l'ha* UCCISO:
> *sì, mancando di fé, gli ha fatto guerra.*
> *Io son lo spirto suo* da lui diviso.
> *ch'in questo* inferno *tormentandosi erra.*   [128.1−6]

> I am not, I am not who I seem by my face: he who was Orlando is dead
> and buried; his most ungrateful lady killed him: thus, by her lack of
> fidelity, she waged war on him. I am his spirit, divided from him, which
> wanders through this hell tormenting itself.

The death and division of the self, the *duplicity* which is folly's
structure, is, according to its victim, caused by *duplicity* as well, the
self-difference of the beloved who pledged faith and then betrayed
it (the word "mancando," "lacking," emphasizes the absence which
is and which *causes* madness). In this sense Angelica's "infedeltà"
corresponds to the Alcinian wiles which lead Ruggiero into a
sweeter self-difference. On the other hand, just as with Ruggiero,
Orlando's own duplicity contributes to his predicament. As you
will remember, the subversive effect that the reversal from XXIII.1−2

---

[93] Cf. Petrarch, *Rime* CXCIX.11−14; *Furioso* XXIII.25.2; 35.5−6; 82.1, 3, 5; 83.5;
90.6; XXXIV.65.4; XL.41.7−8 (echoing XXIV.1).

to XXIV.1–3 has on our faith in God's justice is itself reversed in XXXIV when we learn that Orlando "non può altrui conoscere, e sé manco" ("doesn't know others, much less himself" 65.4) because of his own "infedeltà," his choice of a beautiful "infidel" over Carlo and God. From yet another perspective, however, the fact that Orlando was precisely on the point of returning to Carlo and giving up his quest for Angelica when the madness begins (XXIII.98) prevents us from accepting unequivocally the explanation of folly as divine remedy.

If madness is the doubling of self-difference, provoked in part by Orlando's grudging recognition that he is different from that "Medoro" to whom Angelica has given her love, and consequently different from what he believed himself to be, it is also a state of *undifferentiation* leading to the failure to be recognized for who one is and caused by the recognition that others are just like oneself. It is noteworthy that all of the short episodes in the canto which act as preludes to the great scene involve successful or unsuccessful recognitions, all based on the ability to detect or protect identity by means of name, outer appearance, and other "segni" and "indizii," and beginning with Pinabello's failure in the preceding canto to recognize Bradamante until it is too late, when she has already recognized him (XXII.70–73). The number of such passages in XXIII is startling.[94] The climax of this preparatory sequence comes when

[94] I am again indebted to Mazzotta for this general line of argument. Other scenes of recognition include the following: (1) Bradamante's recognition of her cousin Astolfo, followed by his reciprocation after she tells him her name and shows him her face (XXIII.10); (2) Bradamante's unwelcome recognition of her home and family (21) and failure to escape recognition by them (22–24); (3) her instructions of Ippalca (whose name etymologically describes her true identity) that she chase off any would-be assailants by making them recognize to whom the horse she leads belongs (28–31); (4) the encounter of Ippalca with Rodomonte, in which he counters her identification of the horse's master with a fierce assertion of his own identity (33–37); (5) Zerbino's failure to recognize the dead Pinabello (35, 45) or to identify his killer by the traces left behind (40); (6) the Count Anselmo's desire to identify his son's killer (47) and to recognize Zerbino as such on the basis of "chiaro indizio" (49.8, cf. 50–52); (7) Orlando's recognition of Zerbino as "degno di molta stima" from his outward appearance and as innocent from his "parole" (56); (8) the failure of Anselmo's knights to recognize Orlando (58); (9) Zerbino's recognition of his beloved (63–64) and his failure to realize that she is still faithful to him (65); and (10) Issabella's joyful recognition of him (67), followed by Orlando's (68). Note especially

Orlando encounters Mandricardo. The latter, in virtue of "indizio e segno manifesto" ("plain signs and indices") and "i dati contrasegni" ("the marks described [to him]"), recognizes the former as "colui ch'io vo cercando" ("he whom I seek") and has been following by "vestigi" ("traces") and "fama" (72–74). Orlando, flattered by the chivalric interest in his prowess, responds, removing his helmet, that "se 'l volermi veder ti fa venire, / vo' che mi veggi *dentro*, come *fuori*" ("if desire to see me brings you here, I want you to see the inside as well as the outside" 75.5–6), then invites him to see if (inner) valor matches (outward) "sembiante." What promises to be a "disinterested" combat in the name of honor, however, erupts into a passionately violent hatred when Orlando discovers that Mandricardo has *not* recognized him at all, *qua* Orlando. The complacent assumption that his clothing reflects his physical self and that his physical self exactly expresses an inner identity is suddenly threatened by the realization that name and appearance, not to say name and essence, are scarcely connected at all, and that his inner nobility can be mistaken for basest treachery, his sword Durindana, his property and sign of his proper identity, not acknowledged as *his* at all.[95] The encounter already suggests that Orlando's, or anyone's, identity is to some extent arbitrary and contingent, that he may quickly find himself different from what he thought he was, and no different than anyone else.

After he does fall into madness, he loses all the traits and signs which gave him a distinctive identity, which differentiated him from all others. He is now literally "al sasso indifferente" ("no different than" *or* "indifferent to" a stone, XXIII.111.8); only Astolfo, with the secret knowledge imparted to him by St. John, and (oddly) Fiordiligi, can recognize him. He himself loses the power to differentiate: he can no longer tell black from white, or his former beloved from a mare (XXIX.68, 73); he can no longer distinguish

the frequency of appearance of the following semiotically charged words: "nome"— 10.7, 25.2, 27.4, 30.1, 31.8, 106.5 and 114.3; "indizio," "segno," "vestigio"—32.1, 49.8, 68.7, 72.3 (twice), 72.6, 73.2, 127.1, 136.5. Note also the regular appearances of the following words: "narrare," "faccia," "sembiante," "apparire," "manifesto," and "chi."

[95] For the "proper" in this episode, see again Bonifazi, *Le Lettere,* pp. 109–110, and compare Ossola, "Métaphore et Inventaire," p. 185.

life from death (71–72). It is also, in one sense, the recognition of indifference as much as difference which precipitates the madness. Orlando's pursuit of the ever-fleeing Angelica, like all the pursuits of desire in the poem, is a chase after an unattainable absence, in the deluded belief that it is attainable and is a presence, not merely an imaginative projection of the self's own desires.[96]

What shatters him is a double realization. First he does see that he has pursued not a presence but a phantom of his own creation, just like Sacripante in canto I:

> Quel che l'uom vede, Amor gli fa invisible,
> e l'invisibil fa vedere Amore.
> Questo creduto fu; che 'l miser suole
> dar facile credenza a quel che vuole.   [1.56.5–8]

What a man sees, Love makes invisible to him; and the invisible is made visible by Love. This [Angelica's claim to virginity] was believed because the wretch usually gives easy credence to what he desires.

In these words, which parody St. Paul's definition of faith (Hebrews 11), we first learn that in this world "believing is seeing" as well as the other way around. When Orlando learns it, the tension between the void of subjectivity and the desired object which he hopes will fill that void slackens, and his identity, which existed precisely and only in the space of that tension (as the character "Orlando" exists for the reader only as a narrative tension), disappears. In the second place, however, he also recognizes Angelica as all too present and attainable to another, Medoro. And consequently he must recognize his identity as Angelica's lover as *improper*, open to free substitution on her part. In other words, he is forced to see Angelica not as an object but as a subject, not different than he is in her desires (which partly accounts for why Medoro takes on such Angelica-like qualities in cantos XVIII and XIX).[97]

---

[96] By far the best account of desire in the *Furioso* is Donato's, with all due credit to René Girard's theory of "metaphysical" and "triangular" desire see *Deceit, Desire and the Novel*). See also Carne-Ross, "One and Many," esp. p. 233: "the inconstant beauty which he [Orlando] will pursue is essentially a projection of his own thoughts and needs."

[97] See especially XVIII.166 and XIX.10, 28. This phenomenon was brought to my attention by Walter Stephens.

Angelica, once desirable as "the absence of a presence," thus proves to be both too absent *and* too present. Ironically, by asserting her own selfhood and her own right to choose an object of desire, what Angelica accomplishes is instead a total breakdown of the self/other, subject/object *distinction,* so that in fact while Orlando is "not himself" anymore, neither is he anyone else.[98] Orlando's maddening love is the inverse, but also the double, of Narcissus' fatal passion. If the former, like Echo turned to stone (cf. XXIII.III), loves another who will never be present, the latter is, of course, caught in love of the self. But Orlando's discovery is that Angelica's supposed love for him was merely a vain specular projection of his love for her, and was in this sense a form of "self-love." On the other hand, the most horrifying aspect of Narcissus' plight is that self-love actually is other-love—that precisely as subject and object seem to coincide, the lover fully present to the beloved, they are actually forever alienated from one another.[99] In both cases, the fall into conscious self-knowledge, which travesties the Platonic imperative, leads immediately into a fall out of consciousness into madness or death, as the lover discovers that the beloved other exists as self and that his own self exists only as otherness and lack.

As the lines from 1.56 quoted above suggest, the theme of desire and undifferentiation, of desire as unfulfillable yearning for differentiation, is present from the beginning of the poem, even then centered around Angelica. About her gather a series of apparently stable, identity-conferring, differential oppositions: lover and beloved; pursuer and pursued; male and female; pagan and Christian. On the other side, a shared, unsatisfied desire for her tends to efface apparently radical differences between her several lovers (including Rinaldo, Orlando, Ferraú, Sacripante), notably that between the "pagan" Ferraú and the "Christian" Rinaldo (cf. 1.22). These two first act out their "differences" in combat, but soon enough set them aside to pursue Angelica in tandem. When they do divide up

---

[98] Santoro, "L'Angelica del *Furioso:* Fuga dalla Storia," *Esperienze Letterarie* 3 (1978), no. 3, makes the interesting suggestion that the lovers' attempts to reduce Angelica to mere object contrast with her own (often overlooked, obviously utopian) desire for an independent identity.

[99] On Narcissus, compare Mazzotta, "The *Canzoniere,*" pp. 280–82.

it is only to follow two identical and alternative paths, which are "senza differenzia alcuna" ("without any difference" 23.3). Nor is this the only collapsed opposition in the canto. For instance, Sacripante's male identity is "undercut" in his defeat at the hands of a female knight, Bradamante (60–71). As the next canto broadly hints, Bradamante throws the basic structure of chivalric desire into crisis precisely because she herself acts it out, not as the female beloved but as the lover in pursuit of a *male* object of desire, Ruggiero. It is no accident then that in her meeting with Pinabello she plays the role of "knight errant" while he occupies the place of a "damsel in distress" (ii.30 ff.).[100] We are, moreover, reminded that Anglica herself was recently the pursuer and Rinaldo the pursued, though the magical agency of the Fountains of Love and Hate has now effected a symmetrical reversal of their earlier positions (1.77–79). That reversal, in the terms of Donato's Girardian analysis, and my own, figures the arbitrariness of desire, the "indifference" of subject and object, lover and beloved.

What the plot suggests structurally, the proem to canto ii and the stanzas which follow it make more explicit. The first stanza laments the injustice of love, the fact that it is never reciprocal, that there is never any equivalence between the desires of the interest parties:

Ingiustissimo Amor, perché si raro
corrispondenti fai nostri desiri?
onde; perfido, avvien che t'è sì caro
il discorde voler ch'in duo cor miri?
Gir non mi lasci al facil guado e chiaro,
e nel più cieco e maggior fondo tiri:
da chi disia il mio amor tu mi richiami,
e chi m'ha in odio vuoi ch'adori et ami.

---

[100] The confusion of male and female roles is constant throughout the poem, especially in the characters of Bradamante and Marfisa: e.g., the latter's desire to kill ten men *and* satisfy ten women in a single night (xix–xx); the former's triumph as *both* strongest knight *and* most beautiful lady in the Rocca di Tristano (xxxii). See also the Fiordispina and Ricciardetto episode (xxv) and that of Marganorre (xxxvii). Ariosto shows a tendency to identify himself with women artist-figures— notably Alcina, Melissa, Cassandra. On this topic generally, see John McLucas, "Ariosto and the Androgyne: Symmetries of Sex in the *Orlando Furioso*" (Diss. Yale 1983).

Most unjust Love, why so rarely do you make our desires correspond? How, perfidious one, does it happen that you are so fond of seeing discordant wills in two hearts? You refuse me the easy and shallow ford and draw me into the deepest and blindest bottom—you call me back from one who desires my love and wish that I love and adore one who hates me.

The asymmetry of this relationship seems to be a negative, but in my terms it has a hidden positive side, that of creating the appearance of a difference between lover and beloved. The second stanza, however, though apparently continuing the poet's plaint, actually undermines it radically:

Fai ch'a Rinaldo Angelica par bella,
quando esso a lei brutto e spiacevol pare;
quando le parea bello e l' amava ella,
egli odiò lei quanto si può più odiare.
Ora s'affligge indarno e si flagella;
così renduto ben gli è pare a pare   [2.1–6]

You make Angelica seem beautiful to Rinaldo when he seems ugly and unpleasant to her; when he seemed handsome to her and she loved him, he hated her as much as one can hate. Now he afflicts and torments himself vainly—thus he gets back tit for tat

Love, far from being unjust, has an exact economy and a perfectly symmetrical equality ("pare a pare")—in the sense that the opposition between lover and belover, pursuer and pursued, is constantly being reversed and hence effaced. The principle of undifferentiated parity is, in turn, linked in the same stanza to its etymological relative, *appearance*. Rinaldo may *appear* ugly or may *appear* handsome to Angelica, but the appearances are reciprocally canceling and finally equivalent. Neither is indicative of anything intrinsic to the identity of Rinaldo or to that of Angelica. As 1.56 suggests, the beloved is in the *eye* of the beholder, but not in his/her "I"—desire is what attempts to constitute the self by differentiating it, but it is also what subverts that self. Though Angelica and Rinaldo are by no means indifferent *to* each other, they are undoubtedly in-different *from* one another. And their initial situation points inexorably both toward Angelica's 180-degree role reversal, when she falls for

Medoro in canto XIX, and toward Orlando's crisis of self-difference and undifferentiation which is thereby provoked.

From the perspective of madness as "un-difference," Orlando's silence too makes perfect "sense" (the sense of nonsense), since it refuses the differential structures of language which presume a difference between self and others that requires the bridge of linguistic communication and which operate by virtue of differentiations of every kind (black/white, human/animal, etc.). In spite of this association of madness and silence, however, Orlando's folly, like Ruggiero's, is quite ostentatiously mediated by (poetic) language, as well as being represented within Ariosto's language in "segni espressi" ("clear signs" cf. XXIV.1, XXIX.49). We have already seen that the episode is packed with examples of people trying to locate the truth of their own identities and those of others through recourse to name and "indizii" which are not always as "chiari" as they seem to be. The "sign" of Orlando's madness, by his account, is that he is *not* what he appears to be "in viso," that the *seen* and semiotic is "diviso" from the inner and essential. Thus the "alienatio" which is madness is expressed as, takes the form of, allegory as "alienatio" or "alieniloquium."[101] Moreover, the approach to this condition takes place through a series of interpretations of names, poems, stories, and other "indices," such that language can be seen as the efficient cause of madness.[102] After the "prologue" of Mandricardo's misreading of Orlando's identity, the latter wan-

---

[101] For the definition of madness as *alienatio*, see, for instance, Marsilio Ficino, *Commentum cum Summis Capitolorum* chap. 13 (on *Phaedrus* 243e), in Allen, ed. and trans., *Marsilio Ficino*: "Erret quoque quisquis amorem incontinentem hac propria ratione damnaverit quia sit furor quidam id est alienatio mentis. Est enim preterea et furor aliquis per quem animus alienatur deo raptus super hominem elevatus" (pp. 141–43). For the distinction of madness into two types, see n. 140, below. For allegory as "alienation," see Chapter 3, n. 3, and Dante, *Letter to Can Grande*, in Haller, ed. and trans., *The Literary Criticism*, p. 99, where he derives "allegoria" etymologically from Greek "alleon," i.e., "alienum" or "diversum."

[102] See, first of all, Giamatti, "Headlong Horses, Headless Horsemen," pp. 298–300, and Donato, "Desire," p. 29, on the "conjunction of literature and madness" in the episode. Weaver ("Lettura," pp. 385, 393) suggests that there are at least two more major episodes in which a narration provokes or inflames madness: Bradamante and the Gascon, in XXXII, and Rodomonte listening to the Host's tale, in XXVII–XXVIII. See also Bonifazi, *Le Lettere*, p. 104, on the "furore narrativo."

ders for three days and finally stumbles upon a grove where he discovers the names of Angelica and Medoro inscribed together on the tree trunks in what appears to be her handwriting (102–103). He then finds a poem in Arabic which identifies itself as by Medoro and celebrates his conquest of Angelica (106–110). He goes on to the village where he takes lodging, by happenstance, with the shepherd who knew the two lovers. The shepherd tells him the story of their love "to cheer him up." Finally he produces a bracelet given to him by Angelica (and which Angelica had received as a token of love from Orlando, a "testimonio e segno" ["witness and sign" XIX.37.6]). The progression is from less certain and complete signs to evidence which is increasingly closely linked to its origin, culminating with an eyewitness and, then, Orlando himself as originator of the bracelet's significance.[103]

A few acute readers have discussed the clear link between this sequence and that of Ruggiero *presso* Alcina, both in the pastoral setting and in the focus on literature itself.[104] Specifically, Orlando's "education" in the infidelity of Angelica, by the agency of arboreal inscriptions on a "scorza," recalls the teachings of Astolfo "inalberato" regarding the duplicity of Alcina and shares their association with poetic discourse. And, in one view, it is the "infedeltà" of this language, as of Alcina's, which is the cause of Orlando's madness.[105] From this perspective again one might posit the essential "identity," the indifference, of the two heroes.[106] Both are victims of madness brought on by a divorce between sign and thing;

---

[103] In addition to the almost continuous references to "scritti," "istoria," etc., see XXIII.29, 36, 38, 49, 56, and XXIV.56–58, for further references to narration and folly.

[104] See especially Giamatti, "Headlong Horses, Headless Horsemen," p. 298; Donato, "Desire," p. 30.

[105] See especially Bonifazi, Le Lettere, pp. 107, 109; Ferroni, "L'Ariosto," p. 82.

[106] I have suggested all along that the identities of the two characters are established as functions of one another. In addition, their resemblance is a major threat to the very identities it determines. This is particularly true of Orlando/Roland who is systematically displaced from the center of the narrative tradition. The poem takes its name from him, but in other ways Ruggiero clearly usurps his role: it is Ruggiero, and his destiny, which are the narrative hinges of the main, genealogical, plot; it is he who dominates the concluding cantos; he who defeats Rodomonte in the final conflict. Above all it is he, not Orlando, who is to be the victim of Ganelon's treachery (and it is Astolfo who owns the great horn).

both "express" their madness "allegorically" as a split between name and essence. Madness would thus appear to be caused by, and to *be,* in a sense, poetic misrepresentation, much as Plato's Socrates argues that it is.

While admitting, however, that language (and poetry in particular) is being presented as agent of madness in canto XXIII, I would argue that it does so in a way which departs radically from the main thrust of the Alcina episode: in this case language maddens not because it lies, *but because it tells the truth.*[107] Unlike the typical postlapsarian *locus amoenus,* such as Alcina's island, this one offers signs which reestablish an Adamic-edenic equivalence between *res* and *verba.* If Ruggiero's madness is a scandal for conventional assumptions (whether Renaissance or contemporary) about the possibilities for successful reference, Orlando, on the other hand, seems an impossible stumbling block for those skeptical readers who wish to see the poem as either non- or anti- referential/representational. The true "istoria" of the shepherd sets out, well in advance of the lunar episode, a poetics of literal veracity opposite to that announced by St. John, but no less problematic in its own way. We even notice that Orlando's failed attempts at self-deception were anticipated by Ruggiero's more successful decision to disbelieve the truth about Alcina as it was accurately referred to him by Astolfo. What differentiates this situation from that one is that Orlando cannot finally resist the truth which his reading/hearing/seeing forces upon him and that the consequences are cataclysmic. It is curious to notice how closely the series of excuses the Count invents for disbelieving the evidence corresponds to some of the themes dearest to the hearts and pens of "postmodern" critics of referentiality. He first tries to determine that the proper name is really "improper": that it could belong to an "Angelica" other then "his" (103), or, conversely, that "Medoro" could be just another name for *him* (104). His next

---

[107] Both Giamatti, "Headlong Horses, Headless Horsemen," p. 300, and Weaver, "Lettura," pp. 395, 398, recognize a double threat of madness from language which lies and from language which tells unbearable truths. Neither, I believe, explores sufficiently the consequences of this paradoxical situation both for the poem and poet and for much of the criticism written on it. Bonifazi (*Le Lettere,* p. 110) admits that "è proprio la fedeltà di ciò che è scritto che prova l'infedeltà [di Angelica]" without altering his basic premise about "le lettere infedeli."

attempts to preserve the illusion also depend on the divorce of language from original truth. He tries to imagine that someone envious of Angelica has tried to "defame" her by misrepresenting her name and that, as a consequence, she/he has "molto la man di lei bene imitato" (114.8), i.e., forged her handwriting. What is genuinely astonishing in a poem where self-deception is the rule, and divorce between language and reality its first corollary, is that "poco gli giova usar fraude a se stesso" ("it little avails him to use fraud against himself" 118.1; cf. 103.5–8, 104.5–6, 111.2–3, 114.1–2, 117.7–8).

One might well argue that "deconstructive" attacks on reference, which so elegantly expose "the force of a desire" which "lies" (in both senses) behind most theories of truth-telling,[108] are themselves guided by an equally utopian desire to be *free* from the bonds of reference which "de-term-ine" us and from the limits which history inexorably imposes upon us, to open up into a free play of imagination and desire.[109] How strange to discover that it is not the success but the *failure* of reference which we often desire, because it conceals us from ourselves and others, allows us to write the fictions which sustain us, and permits us, like gods, to project our will onto the world and its inhabitants, giving them the shape that we choose.

Melissa's deconstruction" of Alcina's garden reveals the fairy's attempt to pass off unnatural desire as purely natural, to make the insignificance of a desert stand for the plenary meaning of Eden; it frees Ruggiero from self-deception and puts him on a desert road to sanity (which, however, ultimately leads to further mystification and another imprisonment). It is no coincidence that the revelation of Angelica's infidelity produces a similar result. Orlando tears apart the literary-pastoral scene: filling up the "chiare, fresche et dolci acque" of Petrarchan lyrics, chopping down bookish trees, slaughtering the shepherds of *Arcadia* (XXIII.129–31, 134–36;

---

[108] See, for example, Jacques Derrida, "Signature Event Context," *Glyph* 1 (1977).

[109] This is my interpretation of the "apocalyptic" pages of Derrida's "Structure, Sign, and Play in the Discourse of the Human Sciences," in *Writing and Difference,* esp. pp. 192–93. I do, however, recognize that Derrida takes a certain distance on what he refers to as the "Nietzschean" theory of interpretation, though it still seems to me that he does not quite escape it.

XXIV.5 ff).[110] As he does so, he fulfills, in a way he never antici-
pated, the prophecy of his dream that he too would wander in a
desert of disillusionment, thus "giving the lie" to the narrator's hint
that the dream was merely the product of fear and hope. Unlike
Ruggiero, of course, Orlando's encounter with the truth behind
illusion does not liberate him (even illusorily), but instead produces
a void and a consuming violence. Unlike Melissa's "deconstruc-
tion," Orlando's is not an attack on dangerous mystification, but
instead on intolerable truth. Between them, in a sense, they furnish
an allegory for the project of much contemporary theory.[111] One
critic may argue that Orlando's assault on the poetic forest is the
revenge of a man whose illusions have been destroyed by the facts
inscribed in it. Another might assert, by contrast, that the violence
goes in the opposite direction, that the pastoral landscape is the place
of literary and erotic deception and that Orlando's violence is the
reality principle which exposes it for an empty sham.[112] Both
claims are right: the emphasis falls doubly on the poem as illusion
and as exposer of its own illusion, and there is no simple way of
deciding which function is valued more highly or of establishing
a durable hierarchy between them. Illusion protects Orlando, but

[110] I have adapted a suggestion by Walter Stephens.

[111] A certain Romanticism, for instance that of Giacomo Leopardi, held that
eighteenth-century Reason's "demystification" of myth and poetic illusion was
turning the world of man into a desert of insignificance by revealing the purely
empirical (i.e., random, mechanical) order of existence. It would be no surprise
these days to hear "deconstruction" attacked for the same reason, except that its
target for demystification is that same Reason, now seen as itself the site of myths
and mystifications rather than as their debunker. From this structure, two arguments
can be made: (1) that deconstruction is indeed a way of exposing man's location in
a "desert of insignificance"; but also (2) that, by its attack on Reason, decon-
struction is returning us to a world of myth and fiction on the far side of Reason,
opening up all the possibilities for self-deception and fictive reinventions of the
world, etc., whose loss Leopardi felt so acutely. I would argue that both of these
arguments are justified, and that Ariosto puts his poem too in just such a double
bind of sternly provoking crises in the meanings by which we live and, at the same
time, evading those crises by a retreat into fantasy. It is ironic that Leopardi should
have looked back, in the canzone "Ad Angelo Mai" (ll. 106 ff.), on the world of
the *Furioso* as one of utopian illusion still intact.

[112] Durling, *The Figure of the Poet,* p. 173; Giamatti, "Headlong Horses, Headless
Horsemen," pp. 298–99.

entraps Ruggiero, while the counterpoetry of deconstruction mad-
dens the former and frees the latter.

The poem also makes it clear that this dilemma applies to its
readers, who seem to be at risk either if they fail to see themselves
in Ruggiero (as Ruggiero fails to see himself in Astolfo) or if they
do see themselves in Orlando. Like the Alcina episode, though to
very different ends, cantos XXIII and XXIV draw subtle parallels be-
tween Orlando's interpreting and the readers'.[113] After all, the story
that he gradually unfolds for himself in the forest is the same one
the author related to the reader four cantos earlier. Specifically, the
host's attempt to use the tale of Angelica to soothe his guest seems
to figure the typical pose of the poet-narrator "diverting" his read-
ers. Its unexpected consequences then give reason to fear for the
reader who may identify too closely with the tales told by the poet.
At XXIII.128.8, in fact, Orlando identifies himself as an exemplary
figure for those who put their hope in love. And the narrator, after
having equated himself with Orlando in XXIII.112.3 (and again in
XXIV.3), hints at canto's end that his story might have evil effects
on its readers (as the host's did on his):

> *Ma son giunto a quel segno il qual s'io passo*
> *vi potria la mia storia esser molesta*   [136.5–6]

> I have reached the point which, if passed, my story might be noxious
> to you

He is ostensibly referring to the wearying effect of lengthy narra-
tion; but the context presses the other possibility upon us as well.

Thus if the *Furioso* represents (and embodies) a crisis of self-
knowledge and poetic reference, it is a crisis more extensive and
complex even than was suggested in Chapter 3: not only is truth
in crisis, truth *is* a crisis in itself. It has been argued, by Weaver

---

[113] Giamatti, "Headlong Horses, Headless Horsemen," p. 300: "Orlando in the
wood of words is Ariosto's image for the reader in the poem." Actually he is one
of many. As usual taking opposite sides of the same question, Giamatti would say
that the parallel is constructive and educative, while Donato ("Desire," esp. p. 28)
would say that it dramatizes the inevitable failure of attempts to structure a coherent
self through reading or writing.

and Santoro for instance, that the poem recognizes the dangers of knowing too much and specifically advocates a "wise ignorance" about the faith or lack thereof in others, as for example in Rinaldo's refusal to drink from the chalice (parody of Faith's traditional cup) which would reveal whether or not his wife had remained faithful to him.[114] In other words, one should embrace the view that the greatest illusion is to think that one can live without illusions.[115] But of course the poem furnishes striking examples of the dangers of blind trust in others, as it does of the virtues of ignorance, including: the metamorphic fate of Alcina's former lovers; Bradamante's near-fatal reliance on Pinabello (ii); Rodomonte's quiescent acceptance of Issabella's suicidal lies (xxix); the tale of Ginevra and Ariodante (iv–vi); and so on. One particularly savage and pointed instance comes in canto xxi when the blind faith of Filandro, ironically celebrated in the proem, is manipulated by the devious Gabrina so that he ends up killing the friend to whom he thought he was being loyal and marrying the personification of duplicity and infidelity.[116]

The complexity and subtlety of Ariosto's analysis of the relationship between writing and madness appears most plainly if one compares it to the book most famous for its treatment of that question, Cervantes' *Don Quixote*. The comparison between the *Furioso* and the *Quixote* is traditional, though usually off-target. In the *Aesthetics*, Hegel argues that they share the project of ironically separating chivalry and its literature from the realities of historical existence, of fragmenting a once-cohesive *forma mentis* (when literary chivalry was the product and specular reflection of a sociopolitical system). He then makes a further distinction between the two which clearly

---

[114] Santoro, "La Prova del 'Nappo' e la Cognizione Ariostesca del Reale," *Esperienze Letterarie* i (1976), no. i, pp. 16–18; Weaver, "Lettura," p. 395. Griffin, *Ludovico Ariosto,* p. 87, appositely cites Leonardo da Vinci to the effect that "the perfection of knowing is the cause of folly" (Codex Atlanticus 39ʳ).

[115] Cf. Giamatti, *The Earthly Paradise,* p. 164.

[116] F. Masciandaro, "Folly in the *Orlando Furioso:* A Reading of the Gabrina Episode," *Forum Italicum* 14 (1980), links this episode to Orlando's *furor* but leaves aside the central question of "blind faith" in the canto. See also Bonifazi, *Le Lettere,* p. 109, and Saccone, "Clorindano e Medoro." The *Cinque Canti* lay increasing stress upon the dangers of blind trust in others.

influenced DeSanctis and has been recycled often since.[117] For Hegel, the *Furioso* remains entirely within the domain of chivalric literature, simply heightening and travestying it to the point that it is perfectly detached from any world beyond poetry and its evasive imaginings. By contrast, Cervantes' masterpiece stages the problematic encounter of chivalric literature with history. He writes not a chivalric romance per se, but rather the story of a contemporary reader of such romances, one whose transcendent blindness clashes perpetually against a world from which all magic and nobility have disappeared long since. Cervantes, at least in this view, exceeds Ariosto both in his comic "realism" and in his self-conscious "metaliterary" examination of the unstable relation between poetic fiction, the historical world, and the individual consciousness that wanders between them.

The present discussion of Ariosto's treatment of madness suggests the inadequacy of this hierarchical contrast. Orlando's madness, like the Don's, is provoked by reading, but for what appears to be a diametrically opposite reason: what he reads is not fiction, but fact. On the other hand, as we have also already seen, Ariosto provides just as much evidence for the opposite contention: that we must try to penetrate the fictions and deceptions around us, lest they deprive us of liberty, sanity, or even life, as in the cases of Alcina and Gabrina. By dramatizing not only the power of literary art to madden by disguising reality, but also, inversely and irreconcilably, its potential for inducing folly by revealing intolerable truths, Ariosto gives a more balanced and more complex account of the relationship between literature and insanity than the traditional "Cervantes" to whom he is compared.[118] It is no wonder, then, if Ariosto deploys his chivalric plot now for purposes of aes-

---

[117] G.W.F. Hegel, *Aesthetics,* vol. 1, pp. 591–92, 605; vol. 2, pp. 1107–1108. Pirandello, "L'Umorismo," sets up an analogous contrast. More recently, see Nancy Doyle, "The Artist as 'Artifex Mundi' in Ariosto's *Orlando Furioso* and Cervantes' *Don Quixote*" (Diss. Indiana University 1979). Cf. Valesio, "The Language of Madness," p. 217.

[118] The argument is not that the hierarchy should be reversed, or that the reductive (though longstanding) reading of Cervantes mentioned here is the correct one; it is rather that the conventional opposition is invidious and needs to be rethought, without reference to any intellectual, moral, or aesthetic hierarchy.

thetic evasion, now for those of ethical commentary: he is aware
of the contradictions between those enterprises, but also of those
within them.

Truth is dangerous, but so is ignorance. Poetry lies, but also tells
the truth. And the point is that these two things can never be sep-
arated—lying and truth, infidelity and faith, are always simulta-
neous. The poem is full of cases where faith is mistaken for infidelity
or vice versa.[119] Orlando is in his predicament because he is simul-
taneously too faithful to Angelica and not faithful enough to
Carlo and God. Angelica becomes unfaithful to Orlando only when
she becomes what she has never before been to anyone: namely,
a devoted and faithful lover (excepting the magical attachment
to Rinaldo). Orlando's folly is soon contextualized by a series of
examples of fidelity and infidelity which reflect back upon it. In
Rodomonte infidelity also provokes a kind of madness, but in
this case the hero soon shifts his allegiance, to Issabella, and thus
demonstrates his own underlying inconstancy (cf. XXIX.1.1–4).[120]
Issabella's absolute fidelity, on the other hand, leads her to "lose
her head" literally and grotesquely, as Orlando did metaphorically.
In canto XXVIII, Giocondo seems headed toward madness or death
when he, like Orlando, obtains ocular proof of his beloved's be-
trayal, but regains his equilibrium when he finds that Astolfo's wife,
and indeed all wives, are unfaithful as well. In fact, he "becomes his
name," "giocondo" (XXVIII.39), achieving symbolic integration of
name and being, precisely when he discovers the essential duplicity
of the world and then sets off with King Astolfo on an odyssey of
masculine incontinence and inconstancy. This conflation of con-
flicted faiths is in fact a repeated motif of the poem: it especially
characterizes all of Ruggiero's later tergiversations between faith to
Bradamante and faith first to Agramante and then to Leone, which

---

[119] For example: Ariodante mistaking Ginevra's faith for infidelity, while Dalinda
makes the reverse error with Polinesso; Norandino mistaking Martano for Grifone
and vice versa; Argeo mistaking Gabrina's treachery for sincerity; Giocondo's mis-
placed trust in his wife; Bradamante's readiness to believe Ruggiero has betrayed
her with Marfisa; and so on.

[120] Weaver ("Lettura," p. 385 ff., passim) gives an excellent account of the struc-
tural and thematic points of comparison between Orlando's love madness and that
of Rodomonte (XXVII–XXIX) *and* Bradamante (XXXII). Cf. n. 102, above.

result necessarily in continual breaching of faith (particularly to Bradamante).[121] Bradamante earlier fell into madness when a *false* story convinced her of Ruggiero's infidelity (xxx.75 ff.; xxxII.10 ff.). Later, however, it is she who comes nearest to a resolution of the problem:

> *Basti che nel servar fede al mio amante*
> *d'ogni scoglio più salda mi ritrovi,*
> *e passi in questo di gran lunga quante*
> *mai furo ai tempi antichi, o sieno ai nuovi.*
> *Che nel resto mi dichino incostante,*
> *non curo, pur che l'incostanzia giovi:*
> *pur ch'io non sia di costui tòrre astretta,*
> *volubil più che foglia anco sia detta.* [xLV.101]

It is enough that I be more unyielding than any promontory in keeping faith with my lover and that in this I surpass all women from ancient times to our own. For the rest, I don't care if I lapse into inconstancy, providing that inconstancy is useful to me; as long as I am not forced to take that one [Leone], let me be called more flighty than a leaf.

Remarkably, Bradamante's speech has a double echo which links her both to Filandro, whose constancy is compared to a cliff ("sco-glio") which resists the ocean's batterings, *and* to Gabrina, whose exemplary treachery is compared to the flightiness of a wind-blown

---

[121] Once Atlante has stopped carrying Ruggiero off from Bradamante, Ruggiero himself takes over. In xxv.81–91 he breaks a promised word to Brada-mante in order to go to Agramante's aid. In xxxv–xxxvi Bradamante's fears of his erotic infidelity are dispelled by Atlante's revelations from the grave; but Ruggiero still chooses loyalty to Agramante, though he now knows him to be the son of his father's murderer. The narrator's apology for his dithering (xxxvIII.1–6) is soon belied by the dilemma of having to fight Rinaldo, Bradamante's brother and Agramante's foe (xxxvIII.68–73, 87–90; xxxIx.1 ff.), so that "non sapea egli stesso il suo desire" (xxxvIII.90.2). In xL.61–71 we see yet another debate resolved in favor of Agramante, though the bad faith of this position is exposed by the post-conversion promise that "Bradamante più [non] terrebbe a ciancia" (xLI.49.5). Finally, in xLv, his decision to keep faith with his enemy turned rescuer, Leone, leads him to betray Bradamante by secretly taking Leone's place in a duel with her which wins her hand for the apparent victor. His erroneous desire to "keep faith" is specifically set off against her declaration quoted below.

leaf (xxi.15–16).[122] She promises to be both faithful and unfaithful. And literary reference too is both faithful and unfaithful, one contemporaneously with the other, in a poetic garden which is at once a place of deception and a fount of truth.

iii. *Oneness in Nonsense*

Coming back at last to my initial questions, it is now clear that the relationship of language to truth and reason, on the one hand, and to madness and fiction, on the other, is genuinely troubled on both sides. Orlando's madness may ostensibly have as one of its attributes the absence of speech; nonetheless, language, whether lying or truthful, is implicated in madness, as its potential cause, if not its expression. Under such circumstances there seems to be no possibility of a comfortable equation between *ratio* and *oratio*. On the contrary, there seems to be no room left for anything which is *not* madness. It becomes increasingly difficult to sustain the common critical argument that Orlando's folly furnishes a *negative* proof of the powers of reason, insofar as it is the result of a correctable error. Such claims are inevitably based on the existence of an alternative figure, one of the characters (most often Rinaldo or Astolfo), or the poet himself, whose reasonableness makes up for the gap at the poem's center.[123] The "wise ignorance" of Rinaldo has already been questioned and will come in for more scrutiny later on, as will the assumption that Astolfo successfully cures madness. It is the "figure of the poet," however, whose dominance of and detachment from

---

[122] The Ruggiero-Leone episode is in fact alive with echoes from canto xxi: (1) they alone in the poem share a setting in postclassical Greece; (2) Bradamante's assertions of faith in xliv.61 and xlv.101 echo xxi.15, 16, 45; (3) a character by the name of "Androfilo" (and his symmetrically named wife, "Theodora") appear prominently in xlv, recalling-by-reversing the name "Filandro." More echoes could easily be added to this list. The evidence suggests how the 1532 revisions can be seen as specific palinodic and/or continuatory responses to the first two editions. The same could easily be argued for the Olimpia and Marganorre additions as well.

[123] For Astolfo, see Giamatti. For Rinaldo, see Santoro, "La Prova del 'Nappo.'" Santoro follows the tradition, dating from Toffanin and continued by Montano, which opposes Orlando's "forza" and madness to Rinaldo's canny "sapere" (cf. Chapter 2, n. 116). The opposition is apparently defined in xxvii.7, but already in the next stanza it is said that *both* heroes are mad.

his poetic world has always been the strongest argument for a sanity by, and against, which an inhumanly violent folly can be placed in reassuring perspective. His fluid poetic articulations make the strongest possible case for *oratio* as valuable opponent of *furor*.

As every reader of the *Furioso* knows, the narrator frequently compares his own erotic frustrations and their effect on his sanity to the erosion of Orlando's wits, usually at the most crucial junctures in the poem.[124] Several critics in recent years have drawn from this analogy the conclusion that Ariosto is as much subjected to desire and consequent folly as his heroes, that he makes an exact equation between the "deviation" and error of his narration and their mad strayings through the forest. In this view, far from constituting a single "figure of the poet," he dramatizes the dispersal of an "I" by dividing his personality within itself and among the multiplicity of characters with whom he variously identifies himself.[125] On the other hand, as already mentioned, Croce much earlier suggested that the denizens of the poem are so many partial "figures" for the poetic self, but he made this observation in the service of arguing that these "Many" were gathered up in and under the "One" of an "occhio divino."[126] And his successors have continued to argue that it is precisely because the poet–narrator can see and refer to his own madness that one can say he has escaped

[124] See Durling (*The Figure of the Poet,* p. 160ff.) for an especially useful list, including I.2, IX.1–2, XXIV.1–3, XXX.1–4, XXXV.1–2. To these can be added XXIII.112.3 and XXXIV.85.7–8, plus several references to precarious authorial sanity in the *Satire:* I.10–12; II.142–53; III.19–21; VII.178–81.

[125] Donato ("Desire," pp. 29–30) argues that Ariosto is subjected to desire as much as his characters are, abolishing the "theological concept of the book," creating an equation between desire and loss of self, on the one hand, and errant narrative on the other. Parker continues the exploration of the relation between narrative and psychological error. Bonifazi equates the poet's madness and the "infedeltà" of his writing with the characters' problems (*Le Lettere,* p. xxxiii). For Saccone too, the poet "non è sempre fuori del ballo," though he places him somewhere between Durling's god and Donato's schizophrenic ("Il Soggetto," p. 245). Cf. Chesney, *Rabelais and Ariosto,* pp. 196–97. They were all anticipated by Giovanni Gherardino, quoted by Borlenghi (*Ariosto,* pp. 152–53) who saw the poem as a labyrinth; not Momigliano's magical-imaginative structure, but "un'immagine dell'umano delirio."

[126] Cf. Chapter 1, n. 61.

it and recovered a perspective of *ratio* phenomenologically apparent in a controlled *oratio*.[127] It may be taken as a "segno espresso" of Ariosto's traditionally assumed qualities of equilibrium, balance, sanity, that he can entertain the possibility of madness through a plural and near-chaotic narrative form, just as it might be supposed that it is Tasso's dread of his own encroaching madness that makes him renounce analogy between his characters and himself and confront its risks within a tightly ordered epic structure. Is it not true that Ariosto is the poet who *writes* about madness, but Tasso is the writer who actually is going mad?

It is the famous Ariostan irony, applied by Ariosto to himself, which creates the impression that the poet has mastered his subject and its threat to his own subjectivity.[128] By splitting himself into a madman and the detached critic who views that madness, Ariosto simultaneously moves outside of himself and recovers himself. What then separates this doubling and separation of the self from the division and alienation with which Orlando characterized his own madness? The answer is inevitably *consciousness* and its linguistic expression, the ability to know one's own blindness and articulate one's own proximity to speechlessness (in a grandiose version of the "inexpressability" *topos*). At the very beginning of the poem, when Ariosto first makes the analogy, he gives the impression that the onset of madness is that which most threatens the poetic "ingegno": he will speak of Orlando's madness

> se da colei che tal quasi m'ha fatto,
> che 'l poco ingegno ad or ad or mi lima,
> me ne sarà però tanto concesso,
> che mi basti a finir quanto ho promesso.   [1.2.5–8]

---

[127] Durling, *The Figure of the Poet*, p. 175: "Like Horace, by pretending to be insane and by acting out his insanity, he conveys a strong impression of his real sanity." See also: DeBlasi, "Ariosto," pt. 1, pp. 321, 331–32; DiTommaso, "Insania," pp. 586–87; Jordan, "Enchanted Ground," pp. 159–60, 180; Valesio, "The Language of Madness," p. 234; Montano, "Follia," p. 163.

[128] For DeBlasi, perhaps the first to make this point, Ariosto stands above his poem "guardando da un punto superiore e fermo donde contempla pure se stesso, il suo esser debole e umano, consapevole delle proprie illusioni" ("Ariosto," pt. 1, p. 330).

if she who has almost reduced me to such [madness], who files away
at my little wit, now and ever, will, nevertheless, concede me the time
needed to finish what I have promised.

Poetry goes on, it seems, only as long as madness can be fore-
stalled. And poetic writing itself, taking place in a "lucid interval"
(XXIV.3.4) is thus at least an index of reason and possibly its pre-
server. In contrast to the poet's divided stance of irony is the more
decisive splitting which reduces Orlando to a mere thing without
self-awareness or power of speech. Irony is thus indeed the struc-
tural double of schizophrenia, but is also its opposite and remedy.
As for what has been said about language's agency in madness, one
can argue that it is not poetry itself which is the cause, but Orlando's
reading of it, and in any case it is not the *expression* of a madness
at all. Language is thus tentatively rejoined to reason, and silence
to folly, even though, curiously enough, it is Orlando himself who
articulates his own dilemma, viewing his old, "dead," self as if from
without.

The notion that the representation of madness actually contra-
dicts, denies, and excludes the "reality" of madness, just as it more
obviously does with silence, is a common feature of some very
recent treatments of the language of Folly and of certain key texts
in Ariosto's day as well. Michel Foucault has argued that classical
"reason," by circumscribing madness within institutions and as the
"other" within its own rational discourse, has paradoxically defined
it as alien and placed it safely outside itself.[129] Jacques Derrida, in
criticizing but also extending Foucault's line of argument, suggested
that Foucault's own discourse, which claims to be on the *side* of
madness against political and linguistic repression in the name of
"reason," is in fact still in the business of "making sense" of that
which is the contradiction of sense, articulating in signs that which
has as its "sign" the decline of discourse into gibberish or silence,
like Orlando who "di qua, di là, di su, di giù *discorre*" ("runs here
and there, up and down" XXIV.14.1) as language is punningly re-

[129] Michel Foucault, *Madness and Civilization* (New York: Random House,
Vintage, 1965).

placed by restless physical motion.[130] The Renaissance, of course, had already anticipated the appropriation by reason of Folly's voice. One thinks perhaps of Brant's *Stultifera Navis,* but especially of the *Encomium Moriae,* first published in 1509 and quite likely known to Ariosto, in which "Stultitia loquitur," in her improper person and in the exemplary form of humanistic oration.[131] Notwithstanding the scandal of madness which can speak, it is easy enough to interpret her locutions as the stratagems of the most calm and reasonable of humanistic minds, deployed to master madness by making it say what he wants it to: "I have praised folly in a way not wholly foolish" (Hudson, p. 3).[132]

There is, however, a second way of applying Erasmus to Ariosto. A slightly different reading of the *Encomium* would have it that Erasmus assumes the voice of Folly in order to make his own (Christian) critique of "classical reason," a critique which reveals that what calls itself reason is often sheerest folly and is all the more mad because it fancies itself not to be such.[133] "Stultitia" takes as

---

[130] Jacques Derrida, "Cogito and the History of Madness," in *Writing and Difference,* pp. 31–63. Note that the line quoted echoes *Inferno* 5.43, a canto whose subject is also the relation between desire and writing.

[131] *Encomium* (Miller edition), p. 71. For Folly's parody of humanistic orations, see Walter Kaiser, *Praisers of Folly* (Cambridge: Harvard University Press, 1963), p. 40 ff. See also Hudson's translation. *The Praise of Folly,* for his analytic diagramming of the work into its oratorical divisions (pp. 129–42). For Ariosto's possible debts to Erasmus, see Rajna, *Le Fonti,* p. 547; Salinari, "L'Ariosto fra Machiavelli ed Erasmo"; Ferroni "L'Ariosto," who places Ariosto instead between Alberti and Erasmus; Griffin, *Ludovico Ariosto,* p. 88; and Montano, whose relevance was noted earlier. For the subject of Folly in the Renaissance generally see, first of all, Kaiser and Klein, as well as Joel Lefebvre, *Les Fols et la Folie* (Paris: Klinksieck, 1968) and the collection of essays by different hands in *Folie et Déraison à la Renaissance* cited above for Ossola.

[132] The original is "stulticiam Iaudivimus, sed non omnino stulte" (*Encomium,* Miller edition, p. 68). The Moria-More pun is on the one hand a playful joke at the expense of a learned friend, but it also displaces this explicit praise of madness by madness toward a symbol of rational Christian humanism.

[133] In sec. i of this chapter the possibility of a folly and blindness *in bono,* along the lines of the Christian "credo quia absurdum," was raised. The latter part of the *Encomium* turns increasingly to this Pauline version of Folly (see esp. pp. 186–94 of the Miller edition). The recurrent theme of "reason" which sees madness in others but not in itself is not new with Derrida: it is stated succinctly in the *Encomium* (p.

a particular target the rational ideals of Stoicism, with its aspiration to human constancy and self-sameness, an ideal which is also frequently travestied in the *Furioso*. Since life is multiple and founded on illusion, it is truest madness to aspire to godlike unity and knowledge (not surprisingly, Ulysses and the Giants are his examples of misguided desire for wisdom) or to demystify rationally the deceptive theatrical appearances which allow us to survive and to avoid the consequences of encounters like Orlando's with the "bare facts."[134] "Wise" men in any case are in the business not of clarifying but of turning "black into white" by means of rhetorical and logical skills, duplicating the undifferentiation into which we saw Orlando plunged.[135] The case has been made that for Ariosto, too, reason is another form of self-deception and is inhabited by madness. And the other side of the coin is that folly, at least a certain Folly, is no longer only the *other* of reason, but is an "*alter* reason" with an alternative mode of vision.[136]

---

190) with a significant reference to Plato's allegory of the cave. The same motif can be found in Alberti, *Momus*, p. 131, and even in Castiglione, *Cortegiano* i.viii. See also *Furioso* XXXIV.84–85.

[134] *Encomium*, pp. 104, 112–14.

[135] Ibid., p. 114.

[136] Chesney (*Rabelais and Ariosto*, p. 6) enrolls Ariosto with Rabelais in what Hiram Haydn called *The Counter-Renaissance* (New York: Scribner's, 1950). For Ariosto, according to Chesney, madness is "no longer . . . a figure of *indignitas hominis*, but rather a symbol of humanistic creativity and optimism" (p. 171) and an "inverse wisdom" (p. 173). At other points, she sees him alternating between two accounts of madness—a wise *alter* reason and the violent *other* of reason (pp. 173–75, 193, 199)—and hence as leaving open and ambiguous the dialectic between reason and madness. Her first emphasis, however, falls clearly on positive folly as "esthetic and epistemological unity" and reconciler of contradictions (pp. 203–204). Ferroni is more cautious, placing Ariosto between an Alberti who (he says) keeps reason clearly separate from madness and an Erasmus who has the one contaminating the other and taking its place. He does at one point, however, argue that Ariosto accepts madness as "l'unica forma della propria salute" ("L'Ariosto," p. 87). Ossola ("Métaphore et Inventaire," p. 195) quotes a wonderful passage from Campanella's *Metaphysics* (pt. 1, bk. 1, doubt 9, chap. i. 1) on knowledge itself as a form of alienation and hence of insanity: "ergo scire est alienari. Alienari est insanire, et perdere proprium esse et aquirere alienum; ergo non est sapere res, prout sunt, sed fieri res et alienatio; sed alienatio est furor et insania; tunc enim insanit homo, cum in aliud esse convertitur." See also, of course, Giordano Bruno, *Degli Eroici Furori*. Compare n. 101, above.

Naturally, it is difficult to see how this insightful folly can be stretched to include the inhuman brutality of Orlando running wild. On the other hand, Erasmus himself was obliged to conceive of folly as double, *in malo* and *in bono,* so that the madness of reason would not be confused with madness's reason, so that the *loss* of self could be distinguished from self-transcendence. He was forced, in other words, to relocate the madness/reason opposition, which he had just collapsed, within the domain of madness itself, and in doing so he followed the previously mentioned Pauline distinction between the madness of the philosophers and the redemptive madness of blind Christian faith, adding to it references to Plato's transcendent *furori*.[137] In the *Furioso* one can hypothesize that Orlando's *furor in malo* is countered by the "saggia follia" of Rinaldo in cantos XLII–XLIII, though I have already suggested that this particular episode is offset by others in which the dangers of ignorance are brought to the fore. One may add, in fact, that this episode itself contains a parodic decline from the blindness of true Christian faith in God's glory to a blind faith in (universally violated) martial chastity. The ironic status of this degenerate faith, designed to mask the inevitability of erotic faithlessness, is made clear (1) by the motif of the fidelity-testing chalice (the "nappo," a kind of sixteenth-century dribble glass), which parodies the standard Christian iconographical representation of Faith's cup, and (2) by Rinaldo's hyperbolic comparison of his (deeply hypocritical) temptation to know about his wife's chastity with Adam's unfortunate desire to eat from the forbidden Tree of the Knowledge of Good and Evil (XLIII.7–8).[138] More persuasively, however, the poet's own *furor*

---

[137] See *Encomium* (Miller edition), p. 192: ". . . summum illud praemium nihil aliud esse quam insaniam quandam. Primum igitur existimate Platonem tale quiddam iam tum somniasse, cum amantium furorem omnium felicissimum esse scriberet. Etenim qui vehementur amat, iam non in se vivit, sed in eo quod amat quoque longius a seipso digreditur et in illud demigrat, hoc magis ac magis gaudet." And further on: "Porro quo amor est absolutior, hoc furor est maior ac felicior."

[138] Ferroni ("L'Ariosto," p. 90), like Weaver and Santoro, also sees Ariosto valuing "la saggia follia di Rinaldo" and refers particularly to XLIII.7–8. The two exemplary stories which follow keep the motif alive with repeated allusions to serpents: e.g., 74, 78, 79, 80, 95, 97–105. For the iconography of *fides* with a (Eucharistic) chalice, see, for instance, Emile Mâle, *The Gothic Image* (New York: Harper & Row, 1958), pp. 111–13.

may seem to provide a positive alternative capable of countering and even curing its opposite number. Such a position actually involves a return by the back door to the belief in Ariosto's "humanism of limits," which also posits the existence of a positive, if pragmatic and relativistic, knowledge alternative to Orlando's brutal folly.[139] In order to accept this, I need to show more fully than has been done previously that the poet-narrator actually, systematically, aligns himself with the traditions of positive poetic frenzy, and that his "lucido intervallo" specifically consists of this, rather than of "reason" more conventionally understood. There are at least two such traditions alluded to in the *Furioso,* and two distinct moments which are associated with them.

The most obvious point of reference for a coincidence of poetic wisdom and *furor* is the Platonic tradition of the four *furori,* especially the *furor poeticus,* articulated in the *Phaedrus* and elaborated in the age just preceding Ariosto's by Ficino and Landino. The Platonic view effectively situates man between two general types of madness (one subsumes the four subdivisions mentioned above).[140] There is the madness of the man whose blind desire leads him in pursuit of the earthly simulacra (especially female beauty) as ends in themselves and who loses his true self in the process. On the other hand, as Socrates suggests in both the *Phaedrus* and *Symposium,* the process of ascending out of the "earthly prison" of materiality and into the true spiritual good also involves a madness, in the sense that one transcends the limits of the corporeal self. In other words, madness as alienation from the self can lead in either of two directions, confirming again that Platonism itself can account for what has often been seen as the specifically anti-

---

[139] In speaking of Ariosto's and Rabelais' "ultimate humanistic art" of wise folly, Chesney (*Rabelais and Ariosto,* p. 204) seems surprisingly close to Giamatti, DeBlasi, and others.

[140] See Landino, "Proemio," pp. 141–43, and Ficino in Allen, ed. and trans., *Marsilio Ficino,* pp. 82–85. For references to most of the principal versions of "furor poeticus" in the Middle Ages and Renaissance, see Curtius, *European Literature,* pp. 474–76; Greenfield (*Humanist and Scholastic Poetics*), who discusses it in relation to Dante, Petrarch, Boccaccio, Bruni, Landino, Ficino, Pico, and Poliziano; and Alice Berry, "Apollo vs. Bacchus: The Dynamics of Inspiration," *PMLA* 90 (1975). For the two major divisions of madness, see n. 101, above, and my earlier discussions of Ariosto's possible use of *Asolani* bk. 1.

Platonic folly of Orlando. In fact, Ficino added yet a *third* type of madness, situated between the divine and the bestial, an intermediate and ambiguous "human" madness, which is perhaps the best suited of all for characterizing the status of *furor* in *Orlando Furioso*.[141]

There is only one explicit reference to the *furor poeticus* as agent of inspiration for Ariosto in the entire poem. Because this passage is unique, it is reasonable to argue that it is not representative of Ariostan poetics; but it is equally reasonable to claim that its specialness demands attention and commentary which it has rarely received.[142] After all, one must give some weight to a direct invocation of *furor poeticus* in a poem whose titular theme is madness and whose author declares himself a sometime victim of folly from the beginning. Moreover, the canto which this proem introduces has a decisive structural role in the poem: it inaugurates the extended series of genealogical tributes and brings one of the two main narrative lines (that of Bradamante and Ruggiero) into focus for the first time. In any case, the invocation of apollonian *furor* is as follows:

> Chi mi darà la voce e le parole
> convenienti a sì nobil suggetto?
> chi l'ale al verso presterà, che vole
> tanto ch'arrivi all'alto mio concetto?
> Molto maggior di quel furor che suole,
> ben or convien che mi riscaldi il petto;
> che questa parte al mio signor si debbe,
> che canta gli avi onde l'origine ebbe:
>
> di cui fra tutti li signori illustri,
> dal ciel sortiti a governar la terra,
> non vedi, o Febo, che 'l gran mondo lustri,
> più gloriosa stirpe o in pace o in guerra;
> né che sua nobiltade abbia più lustri

---

[141] Allen, ed. and trans., *Marsilio Ficino*, p. 79.

[142] See especially Durling, *The Figure of the Poet*, p. 131; Ferroni, curiously concurs ("L'Ariosto," p. 91, n. 58). Chesney (*Rabelais and Ariosto*, p. 195) sees the reference as crucial, if partly ironic. Weaver takes the interesting view that the moon "paese delle pazzie e della poesia" hints strongly at a *furor poeticus* which the poet's erotic madness also foreshadows ("Lettura," p. 388).

servata, e servarà (s'in me non erra
quel profetico lume che m'inspiri)
fin che d'intorno al polo il ciel s'aggiri.

E volendone a pien dicer gli onori,
bisogna non la mia, ma quella cetra
con che tu dopo i gigantei furori
rendesti grazia al regnator de l'etra.   [III.1.1–3.4]

Who will give me voice and words fit for such a noble subject? Who will lend wings to the verse so it may soar to the height of my argument? Now I need far greater fury than usually warms my breast, because this part is owed to my lord and sings his ancestral origins: you, Phoebus, who give luster to the great world, see none among all the illustrious lords allotted by heaven to rule the earth with a lineage more glorious in peace or war; nor one which has maintained its nobility for more lustrums—and will maintain it still, if that prophetic light which inspires me errs not, as long as the heavens wheel about the pole. And, if one wished to tell its honors fully, he would need, not my lyre, but that with which you gave thanks to the king of the ethereal realms after the fury of the giants.

As if to reinforce the connection of inspiration and philosophical ascent, the poet mentions the traditional wings of the soul, in words which may echo directly from the *Asolani* (III.viii.canzone, ll. 63–64), where the lover speaks of a need to follow the transcendent beloved upward. Even more striking is the proximity of the proemial desire for loss of self in a poetic *raptus* to the figure of Merlin, whose "profetico spirto" (9.4) clearly corresponds to Ariosto's "profetico lume." Merlin of course goes on to become perhaps the most consistent artist-figure in the poem, but the crucial thing here is his location: in a tomb where dead body and living spirit coexist.[143] The full importance of this image will emerge later on;

---

[143] Mary Farrell ("Mentors and Magi," pp. 66–69) takes this view which in general has found little favor in the criticism but which I support. The prophecies and artwork of Merlin reappear at regular intervals (III, XXVI, XXXIII); they are also recalled whenever Melissa, Merlin's agent, enters the scene; finally, there are a number of figures, including Atlante and St. John, which can be grouped around Merlin in his triple role as artist-prophet-magician. William Blackburn, "Spenser's Merlin," *Renaissance and Reformation/Renaissance et Réforme*, n.s. 4 (1980), provides useful background on the Merlin legend; he errs, however, in trivializing the magician/artist analogy in the *Furioso*.

for now, it is enough to note that the poet's loss of self in *furor* is doubled and reinforced by a motif of a "death of the self" which is the precondition for genuinely significant utterance.

Even as this complex of associations is being assembled, however, there is the usual ironic countercurrent at work. In the first place, the "furor" is not actually in the service of a transcendent subject or spiritual education, but is rather in celebration of a "mundane" political dynasty (however divinely inspired it might be). Less obviously, but more insidiously, it is juxtaposed with another type of *furor*. Stanza 3 contrasts the apollonian fury with that of the giants, a standard opposition which can be found in Pico as well.[144] The only hint that Ariosto's inspiration might partake of the hubristic assault on divinity which this implies is the allusion to the apotheosis of the Este brothers that will be developed more amply in the genealogical review. Later, however, comes an image which suggests that the two madnesses are not so distant after all:

> Terrà costui [*Azzo V d'Este*] con più felice scettro
> la bella terra che siede sul fiume,
> dove chiamò con lacrimoso plettro
> Febo il figliuol ch'avea mal retto il lume,
> quando fu pianto il fabuloso elettro
> e Cigno si vestì di bianche piume [III.34.1–6]

This one will rule with happier scepter the lovely city that sits by the river where Phoebus called with weeping lyre his son who had so badly governed the light: then when the fabled amber was wept and Cygnus dressed in white plumes

The poet ironically situates the Este family at the site of the fall of the Sun's son, Phaeton, and he later makes Alfonso and Ippolito into (Phaeton–like?) imitators of the sun (57.1–4, 58.7–8; cf. 50). Phaeton is Apollo's human offspring, whose hubristic madness in taking a god's place is clearly analogous to that of the giants and whose fiery fall to death gives rise both to apollonian plaint and to the Swan, figure of poetry *and* mortality. Phaeton links Apollo to the giants and thereby threatens the distinction between good and evil madnesses, implicating both the poet and those he cele-

---

[144] Pico, *Oratio* (Garin edition), p. 116.

brates in an alternative vision of dark and deadly folly.[145] Merlin too, though far more subtly, is subject to a certain contamination by the darker side of the history he foresees. Among the enemies of the Este on display, Ezzellino is preeminent: "immanissimo tiranno, / che fia creduto figlio del demonio" ("most appalling tyrant, who will be thought the demon's son" 33.1—2). With exasperating punctuality (verbal and even, perhaps, numerological these words return in canto XXXIII, *now applied to Merlin himself* who is said, in accordance with a traditional legend, to be "del demonio figlio" ("son of the demon" 9.3). Thus if Ariosto does claim for his poem the inspiration of a poetic fury, it is only by locating it in an ambiguous place, suspended between transcendence and loss of self, between angels and demons, between Apollo and the Titans, just as he does later on in the lunar episode.

More promising, perhaps, as a means of rescuing madness as a valuable and evaluative mode of knowledge, is a second tradition, also of Platonic origin, and not always completely separated from the first. In this case, the figure of madness, at least outwardly, is not so much apollonian as dionysian. The focal image of the tradition appears, oddly enough, precisely at the point when Astolfo has succeeded in netting the mad Orlando, subjecting him to a ritual re-baptism, and forcing him to inhale his lost wits from the jar found on the moon (XXXIX.35—61). Orlando's awakening is described as follows:

> *Poi disse, come già disse Sileno*
> *a quei che lo legàr nel cavo speco:*
> *—Solvite me— con viso sì sereno,*
> *con guardo sì men de l'usato bieco,*
> *che fu slegato . . .*   [60.1—5]

---

[145] The image of the "wings of the soul" in stanza 1.3—4 has as its classical precedent the "remigium alarum" of Daedalus' flight (*Aeneid* VI.14—19; see the discussion of this motif in Chapter 3), with all the apollonian associations that cluster around it in that Virgilian context (VI.9, 35, 56, 69—70, 77, etc.). Taken together with the reference to Phaeton's death, it may also allude to *another* mad flight, Icarus', which by chance appears in a relevant passage from Bembo: "o ali che bene in alto ci levate perché, strutta dal sole la vostra cera, noi . . . quasi novelli Icari, cadiamo nel mare! Cotali sono i piaceri [d'Amore]" (*Asolani* I.xxv; Marti edition, p. 48). See *Asolani* II.xv, p. 88, for the "gigantei furori" as well.

Then he said, as once Silenus said to those who bound him in the hollow cave—"Loose me"—with countenance so serene, with a look so much less twisted than usual, that he was unbound . . .

Much recent criticism and scholarship of the Renaissance has attached special importance to the figure of the Silenus. The *locus classicus* for this figure is Alcibiades' comparison of Socrates to the *sileni* in the *Symposium* (215a–b), though Ariosto's most direct source here is Virgil's *Sixth Eclogue* (24). The *sileni* are ludicrous little statues, named for the comical Silenus of the dionysian entourage, which, when opened, reveal unexpected treasures, just as the unprepossessing outer appearance of Socrates conceals staggering intellectual riches. Erasmus picked up the figure, focusing on it in one of the most famous of the *Adagia* (iii.iii.1) as emblem of Christ's comic concealment of deity within a human frame. Perhaps more important, for my purposes, he also uses it in the *Encomium* to suggest that human things are always double, the appearance of one thing always covering its opposite:[146]

> First of all . . . all human affairs, like the Sileni of Alcibiades, have two aspects, each quite different from the other; even to the point that what at first blush . . . seems to be death may prove, if you look further into it, to be life. What at first sight is beautiful may really be ugly . . . ; the disgraceful, glorious; the learned, ignorant . . . ; the joyous, sad; . . . what is wholesome, poisonous. In brief, you find all things suddenly reversed, when you open up the Silenus.   [Hudson, p. 36]

At least two critics have already compared Ariosto's poetics to that of the Socratic or Erasmian Sileni, arguing that the *Furioso* too possesses a counterwisdom within the appearance of folly.[147]

---

[146] *Encomium* (Miller edition), p. 104: "Principio constat res omneis humanas, velut Alcibiadis Silenos, binas habere facies nimium inter sese dissimiles. Adeo ut quod prima . . . fronte mors est, si interius inspicias, vita sit: contra quod vita, mors: quod formosum, deforme: . . . quod infame, gloriosum: quod doctum, indoctum: . . . quod laetum, triste: . . . quod salutare, noxium; breviter omnia repente versa reperies, si Silenum aperueris."

[147] Ferroni, "L'Ariosto," p. 77; Chesney (who also cites the Erasmian passage), *Rabelais and Ariosto*, p. 199. Curiously, neither refers specifically to xxxix.60. Cf. Rabelais, *Gargantua* (i.prologue, 1.3–6; iii.prologue, v.5–25). Note that the Silenus of the *Encomium* is not necessarily the Christian figure of the *Adagia* at all, but in-

By apparently mediating the restoration of Orlando's wits with an image of Erasmian, Christian, folly *in bono,* curing schizophrenia by making a "double man," Ariosto accounts for his own double status as madman and sage and for his poem's division between comic surface and serious concern. The Silenus is in fact the perfect emblem of "serio ludere," as is Socrates, who ends the *Symposium* with the claim that he can reconcile the comic and the tragic in a single author. It may well be no coincidence at all that St. John's hermeneutics of inversion would describe the Silenus perfectly. Through the Silenus madness and reason, truth and fiction, encounter—the one becoming the allegorical outside for the other and vice versa. For the poet as demonically duplicitous Alcina, we can substitute the poet as Silenus, apparently subject to depersonalizing dionysian fury, though full of Socratic and apollonian wisdom.[148] From this perspective only, it would seem, where a wise Folly speaks, can one explain how the *Furioso* envisions both the end of reason and the cure of a certain madness which speaks lucidly. It offers a wonderful image for a poem and a poet which assume the appearance of frivolity and the evasion of all that is serious, even as they live a condition of internal crisis, division, and alienation, and yet make that same division operate from within as the ironic detachment necessary for formulating critical judgments on self and others.

This very attractive picture, nonetheless, still begs the question, begs to be further questioned. Its success depends on averting the dangerous contamination of education by madness through the discovery of a perspective from which oppositions—between outside and inside, insight and blindness, knowledge and *furor*—can be reinstituted and on which they can be firmly grounded. This is so even though we find the Ariosto of the *Satire* saying, with Paul DeMan, that to recognize one's madness is not to have escaped from it:[149]

---

stead simply suggests that any outside, good or bad, hides its opposite number within. See also Giovanni Pico's letter to Barbaro, in *Opera Omnia,* vol. I, p. 354 for an invocation of the Silenus in answer to Barbaro's critique of philosophical style.

[148] For one proto-Renaissance version of the Apollo/Dionysius opposition in poetry, see Petrarch, *Secretum* bk. II, in *Prose* (Martellotti edition), p. 90.

[149] DeMan, "The Rhetoric of Temporality"; cf. *Furioso* XVI.4.

. . . se ben erro, pur non son sì losco
che 'l mio error non conosca e ch'io nol danni.
  Ma che giova s'io 'l danno e s'io 'l conosco,
se non ci posso riparar, né truovi
rimedio alcun che spenga questo tòsco? [IV.35–39]

For, if indeed I err, I am not so blind as not to recognize my error and condemn it. But what good is it to condemn and to be aware of it if I cannot correct it, or find a medicine to expel this poison?

To see, to know, as St. Paul, Ovid, and Petrarch knew, is *not* to choose: "Veggio 'l meglio, et al peggior m'appiglio" ("I see the better and cleave to the worse" *Rime* CCLXIV.136), and the crisis of the will again checkmates the criticism of the intellect.

The success of the recuperative operations on the poem depends in great part, as I have already suggested, on two assumptions: (1) that Orlando's madness is ultimately and convincingly cured, and (2) that Ariosto, via the Silenus and other means, is aligning himself with an Erasmian critique of reason and/or mastery of madness. Both points can be challenged. The cure of Orlando in XXXIX prepares him to make two decisive contributions, of wisdom and of strength, which lead to the war's end: the siege and destruction of Biserta which carries the fight onto pagan ground for the first time; the triple duel which leads to the deaths of Gradasso and Agramante, the focal points, in Rodomonte's absence, of the pagan cause. It is Orlando's renowned "sagezza" which plots the taking of Biserta, and the battle is preceded by due Christian pieties (XXXIX.64–65; XL.9, 11–12); but the battle which ensues is an infernal nightmare in which pagan and Christian alike are caught up in "furor" and "rabbia" (XL.29.4, 31.1, 32.1), and the "pious" victors patently turn the city into a hell with pillaging, burning, and raping which neither Astolfo nor Orlando, for all their wisdom, is able to restrain (XL.32–34). This contamination of wisdom's projects with madness's violence is only a prelude, however, to what happens on the island of Lipadusa.

The turning point in the conflict which pits Orlando, Brandimarte, and Oliviero against Gradasso, Agramante, and Sobrino comes when Gradasso kills Brandimarte, Orlando's dearest friend, with Orlando's own sword, Durindana. Canto XLII begins with Orlando's agonized reaction to what has happened:

> *Qual duro freno o qual ferrigno nodo,*
> *qual, s'esser può, catena di diamante*
> *farà che l'ira servi ordine e modo,*
> *che non trascorra al prescritto inante,*
> *quando persona che con saldo chiodo*
> *t' abbia già fisso Amor nel cor constante,*
> *tu vegga o per violenzia o per inganno*
> *patire o disonore o mortal danno?*   [1]

What stiff rein, what iron knot, what adamant chain, if such exists, will make wrath observe order and measure so it does not run beyond prescribed limits when you see someone whom Love had fixed in your constant heart with a firm nail suffer by violence or trickery either dishonor or mortal harm?

Orlando, whose cure was a binding followed by a loosing, now breaks all bonds and unleashes his ire again.[150] Just like Achilles, with whom his wrath had been implicitly and is now explicitly compared, a first anger which removed him from the camp of his allies (for a similar reason: both are deprived by the commander-in-chief of a female object of desire) is complemented by a *second* (provoked by the loss of a male object of affection) which leads him to destroy the most formidable of their foes.[151] The fall back into *furor* is unmistakable. The first line of the canto is a close echo of the proem that introduced *Ruggiero's* relapse (XI.1.1). Once again a hero is going beyond the "prescritto," caught up in "*inumano* effetto," leaving behind reason's "impero" (2.1, 4; cf. 4.1–2, 6.5–6). And as

---

[150] For the key imagery of binding and loosing, see Giamatti, "Headlong Horses, Headless Horsemen" and "Proteus Unbound," as well as St. Peter at the gates.

[151] Recent commentators seem to have taken rather too seriously Ariosto's disclaimers regarding his knowledge of Greek literature, and have focused on his debt to the Latin classics. The *Cinquecento* commentators, however, quickly saw analogies between the "wrath" of Achilles and various "furori" and "ire" in the *Furioso*. Fornari (*Spositione*, p. 35) equates Agramante's "giovenili furori" with Achilles', and plenty more examples can be found in skimming through the commentators. Rare among the moderns is Petrocchi, "Lettura," p. 283. Orlando's *furor* can also be compared to Aeneas' in *Aeneid* bk. 12, when, *pietas* forgotten, he kills the abject Turnus.

he brutally attacks the unarmed, bleeding Agramante, Orlando is described with a by-now-familiar simile:

> Qual Nomade pastor che vedut'abbia
> fuggir strisciando l'orrido serpente
> che il figliuol che giocava ne la sabbia
> ucciso gli ha col venenoso dente,
> stringe il baston con colera e con rabbia [7.1–5]

Like a Numidian shepherd who has seen the horrid serpent flee slithering, which with poisonous fang had killed his son as he played in the sand, and who grips tight his club with anger and rage

Ironically, a serpent image was applied to the fear of Agramante when, a few cantos earlier, he detected the Christian ships which were about to destroy his fleet (XXXIX.32).[152] The more important precedent is to be found back in canto XXIII itself, as the tormented Orlando tries futilely to sleep:

> Non altrimente or quella piuma abborre,
> né con minor prestezza se ne leva,
> che de l'erba il villan che s'era messo
> per chiuder gli occhi, e vegga il serpe appresso. [123.5–8]

Not otherwise does he now abhor his pillow, nor with less haste does he arise from it than does the peasant from the grass where he lay down to close his eyes when he sees a serpent close by.

Orlando's new *furor* renews both Ruggiero's and his own. Given the sixteen-canto arc over which the first fall into and rescue from madness were acted out, and the elaborateness of the cure staged by Astolfo, it matters very little that Orlando will come to his senses shortly after dispatching Gradasso: there is no longer any way of imagining a cure to folly that would be permanent. The God who rescued Orlando through Astolfo becomes the "Dio vindice" ("vengeful God" XLII.5.1) who willingly plunges him back into

---

[152] For the serpent imagery, see XLII.38, 47, 50, 51, 55, 56, 74, as well as Weaver ("Lettura," p. 395), who links XXIII and XLII–XLIII to the serpent of Genesis. Other relevant passages include I.11, XXX.56, and XXXVII.78. The closest sources of XLII.7 are *Aeneid* II.378–82, and Ovid, *Fasti* II.341–42. Cf. n. 138, above.

blind violence. Almost all the rest of the canto is dedicated to Rinaldo, who just now learns of Angelica's "betrayal" and proceeds to act out, briefly but very intensely, steeped in a slithering mass of serpent imagery, the same sequence of *furor* and its cure which Orlando underwent.[153] The dialectic of madness swallowing reason and vice versa becomes an open spiral which no longer admits of an hierarchy, or of any final closure.

Perhaps one can take this qualification further to suggest that it is "hidden," snakelike, in the scene of the cure itself, in the image of the Silenus, and from there spreads to infect even the privileged position of the poet and his language. My earlier discussion focused on the Silenus of Erasmus partly because it illustrates so well a certain tradition, and partly because it has been the heuristic recourse of the critics wishing to invoke that tradition. The problem is that the recourse is *only* heuristic, because, though a Silenus does appear at the crucial moment, it is *not* the Erasmian Silenus at all. It derives, instead, partly from the *Hercules Furens* (1063–81) and principally from Virgil's *Sixth Eclogue* (24).[154] The echo of the *Furens* comes from the analogous moment in Hercules' story, when the greatest of heroes returns to himself after the madness during which he slaughtered his family (just as Orlando slaughtered a host of innocents and would have destroyed even Angelica). The second, dominant, source seems at first to suggest that Orlando's schizophrenic self-division has been replaced by the salutary duplicity of Socrates' wise irony. Closer inspection, however, reveals that such a reading is problematic, that the Virgilian Silenus is, if anything, a direct polemical counter to the Platonic-Erasmian one. Admittedly this

[153] It is at this point that the opposition of Rinaldo's "sapere" and Orlando's "forza"—based on the conventional "sapentia"/"fortitudo" distinction; see Robert Kaske, "'Sapientia et Fortitudo' as the Controlling Theme of *Beowulf*," *Studies in Philology* 55 (1958)—is finally collapsed. It is Orlando, in any case, who is most often praised by the poet for his wisdom (see n. 90, above), XXVII.7–8 notwithstanding. As Donato says ("Desire," p. 30), "Rinaldo is as mad as Orlando." And in *this* context Orlando's madness pales before Rinaldo's. Both are resolved, but neither settles the larger question.

[154] Parker (*Inescapable Romance*, p. 39) notes the twin sources, the second of which, at least, has long been known. Jordan ("Enchanted Ground," p. 209) points out that Virgil's Silenus is specifically the figure of a poet. It is typical of Ariosto to blend two sources at crucial moments—as in the title and the first line of the poem (echoing *Aeneid* 1.1 and *Purgatorio* 14.109–111).

Virgilian Silenus, too, is duplicitous and, at first, seems to be so in a similarly positive way. The drunken and lustful follower of Bacchus is netted by two young shepherds and constrained to sing. Far from the expected drinking song, however, what comes forth is a brilliantly grand philosophical hymn which stretches from the creation of the world down through mythical history (a Virgilian sketch for the *Metamorphoses*). Virgil's creature apparently bears the same Socratic doubleness as Alcibiades' does, and actually makes a direct link to the poetic art itself. But here the wheels within wheels have wheels within *them* too. Before beginning his chant, Silenus announces loudly that at the end of his discourse he will return to the seductions and carousals which are his true vocation. The conversion from Dionysius to Apollo thus seems more of a strategic response to circumstance than a revelation of inner character. Moreover, and this is the main point, the lucid song which he sings describes not a Platonic or proto-Christian universe whose origin and end are spiritual and divine, but instead appears to derive its main vision from Lucretius. What is presented is a world composed at random and riddled with irrational eros and violence, where Love (as Epicurean lack, not Christian presence) is the moving force equally capable of gathering matter together into form and of wrenching it apart to restore an original, undifferentiated, chaos.[155]

Where the dionysian outside of Erasmus' Silenus contained an apollonian inside, here the apollonian inside, like the skin of Marsyas, is itself torn open, and its voice of control and its clear vision have

---

[155] For the haunted, "Lucretian," side of Virgil in the *Aeneid*, see W.R. Johnson, *Darkness Visible*. For the specific Lucretian echoes in *Eclogue* VI, see Virgil, *Eclogues*, ed. R. Coleman (Cambridge: Cambridge University Press, 1977). In his notes to the poem, Coleman (pp. 183–85, 202, 205) catalogues several direct echoes of Lucretius' *De Rerum Natura*, particularly in lines 31–40 of the *Eclogue* on the formation of the world out of chaos. Coleman also notes that the tradition of a Lucretian reading of the poem goes back to Servius' commentary on the *Georgics* and *Bucolics*. Servius specifically interprets Aegle, the nymph desired by Silenus, as "the Epicurean doctrine of *voluptas*." This is confirmed by Eleanor Leach, *Virgil's "Eclogues": Landscapes of Experience* (Ithaca: Cornell University Press, 1974), p. 234, n. 22: "Servius . . . takes Silenus as a disguise for Virgil's Epicurean teacher Siro, and thus attributes an Epicurean coloring to the song." See Servius, *In Vergilii Carmina Commentarii*, eds. G. Thilo and H. Hagen (Leipzig: B.G. Teubner, 1881–1902), vol. 3, pp. 66–67. Whatever objections or qualifications there may be to this interpretation of the *Eclogue*, we have nonetheless established that it was a traditional one even in Ariosto's day.

as *their* inside a blind chaos, a deafening roar.[156] By what authority then do I forcibly transfer this allusion from Orlando to Ariosto and elevate it to the status of a poetic? I do so because of the associations with poetry and because, more important, this is not the first allusion to Lucretius at a key point in the text. The "lucido intervallo" in which the poet says he writes, the one which separates him from Orlando and bounds madness with *oratio* and *ratio,* is the same as the one attributed by St. Jerome to Lucretius in dismissing the latter's atheistic philosophy as having been composed "per intervalla insaniae."[157] Is Ariosto embracing the Christianized Epicureanism which Valla, and Erasmus too, used as a lever against the Stoics, and as a way of bringing out the side of Christianity which values the natural and the corporeal?[158] It would seem not, since the allusion is to the atheistic Epicureanism reviled by the Church Fathers (and by Dante in *Inferno* 10) and not the "other" Epicurus resurrected, so to speak, by the Renaissance.

Ariosto may, obliquely, be suggesting not that his Silenus and Virgil's are like Erasmus', but that Erasmus' is, surprisingly, like theirs. A comparison of the two proffered readings of Erasmus— that reason appropriates Folly's voice to master it and that Folly appropriates reason's voice for the same purpose—suggests that that text too is caught in a structure *en abyme* where reason contains folly contains reason contains . . . and no final resting place is available.[159] Reason and madness haunt and inhabit each other, and

---

[156] See Berry for the Apollo/Dionysius opposition not as reason/madness, but as two distinct madnesses, associated respectively with the *prophetic* and the *mystical* (or *hieratic*) of the four Socratic madnesses. She points out that the bacchic and the apollonian are combined or juxtaposed through the Silenus of Alcibiades.

[157] The source is St. Jerome's addition to the *Chronology* of Eusebius to the effect that Lucretius was driven mad by a love potion (note the analogy with Ariosto) and, after composing his books during "intervalla insaniae," committed suicide. See *S. Hieronymi Interpretatio Chronicae Eusebii Pamphili,* in J.P. Migne, ed., *Patrologiae Cursus Completus: Series Latina* (Paris: 1844–1864), vol. 27, cols. 523–26. Cf. Saccone, "Il Soggetto," p. 245; Montano, "Follia," p. 163.

[158] See Valla, *De Voluptate* and/or the later versions of it entitled *De Vero Bono, De Vero Falsoque Bono.* For Erasmus, see the *Encomium* and Kaiser's discussion of its use of the Epicureans against the Stoics (*Praisers of Folly,* p. 55 ff.).

[159] Kaiser (p. 92) insists on the ambiguity of *Stultitia*'s discourse, as does Ferroni ("L'Ariosto," p. 76), who perhaps is the more vigorous of the two in exploring the

language sits at the midpoint, unable to ascertain in which it originated. Does this mean that the *Furioso* is purely Lucretian, purely negative: atheistic and alogical? No, the reversals have come too often, and each new perspective proves as precarious as that it just undermined. The question is an open one. The language of the *Furioso* names its distance from a silence which is equally the cover for demonic absence and divine presence, leaving us in the suspended knowledge that neither madness nor reason will ever truly *appear* in language, particularly this language.

Those few who have specifically meditated on the status of silence in the *Furioso* have been equally divided between, on the one hand, associating it with madness (and *oratio* with *ratio*) and, on the other, linking it with reason (while madness dallies with duplicitous speech).[160] How deliberately Ariosto provokes both responses, by situating his language at the juncture of silence and speech, as of madness and reason, can be seen in an episode already recognized as crucial: the "descent from heaven" in canto XIV, which pivots round a search for Silence personified. At first "Silenzio" seems to be on the side of sense and divine will against the pagan onslaught of Babelic "furor" and "rumor" led by the new Nimrod, Rodomonte (71, 109, 117–19, 133–34). God himself commands the Archangel Michael to enlist Silence's aid for the Christians (76), presumably to stifle the "aspro concento" of Rodomonte's cacophonous attack (134.1). On the other hand, God also commands Michael

---

potential consequences of such a situation. The passage on Ariosto quoted earlier from Saccone ("Il Soggetto," p. 243) amounts to the same thing: "la sanità confina con la pazzia: è dietro, o è l'ombra della pazzia."

[160] Ossola ("Métaphore et Inventaire," p. 186) associates reason—which has no need to speak—with silence, and linguistic metaphor with madness, since both are forms of displacement. How this squares with his characterization of folly as the absence of reason and his assertion that the poem itself is "of reason," I am not sure. Chesney (*Rabelais and Ariosto,* pp. 194–95) seems first to adopt Ossola's position, then the other. Valesio sees *this* period of the Renaissance associating madness with silence, with the situation changing later on. For the madness-silence nexus in Ariosto, see also Daniel Rolfs, "Sound and Silence in Ariosto's Narrative," *Renaissance and Reformation/Renaissance et Réforme* n.s. 2 (1978), as well as, especially, a recent essay of Andrea DiTommaso, "Boiardo/Ariosto: Textual Relations and Poetic Integrity," *Stanford Italian Review* 4 (1984). Cf. nn. 90 and 107, above.

to make use of demonic "Discordia," which is specifically presented as the incompatible opposite of Silence (86). Put on the same level as Discord, Silence is reduced to neutral status: it can be used for divine purposes just as can Babelic Discord, but the opposite is true as well. Confirmation of this equivocation comes when Michael looks first for Silence in the monasteries, once the precincts of silent piety, only to find that devotion has been replaced by its opposite, Discord. He also learns that Silence, once companion to saints and philosophers (exemplars of faith and reason), is now the sometimes partner of Fraud, of treachery, of counterfeiting, of theft, of erotic dalliance (88–90). In other words, Ariosto shows how (apparently angelic) Silence might signify Truth and devotion, but might as easily mask Fraud and treachery.[161] Just as "loss of wits" can be either disappearance into bestial madness or exaltation in divine transcendence, so "loss of voice" may cover both the demonic and the divine. Or, to put it as one of Ariosto's commentators did in another context: "when the madman falls silent . . . he is not at all different from the wise man."[162]

Ariosto goes on to give an imagistic, "tacit" account of the relationship between silence and writing which might easily be extended to include his own written representations, especially of God and of Silence. As God prepares to answer Carlo's prayers, He is described as the "Bontà ineffabile" ("ineffable Goodness" xiv.75.1), a *verbal* description which contradicts itself flatly, by naming the unnameable. The joke continues as the silent Word then speaks at length to Michael in human language (75.5–76.6). On the one hand, Ariosto is having a little fun at God's expense. More to the point, however, he is radically subverting his own attempts to put the ineffable into language. It is in this light, then, that one should understand the reference to Silence "scritto in ogni stanza" ("written in every room [or *each stanza!*]" 79.8), followed by the revelation that Silence is there present only in writing, not in fact ("non v'abita più, fuor che in iscritto" 80.8), and by the later description of Silence

---

[161] See also Greene's treatment of the episode in *The Descent From Heaven,* esp. p. 131.

[162] I translate Porcacchi's gloss on iv.10 in the Orlandini edition: "Quando il pazzo tace, non è punto . . . differente dal savio."

in motion as "discoursing" ("discorreva il Silenzio" 97.1) which anticipates the punning play on Orlando's frenzied movements (XXIV.13.1). We know that at least since the *Phaedrus* (274c–277a) writing has occupied an "equivocal" (though equally "non-vocal") position between speech and silence: it is composed of words, but those words cannot talk back to potential interlocutors. Here Ariosto reveals both the *silence* of his language (it cannot name properly), but also its noisy failure to achieve authentic quiet (it gives us Silence, "in name only"). Once again the *Furioso* is left suspended: between silence and speech, truth and fraud, madness and reason, Logos and Babel.

Perhaps the poet's most subtle and yet powerful joke on this score comes when, after establishing the silence of Orlando as a defining characteristic of madness in direct opposition to his own loquacious "lucid interval," he then makes his hero speak while still lost in madness, not once but several times (XXIX.70.4; XXX.5, 6, 7, 11). Moreover, at precisely this moment, the narrator inserts an extended comparison between his own folly and Orlando's which suggests that his poetic language has just expressed an excessive "ira" or "furor" against women, the verbal equivalent of Orlando's physical and mute attack on Angelica:

Quando vincer da l'impeto e da l'ira
si lascia la ragion, né si difende,
e che 'l cieco furor sì inanzi tira
o mano o lingua, che gli amici offende;
se ben dipoi si piange e si sospira,
non è per questo che l'error s'emende.
Lasso! io mi doglio e affligo invan di quanto
dissi per ira al fin de l'altro canto.

Ma simile son fatto ad uno infermo,
che dopo molta pazienzia e molta,
quando contra il dolor non ha più schermo,
cede alla rabbia e a bestemmiar si volta.
Manca il dolor, né l'impeto sta fermo,
che la lingua al mal dir facea sì sciolta;
e si ravvede e pente e n'ha dispetto:
ma quel c'ha detto, non può far non detto.

Ben spero, donne, in vostra cortesia
aver da voi perdon, poi ch'io vel chieggio.
Voi scusarete, che per frenesia,
vinto da l'aspra passion, vaneggio.
Date la colpa alla nimica mia,
che mi fa star, ch'io non potrei star peggio,
e mi fa dir *quel di ch'io son poi gramo:*
sallo Idio, s'ella ha torto; essa, s'io l'amo.

Non men son fuor di me, che fosse Orlando   [XXX.1.1–4.1]

When reason allows itself to be defeated by impulse and by wrath and does not prevent blind fury from pushing either hand or tongue to the harm of friends; if thereafter one cries and sighs, the error is not thereby corrected. Alas, I sorrow and afflict myself in vain on account of what I said at the end of the last canto. But, I have become like a sick man, who, after much patient suffering, gives in to rage and turns to blasphemy. The pain passes, nor does the impulse remain the same which loosed the tongue to evil speech, and he reflects and repents and is regretful, but he cannot unsay what was said. Well I hope, ladies, that in your courtesy you will grant me pardon, since I ask for it. You will excuse the fact that, in a frenzy, defeated by bitter passion, I rave. Lay the blame on my enemy, who puts me in such a state that I could not be worse off and makes me say things for which I am soon sorry: God knows if she is to blame; she knows if I love her. I am no less beside myself than was Orlando

Even this *pentimento* betrays continuing "ira," as the poet launches a renewed attack on his beloved enemy. Thus, in the space of a few stanzas, with studied perversity, a silent madness becomes verbal and verbal lucidity gets drawn into "cieco furore."[163] Even at poem's beginning, in the very passage earlier cited as proof of an alliance of the poet with the "saggi" rather than the "pazzi," Ariosto hints allusively at this paradox. The image of erotic "filing" which erodes sanity and threatens writing is taken from Horace's *Ars Poetica* (291), where the "limae labor" stands for the slow process of crafting the

---

[163] On the importance of XXX.1–3, see Saccone, "Il Soggetto," p. 245. See also XXIX.49.1–2, where the narrator says he wants to "ragionar del conte" (using a word for speech which links it directly to reason) and XXIX.50.1–2, where he then declares "pazzia sarà, se le pazzie d'Orlando / prometto raccontarvi ad una ad una" (suggesting, in contrast, that too much talk would be madness).

verse.[164] Poetry is again involved in the same corrosive attack on reason at the very moment when it seemed to be forestalling or postponing the effect of that attack.

In any case, the truth of madness is hidden in silence, perhaps forever, and we are offered instead, in Ariosto's words, an improper and metaphorical representation of madness. But just as education itself proved to have the structure of metaphor, so too does its opposite: both are structured as displacements of the self, and, through the metaphorical dislocations of the *Furioso,* the poet first opposes then equates them, and it is the self-consuming equation of self-difference. When first discussing the structure of Orlando's madness, I argued that it consisted of a differentiation, a self-division, followed paradoxically, by a state of radical undifferentiation. My account of the structure of Ariosto's poem is not so very different from this: its language (and its poet) is/are split between reason and madness, finally unable to differentiate between the two. Perhaps one passage from the poem, more than any other, can suggest to what extent this is the case. It comes at the dead center of the poem (or rather, next to its center, the center being a blank space between cantos XXIII and XXIV), a few lines prior to the reference to poetry as "lucido intervallo":

> . . . *non è in somma amor, se non insania,*
> *a giudizio de' savi universale*   [XXIV.1.3–4]

> love is nothing, all told, if not insanity, in the universal judgment of the wise

The apparently clear sense of the line—that all wise men universally judge love to produce madness—reinforces the already discarded hypothesis that there is a plane of wisdom from which love and madness can be judged for what they are. But there is a grammatical ambiguity here which prevents any such simple reading. The adjective "universale" could, in theory, modify two other nouns besides "giudizio," i.e., "amor" and "insania," which are presented as equivalents of one another, and are both opposites of "giudizio." One would naturally argue that, for want of other criteria, the closer noun would attract the modifier. But this is verse, and in

---

[164] Durling (*The Figure of the Poet,* p. 160) notes the parallel.

verse there are more kinds of proximity than one. For instance, "insania" is placed at the end of one line, directly "next" to "universale" which ends the following line. What is the result of such a revised reading? That the line now means: "what is love but a universal madness, according to the judgment of wise men." From universal judgment to universal insanity marks the distance from the stable perspective of reason to a madness which engulfs everything (including the "savi"), from the "unity of Truth" to that folly which is "tutt'una" ("all one" 2.2).[165]

It is not uncharacteristic of Ariosto's procedure that the episode of Zerbino's judgment of Oderico later in the canto offers yet another "giro di vite" which qualifies the paradigmatic definition of universal love-madness. On the one hand, Zerbino's clear error in judgment in pardoning his treacherous friend seems further to illustrate the proem. On the other, Oderico, whose bad faith is demonstrated before and after this interlude, pleads that his murders and attempted rape must be excused on precisely the grounds that Love's force is irresistible. He appropriates Ariosto's musings on the inevitability of human folly as a disingenuous pretext for evading Zerbino's condemnation and the penalty of death. The retrospective implications for human ethics and justice are devastating. Finally, the end of canto XXIV (114) and the beginning of XXV (1–2) see yet another shift of position as "Amor" becomes a force for reconciling competing lovers, benefiting the larger (pagan) community. How does one account for these thematic oscillations in the poem? In some ways they are perfectly predictable once the reader has recog-

---

[165] Another equivocation bolsters the first in XXIV.2.4. Love is compared to a "selva" where "conviene . . . , a chi vi va, fallire." Read as "vi va," the line limits love to a restricted group; read as "viva," it includes all humankind (I owe this suggestion to Paolo Valesio). Compare DiTommaso's discussion of the "insania"/ "furor" distinction (cf. n. 80, above). It is interesting, in this regard, that while Durling begins his piece by expounding the unity of the poet-God, he specifically closes it with an intensive examination of the theme of universal madness (*The Figure of the Poet*, pp. 165–66). The "oneness" of madness can be found (but also contradicted) in the *Encomium*, with its references to the universality of folly. See especially Folly's claim of including all creatures within herself and being immune to rhetorical divisions and of being "sumque mei undique simillima" (Miller edition, p. 74, with obvious parodic reference to the Stoic "semper idem"). Nonetheless she also divides herself in two at a later point, as we saw earlier.

nized the basic paradox defined in XXIV.1–3. In others they seem to supersede or stand outside of it. Where is the principle or perspective that makes of these many, one?

It is, in fact, precisely in the half-light of crisis submitted to judgment, judgment beset by crisis, that one should review the theme of the *unity* of the many-faceted *Furioso*. The project of unifying the poem has always been closely matched with the exorcising of folly, the natural assumption being that madness is indeed a demon whose name is "Legion" (Matthew 7:9). And so the poem would seem to say: "il desiderio uman [by now equatable with folly] non è tutto uno" ("human desire is not all one" XIII.50.4). So it *begins* to say here, too: "Varii gli effetti [della pazzia] son" ("Many are the effects [of madness]" XXIV.2.1). The Renaissance, of course, was obsessed by the problem of the discordant departure of the Many from the One and the possibility of their "harmonious" return to it. Not coincidentally, critics of the *Furioso* have been equally obsessive on this question: from Tasso's laments about the poem's lack of oneness and Giraldi-Cinzio's definition of the author as multiform chameleon down to the present day.[166] Modern views range, as we have seen, from defining the poet or narrator as creative deity who, like Pico, gathers together the rent body of universal truth and reduces the mad multiplicity of the poem to perfect *armonia*, to arguing that "the One does not replace but rather is the Many" and that madness is "the ultimate cognitive structure."[167] In be-

---

[166] See Tasso, *Discorsi*, and specifically the passage cited above in n. 67, and Giraldi-Cinzio, cited in Chapter 1. For the "One and the Many" see Giamatti, "Proteus Unbound," and of course Spitzer, *Classical and Christian Ideas of World Harmony*. The best single summation and parody of the tradition that I know of (particularly in relation to the image of the poet-God) is the closing paragraph of Jorge Luis Borges' "biographical" sketch of Shakespeare, "Everywhere and Nowhere," trans. J.E. Irby, in *Labyrinths* (New York: New Directions, 1964), p. 249: "History adds that before or after dying he found himself in the presence of God and told Him: 'I who have been so many men in vain want to be one and myself.' The voice of the Lord answered from a whirlwind: 'Neither am I any one; I have dreamt the world as you dreamt your work, my Shakespeare, and among the forms in my dream are you, who like myself are many and no one.'" Cf. Derrida, "Edmond Jabès," p. 70: "For the work, the writer is at once everything and nothing. Like God. . . ."

[167] The citations are from Chesney, *Rabelais and Ariosto*, pp. 199, 173. For *armonia* of the One and the Many, see Chapter 1, nn. 4–6, above. Ficino, in his *De Amore*

tween the *Furioso* as poem of the One or as poem of the Many comes Saccone's image of poet and text as Orrilo, constantly dismembered and recomposed.[168] Even more central, perhaps, is the role played by *Discordia* personified in canto XIV: first as a subverter of monastic religion, then as the agent of the one true God against the Babelic many. When Michael reappears in canto XXVII, Discord has slipped out from under the angel's not-so-watchful eye and reverted to doing the devil's work. Discordant multiplicity both serves and subverts divine harmony in the *Furioso*. No wonder if it is at the end of canto XIV that Ariosto uses the words "aspro concento, orribile armonia" ("bitter unison, horrible harmony") in such a way as to reflect obliquely on his own poetic "raucousness," the "strange concord" which is also that of his poem (XIV.134). In this, one of the very rare uses by Ariosto of the word so often applied to him, is a suggestion of just how partial those applications have been.[169] The reader, like Shakespeare's Theseus, is always left to ask "how shall we find the concord of this discord?" (*Midsummer Night's Dream* v.i.60).

The assertion that the objects of desire and its effects are many and various is, ironically, followed closely by the claim that "la pazzia è tutt'una" ("madness is all one" 2.1–2), words which seem to support the idea that insanity, not rational harmony, is the principle of "unity" in the poem. This, however, is not madness as illuminating "cognitive structure," but madness whose true oneness lies in its condition of absolute undifferentiation, the disappearance of self into the other, and the disappearance of the self/other

---

(in Allen, ed. and trans., *Marsilio Ficino*, pp. 221–23) shows how readily Ariosto could have brought together the themes of many/one, discord/concord, dissonance/harmony through a unifying poetic *furor:* "Redire quippe ad unum animus nequit ipse unum efficiatur. Multa vero effectus est, quia lapsus in corpus . . . ad corporalium rerum multitudinem respicit infinitam. . . . Totus autem animus discordia et inconcinnitate repletur. Poetico ergo furore primum opus est, qui per musicos tonos que torpent suscitet, per harmonicam suavitatem que turbantur mulceat, per diversorum denique consonantiam dissonantem pellat discordiam et varias partes animi temperet."

[168] Saccone, "Il Soggetto," p. 245; the poem is like "Orrilo scisso: diviso e intero, pazzo e sano, lucido e cieco."

[169] References supporting the more traditional reading of *armonia* in the poem can be found at VIII.29.1–4 and XLII.81.4. Cf. 1.35.7, II.1–4, VII.19.4, etc.

distinction, and of *distinctio* in general, period. Against God's all-embracing Oneness, the poem poses the undifferentiated totality of "insania universale," a genuine *reductio ad absurdum*. Still I would not argue (and how could I?) that the poem systematically substitutes this Oneness for God's or that of "giudizio . . . universale," but that (first syntactically and then semantically) it sets the *two* side by side as possible origins for its plural and improper language and leaves us no criteria to make our decision *in bivio,* at the crux-roads. After all, how can "one" distinguish unity from unity?[170]

It is no accident that the poet frequently shifts responsibility for events in the poem from God's providence to Fortuna's caprice and back again. Usually critics feel compelled to choose one or the other as the prime mover in the poem.[171] One more spectacular syntactic-semantic equivocation shows, however, that no critical choice and separation can finally be made. It too, interestingly, bears directly on Orlando's madness—as Zerbino is being led off to execution, unjustly accused of murdering Pinabello, the narrator comments:

> Ma Dio che spesso gl'innocenti aiuta,
> né lascia mai ch'in sua bontà si fida
> tal difesa gli avea già proveduta,
> che non v'è dubbio più ch'oggi s'uccida. [xxiii.53.1–4]

But God, who often aids innocents, and never abandons whoever trusts in His goodness, had provided such a defense for him that there is no question of his being killed today.

---

[170] In this regard I would juxtapose my text with the last page of Derrida's "Cogito," with its brilliant confrontation between the "crisis" of and in reason and the crisis of and in madness: "Here, the crisis is on the one hand . . . the danger menacing reason and meaning under the rubric of objectivism, of the forgetting of origins, of the blanketing of origins by the rationalist and transcendental unveiling itself. Danger as the movement of reason menaced by its own security etc. But the crisis is also decision, the caesura of which Foucault speaks, in the sense of *krinein,* the choice and division between the two ways separated by Parmenides in his poem, the way of logos and the non-way, the labyrinth, the *palintrope* in which logos is lost; the way of meaning and the way of nonmeaning; of Being and of non-Being" (p. 62). The parallel to my discussion of the crisis/judgment nexus in Chapter 1 is clear.

[171] Farrell ("Mentors and Magi," pp. 96–100) and Blasucci (*Studi,* pp. 165–66) tend to choose God, while Brand (*Ludovico Ariosto,* pp. 120–21) and Santoro ("L'Astolfo Ariostesco") tend in the other direction.

There is a problem of translation here. If the elided word in the second line is "chi," the passage means that God never leaves those who trust Him; He is faithful and worthy of faith. If the elided word is "che," and "che" is even more likely to be elided in Italian than "chi," it means that God never lets anyone trust in Him (or that He does not exist at all!). In the immediate context, the first meaning is supported by Orlando's rescue of Zerbino. The second meaning emerges, however, as we discover the devastating reward Orlando will soon get for his good deed. The implication then would be that God, just like Fortuna as described later on, repays good with evil ("'l ben va dietro al male, e 'l male al bene" XLV.4.3).[172] When the pendulum swings back in canto XXXIV and we are told that the madness was providentially sent, it is already too late, just one more confirmation that no interpretation is ever final, that the poet is as changeable as Fortuna herself. The assimilation of God to Fortuna, and the poet to both, is then only heightened when the reader recalls the motto with which Ariosto closes his poem, specifically echoing XLV.4.3: "pro bono malum," evil for good.

This, then, is the plight of the "figure of the poet," whose perspective of transcendent judgment has been so often set off against the universal folly represented within the poem. He too is, in a sense, caught betwixt and between two universals—"giudizio" and "insania," God and Fortuna—and is neither able to escape the world of his poem nor fully to enter into it. Ironically, the writing of the poem, his immediate relation to it, is what forestalls madness, but it is also his inability to leave behind the condition of error

---

[172] The equivocation is anticipated in XXIII.1.2–3 ("*rade / volte* il ben far senza il suo premio fia") and 2.5–6 ("Dio, che *le più volte* non sostiene / veder patire a torto uno innocente"). Canto XXIII alternates references to God and Fortuna ostentatiously (2.5, 10.1, 11.6, 19.7, 30.7–8, 33.6, 92.4, 109.4). Jordan ("Enchanted Ground," pp. 149–51) lists some crucial references to Fortuna, including the following: "abbia chi regge il ciel cura del resto / o la Fortuna, se non tocca a lui" (XXII.57.3–4). See aslo 1.10.6, XXII.70.6 and 71.5, XXVII.7 and 33ff. (where Fortuna as causal agent is juxtaposed with Michael's divine mission). Another curious equivocation comes in XLIII.175. Fiordiligi, "per l'alma del defunto Dio pregando," is either praying God for the soul of the deceased (Brandimarte) or praying for the soul of the "deceased God," with a hint that her love is idolatrous, and perhaps even with a slap at the basic tenet of Christian theology: Christ's death (and resurrection).

represented by his characters and his narrative technique which makes that madness a permanent threat. He is certainly no poet-God; but the possibility of a resemblance to "quel che 'l tutto vede" ("he who sees all" XXI.32.6–8; cf. XLI.61, passim) lingers temptingly behind one of the two horizons of the poem, the other concealing "quel re che nulla vede" ("that king who sees nothing" XXXIII.116.7). And the two opposite horizons, like all horizons, ultimately merge in a single circle if pursued far enough. It has been said that "the basic action of the poem is . . . seeing clearly, seeing things in all their complexity."[173] This is only half-true, however: the main actions of the poem are seeing and not seeing; and, more often than not, one masquerades as the other.

iv. *"La Vocal Tomba di Merlino"*

The threat to the poet's identity is not simply that he represents accurately his own possible folly; it even penetrates the operation of representation itself as expression or betrayal of the self. The *Furioso* dramatizes itself both as true teacher of historical and psychological truths and as the duplicitous falsifier of them. The poem's rhetoric encloses a number of versions of its author, already fragmented and contradictory among themselves, and tells us that they may be a literal reflection of his "reality" or that they may be the opposite of his allegorically hidden essence. It both refers to him and defers any direct encounter with him. There is no way to decide which is truer: the poem carefully stages its own indeterminate relation to the heart and mind of its creator, for whom it stands both as "afterlife" (in the sense that Latini says to Dante, "let my *Treasure,* in which I yet live, be commended to you" *Inferno* 15.119–20) and as tomb, both as phenomenological realization of self through the objectification of creative expression and as a deadly reification, the sign of its author's eternal absence.

Madness, in fact, is not the only, or even the most serious, threat to the poet's identity and that of his characters. Death, to which Orlando compares his state of incipient folly, and which is the constantly mentioned limit to Ruggiero's historical identity, is also the

---

[173] Durling, *The Figure of the Poet,* p. 176.

demon which the poet flees and defers and the condition of para-
digmatic crisis which he embraces.[174] It is a commonplace of the
criticism that the poet's brilliant strategy of narrative deferral is
directly linked to the deferrals of various crises by his characters.
As Daniel Javitch's witty title, "Cantus Interruptus," clearly sug-
gests, one of those crises is the act of love: the "plaisir du texte"
and the pleasures of desire both thriving on postponement.[175] But
the pleasure principle is not the only one involved. More often
than not the deferrals are of decisive, irreversible, choices and judg-
ments. Ariosto praises Ippolito for deferring "guidizio" on the
accused brought before him, lest he err like Norandino in con-
demning Grifone to death (XVIII.1–3), juxtaposing the postpone-
ment of princely judgment with his own immediately preceding
narrative deferral (XVII.135.6–8).

The most consistent and symptomatic deferrals are those which
impede the choices—conversion, marriage, rule—that will solidify
Ruggiero's identity. As we know from the previous chapter, how-
ever, what is most striking about those choices is that they are all
linked directly, even causally, to Ruggiero's death—not only by
Atlante, but by the Hermit who effects his conversion as well
(XXXVI.64; XLI.54, 61).[176] That conversion is actually precipitated
by his fearful prayer on the point of drowning, which apparently
leads to a miraculous *rescue* of his life (XLI.47–49). He seems at first
to stand in sharp opposition to his pagan comrades, whose desire for
life actually draws them to death (22.7–8). The Hermit's revelation
then partly effaces that opposition. Perhaps even more strikingly,
the episode of conversion is immediately preceded by Brandimarte's
failed attempt to convert his former liege, Agramante, just as he
himself was converted by Orlando in Boiardo's poem (*Innamorato*

---

[174] I take issue here with Saccone ("Il Soggetto," p. 173) and with the whole tradi-
tion of taking the exclusion (not total, in any event) of tragic death from the poem
as a sign that Ariosto is not "seriously" preoccupied with death.

[175] Cf. Roland Barthes, *The Pleasure of the Text* (New York: Hill & Wang, 1975).
Canto X.114–15 is a good illustration of Javitch's point. I disagree that Ariosto is
teaching us the "disappointment" of the inevitable deferral of satisfaction. Quite the
contrary, it seems to me: the deferral of desire is what brings desire to most intense
"jouissance." I do not take issue with the assimilation of deferral to sexuality; I sim-
ply add that deferral in the poem is also of death, and that the two deferrals can be
expected to converge, à la Freud of *Beyond the Pleasure Principle*.

[176] Cf. *Innamorato* II.xxi.54.5; *Furioso* IV.28–38, passim.

II.xxii.10 ff.), an event of which the reader is reminded for the very first time in the *Furioso*. Ruggiero's spiritual metamorphosis is then immediately *followed* by Brandimarte's violent death (99 ff.). In other words, Brandimarte is shown to be Ruggiero's predecessor as pagan convertite just in time to bring home a causal connection between the metaphorical "death of the self" in conversion and the literal demise of the physical person. A close inspection of the whole poem in fact suggests that religious faith and particularly conversion, as well as marriage and amorous fidelity, are almost always linked directly to death—perhaps the most macabre instances being Issabella's decapitation and Fiordiligi's life in the tomb after Brandimarte's death.[177]

Ariosto's narrative deferrals-of-ending mime Atlante's deferrals-of-death throughout the poem, though writing and life alike make conclusion inevitable (the poem which Ariosto continues took as its abrupt ending its author's death rather than a narrative period).[178] And it is not just the death of characters that concerns the poet. Very soon after the first references to Atlante's efforts to put off

[177] Among other notable instances are the death of Filandro, exemplar of faith, and that of Zerbino. The faithful Issabella's death comes soon after her conversion by the hermit. In canto XXXVII the fidelity of Drusilla leads to murder and suicide in a savage travesty of Eucharistic communion. The same can be seen in Olimpia's earlier murder of *her* new husband. For comic relief, there is the "conversion" from fidelity which rescues Giocondo from his death in canto XXVIII. The question then is whether these deaths have the metaphorical force of the "death of the self" in conversion, or whether they are brutal literalizations of that metaphor which drain it of significance. Unlike Fichter, I do not believe this can be easily decided. See also Parker (*Inescapable Romance*, p. 36) on death *or* conversion as the end to human error. I would add only that the two converge in the *Furioso*.

[178] Momigliano long ago and brilliantly described how the "miniature" world of Atlante's castle-labyrinth (IV.32.3−4) is an image of the poem. Parker (ibid., p. 21) recently pointed out that Daedalus, inventor of flight *and* of the labyrinth, unites the two aspects of imaginative flight and stultifying imprisonment which mark the poem with their conflict. And it is Atlante from whom both hippogryph and labyrinth derive. She also pointed out (p. 35) how the two fairies who defer Grifone and Aquilante's deaths are like Atlante deferring Ruggiero's, and like Ariosto deferring the end of his narrative. Thus I cannot fully accept Quint's identification of Atlante as Boiardo ("The Figure of Atlante"). In that reading, Ariosto's ending of deferral, return to history, and acceptance of death as fact expose as utopian Boiardo's poetics of infinite postponement, ahistoricity, and evasion of death. On the other hand, Ariosto actually has Atlante himself intervene to end the delay in Ruggiero's marriage to Bradamante (canto XXXVI) and insists that the *magus* is aware all along

his ward's demise (IV.45), Ariosto juxtaposes the attempts of a minor character to forestall her death by talking and his own (Scheherazade-like) method of narrative deferral (IV.70.5–6, 72.7–8), in what proves to be the *first* of the many canto-ending uses of the word "differire."[179] The necessary failure of that project is signaled then in the next-to-last stanza of the entire poem which contains the *final* use of "differire," one of three crucially placed rhyme words:

> *ma il giovane [Ruggiero] s'accorse del errore*
> *in che potea cader, per differire*
> *di far quel empio Saracin morire*   [XLVI.139.6–8]

> but the youth was aware of the error into which he might fall by deferring the death of that impious Saracen

The fundamental Ruggieran and Ariostan tendencies of "error" and "deferral" are put to rest as the young hero decides that Rodomonte must die.[180] Furthermore, the accumulated symbolic weight of these words reminds the reader that the pagan's violent death is only a prolepsis of Ruggiero's. This, death, is the end of the poet's error too, as the *first* stanza of the last canto taught us. It hardly seems a coincidence that, within a few octaves of the image of the poetic ship coming to port, Ariosto refers to a very different shore: "la scura spiaggia / di Stige" ("the dark shore of Styx" 9.5–6). The poet writes; he revises. But the River of Death still puts him finally to silence. All the deviations and deferrals of characters and author alike halt: the relative absence and continual

---

that he is only postponing the inevitable tragic crisis. There is a play both of differentiation and resemblance between Ariosto and Atlante and closure is problematized both before and during canto XLVI so that "epic" remains in tension with "romance" (Parker) rather than superseding it (Quint).

[179] In VI.2.6–8 Ariosto closes the Ginevra episode by referring to the failure of Dalinda's tormentor, Polinesso, to *defer* death. Canto-ending uses of "differire" are at VI.81, X.115, XI.83, XIII.83, XVII.135, XXIII.136, XXIX.74, XXXI.110, and XL.82. Other more and less relevant uses are at I.21, 23, 71; XIII.42; XVIII.2, 8; XXIV.68; XXV.3, 23–24; XXVI.68, 86, 96, 113, 116, 126; XXX.22, 29, 30; XXXI.26, 49; XXXII.88; XXXIII.48, 89; XXXVIII.90; XXXIX.19, 34; XLV.113.

[180] The rhyme words from XLVI.139.6, 7, and 8 echo XXXVIII.90.2, 4, and 6, where Ruggiero's hesitation in fighting his brother-in-law to be, Rinaldo, is paired with the narrator's deferral of the story.

displacement of desire is exchanged for the permanent absence of the dead.

The plain connection between decisive choice and death raises interesting questions about the poet's understanding of human liberty, centered around the problem of free will. How does one deal with the fact that choice, human "giudizio," is what constitutes the free self, but also what puts it in crisis and finally cuts it off? Ariosto's "solution" is a rather curious one, since its greatest success is in exposing the essential insolubility of the question. For instance, in one of the *Satire* the poet strenuously defends his own *libertà*, much as Atlante, and later the hero himself, protect Ruggiero's. At one point he claims that he refuses to choose either marriage or holy orders because to do so would bind him permanently, forever foreclosing the possibility of choosing the other:

> *Come né stole [di prete], io non vuo' ch'anco annella*
> *mi leghin mai, che in mio poter non tenga*
> *di elegger sempre o questa cosa o quella.*
> *Indarno è, s'io son prete, che mi venga*
> *disir di moglie; e quando moglie io tolga,*
> *convien che d'esser prete il desir spenga.*
> *Or, perché so come mi muti e volga*
> *di voler tosto, schivo di legarmi*
> *d'onde, se poi mi pento, io non mi sciolga.* [*Satira* ii.115–23]

> I desire neither the stole [of the priest] nor the ring to bind me, so [that] I no longer hold it in my power to choose the one or the other. In vain, if I were a priest, would the desire for a wife befall me; and if I were to take a wife, I would have to renounce the wish to become a priest. Because I know how mutable my intentions are, I avoid binding myself in such a way [that] I cannot loose myself if later I repent.

This passage derives directly, it would seem, from one in Valla's problematic treatment of free will in the *De Libero Arbitrio:*[181]

---

[181] Translated by Trinkaus in Cassirer et al., eds., *The Renaissance Philosophy of Man*, p. 168. The original Latin text from *De Libero Arbitrio* (in Garin, ed., *Prosatori Latini*, p. 542) is as follows: "Longe diversum est aliquid posse fieri et aliquid futurum esse. Possum esse maritus, possum esse miles aut sacerdos, numquid protinus et ero? minime. Ita possum aliter agere quam eventurum sit, tamen non aliter agam. . . . Quare rata est praescientia, remanente arbitrii libertate. Haec ex duobus alterum electura est: nam utrumque agere non licet, et utrum electura sit, lumine suo illa praenoscit."

Something that can happen and something that will happen are very different. *I can be a husband, I can be a soldier or a priest, but will I right away? Not at all.* Though I can do otherwise than will happen, nevertheless I shall not do otherwise. . . . Thus [God's] foreknowledge is valid and [man's] free will abides. This [human] will makes a choice between two alternatives, for to do both is not possible, and He [God] foreknows by His own light which will be chosen.

Ariosto echoes this classic discussion of free will, but collapses the first distinction between what *can* happen and what *will* happen. For him, paradoxically, to exercise the freedom of will by choosing between two things which "could be" means to surrender himself to irrevocable destiny, to lose all freedom and die, if not literally, at least figuratively. In fact, as mentioned in another context earlier, Valla himself eventually undercuts the optimistic conclusion of the paragraph just quoted, when he reminds us that if God's *omniscience* can be squared logically with human freedom, His *omnipotence* cannot. Valla turns to religious faith as the only means out of reason's impasse. Ariosto, on the other hand, goes even further. By juxtaposing the words "legare" and "eleggere" in *Satira* ii, he shows awareness of the predicament defined by the double medieval etymology of "religio" as both a choosing and a binding, a *choosing to be bound,* so that every decisive choice is also the negation of choice.[182]

Liberty emerges from the "autobiography" of the *Satire* as Ariosto's supreme personal value.[183] But the freedom of pure imagination, as we have seen, is partial and finally illusory, always

[182] On Valla's self-contradiction, see Trinkaus, *Image and Likeness,* vol. 1, p. 168, and *De Libero Arbitrio,* p. 550 ff. For the etymology of "religio," see Isidore, *Etymologiarum* VIII.2.1–3, as well as Dante, *Paradiso* 3–4. This is another way of accounting for a narrator both free and bound by passion, as DeBlasi sees him ("Ariosto," pt. I, p. 331). Saccone ("Clorindano e Medoro," pp. 119–200) argues that Ariosto neither resists nor critiques, but rather embraces, a chivalric ethics of binding promise which sacrifices the freedom of the will. Cf. XLI.55.3–6 for the Hermit's reproof of Ruggiero for *deferring subjecting* himself to Christ when he was *free* to do so. For a possible analogy between this textualization of freedom/determinism and Ariosto's own life, consider the poet's long deferral of his marriage to Alessandra Benucci, which was partly determined by his "situazione ambigua tra laicato e stato ecclesiastico" (Dionisotti, "Chierici e Laici," p. 60).

[183] See *Satire* I (esp. 168, 262–65), II.151–53, III.1–9, IV.13–18, VI.162.

checked from without (by demanding patrons, for instance) and from within by its obsessive return to the concerns of "reality" and its inability to postpone conclusion indefinitely. And the other freedom, the freedom of the active will, points even more directly to a metaphorical "death" of the self, its subjugation to impersonal institutions—church, state, marriage—and finally to its *literal* death. The contingent space of freedom which Ariosto makes for himself is thus the protraction of the time prior to choice and judgment, entertaining the *possibilities* of moving from imagination to history, but not yet turning them from liberating possibility into oppressive reality: at the *bivio,* the crux, neither before nor after it.[184]

The poet, however, seems to want to have it two ways: both to remain on this side of the ultimate human crisis, death, and to stand safely on the other side looking back (though he can achieve neither, as he himself acknowledges). Frank Kermode has argued that the perspective of literary ending is analogous to the structure of Apocalypse, that point beyond both individual life and history itself from which each can be viewed retrospectively, *figurally* as Auerbach would put it, to recover, uncover ("revelation," "apocalypse") the sense of what has necessarily undergone annihilation in order to be understood.[185] The Christian perspective includes an analogy between the structure of history culminating in Apocalypse and the individual life leading to the *decisive* moment of death (witness Dante's Guido and Buonconte da Montefeltro in *Inferno* 27 and *Purgatorio* 5).[186] Within the confines of life, which Christianity generally sees as a continuing temporal crisis never free from the spectre of a fall away from God and self, conversion offers a metaphorical "death of the self" and a "type" of apocalyptic perspective.[187] By pointing to Augustine's comparison of human life to a song, Freccero can argue that the analogy of poetic closure with conversion, death, Apocalypse, allows literature to mime the

---

[184] Cf. Derrida, "Edmond Jabès," p. 66: "Freedom allies and exchanges itself with that which restrains it," and "Freedom is grounded only if it is separated from Freedom by the desert of the Promise."

[185] Kermode, *The Sense of an Ending;* Auerbach, "Figura."

[186] Freccero, "Dante's Prologue Scene," pp. 1–20; Kermode, *The Sense of an Ending,* esp. p. 25.

[187] Freccero, "Medusa," p. 16; cf. Augustine, *Confessions* XI.29.

eschatological conferral of order and sense both on the individual and on history.[188] In fact, the end of literature, both its closure and its *telos,* would be to bring self and history together under the sign of poetic language and its judgment. The extent to which this complex of analogies is fully legitimate—even for a poem, like the *Commedia,* which literally takes as its own the perspective of eschatology—has been challenged in interesting ways. Its application to the *Furioso* is much more problematic, as I will show clearly when I turn to the final canto of the poem.[189] It is equally true, however, that the poem offers an elaborate account of its own and its author's relation to death and Apocalypse.

The phrase "giudizio universale," in addition to suggesting the human judgment which overcomes madness, also alludes to the Day of Judgment, particularly since there is a comic reference to the "novissimo dí" just five stanzas later (xxiv.6.3–4). I would argue that it is the possibility and/or defeat of such a perspective toward which the poem gravitates, not only structurally but also thematically, from the very first reference to the "giudicio *uman* [che] . . . spesso erra" ("human judgment which . . . often strays" 1.7.2) which has as its explicit counterpart God's Judgment, which never mistakes itself or others (see especially x.15.1–2; xxxiv.1.1–4, 11.3–4). The access of the poet to this point of view is, as we have seen, most nearly realized in the lunar episode, in the analogy he makes between himself and St. John, author of the Apocalypse itself and one of only three humans who never had to cross the boundary

---

[188] *Confessions* xi.28; Kermode, *The Sense of an Ending,* p. 52; Freccero, "Introduction," in Ciardi translation, p. xvii. See also Barbara Smith, *Poetic Closure* (Chicago: University of Chicago Press, 1968). Smith (p. 1) cites Samuel Johnson's famous essay (*Idler* 103) on the "horror of the last," which suggests why poetic ending should be fled as a sign of death as well as embraced as a perspective of meaning and order.

[189] Mazzotta (*Dante,* pp. 314–15) defines well "the paradox of eschatology and history in the *Divine Comedy*" and the "simultaneously closed and open structure of the poem." Parker (*Inescapable Romance,* pp. 51–53) defines the Dantean-Augustinian model of writing, which by ending includes totality and yet opens out onto meaning beyond itself (the paradox defined by the last word of Augustine's text—"it shall be *opened*"—which Parker herself adapts in her conclusion, p. 243). She then specifically contrasts it with Ariosto's open-ended structure, which nonetheless remains somehow self-enclosed. However, the latter poet's dialectic is more potentially, "sensically" Dantean than Parker will confess it to be.

of the "undiscovered country," permanently exempt from "tempo e morte" (cf. xxxiv.58–59, 61; xxxv.29–30). St John's stay in the Earthly Paradise, however, is only temporary and will end when the "angeliche tube" ("angelic trumpets") give the sign that "torni Cristo in su la bianca nube" ("Christ will return on a white cloud" xxxiv.59.7–8). What John goes on to claim for the poets, and for Ariosto in particular, is a role as secular doubles/parodies of Christ in Judgment who can ensure that heroes and patrons "del sepolcro uscirian vivi" ("emerge alive from the tomb" xxxv.24.5; cf. vii.41.7, xxxvii.16.7–8).

I have long since noted how the eschatological perspective of St. John and of Dante is first brought back within the boundaries of time and the confines of human language and then ironically dismissed as falsification in the course of the episode itself. In the following canto we find *another* voice which speaks from an eschatological vantagepoint, but how different its perspective is! The climax of the Bradamante/Ruggiero/Marfisa misunderstanding in canto xxxvi, the most violent crisis to date in the projected union of the two lovers, comes as Bradamante wages furious war against her suspected rival, Marfisa—until Ruggiero's fruitless attempts at peacemaking lead *him* into battle with Marfisa. The scene of the battle turns out to be a grove of cypresses, traditional emblems of death. Within the grove is a tomb. Just as in the previous canto Bradamante battled Rodomonte by the church-tomb erected to Issabella, just as in canto iii she attends to Merlin's prophecy in his cavernous chapel and sepulcher, once again, and now decisively, her quest for Ruggiero leads her to a grave. In fact, when she first set out to avenge her betrothed's supposed infidelity with Marfisa, she specifically donned an "insegna" bearing the image of a cypress to represent desire for death (hers and/or her rival's; cf. xxxii.46–47). Now, in a scene undoubtedly meant to recall Astolfo bemyrtled, one of the funereal trees is struck by a sword, an earthquake shakes the grove, and the tomb suddenly gives voice to a dire warning (58) and a joyful promise. The trees mark the grave of Atlante, dead from sorrow at the prospect of Ruggiero's unpreventable death (64). The perspective of the tomb has reconciled the great *magus* to that dreaded event, for he now intervenes to clarify his adopted son's identity, forestalling a possible fratricide and opening the way to the fatal marriage so long resisted. Ruggiero learns he is the son of a Christian treacherously slain by pagans, as well as the twin brother of Marfisa.[190] The effect is complex: even as Bradamante's desires turn back from death to life, from hate to love, the reader confronts Atlante's entombment and the pledge of a union which guarantees a similar fate for Ruggiero in the near future. Above all, by Atlante's recantation of his former enchantments, the scene constitutes a recognition of the futility of magical and poetic efforts to evade mortality (though, ironically, the fatal marriage is still fully ten cantos off). The link between Atlante and Ariosto, already clear, is made again by the curious association of the cypresses with the printed word ("parean d'una stampa tutti impressi" 41.8) and by the inscription of "brevi carmi" ("brief verses" 42.3, 6; cf. 29.5) on the tomb itself.

The image of poetry speaking, as it were, from beyond the tomb and within the afterlife of a Christian paradise in the lunar episode is thus precisely juxtaposed with another poet-figure whose voice speaks generously from *inside* the tomb and in the assurance of its own "eternal death" of damnation (66), like the heretics in *Inferno* 10, especially the Epicureans, speaking from the sepulchers in which they will be sealed at the Last Judgment (7–15). Once more the poetic project is suspended between salvation and damnation, between the sealed tombs of Lucretius and the empty tomb of Christ. On both sides of the opposition there is an ironic swerve toward the other position. The lunar surface fails to mediate the move from human mortality to eternal life, while St. John links himself to a swanlike "poetry of death." Atlante, for his part, can abandon his Lucretian despair long enough to see himself as an agent of God's will (xxxvi.61.7–8). In fact, the traditional "Atlas," the giant turned to stone mountain by Perseus, stands precisely at the intersection of heaven and earth, keeping the one from crushing the other. It is from this mythic occupation that his roles as astronomer, philosopher, and magician clearly derive, since all mediate the

---

[190] The twinship of Marfisa and Ruggiero undermines Marfisa's claim to phoenix-like uniqueness, and compromises the "individuality" of Ruggiero as well. Canto xxxvi reminds us both of Marfisa's insignia (17–18) and of the fact that Bradamante too is a *twin* (13–14).

encounter of the two orders. When Pico says that the *magus* "marries heaven to earth" he may well be thinking specifically of Atlas.[191] But if Ariosto's Atlante, like his St. John, stands between them, yet he does not unite them, no more than the Heaven of the Moon does. The dialectic of cantos XXXV and XXXVI is rehearsed at the beginning of canto XXXVII, where poetry is figured both as a kind of tomb and as that which may transcend the tomb. The exhortation of women to write reprises the image of literature able to "trar del sepolcro, e far ch'eterno viva" ("raise him from the grave and make him live eternally" 16.8), but also compares *the* exemplary woman poet, Vittoria Colonna, to Artemesia, famed for the magnificent tomb (the "mausoleum") she built for her husband, Mausolus (18).

There is, in fact, a figure in the poem who embodies this predicament far more explicitly and potently than these two do, one who originates a sequence of imagery that spans the poem's length and juxtaposes several distinct approaches to the poet's situation. Only one critic to date has noted that the *Furioso* is punctuated by a series of tombs, as well as other images of depersonalizing restraint and enclosure, each of which forecasts and insists upon the tragic inevitability of death, even as the poem strives to keep that "absence" from entering the present and eradicating the presence of life.[192] The most prominent of these are the burial of Dardinello by Cloridano and Medoro (and the death of the former, XVIII–XIX); the church which Rodomonte converts into a tomb for Issabella and the (Babelic) tower with which he marks it (XXIX and XXXV); the tomb in which Brandimarte is placed and which becomes the scene of Fiordiligi's "life in death." There are other spaces, notably the cave where Orlando first finds Issabella "buried alive," which are metaphorically designated as "tombe" (e.g., XII.90.1–2, 93.7; XIII.31.4). Most important of all, however, is the tomb-church where Merlin lies between life and death, which Pinabello tried to turn into

---

[191] This renowned passage can be found in *Oratio* (Garin edition), p. 152: "ita Magus terram caelo, id est inferiora dotibus virtutibusque maritat." In *Capitolo* XIV.19–20, Ariosto compares himself to Atlas bent under the burden of the heavens. In *Cinque Canti* I.B, 1, 38, he again alludes to Atlas as heaven-touching mountain. Cf. Shapiro, "From Atlas to Atlante."

[192] Chesney (*Rabelais and Ariosto*, p. 158) hints at the importance of the motif. For Alberti on tombs, see Garin, "I Morti."

Bradamante's tomb as well. It inaugurates the series and makes firm the link between Ariosto and Merlin, poetry and the tomb:

> Questa è l'antiqua e memorabil grotta
> ch'edificò Merlino, il savio mago
> che forse ricordare odi talotta,
> dove ingannollo la Donna del Lago.
> Il sepolcro è qui giù, dove corrotta
> giace la carne sua; dove egli vago
> di sodisfare a le, che glil suase,
> vivo corcossi, e morto ci rimase.
>
> Col corpo morto il vivo spirto alberga,
> sin ch'oda il suon de l'angelica tromba
> che dal ciel lo bandisca o ve l'erga,
> secondo che sarà corvo o colomba.
> Viva la voce; e come chiara emerga,
> udir potrai da la marmorea tomba,
> che le passate e le future cose
> a chi gli domandò, sempre rispose.   [III.10−11]

Merlin, the wise magician, whom you have sometimes heard remembered, built this ancient and memorable grotto, where the Lady of the Lake deceived him. Down here is the tomb where lies his corrupted flesh; where he, eager to satisfy she who persuaded him to it, lay down in life and remained in death. With the dead body dwells the living spirit, until he hear the angelic trumpet that banishes him from heaven or raises him up to it, accordingly as he will be crow or dove. The voice lives; and you will hear how clearly it emerges from the marble tomb, for he has always answered whoever asked him of things past and things to come.

We have already shown how closely Merlin is linked with Ariosto as figure of the artist, the "profetico lume" of the latter (2.7) anticipating the "profetico spirto" of the former (9.4), and we can add to that now. He, like Astolfo trapped in the tree, or Atlante bound "de la sua propria catena" ("with his own chain" IV.37.1), or, especially, Ariosto caught in an inescapable crisis of love and betrayal, is the figure of a poet-prophet able to foresee and judge with great clarity and yet unable to make use of his own powers to free himself from madness and death.[193] The "vivid" image, repeated in stanzas 15 and 16, of the disembodied voice emanating from the grave (artistic product of its occupant's own magic, like Atlante's) is reinforced by two images of uncanny life-in-death in the genealogical review that follows. One stanza alludes to the myth of Castor and Pollux, sons of Leda and her divine swan, who take turns dying so that the other may live (50). This image gains force from its close proximity to another swan, Cygnus, whose poetic song laments Phaeton's death and signals the singer's own (34).[194] Even more to the point, this whole sequence is Ariosto's imitation of Aeneid VI, where Virgil has Aeneas meet his dead father, learn of the lives which will spring from him, mourn the death of Marcellus, all in the context of the life-death-life cycle of metempsychosis. If Ariosto is tacitly equating himself with Virgil (56.5–8), however, the emphasis has shifted from life toward death.[195] If Dante speaks from the "oltretomba," if Tasso's epic recounts a quest *for* the tomb, Ariosto places himself within a poem-as-tomb from which a living voice may still emerge.

"La vocal tomba di Merlino" (VII.38.3) is as powerful a portrayal of poem, poet, and problematic presence-as-absence of the one within the other as the *Furioso,* or any poem, has to offer. Neither the eternal life of St. John nor the eternal death of Atlante is proper to Merlin: he is left hanging *between* the crisis of his own death and the Last Judgment which will impose significance on life and death

[193] There are some interesting facts brought out by Graf (*Miti,* p. 69) which suggest potential parallels between Merlin and St. John, including the legend that St. John (exactly like Merlin) was one of the "dormienti" asleep in a cavern near Ephesus awaiting the return of Christ. Farrell ("Mentors and Magi," p. 84) notes that St. John and Merlin are both awaiting the Second Coming.

[194] Concerning III.34.7–8, cf. XLII.92.7–8, where the "plettri"/"elettri" rhyme, with the same mythical resonance, is now used specifically of poets, just before Ariosto coyly represents himself representing his veiled beloved.

[195] Virgil provides a consolidating link between Ariosto and Merlin as one who traditionally combined the roles of poet, sibylline prophet (the "sortes virgiliane"), and necromancer. See particularly Domenico Comparetti, *Virgilio nel Medioevo* (Firenze: La Nuova Italia, 1937–1946), and John Spargo, *Virgil the Necromancer* (Cambridge: Harvard University Press, 1934). For the view of Virgil as "poet of death," see W.R. Johnson.

alike. This insistence on the poet-prophet's blindness to his own fate comes as no surprise from a man who once sketched his own epitaph and included in it these words: "he was unable to tell at all what the future held [for him]" ("non scire haud potuit futura" *Carmina Latina* LVIII.6). Merlin's ultimate destiny as "corvo o colomba" is left absolutely indeterminate "sin ch'oda il suon de l'angelica tromba." Aptly enough, the prophecy Merlin affords Bradamante closes with an allusion to Revelation, just as it opened with one:

> *Statti col dolcie in bocca, e non ti doglia*
> *ch'amareggiare al fin non te la voglia.*   [62.7–8]

> Keep the sweet taste in your mouth and don't be regretful that I don't want to make it bitter for you at the end.

These words, which constitute a refusal to elaborate on the tragic treachery of Don Giulio and Don Ferrante d'Este, clearly echo this Biblical passage:[196]

> And I took the book from the hand of the angel and ate it: and it was sweet as honey in my mouth. And when I had eaten it, my belly was bitter.   [Revelation 10:10; cf. 10:9 and Ezechiel 3:1–3]

The words are significant not only because they come in a prophetic and apocalyptic context, not only because they offer an anticipation of the link between Merlin and St. John, but, most of all, because they remind the reader, even in the process of denying that they do so, of the bitter within the sweet of Merlin's prophecy and Ariosto's book. Sweetly comic evasion masks tragic crisis: for the characters of the book, for the Este family, even for the mortal author himself.

When Ariosto closes his work, one might say, he will be (already has been, *is* forever) sealed in a tomb like Merlin's. The attempt to let the poet, as well as his heroes and patrons, go on living eternally in the act of writing is sabotaged from the beginning by

---

[196] "Et accepi librum de manu angeli, et devoravi illum: et erat in ore meo tanquam mel dulce, et cum devorassem eum, amaricatus est venter meus."

the only *true* prophecy in the book: the prophecy of the author's own death. He goes on speaking to us now, today, but from the crypt he has occupied since 1533 (a crypt which, as chance would have it, has been located since 1801 in the Sala Maggiore of the Biblioteca Ariostea in Ferrara, side by side with the oldest editions of his poem). In the interim space between the most private of crises, death, and the last crisis of all, the Apocalypse, a "viva voce" goes on speaking, naming its own absence from the words which bear its name.

The poem speaks of a crisis which has long since transformed the contingent uncertainty of the relation between writer and text into the permanent disjunction of death. Yet it also clearly gives that crisis its name, passes a judgment, which is *undivided* from that which it designates. This is not quite what Barthes, "after the New Criticism," calls the "death of the author," no more than it is what Augustine sees as the disappearance of the human author of Genesis from words which bear God's own meaning in them.[197] The author is dead but he also lives, has been subjected to time and has overcome it, has been lost in the impersonal structures of language

---

[197] Roland Barthes, "The Death of the Author," in *Image, Music, Text* (New York: Hill & Wang, 1977). See also Michel Foucault, "What Is an Author?" in *Textual Strategies*, ed. J. Harari (Ithaca: Cornell University Press, 1979). For Augustine, see n. 61, above. I have set the two in opposition, but this is not quite the case. Barthes thinks of the work-to-text, author-to-"scriptor," movement as "anti-theological," because it kills off the "Author-God" so that his text and readers may come into their own and into life. Well, he may be murdering the Romantic poet-deity, but his "death of God" anti-theology sounds suspiciously like the "death *and* rebirth" theology which is the essence of Christianity. Augustine too, by the way, sponsors the multiplication of meanings independent of human author, according to a principle of freely playing desire: *caritas*. This is the point when one could return to the metaphor of Renaissance and define Ariosto's life-and-death struggle with it and with the historical epoch it tries to designate. Mario Vitale, *L'Ariosto fra Illusioni e Conoscenza* (Napoli: Giannini, 1969), p. 9, has in fact offered the following brilliant observation: "il poeta, lasciandosi vivere, è sceso nella sua creazione 'vivendo, cioè, e non più vivendo' come diceva Nietzsche, dimenticando se stesso nella sua opera." Rather than Nietzsche, however, we should think of Dante at the bottom of hell: "io non mori' e non rimasi vivo." By identifying himself with Merlin, in a sense, Ariosto places himself at the very bottom of Dante's *Inferno* (34.25), suspended forever at the very moment of conversion, knowing neither whether he will go up or down, or whether he will live forever or die eternally.

(which cannot bear us back to a human origin), and yet has left an irreducible trace within it and upon it. From this most ambiguous of perspectives, the poet finally leaves open both the possibility that no reader will ever raise him from his linguistic coffin *and* the possibility that he too will arise in the presence of the Author of authors, the only critic who could hope to pass a judgment outside of crisis.

v. *Canto* XLVI: *Hippolytus' Horses and the Art of Cassandra*

At the beginning of this study, I introduced, by way of a partial reading of canto XLVI, the problem of the representation of crisis in the *Orlando Furioso,* and of the reading and the writing of the poem as themselves marked by crises which interfere with every approach to that representation. Much like Ruggiero circling back to the point (almost) of his departure, I now return, briefly, to the poem's end in a last effort to review and clarify the aptness and usefulness of thinking of the *Furioso* as a poem both of crisis and of evasion— to situate my reading of the poem between those who see it as a world of pure art (or language), vigorously excluding any serious encounter with the self, and those who have recently begun to argue again for the poem either as defender and promoter of certain "Renaissance" values and concepts or as committed questioner of these.

The ending of the poem can be thought of as simultaneously closing and opening the work (or closing the story to disclose its meaning):[198] closing by resolving all of the crises which have kept the narrative in motion and by bringing the poet to the end of his error-fraught "sea-sorrow" as well; opening by insisting on the marriage of Ruggiero and Bradamante as the beginning of an *historical* movement which leads to the apotheosis of Ippolito (87.4) in the "present" and by reuniting the poet with his friends and cul-

---

[198] See again n. 189, below. The classic response to the poem is Caretti's "L'Ariosto," p. 36: "il *Furioso* ci pare come un libro senza conclusione, come un libro perenne," in which neither comic marriage nor tragic death is a sufficient climax. Recent criticism, emphasizing the epic side of the poem and, for the first time, making serious readings of the last quarter of the poem, *qua* conclusion, now argues (with Quint, Fichter, and even Parker to a degree) for closure.

tural peers. Both Ariosto and Ruggiero are restored to community after long, frenzied, parentheses. The drama that is written and the drama of writing approach a point of coincidence as the "donne e cavallieri" who are the poem's subject are doubled by those who are its readers (notice the echoes connecting stanza 7 with 75, and 8 with 87). And as the text approaches the shore, so too, in a sense, does the shore of reality move toward the ideality of literature, in the image of a present time from which all conflict is banished (Rodomonte, arch-pagan, is also the last pagan, and his death apparently removes all threats to Carlo and Christendom) and with the promise of an ideal "future" consequence, a new golden age realized in Estense Ferrara, deriving directly from that "present." The explicitly celebratory tone of the canto takes its force from these convergences: "comic" marriage and tragic death, individual and community, poetic present/past and historical future/present, poem and audience. Crises are brought under control, while evasions by characters and narrative cease. From this perspective, the representation of crisis has indeed been a fictional pretext for its resolution, while the poem's evasions have been designed to highlight the importance of final return.[199]

Nevertheless, major obstacles stand in the way of an acceptance of this "sunny," apollonian picture of the access of reader, poem, and poet to a standpoint of the end, from which the internal order of the poem can be discovered and extended outward to its readers, its author, its historical context. The first is that, as we have already begun to see, the ending comes not as a climax, but as the fitting anticlimax to a poem which parodies epic beginning *in medias res,* by starting off in the middle of someone else's work. Even though the last ten cantos are packed with clarifying reversals, recognitions, and resolutions, the poem continues to be structured by a principle of deferral, so that every apparent conclusion turns out to be merely proleptic of a *true* closure that never seems to come. The massacre of Pagandom at Biserta does not do it. Nor does the death of Agramante. Ruggiero is particularly adroit at finding one pretext after another for putting off marriage to Bradamante. The last straw would seem to be the Leone addition of 1532 in which Ruggiero,

[199] This is Durling's account: *The Figure of the Poet,* pp. 130-31.

after his conversion and the decision that "né Bradamante più terrebbe a ciancia" ("he would no longer stall Bradamante with idle chatter" XLI.49.5), still manages to find a way of dividing his loyalties and betraying his promise to her.[200]

Among its many other functions, the circle of Ruggiero around the world is a parody of the poetic journey to a conclusive endpoint, a travesty of the universal emblem of completeness. The end turns out to be identical with the beginning, is the Alpha and Omega, not of existence but of absence. Even if Ruggiero *did* now reach mature, coherent selfhood, and it is not clear that he does here or anywhere, the reader has already been predisposed to resist this determination and to challenge the poet's and his/her own desire to make end subsume middle. Instead, the middle subverts the ending, is a proleptic, "prophetic" gloss on the illusory finality of any narrative stopping place.[201] And this subversion is in keeping with the general playfulness of the poet's treatment of narrative time: for example, he often plants within an earlier sequence events which actually happen much later in the poem.[202] The most consistent example of this, however, is the poem-long joke of his "prophecies," culminating in this canto, which actually "predict" the past and the present and even then are likely to falsify them knowingly.[203] The spatialization of narrative time—which normally characterizes and affirms the dominance of the retrospective, inclusive gaze of conclusion—here has the opposite effect, because it happens *throughout*

---

[200] See David Marsh, "Ruggiero and Leone: Revision and Resolution in Ariosto's *Orlando Furioso*," *MLN* 96 (1981), who reads the episode as furthering epic closure. Cf. n. 121, above, for a summary of Ruggiero's dilatory tactics.

[201] Cf. Parker, *Inescapable Romance*, pp. 20, 34–39, 52–53.

[202] This is an oft-remarked-upon phenomenon. Consider, for instance, XIX.42, where Angelica and Medoro meet an unidentified brute (i.e., Orlando) some four cantos before he actually goes mad. Once in canto XXII, we find Astolfo setting out on his journey, which leads to Orlando's cure three months after the madness began, still before it has begun. Then, in XXIV, Fiordiligi is abandoned by the author just as she comes upon the Count at a river. She has herself just left Issabella and the dying Zerbino. When the author returns to her again in XXIX, however, we discover that the river is the one by which Rodomonte has built an elaborate monument in honor of the now dead Issabella.

[203] Even Fichter, who takes the genealogical epic quite seriously, admits that Ariosto is rewriting history with merry abandon (*Poets Historical*, pp. 86–87).

the poem. No fixed temporal hierarchy subordinates beginning and middle to end: any point in the poem can claim for itself "priority" and "finality" both, though in the resulting cacophony, none successfully establishes them. As shown previously in this chapter, Ariosto adopts almost from the beginning (canto III) the "perspective of *an* end," the perspective of life recalled from death, and of death foreseen from life. He redefines the sense of an ending to deny apocalyptic mastery and to assert a suspension between being and nothingness, literature and reality, sense and insignificance. In narrative terms, he scrambles the dichotomy between the diachronic perspective of narration *in via* and the synchronic perspective of conclusion. What is more, he posits as the precondition of poetic/prophetic commentary on history the depersonalization and death of the self, the failure to bridge the separation between personal and public identity. And this, as will now be seen, is equally applicable to the character, Ruggiero, and to the creator, Ariosto.

It is true, as seen earlier, that the "errore" of both is ostensibly brought to an end: the poet's in the first stanzas of the canto, the hero's in the last. But a closer look at XLVI shows that neither career dovetails quite as neatly with the "present" historical moment of the poem's completion (or its reading) as it first seemed to. This final canto too participates in the continuing erosion of genealogical and historical values which should justify the young Ruggiero's marriage and consequent death. It too, as a reading of the first lines suggested, refers allusively and ironically to its own mode of signification and to the process of interpretation by which its meaning will be discovered, distorted, or reinvented. To begin with Ruggiero: he is, in fact, rescued from self-destructive "rabbia" and suicide-by-starvation through the efforts of Melissa and Leone (19, 21, 23–24, passim). Even more impressively, he undergoes a pair of startling recognition scenes which confirm his identity and make it spectacularly public, as he finally wins his bride and with her a regal crown (34, 36, 39, 41, 56–59). Then, in the last stanzas of the poem, he defends and apparently liberates himself from the long-standing charge of infidelity (in this case, to Agramante), even as he once more defers, briefly, his own death by dispatching his accuser in his stead. Still, the specific allusion to Ganelon's soon-to-be-realized plots against his life (67–68) and to his progenitor Hector's similar victimization, which led to the treacherous destruction of Troy itself (82), do ensure that Rodomonte's demise appears rather as prolepsis than as deferral.[204] Moreover, the battle, which should act as a final symbolic resolution of the pagan/Christian conflict, loses its archetypal value because the erstwhile arch-pagan, Rodomonte, has specifically been deprived of the Babelic armor of Nimrod which conferred that role upon him and is consequently helpless against the magical furniture of Ruggiero (119–20). Finally, this same "Herculean" Ruggiero, who has seemingly learned at last to rein in his passions and remain "in sé raccolto" (133.7), has his mythological identity put in doubt once more by yet another assimilation to Anteus (124–25, 133) and by a simile which debases the combat in likening it to a dogfight.[205]

Whatever final confirmation the canto may give about Ruggiero's problems, however, it also offers an apparently full compensation for them: an image of the finest flower of his and Bradamante's "albero genealogico," the glorious life of Cardinal Ippolito d'Este as woven into Cassandra's tapestried pavilion of prophecy. The pavilion, magically transported by Melissa from the court of the Eastern emperor to house the nuptials of her charges, brings the dénoument of Ruggiero's story together with that of the poet: not only does it depict the historical *telos* toward which the hero's career tends, the justification of his life *and* death; it also is a figure of Ariosto's poem *qua* genealogical epic, and images the man who is both the poem's ultimate subject and its most important reader (to whom Ariosto is *subjected*). If courtly "donne e cavallieri" are both denizens of the *Furioso* and its audience, in Ippolito the two roles merge most clearly: he is the source and end of the poem's historical meaning, but he is also the privileged interpreter, the constantly apostrophized patron, for and through whom that meaning should emerge. Through him, therefore, Ariosto might seem to realize two fundamental projects of humanism: the harmonious reconciliation of literature with history (the "impegno civile" of civic

---

[204] See Saccone, "Il Soggetto," p. 241; but compare n. 174, above.

[205] Giamatti ("Headlong Horses, Headless Horsemen," p. 304) cites this episode to prove the ultimate success of Ruggiero's education. Also, note that Rodomonte takes turns with Ruggiero playing the roles of Hercules and Anteus (134–36). Cf. Chapter 2, n. 30, for similar instances.

humanism) and of past with present (the philological excavation and revivification of dead texts and buried cities). And yet, as we are about to see, Ariosto punctures the reputation of his patron in the act of inflating it and abdicates the role of courtly flatterer when he seems most caught up in it.[206]

In canto III, which prophesies the marriage now consummated and outlines the genealogy of which Ippolito is the culmination, the line leading from Ruggiero to the Duke and Cardinal is marked by treachery not only at its beginning but also at its end, with the thwarted fratricidal plotting of Don Giulio and Don Ferrante d'Este. In canto XLVI comes the second, symmetrical, reference to the near-tragic "congiura" (95), which again strikes a dissonant note in its festive context. Still, the emphasis here seems at first differently placed, tending to fall on Ippolito's brilliant success in averting from Alfonso and himself the treacherous ends of the first and second founders (Hector and Ruggiero) of their line. In exposing the plot, the Cardinal is compared to Cicero rescuing the freedom of Republican Rome from the insidious Cataline and his fellow conspirators (95.7–8). In the next stanza he becomes, implicitly, another Caesar who "viene e vede e vince" ("comes, sees, and conquers" 96.8). Not only is he heir to the political and military greatness of classical Rome, he is also the defender of the papacy (96) and himself perhaps destined to become a great pope (90): he potentially unites classical and Christian Rome, temporal and ecclesiastical power, in a grand Renaissance synthesis.[207]

Still, the margins of the canto contain subtle hints that these comparisons are not all in Ippolito's favor. Julius Caesar, one might remember, was himself the victim of a treacherous assassination. More explicitly, and insidiously, an early stanza (6) is given over almost entirely to a rather different image of Caesar: not the triumphant warrior in Gaul, but the crosser of the Rubicon, the man

---

[206] Ariosto's own difficulties with Ippolito were no secret, at least after the Cardinal had departed for Hungary, leaving the recalcitrant Ludovico behind. See especially *Satire* I and II.

[207] For critics who tend to take the encomia of Ippolito and the Este as essentially sincere, see Durling, *The Figure of the Poet*, pp. 137–50; Brand, *Ludovico Ariosto*, pp. 107–114. For contrary views, compare Bonifazi, as well as Kennedy, *Rhetorical Norms*, pp. 140–42.

most responsible for ending the age of Republican liberty which Cicero (among many others) had defended. Ariosto thus subtly continues the early humanist debate over the relative merits of the Empire and the Republic in terms of his own primary valuing of *libertas*.[208] One might even recall that earlier, in the midst of an even loftier paean to divine Ippolito (xxxv.3 ff.), a tacit parallel was drawn between the Cardinal and one of the less pleasant heirs of the Caesarian name: Nero, ravager of his own homeland, murderer of literati such as Seneca and Lucan. Canto XLVI itself strikes another odd note when it specifically mentions the Emperor Constantine's departure from Rome for the East, presumably with an allusion to his (alleged) donation of temporal sovereignty in the West to the papacy (84).[209] In other words, Ippolito's apparently positive yoking of ecclesiastical to secular power is set off implicitly against a catastrophic example of the same.[210] Lastly, the Cardinal is portrayed as being "adored as a god" by his flock (87.4), raising the spectre of a Senapo-like idolatry.

In Ariosto's description of Cassandra's tapestry, Ippolito is first identified as "il più cortese cavalliere" ("the most courteous knight" 81.4) in Hector's noble line. As the paragon of chivalry, or *cavalleria*, with special emphasis on the originary meaning of "horsemanship," the Cardinal stands as the climactic endpoint of the poem's extensive, systematic juxtaposition of the medieval chivalric institutions with the classical literary and philosophical traditions of equine

[208] See Bruni, *Dialoghi*, and Guarino Veronese's letter to Poggio, both in Garin, ed., *Prosatori Latini*, for instances of the polemical use of the two great phases of Roman history (and the two key figures, Scipio and Caesar) in the contemporary contest between monarchy and republic. Note that Ferrara was a bastion of the pro-Caesar camp. See also Salutati, *De Tyranno*, and, for echoes in the High Renaissance, Castiglione, *Cortegiano* IV.xix–xxii, and the "two Machiavellis" of the *Principe* and the *Discorsi*.

[209] When Ariosto refers to Constantine elsewhere, he specifically mentions the Donation pejoratively (XVII.78; XXXIV.80). If there is any recognition of Valla's attack on the authenticity of the gift in the poem, it is only implicit.

[210] It is also worth mentioning that in earlier historical reviews the Este are systematically designated as warriors of the Church *until* we arrive at the time of Alfonso and Ippolito, when the Duke and Cardinal actually did frequent battle against the Pope (cf. III.25, 27, 30, 31, 33, 34–36, 39, 52, 54–56; XXXIII.16, 20, 38–41, 43, 45, 48, 55–56).

symbolism which ultimately derive from the *Phaedrus*.[211] He comes as the last entry in a Renaissance horse show which sets magical romance steeds (Frontino, Brigliadoro, Rabicano, Baiardo, and so on) alongside the mythological Pegasus (and Geryon). Of course it is not merely this epithet, nor his "great" deeds and greater potential, which makes of him *the* crucial point of convergence of *the* most important thematic-imagistic complex in the poem. Rather, it is his name. That name, both in its etymological significance and in its ineluctable associations with the classical myth of Hippolytus, is both perfectly appropriate and corrosively ironic when applied to the ultimate "cavalliere," or horseman. From it emerge the most subtle and most serious problems in Ariosto's presentation of his patron.

The story of Hippolytus, *never* mentioned directly in the *Furioso*, is nonetheless constantly before the reader in the form of an insistent name and a pervasive system of images: imposing itself as the most powerful present-absence in the poem. Ariosto would have known the myth from several sources (as would his readers), most importantly Seneca's dramatization of it in his *Hippolytus*.[212] Given that the Este court was a focal point in the revival of classical drama, that the *Hippolytus* was performed in Ferrara just before a presentation of Ariosto's own *I Suppositi* and during the period of composing the *Furioso* (February 2, 1509),[213] and that the title of the poem derived from a not-unrelated play of Seneca, the poet's intimate acquaintance with the work cannot be doubted. In fact, he clearly makes a few, notable, allusions to the *Hippolytus* in the *Furioso*, most obviously in the repetition by Gabrina-Argeo-Filandro in canto XXI of the Phaedra-Theseus-Hippolytus triangle.[214]

[211] Cf. Chapter 3, sec. vi and relevant notes.

[212] See also *Aeneid* VII.761 ff.; as well as Ovid, *Heroides* V and *Metamorphoses* XV.497–554.

[213] Catalano, *Vita*, vol. I, pp. 86–87.

[214] Gabrina's pretense to Argeo that Filandro raped her also has analogues in the Biblical story of Potiphar's wife and in one of the myths of Bellerophon, but comes most directly from *Hippolytus* 888 ff. In addition: XXV.37.3–8 alludes to *Hippolytus* 119–23 (and is preceded by a mention of Ippolita, XXV.32.1); XIV.5 echoes *Hippolytus* 1123; the Orca in X–XI may be partly derived from *Hippolytus* 1031–54 in addition to its other sources; while Ariadne, classical model for Olimpia abandoned, lost Theseus to none other than Phaedra.

The features of the story most relevant to Ippolito and the poem are the following. Hippolytus, son of Theseus, was a scrupulously chaste devotee of Diana, famed as a huntsman and, especially, as a master horseman. Venus, enraged by his refusal of love, revenged herself by inflaming his stepmother, Phaedra, with a mad passion for him which he repulsed. Phaedra then accused *him* of rape to Theseus, who, believing too readily, called upon the gods to destroy his son. This they did by sending a great sea monster to frighten his horses. The horses ran wild, and their charioteer, for the first time unable to control the reins, was dragged, dismembered, and killed.

The myth is one of several analogous tales containing catastrophic winged flight, or equine violence, or both, which enact poetically what the Phaedran charioteer represents in a philosophical context. Icarus' doomed flight and Bellerophon's fall from the Pegasus are both invoked more or less specifically in the *Furioso*.[215] More important, the myth of Phaeton, with the fatal fall from an un-governed chariot, is not only nearer the *Phaedrus,* but also plays a crucial role in the crucial canto III, where, linked to Ferrara and the Este (34), it may partly serve as a proleptic stand-in for Phaeton's nearest structural sibling, Hippolytus. The proximity of the two stories is such that Seneca made explicit mention of it (*Hippolytus* 1090–92). The myth of Hippolytus, in fact, has by far the most numerous and interesting connections to Plato's dialogue and to the uses Ariosto makes of the Phaedran tradition. The correspondences are such that one might be tempted to see the *Phaedrus* itself as writ-ten in specific relation to some version of the myth, perhaps Euri-pides' own *Hippolytus*. The shared image of wild horses dragging a chariot, common to Phaeton as well, is reinforced by the tempt-ing coincidence of names (Phaedra/Phaedrus) and by the common theme of love-madness.[216]

The importance of these imagistic-thematic elements for the *Furioso* is by now so clear as to require no further comment. And yet, one might still, and rightly, ask *why* one should see Hippolytus in Ippolito when the poem patently refuses to connect the two

---

[215] See especially XXXII.21, XXXV.31, and XXXVIII.16.6; cf. Chapter 3, sec. vi.

[216] In addition, the references in the *Phaedrus* to the Asclepedes and to the medical pretensions and successes, respectively, of rhetoric and philosophy, may allude to the episode of Aesculapius' healing of Hippolytus (270c–d).

openly and makes only glancing references to the myth at all. The reasons are many, however. The discussion of Hercules showed how ready the Este were to trade on the mythological associations of names.[217] Even supposing the improbable—that the name is not intended to evoke the classical hero (though it does, intention or none)—it is also true that the eponymous saint was martyred by being dragged to death by horses. Moreover, even without reference to the myth, the name "Ippolito" carries openly, etymologically, the meaning of "loosed or unreined horse" (fitting epithet and epitaph for a master of horses destroyed by his own steeds). Despite his protestations in Satira VI and elsewhere, Ariosto certainly knew enough Greek, and was sufficiently given to etymological naming, that he could not have avoided making the association for himself. A particularly significant example tells much: the introduction of one "Ippalca" into the poem, whose name reflects her limited function as "conductress of horses" (xxiii.29.8).[218] Add to this the framing context of a forty-six-canto poem whose most obvious theme is love-madness and whose central image is the unreined horse, and which may well be substantially indebted to Seneca's Hippolytus on both counts, and the connection seems inescapable.[219] Why then no more open references? Because an acute, classically trained reader of the Renaissance would need no more and, much more cogently, because the poet would hardly risk the offense to his patron, a man who held the power of life and death in Ferrara, not to mention considerable sway over the poet's purse strings.

Once the possibility has occurred to the reader, however, certain hints in canto XLVI seem designed to press home a link and tease out its curious implications. In the tapestry, Ippolito seems to share nothing more with his namesake than his (ecclesiastical) vocation for chastity and a fondness for the hunt (91). On the other hand,

---

[217] Cf. Gundersheimer, Ferrara, p. 256; and Chapter 2, n. 31, above.

[218] Other significant Greek names include "Filandro," "Androfilo," "Theodora," "Andronica" (and the other cardinal virtues), Ippalca's mother "Callitrefa."

[219] If the ultimate source is the Phaedrus, along with the other texts previously cited, the Hippolytus might be one of the most important mediate sources, perhaps even the principal mediator, given the density of its references to unreined horses and erotic furor. See especially 96, 112, 179, 184, 248, 255, 279, 360–86, 450, 824–28, 891, 1002–1003, 1006, 1054–56, 1068–71, 1075–77, 1082–92, and 1259.

shortly before the viewing of the "prezioso velo," the poet com-
pares Marfisa's abortive challenge to her disguised brother with
Egeus' near poisoning of his disguised son, Theseus, instigated by
his new wife, the treacherous Medea (59). The comparison is mar-
ginally relevant to the situation at hand; but its second, and far
more important, function is to remind us that Theseus later, at the
behest of yet another unnatural stepmother, was more successful
(and less) in bringing about the destruction of his own son. Earlier
still, in the list of those awaiting Ariosto on the shoreline, certain
names may stand out. For instance, in 13.3, we meet one Fedro, so
named because he had once taken the part of Phaedra in a perform-
ance of Seneca's *Hippolytus* in Rome (incidentally making real the
possible Phaedrus/Phaedra connection mentioned earlier). Stanza 4,
line 3, mentions one *Ippolita* Sforza, a reference which would hardly
attract attention or bear connection to Ippolito d'Este, were it not
set so close by a mention of Angela Borgia (4.6), a relative and
attendant of Alfonso's notorious wife, Lucrezia. The nearness of her
name to a derivative of Ippolito's own, and also to a "Iulia" (i.e.,
Giulia, 4.2), might easily have reminded a contemporary reader that
the Cardinal, nominal celibacy notwithstanding, had been the fierce
rival of his brother, Don *Giulio*, in courting this same Angela, and
that this fraternal contest had led him to order the blinding of his
own brother—an order which was actually carried out, with partial
success, less than a year before the famous "congiura" of 1506.[220]
The crime went unpunished by Alfonso and tends to put the sub-
sequent "tradimento" in a different light altogether. And how well
this episode, certainly known to most of the readers listed in the
canto, fits into the *Furioso:* desire of an "angelic" lady which leads
to a "blinding" passion! Of course, Ippolito no longer plays the
part of Hippolytus or sacrificial victim; he is rather the betraying
Phaedra of the piece—a point highlighted (though whether delib-
erately or not I make no claim) by the shifts of gender in the sug-
gestive names of Fedro and Ippolita. One might even remember
that the Hippoliti, Christian saint and pagan hero, were not alone
in being torn to death by horses—this was, oddly enough, also the

[220] Catalano, *Vita*, vol. I, pp. 236–38, 241–42.

punishment administered to Ganelon, Ruggiero's future nemesis, for his treachery in the *Chanson de Roland*.

The invocation of the myth of Hippolytus may thus have two opposite and yet equally deleterious effects on the genealogical encomium: it may suggest that the Este lack the Machiavellian *virtù* or personal force to avoid becoming victims of treachery and to rule successfully in a violent world; or it may suggest that they do possess such force, but only at the cost of sacrificing virtue in the more conventional moral sense to the violence of their own desires. Whichever the case, the problems with the family had already been forecast by the title (with its allusion to mad Hercules destroying his family), bolstered by the subsequent reference to Ippolito as "generosa Erculea prole" (1.3.1).[221] The first line of the poem, "Le donne, i cavallier, l'arme, gli amori," may then seem to echo the Virgilian "arma virumque cano" which introduces the greatest of genealogical epics and the return of the golden age under Augustus Caesar. But it also, and even more closely, echoes from Dante's *Purgatorio* 14.109–111, on the ledge of *Invidia* (*blind* envy), where the words refer to a past time, already remote in Dante's day, when noble chivalric families flourished, and to the fact that they had since fallen into decay and ruin. In other words, even as Ariosto sets the stage for a final "Renaissance" of the heroic literary past in the historical present, he undercuts the possibility of such a connection, implying that it is an utopian hope, a seductive fiction.

As I have argued repeatedly, the meaning of Ruggiero's conversion and marriage, his access to political power, his triumph over demonic force, is his own death by treachery. And the meaning of that death is more violence, more betrayals, more deaths. Like Aeneas, Ruggiero sacrifices himself; but, unlike Virgil's hero, little or nothing is gained by it. By claiming Hector and the ruling house of Troy as ancestors for Ruggiero and the Este, Ariosto seems to be paralleling them with Aeneas and the Augustan Empire. But Aeneas escaped Troy to found Rome, in a grand *translatio imperii*, while Hector died, "a tradimento," leaving his city to utter destruction. The apparent reconciliation of poetry and history in XLVI

---

221 Cf. Chesney (*Rabelais and Ariosto*, p. 111).

is painfully disrupted in two diametrically opposed ways. On the one hand, the transparent fiction of Ruggiero as Este ancestor is complemented by the newly apparent falsehood in the description of the Este brothers as generous, rational, heroic lords. Rather than opening out onto the historical presence of Ippolito d'Este, it instead begins to draw him into itself, hinting, as in the lunar episode, that his "storia" and that of his family are indeed only Ariosto's inventions; trapping him in a "net of Caligorante" which binds him with the equine imagery suggested by his own name. On the other hand, Ariosto is *also* suggesting again, as in the case of Orlando's madness, that his poem *can* refer truly to history—not as ideal *locus amoenus*, but as scene of blindness, violence, and deception where rampant injustice passes itself off as the return of Astrea (III.51) and of the golden age of Saturn, first king of Italy.

Chapter 2 focused briefly on a feature of the Hippolytus story which has so far been omitted here: the "re-memberment" of the young horseman's torn body by another of Apollo's human sons, Aesculapius; the renaming of the reborn Hippolytus as "Virbius" ("twice a man"); his "new life" in Saturnalian Italy. That myth, as used by Boccaccio and others, with its analogues, such as the Horus/Osiris story adapted by Pico, is a perfect figure of Renaissance—whether of the philological reconstruction of the ruined past in the present or of the philosophical recovery of the One out of the Many.[222] In the *Furioso*, however, Ippolito is never transformed by an Aesculapian author into Virbius, but, instead, is linked only to the violence, fragmentation, and duplicity of the first part of the myth. Significantly, when Ferrara is placed according to mythological coordinates, it is not in the Italy of Virbius reborn, but rather at the very site of Phaeton's disastrous and irredeemable fall (III.34).

And just as the historical link noisily forged in the tapestry between Ruggiero and Ippolito is quietly shattered, so too the harmonious encounter of the *Furioso* with its courtly readers is marked by an inner discord. On the one hand, as shown in Chapter 1, the

[222] See Giamatti, "Hippolytus among the Exiles"; Greene, *The Light in Troy*, pp. 164–69, 235, 321 (n. 34); Boccaccio, *Genealogia*, proem (vol. 1, pp. 9–10); Salutati, *De Laboribus Herculis*, vol. 2, pp. 442–44; Pico, *Oratio* (Garin edition), p. 116. Cf. Chapter 2, n. 63, above. As mentioned earlier, Ariosto's Orrilo is a kind of parody of Virbius/Horus.

image of the poem as both map and sea debunks any notion of the poet finding a way out of his work and back to his friends. On the other hand, these "friendly" readers, like those of the tapestry, either unknowingly reduce the *Furioso* to trivial object of pure aesthetic delight or, like Bradamante, misread its references to historical reality as a placid panegyric to a new golden age. In either case, the poem is reduced from referential commentary on the harsh truths of history to an idyllic or idealized fiction, a self-enclosed work of art in the Crocean mode. Ippolito, the patron and privileged reader of the work, is also celebrated in the tapestry for his youthful education in interpreting the "occult meanings" of ancient writings (89.3–4), as well as for his later patronage of philosophers and poets (92). But the darker undertones of the name and of the canto reveal him rather as the man who reputedly and obscenely dismissed the poem as utter nonsense ("tante coglionerie, Messer Ludovico") and who repeatedly turned the poet from his literary vocation toward more "practical" matters, so that, as Ariosto writes, "di poeta cavallar mi feo" ("from a poet [he] made a horseman of me" *Satira* VI.238).[223]

In the last few pages I have said two distinctly different things about the *Furioso*—that its own mode of reference is duplicitous and difficult to penetrate, and that its readers have systematically misread it, blindly overlooking the obvious. Which is truer? Is it the poem's self-satisfied self-containment, its betrayal of its readers by trying to re-create them as part of its own labyrinthine fiction, that has led to its being read as an "unproblematic" avoider of crisis? Or is it the readers, in their various ways, who have themselves done this violence to the poem? Is it a question of Ariosto turning the tragedy of history into negligible comedy, or of the audience systematically misinterpreting tragic truth as comic-ironic fiction? Is the *Furioso* evading crisis, or representing it, or both? These questions can be protracted one more time, though still not fully resolved, by inquiring why it is that Cassandra, of all possible artist-figures, should have authored the tapestry, this "prezioso velo" (84.4).

---

[223] See Catalano, *Vita,* vol. I, pp. 183, 435, for an euphemistic version of Ippolito's supposed slander.

Cassandra's role as last of the surrogate poet-figures is made clear, as it was before in the case of Alcina, by the poetic associations of the veil and by the insistent prior use of tapestry and weaving as metaphors for Ariosto's art.[224] As the possessor of (or, rather, as one possessed by) the "furor profetico" (XLVI.80.4), she caps the symmetrical echoing of canto III at poem's end by recalling both Merlin's prophetic spirit and the poet's Phaedran poetic folly (III.1–3, 9). It is thus clear that, though her presence is appropriate to the project of connecting the Este to Troy, she plays a more complex and "metapoetic" role than that. One might suggest, for instance, that by comparing himself to a woman artist, Ariosto is continuing the poem-long project of collapsing fundamental conceptual differences, including sex roles.[225] Far more obvious, however, is the fact that the mythological Cassandra's poetic-prophetic discourse is of a very special kind: one which, in fact, violently erases the lines between poetry's falsehoods and prophecy's truths.

Cassandra's gift of foresight was granted to her by an enamored Apollo (god of poetry and prophecy both), but was ironically qualified by him when she refused to keep her part of the erotic bargain: she would always predict the truth; but she would never be taken seriously, always be regarded as a fountain of nonsense, a *pazza furiosa*.[226] She prophesies, always futilely, the tragic truths

---

[224] For Cassandra and the veil, see Farrell ("Mentors and Magi," p. 124), who takes it to be a "cheerful" work and "the ultimate reconciliation of history and fiction in the poem." Welles ("Magic," p. 124) sees it as the image of the poem "which we can admire but, without proper instruction, cannot understand." For the veil as figure of poetry see Chapter 3, n. 70. In addition, the work actually contains "scritture" (86.1–2; 98.6).

[225] Cf. n. 100, above. Notice the confluence of male and female poets in XLVI (3, 4, 9, 10, 13, 14, 15, 17). See also XXXVII.1–19 and Durling, *The Figure of the Poet*, for a basic account of the "querelles des femmes" acted out in the *Furioso*. More recently, see Margaret Tomalin, *The Fortunes of the Warrior Heroine in Italian Literature* (Ravenna: Longo, 1982); McLucas, "Ariosto and the Androgyne."

[226] Bembo, *Asolani* III.xv (Marti edition, p. 150) uses Cassandra and Apollo in an interesting simile: "potrassi credere che la natura, quasi pentita d'avere tanti gradi posti nella scala delle spezie . . . poscia che ella ci ebbe creati col vantaggio della ragione, più ritorre non la potendo, questa libertà ci abbia data dell'arbitrio, a fine che in questa maniera noi medesimi la ci togliessimo, del nostro scaglione volontariamente a quello delle fiere scendendo; a guisa di Febo il quale, poscia che ebbe alla troiana Cassandra l'arte dell'indovinare donata, . . . le diede che ella non fosse

which beset her city, her family, and herself, up to and including her own murder. She is "truth with a lying face" in its extreme form; she is the epitome of Silenian "serio ludere," but also its perversion, since the grotesque folly of the surface never yields up its hidden treasures. Her tapestry puts the perfect period to the series of self-subverting prophecies which punctuate the poem.[227] She is the last of the unheeded prophets, the "successor d'Astolfo" as Pier delle Vigne. There is nothing, and no one, in the *Furioso* that better crystallizes the position of its author, who both lies and tells the truth, who flies from both madness and reason, than the figure of Cassandra in canto XLVI. She embodies the poet's mute and resigned protest of his readers' inability to hear and believe him. She stands for his fate as victim of a betrayal—less by those readers than by poetry itself (impersonated by Apollo), which lends its own most serious utterances to trivialization and laughter. If canto XLVI begins by providing an image of poetry closing in upon itself, unable to escape inevitable referential shipwreck, and then shows poetry as a voice crying out unheard in the wilderness, it reconciles the two accounts of poetry through Cassandra. To mistranslate Dante, Ariosto speaks truly "unseeable truths" ("invidiosi veri" *Paradiso* 10.138).

Cassandra also takes us beyond the traditional account of Ariosto the master ironist. It is true that, from the perspective of the privileged reader who recognizes her predicament, the discrepancy between what she says and what her readers hear is precisely ironic. Nonetheless, from *her* own perspective, which Ariosto identifies with *his* own perspective, she is the exact opposite of an ironist: far

---

creduta." Notice how the myth of creation parodies Pico's and how the analogy connects Cassandra to the same problematic of freedom/slavery, blindness/insight that is at the center of our present treatment of Ariosto.

[227] Like the "tedious" troop review in canto X, the various prophecies and *ekphrases* generally deserve more commentary than they have received. Among the "self-subverting" prophecies are (1) the allegory in canto XXVI of beastly Avarizia slain over and over again, but always resurgent (source of Spenser's Blatant Beast); (2) the prophetic warning to French invaders of Italy in canto XXXIII, which proves by its very contents that it will never be heeded; (3) the apostrophe to Italy at the beginning of canto XXXIV which should (like Petrarch's *Rime* CXXVIII and Machiavelli's *Principe* chap. 26) announce a political savior for Italy, but instead ends in a cry of despair.

from saying one thing and meaning another, she always says precisely what she means—but always finds herself mis-taken by her readers. Ariosto's last thrust at his future readers comes in the accurate anticipation that they would confuse him with an omniscient "master of ironies." Of course, by presenting Cassandra explicitly as the author of a celebratory tapestry rather than as a tormented prophetess, and by leaving it to the reader to recognize hidden implications, Ariosto *does,* at the same time, justify the traditional label. In fact, the self-pity and pathos inherent in the poet's equation of his own plight with Cassandra's are not left untouched, no more than Ariosto ever leaves any moment untouched. This touching portrait is countered by another version of the poet's *craft* (in both senses), the one also found in canto XXXV, which shows a writer willing to sabotage the reputation of patrons (like Ippolito) who do not adequately reward their dependents. After all, there is another side to the prophetess: she is betrayed by Apollo, as Merlin was by Vivian, but only because she, in turn, had first been a betrayer, failing to keep her word to the god, like Alcina a willing deceiver.[228] Ariosto indicts his readers, especially the "cardinal" reader, for blindness and/or ingratitude, but he shows as well his own complicity in deception, his own vindictive streak. He reveals himself, like his horsey master, as willing to return evil for good, "pro bono malum," and as the partial author of his own poetic folly.

Vittore Branca speaks summarily for much of recent Ariosto criticism and for large segments of this study as well when he rejects the image of a *Furioso* "solare e apollineo." And yet it would be another error to dismiss those qualities which have long dissuaded readers from taking the poem seriously as purely chimerical.[229] The poem's sunny, nonsensical side will never be fully denied. As

---

[228] It could be shown that the poet links himself not only to Alcina, but also to a series of the most despicable and vicious traitors in the poem—Caligorante and his woven net (XV); the Orco, gross parody of a pastoral shepherd-poet (XVII); Gabrina, hiding evil under a veil of fictive faith (XXI); Marganorre, linked to male poets generally as an oppressor of women (XXXVII).

[229] Brand (*Ludovico Ariosto,* p. 164) says in passing that Ariosto wrote "a serious poem too effectively disguised as entertainment." My point is that there are very interesting reasons for that disguise.

we saw, Ariosto even puts himself under the auspices of Apollo in canto III, albeit (and here the pendulum swings back, and lower) of an Apollo who is the source of a "profetico lume," but also of a darker fury as well, who fathered the "figliuol ch'avea mal retto il lume." He can be a viciously ironic god, capable of burying afflatus in incomprehensible ravings, as he does to Cassandra. Rather than discarding the adjective "apollonian," then, it may prove wiser, at least foolishly wise, to redefine it, with two heuristic (and also polemical) recourses to Nietzsche's famous opposition between Apollo and Dionysius.[230]

In the first place, the "apollonian" poetry of Ariosto is Nietzschean insofar as it expresses not an essential tranquillity, but a desire for and a superficial illusion of tranquillity achieved at great cost and barely covering the horrors of madness and death, the disappearance of both self and social order into an undifferentiated chaos. Apollo, in other words, is the opposite of the Silenus, whose dionysian outside masks Socratic self-possession. But, in a second moment, the Ariostan Apollo, common fount of an illumination and of a poetic madness, belies the dialectic of Nietzsche by making himself, and Cassandra, the ambiguous locus of both dionysian and apollonian qualities.[231] Of course, it is the moon, rather than the sun, which lights up the poem's most famous pages, and which, as I have both asserted and denied, most explicitly figures the poet's enterprise. The multivalence of the moon is that of the *Furioso:* it reflects the sun's light and the earth's darker landscape; is a place of speculative reflection as of imaginative lunacy. Between flight and return, speculation and madness, this is where I hope I have situated the *Furioso.* And so it happens that I find myself in complete agreement with at least this DeSanctian judgment of the poem: "you don't know if it is a serious matter, or a joke."[232]

---

[230] Nietzche, *The Birth of Tragedy*, pp. 59–60, 78, 124–25.

[231] Berry shows that the reason vs. madness distinction between Apollo and Dionysius actually turns into an opposition between two kinds of poetic madness. I believe Ariosto collapses even that distinction. Anyone who has read the magnificent and horrifying description of the apollonian priestess possessed by her god in Lucan's *Pharsalia* (bk. v.86 ff.) will understand that even the classical Apollo was not all song and light.

[232] DeSanctis, "Ariosto," p. 477: "non sai se è una cosa seria o da burla."

BIBLIOGRAPHY

Primary Sources

Alberti, Leon Battista. *Intercenali Inediti.* Ed. E. Garin. Firenze: Sansoni, 1965. First published in "Venticinque Intercenali Inedite e Sconosciute di Leon Battista Alberti," *Belfagor* 19 (1964), 377–98.

—— *Momus.* Ed. and trans. G. Martini. Vol. 13 in the Scrittori Politici Italiani series of the Istituto Nazionale di Cultura Fascista. Bologna: Zanichelli, 1942.

—— *Opere Volgari,* vol. 1. Ed. C. Grayson. Bari: Laterza, 1960.

Alighieri, Dante. *La Commedia, Commento di Cristoforo Landino.* Firenze: 1481.

—— *The Divine Comedy.* 3 vols. Trans. C. Singleton. Princeton: Princeton University Press, 1970.

Allen, Michael, ed. and trans. *Marsilio Ficino and the Phaedran Charioteer.* Berkeley: University of California Press, 1981.

Ariosto, Ludovico. *Lettere.* Ed. A. Stella. Verona: Mondadori, 1965.

—— *Opere.* 2 vols. Ed. S. Orlandini. Venezia: 1730.

—— *Opere Minori.* Ed. G. Fatini. Firenze: Sansoni, 1915.

—— *Opere Minori.* Ed. C. Segre. Milano and Napoli: Ricciardi, 1954.

—— *Orlando Furioso.* 2 vols. Ed. E. Bigi. Milano: Rusconi, 1982.

—— *Orlando Furioso.* Ed. L. Caretti. Milano and Napoli: Ricciardi, 1954.

—— *Orlando Furioso.* Eds. S. DeBenedetti and C. Segre. Bologna: Commissione per i Testi di Lingua, 1960.

—— *The Satires of Ludovico Ariosto: A Renaissance Autobiography.* Ed. and trans. P. Wiggins. Athens: Ohio University Press, 1976.

Barbaro, Ermolao. *Epistolae, Orationes et Carmina.* 2 vols. Ed. V. Branca. Firenze: "Bibliophilus," 1943.

Battaglia, Felice, ed. *Il Pensiero Pedagogico del Rinascimento.* Vol. 3 in I Classici della Pedagogia Italiana series. Eds. E. Lama and L. Volpicelli. Firenze: Sansoni e Giuntine, 1960.

Bembo, Pietro. *Opere in Volgare.* Ed. M. Marti. Firenze: Sansoni, 1961.

Boccaccio, Giovanni. *Boccaccio on Poetry; Being the Preface and the Fourteenth and Fifteenth Books of Boccaccio's Genealogia Deorum Gentilium.* Ed. and trans. C. Osgood. Indianapolis and New York: Bobbs-Merrill, 1956; first published 1930.

—— *Genealogie Deorum Gentilium Libri.* 2 vols. Ed. V. Romano. Bari: Laterza, 1951.

Cassirer, E., et al., eds. *The Renaissance Philosophy of Man.* Chicago: University of Chicago Press, 1948.

Castiglione, Baldassare. *Il Libro del Cortegiano.* In *Opere di Baldassare Castiglione, Giovanni della Casa, Benvenuto Cellini.* Ed. C. Cordié. Milano and Napoli: Ricciardi, 1960.

Erasmus, Desiderius. *Moriae Encomium, id est Stultitiae Laus.* Ed. C.H. Miller. Vol. 4, pt. 3 in *Opera Omnia.* Amsterdam and Oxford: North-Holland, 1979.

—— *The Praise of Folly.* Trans. H.H. Hudson. Princeton: Princeton University Press, 1941; repr. 1969.

Fornari, Simone. *Spositione sopra l'"Orlando Furioso" dell'Ariosto.* Firenze: 1549.

Fulgentius. *Opera.* Ed. R. Helm. Stuttgart: B.G. Teubner, 1898; repr. 1970.

Garin, Eugenio, ed. *L'Educazione Umanistica in Italia.* Bari: Laterza, 1949; repr. 1966.

—— ed. *Filosofi Italiani del Quattrocento.* Firenze: LeMonnier, 1942.

—— ed. *Il Pensiero Pedagogico dello Umanesimo.* Vol. 2 in I Classici della Pedagogia Italiana series. Eds. E. Lama and L. Volpicelli. Firenze: Sansoni e Giuntine, 1958.

—— ed. *Prosatori Latini del Quattrocento.* Napoli and Milano: Ricciardi, 1952.

Haller, Robert, ed. and trans. *The Literary Criticism of Dante Alighieri.* Lincoln: University of Nebraska Press, 1973.

Isidore of Seville. *Etymologiarum sive Originum Libri XX.* 2 vols. Ed. W. Lindsay. Oxford: The Clarendon Press, 1966.

Landino, Cristoforo. *De Vera Nobilitate.* Ed. M. Lentzen. Genève: Droz, 1970.

—— *Disputationes Camaldulenses.* Ed. P. Lohe. Firenze: Sansoni, 1980.

—— *Scritti Critici e Teorici.* 2 vols. Ed. R. Cardini. Roma: Bulzoni, 1974.

Lucian. *Works,* vol. 1. Trans. A.M. Harmon. In the Loeb Classical Library. Cambridge: Harvard University Press, 1913; repr. 1961.

Luiso, Francesco. *Studi sull' "Epistolario" di Leonardo Bruni.* Ed. L.G. Rosa. Roma: Istituto Storico Italiano per il Medio Evo, 1980.

Machiavelli, Niccolò, *Tutte le Opere.* Ed. M. Martelli. Firenze: Sansoni, 1971.

Migne, J.P., ed. *Patrologiae Cursus Completus: Series Latina.* Paris: 1844–1864.

Milton, John. *Complete Poems and Major Prose.* Ed. M.Y. Hughes. Indianapolis: Bobbs-Merrill, Odyssey, 1957.

Petrarca, Francesco. *Prose.* Ed. G. Martellotti. Milano and Napoli: Ricciardi, 1955.

—— *Rerum Familiarum Libri.* Eds. V. Rossi and U. Bosco. Vols. 10–13 in Edizione Nazionale delle Opere di Francesco Petrarca series. Firenze: Sansoni, 1933–1942.

—— *Rime, Trionfi e Poesie Latine.* Eds. F. Neri et al. Napoli and Milano: Ricciardi, 1951.

Pico della Mirandola, Gianfrancesco. *On the Imagination.* Ed. and trans. H. Kaplan. New Haven: Yale University Press, for Cornell University Press, 1930.

—— *Opera Omnia.* Ed. E. Garin. Torino: Bottega d'Erasmo, 1972; repr. of Basel 1573 ed.

Pico della Mirandola, Giovanni. *"De Dignitate Hominis," "Heptaplus," "De Ente et Uno" e Scritti Varii.* Ed. E. Garin. Firenze: Vallechi, 1942.

—— *Opera Omnia.* 2 vols. Ed. E. Garin. Torino: Bottega d'Erasmo, 1971; repr. of Basel 1572 ed.

Plotinus. *Enneads.* 4th ed. Trans. S. MacKenna, revised by B.S. Page. London: Faber & Faber, 1969.

Rabelais, François. *Oeuvres Complètes,* vol. 1. Ed. P. Jourda. Paris: Garnier, 1962.

Salutati, Coluccio. *De Laboribus Herculis.* 2 vols. Ed. B.L. Ullman. Zurich: Thesaurus Mundi, 1951.

Santangelo, Giorgio, ed. *Le Epistole "De Imitatione" di Giovanfrancesco Pico della Mirandola e di Pietro Bembo.* Firenze: Leo S. Olschki, 1954.

Seneca. *Tragedies,* vol. 1. Ed. and trans. F.J. Miller. In the Loeb Classical Library. Cambridge: Harvard University Press, 1917; repr. 1968.

Servius. *Vergilii Carmina Commentarii.* 3 vols. Eds. G. Thilo and H. Hagen. Leipzig: B.G. Teubner, 1881–1902.

Silvestris, Bernardus. *Commentary on the First Six Books of the "Aeneid" of Virgil Commonly Attributed to Bernardus Silvestris.* Eds. J.W. Jones and E.F. Jones. Lincoln: University of Nebraska Press, 1977.

Tasso, Torquato. *Prose.* Ed. E. Mazzali. Milano and Napoli: Ricciardi, 1959.

Valla, Lorenzo. *Scritti Filosofici e Religiosi.* Ed. and trans. G. Radetti. Firenze: Sansoni, 1953.

Varese, Claudio, ed. *Prosatori Volgari del Quattrocento.* Napoli and Milano: Ricciardi, 1955.

Virgil. *Eclogues.* Ed. R. Coleman. Cambridge: Cambridge University Press, 1977.

Secondary Sources

Abrams, M.H. *The Mirror and the Lamp.* New York: Oxford University Press, 1953.

—— *Natural Supernaturalism.* New York: Norton, 1971.

Adams, Hazard, ed. *Critical Theory since Plato.* New York: Harcourt Brace Jovanovich, 1971.

Allen, D.C. *Doubt's Boundless Sea: Skepticism and Faith in the Renaissance.*
Baltimore: The Johns Hopkins University Press, 1964.
—— *Mysteriously Meant: The Rediscovery of Pagan Symbolism and Allegorical Interpretation in the Renaissance.* Baltimore: The Johns Hopkins University Press, 1970.
Auerbach, Erich. *Dante: Poet of the Secular World.* Trans. R. Manheim. Chicago: University of Chicago Press, 1961; first published in German, 1929.
—— "Dante's Addresses to the Reader." *Romance Philology* 7 (1954), 268–78.
—— "Figura." In his *Scenes from the Drama of European Literature.* Trans. R. Manheim. New York: Meridian Books, 1959; essay first published in German, 1944.
—— *Mimesis.* Trans. W. Trask. Princeton: Princeton University Press, 1953; first published in German, 1946.
Austin, John. *How to Do Things with Words.* Eds. J. Urmson and M. Sbisà. 2nd ed. Cambridge: Harvard University Press, 1975; 1st ed., 1962.
Bacchelli, Riccardo. *La Congiura di Don Giulio d'Este.* Milano: Mondadori, 1958; first published 1931.
Bahti, Timothy. "Petrarch and the Scene of Writing: A Reading of *Rime* CXXIX." *Yale Italian Studies,* n.s. 1 (1982), 45–63.
Baillet, Roger. *Le Monde Poétique de L'Arioste.* Lyon: L'Hermès, 1977.
Baldini, Antonio. *Ariosto e Dintorni.* Caltanisetta and Roma: Salvatore Sciascia, 1958.
Barish, Jonas. *The Antitheatrical Prejudice.* Berkeley: University of California Press, 1981.
Barkan, Leonard. *Nature's Work of Art.* New Haven: Yale University Press, 1975.
Barthes, Roland. "The Death of the Author." In his *Image, Music, Text.* Trans. S. Heath. New York: Hill & Wang, 1977; first published in French, 1968.
—— *The Pleasure of the Text.* Trans. R. Miller. New York: Hill & Wang, 1975; first published in French, 1973.
—— *S/Z.* Trans. R. Miller. New York: Hill & Wang, 1974; first published in French, 1970.
Bec, Christian, ed. *Italie 1500–1550: Une Situation de Crise?* Lyon: L'Hermès, 1976.
Bernheimer, Richard. *Wild Men in the Middle Ages.* New York: Octagon Books, 1970; first published 1952.
Berry, Alice. "Apollo vs. Bacchus: The Dynamics of Inspiration." *PMLA* 90 (1975), 88–95.

Bertoni, Giulio. *La Biblioteca Estense e la Coltura Ferrarese*. Torino: Loescher, 1903.

Bigi, Emilio. "Petrarchismo Ariostesco." *Giornale Storico della Letteratura Italiana* 130 (1953), 31–62.

Binni, Walter. *Metodo e Poesia di Ludovico Ariosto*. Messina: G. D'Anna, 1947.

Blackburn, William. "Spenser's Merlin." *Renaissance and Reformation/ Renaissance et Réforme*, n.s. 4 (1980), 179–98.

Blasucci, Luigi. *Studi su Dante e Ariosto*. Napoli and Milano: Ricciardi, 1969.

Bonadeo, Alfredo. "Note sulla Pazzia di Orlando." *Forum Italicum* 4 (1970), 39–57.

Bonifazi, Neuro. *Le Lettere Infedeli*. Roma: Officina Edizioni, 1975.

Borlenghi, Aldo. *Ariosto*. Palermo: Palumbo, 1961.

Bowra, C.M. *From Virgil to Milton*. Toronto: Macmillan, 1945.

Branca, Vittore. "Ludovico non della Tranquillitate." *Veltro* 19 (1975), 75–81.

Brand, C.P. *Ludovico Ariosto: A Preface to the "Orlando Furioso."* Edinburgh: Edinburgh University Press, 1974.

Bruscagli, Riccardo. *Stagioni della Civiltà Estense*. Pisa: Nistri-Lischi, 1983.

Bundy, Murray. *The Theory of Imagination in Classical and Medieval Thought*. Urbana: University of Illinois Press, 1927.

Burckhardt, Jacob. *The Civilization of the Renaissance in Italy*. 2 vols. Trans. S.G.C. Middlemore. New York: Harper, Colophon, 1929; repr. 1958.

Burke, Kenneth. *The Rhetoric of Religion: Studies in Logology*. Berkeley: University of California Press, 1970; first published 1961.

Cantimori, Delio. *Eretici Italiani del Cinquecento*. Firenze: Sansoni, 1939; repr. 1967.

Caretti, Lanfranco. *Antichi e Moderni*. Torino: Einaudi, 1976.

—— *Ariosto e Tasso*. Torino: Einaudi, 1961.

Carne-Ross, D.S. "The One and the Many: A Reading of the *Orlando Furioso*, Cantos 1 and 8." *Arion* 5 (Summer 1966), 195–234.

Catalano, Michele. *Vita di Ludovico Ariosto*. 2 vols. Vols. 15 and 16 in the Biblioteca dell' "Archivium Romanicum" series. Ed. G. Bertoni. Genève: Leo S. Olschki, 1930–1931.

Cerulli, E. "Il Volo di Astolfo sull'Etiopia nell'*Orlando Furioso*." *Atti dell'Accademia dei Lincei, Rendiconti della Classe di Scienze Morali*, series 6, vol. 8 (1932), 19–38.

Chesney, Elizabeth. *The Counter-Voyage of Rabelais and Ariosto: A Comparative Reading of Two Renaissance Mock Epics*. Durham: Duke University Press, 1982.

Chiampi, James. "Angelica's Flight and the Reduction of the Quest in the *Orlando Furioso.*" *Canadian Journal of Italian Studies* 4 (1980/81), 1–25.
—— "Between Voice and Writing: Ariosto's Irony According to St. John." *Italica* 60 (1983), 340–50.

Chiappini, Luciano. *Gli Estensi.* Modena: Dall'Oglio, 1967.

Clements, Robert J. *Picta Poesis.* Roma: Edizione Storia e Letteratura, 1960.

Codino, Fausto. *Introduzione ad Omero.* Torino: Piccole Edizioni Einaudi, 1965.

Comparetti, Domenico. *Virgilio nel Medioevo.* 2 vols. Revised ed. Ed. G. Pasquali. Firenze: La Nuova Italia, 1937–1946.

Contini, Gianfranco. "Come Lavorava L'Ariosto." In his *Esercizi di Lettura.* 2nd ed. Torino: Einaudi, 1974; 1st ed., 1939.

Corsaro, Antonio. "'In Questo Rincrescevol Labirinto': Le *Satire* Garafagnine di Ludovico Ariosto." *Filologia e Critica* 4 (1979), 188–211.

Courcelle, Pierre. "Quelques Symboles Funéraires du Néoplatonisme Latin." *Revue des Etudes Anciennes* 46 (1944), 65–93.

Croce, Benedetto. *Ariosto, Shakespeare e Corneille.* Vol. II of Opere di Benedetto Croce series. Bari: Laterza, 1968; first published 1920.

Cuccaro, Vincent. *The Humanism of Ludovico Ariosto: From the "Satire" to the "Furioso."* Ravenna: Longo, 1981.

Culler, Jonathan. *Ferdinand de Saussure.* New York: Penguin, 1977.
—— "Literary History, Allegory and Semiology." *New Literary History* 7 (1975/76), 259–70.
—— *Structuralist Poetics.* Ithaca: Cornell University Press, 1975.

Curtius, Ernst. *European Literature and the Latin Middle Ages.* Trans. W. Trask. Princeton: Princeton University Press, 1953; repr. 1973; first published in German, 1948.

Dalla Palma, Giuseppe. "Una Cifra per la Pazzia d'Orlando." *Strumenti Critici* 9 (1975), 367–79.

DeBlasi, Giorgio. "Ariosto e le Passioni." *Giornale Storico della Letteratura Italiana,* pt. 1 in 129 (1952), 318–62, and pt. 2 in 130 (1953), 178–203.

DelCorno-Branca, Daniella. *L' "Orlando Furioso" e il Romanzo Cavalleresco Medievale.* Firenze: Leo S. Olschki, 1973.

DeMan, Paul. *Allegories of Reading.* New Haven: Yale University Press, 1979.
—— *Blindness and Insight.* New York: Oxford University Press, 1971.
—— "The Rhetoric of Temporality." In *Interpretation: Theory and Practice.* Ed. C. Singleton. Baltimore: The Johns Hopkins University Press, 1969.
—— "Semiology and Rhetoric." *Diacritics* 3 (1973), 27–33.

Derrida, Jacques. "Limited Inc abc . . ." *Glyph* 2 (1977), 162–254.
—— *Marges de la Philosophie.* Paris: Minuit, 1972.

—— *Of Grammatology*. Trans. G.C. Spivak. Baltimore: The Johns Hopkins University Press, 1976; first published in French, 1967.

—— "Signature Event Context." *Glyph* 1 (1977), 172–97; first published in French, 1972.

—— *Writing and Difference*. Trans. A. Bass. Chicago: University of Chicago Press, 1978.

DeSanctis, Francesco. "Ariosto." *Storia della Letteratura Italiana*. 2 vols. Ed. M.T. Lanza. Milano: Feltrinelli, 1964.

Dionisotti, Carlo. *Geografia e Storia della Letteratura Italiana*. Torino: Einaudi, 1967.

DiTommaso, Andrea. "Boiardo/Ariosto: Textual Relations and Poetic Integrity." *Stanford Italian Review* 4 (1984), 73–92.

—— "'Insania' and 'Furor': A Diagnostic Note on Orlando's Malady." *Romance Notes* 14 (1972/73), 583–88.

Donato, Eugenio. "Death and History in Poliziano's *Stanze*." *MLN* 80 (1965), 27–40.

—— "'Per Selve e Boscherecci Labirinti': Desire and Narrative Structure in Ariosto's *Orlando Furioso*." *Barroco* 4 (1972), 17–34.

Doob, Penelope. *Nebuchadnezzer's Children: Conventions of Madness in Middle English Literature*. New Haven: Yale University Press, 1974.

Doyle, Nancy A. "The Artist as 'Artifex Mundi' in Ariosto's *Orlando Furioso* and Cervantes' *Don Quixote*." Diss. Indiana University, 1979. Abstract in *DAI* 40 (1980), 4016–4017A.

Durling, Robert. *The Figure of the Poet in Renaissance Epic*. Cambridge: Harvard University Press, 1965.

—— "Petrarch's 'Giovene Donna Sotto un Verde Lauro.'" *MLN* 86 (1971), 1–20.

—— ed. and trans. *Petrarch's Lyric Poems*. Cambridge: Harvard University Press, 1976.

Economou, George. *The Goddess Natura in Medieval Literature*. Cambridge: Harvard University Press, 1972.

Farrell, Mary M. "Mentors and Magi in Ariosto and Rabelais." Diss. Yale University, 1976. Abstract in *DAI* 37 (1977), 4395A.

Fatini, Giuseppe. *Bibliografia della Critica Ariostea (1510–1956)*. Firenze: Felice LeMonnier, 1958.

Felman, Shoshana. "Turning the Screw of Interpretation." *Yale French Studies* 55/56 (1977), 94–207.

Ferguson, Wallace. *The Renaissance in Historical Thought*. Boston: Houghton-Mifflin, 1948.

Ferroni, Giulio. "L'Ariosto e la Concezione Umanistica della Follia." In *Atti del Convegno Internazionale "Ludovico Ariosto."* Roma: Accademia Nazionale dei Lincei, 1975.

Fichter, Andrew. *Poets Historical: Dynastic Epic in the Renaissance.* New Haven: Yale University Press, 1982.

Fletcher, Angus. *Allegory: The Theory of a Symbolic Mode.* Ithaca: Cornell University Press, 1964.

Foscolo, Ugo. "Poemi Narrativi." In *Saggi di Letteratura Italiana.* Ed. C. Foligno. Vol. 11, pt. 2, in the Edizione Nazionale delle Opere di Ugo Foscolo series. Firenze: Felice LeMonnier, 1958.

Foucault, Michel. *Madness and Civilization.* Trans. R. Howard. New York: Random House, Vintage, 1965; an abridgment of the 1961 French ed.

—— *The Order of Things.* New York: Random House, Vintage, 1973; first published in French, 1966.

—— "What is an Author?" In *Textual Strategies.* Ed. J. Harari. Ithaca: Cornell University Press, 1979.

Freccero, John. "Dante's Firm Foot and the Journey without a Guide." *Harvard Theological Review* 52 (1959), 245–81.

—— "Dante's Pilgrim in a Gyre." *PMLA* 76 (1961), 168–81.

—— "Dante's Prologue Scene." *Dante Studies* 84 (1966), 1–25.

—— "The Fig-Tree and the Laurel: Petrarch's Poetics." *Diacritics* 5 (Spring 1975), 34–40.

—— "Infernal Inversion and Christian Conversion (*Inferno* XXXIV)." *Italica* 42 (1965), 35–41.

—— "Introduction." In Dante Alighieri, *Paradiso.* Trans. J. Ciardi. New York: New American Library, Mentor, 1970.

—— "Medusa: The Letter and the Spirit." *Yearbook of Italian Studies* 2 (1972), 1–18.

—— "*Paradiso* X: The Dance of the Stars." *Dante Studies* 86 (1968), 85–112.

—— "The River of Death: *Inferno* II,108." In *The World of Dante.* Eds. S.B. Chandler and J.A. Molinaro. Toronto: University of Toronto Press, 1966.

Frye, Northrop. *Anatomy of Criticism.* Princeton: Princeton University Press, 1957.

—— *The Secular Scripture.* Cambridge: Harvard University Press, 1976.

Gaeta, Franco. "L'Avventura di Ercole." *Rinascimento* 5 (1954), 227–60.

Galinsky, Gotthard Karl. *The Herakles Theme.* Totowa, N.J.: Rowman & Littlefield, 1972.

Garin, Eugenio. *L'Educazione in Europa 1400–1600.* Bari: Laterza, 1957; repr. 1976.

—— "Le Favole Antiche." *Rassegna della Letteratura Italiana* 57 (1953), 402–419.

—— "La Letteratura degli Umanisti." In *Il Quattrocento e l'Ariosto.* Eds. E. Cecchi and N. Sapegno. Vol. 3 in the Storia della Letteratura Italiana series. Milano: Garzanti, 1965.

—— *Rinascite e Rivoluzioni*. Bari: Laterza, 1975.

—— *Ritratti di Umanisti*. Firenze: Sansoni, 1967.

—— *L'Umanesimo Italiano*. Bari: Laterza, 1952.

Giamatti, A. Bartlett. *The Earthly Paradise and the Renaissance Epic*. Princeton: Princeton University Press, 1966.

—— *Exile and Change in Renaissance Literature*. New Haven: Yale University Press, 1984.

—— "Headlong Horses, Headless Horsemen: An Essay in the Chivalric Romances of Pulci, Boiardo and Ariosto." In *Italian Literature: Roots and Branches*. Eds. K. Atchity and G. Rimanelli. New Haven: Yale University Press, 1976.

—— "Proteus Unbound: Some Versions of the Sea God in the Renaissance." In *The Disciplines of Criticism*. Eds. P. Demetz et al. New Haven: Yale University Press, 1968.

Gilson, Etienne. *Reason and Revelation in the Middle Ages*. New York: Scribner's, 1938.

Girard, René. *Deceit, Desire and the Novel*. Trans. Y. Freccero. Baltimore: The Johns Hopkins University Press, 1965; first published in French, 1961.

—— *Violence and the Sacred*. Trans. P. Gregory. Baltimore: The Johns Hopkins University Press, 1977; first published in French, 1972.

Goez, Werner. *Translatio Imperii*. Tübingen: J.C.B. Mohr, 1958.

Graf, Arturo. *Miti, Leggende e Superstizioni del Medioevo*. Torino: Loescher, 1892.

Grafton, Anthony. *Joseph Scaliger: A Study in the History of Classical Scholarship*, vol. 1. Oxford: The Clarendon Press, 1983.

—— and L. Jardine. "Humanism and the School of Guarino: A Problem of Evaluation." *Past and Present* 96 (August 1982), 51–80.

Greenblatt, Stephen. *Renaissance Self-Fashioning*. Chicago: University of Chicago Press, 1980.

Greene, Thomas. "*Il Cortegiano* and the Choice of a Game." *Renaissance Quarterly* 32 (1979), 173–86.

—— *The Descent from Heaven*. New Haven: Yale University Press, 1963.

—— "The Flexibility of the Self in Renaissance Literature." In *The Disciplines of Criticism*. Eds. P. Demetz et al. New Haven: Yale University Press, 1968.

—— *The Light in Troy*. New Haven: Yale University Press, 1982.

Greenfield, Concetta. *Humanist and Scholastic Poetics, 1250–1500*. Lewisburg Pa.: Bucknell University Press, 1981.

Griffin, Robert. *Ludovico Ariosto*. New York: Twayne, 1974.

Gundersheimer, Werner. *Ferrara: The Style of a Renaissance Despotism*. Princeton: Princeton University Press, 1973.

Hanning, Robert. "Ariosto, Ovid and the Painters." In *Ariosto 1974 in America*. Ed. A. Scaglione. Ravenna: Longo, 1976.

—— and D. Rosand, eds. *Castiglione: The Ideal and the Real in Renaissance Culture*. New Haven: Yale University Press, 1983.

Haydn, Hiram. *The Counter-Renaissance*. New York: Scribner's 1950.

Hegel, G.W.F. *Aesthetics*. 2 vols. Trans. T.M. Knox. Oxford: The Clarendon Press, 1975.

Heitmann, Klaus. "Insegnamenti Agostiniani nel *Secretum* del Petrarca." *Studi Petrarcheschi* 7 (1961), 187–93.

Herrick, Marvin. *Italian Tragedy in the Renaissance*. Urbana: University of Illinois Press, 1965.

Internoscia, Donato. "Are There Two Melissas, Both Enchantresses, in the *Furioso?*" *Italica* 25 (1948), 217–26.

Jakobson, Roman. "Linguistics and Poetics." In *Style in Language*. Ed. T. Sebeok. Cambridge: MIT Press, 1960.

—— and Morris Halle. *Fundamentals of Language*. 2nd ed. The Hague: Mouton, 1971; 1st ed., 1956.

Javitch, Daniel. *"Cantus Interruptus* in the *Orlando Furioso." MLN* 95 (1980), 66–80.

—— "The Imitation of Imitations in *Orlando Furioso." Renaissance Quarterly* 38 (1985), 215–39.

—— "Rescuing Ovid from the Allegorizers: The Liberation of Angelica, *Furioso* x." In *Ariosto 1974 in America*. Ed. A. Scaglione. Ravenna: Longo, 1976.

Johnson, W.R. *Darkness Visible*. Berkeley: University of California Press, 1976.

Jordan, Constance. "Enchanted Ground: Vision and Perspective in Renaissance Romance." Diss. Yale University, 1976. Abstract in *DAI* 37 (1977), 4337A.

Jung, Marc-René. *Hercule dans la Littérature Française du XVIᵉ Siècle*. Vol. 79 in Travaux d'Humanisme et Renaissance series. Genève: Droz, 1966.

Kaiser, Walter. *Praisers of Folly*. Cambridge: Harvard University Press, 1963.

Kaske, Carol. "Spenser's Pluralistic Universe: The View from the Mount of Contemplation: *F.Q.* i.x." In *Contemporary Thought on Edmund Spenser*. Eds. R.C. Frushell and B.J. Vondersmith. Carbondale: Southern Illinois University Press, 1975.

Kaske, Robert. "'Sapientia et Fortitudo' as the Controlling Theme of *Beowulf." Studies in Philology* 55 (1958), 423–56.

Kennedy, William. "Ariosto's Ironic Allegory." *MLN* 88 (1973), 44–67.

—— *Rhetorical Norms in Renaissance Literature*. New Haven: Yale University Press, 1978.

Kermode, Frank. *The Sense of an Ending.* New York: Oxford University Press, 1967.

Klein, Robert. "Le Thème du Fou et l'Ironie Humaniste." In *Umanesimo ed Ermeneutica.* Ed. E. Castelli. Vol. 3 in the Archivio di Filosofia series. Padova: CEDAM, 1963.

Klopp, Charles. "The Centaur and the Magpie: Ariosto and Machiavelli's *Prince.*" In *Ariosto 1974 in America.* Ed. A. Scaglione. Ravenna: Longo, 1976.

Kristeller, Paul Oskar. *Renaissance Thought.* New York: Harper & Row, Harper Torchbooks, 1961.

Leach, Eleanor. *Vergil's "Eclogues": Landscapes of Experience.* Ithaca: Cornell University Press, 1974.

Lefebvre, Joel. *Les Fols et la Folie.* Paris: Klinksieck, 1968.

Lewis, C.S. *The Allegory of Love.* London: Oxford University Press, 1936; repr. 1975.

—— *A Preface to "Paradise Lost."* London: Oxford University Press, 1942.

Lot, Ferdinand. *Etude sur le Lancelot en Prose.* Paris: Champion, 1918.

Lukács, Georg. *The Theory of the Novel.* Trans. A. Bostock. Cambridge: MIT Press, 1971; first published in German, 1920.

Mâle, Emile. *The Gothic Image.* Trans. D. Nussay. New York: Harper & Row, 1958; first published in French, 1913.

Marinelli, Peter. "Redemptive Laughter: Comedy in the Italian Romances." *Genre* 9 (Winter 1976/77), 505–26.

Marsh, David. "Horatian Influence and Imitation in Ariosto's *Satire.*" *Comparative Literature* 27 (1975), 307–26.

—— "Ruggiero and Leone: Revision and Resolution in Ariosto's *Orlando Furioso.*" *MLN* 96 (1981), 144–51.

Martines, Lauro. *Power and Imagination: City States in Renaissance Italy.* New York: Knopf, 1979.

Masciandaro, Francesco. "Folly in the *Orlando Furioso:* A Reading of the Gabrina Episode." *Forum Italicum* 14 (1980), 56–77.

Mazzeo, Joseph. *Renaissance and Revolution: The Remaking of European Thought.* New York: Pantheon, 1965.

Mazzotta, Giuseppe. "The *Canzoniere* and the Language of the Self." *Studies in Philology* 75 (1978), 271–96.

—— *Dante: Poet of the Desert.* Princeton: Princeton University Press, 1979.

—— "The *Decameron:* The Literal and the Allegorical." *Italian Quarterly* 72 (1975), 53–73.

—— "The *Decameron:* The Marginality of Literature." *University of Toronto Quarterly* 42 (1972), 64–81.

—— "Games of Laughter in the *Decameron.*" *Romanic Review* 69 (1978), 115–31.

McLucas, John. "Ariosto and the Androgyne: Symmetries of Sex in the *Orlando Furioso*." Diss. Yale University, 1983. Abstract in *DAI* 44 (1984), 2784A.

Momigliano, Attilio. *Saggio sull' "Orlando Furioso."* Bari: Laterza, 1928; repr. 1973.

Mommsen, T.E. "Petrarch and the Story of the Choice of Hercules." In his *Medieval and Renaissance Studies*. Ed. E. Rice. Ithaca: Cornell University Press, 1959. Essay first published in *Journal of the Warburg and Courtauld Institutes* 16 (1953), 178–92.

Montano, Rocco. "La Follia di Orlando." In his *Saggi di Cultura Umanistica*. Napoli: Quaderni, 1962. Essay first published in *Follia e Saggezza nel "Furioso" e nell' "Elogio" di Erasmo* (Napoli: Edizioni "Humanitas," 1942).

Murrin, Michael. *The Allegorical Epic*. Chicago: University of Chicago Press, 1980.

—— *The Veil of Allegory*. Chicago: University of Chicago Press, 1969.

Nardi, Bruno. "La Mistica Averroistica e Pico della Mirandola." In *Umanesimo e Machiavellismo*. Ed. E. Castelli. Padova: Liviana, 1949.

Nicolson, Marjorie H. *The Breaking of the Circle*. Revised ed. New York: Columbia University Press, 1960; 1st ed., 1950.

Nietzsche, Friedrich. *The Birth of Tragedy and the Genealogy of Morals*. Trans. F. Golffing. Garden City, N.Y.: Doubleday, Anchor, 1956.

Ossola, Carlo. "Métaphore et Inventaire de la Folie dans la Littérature Italienne du XVIe Siècle." In *Folie et Déraison à la Renaissance*. Bruxelles: Editions de l'Université de Bruxelles, 1976.

L'Ottava d'Oro. Milano: Mondadori, 1933.

Padoan, Giorgio. "L'*Orlando Furioso* e la Crisi del Rinascimento." In *Ariosto 1974 in America*. Ed. A. Scaglione. Ravenna: Longo, 1976. Essay first published in *Lettere Italiane* 27 (1975), 286–307.

—— *Il Pio Enea, l'Empio Ulisse*. Ravenna: Longo, 1977.

Panofsky, Erwin. "'Et in Arcadia Ego': Poussin and the Elegiac Tradition." In his *Meaning in the Visual Arts*. Garden City, N.Y.: Doubleday, Anchor, 1955.

—— *Hercules am Scheidewege*. Leipzig: B.G. Teubner, 1930.

—— "The Neoplatonic Movement and Michelangelo." In his *Studies in Iconology*. New York: Harper & Row, Harper Torchbooks, 1939; repr. 1962.

—— *Renaissance and Renascences*. 2nd. ed. Stockholm: Almquist & Wiksell, 1965; 1st ed. 1960.

Parker, Patricia. *Inescapable Romance: Studies in the Poetics of a Mode*. Princeton: Princeton University Press, 1979.

Parry, Adam. "The Two Voices of Virgil's *Aeneid*." *Arion* 2 (1963), 66–80.

Patrides, C.A. *The Phoenix and the Ladder.* Berkeley: University of California Press, 1964.

Pavlock, Barbara. "Epic and Romance: 'Genera Mixta' in Vergil, Ovid, Ariosto, Milton." Diss. Cornell University, 1977. Abstract in *DAI* 38 (1978), 4148A.

Peirce, Charles S. *Collected Papers.* 8 vols. Cambridge: Harvard University Press, 1931–1958.

Pépin, Jean. *Mythe et Allégorie.* Paris: Aubier, 1958.

Petrocchi, Giorgio. *I Fantasmi di Tancredi.* Caltanisetta and Roma: Salvatore Sciascia, 1972.

—— "Orazio e Ariosto." *Giornale Italiano di Filologia,* n.s. 1 (1970), 3–13.

Pigman, G.W. III. "Versions of Imitation in the Renaissance." *Renaissance Quarterly* 33 (1980), 1–32.

Pirandello, Luigi, "L'Umorismo." In *Saggi, Poesie e Scritti Varii.* 3rd ed. Ed. M. Lo Vecchio-Musti. Verona: Mondadori, 1973; essay first published 1920.

Pool, Franco. *Interpretazione dell'"Orlando Furioso."* Firenze: La Nuova Italia, 1968.

Poulet, Georges. *The Metamorphoses of the Circle.* Trans. G. Poulet, C. Dawson, and E. Coleman. Baltimore: The Johns Hopkins University Press, 1966; first published in French, 1961.

Quinones, Ricardo. *The Renaissance Discovery of Time.* Cambridge: Harvard University Press, 1972.

Quint, David. "'Alexander the Pig': Shakespeare on History and Poetry." *Boundary 2* 10.3 (1982), 49–67.

—— "Astolfo's Voyage to the Moon." *Yale Italian Studies,* o.s. 1 (1977), 398–408.

—— "The Figure of Atlante: Ariosto and Boiardo's Poem." *MLN* 94 (1979), 77–91.

—— *Origin and Originality in Renaissance Literature: Versions of the Source.* New Haven: Yale University Press, 1983.

Rahner, Hugo. *Greek Myths and Christian Mysteries.* Trans. B. Battershaw. London: Burns & Oates, 1963; first published in German, 1957.

Rajna, Pio. *Le Fonti dell' "Orlando Furioso."* 2nd. ed. Firenze: Sansoni, 1900; repr. 1975 (Ed. F. Mazzoni).

Réau, Louis. *Iconographie de L'Art Chrétien.* 3 vols. Paris: Presses Universitaires de France, 1955–1958.

Rebhorn, Wayne. *Courtly Performances: Masking and Festivity in Castiglione's "Book of the Courtier."* Detroit: Wayne State University Press, 1978.

Resta, G. "Il Sogno di Orlando." In *I Metodi Attuali della Critica in Italia.* Eds. M. Corti and C. Segre. Torino: ERI/Edizioni RAI, 1970. Excerpted from "Ariosto e i Suoi Personaggi," *Rivista di Psicoanalisi* 3 (1957), 59–83.

Rodini, Robert and Salvatore Di Maria. *Ludovico Ariosto: An Annotated Bibliography of Criticism, 1956–1980.* Columbia: University of Missouri Press, 1984.

Rolfs, Daniel. "Sound and Silence in Ariosto's Narrative." *Renaissance and Reformation/Renaissance et Réforme,* n.s. 2 (1978), 151–69.

Ruggieri, Ruggiero. *L'Umanesimo Cavalleresco Italiano.* Napoli: Fratelli Conte, 1977.

Russo, Luigi. "Ariosto Maggiore e Minore." *Belfagor* 13 (1958), 628–46.

Saccone, Eduardo. *Il Soggetto del "Furioso" e Altri Saggi tra '400 e '500.* Napoli: Liguori, 1974.

Salinari, Giambattista. "L'Ariosto fra Machiavelli ed Erasmo." In *Rassegna di Cultura e Vita Scolastica* 21 (1957), no. 10, pp. 1–3, and nos. 11–12, pp. 3–5.

Salman, Phillips. "Instruction and Delight in Medieval and Renaissance Criticism." *Renaissance Quarterly* 32 (1979), 303–32.

Santoro, Mario. "L'Angelica del *Furioso:* Fuga dalla Storia." *Esperienze Letterarie* 3 (1978), no. 3. pp. 3–28.

—— "L'Astolfo Ariostesco: *Homo Fortunatus.*" In his *Letture Ariostesche.* Napoli: Liguori, 1973.

—— "La Prova del 'Nappo' e la Cognizione Ariostesca del Reale." *Esperienze Letterarie* 1 (1976), no. 1, pp. 5–24.

—— "La Sequenza Lunare nel *Furioso:* Una Società allo Specchio." *Atti dell'Accademia Pontaniana.* Napoli: Giannini, 1975.

Savarese, Gennaro. "Ariosto al Bivio tra Marsilio Ficino e 'Adescatrici Galliche.'" *Annali dell'Istituto di Filologia Moderna dell'Università di Roma* (1978), 21–39.

Scaglione, Aldo. *Nature and Love in the Late Middle Ages.* Berkeley: University of California Press, 1963.

Searle, John. "The Logical Status of Fictional Discourse." *New Literary History* 6 (1975), 319–32.

—— *Speech Acts: An Essay in the Philosophy of Language.* Cambridge: Cambridge University Press, 1969.

Segre, Cesare. *Esperienze Ariostesche.* Pisa: Nistri-Lischi, 1966.

—— ed. *Ludovico Ariosto: Lingua, Stile e Tradizione.* Milano: Feltrinelli, 1976.

Seigel, Jerrold. *Rhetoric and Philosophy in Renaissance Humanism: The Union of Eloquence and Wisdom, Petrarch to Valla.* Princeton: Princeton University Press, 1968.

Seznec, Jean. *The Survival of the Pagan Gods.* Trans. B. Sessions. Princeton: Princeton University Press, 1953; first published in French, 1940.

Shapiro, Marianne. "From Atlas to Atlante." *Comparative Literature* 35 (1983), 323–50.

—— "Perseus and Bellerophon in *Orlando Furioso*." *Modern Philology* 81 (1983), 109–130.

Singleton, Charles. *Dante's "Commedia": Elements of Structure*. Baltimore: The Johns Hopkins University Press, 1977; repr. of 1954 ed.

—— "In Exitu Israel de Aegyptu." *Annual Report of the Dante Society in America* 78 (1960), 1–24.

—— "The Poet's Number at the Center." *MLN* 80 (1965), 1–10.

Smith, Barbara H. *Poetic Closure*. Chicago: University of Chicago Press, 1968.

Spargo, John. *Virgil the Necromancer*. Cambridge: Harvard University Press, 1934.

Spitzer, Leo. "The Addresses to the Reader in the *Commedia*." In his *Romanische Literaturstudien 1936–56*. Tübingen: Niemeyer, 1959.

—— *Classical and Christian Ideas of World Harmony*. Ed. A.G. Hatcher. Baltimore: The Johns Hopkins University Press, 1963.

—— "Speech and Language in *Inferno* 13." *Italica* 19 (1942), 81–104.

Stephens, Walter E. "Berosus Chaldaeus: Counterfeit and Fictive Editors of the Early Sixteenth Century." Diss. Cornell University, 1979. Abstract in *DAI* 40 (1980), 4584A.

Struever, Nancy. *The Language of History in the Renaissance*. Princeton: Princeton University Press, 1970.

Tayler, Edward. *Nature and Art in Renaissance Literature*. New York: Columbia University Press, 1964.

Thompson, David. *Dante's Epic Journey*. Baltimore: The Johns Hopkins University Press, 1974.

Tietze-Conrat, E. "Notes on Hercules at the Crossroads." *Journal of the Warburg and Courtauld Institutes* 14 (1951), 305–309.

Toffanin, Giuseppe. *La Religione degli Umanisti*. Bologna: Zanichelli, 1950.

Tomalin, Margaret. *The Fortunes of the Warrior Heroine in Italian Literature*. Ravenna: Longo, 1982.

Trinkaus, Charles. *In Our Image and Likeness*. 2 vols. Chicago: University of Chicago Press, 1970.

Tucker, Dunstan. "'In Exitu Israel de Aegyptu': The *Divine Comedy* in the Light of the Easter Liturgy." *The American Benedictine Review* 11 (1960), 43–61.

Turchi, Marcello. *Ariosto, o della Liberazione Fantastica*. Ravenna: Longo, 1969.

Turner, Victor. *The Forest of Symbols: Aspects of Ndembu Ritual*. Ithaca: Cornell University Press, 1967.

Valesio, Paolo. "The Language of Madness in the Renaissance." *Yearbook of Italian Studies* 1 (1971), 199–234.

Vinaver, Eugene. *The Rise of Romance*. Oxford: The Clarendon Press, 1971.

Vitale, Mario. *Ariosto fra Illusioni e Conoscenza*. Napoli: Giannini, 1969.

Waith, Eugene. *The Herculean Hero in Marlowe, Chapman, Shakespeare and Dryden*. London: Chatto & Windus, 1962.

Walker, D.P. *The Ancient Theology*. Ithaca: Cornell University Press, 1972.

—— *Spiritual and Demonic Magic from Ficino to Campanella*. London: The Warburg Institute, 1958; repr. 1975 by University of Notre Dame Press.

Weaver, Elissa. "Lettura dell'Intreccio dell'*Orlando Furioso*: Il Caso delle Tre Pazzie d'Amore." *Strumenti Critici* 11 (1977), 384–406.

Weinberg, Bernard. *A History of Literary Criticism in the Italian Renaissance*. 2 vols. Chicago: University of Chicago Press, 1961.

Welles, Elizabeth. "Magic in the Renaissance Epic: Pulci, Boiardo, Ariosto, Tasso." Diss. Yale University, 1970. Abstract in *DAI* 32 (1971), 461–462A.

Wiggins, Peter DeSa. "Galileo on Characterization in the *Orlando Furioso*." *Italica* 57 (1980), 255–67.

Wind, Edgar. *Pagan Mysteries in the Renaissance*. Revised ed. New York: Norton, 1968; 1st ed., 1958.

Wise, Valerie M. "Ruggiero and the Hippogriff: The Ambiguities of Vision." *Quaderni d'Italianistica* 2 (1981), 39–53.

Yates, Frances. *Giordano Bruno and the Hermetic Tradition*. Chicago: University of Chicago Press, 1964.

Yoeman, Margaret. "Allegorical Rhetoric in *Orlando Furioso*." Diss. University of California–Irvine, 1978. Abstract in *DAI* 39 (1979), 7336A.

INDEX

Authors are indexed only when cited in text or discussed in a note. *Orlando Furioso* is abbreviated throughout as *OF*.

277–78, 285, 286–93, 299–300, 303; sources of, 269, 274, 284, 288–90, 300; as synecdoche for *OF,* 264, 304–305. *See also* Alcina-Logistilla episode, paired with lunar episode; moon

Luther, M., 111–12

Lydia, episode of, 267n

Machiavelli, N., 85, 117, 118–19, 150, 178, 276n; Ariosto's knowledge of, 27

madness: as *alienatio,* 321, 323, 331; and allegory, 321, 323; bestial vs. divine, 321n, 337–39, 341–42, 393; caused by language, 39, 44, 107, 158, 196n, 243, 312, 321–29, 331, 334, 336, 351, 354–55; causes of, multiple, 17, 59–60, 279, 314–16, 321–26, 328–29, 336, 360; cured by language, 51, 102, 261, 332–35, 337–38, 350–51, 353–55; as a death, 314, 334, 341, 361; and death, paired in *OF,* 17, 32, 36, 220, 265–66, 270, 361; as divine cure, 279, 307, 315; humanism subverted by, 35–36, 50, 75–76, 310–12; in *OF* criticism, 102–106; and reason, dialectic, 50–52, 103–106, 108n, 200–201, 284, 306–307, 311, 331–37, 345–48, 350–56, 359, 390–93; Renaissance concepts of, 11, 44, 51, 61, 99, 104, 105, 122–23n, 279n, 321, 335–45, 348–50, 357, 393; as self-difference and undifferentiation, 51, 304, 312, 314–21, 336, 342, 355, 358–59; silence vs. speech of, 35–36, 50, 102, 261, 306, 311, 321, 331, 333–36, 344, 351–54; as synonym of love, 355–56; as unity, 307, 356–59; universality of, 265, 270, 306, 355–56, 359; as wisdom, 32, 61–62, 95, 99, 104–105, 170, 262, 284, 336, 338, 342–44. *See also furor poeticus;* irony, madness and; metaphor, as

structure of madness; Orlando's madness; poet, madness/sanity of; Ruggiero, madness of

Magi, 197, 214

magic, 75, 82, 197, 272, 298; as poetry, 340n

man: ambiguity of, 14, 116, 168–70, 172, 175; as *arbor conversus,* 193; becoming beast, 119, 137, 169–70, 173, 200–201, 215–16, 274, 310–11; concept of, attacked, 72–73, 104, 286; concepts of, multiple, 71, 82n, 83–84; concepts of, secular vs. Christian, 46–48, 53n, 68, 71–72, 153, 187, 278; defined by speech/ reason, 50, 80, 311; as a god, 46–47, 53, 66–67, 72, 74, 169–70, 181, 186–91, 193, 197; as a god, critiqued, 61–62, 96–97, 109, 111–12, 115, 136, 171–74, 212, 223–24, 250, 268–69, 274, 278, 280, 281n, 299, 324, 341, 382; as self-maker, 72–73, 92, 172–74, 276. *See also dignitas hominis;* nature, man and

Mandricardo, 217, 315–16, 321; madness of, 310

Manetti, G., 84, 286, 290n

Many, *see* One, and Many

map: vs. sea, figuring poem, 19, 20, 21–22, 25–26, 41, 260, 289

Marcellus, 373

Marfisa, 281n, 319n, 370

marginality: imagery of in *OF,* 125, 141–42; vs. liminality, 124–25; poetic, 9, 124–26, 165, 240, 304

Maria (contemplation), 117

Marsyas, 349

Martha (action), 117

Martines, L., 19

Matthew, Gospel of, 357

Mazzeo, J., 68, 82

Mazzotta, G., 9n, 124–25n, 143, 155n

Medea, 386

Medoro, 317; as poet, 39, 158, 243, 322

Medusa: as poetic eloquence, 67, 166–67. *See also* Pegasus, and Medusa

Library of Congress Cataloging-in-Publication Data

ASCOLI, ALBERT RUSSELL, 1953–

ARIOSTO'S BITTER HARMONY.

BIBLIOGRAPHY: P.

INCLUDES INDEX.

I. ARIOSTO, LODOVICO, 1474–1533.   ORLANDO FURIOSO.

I. TITLE

PQ4569.A83 1986 851'.3 86–8881

ISBN 0–691–05479–7 (ALK. PAPER)

Albert Ascoli is Assistant Professor of Italian and Comparative Literature at Northwestern University. This is his first book.